TERRORISM TODAY

The Past,
the Players,
the Future

Second Edition

CLIFFORD E. SIMONSEN
JEREMY R. SPINDLOVE

Prentice Hall
Upper Saddle River, New Jersey 07458

Library of Congress Cataloging-in-Publication Data

Simonsen, Clifford E.
    Terrorism today: the past, the players, and the future/Clifford E.
Simonsen, Jeremy R. Spindlove.—2nd ed.
        p. cm.
    Includes bibliographical references and index.
    ISBN 0-13-112293-2
    1. Terrorism. 2. Terrorism—History. 3. Terrorism—Prevention. I.
Spindlove, Jeremy R. II. Title.
    HV6431 .S53 2004
    303.6'25'09—dc21   2003007017

"Lest we forget"

This edition is dedicated to the thousands of innocent victims who died so tragically at the World Trade Center, New York, at the Pentagon, Washington, DC, and on a lonely field in Somerset County, Pennysylvania, on September 11, 2001. Also, to the many brave Paramedics, Police Officers, and Firefighters from the city of New York who sacrificed their lives in valiant attempts to save others.

We shall never forget.

Publisher: Stephen Helba
Executive Editor: Frank Mortimer, Jr.
Assistant Editor: Korrine Dorsey
Production Editor: John Shannon, Pine Tree Composition, Inc.
Production Liaison: Barbara Marttine Cappuccio
Director of Manufacturing and Production: Bruce Johnson
Managing Editor: Mary Carnis

Creative Director: Cheryl Asherman
Cover Design Coordinator: Miguel Ortiz
Cover Image: Reuters New Media Inc./Corbis
Editorial Assistant: Barbara Rosenberg
Marketing Manager: Tim Peyton
Formatting and Interior Design: Pine Tree Composition, Inc.
Printing and Binding: Courier/Westford

Pearson Education LTD.
Pearson Education Singapore, Pte. Ltd
Pearson Education, Canada, Ltd
Pearson Education–Japan
Pearson Education Australia PTY, Limited
Pearson Educaçion de Mexico, S.A. de C.V.
Pearson Education Malaysia, Pte. Ltd

10 9 8 7 6 5 4 3 2 1

ISBN 0-13-112293-2

Contents

Foreword   viii
Preface   x
About the Authors   xviii

PART ONE The Defining and History of Terrorism

1

Chapter 1   Defining Terrorism   3
  Overview   3
  Terrorism: Searching for a Definition   4
  Some Approaches to Defining Terrorism   6
  The FBI Construct   10
  The U.S. Department of Defense (DOD) Construct   10
  Motivations for Terrorists   12
  Terrorism as Criminal Behavior   14

Chapter 2   A Brief History of Terrorism   20
  Overview   20
  Violence and Terrorism   20
  When Did Violence Become Terrorism?   22
  State-Sponsored and Religious Terrorism   23
  State-Sponsored Terrorism as Warfare in The Twenty-First
    Century   29
  Religious Terrorism   30
  The Turks and the First Crusade   32
  State Terror and Genocide   33
  Cyclical Nature of Terrorism   35
  Contemporary Events: Historical Roots   38

PART TWO Terrorism Around The World

43

Chapter 3   North America and the Caribbean   45
  Overview   45
  The United States   47
  Domestic Terrorism   54
  International Terrorism   56
  Puerto Rico   56
  Canada   59
  Cuba   62
  The Dominican Republic and Haiti   64

Chapter 4   Great Britain and Northern Ireland   69

Overview   69
Ireland: A History of Pain and Terror   70
The Irish Republican Army aka (PIRA) Provisional
    Irish Republican Army   78
Continuity Irish Republican Army (CIRA)   81
Republican Sinn Fein (RSF)   82
Real Irish Republican Army (RIRA)   82
Other Irish Terrorist Groups   82
The Troubles   86
Marching Season   88
The IRA and Terror International   92
The Northern Ireland Peace Process   93
The Northern Ireland Police Service   99
Terrorism in Mainland Britain   100
Islamic Politics and Terror in the United Kingdom   103
Britain's Response to Terrorism   105
Countering Irish Terrorism   106
Extreme Right Wing Groups   107

Chapter 5   Western Europe   110

Overview   110
Spain   110
France   117
Al Qaeda in France   121
Germany   122
Italy   132
GAP & NAP   135
Greece and Turkey   137
Greece   137
Cyprus   141
Turkey   141
Belgian Terrorism   145

Chapter 6   Eastern Europe and the Balkans   150

Overview   150
Russia and The Soviet Union   150
Chechnya   160
Georgia   162
Yugoslavia   164
Bulgaria   167

Chapter 7   North Africa and the Middle East   171

Overview   171
Israel and Its Right to Exist   171
Terrorist Organizations   180

Jordan   188
Declaration of Principles   199
Lebanon   200
Syria   207
The Rest of North Africa   208
Morocco   208
Egypt   209
Anwar Sadat 1919–1981   210
Egypt's Islamic Extremists   211
Libya   212
Colonel Muammar el-Qaddafi   212
Pan Am 103   216
Sudan   217
Algeria   217

Chapter   8   The Persian Gulf   225
Overview   225
Saudi Arabia   225
Kuwait   228
Iraq   230
Bahrain   235
Oman   237
Iran   240
Yemen   245

Chapter   9   Northeast, Central and Southern Africa   249
Overview   249
Ethiopia   249
Somalia   250
Uganda   251
Zimbabwe   256
The Democratic Republic of Congo (DRC)   260
South Africa   262
Kenya   268
Angola   270
Mozambique   272
Rwanda   273
Background on the Democratic Republic of Congo   275
Nigeria   277

Chapter 10   Southern and Southeast Asia   280
Overview   280
South Asia   280
Pakistan   282
Kashmir   288

Sri Lanka   291
Afghanistan   294
Burma   298
Southeast Asia   302
Cambodia   302
Thailand   304
Vietnam   305

Chapter 11   Pacific Rim   310
Overview   310
China   310
Taiwan (Republic of China)   315
Japan   316
Philippines   320
Indonesia   323
Australia   326

Chapter 12   Latin America   330
Overview   330
Central America   331
Mexico   331
Guatemala   333
Honduras   335
El Salvador   336
Nicaragua   336
Panama   338
South America   339
Colombia   339
Peru   345
Bolivia and Brazil   349
Uruguay, Paraguay   351
Argentina   353
Chile   354
Venezuela   356
Ecuador   358

PART THREE   Counterterrorism   361

Chapter 13   Countering Terrorism   363
Overview   363
The Roles for Counterterrorism   364
Hijackings   375
Intelligence Gathering   387
Counterterrorism Units   389
Great Britain   389
SAS Associates   392
Australia   392
Rhodesia   392

Republic of Ireland   393
Spain   394
The Persian Gulf   395
France   395
Netherlands   396
Norway   396
Germany   397
Israel   398
Czech Republic   398
United States of America   399
Piracy   400

Chapter 14   Terrorism in the Twenty-First Century   407
Overview   407
Terrorism Gets a Larger Stage   408
Chemical, Biological, and Nuclear Weapons
    of Mass Destruction   411
A New Gulf War?   412
The New Department of Homeland Security   416
Weapons of Mass Destruction (WMD)   419
Nuclear Threats   420
Chemical and Biological Threats   420
Holy Terror   421
Techno Terrorism   423
Pro-Life Terrorism   424
Terrorists for Sale or Exchange   429

Index of Internet Web Sites   437
Index   439

Foreword

It was a pleasant surprise, and somewhat challenging, when I was approached by the authors and asked to write a foreword for this, the second edition of *Terrorism Today: The Past, The Players, The Future*. Especially challenging since the foreword for the first edition had been written by an icon, Sir Brian Hayes, the former head of Scotland Yard's anti-terrorist branch and the United Kingdom's second most senior police officer, in whose venerated footsteps one is flattered to follow.

Nevertheless, having taught with this fine text at the American Military University for several semesters, I have no hesitation and am delighted to write a short passage, and thoroughly commend this book to the student, reader and instructor.

During the past two years, I have subjected it to what is perhaps the ultimate test, which it passed with flying colors... my university students, many of whom are practitioners in the field of anti- and counter-terrorism, some of General Officer rank, special forces, others from some of the thirteen eminent institutions which comprise the US Intelligence community, as well as some few from departments of the UK's Ministry of Defence.

Terrorism Today is a serious work. Its most striking virtue is that it is designed not only to impart the most relevant information, but also to ensure as far as possible, that it is assimilated. Its format is specifically designed for learning and pleasantly absent is the burden imposed by so many dry works on terrorism—that of endless text and blurred, disjointed transitions from one topic to another.

The illustrations, charts and boxes in *Terrorism Today: The Past. The Players, The Future* work well to entrench learning. Terrorism is the business of the police and the military, involving weapons and tactics; choke points and kill zones; victims and targets, and the like—these issues do not sit well in a conventional book format of sparsely illustrated text. This is what makes *Terrorism Today: The Past, The Players, The Future* stand out from a crowd of works currently published about terrorism.

On the technical content, it is very notable for its range, and includes material on terrorism in some of those darker corners of the world that are rarely mentioned in the media. However, most notable in the content is the structure of the material itself; concise and straightforward briefs on the given topics that we need to know, in order to command a good knowledge of the subject. This in itself is a rarity and a far cry from not a few contemporary academic works on terrorism. In *Terrorism Today: The Past, The Players, The Future* the reader will find none of the quite ingenious but frustrating (and often lengthy and inconclusive) dissections of obscure speculation on the terrorism phenomenon. *Terrorism Today: The Past, The Players, The Future* is straightforward, coherent and relevant reading... useful as an easy reference tool, which cannot be said of the majority of terrorism books currently available. This is not a volume that will collect dust.

Terrorism invaded the global public consciousness so rapidly following the events of September 11, 2001 that it might reasonably be compared to the advent of the personal computer—sudden, imposed, universal, and persistent. Most definitely a household word now, terrorism is clearly here to stay and solely conventional wars are very nearly passé in any event. *Terrorism Today: The Past, The Players, The Future* demonstrates this important point well and gives us a good grounding in this ongoing and growing global curse.

This book also conveys the equally valid point that the appellation of *terrorist* is essentially conferred upon specific criminals as a sort of added social stigma (not unduly) or term of derision. Increasingly though, new legislation is tending to establish terrorism offenses in their own right, a sort of new abstract or offshoot, somehow more deplorable than conventional criminality. But murder, bodily harm, conspiracy, explosives offenses, kidnapping and criminal damage, solidly remain criminal offenses, committed by criminals, with or without the title of terrorist.

On the historical aspects (and terrorist events pass most rapidly into history since they are, in these times, frequently superseded by even more violent, sophisticated or spectacular outrages), whatever or whoever you view as linked with or responsible for the proliferation of terrorism— whether it is the likes of Leila Khaled, the KGB, religion, World War I, Osama bin Laden or guerrilla warfare—you will surely find a reference to it in this book.

If written works on terrorism were infrequent until the 1970s, it was comparatively more rare, until recent times, to find any authored outside of the tranquil settings of a university or research institute. This book is clearly a considerable work and assembly of academic research, but importantly, it is constructed by highly experienced and accomplished law enforcement practitioners, who have collectively been involved themselves in some of the world's hot-spots on several continents. They are well able to write with authority—from the receiving end. There can be no substitute for first-hand experience in such matters and this shows through in the text. It is convincing, and written in the straightforward language style that police officers know so well; passionless, matter of fact, accurate and straight to the point.

Were my terrorism library to be confined to three volumes, I would opt for *Jane's Infantry Weapons, the Historical Dictionary of Terrorism,* and *Terrorism Today: The Past, The Players, The Future.*

I hope that you enjoy (and use) this book as much as I have.

Paul Medhurst, Ph.D.
Belvedere, Vienna

Paul Medhurst, a former UK police officer in Surrey and the London Metropolitan district first struck up an interest in terrorism at the 1980 Iranian Embassy Siege in Prince's Gate, London. In the British Army (TAVR), he lectured on improvised explosive devices and the detection of terrorists. Later serving with the UN in the Middle East, Africa and the Indian subcontinent. During the war in Angola he negotiated the release of a UN FAO staff member and himself from armed elements. He is currently a security official and terrorism expert in the United Nation, and teaches courses on terrorism for the American Military University.

Preface

When the authors decided to write the first edition of an introductory text about a subject as complex and rapidly changing as terrorism, it became a daunting task very quickly. The very concept of terrorism includes such a wide range of activities that the most difficult task became how to make a text short enough to be effective for instructors, casual readers and students, but long enough to convince colleagues, professionals and practitioners that it adequately covers an acceptable depth into this fascinating discipline. We must admit that at times it seemed like we were trying to paint a moving bus, with the players, organizations and operations changing faster than the words could be written down.

This second edition, which picks up where the first left off (a few months before 9–11, is also written in an admittedly broad-brush manner, re-examines where terrorism came from, where it is today, and where it seems to be going as we reel from the impact of 9–11, the War on Terrorism and the arrangement of new pieces on the world chessboard. This new world arrangement has need of new and specific countermeasures. The student will soon appreciate that there is no easy answer to the question, "What is terrorism?" It will become apparent, in the course of reading this new edition, that most terrorism actions are committed by poorly articulated groups of fanatics or dissidents, often with conflicting goals and little interface. Of course, there are exceptions to every rule. However, it will be shown that many of these groups are continuing their plans to upset security and safety in the United States and around the globe. The knowledge we have assembled will, it is hoped, stimulate students and others to seek out ways to offer better safety and security to all persons worldwide.

Your authors have attempted to provide a clear overview of many of the sectors and operations that comprise the broad terms terrorism and counterterrorism. We explore some specific subjects and locations in greater depth than others, reduce redundancy and cover as many differences and similarities as possible. The second edition is presented in the firm belief that any learning experience should be enjoyable as well as educational. For the instructor, we offer a text that has been organized and written with the goal of making the planning for teaching and the learning experience as interesting as possible, and effective at the same time. This is accomplished by covering the essentials of the subject and each chapter with a large array of pedagogical tools.

Security is an ancient need for humans, a basic rung on the ladder of Maslow's hierarchy of needs. But never, has America's—and all of mankind's—sense of security been so badly shaken as by the events of 9–11 and by escalating terrorist acts abroad and in the American homeland. As with most fields of human endeavor that are just now entering into an academic discipline, the available material presenting scientific theory, literature and research is not very extensive in the field of terrorism. The Information Age has provided most of the materials we have gathered for this introductory text. They have come from a large range of resources found on government sites on the Internet, along with articles, news clips and textbooks dealing with specific areas of interest. Much of the information and data are current, fresh as this morning's news, from diverse sources. We continue to challenge our colleagues in academia and in the operational security, law enforcement and the military to conduct the basic research, collect the data, and develop the theories that will help us transform terrorism into a true topic for academic development and practical knowledge for those who battle this 21st century scourge.

THE TRADITION CONTINUES

The methodology for textbook development, used successfully in the past for several other introductory texts, will continue to be the foundation for this one. It will build on the comments of readers, instructors and students to provide future editions of this text that work well for all three, such as:

- An engaging writing style, resulting in a book that is highly readable and effective as an informational, teaching and learning tool;
- A balanced treatment of practical examples, technology, history and data from available documents and academic research;
- An eye-pleasing design for easy reading, with features such as clearly understood examples of current and historical photographs, illustrations and other supplemental materials to augment the basic text;
- A systems approach to exploring the varied elements of terrorism, terrorists and the various motives for terrorist groups as a potentially integrated and interrelated series of subsystems;
- An unbiased presentation of a wide range of topics makes for a text suitable for instructors and students from many disciplines and points of view;
- In-chapter and end-of-chapter materials that augment the textual materials with examples of events, persons, stories, terms to remember, review questions and bibliographic suggestions for further reading;
- An Instructor's Manual that features test banks and other aids for the busy instructors, many whom are adjuncts who are tilling the fields of law enforcement, security or the military in a full-time capacity.

ORGANIZATION OF THE TEXT

This second edition is divided into three major parts and fourteen chapters that build from an historical background to predictions about the twenty-first century regarding terrorism. It should be noted that materials have been placed in the body of the text, such as "Terrorism Bytes," "Terrorism Briefs" and "Terrorism Players." And "Terms to Remember," "Review Questions," and extensive "Endnotes" have been placed at the end of each chapter, for their content and applicability to the subject matter being covered. These should be considered as important as the textual materials themselves for presentation and study. The materials selected come from the best and most current available sources in the field. Your authors choose to present them in their original form, or blend them into their own writing to minimize confusion.

PART ONE   THE DEFINING AND HISTORY OF TERRORISM

An in-depth historical look at terrorism and its origins, types and history will provide the student with a background necessary to understand the background of yesterday and the evolution of terrorism today.

Chapter 1   Defining Terrorism

This chapter will set the basic definitions for terminology used throughout following chapters and allow the student to understand and differentiate between terrorist acts and ordinary criminal acts. Defining issues, operational terms, useful typologies, as well as forms and tactics of terrorism will be explored. Terrorism as criminal behavior and its use as a method of action are covered. Such acts as ambush and assassination, arson, bombing, hijacking, hostage taking, kidnapping, blackmail and protection are included.

Chapter 2   A Brief History of Terrorism

In this rather short chapter, the act of violence can be described as a logical progression, but taking place in microseconds in a single individual. Violence perpetrated for ideological reasons and for a systematically promoted cause or complaint is shown to be much different. Pogroms by the Church, the Inquisition, the Holocaust, the PLO, the Phoenix Program, Tiananmen Square and guerrilla warfare are among the examples, which illustrate how individual terrorism can grow into a national or religious crusade. Also explored are the motives and methods employed by individual terrorists or groups with some perceived agenda as compared to the motives of a state for suppressing dissent and revolution. The reader/student is introduced to the concept of state-sponsored terrorism a concept that supports terrorist groups and individual terrorists with weapons, money and supplies to achieve their goals. From the Crusades to the frictions between religions around the world today, this section discusses how these got started and where they seem to be today.

PART TWO   TERRORISM AROUND THE WORLD

The reader/student will be brought up to the events of the twentieth and early twenty-first century in general terms leading to terrorism from both the left and right wings. The right wing factions of various countries and regions will be examined and discussed and the difference shown as to goals and objectives. The left wing factions of various countries and regions will be examined in a similar methodology and contrasted with the right wing's goals and the difference discovered as to goals and objectives. Regions and nations are covered in the investigation of terrorism its many different factions and their interrelationships.

Chapter 3   North America and the Caribbean

The reader/student examines the events leading up to 9–11 and the dots that were not connected to prevent that cataclysmic event and what has happened since. The kinds of terrorists and groups found in Canada are discussed, as is their conflict with their French and English origins. The general types of "home-grown" terrorism in the United States are examined and analyzed to see how they compare with those in other parts of the world of the world. The United States is shown to be no longer free from the violent terrorist actions plaguing the rest of the world thus far, but perhaps not for long. The peaceful and idyllic islands of the Caribbean and Cuba are shown to have been impacted by the drug terrorism trade and use as shipping stops.

Chapter 4   Great Britain and Northern Ireland

The background for the "Irish Problem" is detailed and brought up to date with examples of friction and terrorism on both sides of the issues. This long chapter provides a model for the student in examining the other terror spots of the world. It shows similarities and differences in the use of terrorism in meeting political or religious goals. Ireland and Mainland Britain have been embroiled in the violence of terrorism for more than three decades and the current political processes and the methods employed to reach a solution to the violence are examined. The concern of security forces and the export of terror knowledge to other international terror groups is also discussed.

Chapter 5   Western Europe

The French have used or supported terrorist acts and the student will see that the Germans thrived on terrorism and were led into blind obedience and violence many times. Use of terrorism by the Mafia and Mussolini's fascist thugs shows the changing political patterns of the Italians over the centuries. The turbulent history of Spain from the Inquisition to the fascist reign of terror under Franco is examined, along with the many terrorist activities in Spain, especially those of the Basque separatists. In the twenty-first century Europe is now seen as the target for international terror cells plotting and planning mayhem in other regions as well as their adopted homes.

Chapter 6   Eastern Europe and the Balkans

The sad history of the multiracial, multireligious region formerly known as Yugoslavia is examined from the partisan terrorism and German terrorism in WW II to the divided state that has seen constant interracial and interreligious fighting since its breakup. Terrorism and even genocide will be shown to be main weapons in these battles for ethnic purity. The Russians are examined as having a long history of national terrorism to keep the populace under control, from the Czars to the Soviet Union and the murders of fifty million countrymen by Stalin. Chechnya after the fall of the Soviet Union is shown to be continuing to use tactics of terror.

Chapter 7   North Africa and the Middle East

An examination of an area of the world where terror is the primary weapon in local and international conflicts gives the student the "big picture." Slowly we realize that the conflicts are all similar in that troubled region and that terror is the primary weapon used by either side. The 3000-year battle between the Jews, Christians and Arabs remains to be seen as the hotbed of terrorism and is covered in detail as to the problems faced in this ancient feud for land and minds. Algeria, Libya, Egypt and other hot spots of state sponsored and religious terrorism are covered as well.

Chapter 8   The Persian Gulf

The Persian Gulf states have been involved active warfare or constant terrorism, (religious or political). This most valuable source of the world's petroleum remains a hot bed of violence and terrorism today. The persecution of the Kurds in Iraq, the use of oil revenue to sponsor worldwide terrorism and use the constant threat of the use of nuclear, biological, and chemical weapons stir the pot of terrorism in this area. The Gulf War and Saddam Hussien's constant tricks keep the pot boiling. Efforts to unseat Saddam are shown to lead to another crisis in the Gulf. The struggles for prominence among the states that ring the Persian Gulf are examined in some detail.

Chapter 9   Northeast, Central and Southern Africa

From the long struggle for freedom from apartheid in South Africa to a quite different struggle in Zimbabwe, the Dark Continent is shown to have suffered many trials. The genocide in the Congo, Uganda and Rwanda is explored, as well as the tribalism that divides most regions. The threat of right-wing directed warfare against the new black governments is shown to be a new and escalating problem. The great potential of this region, though it has gigantic problems as well, makes its nations the hope for the future.

Chapter 10   Southern and Southeast Asia

India has a long history of terrorist tactics, as well as nuclear weapons. The war against the British imperial rule taught them that terrorism works. Following independence, India has had to fight many terrorism attacks from religious factions and from rebel causes. Pakistan and India have a longstanding state of war and the Punjab has used terrorism to try to gain independence from India. Afghanistan, the first battlefield of the post-9-11 War on Terrorism is also reexamined. Sri Lanka, formerly Ceylon, has suffered a long and ongoing war of terrorism by the Timal Tigers and other splinter groups, so peace remains far from certain. The terrorism used by the rest of the world is found in many parts of Southeast Asia, and the local conflicts, religious and ideological, seem to echo the themes seen elsewhere on the globe. From the Khymer Rouge in Cambodia to the guerilla fighters in the jungles of Malaysia and Indonesia, terrorism has found a long-term home in Southeast Asia.

Chapter 11   The Pacific Rim

China is shown to have moved past the terror-filled period following the ascension of communism. Terror as a philosophy can be traced back in Chinese history as a viable means to control that vast nation. From the "Huks" (Hukbalahaps), who fought against the Philippine government at the turn of the 20th century, then fought against the Japanese as U.S.-supported Filipino guerillas in World War II and the Japanese occupation, on to the terrorist tactics of the Marcos regime, the history of the Philippines has also shown that terror can be a useful tool in controlling a large and poor country. Japan has been stricken with fanatical terrorism that extends back into history through the occupation of China and the Pacific islands in World War II on up to use of chemical terrorism in the present. Indonesia and Malaysia are shown to have many terrorist groups.

Chapter 12   Latin America

The so-called "banana republics" have suffered with long struggles using terrorism against the people by repressive dictators, as well as terrorism against the governments by rebel causes. Major conflicts are examined in terms of past history and present status. The roles of Mexico and Cuba in these struggles are pointed out to the student. The "other America" is shown to have been rife with terrorist activities for a long time, from the Shining Path of Peru to the "disappeared" in Brazil and Argentina. The drug cartels in Colombia, as well as political upheavals, have shown this region to be very violent and dangerous as suppressive governments invite terrorist organizations to emerge. Mexico is shown to have a long history of terrorism and revolution.

PART THREE   COUNTERTERRORISM

This final part will discuss the kinds of efforts being expended around the world to find ways to deter or discover terrorism and find other ways to deal with it. The final chapter will examine what the future of terrorism might be.

Chapter 13   Countering Terrorism Around the World

Efforts, political and operational, are examined to determine which are effective and which have failed. These range from national paramilitary groups to local activities by regular citizens. The importance of intelligence gathering, the cycle of intelligence, and the proper uses of intelligence against terrorism are studied in detail. The threats to aviation from acts of terror along with maritime piracy will be discussed. Worldwide types of antiterrorist groups and strategies are examined, from the Delta Force in the United States, to the Mossad in Israel, the Special Action Squads in the United Kingdom and many other highly organized and effective agencies. The strategies of the United Nations and regional governments are discussed and analyzed as to their success or failure.

Chapter 14   Terrorism in the Twenty-First Century

The authors will make an attempt to predict the most likely spots where the pressure from terrorism will be found at the start of the twenty-first century, and what possible effects the War on Terrorism will have in the future. This will include looking at the possible and probable threat from Weapons of Mass Destruction (WMD).

ACKNOWLEDGMENTS

How do authors begin to acknowledge those persons whose support, encouragement, assistance and belief in our dream have allowed us to develop, refine, and produce a second edition of a book that attempts to cover an almost encyclopedic, worldwide view of terrorism? To try to acknowledge each of them individually would take several pages and we shudder to think we might miss some of them. The list begins with our families and close personal friends, then our colleagues and international friends in academia, as well as professionals and practitioners in terrorism at the international, federal, state and local levels. Perhaps most important were the efforts of Dr. Paul Medhurst, who was kind enough to review our work and then write for us a wonderful Foreword. Our friend Jaffar Siddiqui provided a point of view that kept us well aware of when we were clearly too far one way or the other. Jaffar even helped by sharing some of his own writings that exemplified how to balance a discussion of blame calling. To each of them and the rest of you we extend our deepest appreciation and gratitude for encouraging and assisting us in putting together a text about this important topic that seems to work.

We would, however, like to single out a few of the special people at Prentice Hall, who helped the authors turn their prose, ideas and concepts for a book about terrorism into a textbook that will greatly assist the users, professors and students alike. First, our senior editor, Frank Mortimer, gets kudos for allowing us to write, and leading us through, this second edition with minimal problems and a lot of positive support. Frank fought for our ideas and listened to our suggestions to use new concepts and techniques, rather than just staying with the status quo. Sarah Holle, our coordinating editor, gets an especially big "thank you." She was a calm in the storm of book writing and got us through the rapids of production in fine style. John Shannon, our production editor, was a calm and professional center in the midst of what could have become a frantic effort to stay on schedule.

The authors also wish to thank the following reviewers: Joe Goldberg, Industrial College of the Armed Forces, Washington, DC; Paul Medhurst, American Military University, Vienna, Austria; Andrew Silke, University of Leicester, Leicester, Great Britain; and Albert Sproule, De Sales University, Center Valley, PA;

We also must offer continuing thanks to the last, but by far not the least, of those who provided support and solace . . . our wives Fran and Esther, and our families, friends and relatives. Special thanks to Glenn Ross for his invaluable support and advice. While they will enjoy with us whatever modest success we may garner with this text, they have also had to put up with the periodic absences and the frequent bouts of frenzied revisions and changes . . . often from long distances on e-mail. His employer, in Jeremy's case, and his clients, in Cliff's case, have been extremely supportive and understanding; thank you, too. We have found out that writing can be a lonely task, especially when it involves such a specific and rapidly changing field, it is often not easy to discuss with anyone else in the frantic throes of creation and revision. We deeply appreciate the understanding and support we have gotten over the past periods of hard work and love you all for understanding and caring.

About the Authors

Jeremy R. Spindlove

Jeremy Spindlove is presently the Regional Director in Loss Prevention, Health and Safety, for a world leader in third party logistics management. He has spent more than thirty-five years in both policing and private sector security operations and administration on an international scale. During his police service in Great Britain he was the first officer on the scene of the IRA bombing of the Horse and Groom Pub in Guildford. During his service as an aviation security expert with British Airways he was assigned to trouble spots in Europe, North Africa and the Middle East, spending two years in Baghdad at the start of the Iran-Iraq war. He also spent several months in Beirut during the Israeli invasion of Southern Lebanon, and saw further duty in Amman, Jordan. He has served as Director of Security at the Vancouver International Airport, Canada; and has written and presented many papers on terrorism and aviation security, and presented a seminar on aviation security to the International Aviation Management Institute at the University of British Columbia; and at the governor of the state of Washington's Annual Conference on Security. He has authored a contributory text on victims of terrorism, titled *Victimology—A Study of Crime Victims and Their Roles,* edited by Judith M Scarzi and Jack McDevitt. He is an active member of the American Society for Industrial Security. Jeremy Spindlove is pleased to have been able to co-author with Professor Simonsen this, the second edition of Terrorism Today, and to have experienced the unique blend of his writing talent with his own personal experiences.

Clifford E. Simonsen, Ph.D., CPP

Presently the President of Criminology Consultants International, Clifford Simonsen has more than forty years of experience in criminal justice, security and law enforcement. As a career Army officer, he retired as a Military Police Colonel. His background includes a Ph.D. in Public Administration, (with an emphasis on criminal justice administration and deviance) from Ohio State University, and a Master's in Criminology from Florida State University. He is also a graduate of the Army War College and the Industrial College of the Armed Forces. Dr. Simonsen is the author of dozens of articles on the fields of crime, criminal justice, delinquency and security and is the author or co-author of several texts in a broad range of disciplines. These include Corrections in America: An Introduction (10th ed.), Juvenile Justice in America (4th ed.), and Private Security in America and Security Administration. Dr. Simonsen has taught at several universities, both full-time and as an adjunct. He is a lifetime member of the American Society for Industrial Security (and a Lifetime Certified Protection Professional). He also belongs to the American Correctional Association, the Academy of Criminal Justice Sciences and the International Association of Professional Security Consultants. Dr. Simonsen is pleased to be co-authoring this second edition with Jeremy Spindlove and sharing in his depth of experience with terrorism on both a local and international scale.

PART ONE
The Defining and History of Terrorism

A young Palestinian stone thrower confronts an Israeli tank at the Karn Crossing Point between Israel and the Gaza Strip. (AP Photo/Laurent Rebours)

1 Defining Terrorism

"Kill one, frighten one thousand."

Sun Tzu

OVERVIEW

Since the events of 9–11, terrorism, if only used as a "bogeyman" phrase, has a constant impact on the processes of major governments and the lives of common people worldwide. Like the sword of Damocles, the threat hangs over all of us everywhere, from the way we conduct our personal lives to the way corporations transact their business, even including the conduct of national and foreign affairs between governments. Fear of terrorism has spawned a massive security industry aimed at protecting individuals, tourists, travelers, institutions and industries. The specter of doom has required the expenditure of huge sums of money to protect us from the threat of dangers by those mysterious arch-criminals we call "terrorists." Since the horrific attacks of 9–11, this threat has become acutely real to citizens of the United States and their allies and friends. In order to travel, especially by air, this threat has forced large delays and drastic changes in our planning, scheduling, security measures and timing for a trip, most markedly for a trip abroad. The television, print and radio news media, both legitimate publications and tabloids, happily respond and immediately inform and frighten us about horrible terrorist acts from around the globe.

Who is this larger than life creature that we call a "terrorist?" What are terrorist acts? Can we protect ourselves against them? How do we define this activity we casually refer to as "terrorism?" Combs discusses this problem:

> ". . . terrorism is a political as well as a legal and a military issue, its definition in modern terms has been slow to evolve. Not that there are not numerous definitions available—there are hundreds. But few of them are of sufficient legal scholarship to be useful in international law, and most of those which are legally useful lack the necessary ambiguity for political acceptance."[1]

The task of trying to define terrorism or terrorist behavior is difficult, but not impossible. The term must be carefully constructed so that it projects the meaning intended. A **terrorist incident** is any violent act that can become a broader threat as the purpose and intention for it becomes better known. What it is, and is not, called hinges on a commonly understood meaning of the term "terrorism." This chapter will lay a foundation that will assist the student throughout the rest of this text.

The student/reader is about to embark upon a journey into the fascinating phenomena of terrorism and terrorists. In order to understand these con-

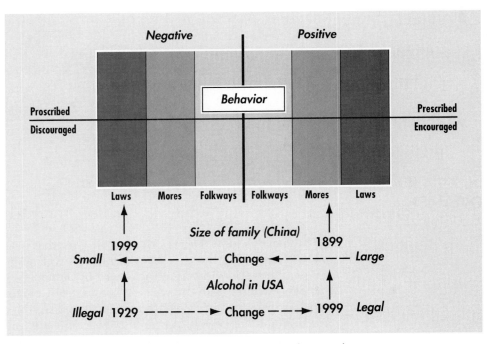

Behaviour changes along the continuum over time, and as conditions vary.

cepts, we must explore together the historical context and specific rules society has developed as a factor in defining the use of criminal and antisocial acts to meet political or social goals. Behavior in social groups, whether they are primitive tribes or complex modern nation-states, can be regarded as points on a simple continuum, as shown in the above figure.

In even the most primitive societies, certain acts or groups of acts have been universally forbidden, discouraged, or **proscribed**. Such acts include murder, rape, incest, kidnapping and treason (or some form of rebellion affecting the social group's safety and authority). By contrast, most societies have encouraged, sponsored, or **prescribed** other behaviors such as having children, marrying, hunting, growing food, and other actions that benefit the common social welfare.

Terrorism often falls into the range of behaviors that are not only violation of **laws,** but violation of the politics and practices **(mores)** of a social group or an organization. Often the violation of codified law requires that a person must call a public safety officer to effect an arrest. All of these aspects are related to the ways that social groups or subcultures chose to respond to transgressions.

TERRORISM: SEARCHING FOR A DEFINITION

It is easy to use the terms "terror," "terrorism" and "terrorist" about acts that shock the senses of reasonable people. The **Reign of Terror** *(Regime de la Terreur),* that took place in France from 1792–1794, has been accepted by most as the first general use of the term terrorism. During that bloody revolution, those who resisted faced arrest, imprisonment and death by guillotine. Most of these actions were without the benefit of trials or legal procedure. Brutal members of the revolutionary group took efforts to eliminate every possible threat to their revolution, eventually seeking out those with even moderate to mild opposition to their cause. Those who considered themselves as possible targets of the revolutionaries finally decided to take counteraction for their self-preservation. On July 27, 1794, members of the Jacobin dissenters murdered Robespierre and his council of supporters. The Reign of Terror, in which over 400,000 "suspects" (including children and women) had been imprisoned, hanged, and guillotined, came to an end. But the seminal concepts of terror tactics as a part of political strategy grew out of these bloody episodes.

From this devastating beginning, terrorism and terrorist acts became defined as the systematic application of violence to establish and maintain a new political or religious system. Such a definition may be difficult to use today, primarily because it fails to separate terrorism from other acts of aggression that use terror as only a small component, not the primary objective of such aggressive behavior.

For example, terror in conventional warfare between nation-states is a natural by-product of the violence and confusion of combat. Military objectives are chosen in order to effect the quickest elimination of the enemy force and the destruction or disruptions of its command, control, communication, support and supply networks. Victory is decided by force of numbers, skill at arms, weapons superiority, strategy and tactics, or a combination thereof. Terror is not intended to be the primary factor in such military actions.

Those soldiers (in war) or citizens frightened into surrender or compliance, but not physically injured, are the real targets of terrorism. Other casualties are easily classified according to the way they were injured or killed. Rosie offers a tentative definition of terrorism for consideration:

"The use and/or threat of repeated violence in support of or in opposition to some authority, where violence is employed to induce fear of similar attack in as many non-immediate victims as possible so that those so threatened accept and comply with the demands of the terrorists."[2]

Within this wordy, but necessarily so, definition we can perhaps work out a methodology for describing the behaviors of terrorists acting from a variety of motives. At the same time, this definition remains neutral with regard to the great variety of individual traits that characterize particular groups. This definition can be applied to political terrorism, revolutionary terrorism, state terrorism, religious terrorism, and others. It eliminates the need for suggesting a particular type of motivation as part of the definition of terrorism and the temptation to infer that all terrorism is politically motivated.

The modern-day **assassin** is today's suicide bomber, or the shooter of doctors and staff at an abortion clinic, or acts calculated to induce fear and anxiety in a wide number of people, a far larger number than those likely to be injured by the acts themselves. The perpetrators of the act believe that such means can coerce a larger group into abandoning certain commercial practices or medical procedures that are the root cause of the acts. These are most definitely acts of terrorism, but are not necessarily considered politically motivated in the larger sense.

This definition of terrorism also excludes acts of violence in which the terror component is incidental or secondary to some other primary objective.

The death of the owner of a major logging company may be the goal of extremists that wish to eliminate his voice or his particular quality of leadership. Or the owner could be about to influence some item of legislation that is opposed to the extremist group's goals. The fear generated by the killing is of secondary importance to the actual silencing of that individual. This act should be labeled "murder" or "assassination," rather than terrorism. If the extremist group that killed this leader were also to issue a statement of demands, however, and threaten that more industrialists and even private citizens would be attacked if demands were not met, then it would be fair to refer to such a group as terrorists.

It is clear that labeling a person or a group as terrorist does not preclude also categorizing that same person as a "madman," "guerrilla," "ideologue," or "revolutionary."

After all, a grocer who plays baseball on weekends can be referred to as a "baseball player," but he has not, however, stopped being a "grocer." Members of the IRA (Irish Republican Army), PLO (Palestine Liberation Organization), or ETA (Euzkadi Ta Azkatasuna) may be seen as **freedom fighters** to their subgroup of the political system. But, to others in the system, they remain "terrorists." Clearly, without some recourse to established definitional parameters, such labels are purely a matter of value judgment. If the person making the judgment does not agree with the objectives of the group using such methods to gain some goal they will be called (with very few exceptions) "terrorists." The group thus categorized immediately denies this, of course, and calls itself a "national liberation army," a "workers army," or similar term. The overwhelming conclusion is that a terrorist group has no legitimacy, and therefore its aims have no validity. The label of "terrorist" then becomes a term of derision, and thus obscures whatever legitimate complaints the group may have.

In order to understand the phenomenon of terrorism, one must always assess the divergent views of what exactly constitutes terrorism and the "definition in use." Reaching a general consensus on the definition of terrorism has generated many debates in the social sciences. It is clear that no single definition seems to satisfy.

Terrorism is a special type of violence. It is a tactic used in peace, conflict and war. The threat of terrorism is ever present, and an attack such as 9–11 is likely to occur when least expected. A terrorist attack, like 9–11, as happened, may be the event that marks the transition from peace to conflict, or war. Combating terrorism is a factor to consider in all military plans and operations. Combating terrorism requires a continuous state of awareness; it is a necessary practice rather than a type of military operation. Terrorism is a criminal offense under nearly every national or international legal code. With few exceptions, acts of terrorism are forbidden in war as they are in times of peace.[3]

SOME APPROACHES TO DEFINING TERRORISM

In addition to the definitions used above, the following are some samples of the diverse definitions used to describe terrorism:

Simple: Violence or threatened violence intended to produce fear or change

Legal: Criminal violence violating legal codes and punishable by the state

Analytical: Specific political and social factors behind individual violent acts

State-sponsored: National or other groups used to attack Western or other interests

State: Power of the government used to repress its people to the point of submission[4]

In his book, *Political Terrorism* (1983), Alex Schmid surveyed 100 scholars and experts in the field and asked for a definition of terrorism. This analysis found two characteristics of the definition: first, an individual being threatened and second, the terrorist act meaning is derived from the choice of target and victims. Schmid's analysis concluded that the following elements are common throughout the 100 definitions surveyed as follows:

- Terrorism is an abstract concept with no essence.
- A single definition cannot account for all the possible uses of the term.
- Many different definitions share common elements.
- The meaning of terrorism derives from the victim or target.[5]

The perpetrators of terrorism may truly believe their cause to be altruistic and serving for the betterment of society. Bruce Hoffman in his work *Inside Terrorism* (1998) states that the terrorist is fundamentally a violent intellectual, prepared to use—and indeed committed to using—force in the attainment of his goals. Hoffman also adds that by distinguishing terrorists from other types of criminals and terrorism from other forms of crime, we come to appreciate that terrorism is:

- Ineluctably political in aims and motives;
- Violent . . . or, equally important, threatens violence;
- Designed to have far-reaching psychological repercussions beyond the immediate victim or target;
- Conducted by an organization with an identifiable chain of command or conspiratorial cell structure (whose members wear no uniform or identifying insignia);
- Perpetrated by a sub-national group or non-state entity.[6]

Once we accept that terrorism is simply a means to an end—nothing more and nothing less—we can apply the term without the inclusion of moral beliefs and sociological-political mumbo-jumbo. The operatives of the PLO are terrorists. But that fact, standing alone, does not mean that their aims and objectives are without some validity. Members of the IRA can be described as freedom fighters, but they must also accept that they are terrorists in their methods of reaching that goal.

It is often easier for one to perceive a long-established, freely elected (even dictatorial, religious, or royalist) regime as "legitimate," than it is to accept that a handful of individuals with views significantly different from those of the majority might deserve the same classification. This is especially so if the methods used by the handful of individuals provoke moral indignation by being horrific actions against a sanctioned "legitimate" target, such as the government. When an indiscriminate "enemy" label is applied to those not actually supportive of a dissenting aggressor's objective, the situation becomes far more disturbing. More so, because the aggressors frequently use violence as a means to their ends. Wearing no uniforms to indicate their presence, they employ weapons that they need not personally fire or activate (mail bombs, car bombs, time bombs, etc.) or unknown aggressors killing unknown victims for reasons that are seldom made clear until after the event.

There will always be some bottom-line considerations, of course, even when the targets are **"acceptable enemies"** in the eyes of many onlookers. Violence against former Soviet-backed regimes, for example, finds more favor among Western observers, even when such strikes are easily defined as terrorist actions. But if the nature of the assault transgresses certain unwritten but widely accepted boundaries of decency or fair play, then condemnation is applied. The downing of a Russian helicopter gunship by elements of Chechen rebels, for example, is more likely to be interpreted (except by supporters of the Russians) as acceptable than the downing of a civilian airliner by the PLO. The deliberate slaughter of armed soldiers in an ambush is more easily accepted than is the slaughter of small children. In descending order, fair game for terrorists or dissenters might be depicted as follows:

1. Military personnel;
2. Government officials;
3. Civilians unconnected in any way with the continuance of the policy against which the terrorist is fighting.

This same attenuated sample list might constitute the basis of a target selection for almost any military offensive. On the other hand, an actual terrorist group would consider the following order to be more appropriate for maximum impact:

1. Civilians unconnected in any way with the continuance of the policy against which the group is fighting;
2. Government officials;
3. Military personnel.

This seemingly illogical order is very logical for terrorism, because maximum fear and anxiety can be generated by attacks against noncombatants. This prioritizing demonstrates to the populace as a whole that the targeted regime is unable to protect them. Such actions are generally a far safer technique for the terrorist group than trying to prove that the regime cannot protect itself. Terror groups will choose outrage and cause revulsion in its target audience in order to maintain the required level of terror and anger against the government.

We should now have a basis for understanding that, while strategies incorporating acts of terrorism in the past centuries have changed somewhat in delivery and methods, the primary purposes of terrorist acts have generally remained constant:

• To bring attention to a perceived grievance or cause by some act or acts that are shocking and attention-getting;

- To use the media by attracting coverage of such acts in order to get the widest possible dissemination of the message;
- To contain reaction by the public at large through fear and intimidation;
- To coerce change and destabilize opponents through the threat of further and continued such acts until the grievances or causes are recognized and acted upon.

Jenkins argued a quarter of a century ago that, ". . . terrorism is theatre; therefore terrorists do not want a lot of people dead . . . they want a lot of people watching and listening."[7] This watching and listening has ranged over the centuries from a few villagers who stood by while terrorists acted or gave their speeches to instant and live television coverage by one of the major networks of the most vile acts, piped into millions of homes. It is seldom that one hears of the barbarous acts committed in Third-World countries on the evening news in other than a passing sound bite. But, let a few thugs take over an airliner from a developed country and the media flock to stand and listen to the demands of the terrorists and broadcast them around the globe. This chapter begins our study of this thing we call "terrorism" and examines the difficulty in deciding just what that means. George Rosie highlights this difficulty:

> Terrorism is a complex, multifaceted, and often baffling subject. The organizations involved have a way of emerging, splintering, disappearing and then reappearing, which makes it very difficult for the average reader to follow. Individuals come and go, are jailed, die, go underground, or apparently vanish. Counter-terror bureaucracies are formed then reformed, names are changed, and leaders are shuffled around as they are promoted, demoted, forced to resign, or put out to pasture. Incidents proliferate across the world, some of which can trigger off a chain of events that will destabilize a whole region and bring nations to the edge of ruin. At the same time major terrorist actions can shock for a short while, and then be quickly forgotten (except by those affected by the inevitable tragedy). Treatises are written, theories propounded, grievances aired, tactics discussed, occasionally to some effect, usually not. Causes are picked up by the world's media, examined, probed, and then all too often overlooked, until the next bomb explodes, or the next airliner is hijacked.[8]

We continue our examination of what terrorism is with a few more commonly used definitions. Acts of terrorism conjure emotional responses in the victims (those hurt by the violence and those affected by the fear) as well as in the practitioners. Even the U.S. Government cannot agree on one single definition. Listed below are a few more common definitions of terrorism:

- Terrorism is the use or threatened use of force designed to bring about political change.—Brian Jenkins
- Terrorism constitutes the illegitimate use of force to achieve a political objective when innocent people are targeted.—Walter Laqueur
- Terrorism is the premeditated, deliberate, systematic murder, mayhem, and threatening of the innocent to create fear and intimidation in order to gain a political or tactical advantage, usually to influence an audience.—James M. Poland

- Terrorism is the unlawful use or threat of violence against persons or property to further political or social objectives. It is usually intended to intimidate or coerce a government, individuals or groups, or to modify their behavior or politics.—U.S. Vice-President's Task Force, 1986
- Terrorism is the unlawful use of force or violence against persons or property to intimidate or coerce a government, the civilian population, or any segment thereof, in furtherance of political or social objectives.—FBI definition
- The calculated use of violence or the threat of violence to inculcate fear; intended to coerce or to intimidate governments or societies in the pursuit of goals that are generally political, religious, or ideological–Department of Defense definition.[9]

THE FBI CONSTRUCT

The FBI seems to have developed a very **useful construct** of what is to be considered as terrorism in the United States. This issue concerns foreign power-sponsored or foreign power-coordinated activities that:

a. Involve violent acts, dangerous to human life, that are a violation of the criminal laws of the United States or of any state, or that would be a criminal violation if committed within the jurisdiction of the United States or any state;

b. Appear to be intended to:
   - Intimidate or coerce a civilian population;
   - Influence the policy of a government by intimidation or coercion;
   - Effect the conduct of a government by assassination or kidnapping.

c. Occur totally outside the United States or transcend national boundaries in terms of the means by which they are accomplished, the persons they appear intended to coerce or intimidate, or the locale in which their perpetrators operate or seek asylum.

Investigating acts of terrorism overseas includes interviewing victims, collecting forensic evidence, and apprehending terrorist fugitives. The FBI coordinates all overseas investigations with the U.S. Department of State and the host foreign government.[10]

THE U.S. DEPARTMENT OF DEFENSE (DOD) CONSTRUCT

Terrorism, as defined by the DOD, is normally considered to be calculated. The selection of a target is planned and rational. The perpetrators know the effect they seek. Terrorist violence is neither spontaneous nor random. Terrorism is intended to produce fear in someone other than the victim. In other words, terrorism is a psychological act conducted for its impact on an audience. It is abundantly clear that the attack on 9–11 was calculated and that the terrorists knew what they were doing, but the impact caused the opposite and awakened a sleeping giant.

The DOD definition, noted earlier, also addresses goals. Terrorism may be motivated by political, religious, or ideological objectives. In a sense, terrorist goals are always political, as extremists driven by religious or ideological be-liefs usually seek political power to compel society to conform to their views. The objectives of terrorism distinguish it from other violent acts aimed at per-sonal gain, such as criminal violence. However, the definition permits includ-ing violence by organized crime when it seeks to influence government policy. Some drug cartels and other international criminal organizations engage in po-litical action when their activities influence governmental functioning. The essence of terrorism is the intent to induce fear in someone other than its di-rect victims in order to make a government or other audience change its politi-cal behavior.

Terrorism is common practice in insurgencies, but insurgents are not necessarily terrorists if they comply with the rules of war and do not engage in forms of violence identified as terrorist acts. While the legal distinction is clear, it rarely inhibits terrorists who convince themselves that their actions are justified by a **higher law.** Their single-minded dedication to a goal, how-ever poorly it may be articulated, renders legal sanctions relatively ineffective. In contrast, war is subject to rules of international law. Terrorists recognize no rules. No person, place, or object of value is immune from terrorist attack. There are no innocents.

The development of bureaucratic states led to a profound change in ter-rorism. Modern democratic governments have continuity that older, charis-matic, royal or inherited governments did not. Terrorists found that the death of a single individual, even a monarch, did not necessarily produce the policy changes they sought. Terrorists reacted by turning to an indirect method of at-tack. By the early twentieth century, terrorists began to attack people previ-ously considered innocents to generate political pressure. These indirect attacks create a public atmosphere of anxiety and undermine confidence in government. Their unpredictability and apparent randomness make it virtu-ally impossible for governments to protect all potential victims. The public demands protection that the state cannot give. Frustrated and fearful, the peo-ple then demand that the government make concessions to stop the attacks.

Modern terrorism behavior and philosophy offers its practitioners many advantages. First, by not recognizing innocents, terrorists have an infinite number of targets. They select their target and determine when, where, and how to attack. The range of choices gives terrorists a high probability of suc-cess with minimum risk. If the attack goes wrong or fails to produce the in-tended results, the terrorists can deny responsibility.

Ironically, as democratic governments become more common, it may be easier for terrorists to operate. The terrorist bombings of the World Trade Cen-ter in New York City, the Oklahoma City Federal Building, the U.S. embassies bombed in Kenya and Tanzania, and the USS Cole in Yemen, leading up to the attacks of 9–11, proved how easy it is for terrorists to operate in a free or de-mocratic world. Authoritarian governments whose populace may have a better reason to revolt may also be less constrained by requirements for due process and impartial justice when combating terrorists.

As national leaders and politicians address terrorism, they must consider several relevant characteristics. First, anyone can be a victim. (Some terrorists may still operate under cultural restraints, such as a desire to avoid harming women, but essentially, there are no innocents these days.) Second, attacks that may appear to be senseless and random are not. To the perpetrators, their attacks make perfect sense. Acts such as suicide bombing in public places of assembly, and shooting into crowded restaurants heighten public anxiety. This is the terrorists' immediate objective. Third, the terrorist needs to publicize his attack. If no one knows about it, it will not produce fear. The need for publicity often drives target selection; the greater the symbolic value of the target, the more publicity the attack brings to the terrorists and the more fear it generates. The media often provide the notoriety, inadvertently, wanted by the terrorists, just by covering the event.

Finally, a leader planning for combating terrorism must understand that he cannot protect every possible target all the time. He must also understand that terrorists will likely shift from more protected targets to less protected ones. This is the key to defensive measures.[11]

MOTIVATIONS FOR TERRORISTS

Terrorists are inspired by many different motives. One could classify them into three categories: rational, psychological, and cultural. Many combinations and variations of these factors may shape a terrorist. Rational terrorists think through their goals and options, making a cost-benefit analysis. They seek to determine whether there are less costly or more effective ways to achieve their individual or group objectives other than terrorism. To assess the risk, they weigh the target's defensive capabilities against their own capabilities to attack. They measure the group's capabilities to sustain the effort. The essential question is whether terrorism will work for the desired purpose, given societal conditions at the time. The terrorist's rational analysis is similar to that of a military commander or a business entrepreneur considering available resources and courses of action. Groups considering terrorism as an option ask a crucial question; can terrorism induce enough anxiety to attain their goals without causing a backlash that will destroy the cause and perhaps the terrorists themselves? To misjudge the answer is to risk disaster. In the case of the attacks of 9–11, it generated a backlash now known as the "War on Terrorism."

Psychological motivation for resorting to terrorism derives from the terrorist's personal dissatisfaction with his/her life and accomplishments. This individual finds a reason to be involved in dedicated terrorist action. Although no clear psychopathy is found among terrorists, there is a nearly universal element in them that can be described as the "true believer." Terrorists do not even consider that they may be wrong and that others' views may have some merit. Terrorists tend to project their own antisocial motivations onto others, creating a polarized "us versus them" outlook. They attribute only evil motives to anyone outside their own group. This enables the terrorists to dehumanize their victims and removes any sense of ambiguity from their minds. The resulting clarity of purpose appeals to those who crave violence to relieve their constant anger. The other common characteristic of the psychologically motivated terrorist is the pronounced need to belong to a group. With some terrorists, group acceptance is a stronger motivator than the stated political objectives of the organization. Such individuals define their social status by group acceptance.

Terrorist groups with strong internal motivations find it necessary to justify the group's existence continuously. A terrorist group must, as a minimum, commit violent acts to maintain group self-esteem and legitimacy. Another result of psychological motivation is the intensity of group dynamics among terrorists. They tend to demand unanimity and be intolerant of dissent. With the enemy clearly identified and unequivocally evil, pressure to escalate the frequency and intensity of operations is ever present. The need to belong to the group discourages resignations, and the fear of compromise disallows their acceptance. Compromise is rejected, and terrorist groups lean toward inflexible positions. Having placed themselves beyond the pale, forever unacceptable to ordinary society, they cannot accept compromise. They consider negotiation dishonorable, if not treasonous.

Such dynamics also make any announced group goal nearly impossible to achieve. By definition, a group that achieves its stated purpose is no longer needed. As a result, success threatens the psychological well-being of its members. Therefore, when a terrorist group approaches its stated goal, it is inclined to redefine it. The group may reject the achievement as false or inadequate or the result of the duplicity of "them." Terrorist groups often suffer from fear of success. One effective psychological defense against success is to define goals so broadly that they are impossible to achieve. Even if the world proclaims the success of a political movement, the terrorists can deny it and fight on.

Cultural concepts also shape values and motivate people to actions that seem unreasonable to foreign observers. For example, Americans are generally reluctant to appreciate the intense effect that cultural factors have on behavior. They accept the myth that rational behavior guides all human actions. It is easy to reject as unbelievable such things as vendettas, martyrdom, and self-destructive group behavior when they observe them in others. There is disbelief that such things as the destruction of a viable state can be done for the sake of ethnic purity, especially when the resulting mini-states become economically unstable.

The treatment of life in general and individual life in particular is a cultural characteristic that has a tremendous impact on terrorism. In societies in which people identify themselves in terms of group membership (family, clan and tribe), there may be willingness to accept self-sacrifice seldom seen elsewhere. At times, terrorists seem to be eager to give their lives for their organization and cause. The lives of "others," even strangers who they perceive as being wholly evil in the terrorists' value system, can therefore be taken without remorse. Other factors include the manner in which aggression is channeled and the concepts of social organization. For example, the political structure and its provisions for power transfer shape and level of violence. In some political systems there is effective nonviolent means for the succession to power. A culture may have a high tolerance for nonpolitical violence, such as banditry or ethnic turf battles, and remain relatively free of political violence. The United States, for example, is one of the most violent societies in the world, yet political violence remains a rare aberration. By contrast, both France and Germany, with low tolerance for violent crime, have long histories of political violence.

A major cultural determinate of terrorism is the perception of "outsiders" and anticipation of their threat to ethnic group survival. Fear of cultural dilution or extermination leads to violence that, to someone who has not experienced it, seems irrational. All human beings are sensitive to threats to their values and beliefs, which they identify themselves. These include language, religion, group membership, and homeland or tribal territory. The possibility of losing any of these can trigger defensive, even xenophobic, reactions.

Religion may be the most volatile of cultural identifiers, because it encompasses values and beliefs deeply rooted in a cultural paradigm. A threat to one's religion puts not only the present at risk but also one's entire cultural past and future. Many religions, including Christianity and Islam, are so confident they are right that they have often used force to make converts or to eliminate nonbelievers. Terrorism in the name of religion can be especially violent and is discussed next in Chapter 2. Like all terrorists, those who are religiously motivated view their acts with moral certainty and even divine sanctions. What would otherwise be extraordinary acts of desperation becomes a religious duty in the mind of the religiously motivated terrorist. This helps explain the high level of commitment and willingness to risk death among religious extremist groups.

TERRORISM AS CRIMINAL BEHAVIOR

The broad range of violent activities that are often labeled as "terrorism" can now be seen as difficult, if not impossible, to define in some simplistic and universal way. There are some specific acts that seem to straddle the behavioral continuum in such a way to cloud the distinctions between criminal acts and terrorist acts. Some so-called terrorist acts are so specific and localized as to be outside the scope of the broad definitions. We shall examine a few of them that seem especially relevant as we enter into a new era of crime and terror for the twenty-first century.

Hostage-Taking

Taking hostages, whether for political reasons or for extortion of funds to support terrorist groups, is a tactic often used. The policy of the U.S. Government, for one, is to make no concessions to terrorists holding official or private U.S. citizens hostage. It will not pay ransom, release prisoners, change its policies, or agree to other acts that might encourage additional terrorism. At the same time, the United States will use every appropriate resource to gain the safe return of American citizens who are held hostage by terrorists.

Hostage-taking is defined under international law (International Convention Against the Taking of Hostages, adopted December 17, 1979) as, "The seizing or detaining and threatening to kill, injure, or continue to detain a person in order to compel a third party to do or abstain from doing any act as an explicit or implicit condition for the release of the seized or detained person. This activity is also a criminal act in most countries around the world, as a part of extortion or kidnapping for profit."

It is generally accepted in the international community that governments are responsible for the safety and welfare of persons within the borders of their nations. Terrorist threats and public safety shortcomings in many parts of the world have caused the United States to develop enhanced physical and personal security programs for U.S. personnel, and to establish cooperative arrangements with the U.S. private sector to help warn and protect business travelers. Bilateral counterterrorism assistance programs and close intelligence and law enforcement relationships have been instigated with many nations to help prevent terrorist incidents or resolve them in a manner that will deny the terrorists political or financial benefits from their actions. The United States also seeks effective judicial prosecution and punishment for terrorists and criminals victimizing the U.S. Government or its citizens and will use all legal methods to these ends, including extradition alone and, hopefully, in cooperation with other governments.

After many serious incidents, the U.S. Government concluded that paying ransom or making other concessions to terrorists in exchange for the release of hostages only increases the danger that others will then be more subject to be taken hostage, ad infinitum. In some very poor nations, kidnapping and ransom are growth industries! U.S. Government policy is to reject any demands for ransom, prisoner exchanges, and deals with terrorists in exchange for hostage release. At the same time, every effort will be made, including contact with representatives of the captors, to obtain the release of the hostages without responding to the demands of the terrorists. United States policy also strongly encourages American companies and private citizens not to respond to terrorist ransom demands. It believes that good security practice, relatively modest security expenditures, and continual close cooperation with embassy and local authorities will lower the risk to Americans living in high-threat environments.

While the U.S. Government is concerned for the welfare of its citizens, it cannot support requests from private companies that host governments violate their own laws or abdicate their normal law enforcement responsibilities. On the other hand, if the employing organization or company of a hostage works closely with local authorities and follows U.S. policy, U.S. Foreign Service posts can be involved actively in efforts to bring the incident to a safe conclusion. This includes providing reasonable administrative services and, if desired by the local authorities and the American organization, full participation in strategy sessions. Requests for U.S. Government technical assistance or expertise will be considered on a case-by-case basis. The full extent of U.S. Government participation must await an analysis of each specific set of circumstances. Again, we see the problems involved with making precise definitions of who can do what in a situation which may or not be terrorism.

Legal Issues in Hostage Taking

Under current U.S. law, 18 USC 1203 (Act for the Prevention and Punishment of the Crime of Hostage-Taking, enacted October 1984 in implementation of the U.N. convention on hostage-taking), seizure of a U.S. national as a hostage anywhere in the world is a crime, as is any hostage-taking action in which the U.S. Government is a target or the hostage-taker is a U.S. national. Such acts are, therefore, subject to investigation by the Federal Bureau of Investigation and to prosecution by U.S. authorities.

Assassination

On 9–11, terrorists like Osama bin Laden and his al Qaeda allies struck a blow to the peaceful (some say "ignorant") bliss of America and have created a justifiable fear that they will strike at the United States again. This fear tended to increase pressure in official Washington and around the talk show circuit to reconsider assassination as a method of solving problems with leaders we consider dangerous. The old argument remains, "How many lives would we have saved if Hitler had been assassinated in 1938?" This argument is strong, and for a long time many countries have ordered "extreme sanction" on leaders of countries or against criminal or terrorist organizations. To cut the head off the snake was considered good response to perceived danger. But ordering an assassination today would mean straying from a long-established policy and practice. This issue is noted in Terrorism Brief 1-1, written after the bombings in Africa, but which has had little mention since 9–11.

Time will tell whether or not the United States can garner the backing of the international community to head into a sure-to-spiral path of assassinations to meet perceived solutions to growing problems. The problem is similar to that of euthanasia: Who decides when a person is so evil or in such bad health that elimination is the only alternative? This issue will have a long discussion period in times when cooler emotions prevail. The situation now evolving in Iraq will show what methods may be used to oust Saddam Hussein, one way or another.

TERROR BRIEF 1–1

Assassination: Needed or Not?

The FBI, which investigated the 1998 U.S. embassy bombings in Africa, allegedly masterminded by Osama bin Laden, says the exiled Saudi multimillionaire undoubtedly will launch another terrorist attack on an American target. How true that turned out to be!

"We can predict with some certainty that we will see a reaction by bin Laden and his organization," FBI Director Louis Freeh told the Senate Judiciary Committee after the investigation. The potential targets are not limited to embassies overseas. "We've identified people in the United States or people who have transited the United States who are associated with him," Freeh said, "Bin Laden poses about as serious and imminent a threat as I can imagine."

Against that backdrop, committee members asked Freeh to consider the legality of assassinating bin Laden and other suspected terrorist leaders. "What is present law with respect to their takedown?" asked Senator Dianne Feinstein (Democrat, California).

Senator Joseph Biden (Democrat, Delaware) stated, "I would very much like a legal memorandum from the FBI, stating whether or not the prohibition against assassination of heads of state applies to organized crime units, and/or terrorist units." While the senators said they were not ready to advocate assassination, even consideration of the idea marked a sharp departure from the longstanding U.S. policy against assassination, a policy driven by pressure from Capitol Hill against the CIA in the mid-1970s.

In an interview after the hearing, Senator Arlen Specter (Republican, Pennsylvania) said the rules forbidding assassinations do not apply to situations in which the United States is virtually at war with an international terrorist organization. "If you're undertaking a military action, there's no limit" on the use of force, Specter said. The United States could send Special Forces to try to arrest bin Laden. There's always the possibility that you'll have a firefight. When you have a warrant for someone's arrest you can use whatever force you have, including lethal force."

In 1976, after extensive hearings that exposed CIA assassination plots, President Ford signed an executive order prohibiting U.S. officials from plotting or engaging in "political assassination." The prohibition was broadened by Presidents Carter and Reagan to state, "No person employed by or acting on behalf of the United States government shall engage in, or conspire to engage in, assassination."

The prohibition is not limited to assassination against heads of state, said Steve Aftergood of the Federation of American Scientists, a Washington-based watchdog group that follows intelligence matters. The legalities of killing a specific person in a military strike are less clear.

Former CIA Director James Woolsey, who also testified before the Judiciary Committee, said, "There's a difference, even though it's a subtle one, between an air strike going at facilities when you know an individual might be there, and going after a single individual."

Still, Woolsey opposed a deliberate assassination campaign. "First of all it's hard to do. The United States isn't very good at it," he cited bungled plots in the 1960s to kill Cuban leader Fidel Castro. "It would make it more likely that one or more groups would come back with an assassination attempt aimed at the U.S. President."

Following the August 1998 U.S. embassy bombings in Kenya and Tanzania, the Clinton administration planned and executed a cruise missile strike on alleged terrorist assets of Osama bin Laden's in Sudan and Afghanistan. The timing of the strikes was pegged in part to intelligence indicating bin Laden would be at the Afghan camps on that day. Officials now believe he had left the site hours before the missiles struck.

"We have to think in a different way than we thought before," Feinstein said. "It's a very dicey thing to get into a situation where you're going to have to employ licensed hit squads. At the same time we need to find ways to be proactive."

Source: John Diamond. "Senators Question Assassination Law." 1996: *Washington Times* (Associated Press, Washington). www.washtimes.com/national/lnbeltway.htm.

Abortion Clinic Violence

When and how does legitimate protest in a free democracy become terrorism? On January 3, 1997, the peace of the new year was shattered by bomb blasts and injuries at the NorthSide Family Services Clinic in Atlanta, Georgia, rekindling fears and memories of the bombing at the Summer Olympics in that stately Southern city. The first blast occurred at 9:30 AM, while the second blast was set and deliberately delayed to catch federal agents, firemen, ambulance attendants, and clinic workers as they responded to the scene, 45 minutes later. The second blast resulted in major and minor injuries and serious damage to the five-story building less than a week before the Twenty-eighth anniversary of the Supreme Court's decision in *Roe v. Wade,* which had legalized abortion. Was this explosion simply individual rage and violence or was it a terrorist act?

As was mentioned earlier, terrorism can be defined as, "the unlawful use of force or violence against persons or property to intimidate or coerce a government, the civilian population, or any segment thereof, in furtherance of political or social objectives." The acts of violence against abortion clinics by those who wish to have the Supreme Court reverse **Roe v. Wade** seem to fall neatly within this definition as well. Terrorism is a technique, a way of engaging in certain types of criminal activity, so as to attain particular ends. It is a process by which a group can create an overwhelming fear for coercive purposes. Such fear will then be raised not only in the immediate victims but also within the broader community or society. Such thinking fits nicely within the parameters of the violence used against abortion clinics by extremist Right to Life movements across the nation. The technique used in the Atlanta Summer Olympics of 1996 bombings is also well known, learned from the methods of terrorist groups like the Irish Republican Army (IRA). At approximately 1:25 AM an explosive device detonated in Centennial Olympic Park, a public park that can be visited by any of the people there to visit the Olympic Games. It is not a secure venue area. This method is referred to as the "congregate effect." The goal is to get people to gather around or near the first bombing and then explode the second or third device with devastating impact. Such planning is not typical of a random act of violence by a single person.

SUMMARY

Terrorism is a complex, multifaceted, and often-baffling subject. The players involved have a way of rising to prominence, splintering, disappearing for years and then reappearing. Counterterrorist bureaucracies are formed then re-formed, names are changed, and leaders are shuffled around as they are promoted, demoted, killed, or forced to resign. Incidents proliferate across the world, some of which can trigger off a chain of events that will destabilize a whole region and bring nations to the edge of ruin. At the same time, major terrorist actions can shock for a short while, and then be quickly forgotten (except by those impacted by the tragedy). Treatises are written, theories propounded, grievances aired, tactics discussed, occasionally to some effect, usually not. Causes are picked up by the world's media, examined, probed, and then all too often overlooked, until the next bomb explodes, the next airliner is hijacked, or a cataclysmic event like the attacks on 9–11. With the various definitions and application of them to specific events, the reader now has a good foundation for the study of terrorism and terrorist acts as the shocking of the senses and promotion of fear and concern around the world. In the next chapter we shall review state-sponsored and religious terrorism from several viewpoints. Terrorist causes are often looked upon as bizarre or weird when seen in the context of the present, but most issues (political, religious, racial or ethnic) have a pattern that needs to be placed in context. We believe that those who understand the historical foundations of the issues that face the free world since 9–11 will never be able to view the evening news in the same way.

TERMS TO REMEMBER

acceptable enemies	**freedom fighters**	**laws**
assassin	**higher law**	**mores**

| prescribed | Reign of Terror | terrorist incident |
| proscribed | Roe v. Wade | useful construct |

REVIEW QUESTIONS

1. Trace the concepts of social response to violence from retaliation through the development of codes and laws.
2. How did the Inquisition contribute to punishment of offenders of those times?
3. What are the advantages and disadvantages of vengeance?
4. Discuss the pros and cons for the use of assassination.
5. What are the differences between criminal behavior and crime?

ENDNOTES

1. Cindy C. Combs. *Terrorism in the Twenty-First Century.* (Prentice Hall, NJ, 1997.) p. 6.
2. Brian Jenkins. *International Terrorism: A New Mode of Conflict.* (Los Angeles: Crescent, 1975.) p. 4.
3. See, for example, the Hague Regulation of 1907 and the Geneva Conventions of 1949.
4. George Rosie. *The Directory of International Terrorism.* (Paragon House. New York. 1987.) p. 7.
5. U.S. Army Field Manual 100-20. *"Combating Terrorism."* Stability and Support Operations. (U.S. Department of Defense, U.S. Government Printing Office, Washington, DC, 1993) Chapter 8.
6. Editors. *"FBI Counterterrorism Responsibilities."* FBI Website, see Internet index. (U.S. Government Printing Office, Washington, DC. Department of Justice, 1996.)
7. U.S. Army Field Manual 100-20. *"Combating Terrorism."*
8. Ibid.
9. Jonathan R. White. 1991. *Terrorism: An Introduction.* Brooks/Cole Publishing California. USA 1991, p. 13
10. Alex P. Scmid. *Political Terrorism,* Transaction Books, Anderson Press. Cincinnati, OHIO, 1983. p. 107–109.
11. Bruce Hoffman, "Defining Terrorism," *Inside Terrorism.* Columbia University Press, 1998. p. 19.

2 A Brief History of Terrorism

If we suppose that humans are by nature wicked, the kindness and love need special explanation. If, on the other hand, we think that the depth of our soul knows only good we must provide an account of wickedness and violence.

John Lachs

OVERVIEW

When did terrorism begin? As noted in Chapter 1, the word "terrorism" was coined during the French Revolution and the Jacobean Reign of Terror. However, that does not mean that individual and group acts of what we might classify as terrorism cannot be traced back into the earliest activities of humankind. This chapter will briefly examine human violence and how it came to be incorporated into the label of terrorism happening today. We shall examine the evolution of humankind into the behavior that we have defined (with some difficulty) in Chapter 1. This will provide the reader with a different perspective on the behavioral aspects of violence as just another point on the "Continuum of Behavior" that was shown in Chapter 1.

VIOLENCE AND TERRORISM

What are the conditions that can generate violence? What is it that allows a person, or group, to apply violence to a situation and believe it to be such a logical or natural response? Violence is the application of great power that results in measurable harm by a conscious decision of the individual applying it. Violence in this sense has had broad usage in the world, demonstrated by the application of great force to achieve specific short-term goals by agents acting alone, in mobs or as part of an organized group of like-minded individuals.

If we think of the paradigm of violence as the fury of a wounded or humiliated man, we can readily see that violence, or something very like it, is not even a uniquely human possession. Animals also release their energies in violent and destructive ways; in fact it is its similarity to the behavior of brutes that makes violence so distasteful to the human mind.[1]

In the earliest social groups the violence could be controlled or quickly dealt with by individual or **group retaliation**. Violent people were considered to be like animals and banished to the wild to live as such. Probably the earliest examples of what might be called terrorist behaviors were those actions intended to frighten another group into running away or surrendering by the threat of violence, such as painting themselves in bright patterns and colors, brandishing weapons and shouting threats, killing enemies and placing their heads on poles, etc. The goal was to so shock the "enemy" that they would either go away or submit to the will of the perpetrators.

Modern societies are composed of diverse religious, ethnic, and racial groupings that often seem out of contact with the ruling structures. Use of one-on-one violence as a way to bring attention to an individual (or group) grievance becomes more difficult. When a public official seems to be inaccessible, a natural temptation for a frustrated constituent is to burst into his or her office, pound on the desk, sometimes with a weapon. Or, to stalk the officials, and seize and shake them at a shopping center . . . or at the extreme even kill them. When an unwilling or uncaring bureaucracy fails to respond to a **perceived grievance**, it can result in some spectacular and destructive act. Shooting a politician or destruction of public property is not a rational choice for the aggrieved person's situation. Motivation to "do something" grows from anger, frustration and hopelessness. The hapless "victim" begins to see all of society as a monstrous machine. It is against this background that the distraught and frustrated person believes a blow must be struck.

Today's global societies tend to consider violence as an attractive, attention-getting solution as most actions are social in nature. There are few constructive, autonomous and well thought out actions open to those not writers, doctors or self-employed professionals. The doing of virtually anything worthwhile usually includes the cooperation with and actions of others. Violence and destruction, however, are among a small number of things available to a single individual. One needs no assistance to shoot at drivers from a freeway overpass, or to drive a car into pedestrians. This natural desire to do something can easily be channeled into a "violent" something. The fast-moving pace of modern society may make one feel that it is critical to do something, whether bad or good. The catch phrase is, "Don't just stand there . . . *do* something!" Violence, precisely because it is usually initiated as an individual decision, is something we can do that leaves us feeling active and involved. The act of violence can be described as a logical progression: (1) **formation of intent**, (2) execution and, (3) immediate consequences, taking place in microseconds in a single individual. The feeling that whatever we do is not something of our own design has been rectified, and replaced by thoughts that are all unique and individually our own.

Violence perpetrated for ideological reasons and for a systematically promoted cause or complaint is much different. Organizations in the business of doing such things frequently suffer from too much discussion and very little action. In the mind of an individual person, being told to do something does not match an act both conceived and performed by that individual. Individuals taking violent action on their own, by contrast, take satisfaction in the self-empowered nature of their individual act. They accept responsibility for their acts; "I did that, with pride." Acts of violence planned and executed by a group always dilutes the credit so that blame is spread so broadly that it fails to satisfy an individual.

For example, Lachs presents a surprisingly positive side to the horrors of war. "Many people report that great danger leads to an exhilaration that renders experience vibrant. Some say they can never recapture the keen sense of being alive they felt in battle, or even when they merely supported the war effort."[2] The oftentimes dullness and predictable regularity of most individuals' daily life seems to validate such claims as believable and natural. Living in a routine and the cocoon of a safe society eventually makes life seem dull. War makes one begin to contemplate death up close and personal, feeling its nearness and finality with crystal clarity. Something akin to this effect happens in connection with violence. In these outbursts, the adrenaline flows in quantity, the eyes focus tightly into "**tunnel vision**" and blood rushes to the brain and other vital organs. Any soldier in combat or policeman in a shootout can describe that effect clearly. This is a drug that is not available on the street or in a pharmacy, but, once experienced, is just as addictive.

WHEN DID VIOLENCE BECOME TERRORISM?

By definition, the **assassination** of Julius Caesar, in 44 BC, was an act of terrorism. This holds true as well, insofar as a modern political assassination is defined, as terrorism.[3] Modern political scientists generally treat assassination as a terrorist act, whether by an individual acting alone (as John Hinckley, in relation to President Reagan) or in concert with a group (as in the attempted shooting of President Ford).

Group terrorism became common as early as the Middle Ages. In fact, the word "assassin" comes from an Arabic term *hashashin,* which literally means "**hashish-eater**." It was used to describe a sectarian group of Muslims who were employed by their spiritual and political leader (the local Caliph) to spread terror in the form of murder and destruction among religious enemies, enhanced with the promise of instant acceptance and transport to Paradise if killed themselves.[4] This promise is similar to the incentives claimed for suicide bombers in the Israel-Palestinian ongoing cycle of violence, and the highjackers of the four airlines used in the attacks of 9–11. Marco Polo's travel journals included lurid tales of murder committed by these assassins. These early terrorists were motivated not only by promises of eternal reward in the afterlife, but also by unlimited access to hashish and other drugs. Even the Crusaders made mention of this group of fanatics and the terror they inspired.[5]

The region from which the original assassins emerged was Persia, the present day Iran. In modern times, the Ayatollah Khomeini became the religious leader of the Shi'ites in Iran during its revolution in the late 1970s. It is widely accepted that the young men in the Iran-Iraq wars were told that they would go directly to Paradise if they fought bravely and died fighting for Allah. Stories from that war claim 15- and 16-year-olds walked in waves into the guns of their enemies, the Iraquis, unarmed and unafraid. The potent combination of religious and political fanaticism is the legacy of the Brotherhood of Assassins.

Islam, Christianity, Judaism and Hinduism are not by doctrine violent religions. And, generally speaking, neither are any of the other major religions. However, the mixture of religion and politics has quite often resulted in violence, frequently against innocent victims, which makes it, according to the definition suggested in the preceding chapter, terrorism. The Middle East, as the home of three major world religions, has been plagued by a variety of violent sects. The creation of violent sects, however, whose blending of religion and politics is similar to the Brotherhood of Assassins, continues to fan the flames of violence. Religion is the "narcotic" which both motivates terrorist actions in its name and deadens their consciences to the slaughter that they inflict on innocent persons.

If terrorist acts were perceived as the way to "right the wrongs" committed by government, then the political assassin was not given universal disfavor. Vidal, a leading French legal scholar, has noted that whereas formerly the political offender was treated as a public enemy, he is today considered as a friend of the public good, as a man of progress, desirous of bettering the political institutions of his country, having the laudable intentions, hastening the onward march of humanity, his only fault being that he wishes to go too fast, and that he employs in attempting to realize the progress which he desires, means irregular, illegal, and violent.[6]

Not until the middle of the twentieth century was the murder of a head of state, or any member of his family, formally designated as terrorism. Even today, those who commit the "political" crime of murder of a head of state can often enjoy a type of special protection, in the form of political asylum.[7]

STATE-SPONSORED AND RELIGIOUS TERRORISM

State terrorism, whether it is internal (against its own people or dissenters) or external (using or funding outside terrorist groups or individuals), offers a real threat to international stability and security. Internal terrorism can often inspire the formation of resistance movements, which often resort to revolutionary or terrorist tactics. This cycle of terror and violence can result in a whirlwind that can suck in all within its reach, innocent or guilty. Exportation of support for external terror, sponsored by **rogue states**, has resulted in the proliferation of terrorist attacks worldwide. Even states whose official policy specifically rejects the use of terror have been guilty of providing financial and operational aid, often clandestinely, to those who would promote terrorism. With the exception of a few states, such as Iran, Iraq and Libya, most have attempted to keep their dealings with terrorists a secret as much as possible.

The Big Seven

President Bush put state supporters of terrorism on notice in his September 20, 2001, address to the joint session of Congress: "Every nation, in every region, now has a decision to make. Either you are with us, or you are with the terrorists." The "Big Seven" of designated state sponsors—Cuba, Iran, Iraq, Libya, North Korea, Syria, and Sudan—clearly heard the President's message. While some of these countries appear to be reconsidering their present course, none has yet taken all necessary actions to divest itself fully of ties to terrorism. Sudan and Libya seem closest to understanding what they must do to get out of the terrorism business, and each has taken measures in the right direction. Iran, North Korea, and Syria have, in some narrow areas, made limited moves to cooperate with the international community's campaign against terrorism. Iran and Syria, however, seek to have it both ways. On the one hand, they clamped down on certain terrorist groups, such as al Qaeda. On the other hand, they maintained their support for other terrorist groups, such as **Hamas** and Hezbollah, insisting they were national liberation movements. North Korea's initial positive moves halted abruptly. Until all states that support or tolerate terrorism cease their sponsorship, whether by choice or coercion, they remain a critical foundation for terrorist groups and their operations. Even though the year 2001 saw a continuation of a slow trend away from state sponsorship as the guiding force behind the overall global terrorist threat, state sponsors still represent a key impediment to the international campaign against terrorism. In certain areas, including Israel, the West Bank, and Gaza Strip, state sponsors remain an important driving force behind terrorism. Iran continues its firm support for Hezbollah, Hamas, and the Palestine Islamic Jihad. Iraq employs terrorism against dissident Iraqi groups opposed to Saddam Hussein's regime. Syria continued its support for Hezbollah and allowed Hamas, the Palestine Islamic Jihad, and other Palestinian rejectionist groups to maintain offices in Damascus. The reactions to the President's message to the "**Big Seven**" were as follows:

Cuba

Since September 11, 2001, Fidel Castro has vacillated over the war on terrorism. In October 2001, he labeled the U.S.-led **War on Terrorism**, "Worse than the original attacks, militaristic, and fascist." When this tactic earned ostracism rather than praise, he undertook an effort to demonstrate Cuban support for the international campaign against terrorism and signed all twelve U.N. counterterrorism conventions as well as the Ibero-American declaration on terrorism at the 2001 summit. Although Cuba decided not to protest the detention of suspected terrorists at the U.S. Naval Base at Guantanimo Bay, it continued to denounce the global effort against terrorism—even by asserting that the United States was intentionally targeting Afghan children and Red Cross hospitals. Cuba's signature on U.N. counterterrorism conventions not withstanding, Castro continued to view terror as a legitimate revolutionary tactic. The Cuban Government continued to allow at least twenty Basque ETA members to reside in Cuba as privileged guests and provided some degree of safe haven and support to members of the Colombian FARC and ELN groups. In August, a Cuban spokesman revealed that Sinn Fein's official representative for Cuba and Latin America, Niall Connolly, who was one of three Irish Republican Army members arrested in Colombia on suspicion of providing explosives training to the FARC, had been based in Cuba for five years. In addition, the recent arrest in Brazil of the leader of a Chilean terrorist group, the Frente Patriotico Manuel Rodriguez (FPMR), has raised the strong possibility that in the mid-1990s, the Cuban Government harbored **FPMR** terrorists wanted for murder in Chile. The arrested terrorist told Brazilian authorities he had traveled through Cuba on his way to Brazil. Chilean investigators had traced calls from FPMR relatives in Chile to Cuba following an FPMR prison break in 1996. But the Cuban Government twice denied extradition requests, claiming that the wanted persons were not in Cuba and the phone numbers were incorrect. Numerous U.S. fugitives continue to live on the island, including Joanne Chesimard, wanted in the United States for the murder in 1973 of a New Jersey police officer and living as a guest of the Castro regime since 1979.

Iran

This Persian Gulf nation remained the most active state sponsor of terrorism in 2001. Iran's Islamic Revolutionary Guard Corps (**IRGC**) and Ministry of Intelligence and Security (MOIS) continued to be involved in the planning and support of terrorist acts and supported a variety of groups that use terrorism to pursue their goals, although some within Iran would like to end this support. Hardliners who hold the reins of power continue to thwart any efforts to moderate these policies. Since the outbreak of the *intifada,* support has intensified for Palestinian groups that use violence against Israel. During the period 2001-2002, however, Iran appears to have reduced its involvement in other forms of terrorist activity. There is no evidence of Iranian sponsorship or foreknowledge of the September 11 attacks in the United States. President Khatami condemned the attacks and offered condolences to the American people. During 2001, Iran sought a high-profile role in encouraging anti-Israeli activity by way of increasing its support for anti-Israeli terrorist groups. Supreme Leader Khamene'i continued to refer to Israel as a "cancerous tumor" that must be removed. Matching this rhetoric with action, Iran continued to provide Lebanese Hezbollah and the Palestinian rejectionist groups . . . notably Hamas, the Palestine Islamic Jihad, and the PFLP-GC with varying amounts of funding, safe haven, training, and weapons. It also encouraged Hezbollah and the rejectionist Palestinian groups to coordinate their planning and to escalate their activities. In addition, Iran provided limited support to terrorist groups in the Gulf, Africa, Turkey, and Central Asia. This support is at a considerably lower level than that provided to the groups opposed to Israel and has been decreasing in recent years. The Iranian Government took no direct action in 2001 to implement Ayatollah Khomeini's **fatwa** (call for death) against Salman Rushdie, but the decree has not been revoked nor has the $2.8 million bounty for his death been withdrawn. Moreover, on the anniversary of the *Fatwa* in February, some hard-line Iranians stressed again that the decree is irrevocable and should be carried out. During Operation Enduring Freedom, Tehran informed the United States that, in the event U.S. warplanes went down inside Iran, Iranian forces would assist downed air crews in accordance with international convention. Iran also worked with the United States and its allies at the Bonn Conference in late 2001 to help in the formation of the Afghan Interim Authority. Tehran pledged to close its borders with Afghanistan and Pakistan to prevent the infiltration of Taliban and al Qaeda escapees. There are, however, reports that Arab Afghans, including al Qaeda members, used Iran as a transit route to enter and leave from Afghanistan.

Iraq

Iraq was the only Arab-Muslim country that did not condemn the 9–11 attacks against the United States. A commentary of the official Iraqi radio station on September 11th stated that America was ". . . reaping the fruits of [its] crimes against humanity." Subsequent commentary in a newspaper run by one of Saddam Hussein's sons expressed sympathy for Osama bin Laden following initial U.S. retaliatory strikes in Afghanistan. In addition, the regime continued to provide training and political encouragement to numerous terrorist groups, although its main focus was on dissident Iraqi activity overseas. Iraq provided bases to several terrorist groups including the Mujahedin-e-Khalq (**MEK**), the Kurdistan Workers' Party (PKK), the Palestine Liberation Front (PLF), and the Abu Nidal Organization (ANO). In 2001, the Popular Front for the Liberation of Palestine (PFLP) raised its profile in the West Bank and Gaza Strip by carrying out successful terrorist attacks against Israeli targets. In

Iraqi women walk in front of poster of Iraqi President Saddam Hussein—
September 17, 2002. (AP Photo/Amr Nabil)

recognition of the PFLP's growing role, an Iraqi vice president met with former
PFLP Secretary General Habbash in Baghdad in January 2001 and expressed
continued Iraqi support for the *intifada.* Also, in mid-September, a senior delegation from the PFLP met with an Iraqi deputy prime minister. Baghdad also
continued to host other Palestinian rejectionist groups, including the Arab
Liberation Front, and the 15th of May Organization.

Meanwhile, Czech police continued to provide protection to the Prague
office of the U.S. Government-funded Radio Free Europe/Radio Liberty
(RFE/RL), which produces Radio Free Iraq programs and employs expatriate
journalists. The police presence was augmented in 1999 and 2000, following
reports that the Iraqi Intelligence Service might retaliate against RFE/RL for
broadcasts critical of the Iraqi regime. As concerns over the facility's security
mounted through 2000, the Czechs expelled an Iraqi intelligence officer in
April 2001. The Iraqi regime has not met a request from Riyadh for the extradition of two Saudis who hijacked a Saudi Arabian Airlines flight to Baghdad in
2000. Disregarding its obligations under international law, the regime granted
political asylum to the hijackers and gave them ample opportunity to voice
their criticisms of alleged abuses by the Saudi Government in the Iraqi Government-controlled and international media. At this writing, the U.N. and the
Coalition nations in the War on Terrorism are working on a hard-nosed declaration to the Saddam Hussein regime that will require him to give total access
to U.N. inspectors after eleven years of dodging full inspections of his suspected sites and others in the development of WMDs, or else face a second
Gulf War led by the United States.

Libya

Following the September 11 terrorist attacks, Libyan leader Muammar el-Qaddafi issued a statement condemning the attacks as horrific and gruesome and urging Libyans to donate blood for the U.S. victims. On September 16 he declared that the United States had justification to retaliate for the attacks. Since September 11, Qaddafi has repeatedly denounced terrorism. Libya appears to have curtailed its support for international terrorism, although it may maintain residual contacts with a few groups. Tripoli has, in recent years, sought to recast itself as a peacemaker, offering to mediate a number of conflicts, such as the military standoff between India and Pakistan that began in December 2001. In October, Libya ransomed a hostage held by the Abu Sayyaf Group, although it claimed that the money was not a ransom and would be used for "humanitarian assistance." Libya's past record of terrorist activity continued to hinder Qaddafi's efforts to shed Libya's pariah status. In January, a Scottish court found Libyan intelligence agent Abdelbasset Ali Mohmed al-Megrahi guilty of murder, concluding that in 1988 he planted an explosive device on **Pan Am Flight 103**, which when detonated resulted in the murder of all 259 passengers and crew on board as well as 11 persons on the ground in Lockerbie, Scotland. Judges found that al-Megrahi had acted "in furtherance of the purposes of . . . Libyan Intelligence Services." His confidant, Libyan Arab Airlines employee Al-Amin Khalifa Fhima, was acquitted on the grounds that the prosecution failed to prove his role in the bombing "beyond a reasonable doubt." At year's end, Libya had yet to comply fully with the remaining U.N. Security Council requirements related to Pan Am 103, including accepting responsibility for the actions of its officials, fully disclosing all that it knows about the bombing, and paying appropriate compensation to the victims' families. Libya's hesitation to do so may have reflected a hope that Megrahi's appeal would overturn his conviction. (On March 14, 2002, a Scottish appellate court upheld Megrahi's conviction.) In November, a German court convicted four defendants in the bombing in 1986 of La Belle Discotheque in West Berlin. In rendering his decision, the judge stated that Libyan Government officials had clearly orchestrated the attack. In response to the court's findings, the German Government called on Libya to accept responsibility for the attack and provide compensation to the victims. Two U.S. servicemen and one Turkish civilian died in the bombing, and more than two hundred persons were wounded.

North Korea

The Democratic People's Republic of Korea's **(DPRK)** response to international efforts to combat terrorism has been disappointing. In a statement released after the September 11 attacks, the DPRK reiterated its public policy of opposing terrorism and any support for terrorism. It also signed the U.N. Convention for the Suppression of the Financing of Terrorism, acceded to the Convention Against the Taking of Hostages, and indicated its willingness to sign five others. Despite the urging of the international community, however, North Korea did not take substantial steps to cooperate in efforts to combat terrorism, including responding to requests for information on how it is implementing the U.N. Security Council resolutions, and it did not respond to U.S. proposals for discussions on terrorism. It did not report any efforts to search for and block financial assets as required by U.N. Security Council Resolution 1373. Similarly, the DPRK did not respond positively to the Republic of Korea's call to resume dialogue, where counterterrorism is an agenda item, nor to the United States, in its call to undertake dialogue on improved implementation of the agreed framework. In light of President Bush's call to recognize the dangerous nexus between weapons of mass destruction and terrorism, this latter failure, with its implications for nuclear development and proliferation, was especially troublesome. In addition, Pyongyang's provision of safe haven to four remaining Japanese Communist League Red Army Faction members who participated in the hijacking of a Japanese Airlines flight to North Korea in 1970 remained problematic in terms of support for terrorists. Moreover, some evidence suggested the DPRK might have sold limited quantities of small arms to terrorist groups during the year. As this book goes to press, the North Koreans have begun to return to the production of nuclear material for use in weapons of mass destruction (WMD). They are a threat to the Korean Peninsula and the region and efforts continue to change their suicidal course to war.

Sudan

The counterterrorism dialogue begun in mid-2000 between the U.S. and Sudan continued and intensified during 2001. Sudan condemned the September 11 attacks and pledged its commitment to combating terrorism and fully cooperating with the United States in the campaign against terrorism. The Sudanese Government has stepped up its counterterrorism cooperation with various U.S. agencies, and Sudanese authorities have investigated and apprehended extremists suspected of involvement in terrorist activities. In late September, the United Nations recognized Sudan's positive steps against terrorism by removing U.N. sanctions. Sudan, however, remained a designated state sponsor of terrorism. A number of international terrorist groups including al Qaeda, the Egyptian Islamic Jihad, Egyptian al-Gama'a al-Islamiyya, the **Palestine Islamic Jihad,** and Hamas continued to use Sudan as a safe haven, primarily for conducting logistics and other support activities. Press speculation about the extent of Sudan's cooperation with the United States probably has led some terrorist elements to depart the country. Unilateral U.S. sanctions remained in force.

Syria

Syria's president, Bashar al-Asad, as well as senior Syrian officials, publicly condemned the September 11 attacks. The Syrian Government also cooperated with the United States and with other foreign governments in investigating al Qaeda and some other terrorist groups and individuals. The Government of Syria has not been implicated directly in an act of terrorism since 1986, but it continued in 2001 to provide safe haven and logistical support to a number of terrorist groups. Ahmad Jibril's Popular Front for the Liberation of Palestine-General Command (PFLP-GC), the Palestine Islamic Jihad (PIJ), Abu Musa's

Fatah-the Intifada, George Habash's Popular Front for the Liberation of Palestine, and Hamas continued to maintain offices in Damascus. Syria provided Hezbollah, Hamas, PFLP-GC, the PIJ, and other terrorist organizations refuge and basing privileges in Lebanon's Beka'a Valley, under Syrian control. Damascus, however, generally upheld its September 2000 antiterrorism agreement with Ankara, honoring its 1998 pledge not to support the Kurdistan Workers' Party (**PKK**). Damascus served as the primary transit point for the transfer of Iranian-supplied weapons to Hezbollah. Syria continued to adhere to its long-standing policy of preventing any attacks against Israel or Western targets from Syrian territory or attacks against Western interests in Syria.[8]

STATE-SPONSORED TERRORISM AS WARFARE IN THE TWENTY-FIRST CENTURY

During the second half of the twentieth century, various countries began to use terrorist organizations to promote state interests in the international domain. In some cases, states have established **"puppet" terrorist organizations**, whose purpose is to act on behalf of the sponsoring state, to further the interests of the state, and to represent its positions in domestic or regional fronts. The patron state provides its beneficiary terrorist organization with political support, financial assistance, and the sponsorship necessary to maintain and expand its struggle. The patron uses the beneficiary to perpetrate acts of terrorism as a means of spreading their ideology throughout the world. Or, in some cases, the patron ultimately expects the beneficiary to gain control of a state, or impart its ideology to the general public.

State-sponsored terrorism can achieve strategic ends where the use of conventional armed forces is neither practical nor effective. The high costs of modern warfare, and concern about non-conventional escalation have turned terrorism into an efficient, convenient, and generally discrete weapon for attaining sponsor state interests in the international realm. Some specific advantages are:

- **LOW COST—FINANCIALLY:** Terrorism offers a relatively inexpensive method of making a point by insurgent groups who lack the finances, personnel or the armament to win against a nation's army on a conventional battlefield. Terrorist tactics also can provide small, non- "superpower" nations a low-cost way to wage war, whether overtly or clandestinely, on a hostile state whose resources provide a serious obstacle to waging a full-scale war.

- **LOW COST—POLITICALLY:** For states, particularly those who can successfully provide and hide clandestine support for terrorist groups, the political cost can be quite low, as long as such support remains secret. On the other hand, profit in arms sales, might become temptingly high. When such support is not too obvious, as with Libya, other nations have often tended to look the other way.

- **HIGH YIELD—FINANCIALLY:** States that are arms dealers to terrorists can usually profit quite handsomely, with little or no political, military or economic impact. Sometimes being caught results in the recall of a couple of ambassadors, but seldom any impact on diplomatic or trade relations.

- **HIGH YIELD—POLITICALLY:** For dissenters who decide to use terrorism as a political weapon, the political currency can be very large in value. This is especially true when the targeted government reaction are not supported by the citizen in the middle and could lead to a regime being ousted from power. Major concessions can then be "bought" when a successful terrorist incident shocks the populace too much.

- **LOW RISK—POLITICALLY AND FINANCIALLY:** Financing of terrorist operations can be much less than for a fully equipped and trained army. And, the individuals carrying out these operations are not subjected to as much risk as would be in conventional warfare. In a successful terrorist operation, the rewards are often very big. For a failed operation, the losses are generally small, unless the failure can be traced back to a state sponsor. The finding of these linkages has become very costly in financial and, more importantly, in political terms.[9]

What deters nations from engaging in this high-profit, low-risk terrorist form of warfare? Nuclear warfare is generally accepted as unthinkable and unconventional or counterinsurgent warfare, as both Vietnam and Afghanistan seem to have demonstrated, and it seems too expensive and unwinnable today.

The U.S. Secretary of State, in May 2002, clearly designated the governments that are supporting state sponsorship of terrorism. Those named were: Cuba, Iran, Iraq, Libya, North Korea, Sudan, Syria and Sudan. These governments have and are providing support to international terrorism, either by engaging in terrorist activity themselves or by providing arms, training, **safe havens**, diplomatic facilities, financial backing, logistic and/or other support to terrorists. The U.S. policy of bringing maximum pressure to bear on state sponsors of terrorism and encouraging other countries to do likewise has paid significant dividends. There has been a clear decline in state-sponsored terrorism in recent years. A broad range of bilateral and multilateral sanctions serves to discourage state sponsors of terrorism from continuing their support for international acts of terrorism, but continued pressure is essential.

In January 1991, President George Herbert Bush informed the U.S. Congress that he was continuing U.S. sanctions against Libya, since the "Libyan government continues to employ international terrorism and to support it, in violation of international law and international rules of conduct."

RELIGIOUS TERRORISM

Were the Crusades simply a form of terrorism done in the name of religion? One definition of "genocide" is as follows:

> . . . a conspiracy aimed at the total destruction of a group and thus requires a concerted plan of action. The instigators and initiators of a genocide are cool-minded theorists first and barbarians only second. The specificity of genocide does not arise from the extent of the killings, nor their savagery or resulting infamy, but solely from the intention: the destruction of a group.[10]

The Crusades were a series of wars in which Christians and Muslims fought to eradicate each other in the Holy Lands to control the area referred to as the **Middle East**. Perhaps this effort to destroy the Muslims does fit the definition. So many wars of annihilation seem to fit this category of genocide. Christians

TERROR BRIEF 2–1

Pan Am Flight 103 (Lockerbie)

In December 1988, a Pan American airliner blew up over the Scottish town of Lockerbie. Two hundred and eighty people were killed in the explosion, most of them passengers aboard the plane, some residents of Lockerbie, whose homes were struck by falling debris. In November 1991, the Americans and the British announced officially that their investigation indicated the following suspects in the bombing: Abdel Basset Ali Mohmed al-Megrahi (former director of security at the Libyan airline and later head of the Center of Strategic Studies in Tripoli) and Al-Amin Khalifa Fhima (director of the Libyan airline office in Malta). According to the U.S. spokesman, the two trained for the attack at a military installation in Libya over a period of three years: "They planted the bomb in a Toshiba brand radio-cassette recorder and exploited their aviation connections to ensure that their bag would be on board Pan Am Flight 103, leaving from Frankfurt. When the passengers changed flights in London, the bag followed." The two were indicted and the U.S. demanded their extradition in order to stand trial in the United States, and threatened to impose international sanc-

tions upon Libya. Under U.S. and British pressure, the U.N. Security Council adopted Resolution 731 calling upon Libya to extradite the two suspects. At this stage it is unclear how the affair will end. It must be taken into account, however, that in order to prevent the incrimination of senior officials in the Libyan administration, traces of the two suspects in the bombing may disappear.

Senior Libyan officials, both within the political establishment and the upper echelons of the military hierarchy, are engaged in developing and maintaining Libya's ties with terrorist organizations around the world. The scope of the vast aid granted by Libya, both in the past and at present to international terrorism, varies according to Libya's international standing and its critical interests at any given time. Thus, when the West increases its pressure upon Libya (whether economic, diplomatic or military), it curbs some of its contacts with the various terrorist organizations. However, when Qaddafi feels the economic or military noose loosening, he immediately renews ties with the terrorist organizations, even publicly flaunting those ties.

considered this area their most holy location and believed that they, not Muslims, should control it. The many wars fought by the Crusaders were ultimately not enough to reclaim the region. But there had been an unexpected positive effect. Western Europeans had left their homes to fight in a distant war and the stories of the returning soldiers encouraged their countrymen to look beyond their own villages for the first time.

The **founder of Islam**, the Prophet Mohammed, died in 632 AD. Abu Bekr became Caliph, or "the one who comes after." Abu Bekr wanted everyone around the world to follow Islam and "to submit to Allah." He then set about to organize, convert, and subjugate the entire world to whom he believed was the one true God, Allah. A century after Mohammed's death, the lands of Islam under Arab leadership stretched from Spain in the west across North Africa and most of the modern Middle East into Central Asia and northern India. The Arabs were great traders, whose influence reached as far as southwest Asia. The Arabs were interested in learning and in other cultures. Western Europe was mired deep in "the dark ages," so-called because the great civilizations of Greece and Rome had fallen. The Arabs, however, had made great advances in mathematics, medicine, and physical science. They provided us with Arabic numerals, which made possible great advances in mathematics (algebra, in fact, is an Arabic word).

THE TURKS AND THE FIRST CRUSADE

The Turks were not originally from Turkey, they were nomadic people from Central Asia known today as Turkmenistan ("land of the Turks"). One Turkish tribe, the Seljuks, began moving into the Anatolian peninsula, or the area we now call Turkey. These Turks were Muslims, but a Christian emperor, Michael VIII, controlled the peninsula. The emperor appealed to Pope Urban II to help him rid Anatolia of "**unbelievers**." The Pope received Michael's call for assistance, but decided to use the situation to advance a more ambitious plan. Jerusalem is considered Holy Land to Christians, Jews and Muslims, but in 1095, the city was controlled by Muslims. The message from Michael presented Urban II with an opportunity to wage a "War of the Cross," or Crusade, and retake the holy lands and eradicate the unbelievers.

The Pope persuaded the knights of Europe to join the Crusades by appealing to their religious convictions. They were told that Muslim Turks were robbing, raping and killing Christian pilgrims journeying to Jerusalem. The Pope suggested the knights fight Muslims instead of continuing to fight one another. Crusaders left their families for a long journey into the unknown. While they did not succeed in ridding the Holy Lands of nonbelievers, the Crusades had other, more worldly benefits:

- An increase in trade with Europe;
- Travels to new lands and learning about new and interesting cultures;
- Spices that allowed food to last longer and taste better;
- The fine cloths manufactured in the Middle East.

The first Crusaders crossed into Anatolia in 1097 AD and reached Jerusalem by the summer of 1099 AD. (They killed anyone along the way who appeared to be "Semitic" in appearance to rid European cities of unbelievers.) When they finally encountered the Muslims, the fighting was fierce and bloodthirsty, and Crusaders killed not only fighting men, but also women and children. The victorious Crusaders quickly established four colonies along the eastern Mediterranean, including one in Jerusalem. A second Crusade was launched when the Muslims recaptured one of the Christian colonies. This time the Muslims were prepared and defeated the Crusaders.

The Christians then recaptured the Holy Lands by the end of the second Crusade, but a Muslim general named Saladin launched a "**jihad**," (an Islamic holy war), and recaptured Jerusalem. Saladin was neither an Arab nor a Turk—he was Kurdish. The Kurds lived between the Turks and Arabs in the mountainous lands of northern Iraq and eastern Turkey, even as they do to this day. When Saladin recaptured Jerusalem in 1187, the Christians launched a Third Crusade, perhaps the most famous, led by King Richard "the Lion-

Hearted" of England. The Christians fought hard in the Third Crusade, but Saladin was able to hold Jerusalem for the Muslims. The two warriors agreed to a truce that left the Muslims controlling the Holy Lands, with Christians free to visit their shrines. Although many other so-called Holy Wars have taken place for countless centuries, the Crusades are considered to be the eight campaigns into the Holy Lands that occurred from 1095 AD until 1291 AD. The following is a listing of those eight major campaigns:

- 1095–1099 The First Crusade
- 1147–1149 The Second Crusade
- 1189–1192 The Third Crusade
- 1202–1204 The Fourth Crusade
- 1218–1221 The Fifth Crusade
- 1228–1229 The Sixth Crusade
- 1248–1254 The Seventh Crusade
- 1270–1291 The Last Crusade

The Muslims regained control over all of the Holy Lands by 1291, but the Crusades became a turning point for Western Europe. The next two centuries, what we now know as the Renaissance, would lead to exciting advances in science, technology and the arts.

Hundreds of wars and attempts at extermination of certain groups of people have stemmed from religious, ethnic and tribal differences since the Crusades. Catholics against Protestants, Jews against Arabs, Sikhs against Hindus, Hindus against Muslims, Tutsis against Hutus, communism against democracies, Kosovo against Serbia, Khmer Rouge against republicans . . . the list goes on and on . . . all with the same religious zeal. The main weapon in these latter day attempts at genocide has been terrorism, using the greatest terror of all, genocide. From the Inquisition to ethnic cleansing, the resulting terror has created deep splits among religions, tribes and ideologies around the world.

STATE TERROR AND GENOCIDE

The state-approved use of its power and resources to terrorize and attempt to liquidate a specific group of citizens, immigrants, religious or ethnic groups has some ambivalence about its proper designator. Raphael Lemkin, in his 1944 book, *Axis Rule in Occupied Europe,* coined the word "**genocide**." He constructed it from the Greek word "*genos*" (race or tribe) and the Latin suffix "*cide*"(to kill). At the end of World War II, the War Crimes Tribunal was at a loss as to what this crime should be called. History was of little use in finding a proper word to fit the nature of the crimes that Nazi Germany had engaged in at the extermination and concentration camps. "**Ethnic cleansing**," has been used in recent years to soften the eradication of specific groups of people. But, hard or soft, the word genocide better describes "the destruction of a nation or of an ethnic group." It implies the existence of a coordinated plan, aimed at total extermination, to be put into effect against individuals chosen as victims purely, simply and exclusively because they are members of the target group.[11]

"Mass murder," the term that was often used at the time, was an inadequate description of the atrocities committed in Nazi-occupied territories. It could not account for the motives, which arose solely from "racial, national or religious" considerations not the conduct of the war. Genocide required a separate definition as it was clearly not just against the rules of war, but a crime against humanity. Raphael Lemkin was the first person to put forward the theory that genocide is not a war crime and that the *immorality* of genocide should not be confused with the *amorality* of war.[12]

The definition of what constitutes a crime against humanity was established at the Nuremberg Trials. However, despite the significance of this, the jurists at Nuremberg had invented nothing new. They were simply advancing Montesquieu's ideas on international law, which he described as "universal civil law, in the sense that all peoples are citizens of the universe." Killing someone simply because he or she exists is a crime against humanity; it is a crime against the very essence of what it is to be human. This is not an elimination of individuals because they are political adversaries, or because they hold to what are regarded as false beliefs or dangerous theories, but a crime directed against the person as a person, against the very humanity of the individual victim. Thus it cannot be categorized as a war crime. Alain Finkielkraut, the French philosopher, pointed out that, it is quite a different thing to be regarded as an enemy than as a particular species of vermin to be systematically wiped out. Genocide is a crime on a different scale from all other crimes against humanity and implies an intention to completely exterminate the chosen group. Genocide is therefore both the gravest and the greatest of the crimes against humanity.

In the same way as in a case of homicide the natural right of the individual to exist is implied, so in the case of genocide as a crime, the principle that any national, racial or religious group has a natural right to exist is clearly evident. Attempts to eliminate such groups violate this right to exist and to develop within the international community. Lemkin's efforts and his single-minded perseverance brought about the Convention for the Prevention and the Punishment of the Crime of Genocide which was voted into existence by the General Assembly of the United Nations in 1948. After stating in Article 1 that genocide is a crime under international law, the Convention laid down the following definition:

Any of the following acts committed with intent to destroy, in whole or in part, a national, ethnical, racial or religious group, as such:

- Killing members of the group;
- Causing serious bodily or mental harm to members of the group;
- Deliberately inflicting on the group conditions of life calculated to bring about its physical destruction in whole or in part;
- Imposing measures intended to prevent births within the group;
- Forcibly transferring children of the group to another group.

The final definition as it stands today is based on four constituent factors:

- A criminal act . . .
- with the intention of destroying . . .

- an ethnic, national or religious group . . .
- targeted as such.[13]

Consequently the word "genocide" has often been used when making comparisons with later massacres throughout the world in order to attract attention by evoking images of the concentration camps and their victims. The inevitable consequences of such misuse of language are a loss of meaning and a distortion of values. For example, there is a great danger in the way the media applied the term "holocaust" to the devastation wrought by the cholera epidemic in Goma, which had the largest concentration of Rwandan refugees in the Democratic Republic of Congo (formerly Zaire). This puts the medical disaster that resulted from the massive influx of refugees as a consequence of the genocide on the same level as the genocide itself, a premeditated mass crime, systematically planned and executed. This has resulted in a double error with the exaggerated emphasis focused on the cholera victims (catastrophe though that was), distracting attention from the real crime already committed. The fact that cholera does not handpick its victims according to their ethnic origin was completely overlooked.

The controversial thousand-plane carpet-bombings that took place over Germany, incendiary and nuclear bombs over Japan, and in more recent times over Vietnam, still claimed their victims in a totally haphazard manner. Intrinsic meaning is lost when words like "genocide" or "holocaust" are used loosely to describe any human disaster with a large number of victims, regardless of the cause. It would be hard to deny that some form of evil has always existed in the world. But if such evil is seen in general, impersonal terms such as barbarism, man's inhumanity to man, chance circumstance or plain hatred, then there are no individual culprits at whom an accusing finger can be pointed. So-called collective blame is just another way of denying the facts. If one uses the definitions above and places them in the context of the larger category of crimes against humanity in general, there have really only been three genuine examples of genocide during the course of the twentieth century; the Armenians by the Young Turks in 1915; the Jews and Gypsies by the Nazis in World War II; and the Tutsis by the Hutu racists in 1994.

CYCLICAL NATURE OF TERRORISM

Terrorist acts have too often created a cycle of violence, with those against whom the terror-violence is first carried out becoming so angered that they resort to terrorism in response. This is clearly seen in the present situation in the Israel/Palestinian dispute in the Middle East and the Northern Ireland "troubles" that have killed thousands of innocent people by countering "their" violence with "our" violence, an "eye for and eye" in an endless circle. Each violent act frequently causes equally violent reactions. When the violence is unselective, when innocent people are victimized by car bombs and random violence, the reactive violence is also likely to "break all the rules" in the selection of targets, and become their own form of terrorist violence. Round and round it goes and where it stops nobody knows, seems to be the theme song of terrorism.

Perhaps the most prominent proponents of individual and collective violence as a means of destroying governments and social institutions were the

Russian anarchists. These were revolutionaries within Russia who sought an end to the Czarist state of the late 19th century. "Force only yields to force," and terror would provide the mechanism of change, according to the Russian radical theorist Alexander Serno-Solovevich.[14]

In the writings of two of the most prominent spokesmen for **revolutionary anarchism**, Mikhail Bakunin and Sergei Nechaev, one finds philosophies often echoed by modern terrorists. Bakunin, for example, advocated in his *National Catechism* (1866) the use of "selective, discriminate terror." Nechaev, in his work, *Revolutionary Catechism,* went further in advocating both the theory and practice of pervasive terror-violence. He asserted of the revolutionary: Day and night he must have one single thought, one single purpose: merciless destruction. With this aim in view, tirelessly and in cold blood, he must always be prepared to kill with his own hands anyone who stands in the way of achieving his goals.[15]

This is surely a very large step in the evolution of a terrorist from the use of a lone political assassin in earlier centuries. Even the religious fanatics of the assassins were arguably less willing to kill "anyone" to achieve a political objective. But this difference may well have existed more on paper than it did in practice. In spite of this written willingness to kill "anyone" who stood in the way, even the Socialist Revolutionary Party resorted primarily to selective terror-violence, and took special pains to avoid endangering the innocent bystanders. The "**Union of Russian Men**" formed to combat the growing revolutionary movement "by all means" was not only sanctioned by the Tsar, but granted special protection by him. This reactionary group engaged in a variety of terrorist activities, including but not limited to political murders, torture, and bombing. The Okrana (the Czarist secret police) also used viscious counterterror against the militant revolutionaries in an unabated attack until World War I began. George Kennon, commenting on the rising tide of "terrorism" in Russia during the last half of the nineteenth century, explained the relationship of state and revolutionary terrorism in this way:

> Wrong a man . . . deny him all redress, exile him if he complains, gag him if he cries out, strike him in the face if he struggles, and at the last he will stab and throw bombs.[16]

Some of the seeds of a more widespread and random terror-violence had been sown in the revolutionary and anarchistic movements of the late nineteenth century. But, by the beginning of the twentieth century, terror-violence was still principally directed toward political assassination. Between 1881 and 1912, at least ten national leaders lost their lives to assassinations. The Haganah, a Zionist underground army, and the Irgun Zvai Leumi, a Zionist militant force willing to use terrorist tactics against the British forces in Palestine, did so, and bombing, murder, and assassination became the order of the day, as British counter-violence met with escalating Haganah and **Irgun** terrorism. (Around and around . . .) When the Irgun bombed the King David Hotel, in which many innocent persons died or were seriously injured, British determination to quell the rebellion waned.

But during the struggle to gain a homeland free of Nazi terror, the Irgun had also committed terrorist acts against the indigenous population. Israel finally declared itself to be an independent state in 1948. Then, some of the dispossessed people within its borders and those who fled to surrounding states began a terrorism campaign against the new nation of Israel, whose terror-

Groups Affiliated with the al Qaeda Network

Uzbekistan

English Name: **Islamic Movement of Uzbekistan (IMU)**

The IMU consists of a coalition of Islamic militants from Uzbekistan and other Central Asian states opposed to the secular regime of President Islam Karimov. Most militants were believed to be in Afghanistan in the winter of 1999-2000, though some may have remained in Tajikistan. Its recruits have been trained in Osama bin Laden's camps in Afghanistan as well as in Pakistan. Training has also taken place in Uzbekistan's Ferghana Valley. The President of Uzbekistan is fully aware of the Islamist threat and has threatened with severe retaliation.

Lebanon

English Name: **Party of God**
Original Name: **Hezbollah**

Radical Shia group founded in 1982 by Iran military intelligence following the Israeli invasion of Lebanon. The organization is closely allied with and influenced by Iran. Since the early 1990s, Hezbollah has demonstrated its ability to conduct terrorist attacks far from the Middle East. An Executive Committee coordinates the four area councils: Beirut, southern suburbs, Bekaa Valley and Southern Lebanon. Its military strategy is allegedly coordinated with Iranian religious and military officials. Remains closely associated with al Qaeda through various training camps and the coordinated drug trafficking efforts operating from the Bekaa Valley and many regions in Afghanistan.

Algeria

English Name: **Armed Islamic Group (GIA)**
Original Name: **Groupe Islamiste Armé,**
Jama'a Islamiya Moussalaha

Militant Islamic fundamentalist group that began violent activities following the cancellation of elections by the Algerian government in 1992 after the Islamic Salvation Front (FIS) won the first round. Many of the members fought against the Soviet Union in Afghanistan as mujahideen (freedom fighters known currently as Arab Afghans), as well as recruiting the underprivileged, "petty" criminals and enraged youths of greater Algiers. The GIA concentrates it's violent operations on urban areas in an effort to gain wider press coverage.

Kashmir

English Name: **Movement of Holy Warriors (HuM)**
Original Name: **Harkat ul-Mujahedeen,**
Harakat ul-Mujahidin

The Harakat ul Ansar was formed by a merger of the Harakat ul-Jihad al-Islami and the Harakat ul-Mujahedin. The merger and its transformation into a terrorist organization came about as part of the Afghan jihad. The HuM is a Pakistan-based Islamic militant group that seeks to end Indian control of Muslim-inhabited parts of the divided region of Kashmir. It changed its name from Harakat al-Ansar to Harakat ul-Mujahedeen in an attempt to avoid American sanctions. Not all factions within HuM seem to be in favor of cooperation with the al Qaeda network.

Philippines

English Name: **Father of the Executioner;**
Bearer of the Sword (ASG)
Original Name: **Abu Sayyaf Group**

Small and radical Islamic separatist group operating in the southern Philippines. It is named after the nom de guerre of its first leader Abu Sayyaf, the name used by Abdurajak Abubakar January-jalani when he fought in Afghanistan. The group split from the MNLF in 1991 under the leadership of Abdurajik Abubakar Januaryjalani who was killed in a clash with the police in 1998. His younger brother, Khadafi Januaryjalani, replaced him as head of the organization. Ramzi Ahmed Yousef, the main suspect in the 1993 World Trade Center bombing, enlisted the ASG in 1991 to become one of the key support groups in a global terrorist network controlled by Yousef.

Java

English Name: **Lashkar Jihad**

The Lashkar Jihad is a Muslim fundamentalist paramilitary organization based in Java, which has threatened to wage a holy war against Christians in Indonesia. It has been responsible for the escalation of violence in the Moluccan Islands where formerly there was no conflict between Christians and Muslim. Some observers believe that the military may have armed the organization, as the fighters use army weapons. Some observers have linked the unrest to the investigations of former president Suharto for alleged corruption and army generals implicated in the 1999 violence in East Timor. While units of the Mobile Brigade (BRIMOB) special police forces chose the side of the Christians, the military fight alongside the Muslims.

Crime & Justice International October/November 2001

Crime & Justice International October/November 2001

Terror Groups associated with Osama bin Laden's al Qaeda Terrorist Network. (Used with permission by *Crime & Justice International*) violence against the Palestinian people sparked a conflict which continues to rend the fragile fabric of peace in the Middle East. Born in bloodshed, violence, and desperation, Israel continues to struggle against the terrorist violence that its very creation evoked.[14]

CONTEMPORARY EVENTS: HISTORICAL ROOTS

Is contemporary terrorism different and, if so, then in what ways? One reason for briefly reviewing the historical pattern and roots of terrorism is to be able to discover whether that pattern remains accurate in the contemporary world. If terrorism today is just like the terrorism of previous centuries, then we can use historical patterns to predict behavior and to construct responses based on successful attempts to combat this phenomenon in the past. If terrorism today is different, however, then historical patterns will be less useful in designing responses, although such patterns may still be of use in understanding the dynamics of the phenomenon. Terrorism has clearly existed before the twenty-first century. What we need to know as we prepare for yet another century is whether new forms of terrorism are that much different from their historical counterparts.

Related to these differences between historical and modern terrorism are important developments in the contemporary world. Modern methods of travel, for example, make it possible to carry out an assassination in the morning in country X and be halfway around the world from that nation within a matter of hours. Modern communications, too, have created a "smaller world." Events in places like Nigeria, Cape Town or Sri Lanka, for instance, are immediately transmitted in a dozen ways to New York City, Seattle or Omaha. Such communications, too, have served to expand the theater and enlarge the audience to which the terrorist plays his drama of death and violence. To catch the attention of America, the third world terrorists need not hijack airliners, fly to New York City and Washington, DC and crash them into the World Trade Center towers and the Pentagon. They need only plant a bomb in any city in the world larger than Mayberry, RFD.

The dramatic increase in the arsenal of weapons available to modern terrorists is also worth consideration. The would-be assassin does not need to rely on a small handgun to eliminate his victim. A **letter bomb** or an envelope containing anthrax can do the job without endangering the perpetrator, as the Unabomber in the United States has demonstrated. The potential for destruction through chemical and biological weapons has not yet been fully tapped, as noted in Chapter 14, although the sarin gas attacks in subways in Japan in 1995 gave ample evidence of the potential for such weapons when used in the very vulnerable mass transit systems of a modern city. Perhaps, until recently, the consequences of using such weapons were too dramatic for most groups to contemplate. But modern technology has certainly put at the terrorist's disposal a vast array of lethal and largely indiscriminate weapons, of which the **sarin toxin** apparently used in Japan represents only a very simple example. With this arsenal, the selection of victims has become devastatingly indiscriminate.

We hope the reader can now see that, as historical precedents for terrorism grow, it becomes very hard to distinguish between legitimate and illegitimate violence. As the nations born out of a climate of violence, such as Ireland

and Israel, become themselves illegitimate, it is increasingly difficult to condemn the terrorist for using methods employed in the struggles for independence and survival. The longer the history of terrorism grows, the harder it is to make a label of "terrorism" stick to the actions of any group or nation.

SUMMARY

If violence begets terrorism then terrorism must be as old as society and began with the first peoples of the Earth. This chapter is not very long. It was deliberately written that way to tweak the curiosity of the reader/student and, hopefully, make them want to learn more. Understanding terrorism without learning something about the history of a terrorist group, individual terrorists and the conditions that spawned them is like eating soup without salt. It feeds the body but is pretty bland and tasteless. Following chapters will involve places, cultures and issues that have strange names and exotic locations, as well as well-known names and places that have been touched by terrorism. Some will be covered in more depth than others. All of them will tell the student something about the social, religious or economic conditions that allowed the cancer of violence to grow into terrorism, whether by the state or by groups of people that have gone beyond the pale. Part Two will take the reader on an exciting and interesting trip around the world, examining the most significant terrorist locations, starting with the problems before and after the attacks of 9–11 in North America and Caribbean and a tour of the major regions of the world. As has been shown in this chapter, the death tolls from the acts of antigovernment terrorists are almost insignificant when compared with terrorism and genocide in the name of the state. Throughout history, from the time of the ancient Egyptians, who killed every member of a defeated army to the "Killing Fields" of Cambodia and Rwanda this has been true. State terrorism in this century alone has resulted in untold millions of deaths. The human rights movements, such as Amnesty International and others, has begun to shine bright light on the depredations committed by nations against their own people. Power and religious fanaticism have driven the kinds of terrorism that resulted in Hitler's holocaust and the conflicts between the Irish Catholics and Protestants, the Jews and Arabs, Shia and Sunni Muslims and the dozens of other conflicts around the globe. Instantaneous television coverage of these atrocities has begun to make the world aware that the most pernicious forms of terrorism are not those used by a single fanatic throwing bombs. In the next part we will explore the regions of the world to let the reader acquire a better understanding of where the causes for terrorism can be found in a large number of nations and cultures.

TERMS TO REMEMBER

assassination	*fatwa*	genocide
Big Seven	formation of intent	group retaliation
DPRK	founder of Islam	Hamas
ethnic cleansing	FPMR	hashish-eater

IRGC	**Pan Am Flight 103**	**rogue states**
Irgun	**perceived grievance**	**safe havens**
jihad	**PKK**	**sarin toxin**
letter bomb	**"puppet" terrorist organizations**	**tunnel vision**
MEK		**unbelievers**
Middle East	**revolutionary anarchism**	**Union of Russian Men**
Palestine Islamic Jihad		**War on Terrorism**

REVIEW QUESTIONS

1. Describe how violence can become terrorism.
2. Explain the three logical progressions that one must follow in order for a violent act to occur.
3. From where did the term assassin originate? Expand on that story.
4. Describe the concept of a "little war" and what it means in comparison with terrorism.
5. Discuss the differences between state-sponsored terrorism and actions by an individual or group as terrorism against the state.
6. What is the difference between state terrorism and state-sponsored terrorism?
7. Discuss the genocide by the Nazis against Jews and how that differs from the genocide in Rwanda.
8. What is your opinion in regard to the use of terrorism against a tyrannical leader?
9. Name the "big seven" states on the Department of State's list that sponsor terrorism.
10. How is terrorism different from violent behavior?

ENDNOTES

1. John Lachs. "Violence as Response to Alienation." *Alienation and Violence.* (Science Reviews Ltd., Middlesex, UK, 1988), pp. 147–160.
2. Ibid., p. 155.
3. Cindy C. Combs. *Terrorism in the Twenty-First Century,* (Prentice Hall, Upper Saddle River, NJ, 1997), p. 20.
4. Ibid., p. 21.
5. See M. Hodgson. *The Order of the Assassins* (1960); B. Lewis, *The Assassins: A Radical Sect in Islam* (1968).
6. B. Harwood, *Society of the Assassin: A Background Book on Political Murder* (London; International Institute for Strategic Studies).
7. Carl Sandburg, *Abraham Lincoln: The War Years* (Cambridge: MIT Press, 1939), Vol. 4, p. 482.
8. Vidal, *Cours de Droit Criminal et de Science Pententiare,* 5th ed. (Paris: Institute de Paris Press, 1916), pp. 110–112.
9. Political asylum is sanctuary or refuge for a person who has committed a crime such as assassination of a political figure. It is granted by one government against requests by another

government for the extradition of that person to be prosecuted for this 'political' crime. Funk and Wagnall's Standard Dictionary, Comprehensive International Ed., Vol. 1, p. 86, col. 3.

10. U.S. State Department of State. *2001 Patterns of Global Terror Report.*

11. In the Information Age, the Internet has become a valuable tool for researchers and authors. Much of the background data contained in this chapter and woven into and throughout this book were extracted from Web sites such as: Amnesty International; The U.S. Department of State *2001 Patterns of Global Terror Report;* The U.S. Departmentof State Background Notes: Geographic Entities and International Organizations; The U.S. Central Intelligence Agency World Factbook and other government sources. We are grateful for the presence of these modern sources and the information they have provided.

12. Central Intelligence Agency World Factbook.

13. Ibid.

14. Ibid.

15. U.S. Department of State, *Country Reports on Human Rights Practices.* 1998.

16. Ralph Lemkin: *Axis Rule in Occupied Europe.* 1944.

17. *Convention for the Prevention and Punishment for the Crime of Genocide;* General Assembly of the United Nations. 1948.

PART TWO
Terrorism Around the World

Flags at half staff—Bayonne, New Jersey. September 12, 2001. (AP Photo/
Chales Krupa)

3 North America and the Caribbean

"We cannot sit home and hope that trouble will somehow pass us by. And if we are going to build the kind of world we want for our children and ourselves we must take the lead in designing it, not wait for others to set the parameters for us."

Madeleine K. Albright

OVERVIEW

Over the last three decades or so, North America's television screens have displayed major terrorist bombings, hijackings and murders taking place in far away lands with exotic names and for seemingly bizarre reasons. Viewers were intrigued by the sound bytes, but most remained complacent and went on with their lives. The prospect of any major terrorist attack in the United States, Canada or the Caribbean was simply unimaginable. Oh, there were some far-out fringe groups of survivalist, ecology freaks, and various types of protesters, but they were thought of as "home-grown," and certainly nothing like the radicals in the Persian Gulf, the Middle East, or South Asia. All that "head-in-the-sand" thinking came to an abrupt halt in February 1993. On that day, the shocking television pictures of terrorist violence came not from Beirut, Londonderry or Jerusalem, but from New York City, at the World Trade Center, the second tallest building in the world! At approximately 12:18 PM, on 26 February 1993, an improvised explosive device in the back of a rental vehicle exploded on the second level of the parking basement. The resulting blast produced a crater, approximately one hundred and fifty feet in diameter and five floors deep, in the parking basement. The structure consisted mainly of steel-reinforced concrete, twelve to fourteen inches thick. The epicenter of the blast was approximately eight feet from the south wall of **World Trade Center** Tower One, near a support column. The device had been placed in the rear cargo portion of a one-ton Ford F350 Econoline van, rented from a Ryder Rental Agency in Jersey City, New Jersey. Approximately 6,800 tons of concrete and steel were displaced by the blast.

The main explosive charge consisted primarily of approximately 1,200 to 1,500 pounds of homemade, (nitrogen-fertilizer based) explosive, urea nitrate. The fusing system consisted of two 20-minute lengths of a nonelectric, burning-type fuse. The fuse terminated in lead azide, as the initiator. Also incorporated in the device and placed under the main explosive charge were three large metal cylinders of compressed hydrogen gas.

The resulting massive explosion killed six people and injured more than a thousand. More than 50,000 people were evacuated from the Trade Center complex during the hours immediately following the blast. The initial inspection on February 27th was described as a scene of massive devastation, almost surreal. There were small pockets of fire, electrical sparks arcing from damaged wiring, and automobile alarms whistling, howling and honking. The explosion ruptured two of the main sewage lines from both Trade Center towers, the Vista Hotel, and several water mains from the air conditioning system. In all, more than two million gallons of water and sewage drained into the tower and was pumped out of the crime scene. America had been given a wake-up call.

In April 1995, yet another terrorism event filled the airwaves and television screens around the world with the image of the **Alfred P. Murrah Federal Building** in Oklahoma City, shattered by a devastating blast. Another huge truck bomb had destroyed that building, leaving 168 people dead and more than 500 others injured. Early reports indicated that the bomber might be from the Middle East, and unconfirmed rumors, prejudice and public anger to a fever pitch. The arrest of Timothy McVeigh and his subsequent trial, conviction, and execution, as well as the arrest and conviction of his friend Terry Nichols, rattled the nerves of the entire nation. When it was revealed that both were members of right-wing local **militias**, it became clear that *domestic* terrorists had planned and committed this terrible act. Those two events and many others since have caused officials in the United States to rethink and reorganize their efforts and perceptions of where terrorist threats really lay. But the dots still had yet to be connected and the public slipped back to everyday life.

Then, on August 7, 1998, two U.S. Embassies in East Africa were, almost simultaneously, rocked by powerful explosions. The blasts took place at almost the same time, 10:30 AM local time in each country. Embassy officials confirmed that the explosions were the result of car bombs detonated near the two embassies, one in the Kenyan capital of Nairobi, and the other in Dar es Salaam, the capital of Tanzania. In Kenya, the explosion toppled the nearby Ufundi Cooperative Bank building over onto the embassy. The blast occurred shortly after the U.S. Ambassador, Prudence Bushnell, met with the Kenyan Trade Minister at the Bank. She was taken from the site on a stretcher, but later found to have sustained only light wounds from flying glass and debris. The bank building, located between the trade center and the embassy, was leveled. Apparently the bomb was placed there, rather than at the embassy itself, because of the embassy's bombproof construction. In Tanzania, another massive explosion left a large crater outside of the U.S. Embassy. An eyewitness stated, "The people at the front of the building didn't stand a chance." The blast occurred near the spot where a gasoline tanker had been observed parked in the embassy parking lot. More than sixty people were killed in that explosion, with at least another five hundred wounded.

No one claimed responsibility for the attacks, and officials stated that they feel certain that the blasts were unrelated to U.S. relations with either of the countries in which the blasts occurred. There was, however, a good deal of suspicion pointing to Osama bin-Laden. The Saudi millionaire and terrorist financier had made repeated threats to attack American targets. There is no doubt that his extensive terror network could have been capable of carrying out the attack, but still the dots were not being connected or a threat to the mainland of the United States anticipated. It was still happening on foreign soil, and these dots were slow to be connected as well. The citizens of the United States went on about their business and memory faded.

THE UNITED STATES

The United States is a very big country, although not as big as most Americans sometime would like to think it is. Actually, it is only half the size of Russia; just three-tenths the size of Africa; one-half the size of South America (only slightly larger than Brazil alone) and a bit larger than China. But it is in fact, about two and one-half times the size of all of Western Europe. The United States, including Alaska, shares a long border with its northern neighbor, Canada, of over 6,000 miles. And to the south it shares another long border, over 2,000 miles, with Mexico. In terms of preventing terrorism, smuggling and drug trafficking opportunities, these borders represent an enormous amount of territory to protect. Then, when you add in the United States coastlines of about 13,000 miles the difficulty escalates rapidly.

In the mid-1990s, international terrorism within the United States was generally not considered to be an issue, or threat, yet. But there were, never the less, events that indicated that, if a foreign terrorist group became angry enough at the United States, and determined enough, with leadership and financing they could create major problems to the infrastructure and population in such an open country.

The levels of terrorism experienced in places with names such as Beirut, Paris, London, Islamabad and Munich did not create major concern or any impact on the American lifestyle. Public credibility about threats from foreign terrorism in the United States is not enhanced when a violent act occurs and the media issues a sound bite; then the talking heads move on to another story; then later reveal that it was not foreign terrorism. It creates confusion. Two especially relevant examples of this syndrome are:

- The bombing of the van of Naval Captain Will Rogers III, who was the former Captain of the U.S.S. Vincennes, the Aegis missile-equipped U.S. Navy warship that mistakenly shot down an Iranian civilian airliner during the Iran-Iraq War;
- The mysterious "Middle Eastern" man who was brought back to the United States for questioning in regard to the bombing of Alfred P. Murrah Federal Building in Oklahoma City.

In both cases, the media jumped to the conclusion that they were terrorist bombings, planned and executed by other than domestic terrorists. Therefore, when facts otherwise surfaced about these two stories, it became more difficult for the public to take credence in, and ignore any material presented by the media in regard to reports of terrorism.

Mainland USA has never been subjected to as much political violence or terrorism as other areas in Europe, the Middle East, Ireland, the Persian Gulf, Africa or South Asia. Some of the few examples are the Symbionese Liberation Army (**SLA**), the Black Panthers, and the Weathermen. Others, such as the Unabomber come to mind. But such **domestic terrorist acts** have been few and far between. On the other hand, the IRA's ongoing slaughter of innocent women and children with car bombs, as the reader will see in Chapter 4, continued to be frequent and unremitting. But, after August 7, 1998, the United States was slowly awakening to the fact that it was no longer immune to larger scale acts clearly identifiable as foreign terrorist acts. The World Trade Center explosion became perhaps only the first salvo of external terrorist and politically motivated activities that attack random victims, intended to incite fear as well as add an external terrorist signature to an act of violence.

But terrorism in the United States is not limited to those with external agendas from foreign sources, as demonstrated by the attack on the federal building in Oklahoma City, Oklahoma. The terrorists in this case were Americans, members of a paramilitary survivalist militia from Michigan. They had responded with a festering anger over the United States government's bungling of the "**Waco Massacre**" of the Branch Davidians, a fringe religious group headed by David Koresh.

America's Home-Grown Terrorism

The United States is not immune to the use of terrorist actions by some of its citizens. We shall now discuss a long history of hate in America. Not the natural discord that characterizes a democracy, but the wild, irrational, murderous kind of hate that has led men and women throughout our history to extremes of violence against others simply because of their race, nationality, religion or lifestyle. Since 1865, the Ku Klux Klan (KKK) has provided a vehicle for this kind of hatred in America, and its members have been responsible for atrocities that are difficult for most normal people to even imagine. Today, while the membership and actions of the traditional and historical Klan declined in the last half of the twentieth century, there are many other groups that go by a variety of names and symbols who are at least as dangerous as the KKK ever was.

Some of these are teenagers who shave their heads and wear storm trooper jackboots, display swastika tattoos, and call themselves Skinheads or neo-Nazis. Some of them are young men who wear camouflage fatigues and

The New Davidian Center—Mount Carmel, Waco, Texas, 2000. (AP Photo/Donna McWilliam)

practice guerrilla warfare tactics at secret locations. Some of them are conservatively dressed professionals who publish materials filled with their bizarre beliefs, ideas ranging from denying that the Nazi Holocaust against the Jews in World War Two ever happened . . . to those with the conviction that the federal government is an illegal body and that all governing power should rest with county sheriffs. Despite their peculiarities, they all share the deep-seated hatred and resentment that has given life to the Klan and terrorized racial minorities and Jews in this country for almost a century and a half.

The Klan itself has had three periods of significant strength in American history: in the later half of the nineteenth century, in the 1920s, and during the 1950s and early 1960s when the civil rights movement was at its height. The Klan experienced resurgence in the 1970s, but never reached its past level of influence. Since then, with access to the Internet, the Klan has become just one element in a much broader spectrum of white supremacist and hate activity. It's important to understand, however, that violent prejudice is not limited to the Ku Klux Klan or any other white supremacist organization. People who have no ties to any organized group, but who share their virulent hatred, commit bombings, assaults, murders and arsons every year.

Knowing about the past is critical to making sense of the present and planning for the future. Historical research explains the roots of racism and prejudice, which sustain the Ku Klux Klan. As for current events, that is an even easier lesson for most minorities who grew up in the racially torn years of the 1950s. Young civil rights activists, working alongside John Lewis, Andrew Young, the late Dr. Martin Luther King, Jr., Julian Bond and many others saw the Ku Klux Klan as an all-too-visible power in many of the places they went to organize voter registration and protest segregation. They knew what the Klan was, and often had a pretty good idea of who they were. They also knew what the Klan would do to them, if they thought they could get away with it.

Now, of course, you can turn on your television set and see people in Klan robes or military uniforms again handing out hate literature on the town square. You can read in any newspaper of crosses again burned in folks' yards, and it seems as if we were back in the 1960s. Some say the Klan today should just be ignored. History, however, won't let us ignore current events. Those who would use violence to deny others their rights can't be ignored. The law must be exercised to stay strong. And even racists must learn to respect the law. The knowledge of the background of the KKK and its battle with the law, points out the current reasons why hate groups can't be ignored. It is not a pretty part of American history—some of the things you read here will make you angry or ashamed, some will turn your stomach. But it is important that we try to understand the villains as well as the heroes in our past, if we are to continue building a nation where equality and democracy are preserved.

Victims of the Klan

The image of a man hanging lifeless by a rope from a tree limb has become a symbol for the worst of Klan violence. Between 1889 and 1941, 3,811 black people were lynched for "crimes," such as threatening to sue a white man attempting to register to vote, joining labor unions, being "disrespectful" to a white man, looking at a white woman or for no reason at all. During the American Revolution, the term "Lynch Law" described an informal court run by

TERROR BRIEF 3–1

The Militia of Montana

The Militia of Montana is an educational organization dedicated to the preservation of the freedoms of ALL Citizens of the State of Montana and of the United States of America.

The best defense against the usurpation of these freedoms by the tyranny of a runaway, out of control government is a well-informed and well-prepared Unorganized Militia of the Citizens of the State of Montana and of the other States of the Federal Union.

> "A popular government without popular information, or the means of acquiring it, is but a prologue to a farce or a tragedy, or perhaps both. Knowledge will forever govern ignorance, and a people who mean to be their own governors must arm themselves with the power which knowledge gives." - James Madison

James Madison and the other framers of the Constitution knew that in the future if our Constitution was not interpreted in the context and according to the history in which it was drafted, we would not have a proper understanding of the original intent of our founding fathers, or in the words of Madison, primary author and the supreme expert on the Constitution:

> "Do not separate text from historical background. If you do, you will have perverted and subverted the Constitution, which can only end in a distorted, bastardized form of illegitimate government."

The Militia of Montana urges the reader of this page to seek out the TRUTH, taking nothing for granted, for it is the TRUTH, which will keep us FREE.

The Distinction between the National Guard and the Constitutional Unorganized Militia

Most Americans today believe that the National Guard is the Militia reserved to the states in the State Constitutions and the Constitution of the United States of America.

Nothing could be further from the TRUTH.

The National Guard did not exist from the beginnings of the Republic until 1903 when it was instituted and created by Congress as the Act of January 21, 1903, known by the name of its sponsor as "The Dick Act".

In 1982 the Senate Judiciary Committee Sub-committee on the Constitution stated in Senate Document 2807:

> "That the National Guard is not the 'Militia' referred to in the Second Amendment is even clearer today. Congress had organized the National Guard under its power to 'raise and support armies' and not its power to 'Provide for organizing, arming and disciplining the militia.' The modern National Guard was specifically intended to avoid status as the constitutional militia, a distinction recognized by 10 U.S.C. 311(a). Title 32 U.S.C. in July 1918 completely altered the definition of the militia and its service, who controls it and what it is. The difference between the National Guard and Regular Army was swept away, and became a personnel pay folder classification only, thus nationalizing the entire National Guard into the Regular Standing Armies of the United States.

All the arms, munitions, armament and equipment of the National Guard is owned and controlled by the federal government, not by "the people" as clearly stipulated in the Second Amendment. The Unorganized Militia consists of all able bodied persons of the nation and of the states between the ages of 18 and 44, and is exclusive of all members of the organized militia, i.e., the Armed Forces of the Federal Government of the United States and of the National Guards of the various states of the Union.

Article II

"A well regulated Militia being necessary to the security of a free State, the right of the people to keep and bear Arms shall not be infringed."

It is of great interest to note that in the ensuing years since this Amendment was ratified that two commas have been inserted, after the words "Militia" and "Arms", providing misconstruction of a very explicit restriction on the legislatures and the government. These commas appear in virtually all presentations of the 2nd Amendment today, including the official NARA presentation. The correct wording as presented to the States for ratification is shown in the "True Bill" and the Original Congressional Engrossing of the Proposed Amendments. Early publications of the Laws and Constitutions of the the United States DO NOT show these commas, i.e. the Bioren and Duane publication, "The Laws of the United States of America, from the 4th of March, 1789 to the 4th of March, 1815," available in the archives of Yale University, and the "The Constitutions of the United States", which I own and cherish, published in 1809 during Jefferson's administration by "Exeter: Printed by Charles Norris & Co for Edward Little & Co. Booksellers & Stationers, Newburyport."

This volume contains the Declaration of Independence, Articles of Confederation, state constitutions for New Hampshire, Massachusetts, Rhode Island (which was still operating under the King's Charter until 1843), Connecticut, New York, New Jersey, Pennsylvania, Delaware, Maryland, Virginia, North Carolina, South Carolina, Georgia, Vermont, Tennessee, Kentucky, and Ohio. It also has the "Government of the Northwest Territory", "An Act to Divide the Northwest Territory into two separate governments", "An Act Concerning the District of Columbia" and supplements, "An Act to incorporate the inhabitants of the City of Washington in the District of Columbia" and supplements, and finally "An Act erecting Louisiana into two Territories, and providing for the Temporary government thereof."

The Bioren and Duane edition of 1815 was published by an Act of Congress. This publication, in five volumes, represents the first authorized edition of the Laws of the United States and the U.S. Constitution issued following the destruction of the Library of Congress and the other records of the government by the British army in 1814. The lawmakers then seated as the Thirteenth Congress authorized the spending for this special edition on February 16th, 1815.

The Founders of our Nation and the Framers of the Constitution were well aware of the dangers of the tyranny and treason of a run-away governmental bureaucracy and had a very PRIMARY reason for the inclusion of the Second Amendment to the Constitution. Let's let them speak for themselves:

"Firearms stand next in importance to the Constitution itself. They are the American people's liberty teeth and keystone under independence. From the hour the Pilgrims landed, to the present day, events. occurrences and tendencies prove that to ensure peace, security and happiness, the rifle and pistol are equally indispensable. The very atmosphere of firearms everywhere restrains evil interference— they deserve a place of honor with all that's good."

—George Washington, Commanding General of the Continental Army, Father of Our Country and First President of the United States, in his address to 2nd Session of 1st Congress.

"The strongest reason for the people to retain the right to keep and bear arms is, as a last resort, to protect themselves against tyranny in Government."

—Thomas Jefferson, Author of the Declaration of Independence, and President of the United States.

"The highest number to which a standing army can be carried in any country does not exceed one hundredth part of the souls, or one twenty-fifth part of the number able to bear arms. This portion would not yield, in the United States, an army of more than twenty-five or thirty thousand men. To these would be

The Militia of Montana (continued)

opposed a militia amounting to near half a million citizens with arms in their hands, officered by men chosen from among themselves, fighting for their common liberties and united and conducted by governments possessing their affections and confidence. It may well be doubted whether such a proportion of regular troops could ever conquer a militia thus circumstanced. Besides the advantage of being armed, it forms a barrier against the enterprises of ambition, more insurmountable than any which a simple government of any form can admit of. The governments of Europe is afraid to trust the people with arms. If they did, the people would surely shake off the yoke of tyranny, as America did. Let us not insult the free and gallant citizens of America with the suspicion that they would be less able to defend the rights of which they would be in actual possession than the debased subjects of arbitrary power would be to rescue theirs from the hands of their oppressors.

—James Madison, principal author of the Constitution, principal writer of The Federalist Papers, President of the United States, Mainstream Revolutionary and Militant.

"What, Sir, is the use of a militia? It is to prevent the establishment of a standing army, the bane of liberty. . . . Whenever Governments mean to invade the rights and liberties of the people, they always attempt to destroy the militia, in order to rise an army upon their ruins."

—Rep. Elbridge Gerry of Massachusetts, spoken during floor debate over the Second Amendment, I Annals of Congress at 750, August 17, 1789

"It is not the function of the government to keep the citizen from falling into error; it is the function of the citizen to keep the government from falling into error."

—U.S. Supreme Court Justice Robert H. Parker, Chief Prosecutor for the United States of America at the Nuremberg Trials

Of those persons which oppose the upholding of the Second Amendment, a principal lobbyist for the "Brady Bill", in an excerpt from the January, 1984 issue of the National Educator, page 3, an article reveals that Sarah Brady is Chairman of Handgun Control, Inc., and while lobbying liberal Senator Howard Metzenbaum about gun control legislation, said to him: "Our task of creating a <u>SOCIALIST</u> America can only succeed when those who would resist us have been <u>TOTALLY DISARMED</u>."

We owe a debt of gratitude to the Historical Society of Wisconsin, for they spent a great deal of time searching for this January, 1994 issue of the National Educator. The Conspirators to form a Socialist New world Government and the United Nations are still at work treasonously subverting the Constitution in order to enslave the Citizens of the State of Montana, The United States of America and the World in a socialist union.

Thank you and Sincerely,
Randy L. Trochmann
Co-founder, Militia of Montana.

Source: Official Militia of Montana Web site www.militiaofmontana.com.

Colonel Charles Lynch of Bedford County, Virginia, who "tried" Tories and criminals in an effort to restore law and order to the frontier. Lynch's punishments consisted generally of fines or an occasional whipping. In the 1850s, "Lynch Law" was used by the KKK and later as a common phrase, to describe the hanging of one of their objects of hate.

Aryan Nation Alliance—October 28, 2000. (AP Photo/Tom Davenport)

Today there is a trend to spread hate and racism by forming so-called "militias" that use the Internet to spread their message of hatred and intolerance. An example of this is shown in Terrorism Brief 3-1, typical of that found on hundreds of Web sites in the U.S. operating under the banner of so-called free speech.

In the late 1920s, in the days of prohibition, gangs and mobsters preyed on society and each other with deadly violence. Mobsters gunning down those who opposed or interfered with their bootlegging traumatized all that witnessed such carnage. These, as it is now clear, were not just criminal, but terrorist acts. Terror strikes at the basic need for safety by anyone that hears about it or observes it. Serial killers are unwitting terrorists when their deeds are publicized and Street gangs in American cities today use **drive-by shootings** as a tactic for creating fear and terror. These demonstrations keep their rivals in check and neighborhood citizens from reporting these and other crimes against their own communities to the police. The same kinds of fear-inducing methods have long been the favorite tactics of the Cosa Nostra. From killings in schools and fast food places to motorcycle gangs terrorizing an entire town, all forms of violence can be utilized as a means to incite terror.

With a population approaching 290 million, the United States remains a "nation of immigrants," people who came to a great and prosperous land, legally and illegally, from the four corners of the earth. They come in hope of finding opportunities for a better life. As far as terrorism was concerned, many of these immigrants escaped from various forms of it to come to a place where such actions were unthinkable. As we have now seen, the history of the United States does not support that premise and many forms of terror have scarred its brief but bloody past . . . and even now mar its present.

The United States has the most powerful, diverse, and technologically advanced economy in the world. It boasts a per-capita annual income that is the highest among all major industrial nations. In this market-oriented economy, private individuals and business firms make most of the decisions, and government buys needed goods and services predominantly in the private marketplace. American business firms enjoy considerably greater flexibility than their counterparts in Western Europe and Japan in decisions to expand capital plant, lay off surplus workers, and develop new products.

Despite a deep dip in the stock market at the end of 2002, in all economic sectors United States firms are at or near the forefront in technological advances, especially in computers, medical services, aerospace and military hardware. However, the advantage has narrowed since the end of World War II. The rapid development of technology largely explains the gradual development of a two-tier labor market. This occurs when those at the bottom lack the education and the professional/technical skills of those at the top and cannot manage to acquire good jobs that have equitable pay, health insurance coverage and other benefits. Probably a growing terrorism threat in the United States is not from foreign, but from dissatisfied domestic purveyors of violence, hate and terror.

DOMESTIC TERRORISM

The face of domestic terrorism in the United States continues to change. The FBI identified a further decline in traditional left wing domestic extremism, and an increase in activities among extremists associated with right wing groups and special interest radical organizations.

Left Wing Terrorism

Over several decades, left-oriented extremist groups posed the predominant domestic terrorist threat in the United States. In the 1980s, the FBI neutralized many of these groups by arresting key members who were conducting criminal activity. The failure of communism and the fall of the former Soviet Union in 1989 deprived many leftist groups of a coherent ideology or tangible support. As a result, membership and belief for the "cause" by these groups waned.

The United States still faces a threat from some left wing extremists, including a few Puerto Rican terrorist groups. Although Puerto Rico voted to remain within the U.S. Commonwealth in 1993, some extremists still plan and conduct minor terrorist acts in order to draw attention to their support for independence.

Right Wing Terrorism

On the other hand, right wing extremist groups, located at the opposite end of the political spectrum, which generally adhere to an anti-government or racist ideology continue to attract. Many of these recruits feel disenfranchised by rapid changes in the U.S. culture and economy, or are seeking some form of personal affirmation. As the American social structures continue to change, the potential for escalating hate crimes by extremist right wing groups is an increasing concern. Of particular note is that many state and local law enforcement organizations consider a broader range of activities and acts as terrorist, or potentially terrorist, than does the FBI. The official FBI statistics do not count many threatening acts by organizations such as the Skinheads, street gangs and drug dealers as terrorist acts. States and municipalities are equally adamant in identifying right wing, (neo-Nazi, the Ku Klux Klan, anti-Semitic, anti-federalist and militias), and issue-specific (antiabortion, animal rights, environmentalist) organizations as major potential sources for supporters of terrorism in the United States.

The burgeoning militia movement in the United States was brought under a blinding light from the admissions of Timothy McVeigh and Terry Nichols. Such paramilitary, rabid antigovernment groups also continue to attract supporters. Several factors have contributed to the increase of this generally antigovernment mood. In a changing political environment, issues such as gun-control legislation, the United Nations' involvement in international affairs, and clashes between dissidents and law enforcement are cornerstones of militia ideology. When you tie in the neo-Nazi zeal and radical philosophies you have an explosive situation. Some militia members firmly believe that the U.S. Government is in a conspiracy to create a "**New World Order**." According to adherents, international boundaries will be dissolved and the United Nations will be allowed to rule the world. Other militia advocates believe that the federal government has gotten either too powerful or simply illegal and out of control. Many of these militants continue to conduct paramilitary training and stockpile illegal weapons in preparation for an armed Armageddon-type of confrontation with the government. A few of these extreme militia members could pose a serious terrorist threat. Counterterrorism efforts by the United States and others will be covered in Chapter 13.

Special Interest Extremists

Special interest extremists continue to conduct acts of politically oriented crime and terrorism. Violent antiabortion advocates were responsible for almost all of these activities. The Department of Justice's Task Force on Violence Against Abortion Providers (**TFVAAP**) decreased the number of abortion-related crimes from the high 1994 levels. Although the number of incidents has declined, the TFVAAP still investigated more than 100 violations of the Freedom of Access to Clinic Entrances (**FACE**) Act. Two of the most prominent abortion-related events in the 1990s included the following:

On February 22, 1995, Dr. Elizabeth Karlin, a physician in Madison, Wisconsin, received two death threat letters. Vincent Whitaker, an inmate at a local county jail who was serving a 67-year sentence for reckless injury with a motor vehicle, later admitted writing the letters. On September 12, 1995, Whitaker was tried and convicted of two counts of the FACE Act and sending threats through the U.S. Mail. On November 21, 1995, Whitaker was sentenced to an additional 63 months imprisonment.

In August 1995, John Salvi—the suspected murderer of two receptionists during a December 30, 1994, shooting spree at an abortion clinic in Brookline, Massachusetts—was declared competent to stand trial. Salvi was charged under Massachusetts's law with the murders of Shannon Lowney and Lee Ann Nichols, and five other counts of aggravated assault.[1] He received a life sentence in March 1996 and died, of possible suicide, in November of 1996.

The Civil Rights Division of the Department of Justice, through the TFVAAP, investigates any instance in which customers or providers of reproductive health services are criminally threatened, obstructed, or injured while seeking or providing services.

INTERNATIONAL TERRORISM

Following the incredibly planned and executed attacks of 9–11, foreign terrorists of every stripe now view the United States as vulnerable and a priority target. Although, as shown by the rapid mobilization efforts in Homeland Defense, terrorists and their supporters continue to live in and travel with relative ease throughout the country. Ironically, the huge U.S. drug-using population continues to help finance terrorism around the world by being a major consumer of the entire spectrum of illegal drugs. These narco-dollars continue to fill the war chests of terrorist groups around the world. Narco terrorists purchase cut-down cocaine shipped from Colombia through Mexico and the Caribbean, brown tar heroin, marijuana, and increasingly methamphetamine from Mexico. The American user is also a consumer of high-quality Southeast Asian heroin from the Golden Triangle. America is a major illicit producer of its own cannabis, depressants, stimulants, hallucinogens, methamphetamine and designer drugs such as Ecstasy. This creates a multibillion dollar need for drug money-laundering centers. And then the cycle repeats.

PUERTO RICO

The Commonwealth of Puerto Rico is closely intertwined with the United States. The island's inhabitants possess all the rights and obligations of United States citizens, except for the right to vote in presidential elections and the obligation to pay federal taxes. The United States also governs the Virgin Islands, Guam, and American Samoa. Puerto Rico is slightly less than three times the size of Rhode Island. Taino Indians, who inhabited the territory originally, called the island Boriken or Borinquen (a word that with various modifications is still popularly used to designate the people and island of Puerto Rico). The Taino Indians, who came from South America, inhabited the major portion of the island when the Spaniards arrived.

While the post-Colombian native language is Spanish, both Spanish and English are now the official languages. Language has been a central issue in Puerto Rican education and culture since 1898. Until 1930, U.S. authorities insisted upon making English the language of instruction in the schools, the intent being to produce English-speaking persons of American culture in the same way this is done in the United States public schools. But strong resistance to the policy finally brought a change to the use of Spanish as the basic school language, English becoming a second language studied by all. In 1991 the Puerto Rican legislature, following the lead of the pro-Commonwealth Popular Democratic Party and the governor, Rafael Hernández Colon, endorsed a bill that made Spanish the island's official language, thus reversing a 1902 law that gave both Spanish and English official recognition. In

1993 the pro-statehood governor, Pedro J. Rossello, signed legislation restoring equal status to Spanish and English for a population of close to 3,900,000. Puerto Rico's population density of 1,100 people per square mile is among the world's highest—only Bangladesh, The Maldives, Barbados, Taiwan, South Korea and the city-states of Hong Kong and Singapore are more crowded.

It is estimated that some 2 million Puerto Ricans have migrated to the United States. Had these people remained in Puerto Rico, the island would be so densely populated that there would be virtually no room for people to live. Because of the massive migration to the mainland, more Puerto Ricans are said to live in New York City than in San Juan.

Besides the slaves imported from Africa (Sudan, Congo, Senegal, Guinea, Sierra Leone, and the Gold, Ivory, and Grain coasts), other ethnic groups brought to work on the plantations joined the island's racial mix. Fleeing Simón Bolívar's independence movements in South America, Spanish loyalists fled to Puerto Rico—a fiercely conservative Spanish colony during the early 1800s. French families also flocked there from both Louisiana and Haiti. As changing governments or violent revolutions depressed the economies of Scotland and Ireland, many farmers from those countries also journeyed to Puerto Rico in search of a better life.

While the Puerto Ricans have had a fairly peaceful existence, there have been some issues that were terrorism or close to it. The biggest included an action where a quasi-terrorist group, the **Macheteros,** blew up eleven jet fighters of Puerto Rico's National Guard near San Juan. Ronald Fernandez, Professor of Sociology and author of *Los Macheteros: The Violent Struggle for Puerto Rican Independence,* has spent the last seven years researching Puerto Rico. He writes of the Macheteros frustrations and susceptibility to lashing out.

On August 25, 1989, Filiberto Ojeda Rios, acting as his own attorney, gave his closing argument to the jury in a U.S. court in San Juan. The indictment, drawn in the name of the United States of America, charged that Ojeda Rios had shot at and assaulted agents of the Federal Bureau of Investigation. President Reagan had appointed the prosecutor, the judge had been appointed by President Carter, and the American flag stood in the courtroom, but the jury was Puerto Rican.

Far from denying his actions, Ojeda Rios embraced them, and asked the jury to uphold the right of the Puerto Rican people to use force, in self-defense, against the unwanted, foreign presence of the United States of America.

There are no American heroes [in this story,] nor is there a happy ending. Yet it is imperative for Americans to know our own contribution to the perpetuation of colonialism. When the sun rose on October 12, 1992, marking 500 years of colonialism, Americans would do well to have taken a look at Puerto Rico and the destruction wrought there in the name of "democracy." The island today has a per-capita income of one-half that of Mississippi, the poorest state in the United States. Its rates of suicide, mental illness, drug addiction, crime, alcoholism, and sterilization of women are among the highest in the world.[2]

The hotly contested issue of the status of Puerto Rico continues. In 1991, in an island-wide vote Puerto Ricans rejected an amendment that would have "reviewed" their Commonwealth status. In the referendum, Commonwealth status was reaffirmed by a very close vote, with Statehood, 788,296 (46.3%);

Commonwealth, 826,326 (48.6%); Independence, 75,620 (04.4%); Nulls, 10,748 (00.7%). This issue has caused a lot of tempers to flair up again, but falls short of forming terrorist groups.

We have seen that the United States still seems to be "the land of the free and the home of the brave." But its very freedom, in a world of terrorism, can be its "Achilles' heel." As the world economic situation continues to destabilize and the American economy stays strong, the gap between those who can get ahead and those who can't widens. Then, as that gap grows, the disenchanted and disenfranchised left and right movements in the United States, and around the globe, will become a more active threat to its peace and tranquility. Chapter 14 goes into great depth as to the efforts to provide coordi-

September 11, 2002. Mourners in the foot print of the Twin Towers (WTC) one year after the devastating attack. (AP Photo/Amy Sancetta)

nated and effective homeland protection for a nation that has felt too secure by being separated by two oceans from international terrorism.

CANADA

Canada defines the extreme northern reaches of North America and extends all the way to the Arctic Ocean. It is a good neighbor of the United States, and Canadians are more like Americans than different from them. This huge country, bordered by the North Atlantic Ocean and North Pacific Ocean, is slightly larger than the United States (it is the second largest country in the world behind Russia), but has a population of only about 30,400,000. The continuous permafrost in the northern territories is a major obstacle to development, along with cyclonic storms that form east of the Rocky Mountains. They are a result of the mixing of air masses from the Arctic, Pacific, and North American interior, which produce most of Canada's rain and snow.

As a member of the British Commonwealth, Canada's Chief of State is Her Majesty Queen Elizabeth II (since February 6 1952), represented by an appointed Governor General. The head of government is the elected Prime Minister. An affluent, high-tech industrial society, Canada today closely resembles the United States in per capita output, market-oriented economic system, and patterns of production. Since World War II, the impressive growth of the manufacturing, mining, and service sectors has transformed the nation from a largely rural and fishing economy into one primarily industrial and urban. Canada started the 1990s in recession, and real rates of growth have averaged only 1.1% so far this decade. Because of slower growth, Canada still faces high unemployment, especially in Quebec and the Maritime Provinces. With its great natural resources, skilled labor force, and modern capital plant, however, Canada will surely enjoy better economic prospects in the future. The continuing constitutional impasse between English- and French-speaking areas is raising the possibility of a split in the confederation, and makes foreign investors somewhat edgy.

As Juliet O'Neill of the Ottawa Citizen, said in 1996, "You're more likely to be struck down by lightning or die in a car crash than find yourself victim of a terrorist attack in Canada." [3] Your authors searched hard and long to find some examples of serious and violent terrorism in Canada but in the Canadians' favor, few such acts were discovered. In the three decades since terrorism has dominated the headlines and the evening news, you can count major international terrorist acts in Canada in single digits. Those which might be considered major terrorist events have been scattered and uncommon. The **FLQ** (*Front de liberation du Quebec*) crisis in 1970 was the first. Second, the mid-1980s Armenian attacks on Turkish diplomats in Ottawa. And lastly, the alleged involvement of Sikh terrorists in the crash of an Air India jet from Toronto that blew up over the coast of Ireland, killing 329 passengers who were mostly Canadians. This incident occurred in June 1985, on the same day as an explosion in the baggage hall at Tokyo Airport from baggage arriving from a Canadian Pacific airliner from Vancouver. The limited data on terrorism and violence showed the criminal use of explosives was at the very low rate of two cases per 100,000 people. It appears that, in "the peaceable kingdom" of Canada, spectacular violence is rare and terrorism is something seen happening on television, to other people in other countries.

The major concern is that Canada may be being used as a base for organizing, fund raising, consciousness raising, transport and logistics for international terrorists from among the many refugees who have come there. These groups range from Tamil Tigers and Islamic fundamentalists to Protestant and Catholic Irish paramilitaries and Latin American and Asian extremists. Canada stays on the alert for homegrown terrorism from what they refer to as, "issue group extremists." Examples of these are animal rights extremists, armed Indians, antiabortion radicals, neo-fascists, bikers and skinheads.

Of course, potential violence and disputes over land and politics, should Quebec someday choose separation in a referendum, is always on the agenda of Canadian counterterrorism agencies. Among tactics used by low-level terrorist groups in recent years are consumer scare threats, mail bombs, shootings, and vandalism. Canada has some problems with illicit production of cannabis for the domestic drug market, where use of hydroponics technology permits growers to plant large quantities of high-quality marijuana indoors. With its links to the Far East and a very long coastline, Canada has a continuing and growing role as a transit point for heroin and cocaine entering the United States market.

Front du Liberation de Quebec (FLQ)

Liberal and extreme thinking young Quebecers were eager for change and the right to establish a separate French-speaking sovereign state within Canada. Terrorism in such a liberal country as Canada has been rare, but the turbulent days of the radical 1960s saw terrorism come to Central Canada in the shape of a separatist movement, the Front du Liberation de Quebec (FLQ). From its beginnings in 1963 its aim was for the separation of the Province of Quebec from what is termed English-speaking Canada. Canada is part of the British Commonwealth and therefore pays allegiance to the Crown. French-speaking Quebec in the 1960s wanted separation and to have their own sovereign country within Canada. The debate on a separation still continues to this day. In the 1960s, the left wing FLQ espoused a workers revolution as a means of achieving that goal. The FLQ, along with many French speaking Canadians, strongly resented the control that English Canada exerted on both politics and the economy in the Province of Quebec. The Parti Quebecois, still a political party today, has actively pursued the agenda of separation.

The political boost that the FLQ needed came from an unexpected direction. On a visit to Montreal in 1967, the President of France, General Charles De Gaulle in what has become a famous speech, ended with the phrase, *"Vive le Quebec Libre"* (Long Live Free Quebec). Throughout the 1960s, Anglophile areas of Montreal were targets for bomb attacks by the FLQ.[4] More than 200 explosions took place between 1963 and 1970, with the Quebec Government and the Federal Government seemingly powerless to intervene. The FLQ used robberies in the traditional fashion of financing their operations and also a reason to hit at Anglophone businesses. The terrorist event, which spelled the end for the FLQ, was the kidnapping of the British Trade Commissioner, James Cross, and the Province of Quebec's Labor Minister, Pierre Laporte. The kidnapping had little value to the FLQ but gave the Prime Minister of the day,

Pierre Trudeau, the weapon he needed to use a firm hand against all subversive elements, not only Quebec, but throughout the rest of Canada as well. The two VIPs were kidnapped in October 1970. The dead body of Laporte was found days later in the trunk of a car. All Canadians were appalled that the FLQ would go to such lengths. The brutal murder turned public and political opinion sharply against them. James Cross was located in a suburb of Montreal by the Royal Canadian Mounted Police (RCMP). After protracted negotiations, the kidnappers were allowed to fly to Cuba in exchange for the release of James Cross. They had also demanded the release of colleagues serving prison sentences for FLQ offenses, but these demands were not given to the terrorists.

One of the founder members of the FLQ, Raymond Villeneuve, was convicted of planting a number of bombs and was sentenced to twelve years in prison. A national referendum held in Canada in October 1995 saw a narrow defeat for the separation movement, however, by then Villenueve had been released from his prison term and was again assisting with a new younger breed of Quebec separatist also hell-bent on tearing up the constitution. The *Movement de Liberation Nationale du Quebec* is deemed extremely small with a couple of dozen die-hard activists, and consists of some former militant members of the now-defunct FLQ.[5] This terrorist movement, the only one of note in normally reserved and peaceful Canada, has shown that this country was not immune to such social violence.

The Canadians woke up to weaknesses in their border security following a frustrated attempt to cross into the United States with explosives to blow up the Los Angeles airport (LAX) control center at the Millennium celebration. The Canadian Standing Senate Committee on National Security and Defense came up with some strong recommendations to close such holes in security:

> The system of electronic passes must be reinforced by the introduction of a proper screening system for port employees that will include police and security background checks. Canada Customs officers testified that they were occasionally subjected to acts of intimidation by dockworkers during patrols, or while engaged in searches.
>
> The widespread theft of containers and the number of break-ins at ports are disturbing indicators of a high level of criminal activity. The Committee was struck by police comments concerning the sizable percentage of dockworkers with criminal records and the seeming lack of concern about this on the part of most Port employers and Port Authorities.
>
> At the Port of Montreal, the Committee was told that roughly 15 percent of longshoremen and 36 percent of checkers have serious criminal records. At the Port of Halifax, police told the Committee that 187 of 500 employees (39 percent) whose records the police checked had serious criminal records. At the Port of Charlottetown, it was 28 of 51 (54 percent). The Committee is certainly concerned with the sizable percentage of employees with criminal records. But it also believes that criminal elements are unlikely to have a zealous interest in countering terrorist activities, and may knowingly or unknowingly engage in acts that assist terrorists. Even their relentless efforts to prevent Port Authorities from exercising control over activities at a port, so that they can go about their illegal activities, plays into the hands of any would-be terrorists who might be deterred by a more effective level of supervision. The Committee is unanimous in its belief that an enhanced capacity to screen port employees for criminal activity, as well as for

security reasons, is essential to reassure Canadians and Canada's trading partners that our ports do not constitute a danger to their well-being. Police expressed concern that unions continue to exercise excessive control over the functioning of ports.

The traditional hiring hall model exemplifies this, whereby employers request the number of employees they need and the union determines who gets selected and where they will work. "The Committee recommends the introduction of a compulsory background screening system at significant ports to identify from among those employees or candidates for employment those persons who are identified by the Canadian Security Intelligence Service as posing a security risk.[6]

International Terrorism in Canada

As detailed earlier, Canada has been viewed by many terrorist organizations as a safe haven for fund-raising for terror operations. Canada's Security and Intelligence Services has openly reported the existence of at least forty foreign terror groups with bases and operations in Canada. Canada was founded on population growth through immigration, so it is therefore easy for a French speaker from a North African country such as Algeria to live, work and operate clandestinely in the Province of Quebec where French is the commonly accepted language, just as it is in Algeria. Following 9–11, investigators discovered interconnected links to immigrants in both the Province of Quebec and closer to the U.S. border in neighboring Ontario. Ahmed Ressam, the man now in custody for the failed plot to bomb Los Angeles Airport to coincide with the Millennium festivities, purchased many of the items required to assemble his home-made bomb from a Vancouver, British Columbia, area supermarket. Ressam was stopped by an alert U.S. Customs agent attempting to cross the border into the State of Washington in a vehicle, on the ferry route from Victoria into Port Angeles. Ressam remains in custody and is rumored to be closely linked to the hijackers of the suicide aircraft used on 9–11.

CUBA

The Republic of Cuba is situated on an island and is the largest country in the Caribbean. It is located between the Caribbean Sea and the North Atlantic Ocean, just 90 miles south of Florida and is slightly smaller than Pennsylvania. The U.S. Naval Base at Guantanamo Bay is leased by the United States and remains part of Cuba, but only mutual agreement or United States abandonment of the area can terminate the lease. This has been a serious bone of contention in United States/Cuban relations for decades. The population of this communist state is almost 11,000,000. Its ethnic makeup is unique and diverse, with 51% being mulatto, 37% white, 11% black and 1% Chinese.

The state is the primary player in the Cuban economy and controls practically all foreign trade. The government has undertaken several reforms in recent years to stem excess liquidity, increase labor incentives, and alleviate serious shortages of food, consumer goods, and services. The liberalized agricultural markets introduced in October 1994, at which state and private farmers sell above-quota production at unrestricted prices, have broadened legal consumption alternatives and reduced black market prices. Government efforts to lower subsidies to unprofitable enterprises and to shrink the money supply caused the peso's black market value to move from a peak of 120 to the dollar in the summer of 1994 to a low of 20–21 to the dollar at the end of 1996. New taxes helped drive down the number of legally registered self-employed workers from 208,000 in January 1996 to 180,000 by December. Havana announced that GDP declined by 35% during 1989–1993, the result of lost Soviet aid and domestic inefficiencies. The drop in GDP was turned around in 1994, when Cuba reported a 0.7% growth. Government officials claimed that GDP increased by 2.5% in 1995 and 7.8% in 1996. Export earnings rose an estimated 40% in 1996 to $2.1 billion. This trend is a good sign that Cuba may be making a move back into the economy of the region. Some say this is largely on the strength of increased sugar shipment to Russia and higher nickel production through a joint venture with a Canadian firm. With the economic recovery, imports rose for the second straight year, growing by an estimated 26% to $3.5 billion. Despite these moves, however, the economy has dropped again and living standards for the average Cuban have not improved significantly.

Fidel Castro

Kim Il-Sung, Deng Xiaoping, Peron, Khrushchev, Kadar, Franco and Tito are all famous dictators who are long departed. But Fidel Castro remains as the longest-serving leader of any country in the modern world. Castro has all but destroyed his country with iron-fisted leadership yet manages to stay in power. Born on August 13, 1926, Fidel Castro led a revolt against the Batista dictatorship and became the President of Cuba in 1959. He remains ensconced in his palace in Havana, seemingly as solidly as forty years ago. Recent data suggest that nearly half the Cuban work force is unemployed and that most Cubans live on a bare subsistence of only 1,400 calories a day. Foreign investment, which peaked at $563 million in 1994, was probably as low as $30 million in 1998. Part of this decline was due to the fall of the Soviet Union. Worst of all, Cuba has lost its long-held position as the world's largest producer of sugar. Barely 3 million tons are being produced, an all-time low.

Castro is a "classic" dictator in that he emerged not from the historical center of his society but from its physical and moral peripheries. His father was a rough and deceitful "Gallego" from the impoverished north of Spain. Like Napoleon the Corsican, Hitler the Austrian, and Stalin the Georgian, who came from similar difficult backgrounds, Castro has a perversely captivating combination of seductiveness and violence. As a boy, he tried to burn down his parents' house and burn up his father's car. Legend says that young Fidel would regularly hang over a canyon while the trains thundered by. Above all, he was always the perfect Machiavellian, naturally mastering every technique of political, physical and psychological manipulation over the Cuban people, his troops and leaders around the world.

When he was at the Jesuit high school, Castro was fascinated with reading about the European fascists. From Mussolini, he took the Italian's hysterical rhetorical gestures. From Hitler, he borrowed the Austrian's lessons in the sociology of revolution. Hitler had created a power base from the alienated and devastated German lower classes. Castro created his own base from the poor workers and farmers. And so, once he marched into Havana in January of 1959, Castro immediately began using his unique system of revolutionary control. He brought down the upper classes, then the middle classes, through seizing their lands and removing their privileges, or simply terrorizing them. He managed to remove any competitors to power, either by sending them to places where they would surely die (Che Guevara in Bolivia, 1967; Frank Pais on the streets of revolutionary Santiago de Cuba, 1957), or when that didn't work, by executing them (General Ochoa in Havana, 1989).

Meanwhile, his military and intelligence organizations assured, and still assure, his physical control over the island. Castro has been extraordinarily adept at using the traditional Cuban fear of the "Miami Cubans" and the hated "Americanos" to hold his own people ignorant and in check.[7]

"Hatred is an element of struggle; relentless hatred of the enemy that impels us over and beyond the natural limitations of man and transforms us into effective, violent, selective, and cold killing machines. Our soldiers must be thus; a people without hatred cannot vanquish a brutal enemy." Thus spoke **Che Guevara** in 1967, one of the most radical of Castro's entourage who was, as mentioned above, sent by Fidel to die in Bolivia. Guevara used hatred or as he put it "relentless hatred" to "impel us over and beyond the natural limitations of man." This use of hatred to encourage the dehumanization of ones enemy is but another manifestation of the doctrine found throughout the centuries to justify mass murder and torture. It has been used to apparently great success in Cuba, keeping Castro in power for more than forty years.

THE DOMINICAN REPUBLIC AND HAITI

These two small countries share an island and have been involved in strife, war, rebellion and terrorism in the Caribbean to some extent, although minor. We shall examine them briefly as a possible source of future problems in that region. First we look at the Dominican Republic.

The Dominican Republic

Noted more for its major league baseball players in the United States, the Dominican Republic is located on the eastern two-thirds of the island of Hispaniola, between the Caribbean Sea and the North Atlantic Ocean. Haiti borders it. It is slightly more than twice the size of New Hampshire, with a population of about 7,900,000. The ethnic mix is a reflection of past developments with white 16%, black 11%, and mixed 73%, who are 95% Roman Catholic.

Economic reforms launched in late 1994 contributed to exchange rate stabilization, reduced inflation, and strong GDP growth in 1995–96. In 1996, there was increased mineral and petroleum exploration, and a new investment law that allows for repatriation of capital dividends has drawn more investment to the island. Upon coming to power in August 1996, President Leonel Fernandez Reyna nevertheless inherited a trouble-ridden economy hampered by a pressured peso, a large external debt, nearly bankrupt state-owned enterprises, and a manufacturing sector hindered by daily power outages. In December, Fernandez presented a bold economic reform package—including such reforms as the devaluation of the peso, income tax cuts, a 50% increase in sales taxes, reduced import tariffs, and increased gasoline prices—in an attempt to create a market-oriented economy that can compete internationally. The legislature, however, has been slow to act on several of the economic measures. The Dominican per capita purchasing power is $3,670, three times that of their neighbor, Haiti. The Dominican Republic has been very quiet in the wake of events of 9–11, and seems to be satisfied with staying out of the kinds of conflicts they have had in the past.

Haiti

The Republic of Haiti occupies the western one-third of the island of Hispaniola, bordering on the west of the Dominican Republic. It is slightly smaller than Maryland but has a population that is predominately black (95%), with mulatto and white making up 5%. These more than 6.5 million people are crowded into one-half the land space of their neighbor, the Dominican Republic. Haitians are predominately Roman Catholic (80%) and an overwhelming majority also practice Voodoo.

One of the poorest countries in the world, about 75% of the Haitian population lives in abject poverty. Nearly 70% of all Haitians depend on the agriculture sector, which consists mainly of small-scale subsistence farming and employs about two-thirds of the economically active work force. The country has experienced little or no job creation since President Rene Preval took office in February 1996. Failures to reach agreements with international sponsors have denied Haiti badly needed budget and development assistance. Meeting aid conditions in 1997 will be especially challenging in the face of mounting popular criticism of reforms.

François "**Papa Doc**" Duvalier was the absolute dictator of Haiti from 1957–71. His nickname came from his career as a physician. He became director general of the Haitian national public health service in 1946 and subsequently served as minister of health and of labor. After opposing Paul Magloire's coup in 1950, he hid in the interior, practicing medicine, until a general political amnesty was granted in 1956. In 1957, with army backing, "Papa Doc" was overwhelmingly elected president. Reelected in a sham election in 1961, he declared himself president for life in 1964. His regime, the longest in Haiti's history, was a brutal reign of terror; political opponents were summarily executed, and the notorious Tonton Macoutes (secret police) kept the populace in a state of abject terror and fear. Under Duvalier, the economy of Haiti continued to deteriorate, and the illiteracy rate remained at about 90%. Duvalier nevertheless maintained his hold over Haiti. His practice of Voodooism encouraged rumors among the people that he possessed supernatural powers. He died in 1971, after arranging for his son, Jean-Claude, "Baby Doc" to succeed him.

Jean-Bertrand Aristide became president of Haiti in December 1990, elected in a landslide, only to be ousted seven months after taking office. He went into exile in Venezuela and later the United States. Three years later, a 20,000-member United States-led multinational force intervened to forcibly disband the army and restore Aristide to power.

President Aristide was a radical Catholic priest who defended liberation theology. He worked among Haiti's poor and was part of a group of progressive priests who opposed the Duvalier dictatorship. Expelled from his religious order in 1988 because of his revolutionary teachings, he became the candidate of a coalition of leftist parties in the 1990 presidential elections and was elected with an overwhelming majority. Party infighting plagued Aristide toward the end of his five-year term, however, and has continued for the new administration of Rene Preval, who took over in February 1998.[8]

In the relative safety of the new U.N.-protected Haiti, Aristide launched a new umbrella movement recently to invigorate and unify the governing Lavalas coalition. Many Haitians still have hopes of seeing Aristide back in the National Palace in the year 2000. Aristide has insisted that his latest efforts are not a challenge to Preval, a friend and activist whom Aristide belatedly endorsed for president last year. By law, Aristide could not seek a consecutive term as president of Haiti.

To emphasize that the appearance of safety in this battered nation is not necessarily reality, in 1998 unknown gunmen opened fire on the National Palace and police headquarters in the latest apparent effort to try to destabilize Haiti's new government. At least one person was killed, a civilian working at the police station, and a policeman was slightly injured. U.N. soldiers and Haitian police officers returned fire but no casualties were reported. U.N. helicopters also took to the air and patrolled the city. There have been death threats against Preval, former President Aristide and several liberal Haitian legislators. The distinctive sounds of gunfire ring out almost nightly in Port-au-Prince, the Haitian capital.

Preval has blamed the attacks on soldiers from the army that ousted Aristide in 1991, which was disbanded after an American-led military intervention restored the exiled Aristide in October 1994. Preval also has speculated that the subversion could be connected to his controversial plan to privatize some state-owned enterprises. The fate of this beleaguered, poor and downtrodden country is far from settled. The state terrorism created by the two despotic Duvaliers, a combination of violence and Voodoo has left a legacy of former state terrorists ready to leap into the vacuum created by the departure of the U.N. operation. Time will tell if this dire prediction will come to pass.[9]

SUMMARY

America's experience with international terrorism and terrorism since 9–11 is a new phenomenon for most of the security forces to deal with. In addition, American paramilitary-style militia, the Ku Klux Klan, hate groups and organized gangs have been around many decades, however it was the last decade of the 20th century that brought the international flavor of the horrors of terrorists bombs home to all North Americans. Whole generations of British, Irish and European city-dwellers have grown up with a daily diet of terrorism at their doorsteps, so the World Trade Center and Pentagon 9–11 bombings placed the United States onto the international targeting map of terrorist attackers.

Much U.S. attention had been given to fringe groups such as the Branch Davidians, militias, the Unabomber, etc. From an international viewpoint the

United States is now seen, and now sees itself, as being vulnerable to attack, particularly from Islamic extremists wherever there are U.S. personnel, military bases and troops, or U.S. business interests. This now, of course, includes anywhere within the borders of the country.

Canada, on the other hand, thanks to its liberal policies on immigration has seen an influx from third world countries of thousands of "refugees." No doubt many of the refugees are genuine, but some have only escaped from the view of their oppressive regimes and continue to foster and promote terrorism from within Canada. The downing of an Air India B747 off the southern coast of the Republic of Ireland on June 22, 1985, with 329 people killed, 82 of them children was the worst-ever single terrorist attack. Most of the people onboard Air India Flight 182 were Canadian citizens. The Guinness Book of Records still lists the Air India disaster as the worst single terrorist attack ever. Canada's only previous brush with an organized attack using terror tactics has been Quebec's experience with the FLQ. Whether the cause of separation will see any resurgence of an FLQ-styled organization is not yet apparent.

Sporadic problems in the Caribbean and Cuba continue to flare and most of the terrorist and insurgent problems in the islands have been as a result of economic downturns and inefficient and corrupt governments. Cuba remains firmly under the control and dictates of Fidel Castro and his power continues to dominate in the region as well as covertly influencing Latin American states.

TERMS TO REMEMBER

Alfred P. Murrah Federal Building	**FLQ**	**SLA**
Che Guevara	**Macheteros**	**TFVAAP**
domestic terrorist acts	**militias**	**Waco Massacre**
drive-by shootings	**New World Order**	**World Trade Center**
FACE	**Papa Doc**	

REVIEW QUESTIONS

1. Describe the terrorist events that brought major international and domestic terrorism home to the United States.
2. Describe the motives of the Canadian FLQ movement and its major acts of terrorism.
3. Why is there a movement on Puerto Rico for independence?
4. Describe the problems in Haiti and why it is having so much trouble surviving.
5. Discuss why Fidel Castro has been able to maintain power in Cuba for so long.

ENDNOTES

1. In this chapter much was extracted from the website of the U.S. Department of State, *1997 Patterns of Global Terror Report.*

2. The U.S. Department of State, *Background Notes: Geographic Entities and International Organizations.* http//www.state.com.

3. Excerpted from *The Ottawa Citizen,* 3rd August, 1996. by Juliet O'Neill, Foreign Affairs.

4. George Rosie, "The Directory of International Terrorism", (Paragon House, New York, 1987), p. 123.

5. Canadian Press—December 3, 1995, "Neo-FLQ Group to fight for breakup." The Internet.

6. http://www.cp.org/Universal Press Syndicate, 1998.

7. Offices of the General Customs Receivership, Santo Domingo, 1907. Courtesy National Archives.

8. The Columbia Encyclopedia, Fifth Edition 1993, Columbia University Press. Licensed from Inso Corporation. Aristide, Jean-Bertrand, http://bartleby.com.

9. Michael Norton. Associated Press Writer, Aug. 19, 1996, Port-au-Prince, Haiti (AP).

4 Great Britain and Northern Ireland

"Everyone uses violence, I am not ashamed of anything I have done"

Martin McGuinness, Northern Ireland Assembly

OVERVIEW

Britain has been no stranger to acts of domestic terrorism in the latter decades of the 20th century and in this chapter we examine with the reader what is still considered to be one of the most successful and ruthless terror groups, the Provisional Irish Republican Army (PIRA) as well as other terror factions operating in both Northern Ireland and mainland Britain. We will examine how terrorists have turned away from the gun, and toward political strategies. Also, we discuss why the events of 9–11 may have exerted a great influence upon the pursuit of peace in Northern Ireland. The Peace Accord of the last decade, the Good Friday Agreement, and the subsequent start of the **decommissioning** of terrorist weapons has played a major part in bringing Northern Ireland much closer to an outbreak of prolonged peace. Whether any ceasefire can be sustained and, ultimately, a lasting peace achieved entirely from the decommissioning actions by the IRA and Loyalist groups is examined. Other disaffected splinter groups, both Protestant and Catholic, involved in the times of "The Troubles" will be examined. Also discussed will be the changes in policing in Northern Ireland. At the start of the twenty-first century, apart from the Irish terror groups, there were only two other active European terror organizations: ETA operating in the Basque region of Spain, and November 17 in Greece. Of great concern to European countries and to Britain in particular, has been the discovery of foreign terror cells linked with Osama bin Laden, which are discussed in this chapter as well. In the wake of the 9–11 attacks on the New York World Trade Center and the Pentagon, we will examine the rise of Islamic radicalism in Britain, reviewing some of the measures being taken to limit and track down those that have become involved with suspected al Qaeda terrorist operations. Britain has become somewhat of a recruiting haven for young Islamic radicals and that will be discussed, as connections in the wider context of the 9–11 attacks and workings of the al Qaeda network.

IRELAND: A HISTORY OF PAIN AND TERROR

Chronology and History of Ireland

The lush green island country of Ireland has a long and rich history, dating back to as early as the twelfth century as shown below:

- 1170 – The first British migrants arrive in Ireland
- 1690 - Protestant William III defeats Catholic James II at the Battle of the Boyne
- 1801 - Act of Union joins Ireland with Britain abolishing the Irish parliament and becoming part of the United Kingdom
- 1916 - Easter uprising starts in Dublin against British rule in Ireland
- 1921 - Irish Free State made up of the 26 counties — 6 northern counties remain as part of United Kingdom
- 1969 - Civil rights marches signal the start of "The Troubles"
- 1998 - Good Friday Agreement
- 1999 — Power sharing under a Northern Ireland Assembly
- 2002 - Martin McGuiness and Gerry Adams take offices in Palace of Westminster (London) but not their Seat in Parliament.

In the early sixteenth century, James I, the King of England, provided land in areas of Ireland to Scottish settlers in hopes of establishing the Protestant church in Ireland, the conversion of the Irish to Protestantism, the forfeiture of their lands, and assuring Protestant ascendancy to the throne of England.

Both William and Mary were staunch Protestants and were "invited" to invade England and seize the throne. In 1688, William, with a predominantly Dutch army, invaded and was rewarded with a bloodless coup. James II fled England for exile in France. By 1689 William and Mary ruled England while James amassed an army in France to oppose them.

In 1690, James II[1] supported by French and Irish armies fought William at the famous **Battle of the Boyne**. James was defeated and Protestant rule prevailed throughout Ireland. The Protestants were the landowners of Ireland while the Catholics held onto a tenuous existence and suffered great deprivations and poverty. Protestants to this day celebrate William's victory over King James' Catholic army. Orange Lodges hold annual marches and celebrations in the Protestant regions of Ireland on July 12th. The first Orange Lodge was founded in Loughhall, County Armagh in 1795.

In 1801, the Act of Union resulted in Ireland becoming part of Great Britain and, in 1886, British Prime Minister Gladstone tabled the first Home Rule Bill for Ireland. Irish Protestants opposed the Bill. The second Home Rule Bill was introduced and resulted in street fighting spreading throughout Ulster.

An Irish journalist named Arthur Griffith founded a political organization called ***Sinn Fein,*** a Gaelic term meaning "we ourselves" in 1905. The

TERRORISM PLAYER 4–1

William III (1650–1702)

Born in The Hague, Netherlands, William is better known in historical terms as "William of Orange." William married his cousin Mary, daughter of James, Duke of York and the heir to the throne of England. James II as King of England provided a son, and to the chagrin of the English Protestants he christened his son a Roman Catholic.

aims of the newly formed Sinn Fein were to aggressively seek self-government. The Irish Republican Brotherhood, or the IRB, was a secret group that wanted total independence and the formation of an Irish Republic. This group was active in Ireland in the early 1900s. In 1912, the Ulster Protestants signed the Ulster Covenant to oppose and resist Home Rule.[2]

In 1914, in spite of strong Protestant opposition, the British Parliament finally passed a **Home Rule Bill**. However, the outbreak of the First World

TERRORISM PLAYER 4–2

Michael Collins (1890–1922)

Michael Collins was the youngest of eight children, born on October 18, 1890, at Sam's Cross, near Clonakilty, Ireland. His father, Michael, was seventy-five years old when he was born and was a staunch nationalist. Michael grew to be an excellent student and was sent to London, where he studied and passed the Civil Service examination. He worked in the GPO (General Post Office) in London. In 1909, he became a member of the Irish Republican Brotherhood and returned to Dublin to play a minor role in the 1916 Easter Uprising. Upon his release from a Welsh prison in 1916 he began to reorganize the republican volunteers, and also set about building his own sophisticated intelligence service for the coming battles. His intelligence network was successful in penetrating the Royal Irish Constabulary and the Secret Service in Dublin. In its efforts to combat Collins' infiltration of the Secret Service, the British put together a counterespionage group called the Cairo Gang to eliminate the IRA volunteers.

Collins' IRA was successful in hitting back and killed fourteen Cairo agents in and around Dublin. The so-called civil war had been going on since 1919, and in July of 1921 a truce was called. Collins was forced by Eamon de Valera to lead the delegation to London for the negotiations. The Irish delegation signed a treaty in December 1921, and as Collins commented to Lord Birkenhead at the time, he may have signed his own death warrant. The treaty was to cause a significant rift in the republican ranks and cause bitter infighting. When Collins returned to Ireland, he was ambushed and killed in west Cork on August 22, 1922 at *Beal na Blath* (the mouth of flowers).

Source: http://www.sinnfein.ie.

War of 1914–1918 prevented it from being put into effect. It would be fair to say that the large majority of the Irish people supported the British in the conflict with Germany. But the republican movement in Ireland, led by Patrick Pearse, viewed the war as an opportunity to gain total independence from Britain. In Dublin on Easter Monday, 1916, fighting broke out but was rapidly suppressed by British troops. Fifteen republicans were executed following the uprising, which came to be known as the "Easter Rebellion." There was little support for the abortive Easter Rebellion, but the prompt execution of the protagonists gained widespread Irish sympathy.

In the general election of 1918, the republicans, who had already gained control of Sinn Fein, won 73 of the 105 Irish seats in Britain's Parliament. The republicans never took their "seats" in London, however, and chose to meet instead in Dublin. They named themselves the House of Deputies (*Dail Eireann*). This body declared publicly that all of Ireland was now independent from Britain on January 21, 1919. The British created "The Government of Ireland Act —1920" and officially formed two separate countries. The result was wide-scale fighting erupting, from 1920 to 1921 in Northern Ireland. As a means of combating the troubles in Ireland, the British government hastily assembled a fighting force, known infamously to this day as the "**Black and Tans**." Black and Tans were World War I veterans and unsuited to the delicate political and military tasks for dealing with urban rebels. They had been trained in the main only for trench warfare. Their lack of discipline did much to alienate them not only from the Irish, but also from the British. They were officially part of the Royal Irish Constabulary (RIC). By 1921, there were over seven thousand Black and Tans operating in Ireland. The Black and Tans burned and rampaged through several Irish villages north of Dublin. This not only shocked the British public, but also brought about their recall from Ireland. The group was then disbanded and withdrawn in July 1921.

As noted above, the Government of Ireland Act divided Ireland into two separate countries. The six counties of Ulster in the north and the three counties of Ulster in the south were one half, and the remaining twenty-three counties the other. The counties in the north accepted the act, and the state of Northern Ireland was formed. However, the republicans in the south rejected the act and bitter fighting broke out between the Irish Republican Army (IRA) and British troops.

In 1921, Britain and the Irish republicans signed a treaty creating the south as a dominion of Great Britain to be called the **Irish Free State**. There was disagreement between the various and sundry republican factions. One group led by Eamon de Valera, one of the icons for the IRA, wanted total separation from Britain and a reunification with Northern Ireland. An opposition group led by Michael Collins[3] and later William Cosgrave was in favor of the treaty.

In 1922, Civil War in Ireland broke out, and continued until the fighting ended in 1923. The warring factions then formed opposing political parties within the Irish Free State. Eamon de Valera became leader of Sinn Fein and William Cosgrave led the *Cumann na nGaedheal* Party. Michael Collins was executed and the Irish Republican Army **(IRA)** was outlawed, but continued to exist to harass and attack British interests.

TERRORISM PLAYER 4-3

Gerry Adams

The oldest of ten children, Gerry Adams was born October 6, 1948, and raised in the Catholic West Belfast District where he still lives with his family. Heavily involved in the civil rights movement of the 1960s, he campaigned rigorously and for his efforts was interned without trial in 1972. After his release he was again arrested in 1973 and 1977. A target for loyalist paramilitary groups both he and members of his family have been attacked. He was elected president of Sinn Fein in 1983 and to the British Parliament as the member for West Belfast. For Adams to take his seat in Parliament would require him to take the oath of allegiance to the monarchy. Gerry Adams is in the forefront of political activity, with ongoing discussions with the Irish government in Dublin as well as meetings with the President of the United States, Bill Clinton, much to the dismay of the British Government. It is a commonly held view point that the official political wing, Sinn Fein, is under the total control and direction of the PIRA. In looking at the statistics relative to the most recent general election it can be clearly seen that The Social Democratic and Labour Party (SDLP), with its leader, John Hume, won 24% of the Catholic vote, compared to only 16% for the Sinn Fein Party. Sinn Fein's share of the vote in the 1997 Republic of Ireland elections was only 4%. Adams, considered to be a skillful negotiator, does at least provide for the opportunity to begin a peace process.

Source: http://wwwsinnfein.ie.

Britain's Vietnam?

Religion has been the battleground, as well as the single most discernable problem, stemming from injustices for centuries. Divided mainly on the lines of dominant Protestant presence over a Catholic majority led to discrimination against Catholics in almost every facet of everyday life, from getting employment to finding housing. Even the police service, the Royal Ulster Constabulary (**RUC**), was almost exclusively Protestant. These civil injustices go back over centuries and are still manifested in Protestant pro-Unionist organizations in Northern Ireland. This imbalance added to the divisions in the North over the last three decades. Despite this, it would ultimately lead to a rebirth of a police force to be divested of its antiterrorism role and bring it back into a community role serving the community as a whole, both Protestant and Catholic. The changes being made to the police force and the removal of the word Royal from its title, as well as other recommendations unpopular with Unionists, who view change as pandering to the Republican movement.

The 1960s saw a decade of tumultuous worldwide changes, with the British Empire giving up its worldwide colonies without a fight. Britain had just quit one of the last remaining colonies, Aden. This was after a total breakdown of law and order, achieved through terrorist violence. The IRA contended that they could topple a British government that would back down if confronted by the kind of violence that had occurred in Aden. As a result of a

Sinn Fein's Gerry Adams (right) and Martin McGuiness, his chief negotiator, at 10 Downing Street, London, October 10, 2002 to meet with British Prime Minister Tony Blair. (PA Photo/Matthew Fearn)

split in the ranks of the IRA the Provisional IRA (PIRA) was formed in 1969 as the clandestine armed wing of Sinn Fein, a legal political movement dedicated to the removal of British forces from Northern Ireland. The Official IRA, which had been in existence at that time for more than forty years, declared a ceasefire in 1972. From that point forward the term IRA has been used for the organization that split in 1969 and developed from the Provisional IRA. A further split in the Provisional movement resulted from the policies of the Sinn Fein leader Gerry Adams between 1994 and 1998. In the fall of 1997 one faction accepting the new Good Friday Agreement, and the other, a newly formed splinter of PIRA, the Real IRA (or New IRA as it's sometimes called), continuing armed resistance to the British occupation of Northern Ireland. Together with the civil rights issues, and the American debacle in Vietnam, the PIRA aimed to make good use of what they considered positive factors. To the PIRA, Northern Ireland was seen as just another British colony waiting its turn for independence from the mother country. With this and recent history in mind, the terrorists believed that the killing of British soldiers would very quickly influence the decision processes of the British government.

The Political Objectives

Before the reader can appreciate and understand the kinds of terror campaigns that have been waged by the IRA, against both the Protestant and British, in Northern Ireland and in mainland Britain, it is important to acquire a basic understanding of the political goals. The IRA of the 1920s was demanding, and continues to demand, one united Ireland and total separation from the United Kingdom. In support of this, the nationalists turned to using campaigns of terror. As noted earlier, the Easter Uprising was probably the first, in a long chain of terrorism incidents and acts throughout the 20th century. To

TERRRORISM PLAYER 4-4

Martin McGuinness

Born into a nationalist family in 1950, he is the second eldest of seven children. He was educated by the Christian Brothers, but left school at age 15. He became involved as an 18-year-old in the civil rights movement in Derry (Londonderry) after October 5, 1968, and joined the Sinn Fein in 1970. McGuinness was elected to the *Ard Comhairle,* Sinn Fein's National Executive, and has played a key role in the support and strategy of ongoing peace negotiations. In 1972, he was Sinn Fein's lead representative in talks with the then British Secretary of State William Whitelaw, in London. In 1982, McGuinness was elected to the short-lived Stormont Assembly. Later that same year he was "excluded" from entering Britain under the terms of the prevention of Terrorism Act. Martin McGuinness is Sinn Fein's chief negotiator and led Sinn Fein's delegation following the PIRA ceasefire on August 31, 1994, in talks with British Minister, Michael Ancram, at Stormont. He also conducted private meetings with Patrick Mayhew as part of Sinn Fein's attempts to persuade the British government to move beyond the impasse involving all-party negotiations. McGuinness and Gerry Adams, Sinn Fein president, met with President Bill Clinton during his visit to Belfast in 1995. McGuinness was elected as Sinn Fein Member of Parliament for Mid-Ulster, but has not taken his seat at the Palace of Westminster.

Source: http://wwwsinnfein.ie.

TERRORISM PLAYER 4–5

Captain Robert Laurence Nairac GC

Robert Nairac was educated at Ampleforth School, one of the leading Catholic private schools in the country. In 1968, he attended Lincoln College at Oxford University where he studied history. Nairac joined the Army and the Grenadier Guards Regiment while still at Oxford. As a young Guards officer he was posted to Northern Ireland and in the mid 1970s acted as liaison officer between the Special Air Service (SAS) and Special Branch (SB). Nairac had a passion for all things Irish and had spent many holidays in the country. Viewed by many of his peers to be somewhat strange and outlandish, Nairac began to immerse himself in intelligence-gathering activities. An officer by day and undercover agent at night! A situation both tricky and extremely dangerous. At this time the SAS were newly on the scene and learning first-hand the difficulties of fighting a terrorist organization immersed and more often protected by the general populace. Nairac certainly lived dangerously and invariably went to meet with Irish contacts without official SAS back-up. On Saturday, May 14, 1977, Nairac left his base at Bessbrook Mill and headed to the Three Steps Public House at Drumintee, a local haunt for members of the PIRA. Full and complete details of what took place in the pub or nearby cannot be reliably confirmed. Nairac's reason for being at this location was to recruit an IRA informer. What transpired and how he was compromised has never been fully explained. Nairac was executed by members of the PIRA at a location just inside the Irish republic. Liam Townson, a PIRA member, was convicted of the execution-style murder and sentenced to penal servitude for life in 1978. Captain Nairac's body has never been found, but PIRA reports suggest that his body was either fed into a meat processing plant or disposed of in an Irish bog. If he was questioned and tortured by the PIRA, it seems that he gave up little if any information. Whether the IRA knew exactly who he was is also not certain. The method and speed of his dispatch tends to lend credence to the theory that those involved were not aware of the value of the man in their possession—had they been it is more probable his capture would have been an immense coup for the PIRA and extensive interrogation would have taken place. The Queen of England posthumously awarded Captain Nairac the George Cross, the highest peace time award for bravery.

Source: 'Bandit Country The IRA & South Armagh', Toby Harnden, Hodder and Stoughton, London 1999. p. 139.

emphasize that point, in the early 1920s the bands of IRA men were relentlessly pursued by the Black and Tans.

Cathal Goulding, the Army Council's Chief of Staff for the IRA, considered and established a viewpoint of shifting the IRA away from violence as the only means to its end. His idea was the formation of both a Catholic and Protestant workers group aimed at the overthrow of capitalism, and achieving one united Ireland. As a result, the end of 1969 found a situation rampant with internal disarray and a split in the IRA ranks. Goulding's ideas offended many Catholics and IRA members who saw themselves as the defenders of the Catholic enclaves of the North. When renewed fighting broke out in 1969, the IRA's lack of weaponry rendered them unable to accomplish their mission and protect the northern Catholics. At a special IRA Convention held in Dublin in

August 1969, it was voted, predominantly by the southerners, to adopt a policy of political activism. Further, to elect Sinn Fein members to the Dublin and British Parliaments. To the men of the north this was viewed as recognition of partition, or "sleeping with the enemy." Led by Sean McStiofain, the Provisional Irish Republican Army **(PIRA)** was formed the following month. John Stephenson, Rory O'Brady, Leo Martin, Billy McKee, Francis Card, and Seamus Twomey led the PIRA of 1969. They believed that physical violence could solve their political problems. Subsequently, splinter terror groups were formed from the original ranks of the IRA. The PIRA was formed as a splinter group from the IRA as well as a smaller group, the Irish National Liberation Army **(INLA)**.

Sinn Fein[4], the name of the political party representing the original IRA, was adopted by the splinter Provisionals as their "political wing." Sinn Fein has risen to prominence over the past three decades as the political party to achieve the goal of separation. However, it must be recognized that the control of the party is exercised through the Army Council of the terrorist group. A sense of fear surrounds this shadowy party, in part because so many of its members have gravitated from the ranks of the PIRA and its Active Service Units.

The PIRA has used terror campaigns to great effect in Northern Ireland against its Protestant neighbors, members of British Army units, and the predominantly Protestant Royal Ulster Constabulary. Indiscriminate attacks on the British mainland took place against a wide variety of targets. These ranged from military establishments to pubs, shopping centers, business districts, airports, and even against the seat of British Democracy, 10 Downing Street, the residence of the British Prime Minister. The object was to successfully attack British military and political targets with the aim of undermining the political will of the government, frightening the citizens and sapping the British economy.

In simplistic terms, the avowed political aim of the Sinn Fein/Irish Republican groups continues to be the removal of British rule and a united Ireland. How could that objective be achieved? In the minds and viewpoints of the IRA of the 1960s, the only way to defeat an enemy was to wage war. After more than thirty years of "the Troubles" there is a glimmer of hope for peace, but must it be "peace at any cost?" The bomb and gun have had the effect of motivating the political leaders on all sides towards a peace agreement. This appears to be achievable but at what cost? More than 3,600 people, both military and civilian, have died during the course of the Troubles. The groups that have split away from the IRA over the last thirty years to form the Provisional IRA, the Continuity IRA, and the Real IRA cannot be seen as having lost total contact with the political organization, Sinn Fein.

To Protestants, the fact remains that both Gerry Adams and Martin McGuiness have had a long association with the IRA, and are viewed as terrorists turned politicians. The political end game has seen the prominent and eventual rise to power of Adams and McGuiness. They now are taking a leading role in negotiations with Tony Blair's British Labor Government. Both men have now been elected to sit in the British House of Commons. However, neither of them has taken their seat to date, as that would require them to swear an allegiance to Her Majesty the Queen, an act they see as repugnant. A landmark date for these two men came on January 21, 2002, when they were

TERRORISM BYTE 4–1

First Deaths of the Troubles

Sunday July 14, 1968:

Francis McCloskey (Catholic), aged 67, died one day after being hit on the head with a baton by a member of the Royal Ulster Constabulary (RUC) during street disturbances in Dungiven, County Derry.

Friday August 15, 1969:

David Linton (Protestant), aged 48, died after being shot by a Republican group during street disturbances in North Belfast.

Friday 15, August 1969:

Gerald McCauley, aged 15, a member of the IRA youth section, *Fianna Eireann,* was shot

dead by Loyalists during disturbances in the Lower Falls Road area of Belfast.

Saturday October 11, 1969:

Victor Arbuckle, aged 29, was the first member of the RUC killed in the Troubles; he was shot by Loyalists during street disturbances on the Shankhill Road in Belfast.

Saturday October 11, 1971:

Robert Curtis, aged 20, was the first British Army fatality. He was shot dead by a member of the Irish Republican Army while he was on foot patrol on the New Lodge Road, Belfast.

Source: Conflict Archive on the Internet http://cain.ulst.ac.uk/events.

greeted in London by British Prime Minister Tony Blair and occupied their new offices in the Palace of Westminster.

THE IRISH REPUBLICAN ARMY aka (PIRA) PROVISIONAL IRISH REPUBLICAN ARMY

Official records do not indicate the exact membership numbers of Northern Ireland paramilitary groups. It is widely believed that the numbers of IRA members reached a peak in the war-torn years of the 1970s at around 1,500–2,000 active members and declined over the next fifteen years until the announced ceasefire in 1994 with a membership probably around 300 to 500. Still considered to be one of the most powerful and effective terror organizations of the last century, the IRA traces its roots in the Easter Rebellion of 1916, in what is now the Republic of Ireland, and gets its name from the first "Volunteers" who fought for a free Irish State. The Provisional IRA was established when the IRA split in December 1969, between the "Officials" and the "Provisionals." Confusion was rampant, as both organizations had a military wing, the "Official" and "Provisional" IRA, and both had a political wing, the "Official" and "Provisional" Sinn Fein. It was the "Official" IRA that declared a ceasefire in the summer of 1972 and, from then on, the term IRA was used for the organization that had developed from the "Provisional" IRA. From a splinter group of a small and badly equipped paramilitary grouping, the "Provisional" IRA developed into a comparatively large, well-financed, well-equipped guerrilla/terrorist organization that has been involved in, what it calls an "armed campaign" for almost three decades. The IRA's development of wider connections, in countries like Libya, Spain, North and South America, for logistical and weaponry support, expanded it into a truly international terrorist organization.

In respect to activities outside of Northern Ireland and mainland Britain, the IRA has been known to have been active in Europe and set up safe houses during the early 1990s for operations aimed at military and government targets in the Netherlands, France, and West Germany. Ease of movement and lack of border controls in the Benelux countries made opportunities for movement that much simpler. Weapons seizures in Europe in the early 1990s, and two active service units (**ASU**) arrests likely slowed down any advances that may have been contemplated by the PIRA for extensive operations in Europe. The PIRA has, more or less, observed the ceasefire put in place since the end of the last decade. No doubt, the strong influence of McGuiness and Adams has been brought to bear as Sinn Fein has used its political machine to edge closer to a peaceful solution after thirty long years of violence. In August 2001, the credibility of the PIRA and Sinn Fein was brought into question when Colombian security forces arrested the PIRA's head of engineering, while developing mortars for the FARC guerillas (see also Chapter 12). Three suspected members of the Irish Republican Army were arrested on August 11, 2001, at Bogotá's El Dorado International Airport, charged with training the Revolutionary Armed Forces of Colombia (FARC) in explosives handling and urban terrorist tactics.

Of the three Irishmen arrested, one was identified as Niall Connolly, who has been in Latin America for at least a decade, according to Colombian and British officials. Since 1996, however, Connolly has lived in Havana under the pseudonym David Bracken. He reportedly traveled frequently to Venezuela, Panama, Nicaragua, and El Salvador, where he is believed to have established contacts with individuals and groups interested in arms smuggling, drug trafficking, and supporting the FARC's expanding insurgency in Colombia. Security forces in Northern Ireland also claimed Connolly was Sinn Fein's contact with Fidel Castro's government in Cuba, and was helping to arrange Sinn Fein President Gerry Adams' eight-day visit to South America. Sinn Fein denied having any relationship with Connolly or knowledge of his activities in Latin America, but Cuba's Foreign Ministry released a statement on August 17, stating that Connolly had lived in Cuba for five years as Sinn Fein's Latin America representative.[5] The fear from Ulster Unionists was that the IRA was on the one hand talking peace and decommissioning, while on the other was conducting training and seeking high-powered weapons.

The other two suspects were identified as James "Mortar" Monaghan and Martin McCauley. Monaghan once was a member of Sinn Fein's ruling executive body. According to Garda Commissioner, Pat Byrne, both men are experts in the design and manufacture of increasingly effective homemade mortars for use against military and political targets in Northern Ireland and mainland Britain. The two are also skilled in the use of mercury-tilt switches designed to blow up people in cars and radio-controlled "command" bombs for use against armored vehicles. These are technologies that would have significantly enhanced the FARC's explosive-handling capabilities. Remote-controlled explosive devices have been a strong feature of terrorist operations over the last two decades in Northern Ireland, particularly in the border regions.

The U.S. Central Intelligence Agency reportedly supplied the Colombian government with satellite footage of the three suspects training FARC rebels inside a demilitarized zone. Colombian officials have described the FARC-IRA link as a "business relationship," in which the IRA trades advanced explosives-handling techniques for illegal drugs, cash or weapons.

The IRA members probably schooled FARC rebels in how to mix high-powered synthetic explosives, in order to extend the range of homemade gas cylinder mortars. The FARC needed to extend the roughly 400-meter range of its homemade mortars because of better defenses at military compounds built with American assistance. This implies the guerrillas are considering attacks on compounds, which typically house U.S. military and civilian defense personnel assigned to "Plan Colombia," an anti-drug initiative.

These IRA arrests were the latest of several recent developments indicating Colombia will soon experience a sharp rise in violence and destruction. Soon after the 9–11 attacks in New York City, David Trimble, the former First Minister of the Northern Ireland Assembly, made the following statement on terrorism in the British Parliament on Thursday, October 4, 2001: "Terrorism is terrorism, and requires no further qualification, so could I ask you (the Prime Minister) to reject the spurious distinction some people seek to draw between international and domestic terrorism . . . recent events all show that the Irish republican movement is part of an international terrorist network and that there is still no sign that it is making the changes required by the Belfast Agreement"[6]. Mr. Trimble was referencing the arrest of the IRA's head of engineering.

It is not surprising that the PIRA has established itself as one of the most ruthless and well-organized terror groups in the last quarter of the 20th century. It has achieved success against significant odds. The modern day Troubles have their origins in the working class areas of West Belfast and Londonderry back in 1969.

The PIRA, by the late '60s and early '70s, had changed dramatically in its makeup. By the end of the 1960s, the Catholic minority was under increasing pressure and assault from Protestant gangs. Catholic enclaves had to be protected against Protestant gangs who were burning and bombing Catholic-housing districts. Born out of necessity and pressure from the authorities, the PIRA evolved from a loosely knit organization to one with a military structure employing geographically based brigades, battalions and companies. The PIRA reorganized to form cells based on the continental cellular structure and better adapted to modern day terrorist activities. Autonomous active service units were formed with these cells and were difficult to penetrate or identify, as each cell had only three to four members. They were given code names and were directed by controllers. It was difficult to operate in the Catholic housing districts of Belfast and Londonderry, as everyone knew everyone else. However, away from Northern Ireland, these cells have proved to be successful paramilitary units in operations against mainland Britain. The PIRA owed much of its thirty years of success to the effectiveness of the cell system, similar to that used by the al Qaeda.

TERRORISM BYTE 4–2

IRA Gun Running

The PIRA has had a long and fertile relationship with Irish Americans either through financial support or even more forthrightly with arms acquisitions. Many weapons being used on the streets of Belfast have their origins in the United States, where gun ownership is as simple as producing a driver's license. Siobhan Browne, an American citizen of Irish birth and living in Florida, met up with Irishman Anthony Smyth in a bar in Florida. Browne knew that Smyth had joined the IRA as a teenager and his friend Connor Claxton had been sent from Northern Ireland to buy guns. Claxton and his Basque girlfriend, Idoia Elorriaga, moved in with Smyth and Browne. Elorriaga was a member of the political wing of ETA the Basque separatist terror group. As Smyth had no Green Card, Browne went to stores in Florida with Smyth to buy guns. The amount of weapons being purchased came to the attention of the Bureau of Alcohol, Tobacco and Firearms when guns were found hidden inside toys in a mail shipment between the United States and Ireland. On July 26, 1999, Browne, Smyth and Claxton were arrested. Prior to her trial, Browne met with a senior IRA official who told her that the gun running had been going on for four years and involved more than fifty IRA 'volunteers.' Browne pleaded guilty and was sentenced to 20 months and a $40,000 fine. Smyth received three years and Claxton four years.

Source: Florida/Naples Daily News: http://www.naplesnews.com.

CONTINUITY IRISH REPUBLICAN ARMY (CIRA)

The Continuity IRA (CIRA) is an offshoot of PIRA and is also referred to Continuity Army Council and the Irish Continuity Army Council. When the Provisionals began moving tentatively towards a peace accord and instituted a ceasefire, a goodly number within the ranks decided to split and to continue the "armed struggle" against the British. CIRA is considered by some analysts to be a military arm of Republican Sinn Fein (RSF), with a membership of about seventy. Any weapons and explosives in the group's possession are likely to have come from PIRA weapons dumps. The CIRA are not currently observing a ceasefire within the terms of the Good Friday Agreement and have continued sporadic operations both in Northern Ireland and mainland Britain. Their activities in Northern Ireland have been predominantly car bomb attacks aimed at buildings and Royal Ulster Constabulary Police stations. Its mainland Britain campaign has included bomb attacks by planting bombs under Hammersmith Bridge, and in July 2000, at Acton Underground Station. In September of that same year, they fired an antitank rocket at the British Secret Intelligence Service (MI5) headquarters at Vauxhall Bridge, London. In February 2001, they left a booby-trap bomb at a British Territorial Army base at White City, London. Their membership is thought to be about attracting dissatisfied members of the PIRA.

REPUBLICAN SINN FEIN (RSF)

This is a breakaway group from Sinn Fein, formed in 1986. The party decided to end its traditional abstention policy and those who opposed the move walked out to form the RSF. The group was lead by Ruairí Ó Braídaigh, former president of Sinn Fein, and Dáithí Ó Conaill, former Chief of Staff of the Irish Republican Army (IRA). At the 1988 RSF Ard Fheis, or annual conference, the party reaffirmed its support for the "armed struggle." RSF rejected the 1993 Downing Street Declaration and is also squarely against the current peace process. There have been claims that CIRA is, in effect, the military wing of RSF but RSF leaders have denied this.[7]

REAL IRISH REPUBLICAN ARMY (RIRA)

RIRA is somewhat smaller in numbers than the IRA at around thirty members. Formed in the Fall of 1997, at the time the IRA was announcing its ceasefire, this breakaway group of Republicans was adamantly against the "peace agreement" and the direction being given by the Sinn Fein leadership of Gerry Adams. Viewed as one of the most dangerous groups in existence after the Good Friday Agreement, one of its most devastating accomplishments was the bomb attack of the Town Center of Omagh, on August 15, 1998 that killed twenty-nine civilians and wounded more than two hundred, the single worst terrorist attack in Northern Ireland history. Following this atrocity, the group was forced to call a ceasefire. In spite of this, the group remains in existence, and gets its support from those not aligned with the peace process. As long as there is a modicum of a deadlock and lack of progress, this group is likely to continue to try to sway support away from the IRA. It operates in much the same way as the IRA has, with bomb attacks on the security forces, commercial locations, and targeting mainland Britain. Its leadership includes Bernadette Sands Mckevitt, the sister of Bobby Sands, an IRA member who died from a hunger strike, and Francie Mackey, a one time Sinn Fein councilor for Omagh. Its weapons and explosives likely come from IRA sources and there is concern that the group is purchasing weapons through Balkan states.

OTHER IRISH TERRORIST GROUPS

Irish National Liberation Army (INLA)

Also known as People's Liberation Army (PLA), People's Republican Army (PRA), Catholic Reaction Force (CRF).

This small terror group is an offshoot of the break up of the IRA in the late 1960s, not accepting of the ideology of either the official IRA or the Provisional IRA. The INLA is considered more Marxist in orientation than the PIRA. Formed in the early 1970s with a relatively small membership of about thirty, it is headquartered in Dublin. Its goals and activities on the terrorist front were centered in and on Belfast and Londonderry. The group's political objectives were the formation of a 32-county Socialist Republic in Ireland, the forced removal by any means, including violence, of British troops from Northern Ireland and the overthrow of the elected government of the Republic of Ireland. The INLA expresses its solidarity with other national liberation and terrorist organizations around the world. Its leadership consisted of Harry Flynn, Gerard Steenson, Thomas Power, and Dominic McGlinchey. McGlinchey, Steenson, and Power were all killed in bitter feuding between INLA and the PIRA in the late 1980s.

The INLA's most audacious act of terror was the 1979 assassination of Airey Neeve, the British Conservative Party spokesman on Northern Ireland. Neeve was killed when a powerful bomb destroyed his car as he was leaving the Houses of Parliament in London. This incident marked the first operation outside Ireland by the INLA.

The group was decimated in the 1980s as a result of the "**supergrass**" trials. The word "supergrass" is an outgrowth of an 18th century slang term "copper" meaning informer, which was rhymed into grasshopper, later shortened to grass. Super was added in the late 20th century to imply informing on a grand scale. In the context of Northern Ireland, the Supergrass strategy involved "reforming" terrorists by allowing them to divulge information about fellow terrorists and current prisoners in court in exchange for a new identity in a new country. Police in Northern Ireland used this strategy in the fight against terrorism and the evidence at that time was admissible in court. Supergrasses were initially responsible for a number of arrests and conviction of Irish terror suspects as the evidence provided was not required to be corroborated. The strategy of this kind of evidence gathering was used through the period of the 1980s but very rarely since then. Uncorroborated testimony is among the more dubious practices in a court of law. These "supergrasses" were designated as such by INLA and PIRA militants as those who informed on their former comrades. By the end of the decade, the problems with admission of supergrass evidence as part of court process led to the release of many imprisoned INLA and PIRA members. The result was a bloody feud between the INLA and PIRA, with many militants killed. The group still remains a brutal and unpredictable organization. The organization was responsible for the murder, in the Maze Prison, of Billy Wright on December 27, 1997, a loyalist Protestant militant. The result of this assassination was a spate of sectarian attacks, in which eight Catholics were murdered. The INLA has been observing a ceasefire since August 1998.

Ulster Volunteer Force (UVF)

Protestant Action Force, Protestant Action Group are also names that it operates under. Considered to be the largest loyalist paramilitary organization, this group is inextricably linked to the Ulster Defense Association and there appears to be no significant ideological difference between them. Over the years, it is believed that more than 40,000 people were members of this Protestant Loyalist organization. Set up to defend and respond to PIRA violence against

Protestants, the UVF was formed in 1912 to respond to the growing demands for Irish independence. When WWI broke out, many UVF members joined up and served in the 39th (Ulster) Division of the British Army. After the war, the returning members were a seasoned force to be reckoned with. Their leader in the 1960s was "Gusty" Spence, who was sentenced to life in prison for the murder of a Roman Catholic. UVF members have been involved in attacks mainly against Catholic civilians and were believed responsible for the simultaneous bombings of Dublin and Monaghan in the 1974 killing of thirty-three civilians. The UVF has been observing a ceasefire since 1994. However, like the IRA splinter groups, UVF has suffered from splits, like the one in 1996 in which disaffected members broke away to form the Loyalist Volunteer Fighters. Active membership of the UVF is likely to be small but with plenty of ready support available should it be required.

Ulster Democratic Party (UDP)

In 1981, the group spawned a political wing, the New Ulster Political Research Group which in turn became the more formalized, elected Ulster Democratic Party. The UDP's political aim is the formation of an independent Ulster. There was considerable infighting within this convoluted organization, which led to a new leadership in the early 1990s. The government banned UDP membership in 1992. Under the terms of Section 30(3) of the Northern Ireland Emergency Provisions Act, 1996, the following loyalist terror groups were proscribed: The Red Hand Commandos, The Ulster Freedom Fighters, The Ulster Volunteer Force and the Ulster Defense Association. Proscribed Republican organizations are: The Irish Republican Army, The Irish National Liberation Army, The Irish Peoples Liberation Organization, Cumann na mBan, Fianna na hEireann, and Saor Eire.

Ulster Freedom Fighters (UFF)/Ulster Defense Association (UDA)

Considered to be the largest of the Loyalist paramilitaries operating in Northern Ireland. The Ulster Freedom Fighters (UFF) has been used as a cover name for the Ulster Defence Association so the two groups can effectively be deemed as one. The UDA was formed in 1971 as an umbrella organization for loyalist groups. At its peak in the 1970s its membership was believed to be around 40,000. Many of the sectarian killings were blamed on the UFF and it was not until 1992 that the UDA became a banned organization and proscribed as such under the terms of section 30(3) of the Northern Ireland Emergency Provisions Act, 1996. Politically aligned with the Ulster Loyalist Democratic Party (ULDP) later to become the Ulster Democratic Party (UDP) with political aims of the formation of an independent Northern Ireland within the British Commonwealth. The ULDP changed its name to UDP in 1989. Along with other Loyalist paramilitary groups the UFF began observing a ceasefire in 1994. The UDP were to be involved in the all-party talks toward the Peace Agreement, however the UFF and UDA broke the ceasefire in late

Ulster Freedom Fighters (UFF) July 12, 2002 on Shankhill Road, Belfast, on the eve of the anniversary of the 'Battle of the Boyne'. (PA STRPA)

1997 and the UDP were expelled from the talks. The UFF and UDA continued sporadic attacks against Catholics and the British government determined that their ceasefire was at an end, in October 2001.

Loyalist Volunteer Force (LVF)

Formed in 1996 as a splinter group of the Loyalist Ulster Volunteer Force, the LVF is a violent, sectarian, anti-Catholic terror group, led by Billy Wright, also known as "King Rat." Republican prisoners, who were believed to be members of the INLA, murdered Billy Wright while he was serving a prison term inside Northern Ireland's Maze Prison on December 27, 1997. The aim of the group is to subvert, by violent means, a political settlement with Irish Nationalists in the Northern Ireland peace process. Although this group was responsible for several deaths in January 1998, by March of the same year they were threatening Protestants who openly supported the Northern Ireland peace process, and following that, declared their own ceasefire to encourage a No vote in the referendum on the Good Friday Agreement.

Red Hand Defenders

Formed late in 1998, this terror organization bands together a conglomeration of loyalists from various paramilitary groups not sympathetic to the Good Friday Agreement. There has been speculation that it may also be a convenient cover organization for members of the LVF and the UDA to carry on operations against Catholic targets while LVF and UDA were claiming to be on a legitimately recognized ceasefire. The significance of this is based on the timing of their emergence and the importance of the Agreement, which allows early release for imprisoned terrorists, but would only apply to organizations adhering to a ceasefire. RHD is believed responsible for the killing of an RUC member during the marching season in 1998 and the death of a Catholic Human Rights Lawyer, Rosemary Nelson, in Lurgan in March 1999.

Orange Volunteers (OV)

A protestant loyalist paramilitary with ties to the Orange Order and was established at the outset of the Troubles. It was, at that time, second only to the UDA and the UVF in size and support. The group was believed inactive by the end of 1980, but its name came up once again in 1998 at about the same time as the Red Hand Defenders. Like other paramilitaries of the time it was made up from those disaffected by the Good Friday Agreement and is likely closely linked with if not drawing on the same membership as the RHD. The operational effectiveness of this 'new' group is not sophisticated and has utilized home-made blast bombs (pipe bombs) and hand grenades. It may be that this small group of dissidents is also involved in crime particularly drug dealing.

THE TROUBLES

There is little doubt that in the early days of **the Troubles** (the fighting between Catholics and Protestants), the PIRA was considered to be more of a nuisance than terrorist threat to the security of a sovereign nation. The current Troubles began with civil rights marches in Northern Ireland. In October 1968, the newly formed Northern Ireland Civil Rights Association organized a march in Londonderry to show its strength and its frustration at the discrimination against them by the Protestant majority. The Catholic minority in the North, probably in copycat fashion of the civil rights marches in the United States, epitomized by the leadership of Dr. Martin Luther King. They started marching for better access to jobs, housing and a fairer share of the economy. But, the marches quickly turned violent. In an attempt to quell the situation, the British government urged the Northern Ireland Prime Minister to make far-reaching reforms to prevent further outbreaks. Without the ability to sway the Unionist politicians, such reforms were doomed. Rioting again broke out in the summer of 1969 and the British government sent troops in to restore order and to protect the Catholic enclaves. By the end of 1970, 153 bombs and incendiary devices had been triggered against Protestant businesses in Northern Ireland.

Turf Wars

Much of the sectarian violence in the early 1970s could be described as turf wars between the warring factions of the IRA, the Irish National Liberation Army (INLA), the Ulster Freedom Fighters (UFF), and the Ulster Volunteer

Force (UVF). Tit-for-tat murders and revenge killings of both Catholics and Protestants were common, driven by pure hatred. This was epitomized by the infamous Shankhill Butchers, a Protestant gang operating in west Belfast with the purpose of intimidating the community and carrying out merciless killings. In those early days there was a real struggle for supremacy in the housing districts and ghettos of west Belfast. The feuding was partly ideological and partly material in that they were fighting for control of the criminal rackets in Belfast and Londonderry. Violence within the various terror groups has been carried out as a measure of discipline within the membership.

Civil Liberty Issues

Civil rights and civil liberties issues in Northern Ireland have aided, confused, and complicated the processes of both peace and terror. In many instances the British government has used human rights violations as a tool, both legislatively and as a method of controlling the violence in Ulster.

The Catholic marches of the late 1960s sparked the rioting and bloodshed that led to larger and larger troop deployments in Ulster at the outset, resulting in the modern day Troubles, founded on civil rights issues. By the start of the 1970s, the British government had made significant moves to curtail the actions of the paramilitary groups with the introduction of internment. This policy had little strategic effect, but gave the PIRA members tremendous sympathy by being seen as "martyrs for the cause."

Internment was introduced in August 1971, as a joint decision of the British and Northern Ireland governments. Its intention was to confine known or suspected IRA terrorists. By removing the Catholic threat from the scene, the action was hoped to defuse any Protestant mobilization. In hindsight, internment failed for the government and created a strong recruiting cause for the PIRA.

During this period, there was a serious issue of how the courts could, and should, deal with terror organizations in Northern Ireland. By nature, the terror campaign also harassed, coerced and intimidated court witnesses, juries, and magistrates. The Diplock Commission[8] was set up to look at ways of dealing with the legal aspects of controlling a terrorist in a free and democratic society. With the aim of ensuring the safety and integrity of the security forces, and giving them the unfettered ability to bring the terrorists before the courts, the Northern Ireland Emergency Provisions Act was passed in 1973. The measures, seen as draconian, served the security services well. The Act provided for:

- Terrorist offenses to be listed as "scheduled" offenses;
- Schedule offenses to be tried by a senior judge sitting alone, with more than the rights of appeal;
- Bail was prohibited for schedule offenses unless granted by the High Court, with stringent conditions attached;
- Persons can be held on police arrests without warrant for seventy-two hours;
- Suspects arrested by the military can be held for four hours;
- Security forces had extensive powers for search and seizure;

- Those arrested for weapons and explosive offenses had the onus of proof reversed, for them to prove their innocence;
- Detention orders could be issued by the Secretary of State, from information gathered by the security forces believing the information and evidence to be valid.[9]

With many convictions for terrorist offenses gathered through this sweeping legislation, the PIRA still managed to make both political and publicity points for their predicament. Once in prison, the terrorist took virtual control of his or her destiny, and intimidated prison officers both inside and outside the confines of jail. Since these laws were adopted in the early 1970s, they have undergone frequent reviews and amendments. In 1988, fifteen years after it was enacted, the Prevention of Terrorism Act, designed to give sweeping powers to security forces in Britain, was challenged in the International Court. The provision within the Act to detain terrorist suspects for up to seven days violated the European Convention on Human Rights.

MARCHING SEASON

Sinn Fein and the IRA are seeking an all-Ireland Republic, as had been proclaimed by the United Irishmen in 1798. The Loyalists, including the entire Orange Order, are determined not to be part of any such republic. It seems almost incredible, to people outside the Province of Northern Ireland, that the act of marching, seemingly so irrelevant to most, should cause such widespread anger and revulsion as well as acts of sectarian violence. Marching in almost military style has been a part of Protestant culture in the North for over two hundred years. The lore and beliefs have been passed from generation to generation. To understand what motivates such sectarian hatred between the Catholics and Protestant communities requires reviewing the historical roots of marching.

Marching season is defined as the time frame between Easter Monday and the end of September with more than two thousand parades held throughout the North. There are, however, specific dates in history that create more flashpoints on the calendar than do other marches. The Protestants celebrate their victory over Catholic King James I, at the Battle of the Boyne, on July 12, 1690, by protestant King William. But, it is more than just the celebration of a victory. To Protestant Orangemen it is the need to display undying allegiance to the Crown and Protestantism. Sometimes referred to as "Orangeism," it could also be described as Ulster Unionism on the march. The Orange Order and the Ulster Unionist Council constitute an integrated political movement that is determined that Northern Ireland will remain within the United Kingdom along with England, Scotland, and Wales, and will never be absorbed by a Catholic-dominated, all-Ireland republic.[10] Both the Orange Order and the *Apprentice Boys* say that marching is an essential part of their Protestant culture. The Apprentice Boys is a Loyalist organization similar to the Orange Order, and they hold an annual commemoration of the ending of the siege of Derry in 1688. The Apprentice Boys march with a Crimson Flag first carried by Protestant supporters of William of Orange who were besieged in Derry by an Irish Jacobite army.

Market Street, Omagh, August 15, 1998. Bomb destroyed city center, killing 27 and injuring 200. (AP Photo/Paul McFlaire)

The challenges to peace during marching season are many, as the long established routes wind their way through Catholic strongholds such as the Garvaghy Road in Portadown and the Lower Ormeau Road in Belfast. Both areas have been rife with outbursts of violence in recent years. The Independent Commission on Policing in Northern Ireland made recommendation in 1998 that it should be a condition for the approval of a parade that the organizers should provide their own marshals. Then, the organizers and the police should work together to plan the policing of such events. This should include, as appropriate, representatives of the neighborhoods involved along the parade route. Whether in reality this can happen, time alone will tell. There is so much hostility toward marching by the Catholic communities, through which

TERROR BRIEF 4–1

1998 Omagh Bombing Arrests

In April 2002, police in the Republic of Ireland arrested two men as part of an investigation into the 1998 bombing in Omagh that killed twenty-nine people. The two, one aged 45 and the other 33, were detained in the Irish Counties of Monaghan and Louth, close to the border with Northern Ireland. The men can be detained for up to 72 hours without charge under Section 30 of Ireland's Offences Against the State Act. A woman pregnant with twins was among the twenty-nine people killed when the dissident Republican guerilla group, the Real IRA, detonated a 500-pound bomb in the market town of Omagh on a busy Saturday afternoon in August 1998. Only one person has so far been convicted in this atrocity—the single bloodiest act in Northern Ireland's thirty year conflict.

Source: Crime and Justice International April 2002 Criminal Justice Center, Sam Houston State University, Huntsville, Texas, Vol. 18, Number 61.

Protestants demand the right to march, that it would take but one small incident to provoke an outbreak of sectarian violence.

The Loyal Orange Institution, or Orange Order, was founded in 1795 after a Protestant victory at Loughgall, County Armagh. This is referred to as the "Battle of the Diamond." In September 1795, several hundred Defenders (Catholics) assembled at a crossroads called The Diamond, near Loughgall in County Armagh. They had come to attack the house of one Dan Winter where, they were convinced the "Peep-o-Day" Boys (Protestants) stored their guns and met to conspire against the Catholics. The Battle of the Diamond, on Monday, September 21, lasted a brief fifteen minutes. The Peep-o-Day boys suffered no losses but as many as forty-eight Defenders were said to have been killed. The first Orange Lodge was established that evening. One James Sloan, an Innkeeper became the first Grand Secretary, with power to issue warrants to whichever group of Protestants wanted to follow his rule and set up Orange Lodges. They were required to swear an oath of allegiance to: "His Majesty King George III, and his successors so long as he and they support the Protestant ascendancy"[11]

Sectarian Violence

The terror groups on both sides of this complex situation have focused on the police and the military as so-called legitimate targets. The long-established hatred and revulsion of some Catholics for Protestants, and vice versa, has caused the senseless deaths of many innocent civilians. Killed purely for their religious affiliations, whether they are from PIRA or a Loyalist paramilitary, tit-for-tat killings have been a hallmark of Northern Ireland's history through most of the twentieth century and into the twenty-first. (An obvious

TERRORISM BYTE 4–3

The Right to Education

The small Protestant enclave of the Ardoyne district of west Belfast, where residents claim no Catholics are welcome until attacks on their own homes end, has seen Protestant extremists hurling a homemade bomb at schoolgirls and their parents as they make their way to Holy Cross Primary School. On September 5th and 7th 2001 Protestant loyalists threw not only verbal abuse and stones but also the bomb, which injured four members of the RUC. The Ardoyne district is where Protestant and Catholic clashes began and the house burning and rioting that started thirty years of conflict for Northern Ireland.

Source: The Protestant retreat: The Economist September 8th 2001, pp. 59.

parallel is the conflict between Israelis and Palestinians.) The start can be dated as far back as June 17, 1922, when the IRA issued an order for the destruction of property owned by Orangemen. According to police reports, at 2:30 that morning, IRA men executed six unarmed Protestants and a policeman. The attack was motivated purely along religious lines and had no significance in the struggle for the IRA. In 1976, a similar but far more gruesome attack took place in the Kingsmills area in South Armagh and claimed the lives of ten Protestant workers who were stopped on their bus ride home from work, taken from the vehicle and executed in a hail of bullets by members of the PIRA.

It would be extremely unjust, however, to cast Northern Ireland as a Province where Catholics and Protestants all hate each other, as this is far from true. Many Catholics work alongside Protestants in all levels of society, but both sides have been targeting innocent civilians, both Catholic and Protestant. Marching season, as discussed above, is also a time where sectarianism comes into play. Protestants have viewed the treatment of Sinn Fein and the republican movement as an erosion of their own political and economic power base. As they lose ground this violence, sectarian in nature, has begun to spread. In 2001, in the weeks leading up to 9–11, Protestants pelted Catholic primary school children with rocks and verbal abuse, as they made their way to school through the Protestant Ardoyne district of Belfast. These scenes were more reminiscent of an earlier age in the southern states of the United States involving bussing of black students to school. The Holy Cross school in the Ardoyne district has been there for more than thirty years but what has changed is the demographics of the area around it. Mainly a Protestant area when the Troubles began, many of the middle-class Protestants moved away. Over the last decade, more Catholic families inhabit the area, to the chagrin of Protestants.

THE IRA AND TERROR INTERNATIONAL

The Sinn Fein and Irish republican terror groups have a problem, and that problem is credibility. The requirement to decommission weapons is all-important to the peace accord. Although some decommissioning has taken place, there is now the double standard of the IRA turning in the old and actively securing new weapons. In May 2002, the IRA purchased a quantity of Russian-made AN-94 assault rifles. In April of 2002, the Israelis identified pipe bomb devices made by IRA terrorists in Palestinian hands. Paul Collinson, a former officer with the Royal Engineers Bomb Disposal, now working for the Red Cross at the Jenin refugee camp, comments, "The pipe bombs I found in Jenin are exact replicas of those in Northern Ireland. The size of bomb, the way they put the nail in, the way of igniting it with a light bulb filament, where they drilled the holes through, the use of a command wire and the means of initiating the bomb; these are all the same."[12] As we can tell from this report the IRA continues to ply its terrorism trade on an international scale, not only in the Middle East but as mentioned earlier, in South America. This broader involvement of the IRA on the international stage was also a focus of the U.S. House International Relations Committee. A report from this committee came to the conclusion that Irish, Iranian, Cuban and Spanish terror groups had probably been sharing techniques and honing their terror skills, and using illicit drug proceeds as payment. Gerry Adams as the President of Sinn Fein not surprisingly turned down an invitation to testify before the Congressional committee on the topic.

How closely linked are Sinn Fein and the Irish terror groups? There is little doubt that Adams and McGuinness have the ability to exert significant pressure, whether direct or implied, on the workings of the PIRA and the Army Council. In early 2002, a daring raid was made on the Northern Ireland Police Special Branch offices at Castlereagh. The IRA managed to seize highly confidential documents, naming police informants and undercover operations. To most observers in the security services, it is highly probable that this information and its seizure were ordered by the PIRA Army Council. In its quest for a peace deal with the men of terror, is it possible that the Labour Government of Tony Blair is appeasing them to far greater an extent than is really acceptable? Most, if not all, terror groups only come to the table to talk peace when they are in such a desperate situation that signing a deal, or calling a ceasefire, is all that is left to them. In 1994, the IRA called a ceasefire, not when they were winning the battle, but were in point of fact losing it. Both Adams and McGuinness are notable survivors. So, it is highly likely that there is a lot of double-talk as well as double standards. In order to control the dissidents within the republican movement it would seem wholly logical for the IRA to continue as before, however allowing Sinn Fein the freedom to express concern, sometimes outrage, and more frequently denial of knowledge of IRA activities when it comes to the thorny topics of bomb making and weapons acquisition.

There are many differences between the struggle for peace in Northern Ireland and the struggle for peace in the Middle East. In Israel and the occupied territories, two sides are attempting to ensure their own survival. On one side is Israel, supported by the political and economic strength of the United

States. On the other are Palestinian people living in squalid refugee camps. They view their situation as hopeless, and resort to violence and suicide attacks. Until there is a political will to settle the issue of a homeland for the Palestinians and security for Israel, there is no likelihood of any cessation of violence. In Northern Ireland there are still many political problems to be resolved as well as centuries of fear and distrust standing between Catholics and Protestants. However, for Northern Ireland there is a tunnel and there is light at the end of it. For the Middle East, the light has yet to be turned on.

THE NORTHERN IRELAND PEACE PROCESS

It seems almost inconceivable, but entirely probable, that the devastation of the 9–11 attacks on New York's World Trade Center prompted the terror groups, particularly the IRA, to begin decommissioning and head towards peace.

It is generally agreed that the peace process was developed from a combination of factors:

- A realization by both the IRA and the British Army that the war could not be won militarily, and the decision by the IRA to develop politics, through its political party Sinn Fein, as an alternative way to fight for its political goals;
- The willingness of the Social Democratic Labour Party (SDLP) to engage with Sinn Fein in pursuing common nationalist political goals by peaceful means;

Reverend Ian Paisley—Democratic Unionist Party. (AP Photo/Brian Little)

TERRORISM PLAYER 4–6

The Reverend Ian Paisley

Ian Paisley is the leader of the Democratic Unionist Party of Northern Ireland. The Reverend Paisley is also Moderator of the Free Presbyterian Church, a sect he founded in 1951 which now accounts for 20,000 members and 30 churches. He first came to prominence in 1963 when he organized a protest march against the decision to lower the Union flag at Belfast City Hall to mark the death of Pope John XXIII. In the 1960s, he led marches, demonstrations and rallies all over Northern Ireland and was repeatedly sentenced to prison for unlawful assembly. Paisley has a now-famous battle cry "No surrender" in his hard line Protestantism, loudly proclaiming opposition to any and every concession offered to the Catholic community in Northern Ireland. He is a staunch opponent of the Good Friday Agreement, which he denounced as treacherous.

Source: CNN Inside Specials–Northern Ireland http://europe.cnn.com/SPECIALS.

- A changing social and economic context in which many of the discriminations against Catholics were addressed, and in which a legal and social infrastructure to address issues of inequality, equality, and respect for diversity, began to be developed;

- An increased willingness by many within civic society, for example among business, trade union, and community groups, to actively engage in process of contact and political leverage for peace;

- The development of some new (albeit small) political parties by the Loyalists, and by the Women's Coalition, which enabled some new thinking on the political landscape;

- A changing international context, including proactive involvement from the U S government, and many U.S. businessmen and politicians, as well as assistance with developing peace processes from South Africa.[13]

In August of 2001, the **Good Friday Agreement** was on the verge of collapse. The IRA had failed to follow through on its decommissioning of weapons. Strangely, the terror events of 9–11 in the United States appear to have had a sobering effect on the men of violence in the troubled region of Northern Ireland. After more than thirty years of the Troubles, with endless bombings and more than 3,000 killed in sectarian violence, both main players—the British government which has endured with an occupying army in the North for over three decades, and the Irish republican terror organizations—eventually came to the conclusion that the fighting must end. From the terrorist standpoint, the use of the gun—albeit used to good effect—has not had its desired effect of removing British occupying forces from Northern Ireland. Early attempts at peace settlements in both the two decades preceding the Good Friday Agreement had been doomed to failure and Direct Rule from Britain had returned. As history moves forward the events that would hinder any lasting peace have principally been the decommissioning of weapons in the possession of the paramilitary groups and the IRA's probable involvement in Colombia and Middle East terrorism. For many decades the romantic image of Irish freedom fighters taking on the Brits was lore in the Irish American communities of both New York and Boston. The effect of first-hand terrorism, live and on television, on the U.S. has required a fundamental shift in attitude to decommissioning of weapons by the IRA. The IRA has received enormous amounts of financial aid from U.S. organizations and groups in support of their cause, however with the aftermath of 9–11, the romantic view of many Americans faded very quickly.

It could be argued that with the new War on Terrorism, those supporters of the republican movement could not fathom why republican groups, namely the Provisional IRA, would need to stockpile such large amounts of ammunition. At the end of the day they could only be used against the U.S. staunch supporter in the war on terror, Tony Blair and his Labour Government. A large amount of weapons and explosives have been stockpiled through the last two decades of the twentieth century from arms shipments from state sponsors of terrorism in the shape of Colonel Qaddafi of Libya. This would surely be repugnant to an American public still reeling from the effects of 9–11. With no decommissioning, the PIRA monetary support would likely dry up, or in any case certainly be significantly diminished by not doing so.

At the end of October 2001 the IRA, under the scrutiny of the Independent International Commission on Decommissioning (IICD), "put beyond use" (a term used by the IRA to signify destruction) a large quantity of weapons and explosives. This may be viewed as a landmark event giving the British Government a further opportunity to announce the removal and closure of army watchtowers along the border with the Republic. These moves would hopefully move the 1998 Good Friday Agreement forward in its implementation process.

In trying to understand why decommissioning happened at this point in time one can look at the arrest in Columbia along with FARC guerillas of two senior members of the republican movement. This can only have been an embarrassment to the Sinn Fein leadership and something that would likely damage relations between the republicans and their U.S. support networks. On the other side of the equation, the Ulster Democratic Unionist party under the leadership of the Reverend Ian Paisley was not satisfied with the manner in which the destruction of the weapons and explosives had taken place and were demanding a full listing of weapons destroyed. The peace process, starting with the Good Friday Agreement, has stumbled along for almost four years. The aim of a coalition of parties to lead what might be termed a joint assembly made up of all 'interested' parties, including the political wing of the Irish Republican Army, Sinn Fein. The inclusion of Sinn Fein and the perception that its leaders still have links and some form of influence over IRA activities has had a severe impact on the power sharing process. Unionist parties will not work out a government with Sinn Fein, so long as the Provisionals retained possession of their weapons and munitions.

Whether the amount of weapons decommissioned will be enough for all parties to come to a power-sharing consensus is of course yet to be realized. However, so long as weapon decommissioning continues and the ceasefires hold, then a power-sharing government for Northern Ireland may just become a reality in the near future, with both Republican groups (Catholics) and Unionists (Protestants) finally succeeding in an enduring peace.

On October 23, 2001, the IRA issued the following statement to the British Broadcasting Association (BBC) on the subject of disarmament:

> "The IRA is committed to our republican objectives and to the establishment of a united Ireland based on justice, equality and freedom. In August 1994, against a background of lengthy and intensive discussions involving the two governments and others, the leadership of the IRA called a complete cessation of military operations in order to create the dynamic for a peace process. "Decommissioning" was no part of that. There was no ambiguity about this. Unfortunately there are those within the British establishment and the leadership of unionism who are fundamentally opposed to change. At every opportunity they have used the issue of arms as an excuse to undermine and frustrate the process. It was for this reason this decommissioning was introduced to the process by the British Government. It has been used since to prevent the changes that a lasting peace requires. In order to overcome this and to encourage the changes necessary for a lasting peace, the leadership of Oglaigh na hEireann (IRA) has taken a number of substantial initiatives. These include our engagement with the Independent International Commission on Decommissioning (IICD) and the inspection of a number of arms dumps by the international inspectors, Cyril Ramaphosa and Martti Ahtisaari. No one should doubt the difficulties these initiatives cause for our volunteers, our supporters, and us. The political process is now on the point of collapse. Such a collapse would certainly, and eventually, put the overall peace process in jeopardy. There is a responsibility upon everyone seriously committed to a just peace to do our best to avoid this. Therefore, in order to save the peace process, we have implemented the scheme agreed with the IICD in August. Our motivation is clear. This unprecedented move is to save the peace process and to persuade others of our genuine intention".
>
> *Signed*
> *P. O'Neill*[14]

The "Agreement" is a document that goes a long way in addressing political, social, economic and judicial inequalities that to many would seem to have been root causes of the thirty years of the Troubles. Three of the most common points have been cause for not just debate, but also at times the near breakdown of the whole agreement. The following sections taken from the Agreement form some of the most contentious points:

Prisoners

1. Both Governments will put in place mechanisms to provide for an accelerated programme for the release of prisoners, including transferred prisoners, convicted of scheduled offences in Northern Ireland or, in the case of those sentenced outside Northern Ireland, similar offences (referred to hereafter as qualifying prisoners). Any such arrangements will protect the rights of individual prisoners under national and international law.

2. Prisoners affiliated to organizations that have not established or are not maintaining a complete and unequivocal ceasefire will not benefit from the arrangements. The situation in this regard will be kept under review.

3. Both Governments will complete a review process within a fixed time frame and set prospective release dates for all qualifying prison-

ers. The review process would provide for the advance of the release dates of qualifying prisoners while allowing account to be taken of the seriousness of the offences for which the person was convicted and the need to protect the community. In addition, the intention would be that should the circumstances allow it, any qualifying prisoners who remained in custody two years after the commencement of the scheme would be released at that point.

4. The Governments will seek to enact the appropriate legislation to give effect to these arrangements by the end of June 1998.

5. The Governments continue to recognise the importance of measures to facilitate the reintegration of prisoners into the community by providing support both prior to and after release, including assistance directed towards availing of employment opportunities, re-training and/or re-skilling, and further education.

As mentioned earlier the decommissioning of weapons by paramilitaries has been a major stumbling block for politicians particularly from the Unionists.

Decommissioning

1. Participants recall their agreement in the Procedural Motion adopted on 24 September 1997, "that the resolution of the decommissioning issue is an indispensable part of the process of negotiation", and also recall the provisions of paragraph 25 of Strand 1 above.

2. They note the progress made by the Independent International Commission on Decommissioning and the Governments in developing schemes that can represent a workable basis for achieving the decommissioning of illegally-held arms in the possession of paramilitary groups.

3. All participants accordingly reaffirm their commitment to the total disarmament of all paramilitary organizations. They also confirm their intention to continue to work constructively and in good faith with the Independent Commission, and to use any influence they may have, to achieve the decommissioning of all paramilitary arms within two years following endorsement in referendums North and South of the agreement and in the context of the implementation of the overall settlement.

4. The Independent Commission will monitor, review and verify progress on decommissioning of illegal arms, and will report to both Governments at regular intervals.

5. Both Governments will take all necessary steps to facilitate the decommissioning process to include bringing the relevant schemes into force by the end of June.

Security

1. The participants note that the development of a peaceful environment on the basis of this agreement can and should mean a normalization of security arrangements and practices.

2. The British Government will make progress towards the objective of as early a return as possible to normal security arrangements in Northern Ireland, consistent with the level of threat and with a published overall strategy, dealing with:

    (i) The reduction of the numbers and role of the Armed Forces deployed in Northern Ireland to levels compatible with a normal peaceful society;

     (ii) The removal of security installations;

    (iii) The removal of emergency powers in Northern Ireland;

    (iv) Other measures appropriate to and compatible with a normal peaceful society.

3. The Secretary of State will consult regularly on progress, and the response to any continuing paramilitary activity, with the Irish Government and the political parties, as appropriate.

4. The British Government will continue its consultation on firearms regulation and control on the basis of the document published on 2 April 1998.

5. The Irish Government will initiate a wide-ranging review of the Offences Against the State Acts 1939–85 with a view to both reform and dispensing with those elements no longer required as circumstances permit.

Before discussing the new police service now established in Northern Ireland, the following is the extract from the 1998 Agreement:

Annex A

Commission on Policing for Northern Ireland

Terms of Reference

Taking account of the principles on policing as set out in the agreement, the Commission will inquire into policing in Northern Ireland and, on the basis of its findings, bring forward proposals for future policing structures and arrangements, including means of encouraging widespread community support for those arrangements.

Its proposals on policing should be designed to ensure that policing arrangements, including composition, recruitment, training, culture, ethos and symbols, are such that in a new approach Northern Ireland has a police service that can enjoy widespread support from, and is seen as an integral part of, the community as a whole.

Its proposals should include recommendations covering any issues such as re-training, job placement and educational and professional development required in the transition to policing in a peaceful society.

Its proposals should also be designed to ensure that:

- The police service is structured, managed and resourced so that it can be effective in discharging its full range of functions (including proposals on any necessary arrangements for the transition to policing in a normal peaceful society);
- The police service is delivered in constructive and inclusive partnerships with the community at all levels with the maximum delegation of authority and responsibility;
- The legislative and constitutional framework requires the impartial discharge of policing functions and conforms with internationally accepted norms in relation to policing standards;
- The police operate within a clear framework of accountability to the law and the community they serve, so:
- They are constrained by, accountable to and act only within the law;
- Their powers and procedures, like the law they enforce, are clearly established and publicly available;
- There are open, accessible and independent means of investigating and adjudicating upon complaints against the police;

- There are clearly established arrangements enabling local people, and their political representatives, to articulate their views and concerns about policing and to establish publicly policing priorities and influence policing policies, subject to safeguards to ensure police impartiality and freedom from partisan political control;
- There are arrangements for accountability and for the effective, efficient and economic use of resources in achieving policing objectives;
- There are means to ensure independent professional scrutiny and inspection of the police service to ensure that proper professional standards are maintained;
- The scope for structured co-operation with the *Garda Siochana* and other police forces is addressed; and
- The management of public order events, which can impose exceptional demands on police resources, is also addressed.
- The Commission should focus on policing issues, but if it identifies other aspects of the criminal justice system relevant to its work on policing, including the role of the police in prosecution, then it should draw the attention of the Government to those matters.
- The Commission should consult widely, including with non-governmental expert organizations, and through such focus groups as they consider it appropriate to establish.
- The Government proposes to establish the Commission as soon as possible, with the aim of it starting work as soon as possible and publishing its final report by Summer 1999.[15]

THE NORTHERN IRELAND POLICE SERVICE

Historically, the Royal Ulster Constabulary has disproportionately been comprised of Protestants and Unionists with the total percentage of Catholics comprising about 7% of the overall membership. Over the last thirty years, the RUC has been identified with political control formerly from the Unionist government in Stormont and latterly during the period of direct rule from Westminster, not as upholders of law but as defenders of the state, and the nature of the state itself has remained the central issue of the political argument.

In 1998 the British government appointed former Governor of Hong Kong, Chris Patten, to head the Independent Commission on Policing in Northern Ireland. The results of the commissions report made 175 recommendations for change. When the recommendations were presented, the Sinn Fein party was adamant that the only way forward for the Peace Accord was a full implementation of all the recommendations, including the striking of the word Royal from the police title. The former RUC has survived a torrid thirty years of strife and assault from the republican terror groups. The force has always had a predominantly Protestant flavor to it and has lost some 300 officers murdered by terrorist acts and more than 9,000 have been injured during this time frame. Policing in the north cannot be likened with any other police force operating in a western democracy. It has had to handle terrorist incidents like no other force, as part of every day policing which can hardly be considered the norm in western civilization. In 1985, INTERPOL stated that the RUC was the most dangerous force in which to serve even surpassing Colombia. The Patten Report, entitled "A New Beginning: Policing In Northern Ireland" produced a report that covered every region of the force from recruitment, IT, size of force, composition by religious affiliation, culture and ethos, public order policing, and human rights. The aim of the recommendations to be adapted was to attract and sustain support for the new organization from the entire community. The problems faced by the police service in Northern Ireland are in a sense unique in a divided society, with its own particular history and culture. But many are similar to those confronting police services in democratic societies elsewhere. The Independent Commission studied policing in other countries, and while they could discover no model that could simply be applied to Northern Ireland, they were able to find plenty of examples of police services wrestling with the same sort of challenges. The challenge for the police service in the North was how could they be accountable to the community they serve if their composition in terms of ethnicity, religion, and gender is vastly different to that of their society. In the words of the founder of the British police service, Sir Robert Peel, the police service's main objective is the prevention of crime rather than the detection and punishment of offenders. The end of the 1990s focused the debate in Britain on policing as it affected ethnic minorities and communities and the police service's relationship with those communities. There is obviously no perfect model for Northern Ireland and there is no example of a country that, to quote one European police officer, "has yet finalized the total transformation from force to service." The commitment to a fresh start gives Northern Ireland the opportunity to take best practice from elsewhere and to possibly lead the way in overcoming some of the toughest challenges of modern policing.[16]

TERRORISM IN MAINLAND BRITAIN

The Angry Brigade

British politicians and the public have suffered under both the threat and the reality of indiscriminate terror acts by the IRA since the early 1970s. Almost totally forgotten by many, however, is a small terror group that came to life in the 1960s, the decade that saw the Beatles, widespread drug use, and fundamental changes in societal views and values. The Angry Brigade is Britain's only noteworthy homegrown terror group.

One of the earliest workers' movements was the Chartist Movement, which started in the 1830s. Prior to this there were other forms of autonomous revolt by workers in the textile mills of the Midlands and the North of England. As a result of threatened job losses due to industrialization, workers formed into armed groups of both employed and unemployed workers. They rioted and caused property damage.

Few may recall the Angry Brigade, however, the group was real and did exist. The members of this group were dissimilar in almost every facet to the Irish terrorists and had no clearly defined enemy to focus on other than wealthy middle class conservatives running business corporations. Unlike the terrorist groups waging war in both Northern Ireland and the mainland, the Angry Brigade was a loosely formed group of communist-style, workers' party members. The philosophy of the Brigade was that of a militant prolabor, left-wing revolutionary movement.[18]

The Angry Brigade came to some prominence in the late 1960s and little has been heard of the group since the main protagonists were jailed in 1971. The group could be termed a copycat, and likened itself to the Weathermen in the United States, and, in a latter period, to the German terrorist group led by Baader and Meinhoff. With no military knowledge or background, the Angry Brigade espoused Marxist theories in the hope that workers would find them acceptable. Britain in the 1960s was a changing society in a great many respects, with a strong Conservative government under Alec Douglas Hume. Modernization and growth in the factories, particularly in the auto industry and the dockyards, was the order of the day. The leaders of the Angry Brigade sought to change government policy and usher in a new era of socialism by murdering politicians and bombing public buildings.

Activists or Terrorists?

As pure activists in a worker's party struggle against the perceived enemy, the state and big business, the Angry Brigade issued communiqués and proclamations stating their cause. The Brigade hoped to gain recognition by professing support for the Irish nationalist movement and such mirror-image revolutionaries as the SLA in the United States. Closer to home, the group espoused support for the activities of the Red Brigade in Italy and the German Red Army faction. There is no recorded information that the group received any support, either of a financial or military nature, from either of these terrorist organizations. What is certain is that the Brigade caused explosions aimed primarily at political and business figures. They were hunted down by Britain's Metropolitan Police force and prosecuted for their terrorist and criminal acts. The Angry Brigade's members believed that they were engaged in a workers' struggle that could only come to fruition if the working masses rebelled against their masters. This altruistic goal was never realized, however, possibly due to the atrocious nature of the Brigade's attacks.

Angry Brigade Terrorist Acts

The Angry Brigade is believed to have been involved in a number of bombings in London aimed at banks, corporations and foreign interest businesses, such as the Bank of Bilbao. The Brigade supported the Basque separatists in Spain. What this group hoped to achieve by attacks on the homes of the Commissioner of the Metropolitan Police, and a member of Parliament is unclear. Certainly these actions demonstrated an ability to coerce and intimidate, but their overall effectiveness can be dismissed as having minimal effect in making any changes in the political arena. Unlike the PIRA, the Brigade had no political machinery, similar to that of Sinn Fein, or any media support. The Angry Brigade was broken up through a series of arrests in 1971. The ringleaders, who became known as the Stoke Newington Eight, were sent to prison for long terms in 1972. The group still remains one of the only examples of homegrown, or internal terrorism, in Great Britain.

Wales and Terror for the Tourist

To a casual observer, the region of the United Kingdom known as Wales seldom conjures up visions of terrorist activity. In fact, Wales is better known for its tourist attractions at Caernavon Castle, the Mountains of Snowdonia, Welsh choirs, famous actors, mining and the sport of rugby. So, is Wales a nest of terror groups or a convenient hiding place for the indigenous terrorist? Over the past three decades there has been the odd discussion of an independent Welsh homeland, which occasionally has been brought to the attention of Britons by random acts of arson. These acts were usually aimed at unoccupied holiday homes and cottages in the Wales countryside. Claiming responsibility for these acts of arson is a group calling itself the *Miebion Glyndwr,* or Sons of Glendower. This group takes its name from Owen Glendower who was a Welsh leader from the fifteenth century who vowed to fight the English and their rule over Wales. The arson attacks upon remote cottages resulted in more than one hundred having been destroyed since the first attack in 1979. The group appears disorganized and factional, with no political platform for their support. About twenty Welsh activists have been convicted and jailed for some fifteen of the attacks. There appears to be little significance to the arsons and no clear links between them. A group calling itself *Cadwyr Cymru* (the Defenders of Wales) has claimed responsibility for some of the arsons, but many might well have been committed for insurance purposes.

Scottish Nationalism (APG)

The desire for separate representation by an assembly different from that at the Palace of Westminster has not been the sole province of Irish nationalism or Welsh nationalism. The 1970s were a period of change in the northern part of the British Isles as well. At that time there was a strong political desire for Scotland to have its own assembly and a measure of autonomy separate from Westminster. In support of these aims, although fervently denounced by Scottish Nationalist parliamentary candidates, the APG was formed. In an attempt to further their cause, the APG planned a series of bank robberies in Scotland and England, and were caught planning to break into a military arsenal. The group was tried and sentenced on charges of conspiracy in 1975. At the trial, it was revealed that some of the APG members had gained their military experience in the service of the British Army and were experienced in counterinsurgency tactics. The official Scottish Nationalist party scorned efforts that they believed could only detract from the legitimacy of the party. Little has been heard from them since that time.

Animal Rights Militia

Animal rights activists have been prevalent in Great Britain for several decades, but this is the only one of their many groups to have moved toward terror tactics and bombings, aimed at companies and research institutes. In 1986, bombs were planted under cars and at the homes of prominent research scientists and animal importers. Although adequate warnings were given, this marked a trend towards violent action by this group. This group, while perhaps using what could be terrorist tactics, are still considered more like criminals than true terrorists. The new **Anti Terrorism Act of 2000** although logically aimed at curbing the IRA and other Northern Ireland terror groups could also be focused on the Animal Liberation Front an activist organization that is believed responsible for a number of bomb attacks against animal research establishments and the agricultural industry. Attacks on fast food establishments in Belgium appear to have been the work of the same group.

ISLAMIC POLITICS AND TERROR IN THE UNITED KINGDOM

With a *fatwa* (religious decree) proclaimed on 9–11 by Osama bin Laden against the United States, one has to question the number of movements based in the capital that give support to terror organizations. A brief look at those groups indicates that London—recently referred to in the print media as "Londonistan,"— is home to the following organizations with political affiliations to suspect groups and state sponsors of terror:

- An Islamic Palestine group (*Fillisteen al-Muslima*), located in London; produces a magazine in support of the Hamas movement;
- The Emigrants *(al-Muhajiroun)*, a group led by Syrian supporters of attacks against the United States;
- Islamic Liberation Party (*Hizb-ut-Tahir*), a student group that has been banned in Arab countries;
- Islamic Observation Center, located in the middle of London, this group is linked with extremist movements in Egypt;
- Islamic Salvation Front (*Front Islamique de Salvation*), a banned Algerian terror group that publishes a newsletter from a base in the west of London.

There is no doubt that the role played by some of the Islamic Front movements in attacks against American interests will lead Britain's Special Branch to consider taking remedial action to investigate these groups and their ties to terrorism. Over the last three to four years, Britain has been viewed as a one of Europe's most liberal societies, therefore attracting a number of dissident groups to its shores for fundraising and other activities. Members are often from terrorist organizations that appear on the U.S. State Department list of overseas terrorist organizations; these groups include *Gama'a al-Islamiyya, Hamas,* Shining Path, the Liberation Tigers of Tamil Elam, *Hezbollah* and the Kurdistan Workers Party. All these groups had been actively recruiting and raising funds freely in the United Kingdom until September 11. In the aftermath of the attacks, Britain introduced tough new emergency powers to arrest and hold suspected terrorists without charge. Al Qaeda is a relatively modern day phenomenon that has been in existence a little over a decade and only became synonymous with terrorism in the days after 9–11. It is clear, and becoming clearer, that the reach and spread of al Qaeda throughout the world and particularly on the European continent is posing one of the most significant risks to Western democracies. Over the last ten years, London has become a haven for young Muslim immigrants as well as asylum seekers. With few prospects for work, they have managed to adapt to the generosity of a welfare state that provides for their physical well being. However, many have resorted to attending institutions such as the **Finsbury Park Mosque** where many observers would say that they were brainwashed into organizations such as al Qaeda and then sent throughout the world to carry out *jihad*. Evidence has been uncovered linking Richard Reid, who attempted to detonate an explosive device in his shoes on board a U.S. transatlantic flight in December 2001, with Zacarias Moussaoui, the so called twentieth hijacker (9–11) as well as the millennium bomber Ahmed Ressam. A mosque is a holy place of worship and the Finsbury Park Mosque is one of the largest in London and is open to worshipers as well as casual visitors. The one-eyed, hook-handed Imam Sheik Abu Hamza is outspoken in his support for Osama bin Laden and in a television interview made no apologies or showed the least amount of remorse for the 9–11 attack on the World Trade Center. So is Finsbury Park a fertile and covert breeding ground for al Qaeda? The mosque itself attracts many Muslims from the diverse ethnic communities in the area, namely, Pakistanis, Bengalis, Egyptians and Algerians. Abu Hamza is himself an Egyptian and has been in the United Kingdom for more than twenty years. His presence is no doubt imposing, a missing eye and a hook in place of his right hand, to young and impressionable Muslims who would see little future for themselves in the western democracies and be easily indoctrinated by the Imam and his cohorts. A Canadian Broadcast Corporation documentary on recruiting al Qaeda in Britain focused squarely on the Mosque in Finsbury. The detailed exposé included hidden videotaping of recruiting activities inside the mosque, as well as videos of terror training tactics, such as how to slit a person's throat. The problem for British police lies in its inability to pinpoint any crime that the Imam may have committed.

Muslim leader—Sheikh Abu Hamza speaking to members of Muslim group Al-Muhajirunn during their rally in London's Trafalgar Square—August 25, 2002. (PA Photo)

On the international scene, Great Britain continues to be the strongest ally of the United States in its war on terrorism. This therefore adds Britain and its citizens to the list of legitimate targets as far as al Qaeda terrorists are concerned. Whether sympathizers or members or cells exist in Britain is not clear. In the United States-led attacks on the Taliban and al Qaeda in Afghanistan, the presence of British citizens operating with the Taliban/al Qaeda was uncovered. The London Daily Telegraph newspaper carried the news that three Britons from the Tipton area had been seized in Kandahar. The romantic nature of young men to seek opportunities to fight for a cause or for money (mercenary) is not a new phenomenon. British, American, French, German, and Belgian men operated extensively in African countries during the 1960s and 1970s as mercenaries, so it is not surprising to find those from the Indian subcontinent who have grown up as migrants in Britain, finding some romantic pull to return and fight for a "holy cause." How deeply rooted any cells of al Qaeda, or other terror groups may be, will only be revealed with massive efforts of the British Intelligence and Police Special Branch. No doubt the activities and members frequenting mosques not only in Finsbury Park but in areas of the Midlands will come under the scrutiny of intelligence services.

BRITAIN'S RESPONSE TO TERRORISM

As has been shown earlier, judicial processes were already the primary weapon used against the terror groups in Northern Ireland, and Britain's early response in sending in the troops to protect Catholics from Protestants did not have the desired effect. The PIRA was up against the entire intelligence resources of a major western government, and those resources were significant. The brigade and battalion structures of the PIRA, established at the latter end of the 1960s, became targets for penetration by the RUC. Informants were placed within the organization and several senior IRA members were arrested. As noted previously, the PIRA remodeled their battalions into smaller cells, in which only a minority of people knew who was who. The British Government was prepared to meet violence head on with their special antiterrorist force, the SAS.[17]

Responding to Irish terrorism has prompted the British government to introduce the new Anti Terrorism Act of 2000, which came into force in February of 2001. The aim of this piece of legislation was to put a stop to the emerging trend of terror activity within Britain and also by its nationals in Asia and the Middle East. The Act also took aim at international terrorism and in particular the presence of the previously mentioned terrorist organizations, which was causing serious embarrassment to the British. The new law allows the government to ban groups and criminalize fund raising as well as their political activity. Religious and ideologically motivated acts are also included in the legislation's definition of terrorism. The main thrust of the legislation is:

- Criminalizing fundraising for terrorist groups;
- The interference with or disruption of electronic systems;

- The possession or dissemination of information facilitating terrorist activity;
- Meetings of three or more persons with the purpose of encouraging support for a proscribed organization or furthering its activity.

In reflection upon 9–11, the legislation was also aimed at those Britons involved with attacks overseas. For instance, the British press reported that in December 2000, a British Muslim from Birmingham, England, is purported to have conducted a suicide attack on an Indian Army barracks in Srinagar, as well as a Briton plotting a terrorist attack earlier the same year against Israel.

COUNTERING IRISH TERRORISM

The advent of terrorism saw the wide-scale development of anti-terror measures being utilized by the British Government against the terror groups in Northern Ireland. Never before in its modern history had a British peacetime government had to deal with internal terrorist activities on the scale that emerged from Northern Ireland. On many occasions Britain has met violence with violence and has had some innovative ideas to counter the terrorists. Among those innovations are its shoot-to-kill policy, internment, removal of a defendant's right of silence during judicial proceedings, and the prohibiting of news media broadcasting statements of PIRA and Sinn Fein. With the "Irish question" still not answered after more than three decades of political and **sectarian** violence, one has to question how effective the countermeasures have really been. The hostility shown by and to Margaret Thatcher helped to feed the terror campaign against British economic, military and political targets. She constantly reiterated that she would "never give in" to the IRA. Each side's inability to achieve military victory should be obvious to the other. The lessons for the rest of the world from Northern Ireland's conflict would seem to be the following:

- Authorities must pursue every effort to make political compromises with dissidents before violence becomes institutionalized.
- The authorities cannot achieve a military victory over terrorists and still maintain civil liberties and democratic institutions.
- Counterterror techniques by authorities that kill, injure, or frighten noncombatants provide support for terrorist groups. Indeed, revolutionary terrorist groups depend on the authorities to perpetrate provocation and outrages against noncombatants.
- Terrorist groups can be devastatingly effective with very few members, given the worldwide availability of sophisticated weapons and explosives.
- Terrorist groups can sustain community support by using both the latent sympathy of citizens, as well as intimidation.
- Even the most technologically sophisticated, well-organized, well-financed, and highly motivated counterterrorist methods can be frustrated by a small group of terrorists with some community support.[18]

There have been notable successes by Britain's counterterror organizations. The Special Air Service Regiment, which continued to thwart and strike at republican terrorists through the 1980s and 1990s, was instrumental in preventing terrorist attacks and setting up offensive traps resulting in the capture and often the death of terrorists.

EXTREME RIGHT WING GROUPS

The issues of immigration and violence by right wing groups against immigrants are not new phenomena for Britain. Hate crimes have been prevalent throughout the last 30 years of the 20th Century. The British National Party has a political agenda, which demands Britain become independent from Europe and stops the influx of immigrants and also calls for the deportation of criminal and illegal immigrants. While this party maintains this stance it has attracted a hooligan element that attacks indiscriminately against persons of foreign origin. The loosely knit group at the center of these attacks is associated with football violence, namely Skinheads. Skinheads first appeared in Britain around the early 1970s and could be found in almost every city in the country, definitely a cult rather than an organization with any political aspirations. Easily spotted, the Skinhead youth has changed little from those early days of the '70s: shaved heads, tattoos, checked shirts, blue jeans and steel toed 'bovver' boots in the Doc Martens style and sporting Nazi insignia. They appeared as angry young men, symbolizing a tough working class background. The Skinheads were known for their violent rampages and became synonymous with extreme nationalism. Their favored targets for violent attacks were Jews, homosexuals and Asians. The style of dress soon went out of fashion, however a hard-core albeit small movement much along the lines of neo-Nazi exists today. Their hate attacks target Jewish cemeteries and Asian shopping areas. Many of the attacks appear random in nature, but there is a belief that some attacks involving English soccer clubs is planned in advance. Their presence and aggressive language is often seen at marches and parades with the British National Party although there is no evidence to suggest that any are members. The ebb and flow of this cult-like movement has endured for almost thirty years and has spread its aggressive attitudes towards Jews and immigrants across Europe and North America.[19]

SUMMARY

Britain has waged a long-standing fight with domestic terror and a few brushes with international terrorism. The success of the SAS rescue at the Iranian Embassy in London in the early 1980s showed terror groups throughout the world that Britain was not going to tolerate, let alone negotiate with terrorists on its soil. Measuring the impact of 9–11 events on peace in Northern Ireland is uncertain as events worldwide unfold. What is undeniable is that in October 2001 the PIRA, under the auspices of the International Commission for Decommissioning, decommissioned some, but just a fraction of their weapons and explosives. Many experts believe that the cache of weapons and explosives under the control of the PIRA, garnered from countries such as Libya in the 1980s, is sufficient to supply a small country's army. This has to be viewed in a much broader context, for the American public, so traumatized by the horror of 9–11, it was inconceivable that the Irish communities in the United States would or could be seen to support a terrorist organization such as the IRA through Northern Irish Aid charities, long a front for funding and fund-raising for the terrorists. With funding drying up from its usual sources, the PIRA had little choice but to begin the decommissioning of its weapons. Added to this, the unsettling news that an IRA official had been arrested in Colombia with FARC rebels muddied the waters, the man in question being an expert in mortar bombs and remote control devices. Damage control was very much on the minds of the Sinn Fein leadership, with no desire to see the entire peace protocol collapse. With Irish terror possibly on the wane and with the political fortunes of the Tony Blair government riding on a Northern Ireland Peace Agreement, the fight against international terror will be the future focus. With so many immigrants from the Indian subcontinent and Africa, the challenges for rooting out terrorist factions with links to Islamic fundamentalist groups has never been greater. However Britain has the necessary terrorist legislation in place to deal with those activists found engaged in terror planning and funding.

TERMS TO REMEMBER

Anti Terrorism Act 2000	**Home Rule Bill**	**RUC**
ASU	**INLA**	**sectarian**
Battle of the Boyne	**IRA**	***Sinn Fein***
Black and Tans	**Irish Free State**	**Supergrass**
decommissioning	**Northern Ireland Police Service**	**The Troubles**
Finsbury Park Mosque	**PIRA**	
Good Friday Agreement	**RIRA**	

REVIEW QUESTIONS

1. Describe the role of the Real and Continuity Irish Republican Army groups in attempting to subvert the Peace Agreement.
2. Discuss the role played by Sinn Fein and its efforts to decommission weapons.
3. What role does the PIRA play in international terrorism?
4. Discuss the level and types of international terrorist groups at work in London.

ENDNOTES

1. *The World Book Encyclopaedia,* Volume 11, p. 25, World Book Inc. 1990
2. *The World Book Encyclopaedia,* Volume 10, p. 427, World Book Inc. 1990
3. Ibid.
4. Ibid.

5. Strategic Forecasting http://www.stratfor.com/standard/analysis_view.php.

6. BBC News Service, October 4, 2001, 13.09 GMT.

7. Terrorism a Historical and Contemporary Perspective, Olsen-Raymer, Gayle, p. 197, American Heritage Custom Publishing, New York, 1996.

8. *The Diplock Report: Report of the Commission to Consider the Legal Procedure to Deal with Terrorist Attacks in Northern Ireland.* Cmnd. 5185 (London: HMSO, 1972) p. 13.

9. Terrorism an International Journal Volume 11, Number 4 1988, *Stretching the Boundaries: The Control of Dissent in Northern Ireland,* Jim Smyth, Department of Social Studies, Queens University, Belfast. pp. 289–295 Taylor and Francis, 1988.

10. *The Orange Order, 1795-1995,* Andrew Boyd 1995. www.history.com.

11. Ibid.

12. The Weekly Telegraph, London, p. 13, May 7, 2002.

13. CAIN website http://cain.ulst.ac.uk.

14. IRA Statement on Decommissioning: www.cnn.com/world.

15. Extract Northern Ireland Peace Agreement: http://www.nio.gov.uk/agreement.htm

16. Extract 1.3 and 1.4, pp. 2, 3 'A New Beginning in Northern Ireland'. The report of the Independent Commission on Policing for Northern Ireland, Crown Copyright 1999, Norwich UK.

17. Jonathan R. White, *'Terrorism and Introduction',* Brooks/Cole Publishing, pp. 220–221.

18. Terrorism an International Journal, Volume 12, Number 1 1989, J. W. Soule,'Problems in Applying Counterterrorism to Prevent Terrorism: Two Decades of Violence in Northern Ireland Considered.

19. Anti-Defamation League. The Skinhead International, A worldwide survey of Neo Nazi Skinheads, New York ADL 1995. ADL, 823 U.N. Plaza New York. http://www.nizkor.org/hweb/orgs/american/adl/skinhead-international.

5 Western Europe

The campaign to eradicate terrorism has reached a new stage. It will be pursued on many fronts with determination and patience. The Alliance stands ready to play its role.

Lord Robertson, Secretary General NATO

OVERVIEW

In this chapter the authors will examine how the Euzkadi Ta Azkatasuna (ETA) terror organization in the Basque Region of Spain, has continued its bloody bombing campaign in spite of an earlier cease-fire agreement and concessions in areas such as local government and education. France still contends with sporadic attacks from dissident Algerian factions as well as the homegrown Corsican terrorists. Germany, unused to being viewed as a terror haven, is firmly on the map in that regard as the launching pad for the planning by some of the suicide hijackers of 9–11. Germany has also been contending with terror of a subtly different kind from that of secretive al Qaeda cells. In this chapter there is also a discussion of terror by hate groups aimed at ethnic minorities by neo-Nazi skinhead factions. In the wider battle for the suppression of terrorist acts we shall also examine the role played by the European countries in freezing monetary assets of terrorist support networks, as related to the events of 9–11. Italy has also seen the effects a free society has on the abilities of terror cells to propagate and pursue their ugly trade of terrorism. In Greece, terrorism has been the province of the shadowy **November 17** group. Until the spring of 2002, authorities had made no headway in managing to arrest any of its members.

SPAIN

Spanish Nationalism and the Basques

The Basque region of Spain spills across the Pyrenees and into southern France. It is estimated that half a million Basques live on French soil and approximately two and a half million live within the borders of Spain. Historical facts about the initial origin of the Basque people are uncertain, however it is known that they have been in this region since before the Gauls and Iberians settled in Spain and France. The Basques have their own language, which is not derived from any other European language or dialect, called Euskera. With their population size it would be logical to expect that they might be a self-governing principality not dissimilar to Monaco. However, the Basque people do not have their own homeland and, in similar fashion to the Irish Republicans, have been fighting for self-government of their own homeland since the first quarter of the 20th century. General Francisco Franco came to power during the Spanish Civil War that took place between 1936–39. He ruled Spain as a dictator until his death in 1975. In the intervening years since then, Spain has achieved tremendous economic growth.

Basque Separatism

As the 20th century drew to a close, there were only two European regions of nationalist conflict. Of course, the most notable and most documented has been the terrorist campaign for separatism from England, waged in Northern Ireland. However, the Basques of the Pyrenean region of Spain have long waged their own internal struggle for a national identity. The Basques have not had a separate homeland or separate autonomy since the 12th century. Amazingly, they have managed to maintain and protect their own language and culture over the centuries. General Franco's approach to dealing with the Basque Nationals was to suppress them at all costs. He incorporated the Basque region into Spain at the end of the Spanish Civil War and outlawed their culture and language. Franco's actions led to a rebirth of Basque nationalist fervor in the late 1950s. Spain continues to suffer from the scourge of terror attacks perpetrated by a frustrated ETA. In 1999, ETA broke its "unilateral and indefinite" cease-fire and recommenced its bombing and assassination campaign. Since the turn of the century, attacks have increased and like those attacks by Irish republicans, the Basque separatists favor the indiscriminate use of remotely detonated bomb attacks in public places to make their point, as well as assassination of local and state officials. Following the 9–11 attacks in New York and Washington, the U.S. Government, which has re-designated ETA every two years as a Foreign Terrorist Organization, went a step further. In October 2001, when ETA was designated under the President's September 23, 2001 Executive Order 13224, ETA was designated as a "Specially Designated Global Terrorist Organization." The Executive Order was specifically aimed at those persons and groups that provide financial support and assistance to terrorist groups. More specifically, the order further blocked property and prohibited transactions with persons that commit, threaten to commit, or support terrorism. In February 2002, the U.S. Department of the Treasury designated twenty-one Spanish nationals under Executive Order 13224. These individuals were designated as members of, assisting in, sponsoring, or providing financial, material, or technological support for, or financial or other services to, or in support of ETA's acts of terrorism, and are otherwise believed to be acting for or on behalf of. These twenty-one individuals were designated by the European Union on December 21, 2001 for their involvement in terrorist acts.[1]

Euzkadi Ta Azkatasuna (ETA)

In 1959, the Basques formed ETA (Basque Fatherland and Freedom) and it was dedicated to promoting Basque independence. The ETA was not originally formed as a terror group but, with Franco's viscious oppression of the Basques, the group was more or less compelled to retaliate with like violence. ETA, like the IRA, gains its membership support predominantly from the working classes. Those members come from regions that identify with the strong ethnic identity of the Basque people. The members are invariably young, frustrated nationalists with a sense of frustration at their lack of autonomy. The majority of Basques favor nationalism but do not support the terrorists' violent "any means to an end" approach to reaching a political goal of self-government and determination. The ETA has, over the past 25 years, been a fragmented organization that has seen several offshoots of the original group formed.

A political report, commissioned in 1986 by the Basque regional government, describes the **Basque** region as being susceptible to political solutions. It also described ETA as, "an unfortunate child of the Franco dictatorship." Much of the report suggested political solutions such as how to accommodate Basque nationalism within the framework of Spain and the European Economic Community (EEC). One of the recommendations was that Basque terrorists, who under Spanish law were tried in Madrid "special" courts, should in fact be tried in Basque courts. And, policing of terrorists should come under the control of Basque police and not Spain's National Police.[2]

Since its inception in the 1950s, the ETA has been riddled with internal squabbling and bitter dissension. The group split apart in 1966, into what was known as ETA-*Zarra* (or old ETA), and ETA-*Berri* or young ETA. ETA-*Zarra* divided into two subgroups, ETA-5 and ETA-6. The ETA subgroup, ETA-5 divided further into ETA-Military and ETA-Politico Military, and the most hardened and seasoned campaigners for armed action come from the subgroup ETA-Military.[3] The splits have caused confusion and consternation among the Basque people as to whether or which of these proliferating schisms to support or oppose.

"Actions Unite—Words Divide" is the slogan adopted by **ETA-Military**, and their terrorist members adopted the same cell-like structure as used by the Provisional IRA terrorists on active service unit duties. ETA-Military commandos or *irurko* were made up of three-man cells. "Sleeping commandos" were organized in the late 1970s by the ETA Military commander, Miguel Apalategui.[4] The "sleepers" were called up from the Basque community to perform one single terrorist act and then returned to their jobs in relative anonymity. To finance their terror campaign, the ETA used robbery and extortion as their main means of sustenance.

Development of the ETA Organization

ETA's growth and its youth movement can be traced back to the Basque Nationalist Party (PNV). The party had been an exiled force since Franco's defeat of Spain's Republicans in the 1939 civil war. The PNV operated as a government in exile, another group to be based in France. The Basque youth movement was determined to ensure that their language and culture would not die. ETA's political standpoint was purely democratic. In 1957, a group of young Basques traveled to France to try to convince the government in exile to resort to an armed struggle against General Franco. The PNV leader, Jose Maria Leizaola, and his government rejected the idea. The first assembly by ETA came about in May 1962. The small group of university students and activists gathered to discuss how to go forward with their ideals. Much of what they discussed at that first assembly was the example set by other groups struggling for national identity against such regimes as Fidel Castro in Cuba and others struggling against colonial masters in Africa and the Middle East. This became the first steps along the road toward terrorism by the ETA. Determining not to be easily captured by police they set up the three-man cell structure and defined ETA as " a revolutionary movement of national liberation."

The works and writings of Mao Tse-tung were to play a significant role in the ETA organization. Impressed by Mao, a young Basque named Jose Ortiz studying in Paris attempted to rouse others in ETA to the same level of influence that he had found in his readings of Mao. Then, the second ETA assembly in 1963 set about attempting to rid itself of Maoist influences. No split occurred as a result of the second assembly. Shortly thereafter, the Maoist militants within the organization produced their own mini-manual, *Insurrection in Euskadi.* The tract brought forward the Basque determination to embark on a war of revolution. A third assembly in 1964 broke with the old, established nationalist PNV and, influenced by the Maoists within ETA, redefined the group as being anticapitalist and anti-imperialist. An ETA leader defined the new direction: "The primacy of the human person and of his rights was the basis for any political action." As the ETA ideology veered to the left, the French Government took action against ETA founding members on French territory and removed them from the frontier region with Spain.

Eustakio Mendizabel Benito headed the ETA at the start of 1970. Benito's group was known as the military front of ETA. He believed passionately in his homeland for the Basque people and preserving their language and was deeply concerned about the future. Benito financed his terror operations, like so many other such groups, by resorting to criminal activities like armed robbery, extortion and kidnappings. The group had no training in the art of weaponry or the use of explosives. They actively purchased arms through the

A Madrid car bombing in April, 2002, had all the hallmarks of the Basque Separatists group ETA. (AP Photo/Denis Doyle)

underground arms networks and bought, as their first consignment, 500 Firebird parabellum weapons. They also stole explosives from local factories and quarry operations.

ETA members are known to have received training from the Popular Front for the Liberation of Palestine (PFLP) at their training base in South Yemen. One of the ETA's most audacious acts was the assassination of Luis Carrero Blanco. Carrero Blanco was vice president of Spain under General Franco from 1967 until his assassination on December 20, 1973. When General Franco stepped down from office in June of 1973, Carrero Blanco succeeded him as Prime Minister of Spain. ETA has become more advanced and well equipped, and has formed alliances with FARC (Colombia) terrorists and members of the IRA (Northern Ireland). While the public face of the IRA would wish the public to appreciate their moves to decommission all weapons and explosives, their terror arsenal is being replaced with explosives provided by ETA. One can only make the obvious assumption that the explosives have been traded for the bomb-making expertise that is a renowned hallmark of the IRA.

New Century—New Campaign

The previously observed ceasefire, which ended in 1999, had probably been misread and likely misunderstood by both the Spanish Government and the popular press. It was widely reported that ETA was on its knees and ready to capitulate. At a secret meeting between ETA and the Spanish Government in 1999, it was presumed by the government's part that ETA was ready to deal. However, what took place at that meeting has never been revealed. In fact, the ETA quickly resumed hostilities against the Spanish government. Similar ceasefires have taken place in Northern Ireland and many observers have felt that these ceasefires, far from being the death knell for the terrorist, is a time for covert rebuilding and recruiting new blood into this type of organization.

ETA, in a manner similar to the Irish terrorists, was supported by a newly founded political organization. The Basque socialist coalition known as the **Herri Batasuna** (peoples unity) **Party** is led by Arnoldo Ortiz and officially denies any links or involvement with the ETA terrorist organization. Most likely, as a furtherance of the EU and U.S. actions in denouncing ETA and it supporters, the Spanish Government voted in July 2002 in favor of banning parties considered to be supporting terrorism. Throughout the spring and early summer of 2002, the ETA terrorists embarked on a prolonged terrorist campaign, targeting Spain's lucrative tourist industry. The proposal to ban the Herri Batasuna Party could motivate nationalistic Basques to resort to violence against the government. The president of the mainstream Nationalist Party and also one of the fathers of Basque nationalism, Xavier Arzalluz, commented publicly, "The time has come to fight for the independence of the Basque region in the streets." Ostensibly the appeal, which sets the Herri Batasuna Party apart from others, is that it conjures up memories of the repressive regime under General Franco. The legislation being proposed has the markings of a bygone era to it. Herri Batasuna's political influence is likely to carry along with it some 200,000 voters, many of whom could become willing supporters of the separatist movement. Many observers compare the ETA movement to the Irish Republican Army and its Troubles in Northern Ireland. ETA's campaign has actually been markedly different from the IRA, as it specializes in kidnappings and extortion. This has never been a trademark of the Irish terrorist. The future for ETA is not good.

Although they continue an aggressive campaign, their public support base even in their own region has diminished. ETA can be termed an ultranationalist movement that, having won concessions, is still not satisfied until it can be granted a Basque homeland separate from Spain. However, outlawing Herri Batasuna won't stop ETA from exploding more bombs and assassinating more Spanish officials. In fact, it could have the opposite effect of attracting more radical support for ETA among Basque nationalists.

In spite of the fact that large numbers of the Herri Batasuna Party have been arrested for their involvement and support of ETA attacks, the party continues to maintain its position by publicly stating that it has no ties, neither institutional nor political to ETA. The Spanish Judge *Baltazar Garzon* has stated that Herri Batasuna is inextricably linked to legal groups and organizations that continue to provide economic and political support to ETA. From this it finds new recruits for the possibly ailing ETA ranks. Although there are no estimates of ETA strength it still continues to use indiscriminate bombings.[5]

Opposition to ETA

Accion Nacional Espanila (**ANE**), Spanish National Action, was a right wing terror movement specifically aimed at Basque separatists. The group was formed in the 1970s and operated against the Basques in the regions of northern Spain. The group is known to be responsible for reprisal killings of ETA terrorists and sympathizers, and has also been active in bombings on both sides of the Spanish border.

Spanish and French cooperation in 2001 combined to produce results, leading to the arrests of thirty-seven ETA members residing in France. Going along with the United States in its war against terror, the French agreed to extradite immediately to Spain any ETA members who had warrants issued against them. In the past, the stumbling block for the French had been the political issue surrounding nationalism, which invariably led to interminable delays in the extradition process.

Spain has been effective in combating terrorism with its paramilitary Special Operations Group (*Grupo Especial De Operaciones*, **GEO**). GEO is part of the Spanish National police and is stationed in Guadalajara near the capital, Madrid. The GEO has special response capabilities and is responsible for VIP protection duties, as well as countering and responding to terrorism. Designed, set up and organized along the lines of many other special counterterrorism units throughout Europe, GEO is specifically focused on dealing with terrorists' attacks, including hijackings of aircraft as well as maritime threats and hostage taking. The GEO can also be utilized in a support role for Spanish police operations outside the realm of terrorism and is active in protecting visiting heads of state and providing security for high profile events such as the Olympic Games held in Barcelona in 1992.

GEO has had some noteworthy successes over the last decade. It was responsible for foiling the assassination attempt on King Juan Carlos in 1995, as well as an attempt by ETA to attack the Barcelona Olympics in 1992. GEO remains the foremost threat to terror cells and activity on the Spanish mainland.

Frente Revolucionario Anti-Fascista Y Patriotico (FRAP)

Although little known today, Spain suffered from other terror groups, one of which was the left-wing Maoist group **FRAP**.[6] In an ironic twist, FRAP received worldwide recognition when several of its members were sentenced to death in 1975, for the killing of a Spanish policeman in Madrid. The worldwide outcry led to demands for Spain to be thrown out of the United Nations. Unmoved by these outbursts for clemency, the Spanish government followed through with the executions as planned on September 27, 1975.

Grupa De Resistencia Antifascista Primo Octobre

The Anti Fascist Resistance Group of October First (GRAPO)[7] was another left wing terror group active in the 1970s at about the same time as FRAP. Four Spanish police officers were killed in a retaliatory action over the execution of five left wing terrorists. From this action on October 1, 1975, they take their name. GRAPO are also responsible for at least one attempt on the life of King Juan Carlos of Spain. The group was led by Juan Carlos Delgado de Codex, until he died in 1979 while attempting to evade arrest.

Post 9–11

Spain has embraced the global assault on international terrorism and strongly supports mutual assistance as a strategy to deny safe haven to terrorists. Mutual agreements and cooperation with the French has enabled both countries to root out ETA suspects on the French side of the border. Spain has also been responsible for the break-up and arrest of two suspected al Qaeda-affiliated cells in late September and November of 2001. In July 2002, the Spanish police continued to chase down suspected al Qaeda members operating on the Spanish mainland. It is alleged that three men arrested were of Syrian origin, two were naturalized and the third held Spanish residency.

The Spanish Police captured the men and found videotapes from a visit to the United States in 1997 in their possession. The footage shows varying angles of the New York World Trade Center towers. The Spanish Interior Minister, Angel Acebes, has stated that the footage "was obviously not what a tourist would make." In addition, other high-profile locations had been taped, including the Golden Gate Bridge in San Francisco, The Sears Tower in Chicago, The Empire State Building, and a high density theme park at Disneyland in California. While this footage was filmed some four years prior to the 9–11 attacks, it gives considerable weight to the theory that al Qaeda is very well organized and plans are made in meticulous detail and far in advance. Pictures of the bridges focused especially on their supports, while another two videos showed violent Mujahideen "terrorist training," fighting and suicide bombers.[8]

The wider prospects for international terrorism in Spain have focused mainly on Algerian nationals residing in or visiting the country. Spanish authorities have, since 9–11, made some significant headway in this respect. Mohammed Atta, one of the 9–11 suicide pilots, met with an Islamic cell operating in Madrid in the summer of 2001. Atta's motives and his activities in Spain have not been established, but one may draw the inference that he was meeting and planning strategies for terrorist attacks. Spanish authorities have established that Atta tried to visit an Algerian serving a prison term for forgery. In trying to determine how widely spread the Osama bin Laden network is, Atta would seem able to give the most direct evidence of links between activities in France, Spain and the United States. Atta was present in Spain at the same time as Tunisian immigrant and former pro soccer player, Nizar Trabelsi, who was later arrested in a plot to bomb the U.S. Embassy in Paris. If Atta met with Trabelsi, then the next rational conclusion would be that the attacks in New York and Washington were to be coordinated with bombing attacks in Europe.[9] As the investigation and links continue to be investigated, the widespread nature of the cell structure in Europe appears to infect France, Spain, Italy, Germany, the Netherlands as well as Eastern European countries. Spain's significance on the terror map also indicates that Ahmed Ressam visited Spain prior to his arrest in the plot to blow up the Los Angeles International Airport on New Year's Eve, 1999.

FRANCE

A Long Acquaintance with Terrorism

On the face of it, France has not seen the same level of terrorist activity as other major European nations. This does not imply that France has been left out of the problems facing other governments in dealing with terrorists. However, Euroterrorists and Middle Eastern terror groups have always needed bases, not only safe houses, but also safe countries from which to mount their terror campaigns without too much political and police interference. The country of choice for many groups has often been France. From a strategic point of view, terror groups have considered France an ideal location from which to strike, then return to hide. It has borders with Spain, Italy, Germany, Switzerland, Belgium and Luxembourg, plus an efficient transportation network of roads, air, sea and rail systems.

France has not been immune to terror, and the history books are full of atrocities perpetrated during the French Revolution. (As noted earlier, the word terrorism was born from that time.) What needs more consideration and discussion is the type of terror groups that utilize France for their base of operations and their reasons for doing so. In this section we will discuss specific groups that have successfully used France as a base to mount terror operations and even to carry on turf wars outside their own countries.

Terrorism means different things to different people. The German Federal Republic used the legal process to combat terrorism, considering terror-

TERRORISM PLAYER 5–1

Maximilien Robespierre (1758-1794)

Born in Aras, France, this comparatively young man came to power during the French Revolution (1789–1799). He was well educated and became a successful lawyer. After Louis XVI was arrested in 1792, Robespierre was elected to the National Convention, which was a national assembly deigned to take over the governing of France. He swiftly removed all his opponents and was then elected to the Committee of Public Safety in 1793. Any disagreement with the committee was considered treachery. This period of time in the French revolution was termed the Reign of Terror. His philosophy was influenced by the teachings of Jean Jacques Rousseau, who argued that the right to govern came from the people. During the Reign of Terror, thousands of his countrymen and women were arrested as suspected opponents of the revolution and subsequently executed. The Reign was necessary to defend and "purify" the revolution. Robespierre instilled so much fear in those around him, that by July 1794, it became a question of kill or to be killed, and he succumbed to the guillotine like many thousands of Frenchmen during this period.

Source: The World Book Encyclopaedia. (World Book Inc. U.S.A 1990), Robespierre p. 370-371, Volume 16.

ism as the use of criminal acts for political purposes. Without belaboring the topic of definition, the student may want to consider that terrorism can easily be termed an import-export industry.

The PFLP in France

In the late 1960s and 1970s France became a European safe haven for the beleaguered terrorist organization, the Popular Front for the Liberation of Palestine (PFLP). The PFLP was one of the most militant and aggressive Palestinian groups linked to the Palestine Liberation Organization (PLO). Wadi Haddad controlled and led the 'external operations' from a secure base in either South Yemen or Aden and directed their operations in Europe. The organization had set up safe houses in Paris for their planned attacks in Europe. The audacious attacks carried out by this group include some of the most spectacular attacks in recent history. The attacks at Zurich Airport in 1969, the Dawson Field Hijackings in 1970 and the attack on OPEC (The Organization of Petroleum Exporting Countries) headquarters in Vienna in 1975 led by Illich Ramirez Sanchez better known as **Carlos the Jackal**[10], now residing in a French prison cell.

The justification for terrorism can be argued vigorously. However, since the end of the World War II, the use of terror as a means to an end has had several primary benefits: local and, in most cases, worldwide attention for a specific cause or causes; as an outlet for political impotence and frustration; and to carry out combative measures for countries or states not in the financial position to take direct action themselves. In the political arena, the last would occur where a state did not wish to take direct confrontational action but rather use the cloak of terror, for which it could always deny involvement after the event. The Palestinian cause will be dealt with under a separate chapter, however many organizations like the PLO, and various offshoots, used France in the 1960s and 1970s as a base of operations.

Japanese Red Army

Also prominent in France, from the field of terrorism in 1970s, was the Japanese Red Army terror group. The group was pledged to a worldwide Marxist revolution. It has actively supported and was very involved in the Middle East struggle for the Palestinians.[11] The group was formed in the early 1970s and is based on feudal Japanese samurai warrior traditions, as well as Marxism. The group operated throughout the world and has been involved in major international terror attacks in support of the Palestinian cause. The group participated in the ferocious attack on Lod Airport in Israel,[12] killing Puerto Rican pilgrims in the departure lounge. This group murdered two U.S. sailors in Italy in 1988. In continuous worldwide support of their Palestinian brethren, they also hijacked an airliner and held the passengers hostage, demanding the sum of $6 million in ransom.

Action Direct (AD)

Having discussed France as a center of operations for international terrorism, we should note that it has had its own brand of internal terrorists. Action Direct was a Marxist terrorist group unlike many of its other European and Middle Eastern counterparts. It evolved, not out of the 1960s, but the late 1970s and early 1980s. Considered a left wing revolutionary group, it began as a communist revolutionary organization and then restricted, or limited, its focus to virulent anti-American sentiment. With its strong views on American interference in European affairs, it adopted the anti-American rhetoric of the Palestinian cause and began to attack Israeli and Zionist targets as well as those associated with capitalism and imperialism, such as **NATO** (The North Atlantic Treaty Organization). France had withdrawn from NATO in July 1967. As Action Direct evolved, it began to build a network of other left-wing terror groups operating in Europe, particularly in Germany, France and Belgium. The Communist Combatant Cells (CCC) in Belgium,[13] the Red Brigade in Italy, and the German-based **Red Army Faction** supported Action Direct's campaign against NATO. Thus, with its original base in Paris, Action Direct also became an international terror organization.

There is some skepticism in official quarters that this group had to feed off and be supported by the other left wing groups. It must be noted that since the unification of East and West Germany, the level of left-wing violence and terror has stopped. This, however, does not indicate that the group has split up or disintegrated, and Action Direct will most likely continue in some form to espouse and support its philosophical goals.

Alien Invaders

To say that French soil had been invaded from a far-away planet would not be a correct assessment in any shape or form. However, in recent times it has been the breeding ground for unwelcome guests from the European and Middle East theaters of terrorist conflict. On the home front, there has been the FLNC (*Front de la Liberation Nationale de la Corse*), a group of Corsican separatists, as well as the extreme left wing AD group. Another is the ARB (*Armee Republicaine Bretonne*). The ARB and the FLNC are distinct in their aims as compared to the AD. They are purely regional French factions with goals of local autonomy. Action Direct, on the other hand, has somewhat fuzzy international ideological goals. Confusingly to the casual or the uninformed observer, Action Direct has gone after anti-Jewish interests, which one would normally associate with the extreme right wing as opposed to the extreme left. France's tolerance for the number of groups active within its borders is probably born out of their own realization of how the French Republic was created. This tolerance has led many other groups to use Paris as a primary base for internal and external operations. The Corsican Army (*armata corsa*) terrorist organization, on the other hand, has its roots in the criminal classes of Corsica and seems to function partly on the nationalist scene and partly with the criminal side of life. It does however denounce the mafia style activities that engross some of the nationalists on the Island of Corsica. Armata Corsa seeks to create an island state independent from France, and also the return of Corsican terrorists imprisoned in mainland France. The group has been mainly involved in attacks against public figures and buildings as well as tourist locations, and concentrating nearly all the attacks on the island itself.

With the disintegration of the Empire of the Shah of Iran, students in Paris took control of the Iranian Embassy to show their support for Ayatollah Khomeini. The city was a tolerant host to both sides, with both pro- and anti-Khomeini supporters in evidence and making their protests public. Both groups clashed during a street protest. Another region of Europe is also represented in France and that is the group called ASALA. This group of exiled Armenians was intent on promoting their cause and airing their grievances against the Government of Turkey. Their grievances go back in history to 1915–1922, when more than one million Armenians were massacred. Headquartered in the Middle East, believed to be mainly in Beirut, their actions are attention seeking and aimed at securing a homeland of their own. Most Armenians lived within former Soviet bloc countries.

By far the most aggressive groups operating out of Paris have been the **PLO** (Palestine Liberation Organization) and the Algerian Islamic terrorist group known as the GIA (Armed Islamic Group). The PLO's headline-catching events included the rocket attack at Orly Airport, when in broad daylight two Lebanese Palestinians calmly parked their car near the runway, and armed with an RPG-7 rocket launcher, fired at an El Al flight taxiing for take off. The rocket missed the El Al aircraft and hit an empty Yugoslav jetliner.[14] The two terrorists escaped capture at the airport. Not to be outdone by the failure, a further attack was again scheduled for Orly Airport six days later. By this time the airport was strongly protected by military security. The group entered the airport with an assembled bazooka, much to the astonishment of the armed police, and a furious gun battle between police and terrorists ensued amidst hundreds of passengers and spectators in the airport building.

As for the GIA, their actions in France in the mid 1990s saw attacks on the Paris Metro subway system. Approximately five million Muslims live in France out of a total population of 58 million. GIA's actions in France resulted in bombings throughout 1995 and, in July of that year, a gas canister bomb exploded in the subway, killing seven and injuring eighty-six. Algeria, a former French colony, had been fighting a rising tide of Islamic radicalism. Rather than accede to it, the Algerian government, at that time under Liamine Zeroual, used military force to repress GIA. Because of its support for the Algerians, the French thus became a legitimate target for the GIA, who hoped to force France to withdraw its support for Algeria. Aircraft hijackings by GIA terrorists seem to almost predict the tragic events of 9–11. In December 1994, armed terrorists disguised as police officers boarded an Air France jet in Algiers and hijacked it to France. The aircraft was reportedly packed with explosives to be detonated over the capital city, Paris. The aircraft landed in Marseilles and was stormed by members of the crack anti-terror group GIGN (Groupe d' Intervention de la Gendarmerie Nationale) which ended the 54-hour siege and culminated in the death of three of the hostages and all of the terrorists.

Since the events of 9–11, the French government has been unstinting in its support of the war on terrorism. French officials expressed their determination to eradicate the "perverse illness" of terrorism and have offered military and logistics support. France played a leading role and supported the invoking of Article 5 of the U.N. Treaty, which covers the mutual-defense clause. As part of Operation "Enduring Freedom," the French provided logistical support with her army, navy and air force. In April 2001, Fateh Kemal was sentenced in Paris for operating a support network believed linked to al Qaeda. He was sentenced to eight years in jail. The French were able to establish links between Kemal's operatives and Ahmed Ressam the millennium bomber arrested by U.S. Customs agents crossing from Canada into Washington State with a bomb intended for Los Angeles International Airport. On the day before the 9–11 attacks, the French authorities began to investigate a group linked to al Qaeda with plans to attack U.S. targets in France. The group's leader, Djamel Beghal, was extradited from the United Arab Emirates (UAE) to France in October 2001 as part of that investigation.

Four million dollars was frozen by the French authorities under the Executive Order 13224, to prevent the support of terrorist activities, in particular, by assets of the former Taliban government of Afghanistan. Although France has been a strong U.N. ally, the desire by the United States to seek the death penalty for Zacarias Moussaoui, the only man arrested in connection with the 9–11 attacks, has meant a lack of cooperation between the French intelligence services and the United States. In spite of this the French have been party to counterterrorism discussions at the G-8 summit meetings.[15]

AL QAEDA IN FRANCE

With the close ties of France to the North African continent during its colonialist era, it is not surprising that many immigrants from Morocco and Algeria ended up in France. The planning and recruiting for 9–11 did not take place in Muslim countries, but mainly on the continent of Europe, in Germany, France and England in particular. The security and intelligence failures can be linked back to Europe and a failure to follow up on specific intelligence reports from the French security services. As for al Qaeda, most of its French cells were second-generation immigrants, and as investigations have shown, (particularly in Germany after 9–11) most of the combatants showed little or no interest in Islam in their own countries. It seems the seeds of Islamic Radicalism may have been sown in the mosques of Europe. Radical Islamic beliefs are not the sole domain of Muslims. Richard Reid, the shoe bomber, and two French native brothers, David and Jerome Courtailler, are converts to Islam. Lionel Dumont, a French citizen from the northern French town of Roubaix, was also a convert to Islam and saw military service with the French in Somalia. In the early 1990s, he went to the former Yugoslavia and joined a mujahideen group, the *Takfir wal Hirja,* in Bosnia. He returned to France and formed an organization with others from the North African communities, called the Gang of Roubaix, which was involved in several terrorist attacks. His links to al Qaeda have never been confirmed, and so far he has evaded arrest from French authorities.[16]

If hindsight is always 20/20, then intelligence sources on both sides of the Atlantic should have picked up on the activities and involvement of Zacarias Moussaoui. The French intelligence track nearly all North Africans traveling from France to either Pakistan and/or Afghanistan. British newspapers reported that the French Directorate of Territorial Security repeatedly informed their counterparts in Britain that Zacarias Moussaoui who was residing in London in the early 1990s, had made trips to both Afghanistan and Pakistan. Further, he was considered to be involved in terrorism. As part of the investigation into the murder of three French Consular staff in Algeria, Moussaoui's name was found in an address book that was seized. Unfortunately, the information provided to the British appears to never have been acted upon.[17]

The FBI had been warned, in advance of 9–11 attacks, that Moussaoui was associated with Osama bin Laden. Moussaoui was arrested on an immigration violation, but the French intelligence report was never acted upon.[18] Zacarias Moussaoui was born in France and, like other suspects arrested in Germany, was not known as an Islamic extremist. In 1992, he went to England and shared an apartment with the French Courtailler brothers while he studied for a degree. Sometime during this period he came under the spell of the fanatical Muslim cleric, Abu Qatada.

GERMANY

A History of Fascism, Terrorism, and Democracy

Historically, Germany has survived two World Wars, been divided into two nations, paid the price of Nazism as well as communism and at the end of the twentieth century rose again as a major industrial power in Europe and a democracy. The history books clearly define the years between the two World Wars as being economically harsh for Germany. This section will deal with the rise of terrorist groups in Germany. However, it is relevant to look back at

Richard Reid aka the Shoe Bomber attempted to ignite an explosive device on board an American Airlines Flight from Paris to Miami—December 22, 2001. (AP Photo/Elise Amendala)

some significant periods of the twentieth century affecting the German people as well as their neighboring countries.

Between the two world wars, Germany saw the rise of the Nazi Party and the rise to ultimate power under the leadership of the former Austrian Corporal, Adolf Hitler. Germany was humbled by its reparation payments, and crippled by the devastation of the dismal worldwide Great Depression of 1929; the German populace faced massive unemployment and starvation. The reparation repayment was renegotiated under the terms of the Young Plan. Hitler campaigned long and hard throughout Germany against the Plan. By July of 1932, the Nazi party held 38% of the seats in the German Parliament (*Reichstag*).[19]

TERROR BRIEF 5–1

Takfir Wal Hirja

In Egypt of the 1960s, the Islamic ideology *Takfir wal Hirja* began to win adherents among extremist groups. Shukri Mustafa, an agricultural engineer, led one of the groups, the Society of Muslims. Mustafa denounced other Muslims as unbelievers and preached a withdrawal into a purity of the kind practiced by the Prophet Muhammad when he withdrew from Mecca to Medina. The ideology is particularly dangerous because it provides a religious justification for slaughtering not only unbelievers, but also those who think of themselves as Muslims. *Takfir Wal Hirja* was a sort of Islamic fascism. Roland Jacquard, a preeminent European terrorism expert, says flatly, "Atta was Takfir." It is not just soldiers of al Qaeda who may be following the Takfir line. Mustafa was executed in 1978, but his ideas lived on; the beliefs of al-Zawahiri's al Jihad were dominated by Takfiri themes. Azzam Tamimi, director of the Institute of Islamic Political Thought in London, says of Zawahiri, "He is their ideologue now . . . His ideas negate the existence of common ground with others."

Source: Time Magazine Special Report November 12, 2001.

Hitler's passionate, self-appointed mission was to lead the badly depressed Germany back to greatness, rid it of communist and other influences, and purge the society of its ills. To achieve this, he had to gain absolute power and control. In 1933, Paul Von Hindenburg, then President of Germany, proclaimed Hitler as Chancellor (Prime Minister). With total control, he then proclaimed his government as the Third Reich. With that, Germany's dictator began his own reign of terror on the German people. By the end of July 1933, through legal processes, Hitler had destroyed the German constitution and outlawed freedom of the press, unions, and all political parties with the exception of the National Socialist Party (the "Nazi" Party). His own breed of police, the dreaded Gestapo, hunted down all opponents of the government. Many were arrested on suspicion alone, and were jailed or shot.

The Nazi used terror-like tactics to not only gain, but also to keep control over the populace. All German children, both boys and girls, were required to join the Hitler Youth or the Society of German Maidens. These children of Germany were indoctrinated into the Nazi philosophy and military discipline and were used as spies to inform on family members that did not embrace the Nazi doctrines. A sophisticated network of spies monitored and reported on the German people and fostered an atmosphere of not only physical but also psychological terror.

Germany's New Order

There have been hundreds of accounts, books and films about Hitler's "Final Solution" for the Jewish problem. His belief was that the German people were a genetically superior race and that his country had to be purged of the impure, non-Aryan peoples. Those groups singled out for special treatment were Jews, gypsies, Poles, homosexuals and Slavs. The term "Holocaust" is widely used, and defines the mass murder of over six million Jewish people. Hitler and his Nazi party members began their reign of terror on the Jews as early as 1933, almost immediately after Hitler came to power. Sometime in early July 1933, (the date has never been precisely confirmed), beginning around the ninth of the month and lasting for about forty-eight hours, Nazi Party members destroyed thousands of Jewish businesses and synagogues throughout Germany, killed dozens of Jews and sent almost 40,000 to concentration camps. The night is referred to as *Kristallnacht* (night of the broken glass).

When the German armies rolled across Europe, a similar fate awaited Jews in those countries that were conquered by Germany. Names of camps that today strike fear and loathing and sheer terror for the nature of the atrocities committed are Belsen, Auschwitz, Buchenvald, Dachau and many others. Hitler's unique brand of terror, which accounted for the mass murder of millions of Jews and other persons who failed to fit his Aryan picture of perfection, was a means to an end. The Nazi leadership saw it as the cleansing of a nation and those it conquered. Such use of political terrorism must be considered a weapon of psychological warfare.

Post World War II and Terrorism

After the end of World War II, a long period of rebuilding and healing took place. By the 1960s the Federal German Republic was experiencing three different types of terrorism. The first, left wing terrorism, came about from the imported views of radical students and their opposition to the U.S. war in Vietnam. Right wing terrorists opposed to the left wing radicals as a continuation of the anti-communist past countered this. Criminals also adopted the terror group's actions and copied and mimicked their attacks for personal, criminal gain. The 1960s were a period of widespread student revolt and protest, although in Germany there was no real catalyst to take the protests to the next stage. Student protests were the order of the day on many university campuses in Europe and the United States as a platform for anti-Vietnam War protests. Modern terrorism, particularly in Germany's case, has been typified by indiscriminate violence, sensationalized by the murder of innocents.

The student body of left wing radicals at the Berlin Free University, in somewhat of a copycat style, protested against American involvement in Vietnam. Although the protests were restricted mainly to marches and the distribution of leaflets there was not a catalyst in place to take any serious action at a higher level that would involve violence directed at the authoritarian government. Two main protagonists came to the forefront of the student protests, Andreas Baader and Gudrun Ensslin.[20] As on many university campuses of the 1960s, both communism and Marxism were prevalent. This was also the case at the Berlin Free University. Baader, Enselin and later Meinhof, were all committed Marxists. Out of the Berlin University was developed the **Red Army Faction**. The RAF was led by Gudrun Enselin and by the free-wheeling Andreas Baader, who presented more of a playboy image than that of a terrorist.

Red Army Faction (RAF)

This group of committed Marxists sought to engage the United States in a combative role by extending the Vietnam War to German soil. This they achieved by attacking U.S. interests in West Germany, and particularly U.S. servicemen and military bases. Many books describe Andreas Baader as more of a delinquent and a follower than a committed terrorist. He seemed in many accounts to draw pleasure from being at the center of an infamous criminal network. To finance their program of violence, the group resorted to a series of bank robberies and other crimes.

The igniting factor in sparking this group into action on a grand scale was in fact an eloquent German lawyer, Horst Mahler, who joined the student movement to give it impetus towards violent action. In 1968, Ensslin and her boyfriend Baader attempted to destroy two Frankfurt department stores with firebombs. They were both captured and sentenced, and a year later temporarily released during an amnesty for political prisoners. When the amnesty was over, they fled to France as fugitives. They returned to West Germany to join with Horst Mahler, but Baader was again arrested. At this point in the group's development, Ulrike Meinhof came into the picture. Meinhof was the editor of an underground newspaper called *Konkert*.[21] The paper had been launched in the 1950s, sponsored and supported by communist groups in East Germany. Meinhof is reputed to be a close friend of Gudrun Ensslin and it was Ensslin who persuaded Meinhof to assist in the breakout of prison of Andreas Baader. The jailbreak on May 14, 1970, resulted in changing the name of the group to the Baader-Meinhof Gang. Over the following two years, Meinhof spent time in Jordan not far from the capital Amman being trained in weaponry by the Palestinians. Meinhof and colleagues became skilled in the use of what was to be their favorite weapon, the Kalashnikov, (better known as the AK-47 assault rifle). Having received their training from the PLO, the group went into action and was involved in the attack on the Organization of Oil Exporting Countries (OPEC) headquarters in Vienna, Austria on December 21, 1975. The RAF were at this point joining forces with a group calling themselves the "**Arab Revolution**," a cover name for The Popular Front for the Liberation of Palestine (PFLP).[22]

Ilich Ramirez Sanchez, better known as Carlos the Jackal, led the assault on the OPEC building. This attack, although targeted against the oil producing

---

TERRORISM BYTE 5–1

BMW for Baader Meinhof Gang (BMG)

In order to finance their group's operations, Andreas Baader insisted on carrying out robberies in the grand style. He instructed his accomplices to steal exotic cars for their getaways. The car of choice was nearly always the BMW. This model of vehicle was so frequently used by the gang that it became nicknamed the Baader Meinhof Wagon (BMW). Their notoriety became a superb marketing tool for the German car manufacturer.

countries was more a case of raising money than having a significant political impact. The Saudi Arabian and Iranian Governments are believed to have paid a ransom of $50 million for the safe return of their nationals. Among the five strong groups that attacked the building were two German terrorists, Gabrielle Tiedermann and Hans-Joachim Klein. During a gun battle with Austrian security officers, Klein was seriously injured. No political demands were made except the demand that the Austrians broadcast a political statement for the Baader Meinhof group. The Austrians allowed the terrorist and a number of the hostages to fly to Algiers and then to Tripoli. The large amount of ransom money was transferred to a bank in Aden to bankroll further terrorism.

The Perpetuation of a Cause

German authorities arrested the principals of the Baader Meinhof group, which by then numbered about one hundred active supporters. In 1972, Baader, Meinhof and Enselin were all sentenced to long prison terms. The group was housed in the maximum security Stammheim Prison. Ulrike Meinhof, suffering from acute depression, hanged herself in her prison cell, May 9, 1976. As for the remainder of the group, it is something of a controversy as to how they met their ends. On the night of November 18, 1977, several members of the Baader-Meinhof group died from self-inflicted gunshot wounds in their prison cells.[23] Many have asked how guns could have been smuggled into a top security prison. The most likely answer to that is that lawyers for the group brought them in to attempt a breakout.

The deaths coincided with news of a dramatic rescue by the antiterrorist GSG-9 in October 1977. The GSG-9 stormed a Lufthansa aircraft at Mogadishu, Somalia, killing three hijackers and rescuing the ninety passengers. It would seem to be entirely logical that the Red Army Faction, or as they were usually called, the Baader-Meinhof gang, would cease to exist. However, it exists to this day and its growth has not been stemmed by arrests of prominent members over the past two decades. With arrests of successive leaders and gang members, the RAF has continued to rise like a Phoenix from its own ashes. It is believed that in both the 1970s and 1980s this was due in part to an elaborate communications system and network setup between the imprisoned terrorists, their lawyers and the activists still working for the cause. Public opinion soured toward the RAF in 1977, an opinion that had generally held them up as romantics fighting for a misunderstood cause. This was naturally embellished by the popular press, which continued to sensationalize the group's criminal activities and misdeeds. However, the previously mentioned hijacking of a Lufthansa airline to Mogadishu, Somalia, by terrorists supported by the RAF resulted in the murder of the aircraft's pilot Jurgen Schumann. This single act helped turn public opinion against them.

The RAF probably reached the pinnacle of its terrorist existence toward the end of the 1970s. The group was responsible for the assassination of the West German Attorney General, Seigfred Buback, and Hans-Martin Schleyer. They went so far as to attempt to murder the head of NATO in Europe, U.S. Army General Alexander Haig. The RAF were still active in the 1980s and by then had joined forces with a little-known German terror unit called the June Second Movement and another called the Red Cells. Little is known of their members or their numbers; however, it seems likely that the groups continue to operate independently of each other. The significance of the date, June 2nd, is in remembrance of Benno Ohnesorg who was killed on that date in 1967, during a student protest that turned into a riot. The most notorious act carried out in their name was the abduction of Peter Lorenz, a candidate for the post of Mayor of West Berlin. The ransom paid was the release of four of their compatriots who were then flown to South Yemen. The group was abandoned in the early 1980s, with most of its members joining the RAF.

Reawaking of Germany's past

Germany has relied on the influx of foreign immigrant workers in the post World War II era for the purposes of rebuilding its infrastructure. 2001 celebrated forty years since the introduction of the "*Gastarbeiter*" program which saw Turkish immigrants brought into Germany for menial labor. Advocates in Germany have been openly hostile to immigration policies, especially since 9–11. If the advocates of restriction on the movement of labor are successful it will likely have a negative impact on the long-term economical viability and growth of the European Union. Integration by large numbers of immigrants to German society over the last three decades has failed. A study conducted by the University of Bielfeld in 1997 showed that about one quarter to one third of young Turkish Muslims in Germany were prepared to use violence in the name of Islam.[24]

Anti-Semitic behavior and phobia still lurks as a haunting reminder of Germany's past. Invariably the message and threats of belligerent intolerance come from German Skinhead factions. It would be incorrect to label every Skinhead as a racist as many are from varying religious denominations who are non racist and who are not purveyors of hate crimes. Much of the bigoted violence in Germany has been directed against foreign workers, particularly Turkish immigrants, however, throughout the 1990s, Jews became the Skin-

TERROR BRIEF 5–2

Hanns-Martin Schlayer

Hanns Schlayer was a prominent German executive kidnapped during the dangerous years of the 1970s when the Baader-Meinhof gang was wreaking terror and mayhem in Europe. He was kidnapped by members of the Rote Armee Fraktion (RAF). His vehicle was attacked in the suburbs of Cologne and his four bodyguards were murdered at the scene. Schlayer was to be used as a bargaining chip for the release of ten RAF members and Andreas Baader of the Baader-Meinhof group.

The demand for the release of the prisoners was further highlighted with the hijacking of a Lufthansa airliner by four Palestinian terrorists. The German GSG-9 ended this hijacking at Mogadishu, Somalia, when the elite anti-terror unit stormed the aircraft. Subsequently Hans Schlayer was shot and killed. None of the prisoners were released and Andreas Baader shot himself in his prison cell with a weapon smuggled into the prison.

heads' target of choice. Year after year since 1990 there has been a steady increase in the number of hate crimes associated with Skinheads, and attacks on members of Jewish communities. Skinheads are easily recognizable by their close-cropped hairstyle, shortened denim-style jeans and "Doc Martens" style boots. Skinheads usually operate in gangs and much of their hatred and violence is spewed after bouts of binge drinking. The gangs roam the streets looking for likely victims to attack. The collapse of the communist regime in East Germany significantly affected the Skinhead situation. The emergence of the eastern Skinheads radicalized the movement in both numbers and militancy. Skins tended to move in with the extreme right wing movements in Germany, namely Michael Swierczek's National Offensive, Frank Huebner's German Alternative, The National Front, and Christian Worch's National List.

German authorities were originally either slow or reluctant to respond to the right wing threats being posed by the Skinhead's hate movement and propaganda; however in the last decade the German authorities have banned some of the Neo-Nazi groups and confiscated their propaganda materials. Skinheads have traditionally not aligned themselves with any particular political party, as they are viewed as part of the "system." Skinheads are most likely to be those in their teens and early twenties. Skinheads also view imprisonment as a badge of honor and there is evidence that Skinheads are receiving a thorough indoctrination in neo-Nazi ideology at **"comradeship evenings"** held in prison. Much of this is provided by the Relief Agency for National Political Prisoners and their Dependants, a right wing group that sends a steady stream of propaganda to incarcerated neo-Nazis and Skinheads.[25]

Germany Into the 21st Century

The unification of Germany, which was one of the most unexpected turning points in Germany's history, brought with it doubts about a new Germany's ability to cope with the depression and despair suffered by its people in the former East Germany. By the end of 1997, there were growing signs in German cities of right wing neo-Nazi groups in the form of Skinheads, as mentioned above, fostering hate campaigns against foreign immigrants living in and coming to the new Germany. With most European communities lowering the barriers on movement between countries and with the fall of the Soviet Union, many thousands of ethnic groups surged westward for a "better life." What they found in Germany was a growing resentment, mainly by extreme right wing groups, to the rising tide of outside ethnic groups seeking jobs in an already struggling economy. The Skinheads and others saw the immigrants as being responsible for the high rate of unemployment and the economic conditions. In many cities, extremists took the law into their own hands and, in shows of nationalist strength, set about abusing and intimidating immigrants.

In some cities, by the spring of 1998, immigrants had virtually disappeared from the community, having been frightened away by the fearsome onslaughts of neo-Nazism. No specific group or organized terror campaign is being sustained, although special police units are being utilized to break up obvious gangs of Skinheads. No one can predict how far Germany will regress towards a neo-Nazi influence, or whether this type of incident is a mere pothole in the road to unification. What most are watching for from the German government is a signal that it fervently opposes the nationalist movements.

Neo-Nazi Demonstration—Leipzig Eastern Germany, November, 2001.
(AP Photo/Eckehard Schulz)

However, with a growing number of incidents involving ethnic groups and neo-Nazi influences at various levels inside Germany's military, it is no surprise that there is a feeling of unease and terror in those who see the unsettling prospect of a rise in the nationalist movement all over again.

Al Qaeda and Germany

Post 9–11, Germany has come to the realization that it has become not only a safe haven but also a recruiting country for radical dissident Muslim youths. Imams in Germany's mosques were calling for a jihad against the United

States. Students from North African and Middle Eastern countries were studying in university campuses throughout the country. Evidence points to Germany as being a staging post for Islamic extremists wanting to gain access via forged travel documents to North America, either directly or through Canadian ports of entry. This is a practice that has been ongoing for more than twenty years. Many questions still remain, one of the most baffling ones being, "Why did the intelligence communities fail to detect the planning for September 11?" Undoubtedly a very tough question, as we will see elsewhere that the signs were there, the information on certain activities of groups and individuals was available. Clearly, it simply was either not recognized as significant, ignored or both.

Intelligence gathering and covert activities by western governments was not at Cold War levels and although the intelligence community and security services recognized the threat of al Qaeda, they probably underestimated the tactical capabilities of the group to strike deep into the heart of America. Germany had been more preoccupied with domestic issues and the revelation that planning for 9–11 had taken place within their country came as a surprise to most Germans. Two prominent members of the 9–11 hijackers, Mohammed Atta and Marwan Al-Shehhi, who are believed to have been the pilots that flew the aircraft into the two World Trade Center towers, spent a significant amount of time in Germany. Atta had studied at the Hamburg University for eight years, during which he appears to have attracted no suspicions from German authorities. He was not openly hostile and did not espouse radical or extreme Islamic views, at least not publicly. Since the fall of the Third Reich and Germany's rebuilding, the German government has been reluctant to interfere with individual rights and civil liberties. In Atta's case, subsequent investigations have revealed that he developed a small religious studies group that is now suspected of being a cover for his principal terrorist planning operations.

In Germany, a religious freedom law forbids the government from banning or restricting any group that it recognizes as a religion. Scientology is restricted under this law, as Germany has ruled that this is in fact a commercial enterprise not a religion. As in the United States, prosecutors must overcome a high standard of evidence to effect a prosecution. The German ability to gather and disseminate intelligence within its borders is also somewhat self-defeating. Law enforcement is decentralized, so police in one of Germany's sixteen states may not share information regularly with police in another region. Germany rarely conducts nationwide criminal investigations or passes information from international agencies to local police.[26]

The third pilot involved in the 9–11 attacks also spent considerable time in Germany. Ziad Zamir Jarrah was born in the infamous Bekka Valley in Lebanon, a stronghold of Hezbollah extremists. Jarrah and his immediate family were not religious fanatics by any means. His family appears genuinely shocked and surprised that their son would be involved in a suicide attack on the United States. Jarrah received a monthly allowance from his father that was more than adequate. However, Jarrah's involvement may have stemmed from his involvement and friendship with local radical Muslims when he moved to Aachen. These radical Muslims were involved in fund raising through local mosques for the Hamas terror group to aid the suicide missions in the Middle East.[27]

As part of the coalition against terrorism, Germany has also banned a network of radical Islamic groups centered on the Kaplan organization based in Cologne. German police raided some two hundred residences in seven separate German states in connection with the ban and seized the headquarters of the Kaplan group. Metin Kaplan, the Caliph of Cologne, is serving a prison sentence for calling for the murder of a rival religious leader. German authorities have characterized the Kaplan group as being anti-semitic and anti-democratic, and have also banned Kaplan's associated foundation, the "Servants of Islam" as well as other groups totaling 1,100 members.[28]

ITALY

After World War I, Italy under Mussolini had violently suppressed and oppressed the Italian Communists. By 1954 the country was the most likely to turn communist in the West. With the cessation of hostilities and the formation of democratically elected government in Italy, the opportunity naturally presented itself for the communists to come to the fore. What the student will learn is that a strong communist indoctrinated left wing group would rise up with some fairly imaginative goals to steer Italy onto a different path than that established by the allied powers. As the new millennium arrived the transnational terrorism from al Qaeda and its associated cells became a frustrating reality for the Italian government and security services. Terrorist plots were to be planned and executed by foreign terror operatives residing in Italy.

Terrorism and Italy

The only significant terrorist movement to emerge from Italy has been the Red Brigade, which has its origins in the early 1970's and grew from an established left wing political party, The Metropolitan Political Collective. Their aim was to bring about a communist revolution in Italy that they believed would spread throughout Europe. At the other end of the spectrum was a smaller and little known group, the Ordine Nuove (New Order), which was an extreme right wing, fascist movement. In similar manner to the Red Brigade Ordine Nuove embarked on a campaign of terror to establish their goal of a strong Italian state, supported by a powerful fascist structure. Throughout the 1970s both groups used the bombings and assassinations as their modus operandi and it was not often evident which group was responsible for specific acts of terror. Observers believed that some of the attacks although credited to one group could well have been done by the other in order to discredit them.

The Red Brigade (RB)

The RB has its fundamental origins, like many other left wing movements, on the Italian university campuses in the latter half of the 1960s. The group might be considered as a fledgling of the World War II *Volante Rosse,* formed during the campaign against Nazi Germany as a communist resistance movement. It continued its campaigns until the end of 1949 and had continued links to the Italian Communist Party, no doubt spawning the next generation of left wing extremists to emerge on the campuses of the 1960s.

Following the end of World War II, Italy moved toward a governing style modeled on the political and economic example of the United States. During the years from 1950–62 the industrial growth and success of the Italian Government lay in the hands of coalitions of political parties, the Republicans, Liberals, Social Democrats and Christian Democrats, all apparently trying to move beyond the fascist past. While exploiting the need for industrial growth and foreign trade, Italy had neglected the social structure of the country. The bubble burst in 1968 with a cultural-style revolution in the universities and schools, and was quickly followed in 1969 with the worst union unrest in the industrialized north that Italy had ever experienced. The unions could not be placated and factories were seized and occupied. Workers and management were intimidated and attacked. All this became the fertile ground for the emerging RB.

The founding members of this organization came from the Sociology Department of Trent University, Renato Curcio and Margherita Cagol.[29] The RB began to target the symbolic nature of the Italian state by attacking senior executives, politicians and parts of Italian society perceived as being repressive by nature. RB did not burst on to the Italian scene but rather confined itself to incubation largely in Milan's industrial heart. It was a time, from 1969–72, of building, training and testing of its avowed objectives. Minor fire bombings and destruction of civil property was the order of the period. The RB support structure outside of Milan at this time was considerably weak. From 1972–74, the RB entered a new phase where it began to expand to the adjacent areas of Turin and Genoa and experimented in kidnapping and extortion. During this same time frame, Italian security forces were able to capture Renato Curcio after a gun battle, in which his wife, Margherita Cagol, was killed. Observers at that time predicted the imminent demise of the Red Brigade, but they were far from reality. The next generation of RB was on the scene and ready to continue the fight to the Italian Government and society in general. The RB has to some length emulated the tactics laid out by Carlos Marighella in his *Mini Manual of the Urban Terrorist,* in 1969. Attention to detail and technical knowledge as well as logistical and intelligence information became a hallmark of the RB. Contained in the *Mini Manual* is Marighella's definition of assaults:

- Assault is the armed attack, which we make to expropriate funds, liberate prisoners, and capture explosives, machine guns, and other types of arms and ammunition.
- Assaults can take place in broad daylight or at night.
- Daytime assaults are made when the objective cannot be achieved at any other hour, as for example, the transport of money by the banks, which is not done at night.
- Night assault is usually the most advantageous to the urban guerrilla. The ideal is for all assaults to take place at night when conditions for a surprise attack are most favorable and the darkness facilitates flight and hides the identity of the participants. The urban guerrilla must prepare himself, nevertheless, to act under all conditions, daytime as well as nighttime.

Kidnapping as a part of the terrorist arsenal is well demonstrated in Italy through the 1970s and perfected by the RB. Mainly symbolic in its action, it did go beyond kidnapping prominent business personages when it kidnapped Genoa's assistant Attorney General Mario Sossi. The RB demanded the release of RB prisoners from jail and in particular Renato Curcio. Sossi was held captive for a month before his release. The concessions received from the Government were the promised release of RB members. However, the Attorney General would not permit the release, which had been bargained under duress.[30] The RB also believed that the concessions they received had sufficiently undermined the state. On June 8, 1974, the RB struck down Genoa's Attorney General Francesco Coco in an armed ambush, which had a twofold effect. The first was a confirmation of the RB's retaliatory ability against the figure that had blocked their earlier attempts to free their colleagues, and second, their threats to selected jurors in the Turin trial of Curcio led to a delay in the trial. Further attacks on members of the bar association had the desired effect of delaying the trial. The intimidating effect of terrorism was working well.

RB Structure

As seen with many other urban terrorist organizations, the RB based its operating habits on the cell structure to prevent infiltration and detection. Working from large industrial areas, it had widespread support among the working classes, who provided food and support to the group. Total membership, either active or passive, has been hard to ascertain. It is believed there were more than five hundred active members, with a support structure possibly in the thousands. It seems likely that by the last decade of the century the RB was reduced to around fifty active members. With its communist Marxist/Leninist ideology, its early support would have come from the Soviet Union, which in the Cold War years would have provided succor and support for such organizations operating in the West. After all, any activity likely to disrupt a democracy would be to their advantage.

Kidnapping

Italy has perfected the art of kidnapping and in fact, enhanced it, with corporations able to get kidnap insurance, turning it into a growth industry. This shortsighted provision made it possible for kidnappers to get their money and for those who were kidnapped to be released, and everyone went away content. The RB, on the other hand, kidnapped for different reasons and rarely for money. Two kidnappings stand out for their sheer audaciousness and the brutality with which they ended. These two kidnappings were significant watersheds for the RB. The first, which resulted in nothing more than the symbolic execution of the president-elect, was to turn public opinion against the RB. Several communiqués were issued prior to his murder and the RB made every effort to exploit the media coverage of this atrocity. During Aldo Moro's captivity the RB showed its strength of purpose and its ability to continue with other operations and carried out two murders and six shootings in Rome, Turin, Milan and Genoa, in spite of the massive police search and crackdown on the RB and any known members.[31] It was a significant demonstration of the RB's ability to conduct several simultaneous operations.

The release of General James Dozier was the first successful rescue of a kidnap victim from the RB by members of the Italian police. By the mid-1980s, the number of terrorist incidents committed by RB was into single figures following a significant decline in support from the left. By the mid-1990s the group was distributing communiqués to indicate a cessation of all operations. How and what role RB will continue to play into the next century is at present unclear. However at the end of 1998, the group were not functioning.

GAP & NAP

Two other groups were on the fringes of the Italian terrorism scene in the 1970s, and modeled themselves on the same style of clandestine activities and systematic violence as the RB. The Partisan Action Group (GAP) originated in Milan at about the same time (1969) as the RB. Their inception is believed to have involved the wealthy Italian publisher Giangiacomo Feltrinelli who was the paymaster and group sponsor. Feltrinelli believed that right wing extremism was on the rise and a return to fascism was a real possibility. He believed that the only way to confront the risk was to form an urban guerrilla movement. His approach was to form the GAP, a resistance/partisan movement modeled on the resistance fighters of WWII. This model differed from that of the RB, which probably accounts for the non merging of the groups in the early days[32] In the days of student and union unrest which had also spread to Italy's prison system another movement sprang up. The Armed Proletarian Nuclei (NAP), came to life from a left wing prison movement, the Movement of Proletarian Prisoners and the Ongoing Struggle (Lotta Continua).[33] Unlike the RB, they gained little acknowledgment. Coming from the ranks of Naples prison inmates, the membership immediately began the "armed struggle," financing of which was done primarily by bank robberies. Their main base of operation started in Naples and spread to Rome, using explosives to bomb prisons and also attacking prison officials. Unlike the RB all the members were easily traceable from their criminal records, and their *modus operandi* coupled with their lack of attention to their own security resulted in numerous arrests of the protagonists. With no ideological base, their recruitment of the criminal elements led to their eventual downfall with the remainder of the membership joining the ranks of the RB. Throughout the terror campaigns, the majority of the targets were either political or paramilitary by nature. Indiscriminate attacks against the Italian populace were uncommon.

The Mancino Law

Decree number 122, issued by the Italian Government in 1993, was an emergency measure to control, restrict and limit attacks of a racial nature. Two months later it was transformed into Law No. 205 by then Interior Minister Nicola Mancino. The law enabled the state to prosecute individuals for "incitement to violence for a broad range of *hate* crimes," which included the use of symbols of hate.[34] Hundreds of youths have been charged under this legislation. Two Italian names have become associated with hate crimes in Italy: Maurizio Boccacci a skinhead organizer and Dr. Sergio Gozzoli an outspoken anti-semite and a Holocaust denier.

Skins Organizations

The Italian Skinheads had, by the early 1990s, organized themselves under the leadership of the *Movimento Politico Occidentale* (MPO, Political Movement of the West), founded by Maurizio Boccacci and headquartered in Rome. The group has links to other far right skinhead groups in France, Germany and Great Britain. A notable incident that was bound to become a flash point was the painting of yellow stars on more than one hundred Jewish businesses and shops in Rome. Jews attacked MPO skins as a result. The MPO has been banned by the government but has since renamed itself with the fascist trappings of *I Camerati,* a term used by Mussolini to address his fascist followers.[35]

In its effort to become more politically acceptable, at a convention of the neo-Fascist Movimento Sociale Italiano (MSI, Italian Social Movement), the delegates voted to move towards the mainstream political parties and to dissolve the MSI. They merged with Alleanza Nazionale (National Alliance), and it was hoped this would make the overall far right movement more respectable. The delegates also agreed on a strong position against anti-semitism. The extremists in the organization—many of them skinheads—broke away from the alliance and reestablished a version of the MSI.

Ideology

The Italian skinhead ideology and that of the far right extremists echoes the sentiments of a past generation of neo-fascists. Their ideology is loosely based on the following:[36]

- The denial of Nazi genocide against the Jews—"historical revisionism";
- Fear and hatred of foreigners, based on the myths of Aryan purity and supremacy;
- The fear and demonization of the Jews in a context of a sinister plot to run the world.

With the breakdown of the symbolic and all-too-real Berlin Wall, the influx of Russian and eastern nationals to the west—particularly Germany and Italy—has fuelled the far right into action. Sporadic action between skins of the far right and ethnic and minority groups will continue in Italy into the new millennium.

International Terrorism

Italy has been no stranger to acts of terrorism, with the result that post 9–11 Italy with its excellent police and intelligence services has not only aided the U.S.-led war on terrorism by its military contributions, but had success in tracking down and arresting suspected al Qaeda cells. International terrorism requires funding and the Italian government in the weeks after 9–11 established the Financial Security Committee comprising senior ministry officials from Finance, Justice and Foreign Affairs aiming to stem the flow of funding to terrorist groups in Europe. Even prior to 9–11, Italian security services had targeted such institutions as the Islamic Cultural Center in Milan because they suspected that an al Qaeda lieutenant, Sami Ben Khemais Essid, who had spent time training as a terrorist recruiter in Afghanistan, was active in Italy. The Italians were monitoring the Cultural Center to discover evidence of traffic in arms and explosives and discovered that Ben Khemais was in fact in contact with other extreme terrorist groups throughout Europe.

Some of those seen at the Cultural Center included terrorists associated with the New York World Trade Center bombing in 1993 and the bombings of the U.S. Embassies in Tanzania and Kenya in 1998. The apparent ease with which international terror groups, and particularly those associated with Osama bin Laden, have been able to operate with comparative freedom is a lesson that security services are now beginning to appreciate. Ben Khemais was sentenced to eight years in prison for his activities. His activities also give us an insight to what may be al Qaeda's next style of terror attack. During the investigation Italian police intercepted a conversation with Khemais which detailed the use of a deadly poison gas attack.

GREECE AND TURKEY

Terrorism is no stranger to these two countries; however, the actions of their respective indigenous terrorist groups is restricted for the most part to actions within the country rather than outside in the international arena.

GREECE

Revolutionary Organization November 17

Twenty-three assassinations, 345 bombings and no arrests after 27 years has led the rest of the West to view the Greek attitude and inability to prevent and deter terrorism with a fair amount of cynicism. Considerable pressure from the European Union has been placed on Greece with concern for security of the Olympic Games in Athens in 2004.

The November 17 Group has operated in Greece with what seems like total immunity. Police and security services had been unable to identify or arrest any members of the organization. This group of left wing extremists have to be considered Marxist-Leninist, anti-imperialist, anti-United States, anti-

Europe and anti-NATO. November 17's first action and the first time it came to world attention was the assassination of U.S. Diplomat Richard Welsh in 1975. Until 2001 The group came together out of the university campuses of Greece much like other left-wing groups in the 1970s. The actual date, **17 November**, (1975) is the commemorative date of the attack on the NTUA (National Technical University of Athens) students by the military and police under the control of the ruling colonels. On that date, several student activists were killed and many captured and tortured. The military junta of the colonels lasted only a few months before it was overthrown. The actual membership number is not known but it can be assumed that it is a small group, with approximately twenty to thirty hard core members. Unlike other groups, it did not take part in low-level operations to test its own ability; rather, it burst onto the world stage with a notable terrorist attack on a diplomat from a major foreign power.

Like its Italian counterparts, the November 17 Group members are extremely Marxist/Leninist in their ideology. In its early years, there were relatively few attacks by this group; in fact, between 1975–1985, November 17 carried out only six attacks. Perhaps the length of time between operations was relative to the fact that police arrested no one. This failure is a sad reflection on the internal workings of the Greek government and its security services. Over the last twenty years, 61 deaths have occurred, with 250 injured from a total of 345 bombings. Not one terrorist has ever been arrested and charged with offenses in connection with these incidents.

The group did expand operations after 1985, and by 1990 had carried out about forty attacks including, bombing, assassinations and shootings, targeting U.S. military personal based at NATO bases in Greece, Greek industrialists, and politicians. The group has been severely critical of the Greek government on its position in respect to U.S./NATO bases in Greece as well as Greece's membership of the EEC (European Economic Community), and therefore the largest number of attacks carried out by the group are directed at internal targets and foreign targets residing on Greek soil. To ensure that no other group claimed responsibility for their terror acts, a handgun of the same caliber was used in consecutive attacks against Greek targets.

The group views itself as the people's vanguard, there to lead the fight on behalf of the working class and to take up the armed struggle. It makes its point with ideological communiqués and actions in support of the cause and its attacks appear geared to making the subverted classes more abstractly aware of what is taking place in the political and economic processes in the country. The group holds the United States responsible for complicity with Turkey over the Cyprus crisis, thus making the United States a legitimate military target in its relentless war of the oppressed. The group's early attacks were primarily symbolic; the first was against the United States and subsequent attacks were against the Greek police hierarchy and representatives of the Greek military junta. An example of the hatred towards the United States can been seen from the content of one of the November 17 communiqués:

> "The American military forces in our country are an occupation force, and we are going to hit anybody who is a member of it or an agent of its secret services. These actions are going to continue and are going to increase until the last Turkish soldier leaves Cyprus and the last American soldier leaves our country."[37]

In its internal struggle with domestic terrorism, the break for Greek authorities came in 2002 with a botched bombing attack, which seriously injured the terrorist bomber. As strange as this would seem, this is the first terror suspect that Greek authorities have been able to apprehend who is a member of November 17. The bomber in this instance was Savas Xiros, who was carrying a bomb that detonated prematurely as he approached the ticket office of a hydrofoil company in Piraeus. In the explosion, Xiros lost a hand and was blinded. The ensuing investigation found a .38 Smith and Wesson revolver in his possession, which had never been fired, but its rightful owner was a Greek police officer killed in a 1984 robbery. The bomber's fingerprints also matched those on the getaway car used in the assassination of a British/Greek tycoon. Greek police have had and continue to have a mutual assistance program with both the British police and the FBI as a result of the Greek government signing a joint memorandum on combating crime.

On the speculative front, Greece had remained as the only European country unable to follow in the footsteps of Germany in crushing the Red Army Faction, Italy, the Red Brigade, and France, its Action Direct. For European observers, the November 17 group had its roots in the popular socialist opposition to the military dictatorship that ruled Greece from 1967–1975. Former Greek Premier Andreas Papendreou was thought to have been involved in the group's initial formation, and Xiros at the age of 40 would at best be a second-generation member of the group. Greek police may benefit from the mistake by the members of November 17 and, with the guidance of their U.S. and British police resources, may begin to dismantle what has been for the Greek public a shadowy organization operating with seeming impunity.

Espanastatikos Laikos Agonas (ELA)

The second most destructive group operating on Greek soil Espanastatikos Laikos Agonas (ELA, Revolutionary Peoples Struggle), is also committed to the overthrow of the Greek system and is a violent Marxist-Leninist organization. That is where the similarity between it and November 17 probably ends. It also grew out of the university campuses of the 1960s and early 1970s. Its fundamental aims and philosophy were directed at the state, imperialism and capitalism, most if not all of its targets for terror were of a symbolic nature. Unlike the secret nature of November 17, which seeks to communicate its position via communiqués, ELA actually utilizes and operates an underground newspaper to forward its aims and political viewpoint. In May 1990, ELA announced that it had merged with another left wing group, the Revolutionary Organization 1 May. Up to this point the strategy of the ELA had been to avoid death and injury to Greeks as well as foreigners on Greek soil. It had conducted a low-level style of campaign and had not ventured into the more glamorous world of remotely detonated bombs. A communiqué to the Greek government in 1993 appeared to be the turning point in its violent methods in its dealings with the state. It perceived all police officers to be the "local representatives of the CIA."[38]

On September 19, 1994, the ELA remotely detonated a bomb alongside a police bus, killing one and injuring ten others as well as a passerby. No warnings were given by ELA, which had previously been a signature for the group.

Detonating the bomb without prior warning signaled a new and more virulent strain in Greek terrorist behavior. Successive and continuous failures by the Greek government to effect any cohesive response to domestic terror has allowed the organizations to continue to operate with impunity. While neighboring countries in Europe, Germany, Italy, France and Belgium had, for the most part, decisively dealt with left wing violence and terrorist threat with a strong and dedicated response force established by powerful political mandate, it seemed to be lacking in Greece until 2001.

Much of the blame for the lackluster efforts of the Greek police must rest on the shoulders of those in political circles. The ruling Pasok party has held onto the reigns of power in Greece for the last two decades. There was a break, however, in this chain in 1989 when the New Democracy party came to power and remained there until 1993. When the Pasok party returned, one of its first actions was to abolish the anti-terror legislation enacted by its predecessors only to reintroduce it in a slightly changed format in 2001.[39]

Revolutionary Cells/Revolutionary Nuclei (RN)

Revolutionary Cells and also known as Revolutionary Nuclei (RN) has its beginnings from a wide spectrum of anti NATO, anti United States and anti European Union left-wing groups in the mid 1990s, and the group is believed to be the successor to the ELA. As ELA has not been credited with any attacks since 1995. It is thought that RN from the manner and style of its communiqués showing much of the same style as used by ELA has now taken its place. The attacks perpetrated by RN in the 1990s were considered low level and aimed mainly at companies having NATO defense contracts as well as Greek Government buildings. The RN has been most active in the Athens area and has also targeted European banks. The size of this terror group is believed to be relatively small drawing support mainly from the Greek militant left.

Minor Terrorist Groups

An increase was noted in terrorist actions in 1998, not only against the state but also at Jewish and anti-Semitic groups, foreigners as well as politicians. The source of the terror appears to be previously unheard-of organizations operating in Greece. Firebombing has been the hallmark of the attacks, which have been aimed at vehicles and buildings. The government of Greece has indicated that these attacks are coming from various quarters, the New Group of Satanists, the Children of November, the Anarchist Street Patrol, and Conscientious Arsonists, all previously unknown before 1998. With the ineptitude of the Greek security services already a well-established fact, only time will tell if the newly formed special task force of more than 1,000 undercover police officers will be effective. As Greece depends heavily on its tourist trade for much valued foreign currency, this style of attack, which seems so indiscriminate, will do a lot to drive that trade elsewhere.

CYPRUS

Situated in the eastern Mediterranean Sea, this small island has a population of some 650,000 people, and consists of 78% Greek-Cypriots, 18% Turkish-Cypriots and 4% Maronite and Latin-Cypriots. The Turks and Greeks lived together on the island for the last five centuries, and mosques and churches can be found almost side by side in many communities.

EOKA

Cyprus had been under the control of the British Empire, which by the 1950s was well into its decline. The majorities of the people of Cyprus were of Greek origin and in the 1950's were under the leadership of the Greek Cypriot Archbishop Makarios. Similar to the operations of the Stern Gang in Palestine the **EOKA** terrorist organization began to strike at the occupying influences of Great Britain. EOKA (The National Organization of Freedom Fighters) was established in 1954 as an underground movement with the blessing and approval of Makarios. The revolt began in earnest with the bombing of the Cyprus Broadcasting Station on April 1st 1955. By 1955, the British Government had declared a state of emergency on the island and the Archbishop went into exile. Following talks with both Turkey and Greece, the British agreed to grant the island independent status. In 1960, the Republic of Cyprus was born under the leadership of Makarios.

On July 20,1974, Turkey invaded the island, ostensibly to 'protect' the minority Turkish-Cypriot community. The international community condemned the action. The U.N. Resolution 353, adopted on the day of the invasion, called for all states to respect, "the sovereignty, independence and territorial integrity of the Republic of Cyprus." It further demanded an immediate end to foreign military intervention in the Republic of Cyprus. Turkey ignored the United States and the international community and seized control of at least one third of the Republic's territory and since then has engaged in a type of terrorism that we know as "ethnic cleansing." More than 1,600 Greek Cypriots are still unaccounted for following the invasion and more than 20,000 lost their homes and possessions. This is a constant and festering sore for the November 17 terrorist group that continues to blame the United States for failing to act on behalf the Greek Cypriots.

TURKEY

The history of the Turkish Ottoman Empire stretches back to when the Ottoman Turks invaded and captured Constantinople in 1453, bringing an end to the Byzantine Empire. The Ottoman Empire stretched across Eastern Europe and into regions of the Middle East as we know it today; it stretched as far south as the western reaches of Saudi Arabia and to Yemen at the southern end of the Red Sea. Its conquests stretched through North Africa from Cairo in the east and Algiers in the west. By the dawning of the eighteenth century, the Turkish Empire was commonly termed "the Sick Man of Europe," and was beginning to lose its huge territorial gains of the previous centuries. The Empire lost Algeria to French rule in 1830 and, by the latter part of 1880, Great Britain had taken control of Cyprus and Egypt. France seized Tunisia in 1881. With a crumbling empire, the Turks had to contend with disruptions on the home front as well, ruled by the dictatorship of Sultan Abdul-Hamid II. His rule was one of fear and violent repression of religious groups, and stimulated the first covert organization set up to oppose the dictator. The Young Turks, as they were known, were dissatisfied students and disaffected military personnel opposed to Hamid. The group staged a successful coup in 1908 with the aim of restoring democracy to Turkey. The replacement for Abdul-Hamid was his brother Mohammad V. The Young Turks had envisioned returning the Ottoman Empire to its former greatness, however the populace were less concerned with aspirations toward empire building and more concerned with their own democratic rights and freedoms. With the Empire crumbling, Turkey entered World War I on the side of Germany, in the hopes that it would win back much of its losses of the past half century.

Kemal Ataturk

As has been witnessed throughout history, many inspirational freedom fighters or military heroes with nationalist aspirations have risen to take control over and to form popular governments. Mustafa Kemal was one such leader whose origins in the Turkish military and his exploits as a natural leader of men brought him to the forefront of politics in Turkey. He formed the provisional government in 1920 after the invasion of the country by forces from Britain, France and Greece. The Ottoman government was unable to protect the country, so the country turned to its nationalist leader, Kemal. The Sultan's powers weakened and the Nationalists grew stronger and were able to forcibly evict the Greeks from Turkish soil. They then sued for peace with the Allies. Turkey as we know it today is formed around the boundaries outlined in the Treaty of Lausanne signed by the nationalists in 1923. The word "Ataturk" is the surname given to Kemal and means father of the Turks.[40] Kemal ruled as President of Turkey until his death in 1938. Turkey did not repeat its mistake of joining on the side of Germany at the outbreak of World War II and managed to keep out of the war; with Germany's defeat, Turkey joined the United Nations in 1946.

Turkey has witnessed many changes in government since the end of World War II ably assisted by a strong military intent on keeping to the democratic principles established so long ago by Kemal. Turkey has had an uneasy peace with its Greek neighbors, which nearly erupted in an all-out war, when Turkey threatened to invade Cyprus in 1964.

Revolutionary Left (*Dev Sol*)

A left-wing Marxist group that has its origins in the Turkish Peoples Liberation Army split off in the late 1970s to form ***Dev Sol***. It's a vehemently anti-NATO group as well as anti-United States. The aims of this group are to foster an uprising or popular national revolution amongst the Turkish working

---

TERRORISM BYTE 5–3

Istanbul Airport Attack

On August 11, 1976, members of the Popular Front for the Liberation of Palestine attacked the passenger terminal at Istanbul International Airport, killing four and injuring a further twenty. The attack took place at the boarding gate for an El Al Israeli airline departure. The attack resulted in the death of one of the hijackers—a Japanese member of the gang—one escaped, and two were detained. The claim for this action was retaliation for the Israeli hostage rescue at Mogadishu airport.

Source: George Rosie, The Directory of International Terrorism, Paragon House New York 1986.

---

classes. The group is financed primarily from criminal activities carried out in Turkey from armed robberies and extortion from businesses.

During the 1980s, the group restricted its area of operation to the domestic scene, mainly in Izmir, Istanbul and Ankara. With the Middle East crisis and the Desert Storm operation against Iraq, the group began attacks on United States military personnel. The group launched a rocket attack at the United States Consulate Building in Istanbul in 1992. Since the early 1980s, the group has suffered from internal factional fighting and has carried out limited operations at home. From the training perspective it is believed that the membership, which is considered to number several hundred, received training and indoctrination at Palestinian camps from radical Palestinians. By the end of 1998, this group was not particularly active in Turkey, but indications are that it is beginning to resurface and may threaten U.S. commercial interests as well as Turkish government figures.

Kurdistan Workers Party (PKK)

The leadership and organizer of **PKK** originated from the student movement at Ankara University. Abdullah Ocalan, the leader, now behind bars in Ankara but still the leader, set up the organization with the specific aim of liberating the Kurds. Ocalan was considerably brutal in his methods and fostered his version of terrorism on his own followers and fellow Kurds. Executing the dissenters usually put down any dissent in the group, and it is believed that Ocalan killed more than 10,000 Kurds during the 1980s. His actions had some sobering effects on the Kurdish people. It showed them that PKK was strong and that the people should side with them in the struggle for freedom from Turkey; it also meant that failure to actively support the movement was perceived as being on the side of the Turks. Therefore, violent action will speak louder than words. Operating in southeastern Turkey, this Kurdish terror group seeks to set up a Kurdish state fashioned on Marxist lines. Mainly composed of Turkish Kurds, PKK has been in operation since 1974 and have been involved in what would best be described as insurgent activities.

As was seen previously, many Turks have migrated to Germany throughout the last 40 years and this in part adds to the financial viability of the PKK. PKK has been responsible for the deaths of at least 35,000 people through its fifteen years of insurgency. In order to finance its operations it uses a variety of tried and tested methods. It is involved in the lucrative trade in illegal immigrants from Iraq into European centers. In addition, the PKK also controls a lucrative portion of the drug traffic from the East into Europe. Its other levels of fund raising include extortion from Kurds residing in France, Germany, Belgium and Romania. The PKK is also the recipient of state sponsors, such as Iran and Syria. From Syria's perspective the destabilization of the Turkish regime plays an important role in economic terms. Although a recent agreement between the two nations was signed in 1998. Animosity has existed for many years between the two countries and the Adana Agreement of 1998 was supposed to restrict PKK activity in Syria. It seems however to be of little effect and PKK operatives continue to plan and execute operations from bases in Syria.

From a wider viewpoint, Turkey's support for the U.S. war on terrorism will not have endeared themselves to the Syrian regime, nor for their support of Israel. As talk in Washington in mid-2002 centers on the Iraqi regime of Sadam Hussein, the launching point for a coalition-led attack would likely center around Turkey. At present the options are limited, as Saudi Arabia appears unwilling to allow U.S. forces to attack Iraq from its bases in Saudi. Any NATO military presence in southeast Turkey would likely come under threat from PKK forces. As the war on terrorism continues, PKK was declared a "terrorist organization" by the European Union in May 2002. PKK continues to receive support from Iran and also maintains bases in the Bekka Valley, Lebanon. Abdullah Ocalan, imprisoned under sentence of death in a Turkish prison, declared in 2000 that his group, the PKK, which has for so long sought an independent Kurdish state through violent struggle, had changed its stance and would now seek, through a political campaign, only guarantees of Kurdish political, economic, social, and cultural rights in a democratic Turkey. Also active in Turkey is Turkish Hezbollah, an extreme Islamic movement comprising Sunni Muslims. However, a government crackdown on this group has severely curtailed its operations, but as in other areas of the Middle East, the group does use the suicide mission as a means of assassination of specific targets, mainly members of the police and government.[41]

Armenian Terrorism

Like the Kurds, the ethnic Armenians of northeastern Turkey have, since 1974, been fighting for their own homeland and autonomy in the region. Two terror groups have come to the fore, the **Armenian Secret Army for the Liberation of Armenia (ASALA)** and the Justice Commandos of the Armenian Genocide. Both groups have targeted diplomats from Turkey in Europe and the United States as part of their terror campaign. Their attacks became more violent when they started to detonate bombs at airports in the 1980s. They set off a bomb at Orly Airport in France adjacent to the Turkish Airlines check-in counters, killing ten and wounding more than seventy in the process. The leader of ASALA, Hagop Hagopian, was shot to death on an Athens street in 1988 and since then the group has been a silent force.[42]

The Nationalist Threat

The **Turkish Revenge Brigade** is a previously unknown group that sprang up in 1998 in opposition to Kurdish movements. Considered to be ultranationalist the group has targeted Kurdish and left-wing journalists actively who support the Kurdish movement. In May 1998, two members of the group attempted to assassinate a leading Turkish human rights activist, Akin Birdal. The motive for the attack is uncertain, but the head of the Human Rights Association claimed at the time that Birdal had received prior death threats and had asked for protection from the government, but to no avail. How the nationalist movement will develop and who is backing and financing its operations is unclear. No doubt, previous reports of Turkish death squads and their involvement earlier in the decade come back into question.

BELGIAN TERRORISM

Belgium, and its involvement with terrorism, was of considerable internal concern during the 1980s. A country known for a stable democracy and with a population of only 10 million, political violence had been unheard of in comparison to the troubles besieging its neighbors. Belgium terrorism was not widely publicized by the world press and probably received little or no mention by the U.S. press. Belgium has also received little or no mention by experts reviewing European terrorist threats. However, terrorist incidents have taken place on Belgium soil from external terror groups. PLO terrorists from the Black September group hijacked a Belgium state (Sabena) airliner to Israel in 1972, and PLO terrorists also attacked the Iraqi Embassy in Brussels in 1978.

The source for internal troubles appeared to rise from the direction of neo-fascist terror gangs, who up until the 1980s had not been active but had aligned themselves with other terror groups in Europe. Considered to be more of a criminal gang element more on the outer fringes of violent political struggle were the right wing **DARE**, the New Force Party and the West New Post. All were considered extreme fascist movements, but which had been nonviolent in comparison to those of the rest of Europe.

Belgium is a country unfamiliar with violent armed robberies so when an outbreak began in 1982, the country was gripped in panic. Terrorism in its ugliest form was on their doorstep. The Belgium press, who nicknamed the group the "Mad Killers," sensationalized the first attacks. Most of the early attacks were aimed at a supermarket chain, and weapons were used. Timing and planning were a hallmark of the operation, and the gang readily killed numerous innocent bystanders. Armed with semiautomatic weapons and wearing bulletproof vests, the group members escaped with limited amounts of cash, which gave the authorities grave concern as to the real motive for the attacks and killings. The Belgians were unable to determine where the threat was coming from, either the left or the right. Terror was causing a crisis in the government and panic in the country, with innocent bystanders being killed. After all, this was not the United States but a hitherto quiet mainstream European country.

Revolutionary Front for Proletarian Action—FRAP

The terms revolutionary and proletarian are often used as much by European neo-Nazis as they are by leftist groups. Contemporary Nazis also hate European links to the United States. FRAP's first action on April 20th 1985, a date universally celebrated by European Nazis as the birthday of Adolf Hitler, was a bombing attack on the North Atlantic Assembly (NAA) in Brussels, and was followed the next day by an attack against the offices of AEG-Telefunken. The first reaction by authorities to these attacks and also from the media was that it was the work of an ultra-leftist group. The initial arrests were made from among members of leftist groups in Belgium. The attacks on these two establishments suggested that FRAP was as likely to be have been rightist as Communist, although the ambiguous circumstances of these attacks mean that it would be the left that would be stigmatized.[43]

Fighting Communist Cells (CCC)

The **CCC** came into being at about the same time as the so-called Mad Killers. How and where they originated was a mystery and there was considerable speculation that the membership included members of the Belgium state security and agents of the far right. With no historical traditions for terrorism and violence it seemed strange for this movement to emerge in Belgium so successfully. It was represented as a left wing organization with affiliations with the other left wing European groups, Action Direct, and the Red Brigade.

The leader of the CCC was Pierre Carette who had a radical history but was determined to be of no real significance as a leader. Carette and the CCC began their short-lived campaign when in October 1984 they attacked offices belonging to Litton Data Systems and two months later followed with another attack on a NATO oil line near Brussels. Other attacks took place against symbolic property targets in Brussels and Antwerp. Carette was arrested following the death of two firefighters in a bomb attack in Brussels. Carette's arrest spelled the termination of the CCC. It is still not clear who or what was involved in the destabilizing attempt of Belgium. Was it all an attempt by the left, or was it some other form of terrorism with an as yet undefined rationale? Whatever the case, there are some underlying aspects to the Belgium political structure and scene that the student would do well to study. One should not dismiss a theory that an agent provocateur may have been involved in the Belgian experience.

The perceived or real threat that overpopulation from immigration may have on an otherwise liberal society is evidenced in the assassination of Pim Fortuyn, a blunt speaking anti-Muslim politician, who has become better known in death than he was in life. "The Netherlands is full" was one of his famous slogans. His viewpoint criticized the fact that the Netherlands was home to 800,000 Muslims from Turkey and Morocco. He referred to Islam as a "backwards" religion that censored free thinkers, mistreated homosexuals and women. His assassination, the first to happen in Holland in three hundred years, has generated a wide spread sympathy for his style of free speech. Perhaps surprisingly it was not at the hands of a fanatical Muslim extremist that he met his death in a hail of bullets. His murderer was Volkert van der Graaf, an animal rights activist; however, his motives for assassination are not readily clear. Pim Fortuyn's party now occupies a position in the center right coalition government and oversees immigration policy.

SUMMARY

Western Europe maintains an important position in the global fight against terrorism. Many of the homegrown terror groups cease to exist, particularly in France and Germany. Italy, on the other hand, continues a relentless battle with the separatist ETA as the group strives for its form of independence. The true meaning of international terror for many if not all the countries listed in this chapter has come to light in their experience with Islamic extremists, either involved in 9–11 or the possibility of chemical and other attacks against U.S. interests. As allies of President Bush's 'War on Terrorism,' many European nations will now be continuing to focus on transnational terrorism, a likely hallmark of the twenty-first century.

REVIEW QUESTIONS

1. Discuss why authorities have been unsuccessful in tracking November 17 until recently.
2. Discuss the association between Germany and the events of September 11, 2001.
3. Contrast the ETA campaign and its lack of success with that of the Irish nationalist groups.
4. Discuss the rise of neo-Nazi hate groups and the reasons behind their rise to prominence.

TERMS TO REMEMBER

ANE	comradeship evenings	NATO
Arab Revolution	DARE	November 17
Armenian Secret	Dev Sol	PKK
Army for the Liberation of Armenia (ASALA)	EOKA	PLO
	ETA-Military	Red Army Faction
Basque	FRAP	Turkish Revenge Brigade
Carlos the Jackal	GEO	
CCC	Herri Batasuna Party	

END NOTES

1. U.S. Department of State Information Programs (usinfo.state.gov) website.
2. The Internet. Intel brief courtesy U.S. Department of State Archives on ETA. http://www.state.gov/s/ct/nls.
3. William Gutteridge. (Ed) "Contemporary Terrorism," an article by Peter Janke, The Institute for the Study of Conflict, 1986, p. 152. Facts on File Inc.
4. George Rosie. *The Directory of International Terrorism.* Paragon House, New York 1987. p. 111.
5. Strategic Forecasting "Spain: Move to Outlaw Separatist Party May Fail" July 5th 2002. www.stratfor.com/premium/analysis.
6. George Rosie. *Directory of International Terrorism.* Paragon House, New York p.135.
7. Pino Arlacchi. *Men of Dishonor,* William Morrow and Co. Inc., New York p. 27.
8. Spain Arrests Al Qaeda Suspect with WTC Footage Tue Jul 16,12:31 PM ET By Chris Brown – BBC News http://news.bbc.co.uk.
9. Elmar Thevessen and Ulf Röller, "Das Netzwerk des Terrors," *ZDF* (German TV), 10/24/2001.
10. David Yallop. *Tracking the Jackal.* Random House Inc. New York 1993. pp. 48/9.
11. Philip Jackson. "Under two flags: Provocation and Deception in European Terrorism," *Terrorism an International Journal* (Taylor and Francis, New York, 1988), p. 280 Volume II.
12. Grant Wardlow. *"Political Terrorism, Theory, Tactics and Counter-measures"* (Cambridge University Press, London, 1982) p. 38.
13. Philip Jenkins. "Strategy of tension: The Belgian Terrorist Crisis 1982–1986" *Terrorism an International Journal,* Taylor and Francis, New York, 1990, p. 299 Volume 13.
14. Yallop. Tracking the Jackal, p.98 David Yallop: Random House Inc. New York 1993.
15. U.S. Department of State website – Patterns of Global Terrorism. http://www.state.gov.
16. "Gang de Roubaix: La Jeunesse de Dumont à l'Etude," TF1.Fr (French TV), 4 October 2001; "Bin Laden's Invisible Network," *Newsweek* (International Edition), 29 October 2001, p. 50.
17. Adam Sage and Daniel McGrory, "French Agents Knew of Hijack Suspect in 1994," *The London Times,* 3 October 2001, p. 4.
18. "Moussaoui," *BBC World,* 13 December 2001; *CNN Inside Europe,* 16 December 2001.
19. *The World Book Encyclopaedia.* World Book Inc. 1990, p.254, Volume 9.
20. Richard Huffman. Motivations from an Internet article: Terrorist motivations 1997. www. Baader-meinhof.com/student/resources.
21. Ibid.
22. George Rosie. *Directory of International Terrorism.* Paragon House, New York, 1986, p. 220.
23. Ibid.
24. The Mackenzie Institute Occasional paper by Emerson Vermaat and Wilhelm, Heitmayer, Joachim Muller, and Helmut Schroeder, *Verlockendere Fundamentaliismus. Turkische jugendliche in Deutschland* (Frankfurt am Main: Suhrkamp, 1997) pp. 128–131.
25. Anti-Defamation League: A worldwide survey of Neo-Nazi Skinheads. New York: ADL, 1995 New York, NY (The Nizkor Project: www.Nizkor.org).
26. *USA Today,* Monday November 26, 2001, Donna Leinwand: *Germany tightens security in sleeper search.* p. 13A.
27. Emerson Vermaat, The Mackenzie Institute, Toronto Canada. pp. 128–131.
28. U.S. Department of State, Patterns of Global Terrorism, released by the Office of Coordinator for Counterterrorism, May 21st 2002, Europe Overview.
29. Gutteridge. Contemporary Terrorism, A Challenge to Italian Democracy, William Gutteridge (Ed) by Vittorfranco S. Pisano. The Institute for the Study of Control London, 1986 p. 167.
30. Ibid. p.177.
31. Ibid. p. 182.
32. Ibid. p. 184.
33. Ibid. p. 184.

34. Anti Defamation League website, *The Skinhead International,* a Worldwide Survey of Neo-Nazi Skinheads. New York Anti-Defamation League 1995 www.nizkor.org.

35. Ibid.

36. Ibid.

37. Andrew Corsun, "Revolutionary Organization November 17 in Greece," *Terrorism an International Journal,* (Taylor and Francis, London 1991), Volume 14, p. 86.

38. G. Kassimeris, "Greece: Twenty Years of Political Terrorism," *Terrorism and Political Violence,* Frank Cass, London 1995. p. 81 vol.7.

39. Jane's Terrorism and Security Monitor, Ed Stephen Ulph, July 2002, "Greece finally takes on 17N", Janes Information Group, p. 4–5.

40. *World Book Encyclopaedia.* World Book Inc. USA 1990, p. 511 Volume 19.

41. U.S. Department of State, Patterns of Global Terrorism 2000, 2001 http://www.state.gov.

42. Ibrahim Cerrah and Robert Peel. "Terrorism in Turkey," *INTERSEC.* England 1997, p. 19, vol. 7.

43. Philip Jenkins. "Strategy of Tension": The Belgian Terrorist Crisis 1982–1986", *Terrorism an International Journal,* (Taylor and Francis, London 1990) p. 304.

6 Eastern Europe and the Balkans

"Terrorism has declared war on us, the people of Russia."

Former Russian President Boris Yeltsin

OVERVIEW

Terrorism in the former Eastern Bloc and in the Soviet Union and Russia is not a new phenomenon in those countries. Its colorful and sad history is depicted in the stories by novelists of the nineteenth century, much as by the novelists of this century under the yoke of the Soviets. Count Leo N. Tolstoy, who wrote *War and Peace* in 1869, captures the fire and horror of the French invasion of Russia in 1812. Reforms made by Czar Alexander II were strongly opposed by his son Alexander III, who succeeded him after his assassination. It was this repressive approach that slowly nurtured the seeds of revolt in Russia, that were at first written about as themes of desperation, discontent and bitterness by the many great novelists and intellectuals of that era.

In this chapter the authors review the early terror theories at work in Russia and the Slavic states and we will see the manner in which the Soviet Union fostered state-sponsored terrorism on an international scale. Many of the nineteenth-century Russian writers like Maxim Gorki wrote short stories and plays that reflected the theories of a communist state in Russia. The early seeds of terror grew out of the appalling conditions under which the people of Russia existed under the Czars and out of a need for social change and the overwhelming will of the people to see change. We shall start with the most well-known events and work down to the others in the central and eastern parts of Europe. Bringing this chapter into focus with the twenty-first century we will find how the 'War on Terrorism' is played out in the Chechen Republic and how the actions of so-called Chechen rebels is deemed terrorism by the Russian Government.

RUSSIA AND THE SOVIET UNION

Narodnaya Volya (NV) (1878–1881)

Roughly translated, Narodnaya Volya[1] has the meaning "**the people's will.**" This highly effective terrorist organization was only in existence for four years. The group grew out of other disaffected Russian movements that were clandestine in nature and formed by the intelligensia. Hard-liners out of several of these groups formed the Narodnaya Volya. As with many current terrorist organizations, the NV used terrorism as a means to a political end. With the aim of causing so much distress and turmoil to the ruling Romanovs, the group hoped that their actions would shake the Russian Empire's political foundations. Numbering more than five hundred and with some fifty or more extremists drawn from the ruling upper class of Russian society, they set out to overthrow the tyranny of the Czars. They sentenced Czar Alexander II to death, and made several unsuccessful attempts on his life.

One of the most fanatical members of the NV organization, 27-year-old Sophia Ptrovskaya, succeeded in planting a bomb that killed the Czar in 1881. In addition, the NV was also responsible for the death of General Mezentsev, head of the Third Section of the Czarist OKHRNA and also the governor general of Saint Petersburg. The NV were hunted down and arrested by Czarist authorities, and terrorism in Russia diminished over the next two decades. The NV was to have a profound effect on Russian history. The inspiration for Lenin to form the Social Democratic Labour Party was born out of NV. Lenin's views of and appreciation for NV taught him an important lesson: that a revolutionary organization cannot be limited to terrorism, but must seize total autocratic and bureaucratic power. The NV symbolized the general social crisis that existed in nineteenth-century Russia, and much later during the Bolshevik revolution, which replaced the old order in Russia. Terrorism faded with the passing of the NV, until the formation of the Social Revolutionary Party at the turn of the twentieth century. Members of NV took extreme care in planning and carrying out their assassinations to avoid killing innocents in the process. The targets for retribution were those deemed guilty of acts of corruption and other acts against the people.

Terror and revolution are two words that would be used frequently and interchangeably for Russians over the first twenty years of the twentieth century. In 1902, the Minister of the Interior was assassinated. The objective for terrorism in early twentieth-century Russia was to awaken the masses to the potential for revolution and social change. The philosophy of this approach is seen today in struggles in other regions of nationalist conflict where the intent is to attempt coercion and motivate the masses to revolt and overthrow the existing authority.

Within the Social Revolutionary Party was a terror sub-group that was given autonomy under the Party, ***Boevaya Oranisatsia*** (BO, or the Fighting Organization). It can be argued that whereas the NV was more aligned with the

TERRORISM BYTE 6–1

Bombing of Kaspiysk

In Russia the term "bandit" is used in place of "terrorist," which was how Russian President Putin described the assailants who planted a remotely detonated mine in the main street of the southern city of Kaspiysk, near the border with Chechnya on Thursday May 9, 2002. The remote-controlled device was exploded during a celebration parade commemorating the defeat of Nazi Germany. Lenin Street was packed with veterans and school children and the blast killed thirty-five and seriously injured more than one hundred and fifty. Russia will continue to experience problems from Islamic separatists and fanatics in this long-suffering region of Eurasia.

Chechen gunman lies dead outside Moscow theater October 26, 2002, after it was stormed by Russian special forces. Over 200 hostages and about 30 rebels died when gas was pumped into the theater to end the siege. (AP Photo/Gazeta)

educated Russian hierarchy, the BO appealed to a wider Russian audience. Within the revolutionary movement widespread dissent continued over the use of terror tactics, and with the emergence of the class struggle, terrorism as a weapon of the period became redundant.

Mikhail Bakunin, the brilliant Russian orator, traveled widely throughout Europe promoting his ideals for revolutionary change. They were based on the destruction of the prevailing social order as it existed in Russia. His approach to anarchy conflicted greatly with that of Marx, and the two were bitter rivals. Bakunin put forward no useful or thoughtful ideas for a future social order and was seen by Marx to be a dangerous fanatic. Bakunin's view was that the state had to be overthrown where as Karl Marx believed that it was capitalism

TERRORISM BYTE 6–2

Bloody Sunday

Czar Nicholas I was to be the last ruling monarch of the Russian Empire. Considered weak and superstitious, he had a total dislike for politicians and the intellectual elite. Following Russia's defeat in the Russo-Japanese war, thousands of protesting peasants and workers marched into Palace Square. The event started out peacefully enough, however, crowd members carrying icons of Czar Nicholas had hoped to get his attention. The chief of police ordered his men to open fire on the group, which resulted in hundreds being massacred. This day, January 9th, 1905, is remembered as Bloody Sunday.

that had to be purged. Marx's theory and ideology was that violence was necessary to transform the nature of the working class, and that violent insurrection was the only means by which society could be changed.

Opposition to the rule of the Bolsheviks, following their rise to power in 1917, came from the intelligensia as well as from opposition newspapers. The Russian republics were involved in a civil war between the years 1918–21. In March 1918, Lenin dissolved the Constituent Assembly when it failed to recognize the leadership of the **Bolshevik** government. The protests of the Left Socialist Revolutionary Party went unheeded by Lenin and so the group withdrew from the coalition. The Bolsheviks began a period of terror and repression against all groups that voiced opposition. Arrests were made of hundreds of artists and intellectuals who were simply aghast at the attitude of the Bolsheviks and had expected a society based on freedom after the overthrow of the Czarist Government. The Bolsheviks dealt with nationalists, Menscheviks, social revolutionaries as well as members of the intellectual levels of society (professors, writers and artists) in the harshest manner. The church in Russia also became a target of communist terror and oppression. A systematic campaign by the communists to deny the Russian Orthodox Church any voice in the Soviet Union started in the 1920s, and by the year 1939 all the clergy and many of the church's followers had been shot or sent to forced labor camps. Of the 50,000 churches only about 500 remained open.

Joseph Stalin

To many, the very name Stalin conjures up scenes of sheer despotic terror. In the first quarter of the twentieth century, his name was almost synonymous with the word terror. This chapter is not designed to teach the student the fundamentals of the Russian Revolution but to explain that the intricate use of terror tactics as practiced by Lenin's Bolsheviks had the unspoken support of the party. Were the Bolsheviks considered terrorists or were they revolutionaries fighting for their political beliefs to achieve a Soviet Republic? In hindsight and because popular movies such as Dr. Zhivago seem to glory in the hostility and man's inhumanity to his fellow man, do we therefore consider the Russian Revolution a result of effective terrorism? In later years, and specifically during the Cold War, the United States and NATO allies viewed the USSR as the prime exporter and sponsor of modern-day terrorism. The notorious terrorist, Carlos the Jackal, is believed to have received his indoctrination, training and funding from the Soviet Union. Although there is evidence that he did receive part of his university education there, no substantive evidence shows that the Soviet Union in fact sponsored him.

Josef Vissarionovich Dzhugashvili adopted the name "Stalin," which is a Russian word meaning of steel. Following the death of Lenin, Stalin became the absolute ruler of the Soviet Union from 1929 until he died in 1953. As a young man, he earned a scholarship to study theology but was subsequently expelled for preaching Marxist idealogies. He was a strong political supporter of Bolshevism throughout Europe, and is credited with being the first editor of *Pravda,* the newspaper voice of the communist party. Stalin used extreme measures on the Russian population to ensure absolute and blind obedience to his will; any who opposed him were summarily dealt with and either shot or sent to labor camps in Siberia. This form of state terrorism was carried out by his head of the secret police, Laurenty Beria, whose very name struck terror in the hearts of the Soviet citizens.

Secret Police

In many states where suppression of the masses by deliberate terror takes place, there is a need for a sanctioned police force or other security network to do the bidding of the dictator. Apart from Adolf Hitler, there have been few other world leaders that have slaughtered and sent to labor camps so many of their own countrymen as Stalin. The communist regime under Stalin viewed any dissent against the party as a repudiation of the proletarian struggle and a violation of Marxist-Leninism ideology. Therefore, a threat to these guidelines was a threat to the very existence of the authority of the state. To this end the Bolsheviks, and then the communists, relied heavily on a strong political secret police to secure and maintain their rule. The original secret police, called the **Cheka**, were formed in 1917, with the intention that they be disbanded after power had been consolidated by the Bolsheviks under Lenin. The first chief of this secret police force was Feliks Dzerzhinskii, who had the power under the Bolsheviks to investigate "counterrevolutionary" crimes.

Much has been written of the Russian Revolution and few would argue that the results of the October Revolution would be felt for decades to come, even though the Soviet Union has gone into the dustbin of history. Again, the difficulty of defining what actions were terrorism becomes apparent. There is no doubt that the actions of the Social Democrats of the Lenin era were terroristic in attitude and nature. However, when viewed and portrayed as a class struggle or for worker rights, why are these conflicts now termed revolutionary actions? Is it the popular belief that where a mass or common populace supports a cause, whether they be righteous or not, these activities are no longer referred to as merely terrorist acts but rather a full-blown popular resistance or revolution?

In the latter part of the twentieth century, western governments have actively criminalized terrorism and created legislation to deal with specific acts of violence against the state, including the banning of terrorist-linked, backed or supported groups. Might it therefore be correct to rationalize that a popular revolution exists within the borders of Spain (ETA) or in Northern Ireland (IRA)? As we strive to continually master what terrorism means in each specific category and indeed each country, it becomes less and less clear to define. In Afghanistan, following the Soviet invasion of that sovereign state, no doubt the rebels fighting for the freedom of their country from the mountains around Kabul would most likely be termed as terrorists by the Soviet Union. It is equally fair to believe that to the Afghans these "terrorists" were better described as "freedom fighters." It is now more than ironic that one of those freedom fighters who was provided support in the form of training from both the United States and Britain, would turn and bite the hand that fed him. We are, of course, referring to Osama bin Laden. The training received by Afghan freedom fighters from Special Forces groups from the United States and Britain's Special Air Service Regiment (SAS) equipped them admirably for covert style operations against their new "enemies" in the West. Some of those fighters no doubt were involved with the Taliban regime and al Qaeda, against the coalition forces in 2001 and early 2002.

TERROR BRIEF 6–1

Where are the Russian Suitcase N-Bombs?

The nightmare scenario of terrorists acquiring Russian suitcase-size nuclear weapons took a dramatic turn when the Kremlin implicitly admitted that the bombs exist, and some may be missing. Until now, persistent rumors of the existence of the small, portable bombs have been vehemently denied by Moscow, with even Premier Viktor Chernomyrdin shrugging off the claims as an "absolute absurdity."

But Professor Alexei Yablokov, who first disclosed the existence of the sophisticated device, was quietly co-opted by the Russian Defense Council to devise new legislation to control the weapons. He was secretly summoned to the Kremlin and ordered to help draft a presidential decree to coordinate the location of "compact nuclear weapons," bring them under secure control, and arrange for their speedy destruction. The Yeltsin government's decision to bring in the professor is a tacit admission that the suitcase bombs exist, and that they may exist outside secure controls representing a genuine international security risk.

It was Yablokov, a distinguished ecologist, academician and former special adviser to Boris Yeltsin, who first alerted the world to the danger posed by these bombs, ideal portable terrorist weapons. He told a U.S. Congressional committee that he was absolutely certain they had been built as he had met someone involved in their construction. He told the press that while there was no certainty that any of the bombs were unaccounted for, there were indeed "some suspicions." He stated, "I won't say how many I think have gone missing, you

will publish it and scare the whole world. It is a question of units not dozens."

Congressman Curt Weldon as Chairman of the House of Representatives National Security, disclosed that General Alexander Lebed had told him of his own concerns about suitcase nuclear weapons. General Lebed, who in his brief six months in government was charged by President Yeltsin to review nuclear security, said that adequate ccounts were made for only 48 out of 132 known bombs. He suspected that the Ministry of Atomic Energy, without the knowledge of the Defense Ministry, might have built some of the weapons for the KGB. Small, tactical nuclear devices may have long been deployed on both sides of the Cold War trenches. The U.S. military is believed to have as many as six hundred atomic demolition munitions (ADMs) some of which are known to troops as "satchel bombs." The weapons were intended for Special Forces to use behind enemy lines for blowing up key infrastructures such as airports and roads. Similar equipment is suspected to have been issued to Soviet Spetznaz units as part of the approximately 25,000 tactical nuclear weapons in the Red Army's armory.

In 1995, rumors swirled around Moscow that Chechen rebels had acquired two such bombs in Vilnius, Lithuania. According to the Russian nationalist paper, *Zavtra,* the weapons were bought for $1 million, and all those associated with the transaction were later murdered to ensure secrecy. The correspondent who wrote the article was subsequently abducted and threatened with death if he pursued the story, which was later withdrawn by *Zavtra.*

Source: Ivo Dawnay. "Russia loses its suitcase N-bombs", *The Sunday Telegraph,* (London, The Telegraph Press, November 9, 1997).

The Great Terror

Throughout modern history there have been many dictators who have purged their respective societies of all opposition from within their own political structures as well as on the outside. The murder of a senior Politburo member on December 1, 1934, was to set in motion a chain of events that resulted in the Great Terror. **Sergei Kirov** was leader of the communist party in Leningrad, and an influential member of the ruling elite. Popular as he was in Leningrad in support of workers' welfare, he disagreed with some of Stalin's policies, and although not thought to be a threat to Stalin, he had been approached by some party members to take over as general secretary.[2]

Did Stalin, who was having doubts about the loyalty of the Leningrad apparatus, possibly perceive him as a threat? It seems entirely possible that the NKVD (The Peoples Commissariat for Internal Affairs) could well have planned Kirov's murder on Stalin's instructions. Using the murder of Kirov as the excuse he needed to crack down hard and to purge the Leningrad Party structure, Stalin introduced wide-sweeping laws that resulted in millions of Russians being arrested. This purge lasted for approximately four years and Stalin never again visited Leningrad. This four-year period saw millions sent to Russian labor camps as well as summary executions and show trials. To say the Russian populace was terrified would be considered an understatement. In view of the terror tactics of Stalin, his complete and total domination of the Russian people was further enforced by forcibly resettling more than one million people mainly Muslims from the Northern Caucasus region and the Crimea. Ethnic Tartars, Chechens, Meskhetians, Kalmyks as well as Bulgarians, Greeks and Armenians from the Black Sea coast were deported.

These deportations took place during and after World War II, with the excuse that they were collaborators with German occupying forces. The forced deportation took place with the use of cattle cars reminiscent of German deportation to forced labor and extermination camps of Jews and Gypsies. The destination for the deportees was Uzbekistan, Siberia and Kazakhstan—names that today have a ring of familiarity to them. By the mid-1950s the forced deportations were denounced by Nikita Khrushchev; however, many were still not permitted to return to their native homeland until after the breakup of the Soviet Union in 1991.

Estonian Guerrilla Movement 1944–1955

One terror or guerrilla group that existed after the collapse of the German Axis was an Estonian movement called the *Metsavennad,* meaning "guerrilla." With the retreat of the German Army, many Estonian soldiers who had been drafted into the German Army attempted to escape the discipline of Stalin, either by leaving the country or fleeing to the forest region of Estonia. These men were known as "brethen." Not only Estonians but deserting Germans also joined the movement. The movement is sparsely written about and they formed a protective band around Estonians to prevent violence meted out by the Soviets. The group was well equipped with an abundance of weapons, and was also supported by those who sought revenge against the Soviet Union for previous forced deportations associated with collectivization in March 1949.

The cause was the ultimate independence of Estonia and although this was realized to be a fruitless gesture against the might of the Soviets, the group obviously hoped for some relief and withdrawal of the Soviets, possibly with another European theater of war. A post-Stalin amnesty in 1955 saw the movement virtually disappear.

"School for Terrorism"

Also known as "**Killer College,**"[3] Patrice Lumumba University is located near Moscow and was established in 1961 as the Soviet Union's educational contribution to the Third World countries of Africa and Asia. It was to this university that the infamous terrorist Ilich Ramirez (Carlos the Jackal) received his postsecondary education. The Venezuelan Communist Party sponsored the admission of Ilich and his brother Lenin to the University. Partying seems to have been a big part of their curriculum while in Moscow, and on several occasions, they went afoul of their Soviet Army and KGB minders. Illich was arrested while demonstrating for the cause of thirty Iranian students who had had their passports seized by the Shah's government. Although they were sponsored by the Venezuelan Communists, neither Illich nor Lenin was a member of the party. Their continuous confrontations with the orthodox members of the Venezuelan Communist Youth movement at the university lead to their grants being suspended and their subsequent expulsion. Though there have been many books and articles written about Carlos the Jackal, whether the **KGB** recruited him during the period he spent in Moscow will probably never be known. On his own admission after leaving the Soviet Union in 1970 his next stop was the melting pot of international terrorism, Beirut.

Into the Millennium

With the breakup of the Soviet Union, and with many of the Russian republics seeking to go their own way and separate from the new Russian Federation, Russia found itself in somewhat unfamiliar waters at the end of 1998. No longer controlled by the communists and with its people sampling capitalist fare, Russia saw many disaffected youth leaning towards right wing nationalism. In the summer of 1998, Boris Yeltsin was openly commenting in press reports about the right wing nationalist threat. What was surfacing in Russia, now subject to rampant unemployment, had already surfaced in a unified Germany. Russian youth were beginning to blame immigrants and Jews for the lack of jobs and the country's woes. Hate crimes and other actions were now commonplace in Russia. Had Russia gone full circle in the last one hundred years? At the turn of the last century, Russia was in turmoil with the uprising of the worker classes, and it is possible that this situation may be repeating itself.

The former Soviet Union has seen more freedom of the press to report on issues and incidents as they occur in everyday life than ever before, and this may become part of the lifeblood of any terrorist group starting up in Russia. Under communist domination, the government-controlled media rarely reported on anti-Soviet acts. Without these restrictions, a key component in any terrorist arsenal is the ability to bring activities to a wide audience. In the democracies of the West, acts of terror and sabotage have received banner headlines. With suppression of the press, there can be little fertile support for any type of terrorist activity. There has been little press freedom to report the extent of activities by Russian forces in Chechnya, and Russia continues to blame Chechen rebels for bomb attacks in Moscow and continues to use this as either a valid reason or excuse to carryout military operations against the state. Chechnya is a small landlocked state with a predominantly Muslim population of approximately one million. During the last three years more than 100,000 Chechens have died in the fighting with Russia. Russian President Vladimir Putin was quick to support George Bush and his declaration of a war on terrorism. As for the problems and how to deal with the breakaway republic of Chechnya, Putin and his government took this as tacit approval to continue a legitimized attack on Chechnya.

The U.S. administration, to ensure support for its role in attacking terrorism on a worldwide basis, has effectively ignored the issues surrounding the Russian actions in the South Caucasus area. With the Cold War over, the enemy is no longer the Soviet Union. Times have changed dramatically and the threat now comes from a worldwide terrorism advanced through the hate and malice of fighters immersed in the Muslim faith with extremist Islamic slants to their actions. The regions of Dagestan and Chechnya are homes to countless numbers of Muslims, however the threat perceived by Russia is vastly different than for that of western democracies from Islamic extremists. Chechens are fighting for their own independence from their former Russian masters and Russia continues to use its military in its campaign to regain control of the region. Chechnya remains an unsettled region and Russia can continue to expect the unexpected from the Islamic Mujahideen, formerly under the control of Chechen Mujahideen leader Ibn al-Khattab. Russian Special Forces killed al-Khattab in April 2002. He was a Chechen of Saudi origin and was the conduit to and intermediary for funds from "friendly" Arab states to finance his attacks, primarily against Russian military targets. Considered a legitimate target due to the town being part of a Russian military garrison, Kaspiysk was attacked previously in 1996 when an apartment building was blown up killing 68 members of the border guard and their families. Many observers note that the United States has found it expedient to ignore Russian atrocities in order to gain support for President Bush's "War on Terrorism." Maybe it is this policy of ignoring the friend's action and condemning the enemy's that wins the United States more enemies for future acts of terrorism. This observation and criticism could also be levied at the U.S. policy, or lack of a distinct policy, for the Middle East in 2002.

Russia–Free Market Economy and the Russian Mafia

Russia became a so-called democracy following the breakup of the Soviet Union. What, one must ask, happened to the KGB after the breakup? Organized crime in the Russian Federation was on the rise, with a police force ill equipped to respond. Interpol, on the other hand, was hard at work tracking the exploits of more than four hundred Russian international criminals, while the Office of International Criminal Justice estimated at least 4,000 organized crime syndicates operating in the Federation by 1996.

TERROR BRIEF 6–2

Apartment Bombings, Moscow

Three hundred civilians died in the first two weeks of September 1999 in bomb attacks targeting civilian apartment blocks in Moscow. Russian authorities place the blame for the devastating attacks on Islamic extremists based in the rebel republic of Chechnya. A massive police presence and sweeping checks of commercial properties has reaped some results. Police claim to have discovered 3.5 tons of explosives in a building on the outskirts of Moscow.

Source: Eighteen Die as fourth bomb blast rocks Russia: http://www.telegraph.co.UK September 17 1999.

With the breakup of the Soviet Union came the dissolution of the Soviet intelligence service (KGB). Their agents, however, did not fade into oblivion. Scratching the surface of Russian bureaucracy will uncover layers, like a Russian doll, of control dominated by former KGB operatives, many in local government and politics. Organized crime syndicates in the Russian Federation in collaboration with former KGB officers is probably a major factor in a booming trade in Soviet-made weaponry, not the least of which are nuclear capability products.

The Russian "Mafia's" links with former KGB operatives have led to the escalation of weapons sales to terror groups, and the Russian Mafia has moved from purely internal criminal activities to the exporting of terrorist weapons with mass destruction capability. Weapons of mass destruction have been on the market to the highest bidder and some of these sophisticated weapons have reached the hands of Third World countries. The potential for global conflict from these sales is yet to be realized and should not be minimized.

At the end of 1998, Russia was at the crossroads, on the road to reform, or possibly taking the long and winding path to anarchy and corruption. The lawless society in Russia has led criminal elements to feed on the possibilities of controlling the state and reaping the rewards from corrupt politicians. With the criminal element playing so large a part in the proceedings of daily life in Russia, it is no wonder that these elements will stop at nothing to achieve their goals. With the economy crumbling, any reform-style politician would be a target in 1998 Russia. On November 22, 1998, the staunch pro-democracy parliamentarian Galina Starovoitova, who was a vocal campaigner for human rights and against political corruption, was murdered in a scene reminiscent of a James Bond movie. She was shot three times in the head at close range as she entered her apartment building. Her campaign was instrumental in exposing corrupt local politicians, and it is believed that this led to her assassination. Starovoitova was well respected but in a minority of democracy reformers. The killing was done in a very professional manner and has the hallmarks of a gangland-style execution. In a country where few women rise to the heights of local and national politics, her passing is something of a watershed for Russian politics. What the outcome will be is uncertain, but the grip of the underworld on Russia seems to be excruciatingly strong. It was brutally summed up at her graveside by Yevgeny Primakov, the Russian Prime Minister, when he commented that the country was, "drifting towards fascism."[4]

Democracy, Free Market Economy and the Rule of Law are not words or statements that go hand in hand with everyday life in Russia in the new millennium. The widespread corruption that continues to manifest itself in both private and public organizations is as rampant as ever. Organized crime covers vast areas of the economy from diversion of collected revenues—a form of money laundering—and the defrauding of overseas aid donors. The illegal trade in arms dealing and the concern that al Qaeda followers would like to acquire nuclear capability suggest that Russia may be a possible source for such weaponry. Remember, too, the newspaper reports that handheld nuclear missiles are missing or unaccounted for. In either scenario, the threat from their mere existence will have many governments concerned. Many terrorist organizations—not just the Chechens—would welcome having this type of capability, even if it was only a threat.

CHECHNYA

A Mixed Background

The Czars began a three-hundred-year attempt to subjugate the Northern Caucasus in 1560. By 1585, Chechnya and other areas of the Caucasus had been conquered by the Ottoman Empire and represented its northern reach into what has become modern Russia. Under Ottoman rule, the Chechens adopted Islam. Russia continued its attempt to capture the area and finally forced the retreat of the Ottomans by 1785.

After winning the Caucasian war (1817–1864), the Russians deported hundreds of thousands of Chechens. In 1877, 1920, 1929, 1940 and 1943 the Chechens made unsuccessful attempts to rebel against the czars and then the communists. While most of the Chechen males were fighting against Hitler in the winter of 1943–44, Stalin ordered that Chechnya be obliterated. Villages were burned, 500,000 people were deported to Kazakhstan and Siberia and their land was given to non-Chechens. In 1957, the Chechens were allowed to return to their homeland. Dzhokhar Dudayev seized power in Chechnya in August 1991. After a popular vote elected him president that November, Dudayev declared independence from the Soviet Union, just a month before its collapse.

Problems in the Caucasus

In February 1994, Russian President Boris Yeltsin and President of the Republic of Tatarstan, Minitimir Shaimiev, initialed a treaty delineating a division of powers between the Russian national government and the government of Tatarstan. The treaty afforded Tatarstan a considerable amount of autonomy, and was welcomed by Yeltsin's Nationalities Minister, Sergei Shakhrai, as a "breakthrough." Kabardino-Balkaria and Bashkortostan followed in short order. These treaties represented a fine-tuning of Russia's evolving federation relations, the basic framework of which had been established by the new Russian Constitution of December 1993. The consolidation of Russia's territorial integrity was essential to prevent another Afghanistan failure to control the huge group of Islamic states within and without the vast Russian borders. Above all, there was the explosive situation in the North Caucasus. There, among other problems, the breakaway republic of Chechnya continued to refuse to consider itself a part of the new **Russian Federation**.

Moscow's previous response to Chechnya's challenge amounted to a policy of benign neglect toward Chechnya and its President, Dzhokhar Dudayev. Moscow allowed the republic to go its own way and even attempted periodically to enter into negotiations with Dudayev. The Russian government repeatedly asserted that under no condition would force be used to resolve their differences with the republic and expressed the hope that these treaties would serve as a model for finding a negotiated solution with Chechnya.

Even as words of encouragement were being spoken, Moscow began stepping up financial and military support for opposition forces to the government in Chechnya. Fighting in the republic intensified over the summer, leading to a major attack on Grozny in November by the combined forces of the Chechen opposition in an effort to overthrow Dudayev. Despite support from helicopters and aircraft with Russian markings, the attack failed. A little more than a week later, President Yeltsin issued a decree authorizing the government, including the military, to take all necessary steps to disarm "illegal armed formations" in the republic. Two days later, 40,000 Russian troops poured into Chechnya. It was a debacle and the Chechen rebels were able to send the demoralized Russian Army home in defeat.[5] In August 1994, the Russian government began military action to stop Chechnya's secession. Russian troops began aerial bombing and attacked the capital of Grozny in December and again in February 1995. Subsequently, the rebel Chechen government moved to the hills and Chechnya was put under an armed Russian occupation.

Regardless of whether Russia had a right to use force to defend its territorial integrity against Chechen secession, it is now clear in hindsight that the invasion was a terrible error. The viciousness of the war made it inconceivable that Chechnya will ever become a "normal" member of the Russian Federation, even if it is granted considerable autonomy and a treaty-based relationship with Moscow like that with Tatarstan. The hostility of the Chechen people toward Russia, deeply rooted before the conflict, has been immeasurably intensified by the brutality of the war and will not be ameliorated by Moscow's promises of financial aid to reconstruct the republic, assuming that Moscow is in a position to deliver on these promises, which it probably is not.

Moscow continues to make the full application of its constitution on Chechen soil as a condition of peaceful existence. With that caveat, the republic will remain a terrible burden on the Russian people, a political nightmare for whatever party is in power in Moscow, and a major and possibly decisive impediment to the preservation of Russian democracy.[6]

Chechnya is rapidly deteriorating into a state of civil war. In 1998 the beleaguered President, Aslan Maskhadov, was the focus of terrorist attacks by opposition forces. The Chechen situation remains tense as we go to press. It is doubtful if conditions there will improve as the U.N. focuses elsewhere in 2003.

Current Situation

Chechnya continues as a threat and a painful thorn in Russia's side. The fighting continues amid atrocities being committed by Russian troops in Chechnya. The Russian military in May 2002 openly proclaimed that they were clamping down on the vicious attacks of its soldiers against Chechens, however this proclamation seems not to have been entirely heeded by the soldiers themselves. Two weeks later, Russian soldiers seized five young men and methodically knifed them to death.[7]

The Russian army has now managed to fight two separate wars in Chechnya, the last ending in 2000. Chechens remained undaunted and throughout 2000 the war was still being taken to the Russian public. Bomb attacks continued in Moscow, the **Pushkin Square** bombing on August 8, 2000, that was detonated at the height of the evening rush hour, injuring more than ninety and killing twelve. On the same day, Chechen fighters killed twelve Russian soldiers in Eastern Chechnya. Whether the bomb came from Chechen militants or warring factions of the Russian Mafia has not become clear. The guilty party, from a Russian viewpoint, would necessarily be the Chechens. Chechnya barely functions and suffers from a ferocious economic embargo from Russia, which has seen most of its infrastructure either destroyed or decaying.

How many times have we heard the expression, "the world has changed since September 11"? Russia is now a staunch alley of the West, is friendly with NATO countries, and has provided logistical and tactical support to U.S. coalition troops engaged in fighting and deposing the Afghan Taliban regime. Even five years ago that kind of cooperation with the Russians probably would have been unthinkable, let alone believable. Russia also plans to establish a regionally deployed 'Rapid Response Force' in Kyrgyzstan ostensibly to fight against extreme Islamic rebels/terrorists/fighters. Establishing such a response force will allow the Russian military to be deployed more widely and also to regain some of its self respect. This Central Asian force, which will be located in the heart of Eurasia and likely staffed and commanded by Russian officers, will be supported by the other Eurasian signatories to the Collective Security Treaty of 1992, who agreed in May to coordinate their military tactical strength against the threat of insurgency from radical and extreme Islamic threats.

GEORGIA

The Pankisi Gorge area in Georgia is described at best as a lawless region and home to bandits, Arab and Chechen terrorists. This area, which sees little or no control exerted over it by the Government of Eduard Shevardnadze, could be a fertile region for terrorist training camps and for Chechen terrorists to launch attacks against Russian targets. The government in Georgia counts among the least stable in the entire Eastern-bloc region. Terrorism and controlling the scourge of the Pankisi Gorge is a problem not easily solved. The mere threat and obvious presence of Islamic extremist terrorists functioning in the area does nothing to assist the United States in its wider war on terror. As time passes, attempts by the government to crack down on this region have at best been weak and at worst downright pathetic.

Cache of weapons and explosives on display after Moscow theater siege October 26, 2002. Rebels were demanding an end to the war in Chechnya and had held 700 people hostage. (AP Photo/Alexander Zemlianichenko)

In the summer of 2002, Shevardnadze announced that his security forces would be cracking down on terrorists and others in the region of the Gorge. Following that announcement, troops moved into the region and a further proclamation from the Ministry of the Interior was released that simply stated "the information on the presence of a large number of armed terrorists is invalid." The Pankisi Gorge is tough terrain for troops and security forces, so it is highly likely that with the advance warning from the government, any terrorists have gone to ground. Human intelligence coming from this region indicates significant numbers of Islamic extremists operating in the Pankisi Gorge so the Georgian claims may be out of line with the reality for this area. The presence of Islamic militants, particularly Chechens, has been an ongoing issue since the mid 1990s. The national TV station in Georgia announced in August 2002 that the Pankisi region was home to a few al Qaeda sympathizers and criminals and bandits. This seems out of context with other intelligence that has come out of this region.

After 9–11, the Georgian president supported the United States-led War on Terrorism. Earlier in the year, the United States sent special ops troops to train in Georgia to make sure the local forces were able to respond to and root out terrorists in the Pankisi region. What has turned out to be a fiasco can be blamed on many variables, including corrupt officials, and the fear of reprisals from Chechen crime groups who are somewhat aligned with the Chechen extremists, and who are certainly capable of targeting officials in Georgia for reprisals.

With no serious outcome to the attempt by the Georgian security forces to crack down or otherwise disperse any terrorists makes the region a prime location for Islamic militants to continue to regroup and train for future operations. The reality appears to be that al Qaeda can operate with impunity in the republic of Georgia. As for diplomacy and the need to trade off political hot potatoes, the Government of Russia has sought to have a free hand in handling its Chechen problems without interference from the United States, in exchange for Russia's support of the American campaign against Iraq.

YUGOSLAVIA

From World War I to Ethnic Cleansing

Yugoslavia as a nation was established by the League of Nations out of the union of territories dating back to the end of World War I in 1918. Bordered on the east with the Soviet Bloc countries of Romania, Hungary and Bulgaria, the Communist State of Yugoslavia encompassed six separate republics mainly founded on their ethnic or religious background. The area in question has been populated for at least 100,000 years.[8] The first groups of Slavs moved to the area in around the fifth century. They migrated from regions now known as southern Poland and the republics of the Russian Empire. Differing groups

Map of border region—Kosovo/Serbia/Macedonia.

of Slavs formed their own enclaves and independent states. Serbians founded Serbia and Croats founded Croatia; however, from about 1400 onwards the southern Slavs were ruled by foreign powers.

The Turkish Empire controlled Serbian areas, while Hungary and Austria ruled Slovenia and Croatia respectively. As the centuries moved by, the desire for a united region became a goal of Slovenia and Croatia. The movement to unite sparked an incident that was to change the destiny of Europe and the fate of millions. On June 28, 1914, in Sarajevo, a Serbian terrorist named Gavrilo Princip from Bosnia assassinated the **Archduke Franz Ferdinand** of Austria-Hungary. Because of pacts between European nations this single terrorist act fueled the start of the Great War 1914–1918. Yugoslavia was so named by King Alexander I, in 1929. The King ruled briefly as an absolute dictator, however dissident Croats terrorists assassinated him in 1934.

To say that modern-day terrorism played a part in the structure of a nation such as Yugoslavia would not be far from the mark. Two resistance groups fought against each other as well as the occupying Germans during World War II. The partisans led by Josip Tito and his communist party, and the Chetniks who supported the monarchy under King Peter.

By the end of World War II, the **partisans** (terrorists?) under Tito established a communist government and on November 29, 1945, the region became the Federal Peoples Republic of Yugoslavia, thus abolishing the monarchy and sending King Peter into permanent exile. As will be seen throughout, many dictators have felt the need to dominate and destroy all opponents of the regime. Yugoslavia under Marshall Tito was no different, and opponents of the communist government were either imprisoned, killed or exiled. Tito declared a one-party communist state. Although a communist state in its own right, Yugoslavia was not a puppet of the Soviet Union. In fact, after the late 1940s, Yugoslavia and the Soviet Union severed ties to one another. During the Cold War, Yugoslavia became a moderate voice.

Modern Day Problems

The people of Yugoslavia split on ethnic lines into the six republics, with Slovenia in the north, and Croatia on its southern border. To the south of Croatia is the area of Bosnia-Herzegovina. Immediately to the east are Serbia and Montenegro. Civil strife between these ethnic regions has, until recently, not been cause for serious concern. Although nationalist tendencies have been in the forefront of Yugoslavia's political history for the last quarter of the twentieth century, they had not erupted into violent conflict until the civil war of the 1990s. Under the rule of Marshall Tito, the country and its republics had been forced to keep their nationalist feelings in check. Tito's aim was to do away with old ethnic divisions and create a social revolution. When Tito died in 1980, the old nationalist desires of the republics were reborn to a certain extent. Up to this time Serbs, Croats and Muslims had lived side by side in peaceful coexistence.

With tough economic times upon them, the Yugoslavs protested Communist policy and began to demand changes to a political system that had failed to permit other political parties. Nationalism was therefore on the rise for the six republics of Yugoslavia.

TERROR BRIEF 6–3

Genocide and Ethnic Cleansing

Genocide, as detailed by international convention in 1948, is a crime. It is defined as the mistreatment or extermination of national or religious groups, generally attributed to a government practice rather than to an individual. *Genos* in Greek means "race" or "tribe". The Latin word *cide* has the meaning "killing." What has been happening in modern day Yugoslavia has been just that, genocide, but more often referred to as "ethnic cleansing." Yugoslavia has a broad spectrum of ethnic and religious groups, and the recent fighting and killing is all about ethnicity, self-determination and land. In Bosnia, ethnic cleansing carried out by the Serbians against Muslims and Croats was done to drive those ethnic groups from the disputed areas, and leave behind a racially pure Serbian region. The terror that this caused was enough to force the population to leave and become refugees. While Aushwitz and Buchenvald were synonymous with the atrocities and terror of the Germans and the genocide practiced on the Jews of Europe, so too will names like Kosovo pass into the history books as examples of terror practiced on ethnic groups. Serbian control of Kosovo was little challenged by the Kosovo Liberation Army (KLA). However, the KLA was not a particularly large force or even a serious threat to the Serbian authorities. The group garnered support from the villages, and it is believed that they were not well organized and amounted to about one hundred in strength. The Serbian police, on the other hand, numbered more than 100,000, with support from the federal army for logistics and weaponry. The KLA was a small destabilizing factor in Kosovo Province.

Acts of political terrorism in the region have been mostly nonexistent. What has been occurring is a bloody civil war, pitching neighbor against neighbor, almost a Balkan version of Northern Ireland. All sides in this conflict, however, have used different tactics from those used in the Northern Ireland conflict. Reports out of the various regions cite incidents of "ethnic cleansing," a sanitized term for such extreme measures as the extermination of whole villages. This region of nationalist conflict and resulting civil war has not had the hallmark of terrorist activity as has occurred in other areas, as we shall see in Palestine. One exception was the attempted assassination by bombing of Kiro Gligorov, President of Macedonia, an event that had the clear markings of terrorist action.

The hatred between the Albanians and Serbs was illuminated by the reported atrocities by both sides. In all respects conflict had turned into a regional war. The lightly armed freedom fighters as they were termed, not terrorists, were up against tanks and heavy artillery. Through the period of the last decade, the Serbian government of Slobodan Milosevic had been criticized for its treatment of ethnic minorities, especially in the minority dominated areas of Vojvodina, Sandak and Kosovo.[9] Milosevic came to power in 1989 and played a dominant role in the conflicts in both Bosnia and Croatia supplying both military and financial support to the Serb nationalist campaigns in the two republics. Milosevic supported proposals from the international community for a brokered peace plan in 1994, however, it was not well received by the Bosnian Serb leadership. This failure prompted Milosevic to close the border between the two republics. In 1995 Milosevic signed the Dayton Peace Accord with Bosnian President Alija Izetbegovic and Croatian President Franjo Tudjman. Full diplomatic relations were restored the following year between the former Yugoslavia, now the Federal Republic of Yugoslavia (FRY) and Bosnia Herzegovina. As for the region of Kosovo it had resisted the Serbian government since the province lost its autonomy and the formation of the KLA in the mid 1990s began to target and attack the Serbian police. The response was swift as the Serbian police and Yugoslav military attacked the ethnic Albanian community in early 1998, forcing nearly a quarter of a million to flee from their homes. At this point the representatives from the North Atlantic Treaty Organization (NATO) threatened to use force to curb the brutal assault by Yugoslavian forces against the ethnic Albanians. Throughout much of 1998 and into early 1999 peace talks were attempted but failed resulting in a NATO force led by the United States initiating a bombing campaign against Yugoslav military targets. This had the opposite effect on the Milosevic government, which intensified its campaign by burning entire villages and forcing the ethnic minority Albanians in Kosovo to flee to Albania, Montenegro and Macedonia. Six hundred and fifty thousand were forced from Kosovo between March 1998 and April 1999.[10] Many unsubstantiated reports of brutal treatment, rape and torture of civilians in the Albanian region of Kosovo were beginning to emerge when by June 1999 the Serbian government agreed to a peace plan for Kosovo. NATO's bombing campaign was suspended on June 10, 1999 and the United Nations Security Council authorized peacekeepers to enter the province. Milosevic lost the federal presidential election in September 2000 to a candidate of a coalition of opposition parties called the Democratic Opposition of Serbia (DOS). In December 2000 DOS won one hundred and seventy-six of the two hundred and fifty seats in Serbia's National Assembly. In March 2001 the Serbian government arrested Milosevic on charges of abuse of power and embezzlement and in June the same year following pledges of economic support to the tune of one billion dollars by western governments. Milosevic was extradited to the International Criminal Tribunal for the Former Yugoslavia (ICTY) in The Hague, The Netherlands to stand trial for war crimes.[11]

The actions of the Serbian government almost mirror the Nazi tactics of World War II, with the rounding up and arrest of those who have given any assistance to the so-called rebels. Those arrested have been doctors and aid workers, lawyers and journalists.

BULGARIA

State-Sponsored Terrorism

The debate on the level of effort conducted by Moscow in the arena of state-sponsored terrorism can be theorized at length; however, there is considerable belief that its communist neighbor Bulgaria was active in this area, possibly on its behalf. The extent of Bulgaria's involvement in state-sponsored terrorism is an issue worth discussion. During the Cold War, Moscow's attempts to destabilize the western democracies involved the use of terror tactics against not only nations but also symbolic personages. In Rome, Italy, on May 13, 1981, a Turkish Nationalist attempted to assassinate Pope John Paul II in St. Peter's Square. The Pope was shot and his would-be assassin arrested. The ensuing investigation uncovered a link to Bulgaria; the Pope's assailant **Mehmet Ali Agca** is believed to have had an accomplice in place to aid in his escape from Italy. The accomplice, Oral Celik, escaped capture by leaving the country in a Bulgarian Embassy diplomatic truck. The following year, a Bulgarian State Airline official was charged in Rome in connection with the assassination attempt.[12] Further evidence of Bulgaria's complicity to export terror is seen in the actions of Sallah Wakkas, a Syrian national operating in Athens. He had purchased more than $50 million worth of Soviet-made weapons and ammunition from a Bulgarian weapons company, **KINTEX**.[13]

Further involvement was uncovered when Greek customs seized a ship en route to North Yemen in 1984. The contents of a consignment of oil tankers revealed huge quantities of weapons and ammunition. The ship's cargo of trucks had been consigned by the Bulgarian State cargo agency, Bulfracht, while the paperwork for the consignment was produced by Inflot, the Bulgarian state shipping agency. It must be assumed that this arms shipment was destined for the Palestine Liberation Organization training camps in North Yemen. One must assume that these were just an example of many other shipments that were not intercepted. In addition, Bulgaria's involvement in drug trafficking has been fairly well documented. Drugs of course can be used in the sale or barter for weapons and explosives. KINTEX of Bulgaria has been a supplier of heroin and morphine to Kurdish dissidents in Turkey, and these drugs have been used to trade for weapons.[14]

The Bulgarian tactics of inflicting terror on its own subjects and also striking out at dissidents in European locations, came to sudden and painful light with two attacks on Bulgarian dissidents in Paris and London. On August 26, 1978, a Bulgarian defector to the west and a former well-known television personality, Vladimir Kostov, was jabbed with a poison-tipped umbrella, laced with the poison **ricin.** He survived the attack, but an incident in London involving the same method, against outspoken novelist and playwright, Georgi Markov, resulted in his death.

Further evidence of the Bulgarian attempts at destabilization revolves around their shadowy involvement in the kidnapping by the Red Brigade of the American NATO General, James Dozier. From evidence deduced by the examining judge at the trial of the Red Brigade ringleader, Antonio Savasta, Bulgaria played a part in the interrogation of the general, as well as offering logistical and training support to the Red Brigade.

SUMMARY

Russia as we know it today has undergone enormous change. The Cold War is over and Russia and the United States are on friendly terms in the War on Terrorism. No longer is it a communist-dominated federation; no longer is it the great bear of the east that wielded so much power and influence in the world due to military strength. No longer does it have the respect of its neighbors or its enemies! Russia is, at the end of the twentieth century, a country in turmoil. Its social and economic problems are clear for all to see. A monetary system in tatters and an economy in ruins are being bailed out by the International Monetary Fund. The hopes and fears of a nation rest on how the political games are played out. Many questions are as yet unanswered. What is certain is that Russia is experiencing levels of organized crime with Russian Mafia-style syndicates permeating all levels of the Russian society. Drugs and weapons are freely available, and a dissatisfied and poorly paid military machine has ground to a halt. This military machine, however, has access to weapons of mass destruction. Some are missing; who has them and who controls them is open for discussion. The possibilities are endless for a criminal with access to this kind of weaponry. Chechnya has problems of its own making. This Russian state seems headed towards Islamic fundamentalism, and the shadowy terrorist group Hezbollah, with sponsorship from Iran, has set up active cells around the world with ruthless efficiency. Whether what we are seeing in Chechnya is terrorism or an all-out fight for a country's survival is an open question, and certainly since the events of 9–11 the Russians have seized the opportunity to use military excesses to press home any advantages they can against the rebel state, under the banner of a War on Terrorism. The region of Macedonia has been devastated by sporadic wars within its borders; the term "ethnic cleansing" is now used to describe the mass murder of a particular ethnic group. The Kosovo Liberation Army lives to fight another day, and its Albanian support in the region is strong. No doubt in the years to come, if the direct fighting ends and some form of lasting peace can be achieved, there is no doubt that sporadic violence, bombings and assassination will be a pattern of daily life in these areas. Wars fought on ethnic lines, where the wounds run deep, take decades to heal. This particular wound is wide open and bleeding.

TERMS TO REMEMBER

Archduke Franz Ferdinand
Boevaya Oranisatsia
Bolshevik
Cheka
KGB
Killer College
KINTEX
Mehmet Ali Agca
Partisans
Pushkin Square
Russian Federation
Sergei Kirov
Stalin
The People's Will

REVIEW QUESTIONS

1. Discuss the reasons for the Great Terror.
2. Describe how Joseph Stalin controlled the Russian people and the military.
3. What do think is meant by a "scorched earth" policy in the Serbian area of the former Yugoslavia?
4. Discuss what the events of 9–11 have meant for Russia's war on terrorism.
5. Discuss the reasons for the NATO campaign in the former Republic of Yugoslavia.

ENDNOTES

1. *The New Encyclopaedia Britannica,* volume 8. Encyclopaedia Britannica Inc. USA, 1985, p. 298.
2. The Internet. "Secret Police," *Revelations from the Russian Archives,* Library of Congress, 1996. http://leweb2.loc.gov/cgi-bin/query.
3. David Yallop. *Tracking the Jackal,* Random House, 1993, p. 20.
4. "Russia's criminal class delivers a fatal blow," *The Vancouver Sun,* November 27, 1998, p. A21.
5. Edward Walker. "The Crisis in Chechnya." *Center for Slavic and Eastern European Studies Newsletter.* Spring, 1995.
6. Edward Walker. "What's Next in Chechnya." *Association for the Study of Nationalities.* http://www.nationalities.org.
7. *U.S. News & World Report,* May 27, 2002. Putin's War, p. 26.
8. Araminta Wordsworth. "Sinking further in a morass of brutality," Canada's *National Post,* Newspaper. Thursday, December 10, 1998, p. A15.
9. Serbia History-Encarta online Encyclopedia http://encarta.msn.com.
10. Ibid.
11. Ibid.
12. Clare Sterling, "Bulgaria Hired Agca to Kill Pope," *New York Times,* June 10, 1984.
13. Philip Sherwell. "NATO planes strike on Kosovo," *The Weekly Telegraph,* The Telegraph Group Ltd., June 9–15, 1998, p. 19, issue #359.
14. "Bulgarian Connection to Illicit Arms Trade," *Wall Street Journal,* August 10, 1984.

7 North Africa and the Middle East

"Clearly substantial resettlement of the Israeli civilian population in occupied territories, including East Jerusalem, is illegal under the Geneva Convention. . . . Indeed the presence of these settlements is seen by my government as an obstacle to peace".

William S. Scranton: Former U.S. Ambassador to the U.N., 1976

OVERVIEW

Peace and terrorism are two very familiar words when used in the context of the Middle East, especially when it involves Israel and the Palestinians. The peace accords and the innumerable sessions proclaiming a new round of talks to resolve the question of a Palestinian homeland and Israeli security will be examined with some detail in this chapter. The resistance to the presence of Israeli settlers in Palestine and the effect this policy has on Israel's security and response by the men of terror in Palestine will also be discussed. Israel's right to exist and the threats and assaults it has had to withstand for over half a century form much of the basis for terror attacks and extreme Islamic movements that have been spawned with an ultimate goal being the destruction of the Jewish state. For the Palestinians, it is issues surrounding their rights and freedoms, justice as well as land; Palestinians have been depopulated and to all intents and purposes terrorized out of their homes to make room for the Jewish settlers, which has persisted contrary to international law for half a century. Syria, under the new leadership of the son of the late President Assad, will be discussed. Although this state has not been directly involved in terror, the country is home to various terror organizations that continue to ply their hateful trade, predictably against Israel and the West.

ISRAEL AND ITS RIGHT TO EXIST

The continuing violence which is the Middle East crisis—seen daily in the news media—resonates with the issues surrounding the "security" of the State of Israel and "hope" for the Palestinians, in the words of President George W. Bush. Pro-Israel lobbyists in the United States contend that, "U.S. aid to Israel enhances American national security interests, by strengthening our only domestic ally in an unstable and vital region of the world." However, the fact is that 17% of the entire U.S. foreign aid budget goes toward support of Israel, which does not include the $2.5 billion received in military support.[1] The ongoing issue surrounding the building of Israeli settlements in Palestinian

Authority areas continues. Since 1967, Israel has continued to create settlements in the territories. ". . . .*the creation of a viable Jewish state . . . . In an adequate area of Palestine instead of in the whole of Palestine would be acceptable,*" stated President Harry S Truman in 1946.[2] The question of inflexibility on behalf of Israel and the question of Palestinian refugees must not be viewed as a new phenomenon. As far back as the creation of Israel, the United States has been fielding the criticism and often the blame for Israel . . . "her belligerence and her arrogance for cold-bloodedness of her attitude toward refugees."[3] The question of Palestinian statehood remains as much in focus today as it was half a century ago. In 1948, once the United States and Britain appreciated that the 1947 U.N. Partition Plan had failed, they concluded that the best political solution—for both the United States and Britain—was to completely deny the Palestinians their own state. Under this Anglo-U.S. strategy, the Palestinians would simply disappear by being absorbed in neighboring Arab states, mainly Transjordan, as it was then known, it is now called the Hashemite Kingdom of Jordan.[4] Land is not the only issue surrounding the Palestinian/Israeli problem, but the retention of land seized beyond the U.N. mandate in 1947 and also following the six-day war remains a continuing stumbling block along with civil rights, freedoms and liberty for Palestinians.

Early History

The Jewish people (Hebrews) settled in the region of Palestine about 1200 years before the birth of Christ. From about 70 AD to 700 AD the region was under the control of the Romans who dispersed most of the Hebrews from the region. With the collapse of the Roman Empire, the Ismaelites (Arabs) settled the region and remained resident until the Turkish (Ottoman) Empire subjugated them in 1516.

Political Considerations

In order to fully appreciate the complexities of this unique region one must first look at what took place due to imperialist influences and designs on this region at the time of World War I. By the latter part of the 1800s, the Ottoman Empire, controlled by Turkey, was in total disarray and internal factional disturbances were continuing within the realm as Turkey's influences waned. The Turkish Empire bordered Persia, which was under the imperialistic controls of the Russians and British. The dwindling Turkish Ottoman Empire comprised a significant section of the Arab territories of the Middle East and this area was, by the start of World War I, an area ripe for the plucking. Britain most certainly had designs on the Arab lands as did the French and Russians. As Turkey was fighting on the side of the German Empire against Britain and France, it suited Britain to turn the Arabs against the Turks. In order to sustain the Jews on the side of Britain, the British Government issued the **Balfour Declaration**, named for the British Foreign Secretary, Arthur James Balfour.

The Declaration reads as follows:

> "His Majesty's Government view with favour the establishment in Palestine of a national home for the Jewish people, and will use their best endeavours to facilitate the achievement of this object, it being clearly understood that nothing shall be done which may prejudice the rights of non-Jewish communities in Palestine, or the rights and political status enjoyed by Jews in any other country."

This Declaration, from the British point of view, was to win support for the war from Jews in Europe and more particularly in the wealthy Jewish neighborhoods in the United States. The Jews viewed this as tacit agreement for their own homeland in Palestine, while the Arabs read a different meaning into the wording. The Arabs believed that they had to agree to any terms put forward before an agreement on self-determination of lands for the Jews was realized. The Arabs fought in the belief that they were assured independence; the Jews in Palestine offered to raise troops to fight on the side of the British.

With the promise of independence to both Zionists and Arabs alike, the British Government had unwittingly sowed the seeds for an almost ceaseless succession of wars. In the decades to come, the Jews and Arabs would fight conventional wars that would then turn into what is now modern-day terrorism, a situation that endured for the remainder of the twentieth century. With the two groups focused on fighting the Turks, Britain had achieved its immediate aim of control of the region and was assured support from both. It was a short-sighted political decision which, it will be seen, left the Middle East with the distinction of being a home base and fertile breeding ground for future generations of terrorists. To many people, the very name "Palestinian" is synonymous with terrorism. This adequately portrays the immense problem that beset this area of the Middle East. British strategic aims at the end of World War I were to solidify a friendly presence in Palestine to ensure protection of its routes into Africa and to the East into India. Of major importance in this would be the Suez Canal and the major shipping route from the Indian

TERRORISM PLAYER 7-1

The Earl of Balfour (1848–1930)

Arthur James Balfour was born in Scotland and educated at Eton College and Cambridge. He was elected to Parliament in 1874. Prime Minister of Great Britain from 1902–1905, he was for twenty years the leader of Britain's Conservative Party. As Foreign Secretary in the Government of David Lloyd George, he issued the Balfour Agreement of 1917, which declared and supported a Jewish homeland in Palestine.

Source: World Book. *World Book Encyclopaedia,* Volume 2. p. 40.

Ocean to the Mediterranean. The British set up Arab kingdoms after the war, and in such a fashion that strong traditional family groups controlled them. Emerging were the states of Saudi Arabia, Iraq and Syria.

Settlements and Terror

Israel's history is founded on its struggle to exist in a hostile environment, surrounded by unfriendly neighbors and Arab refugees. Since the 1948 Arab-Israeli war, the areas occupied by Israel have seen countless incursions by Arab refugees particularly from Jordan and Egypt. Many of these incursions were raids by "foraging" Arabs returning to their home villages, stopping en-route to rob and steal. Many attacks on civilians in Jewish-occupied regions resulted, and it is from these early incursions that the Israelis initiated various response mechanisms. In order to prevent and deter such actions, the Israelis adopted a policy of destroying abandoned Arab villages along the border region and establishing Israeli settlements in their place. With the numbers of dead Israeli civilians running into the hundreds by 1953, the Israeli Government established **Unit 101,** which can be defined as a special operations/commando type of retaliatory unit. This unit was commanded and led by Ariel Sharon on orders from Prime Minister Ben Gurion in August 1953. The Unit drew much criticism due to deaths of innocent civilians, in particular the **Qibya Operation,** which left almost seventy civilians dead. However, its decisive style of action developed in its later attacks against heavily guarded military objectives became one of the fundamental cornerstones in the development of the Israeli Defense Force (IDF). The brutal nature of the attacks mainly against civilian targets eventually led to the abandonment of Unit 101 in 1954, integrating it into the 202 Paratroop Brigade. The Israeli government refused to sanction attacks against civilian targets. Unit 101's belief was that the villages being attacked were hideouts for terrorists. These actions, led by General Ariel Sharon, have come back to haunt the leader who is now the Prime Minister of Israel, and the intifada actions of 2000–2003.

The Stern Gang

The so-called "Stern Gang," was an extreme right wing organization founded by Avraham Stern in 1940 as a split off from the Irgun. Irgun was a Jewish terrorist group organized in the 1930s to defend the Jewish settlers from Arab attacks, and after World War II used their skills to attack the British in Palestine. Their vicious attacks ended with the massacre of two hundred and fifty Arab civilians at Deir Yassin outside Jerusalem in 1948. This single action prompted Israeli Prime Minister David Ben Gurion to call for Irgun to be disbanded and to be absorbed into the Haganah Army which was the forerunner to the Israeli Defence Forces. Stern was killed by the British forces in 1944, but the gang continued under the leadership of Israel Eldad, Natan Yellin-Mor, and Yitzhak Shamir, who became the Prime Minister of Israel 40 years later.

Two notable assassinations are credited to the Stern Gang. On November 6, 1944, they killed the British resident Minister for the Middle East, Lord

TERRORISM BYTE 7–1

Carlos the Jackal

Ilich Ramirez Sanchez, alias Carlos the Jackal, has reportedly issued a call for "protracted people's war, without boundaries" to be directed against Israel and the United States. According to press reports, Carlos wrote the letter to George Habash, the Damascus-based head of the Popular Front for the Liberation of Palestine (PFLP), following the death of Abu Ali Mustafa in Ramallah. According to the Reuters news service, Sanchez's lawyers released the letter to the media and confirmed its authenticity. "The deceitful 'peace process' has come to a pitiful demise. People's resistance in Palestine, armed operations worldwide, are the alternative to surrender," Carlos wrote. According to European press sources, Sanchez signed the letter, "Allahu Akhbar!" and "Yours in Revolution." Carlos is currently serving a life sentence in a French prison for the 1975 killing of two French intelligence agents.

Source: www.emergency.com–ERRI Counter Terrorism Archive.

Moyne, and the U.N. Special Mediator for Palestine, Count Folke Bernadotte on September 17,1948. The *Deir Yassin* massacre in 1948 also involved the Stern Gang, but the much larger Irgun was the main perpetrator of that massacre. Both Stern and Irgun were in existence prior to the formation of the State of Israel and both sought the formation of the Jewish State through actions that are considered terrorism and which were mainly directed against the British mandate in Palestine. The Stern Gang's terror attacks were against the British and not the Arab communities. Discussion of the approaches made by Stern to the Nazis is controversial due to their very abhorrent nature; maybe it was a case in 1939 that his enemy's enemy was therefore Stern's friend. Stern could likely only consider this in terms of the liberation of the region from British control.

Israeli land acquired during the 1967 Six-Day War dramatically altered the borders of Israel. As a result, Israel now controlled, at the brief war's end, some 20,870 square miles of newly acquired territory. Israel's original size, under the 1947 U.N. Partition Plan, was limited to 5,900 square miles, and had been added to following the fighting in 1948 to a total of 7,800 square miles. The new total of land under Israeli control in 1967 grew to 28,870 square miles, nearly five times its original size.[5] Settlements continued to be created and Palestinians were dispossessed of their land as Israel continued its expansionism. Condemnation of Israel for its actions came from the United Nations in the form of Resolutions, which in most cases were vetoed by Israel's staunchest ally, the United States. However, in March 1976 the United States finally condemned these settlements as being both illegal and an obstacle to peace. But, by the time of the U.S. declaration, there were about sixty-eight settlements in the territories, not counting Jerusalem. In condemnation of the Israeli action William W Scranton, U.S. Ambassador to the United Nations, informed the Security Council:

"Next I turn to the question of Israeli settlements in the occupied territories. Again, my government believes that international law sets the appropriate standards. An occupier must maintain the occupied areas as intact and unaltered as possible, without interfering with the customary life of the area, and any changes must be necessitated by the immediate needs of the occupation and be consistent with international law. The Fourth Geneva Convention speaks directly to the issue of population transfer in Article 49. . . . Clearly then substantial resettlement of the Israeli population in the occupied territories, including East Jerusalem, is illegal under the convention and cannot be considered to have prejudged the outcome of future negotiations between the parties or the location of the borders of states of the Middle East. Indeed, the presence of these settlements is seen by my government as an obstacle to the success of the negotiations for a just and final peace between Israel and its neighbors."[6]

Israeli expansion has continued in spite of these words spoken twenty-seven years ago. The Palestinians are under the control of Israeli military occupying forces in the West Bank. This of course does nothing to assure Israeli peace and, in the words of Scranton, the settlements are an obstruction to a peace accord. In February 1989, Prime Minister Yitzak Rabin assured a "Peace Now" delegation that negotiations (with the Palestinians) were only "low level discussions" that avoided any serious issues and granted Israel "at least a year" to resolve the problem (presumably by force). Rabin further stated, "The inhabitants of the territories are subject to harsh military and economic pressure, in the end they will be broken".[7] The peace accords of the 1990s that were drawn up, in Oslo in particular, have been so encumbered as to make it virtually impossible to determine what concessions if any had been made by Israel. This is due directly to the conditions, entailments and qualifications to such a point Palestinians could not feel that they enjoyed even a semblance of self-determination. From the above it is not difficult to see why terrorism has been seen as a tool, and likely viewed by Palestinians as the only tool; they have to make their views and issues clear. Not only to the Israeli public, but also to the world. Maybe the actions of suicide terrorists on 9–11 were seen as an opportunity for the Israeli government to bury the intifada once and for all. In the week following 9–11, the Israelis took their war on terror directly into Palestinian territory. The Israeli army killed twenty-eight Palestinians and mounted sixteen incursions into Palestinian Authority areas. The response to the swiftness of the Israeli attacks and incursion forced Arafat to declare a ceasefire on all fronts and expressed readiness to enlist in America's coalition for "ending terrorism against unarmed innocent civilians." Following this the Palestinian Authority leader warned Islamic Jihad, Hamas and others not to give "pretexts" that would aid Mr. Sharon's designs.

Although they heeded the call from Arafat and ended the firing on Jewish settlements from Palestinian areas, they did not agree to end armed actions in defense of Palestinian towns still under occupation. These groups also affirmed that they would respond if Israel acted against them or their people. On September 24, 2001, the Israeli army established a twenty-mile "closed military zone" along the West Bank's northern border with Israel. This was ostensibly established to prevent suicide bombers infiltrating into Israeli territory.[8]

Regional Map Israel—Gaza Strip/West Bank.

The latest test of the Israeli's will came in the surprising events of September 2000, which triggered the second intifada uprising, attacks by suicide bombers and rioting that has continued off and on through 2002. The latest intifada began on September 29, 2000, the Muslim day of prayer. Israeli Prime Minister, Ehud Barak, dispatched a military force, led by Defense Minister Ariel Sharon, to the Al Aqsa compound. Sharon strode into the *Haram al-Sharif* (The Noble Sanctuary) in what was designed to be a gesture to assert his rights as an Israeli to visit this Muslim holy place. It was this single act that seems to have sparked the beginning of the second intifada. Sharon can hardly be described as a statesman whose actions were likely to endear him to Palestinians in general. His reputation was mainly due to his checkered career, in particular his questionable involvement in the Sabra and Shatila refugee camp massacres in Beirut in 1982.

Throughout the latter half of 2001 and throughout 2002 the Israeli government held the Palestinian Authority's leader, Yassir Arafat, personally responsible for terrorist and suicide attacks against Israel. Israel adopted the military option to attack specific "terror" targets inside the Palestinian controlled areas. In January 2002 the Israeli Air force used F-16s in dropping bombs on Arafat's compound in Ramallah. Most of the military actions had been in response to Palestinian suicide attacks against Israeli targets. Israel also used targeted assassinations to deter, destroy and remove Hamas militant leaders with much success.

Irgun Zvaileumi (NMO, National Military Organization)

The **NMO** was an umbrella organization, and Stern's group came within its sphere of influence. Over the years of the mid 1940s Stern broke away almost completely, and the Night Squads were under the control of a terrorist, in the view of the British, named Menachem Begin. The term Special Night Squads originates from an invention of the British Army in Palestine in 1938 when Orde Wingate set up plans using British soldiers, members of Haganah and the Jewish Settlement Police to combat nighttime incursions by Arabs into northern Palestine. Irgun operated exclusively in Palestine as a Jewish group for the establishment of a modern day Israel. Their main targets were the resident Arab Palestinians and the occupying British Army in Palestine. Bombings were the order of the day and the two pronged attacks were designed to have two legitimate aims for the Jews. The first was to destabilize the British presence in the region and make it costly for the British to retain a presence. As seen above, the effect on the demoralized Palestinians was to produce a mass exodus from the area. Several notable members of Irgun played an important role over the following years in the development and political status of Israel. These included Menachem Begin, who would one day become Israeli Prime Minister, the charismatic Moshe Dyan, later to become Chief of Staff, and Ariel Sharon. The second, more obvious reason was to make life in Palestine extremely unpleasant for the Palestinians. With the agreement on partition by the United Nations, the terrorists of the Irgun began to immediately attack and kill Arab families and individuals who remained in the Jewish sector.

The Continuing Threat to Israel from Terrorism

The difficulties in realizing why peace cannot be found under the efforts of any of the Peace Agreements of the last decade, and those being lauded as this is written, is the credible threat of Hamas and its long-stated aim of the destruction of Israel. Maybe if the Hamas Charter was not so implicit, it could be a viable alternative to the Palestinian Authority to negotiate with Israel, however it is inconceivable that Israel would desire to 'sit down' and bargain for peace with a group whose avowed mission is Israel's destruction.

The following groups have been involved in modern day terrorism since the 1960s and they and their spin-off groups pose the most serious threats to Israel's security. Much is made of Ariel Sharon's insistence in 2002 that there be a cessation of terror attacks for at least a week before Israel will consider any negotiations with the Palestinians. Hamas continues to threaten suicide attacks against Israel, and Israel, the most powerful military force in the region, continues to target Hamas operatives in Palestine—creating a cycle of bloodshed and violence that will continue for decades to come. The ability of Yasir Arafat to make any solid headway in controlling, arresting and prosecuting terrorists from the various subgroups in the region has been exacerbated by the Israeli military stranglehold on the occupied territories and the destruction of the Palestinian economic infrastructure. That is not to say that if the military options on the Israelis' side had not taken place, Arafat would have succeeded in curtailing the suicide attacks against Israeli targets. In fact the opposite is the more likely scenario.

Ariel Sharon

Ariel (Arik) Sharon (Shinerman) (born September 27, 1928 -) became the Prime Minister of Israel on February 17, 2001. Sharon was born in Kfar Malal in 1928. In 1942, at the age of 14, he joined the Haganah. At the creation of Israel (and Haganah's transformation into the Israeli Defense Force) Sharon was a platoon commander in the Alexandroni brigade. He was severely wounded in the Second Battle of Latrun, but healed from his injuries. In 1949 he was promoted to a company commander, and in 1951 to an intelligence officer. He then took leave to begin studies of history and Middle Eastern culture at the Hebrew University of Jerusalem. A year and a half later, he was asked to return to active service in the rank of major, as the head of the new Unit 101.

On its own right, during the first five months, and as a part of a paratroop brigade for two more years, the unit completed a series of daring raids that helped restore Israeli citizens' morale and renew the Israeli deterrent image. However, the unit was also criticized for initially targeting civilians as well as the Arab armies, resulting in the widely condemned Qibya Operation in autumn of 1953, in which more than sixty Jordanian civilians were killed in an ambush of Arab Legion forces. The investigation showed that the order to maximize casualties was not given by Sharon, but by one of his superiors. Shortly afterwards, Unit 101 was merged into the 202nd Paratrooper Brigade (Sharon eventually becoming the latter's commander), which continued to attack military targets only, culminating with the attack on Kalkiliya Police in autumn 1956.

Sharon was a member of the Knesset 1973–1974, and again from 1977-present. In 1975–1976, he served as the security adviser to Prime Minister Yitzak Rabin. He then served as Minister of Agriculture (1977–1981), and as Defense Minister (1981–1983) in Menachem Begin's Likud government. During the Israeli invasion of Lebanon in 1982, while Ariel Sharon was Defense Minister, a massacre of several hundred Palestinians in the Sabra and Shatila refugee camps in Beirut was carried out by the Phalanges, a Lebanese-Christian militia allied with Israel. The Kahan Committee investigating the events of Sabra and Shatila recommended in early 1983 the removal of Sharon from his post as Defense Minister for reasons of negligence, though not complicity in the planning of the massacre.

Some have disagreed with the conclusions of the report. In 1987, *Time Magazine* published a story implying Sharon's direct responsibility for the massacres; Sharon later won a libel case against them. In early 2001, relatives of the victims of the massacre began proceedings in Belgium to have Ariel Sharon indicted on war crimes charges.

Prime Minister Begin dismissed Sharon; however he remained in the successive governments as a Minister without portfolio (1983–1984), Minister for Trade and Industry (1984–1990), and Minister for Housing Construction (1990–1992). In Benjamin Netanyahu's 1996–1999 government, he was Minister of National Infrastructure (1996– 1998), and Foreign Minister (1998–1999). Upon the election of the Barak Labor government, he became leader of the Likud party. After the collapse of Barak's government, he was elected Prime Minister in February of 2001.

Source: Wkipedia Encyclopedia.

Ariel Sharon, Israel's Prime Minister throughout most of the period of
Palestinian conflict, 2001–2002. (AP Photo/Gali Tibbon, Pool)

TERRORIST ORGANIZATIONS

Palestine Liberation Organization (PLO)

In May 1964, 422 Palestinian national figures met in Jerusalem under the
chairmanship of Ahmad Shuqeiri and, following an Arab League decision,
founded the Palestinian Liberation Organization (PLO). It laid down the foundations and structure of the **PLO** and in the early years followed pan-Arabic
ideology. The PLO was set up as an umbrella movement for a large number of
varied interest groups of the Palestinian people. This organization was regarded by many, the Israelis in particular, as a terrorist organization. The early

PLO was not a cohesive organization and contained a broad spectrum of moderate to extremely radical political viewpoints. The militant members of PLO were known as **fedayeen** (warriors), prepared to die for Allah. With such diverse opinions, the PLO soon became splintered and factional. This internecine struggle was much like the many republican factions to be found in Northern Ireland.

The PLO's driving philosophy was the restoration of Palestine, the destruction of Israel as a nation state, and the recreation of an Arab state in former Palestine. The PLO is loosely organized under three headings: the Executive Committee, the Central Committee and the Palestine National Council. The Executive Committee coordinates the major terror activities while the Central Committee acts as an advisory structure to the Executive Committee. During the 1960s, PLO guerrilla groups carried out sporadic attacks against Israel. However, the organization lacked a strong leader for its political and operational activities. During this period, the PLO operated from bases inside the **Hashemite Kingdom** of Jordan, ruled by British-educated King Hussein. There, Yasir Arafat laid the groundwork for his operations among the Palestinians in Kuwait. In 1964, Arafat began to take control of the PLO and turn it from a weak political movement to one that would be recognized as the one true body to represent all the Palestinian people. By 1974, the Arab nations had recognized the PLO as "the sole, legitimate representative of the Palestinian people." In the same year, the United Nations similarly recognized the PLO, with Israel being the exception, of course.

Like all good political and terrorist organizations, Arafat's PLO had a senior security advisor, Ali Hassan Salameh, (a.k.a. Abu Hassan), the "Red Prince." The Israeli intelligence agency, Mossad, believed him to be the PLO member responsible for planning the Munich Olympic Games massacre. The then Prime Minister of Israel, Golda Meir, set Mossad the task of tracking

TERRORISM PLAYER 7–3

Yasir Arafat

His real name is Abdel-Rahman Abdel-Raouf Arafat al-Qudwa al-Husseine, born into a Sunni Muslim family in 1929. His actual birthplace is something of a mystery and is possibly either Egypt or Jerusalem. He studied engineering at the University of Cairo and while there met Palestinian activists Salah Khalaf and Khalil Wazir. With these young activists, he co-founded the terrorist/guerrilla movement **FATAH** in October 1959. Following the humiliation of the 1967 Six-Day War, there was little military left with which to attack Israel. Arafat's fedayeen set up bases in Jordan from which they continued to attack Israel. There were few options open to the PLO other than terrorist-style hit and run tactics. Today Arafat remains chairman of the PLO and hangs on tenuously to a sort of power that is permitted to exist under the control of the Israeli Defense Force. Throughout most of 2002, Arafat was virtually under house arrest in his PLO headquarters in Ramallah surrounded and bombarded by Israeli tanks and artillery. His power and the whole infrastructure of the Palestinian Authority has been virtually demolished.

Palestinian authority leader Yasir Arafat at his Ramallah office, November 4, 2002. (AP Photo/Nasser Nasser).

down the man responsible for the attack, wherever he might hide. The search lasted seven years. In their attempt to assassinate Salameh, the trackers killed an innocent Moroccan bartender in Lillehammer, such was their fervor to exact retribution on the PLO. Salameh met his end dying as he had lived, when a remote-controlled bomb detonated in a stationary vehicle as he drove by with his bodyguards. The attack took place in Beirut on January 23, 1979.

Arafat worked tirelessly to steer the PLO towards legitimacy as a political organization. In 1988 he took a monumental step in announcing the right of Israel to exist and renouncing the further use of PLO terrorism. This commitment from the man who spoke for the displaced Palestinians moved Israel toward discussions on Palestinian self-rule. Young Palestinians, frustrated with the slow progress toward self-rule in a homeland of their own, have increasingly turned to Hamas or Hezbolla for leadership.

On September 13, 1993, (in Oslo) the **Declaration of Principles** between the Israelis and the Palestinians was signed. Palestinian groups formerly under the umbrella of the PLO, such as the Popular Front for the Liberation of Palestine (PFLP) and the Democratic Front for the Liberation of Palestine-Hawatmeh (DFLPH), suspended their participation in the PLO in protest and continued their campaigns of violence not only against the Israelis but also Americans and members of Arafat's PLO. Arafat remains the PLO leader in the region but has been the specific target of Israel almost unceasingly since 9–11. He has endured under house arrest in his own compound for much of 2002. Israeli raids into Palestinian areas such as Ramallah and Jenin to rout out terrorists targeting civilians, continued unabated in spite of international condemnation for the use of military hardware in the West Bank and Gaza regions. By the middle of the year 2002, Arafat was still hanging on as leader of the PLO but facing mounting challenges from Hamas militants. The likelihood that a Palestinian/Israeli accord could be brokered between Sharon and Arafat has to be questioned. Both men have a long history of serious mistrust for the other. Sharon's long-remembered direct or indirect involvement with Christian militias in the Sabra and Shatila camp massacres does nothing to ease the dangers for peace in the region. Any democratic reforms in the Palestinian Authority appear doomed under Arafat's regime.

Arafat tends to operate more as a dictator than a democratic leader. Some two years after an agreed deadline for democratic elections to be held, Arafat has blamed the delay on the Israeli occupation. He states frequently that this must end before elections can take place. There have been sustained calls for the removal of Arafat both by the Israelis and the U.S. government. However, there is no ready heir apparent and, whoever that may be, the person would have to be prepared and willing to renounce terrorism as a start and also have the support and power to negotiate with the Israelis. Even when the PLO and the Israelis approach ceasefire talks, there is always Hamas willing to continue the violence.

Al-Fatah (or Al-Asifa)

Al-Fatah is the fighting organization within the PLO, which actually predates the PLO by six years. Under the leadership of Yasir Arafat it took total control of the PLO after the debacle of the 1967 Six-Day War. It is considered the largest terrorist group marching under the PLO banner. It is estimated to have a force of up to 15,000 fedayeen, financed mostly from support to the Palestinian coffers by wealthy Arab states. **Al-Fatah**, however, has never managed to prove itself as a military machine against the Israelis in spite of its size and support structure, not even in the occupied territories of the Gaza Strip and the West Bank region of Jordan. It was neither able to prevent the Jordanian

TERRORISM BYTE 7–2

Palestinian Suicide Bomber Profile

The profile of a Palestinian suicide bomber during the suicide campaign of 2002 directed mainly at Israeli civilian targets is remarkably consistent. They have been shown to be in an age ranging from eighteen to thirty five, educated and mainly male. Female bombers who emerged in January 2002 tended to come from the lower level of the social ladder, and some were divorcees. The males stood out as extreme worshippers at their mosques and viewed such attacks as the path to glory.

Source: The Science of Terror, Stewart Bell. National Post Canada, May 20th 2002 pBL2.

army from forcibly removing the PLO from its Jordanian training camps around Ajlun and Jerash in 1970, nor could it prevent a repetition in Lebanon when the PLO were swept out by an Israeli invasion force in 1982.

An Al-Fatah terror wing, calling itself **Black September**, commemorated the eviction from Jordan in its name. They were to become legendary for their vicious attack at the Munich Olympic Games village and the massacre of Israeli athletes. Black September is an operational military arm of Fatah. As a result of the Munich Olympics massacre, the prominent members of the squad involved were hunted by Mossad all across Europe and "disposed of" by assassination.

TERROR BRIEF 7–1

Munich Olympic Games 1972

Masterminded by the Palestinian Abu Iyad, the head of the Palestinian intelligence network, the attack on Israeli athletes in the Olympic Village shocked and outraged the world. The attack was carried out by Black September terrorists. The terrorists broke into the village and during the initial attack two members of the Israeli team were shot dead. All the Black September terrorists carried AK-47 assault weapons. Their demands were for the release of 234 Palestinians held in Israeli jails and also members of the Baader-Meinhof Gang, Red Army Faction and specifically Kozo Okomato from the Lod Airport massacre in May 1972. The Israeli Government refused to negotiate with the terrorists. However, after long hours of negotiations with German authorities the terrorists and their remaining hostages were flown by helicopter to Furstenfeldbruk Airport where an aircraft was being readied to fly them to Cairo. What happened next caused a major turnaround in how hostage-taking would be handled in the years ahead. The Bavarian Police opened fire on the terrorists while they still controlled the hostages; the resulting bloodbath left all the hostages dead. So appalling was the carnage from this failed police operation that radical changes would take place stressing significant emphasis on special forces to handle any future incidents.

Source: Richard Clutterbuck. *Guerrillas and Terrorists,* (Ohio University Press, 1980), p. 82.

In spite of the extensive Mossad operation in Europe, Black September rebounded to flourish as the defense arm of Al-Fatah, protecting it and Arafat from the extremist groups sponsored by Syria and Iraq, who were funding Adu Nidal's Black June.

During the sixties and the seventies, Al-Fatah offered training facilities to a wide range of Middle Eastern, European, Asian and African terrorist organizations, as well as insurgent groups. In David Yallop's account, *Tracking the Jackal,* he confirms that one such terrorist movement of the early seventies included the notorious West German Baader-Meinhof Gang.[9] Reciprocal arrangements within these groups allowed for terror operations to be carried out in each other's names throughout the world. It also helped with the financial support required to maintain its operations. It is estimated that Al-Fatah numbers about 7,000–8,000 trained members. Like the Palestinian people as a whole, Al-Fatah is spread throughout the Middle East, but is primarily headquartered in Tunisia. Al-Fatah has been provided with aid from Saudi Arabia, Kuwait and some of the other Arab states in the Persian Gulf region. Al-Fatah members have likewise received training from the former U.S.S.R as well as former communist Eastern Bloc countries.

The tangled web of Middle East terrorism does not start and finish with the PLO. As time goes on and attitudes change, either they soften or harden in their fundamental approach to Israel and its supporters. The PLO, like most organizations that are divided over a wide area, will have many different points of political view. Sabri al-Banna was extreme in his belief that the enemy must be attacked on all fronts, the enemy being Israel, and wavering from that belief was contemptible in his eyes. Al Banna and his supporters split from Fatah and he moved to Iraq in the early seventies.

Abu Nidal Organization

Abu Nidal is the cover name for Sabri al-Banna. The group also uses the following names:

- Fatah Revolutionary Council
- Arab Revolutionary Council
- Arab Revolutionary Brigades
- Black September
- Revolutionary Organization of Socialist Muslims

Similar to the splits in the Irish Nationalist movement, the ANO split from the Al-Fatah organization of the PLO as al-Banna believed Arafat's approach to dealing with Israel was softening, with Arafat tending to become more moderate in his approach to Israel. This was most definitely not to al-Banna's liking and in 1974 he and his supporters left Al-Fatah and set up headquarters in Baghdad, Iraq. The Abu Nidal Organization is now recognized as one of the bloodiest terror groups operating in the Middle East. It certainly became a truly international terror operation by expanding its horizons and ability to strike at its enemies wherever they might be throughout the globe.

Easily recruited, al-Banna was drawn to Baghdad most likely because of what is termed its rejectionist approach to those Middle East countries that favored a peace deal with Israel. Rejectionism is a Middle Eastern political term meaning unilateral refusal of any peaceful settlement with Israel. Iraq would be considered one of the most extreme rejectionist states and one that would not sanction any such deals with Israel. This also had the effect of alienating those states in favor of moderation, such as Jordan and Egypt. Al-Banna's goals can be simply summarized: first and foremost, the destruction of Israel, secondly, control of the PLO with the support of the rejectionist Iraqi government. It seemed to suit Iraq to have a terrorist group within its boundaries that would do its bidding in return for bases and logistical support. al-Banna, under the protection and watchful eye of the Iraqis, trained about two hundred fighters for their joint cause.

To accomplish his goals al-Banna believed that by creating terror on a world stage rather than just a Middle East one, he could meet his goals. His ruthless approach to terrorist actions and atrocities focused the world media and political attention firmly on the regional problems. Abu Nidal has carried out attacks in at least twenty countries and is responsible for the deaths of over nine hundred people. The group has not just targeted Israel. The United Kingdom, the United States, France and those moderate Palestinians with the temerity to seek a peaceful settlement with Israel have been hit as well. Many of Abu Nidal's attacks were spectacular in their audaciousness. The Abu Nidal group credits itself with the assassination attempt on the Israeli Ambassador outside the Dorchester Hotel in London, in June 1982. In broad daylight, a young Arab later identified as the nephew of Sabri al-Banna walked up to the ambassador and shot him in the head at point blank range. The ambassador, Shlomo Argov, was seriously injured. His assailant was also injured by members of the Metropolitan Police Diplomatic Protection Group. This single terrorist attack precipitated an "eye for an eye" response from the Israelis.

The PLO, under Yasir Arafat, denied any involvement in the attack. However, this was insufficient cause not to attack, from the Israeli viewpoint. Terrorism begets terrorism. Israel's response was a military hard line. The Israeli air force mounted a bombing raid on Palestinian camps in Beirut, Lebanon with a death toll estimated at fifty persons and two hundred injured. It has been speculated that this same act provided the Israelis with the excuse to conduct a full-scale invasion of southern Lebanon to purge the region of PLO fighters. The invasion commenced two days after the attack on Argov, and was termed "Operation Peace for Galilee." The action was to destabilize Lebanon and force the PLO to flee the country to Syria, Tunisia and Iraq. Comparisons can easily be drawn to other assassinations which precipitated a war or invasion, notably the death of the Arch Duke Franz Ferdinand, which started World War I. As the strength and notoriety of Abu Nidal increased so too did the international flavor of the training camps in and around Baghdad. These training centers attracted the radical European elements wishing to learn the trade of murder and mayhem.

Some Significant Incidents

Abu Nidal was successful in attacking aviation targets. In light of 9–11, below we list two such attacks dating back to 1985:

December 27 —Rome Airport 08:15

Leonardo Da Vinci Airport is situated on the outskirts of Rome and is the principal international airport in Italy. At 08:15 four young Arabs threw hand grenades at a line of passengers waiting in the check-in line for the El Al flight. El Al's check-in desks are flanked by those of TWA. The four Arabs then opened fire with Kalashnikov AK-47 assault rifles on the American and Israeli passengers waiting in line. Other passengers, including Greeks, Mexicans and two Arabs were killed in the attack. El Al has a record of being proactive in aviation security, and at Rome airport their armed security staff returned fire, along with Italian police and killed three and injured one of the terrorists. Fifteen passengers were killed and seventy injured.

In view of the fact that the terrorists were Arabs, the PLO was immediately denounced as having orchestrated the attack. In this instance Abu Nidal was the likely culprit, however, the incidents in Rome and Vienna were most likely aimed at discrediting Arafat and the PLO. Both Austria and Italy were well disposed to the Palestinian cause and this action would have been designed to turn those countries against Arafat.

December 27 — Vienna Airport 08:15

Timed to coincide with the Rome attack, the injuries were less in Vienna than in Rome with two dead and forty-six injured. The terrorists used the same *modus operandi* as their colleagues in Rome. However they were able to fight their way out of the airport and escape temporarily by car, pursued by Austrian police. A gun battle followed and one of the terrorists was killed and the remaining two surrendered. Again, informed experts put this attack down to Abu Nidal and his attempt to discredit Arafat.[10]

The **Abu Nidal** group has shifted bases periodically from Iraq to Syria and has also had bases in Lebanon and Tripoli. Its presence has also been noted in the Sudan. Its support network and financial aid comes primarily from Iraq and Syria, and more recently from Libya. Reports of Sabri al-Banna's death came on August 19, 2002, through Middle East news reports that he died of gunshot wounds in Baghdad. He was reportedly suffering from leukemia and it is not known whether his death was murder or suicide.

Popular Front for the Liberation of Palestine (PFLP)

The **PFLP** was founded under the umbrella of the PLO in 1967. Its co-founders and leaders were George Habash and Wadi Haddad. George Habash was born in Lydda, Palestine, in 1925, of a wealthy family that followed the teachings of the Greek Orthodox Church. When the British Mandate on Palestine ended in 1948, he was studying medicine at the American University in West Beirut. He and his family became refugees overnight and fled to Jordan. Wadi Haddad was born in Safad, Galilee, in 1939.[11]

After completing his studies, Habash set up a clinic with another Palestinian from the Greek Orthodox Church, Wadi Haddad, in Amman. It might seem strange to the casual observer that two committed doctors trained to save

Sabri al Banna was eleven years old in 1948, when the Israeli War of Independence tore him and his family away from their home in Jaffa near Tel Aviv. Al Banna became known as Abu Nidal or 'father of the struggle'. In 1967 while working as a teacher he joined Yasir Arafat's Fatah guerrilla group and later became the PLO representative in Khartoum. He split from the PLO over the PLO's policy of pursuing a settlement with Israel and went on to form the Fatah Revolutionary Council, which planned to reclaim Palestine through an armed Arab revolution. His initial targets were Israeli and U.S. airlines. In 1973 five members of Abu Nidal's organization attacked a Pan Am jet at Rome airport setting it on fire and in 1974 blew up a TWA airliner over the Aegean Sea killing all on board. Much of the financial support for his group came from Iraq, Libya and Syria until 1987. His organization disintegrated from internal dissent following the shooting of a Jordanian diplomat in Beirut in 1994. His last years were spent in Baghdad where he died in suspicious circumstances or from leukemia.

Source: Bin Laden of the 80's Found Dead, from article by Stewart Bell, Canada National Post August 20th 2002, p A3.

lives should organize a terrorist group destined to take them. They were both committed to the belief in the 1950s that Gamall Abdel Nasser was the best hope for the liberation of Palestine. Both were extreme left wing Marxists. In 1957, Nasser's supporters came close to toppling the Hashemite monarchy in Jordan, however King Hussein was able to defeat the uprising. Habash and Haddad fled and relocated their base of operations to Syria. The PFLP grew out of the Arab Nationalist Movement, which the two men had set up. Both viewed Yasir Arafat with total disdain and loathing for his involvement with the imperialist United States and for his efforts at appeasement of the Israelis. Their philosophy espoused pure terror and was born of the rationale that Israel won its prize by terror so Arabs should gain Palestine back with similar terror tactics.

Al Aqsa Martyrs Brigades

This group, unlike Hamas, does not strive for an Islamic state in Palestine but rather it uses Islam as a weapon to inspire its struggle for an independent Palestine. The movement is linked to Yasir Arafat's Fatah faction and is responsible for many bombs and shooting attacks against Israelis both in the occupied territories and Israel itself.

JORDAN

The Kingdom of Jordan has been a 'refuge' for thousands of displaced Palestinians from West Bank villages for the last four decades. Considerable support probably exists among the Jordanians with sympathies to the Palestinian

TERROR BRIEF 7–2

Israel's Deadly Conflict—Suicide Bombers

January 27, 2002 – A female suicide bomber dies when she detonates a bomb in a shopping mall in East Jerusalem, killing two shoppers

February 16, 2002 – In the town of Karnei Shomren, two teenagers are killed and thirty injured by a suicide bomb attack.

March 2, 2002 – Two babies among the nine killed in a suicide bomb attack in an ultra-orthodox area of Jerusalem. The bombing was believed in retaliation for the Israeli attacks on Palestinian camps that resulted in the death of thirty civilians.

March 9, 2002 – Eleven dead and fifty injured in suicide bombing of a West Jerusalem café. The following day, Israeli jets attacked Yasir Arafat's headquarters.

March 27, 2002 – Twenty are killed and one hundred and thirty wounded by a suicide bombing at a Passover celebration in an hotel in Natanya.

Source: The Independent, March 30th 2002.

cause. Jordan became a safe haven for the Palestinians after the creation of Israel, but problems often arose with so many extreme elements actively embroiled in terrorist campaigns against Israel. The PFLP had training camps within striking distance of Jordan, and for the leadership of the PFLP the King of Jordan himself became a target. There were open confrontations in the streets of Amman between fedayeen members and the late King Hussein's troops. Haddad and Habash were desperate to get the "Palestinian Question" into the focus of world attention. Terror on a grand scale would do that for them. It is not certain whether the two men were actually in concert over the operation, but in July 1970, Haddad was in Beirut with Leila Khaled, a committed member of PFLP planning what has been recorded as one of the most spectacular hijacking events of this century. The hijacking of international airliners to Dawson's Field in Jordan provoked a reaction around the world, and the travelling public experienced the start of passenger screening security at airports worldwide.

Hijacking of Airliners: A New Tactic?

Over the last forty-five years of this century there have been so many attacks of a terrorist nature that it is sometimes hard to recall them. The spectacular ones seem to be held in our mind: the Munich Olympic games massacre, the Iranian Embassy siege in London, the destruction of the U.S. Marine barracks in Beirut, the Oklahoma bombing, Pan Am 103 over Lockerbie, the Air India bombing off the coast of Ireland and of course the New York World Trade Center and the Pentagon attacks are etched in our memories. Hijacking of airliners and the taking of hostages have the immediate ability to focus world attention through media coverage.

The actions of the PFLP almost led to a civil war in their adopted base of Jordan, and certainly led King Hussein to forcibly remove the PLO from its territory. The hijackings were audacious for their sheer nerve, daring and lack of any respect for international convention. The first hijacking took place on a TWA Boeing 707 at 11:50 A.M. on September 6, 1970, en route from Frankfurt, West Germany, to New York. The airliner had a full complement of crew and 145 passengers when it was seized in the skies above Belgium and the pilot ordered to fly to Jordan. At about the same time, a Swissair DC 8 with a similar number of passengers and crew was seized over France and flown to the same location, Dawson Field, Jordan, as the TWA airliner. At about 2:00 P.M., an attempt was made to hijack a third airliner belonging to El Al en route from Tel Aviv to Amsterdam. Due to confusion at check-in, the hijack team was reduced to three members, including Leila Khaled, Patrick Arguello and a third Arab. When the pilot refused to obey the instructions, a violent fight ensued and a flight attendant was shot, and an Israeli sky marshal killed one of the hijackers. Khaled and Arguello were overpowered and the aircraft landed at London's Heathrow Airport. Arguello and Khaled were arrested and taken to a secure Metropolitan Police station in South London. The remaining members of Khaled's group failed to make the flight, then hijacked a Boeing 747 operated by Pan American Airlines. The airliner flew to Beirut, where it refueled and went on to Cairo. The PFLP blew the aircraft up on the ground at Cairo airport after the crew and passengers were taken off. This action by the PFLP, though aimed at the international arena, was a statement to the Egyptian government about its acceptance of the Middle East peace agreement. With hostages numbering about three hundred being held in Jordan, the PFLP laid out their demands to the international community.

The hijackers demanded the release of the three members of the PFLP who had been jailed for the attack on Zurich Airport, and who were presently languishing in a Swiss jail. They also demanded the same for terrorists being held in West Germany for the Munich Airport attack. Their third demand involved Leila Khaled's release from police custody for attempting to hijack an El Al airliner over Europe. Edward Heath's government was in utter turmoil over how to deal with this problem, so the PFLP gave them another nudge by hijacking a BOAC VC-10 and adding one hundred and ten British passengers to their hostage list. After heavy pressure and diplomatic talks, the PFLP moved the hostages to the comfort of Amman, Jordan. Over the next two weeks the hostages were moved around Amman in small groups before all were released on September 30, 1970. The PFLP had previously destroyed the British, Swiss and American Airliners at Dawson Field before the watchful lenses of the world's media.[12] Aerial terrorism had been born and imprinted on the air traveler's psyche.

The last British hostages were released on the same day that Leila Khaled was flown out of the United Kingdom and back to the Middle East. Israel has always steadfastly refused to negotiate with terrorists, and they strongly criticized the Western powers for giving in. Britain never made that mistake again. These events pushed the Middle East to the brink of war and a possible confrontation between the two superpowers. The Bonn Summit conference of major Western powers met in 1978 and agreed to sanctions against states that aided and abetted the hijacking of aircraft. The countries agreeing were the United States, United Kingdom, Canada, France, Italy, Japan, and West Germany.

The Gaza Strip

The Gaza Strip[13] is an area of 140 square miles. It is home to over 830,000 Palestinians and between 4,000 and 5,000 Israeli settlers. The Palestinian population is concentrated in four cities and eight refugee camps. Ninety-nine percent of the population is Sunni Muslim. Although Gaza City is one of the oldest cities in the world, the borders of the area we know as the Gaza Strip were only created in 1949. With the end of the British mandate in Palestine and the resulting Arab-Israeli battles, eventually two thirds of this area was claimed by Israel. The remaining third was claimed by Egypt. After the creation of the Gaza Strip, more than 250,000 Palestinians escaped from the fighting in other areas of the Middle East came to settle there. Since that time Israel has refused to allow those Palestinians to return home, in defiance of U.N. Resolution 141. Most of the inhabitants of the Gaza Strip today are descendants of this group.

So many Palestinians now live in the Gaza Strip that 99% of the population lives on land that is almost 40% controlled by the Israelis. It is not surprising that attacks against Jews by Palestinians are commonplace. Al Fatah has now found a political rival in the Palestinians of Gaza. The Islamic Resistance Movement or Hamas has extensive support in the Gaza Strip and the West Bank areas.

Hamas

Ahmad Rashad a Research Associate at the United Association for Studies and Research puts the **Hamas** popularity down to several factors:[14]

- Hamas calls for the liberation of all Palestine;
- Its reputation as an efficient organization;
- Its honesty and lack of corruption;
- Hamas has been resilient to Israeli crackdowns;
- Daring and successful attacks at Israeli military targets;
- Home-based leadership within the occupied territories, as opposed to the PLO's expatriate direction.

Whatever social or political aspiration it may have for the people of Palestine has to be questioned in relation to its neighbor Israel. The Hamas charter speaks to its aims and concepts. Some of the highlights of the charter are as follows:

> "Israel will exist and will continue to exist until Islam will obliterate it, just as it obliterated others before it."
>
> "The Islamic Resistance Movement believes that the land of Palestine is an Islamic Waqf consecrated for future Moslem generations until Judgment Day. It, or any part of it, should not be squandered: it, or any part of it, should not be given up."
>
> "There is **no solution** for the Palestinian question except through **Jihad.** Initiatives, proposals and international conferences are all a waste of time and vain endeavors."

Sections of the Hamas Charter

The entire charter has not been reproduced here, however some of the articles have. They are worthy of review as they are pertinent in the ongoing events in the Palestinian/Israeli conflict.

Ideological Starting Points

Article One:

The Islamic Resistance Movement: The Movement's programme is Islam. From it, it draws its ideas, ways of thinking and understanding of the universe, life and man. It resorts to it for judgement in all its conduct, and it is inspired by it for guidance of its steps.

The Islamic Resistance Movement's Relation With the Moslem Brotherhood Group:

Article Two:

The Islamic Resistance Movement is one of the wings of Moslem Brotherhood in Palestine. Moslem Brotherhood Movement is a universal organization which constitutes the largest Islamic movement in modern times. It is characterised by its deep understanding, accurate comprehension and its complete embrace of all Islamic concepts of all aspects of life, culture, creed, politics, economics, education, society, justice and judgement, the spreading of Islam, education, art, information, science of the occult and conversion to Islam.

Article Four:

The Islamic Resistance Movement welcomes every Moslem who embraces its faith, ideology, follows its programme, keeps its secrets, and wants to belong to its ranks and carry out the duty. Allah will certainly reward such one.

Article Six:

The Islamic Resistance Movement is a distinguished Palestinian movement, whose allegiance is to Allah, and whose way of life is Islam. It strives to raise the banner of Allah over every inch of Palestine, for under the wing of Islam followers of all religions can coexist in security and safety where their lives, possessions and rights are concerned. In the absence of Islam, strife will be rife, oppression spreads, evil prevails and schisms and wars will break out.

How excellent was the Moslem poet, Mohamed Ikbal, when he wrote:

"If faith is lost, there is no security and there is no life for him who does not adhere to religion. He who accepts life without religion, has taken annihilation as his companion for life."

STRATEGIES AND METHODS

Strategies of the Islamic Resistance Movement: Palestine Is Isalmic aqf:

Article Eleven:

The Islamic Resistance Movement believes that the land of Palestine is an Islamic Waqf consecrated for future Moslem generations until Judgement Day. It, or any part of it, should not be squandered: it, or any part of it, should not be given up. Neither a single Arab country nor all Arab countries, neither any king or president, nor all the kings and presidents, neither any organization nor all of them, be they Palestinian or Arab, possess the right to do that. Palestine is an Islamic Waqf land consecrated for Moslem generations until Judgement Day. This being so, who could claim to have the right to represent Moslem generations till Judgement Day?

This is the law governing the land of Palestine in the Islamic Sharia (law) and the same goes for any land the Moslems have conquered by force, because during the times of (Islamic) conquests, the Moslems consecrated these lands to Moslem generations till the Day of Judgement.

It happened like this: When the leaders of the Islamic armies conquered Syria and Iraq, they sent to the Caliph of the Moslems, Umar bin-el-Khatab, asking for his advice concerning the conquered land—whether they should divide it among the soldiers, or leave it for its owners, or what? After consultations and discussions between the Caliph of the Moslems, Omar bin-el-Khatab and companions of the Prophet, Allah bless him and grant him salvation, it was decided that the land should be left with its owners who could benefit by its fruit. As for the real ownership of the land and the land itself, it should be consecrated for Moslem generations till Judgement Day. Those who are on the land, are there only to benefit from its fruit. This Waqf remains as long as earth and heaven remain. Any procedure in contradiction to Islamic Sharia, where Palestine is concerned, is null and void.

"Verily, this is a certain truth. Wherefore praise the name of thy Lord, the great Allah." (The Inevitable—Verse 95).

Homeland and Nationalism from the Point of View of the Islamic Resistance Movement in Palestine:

Article Twelve:

Nationalism, from the point of view of the Islamic Resistance Movement, is part of the religious creed. Nothing in nationalism is more significant or deeper than in the case when an enemy should tread Moslem land. Resisting and quelling the enemy become the individual duty of every Moslem, male or female. A woman can go out to fight the enemy without her husband's permission, and so does the slave: without his master's permission.

Nothing of the sort is to be found in any other regime. This is an undisputed fact. If other nationalist movements are connected with materialistic, human or regional causes, nationalism of the Islamic Resistance Movement has all these elements as well as the more important elements that give it soul and life. It is connected to the source of spirit and the granter of life, hoisting in the sky of the homeland the heavenly banner that joins earth and heaven with a strong bond.

If Moses comes and throws his staff, both witch and magic are annulled.

"Now is the right direction manifestly distinguished from deceit: whoever therefore shall deny Tagut, and believe in Allah, he shall surely take hold with a strong handle, which shall not be broken; Allah is he who heareth and seeth." (The Cow—Verse 256).

The Three Circles:

Article Fourteen:

The question of the liberation of Palestine is bound to three circles: the Palestinian circle, the Arab circle and the Islamic circle. Each of these circles has its role in the struggle against Zionism. Each has its duties, and it is a horrible mistake and a sign of deep ignorance to overlook any of these circles. Palestine is an Islamic land which has the first of the two kiblahs (direction to which Moslems turn in praying), the third of the holy (Islamic) sanctuaries, and the point of departure for Mohamed's midnight journey to the seven heavens (i.e. Jerusalem).

"Praise be unto him who transported his servant by night, from the sacred temple of Mecca to the farther temple of Jerusalem, the circuit of which we have blessed, that we might show him some of our signs; for Allah is he who heareth, and seeth." (The Night-Journey—Verse 1).

Since this is the case, liberation of Palestine is then an individual duty for very Moslem wherever he may be. On this basis, the problem should be viewed. This should be realised by every Moslem.

The day the problem is dealt with on this basis, when the three circles mobilize their capabilities, the present state of affairs will change and the day of liberation will come nearer.

"Verily ye are stronger than they, by reason of the terror cast into their breasts from Allah.

This, because they are not people of prudence." (The Emigration—Verse 13).

The Jihad for the Liberation of Palestine is an Individual Duty:

Article Fifteen:

The day that enemies usurp part of Moslem land, Jihad becomes the individual duty of every Moslem. In face of the Jews' usurpation of Palestine, it is compulsory that the banner of Jihad be raised. To do this requires the diffusion of Islamic consciousness among the masses, both on the regional, Arab and Islamic levels. It is necessary to instill the spirit of Jihad in the heart of the nation so that they would confront the enemies and join the ranks of the fighters.

It is necessary that scientists, educators and teachers, information and media people, as well as the educated masses, especially the youth and sheikhs of the Islamic movements, should take part in the operation of awakening (the masses). It is important that basic changes be made in the school curriculum, to cleanse it of the traces of ideological invasion that affected it as a result of the orientalists and missionaries who infiltrated the region following the defeat of the Crusaders at the hands of Salah el-Din (Saladin). The Crusaders realised that it was impossible to defeat the Moslems without first having ideological invasion pave the way by upsetting their thoughts, disfiguring their heritage and violating their ideals. Only then could they invade with soldiers. This, in its turn, paved the way for the imperialistic invasion that made Allenby declare on entering Jerusalem: "Only now have the Crusades ended." General Guru stood at Salah el-Din's grave and said: "We have returned, O Salah el-Din." Imperialism has helped towards the strengthening of ideological invasion, deepening, and still does, its roots. All this has paved the way towards the loss of Palestine. It is necessary to instill in the minds of the Moslem generations that the Palestinian problem is a religious problem, and should be dealt with on this basis. Palestine contains Islamic holy sites. In it there is al-Aqsa Mosque which is bound to the great Mosque in Mecca in an inseparable bond as long as heaven and earth speak of Isra' (Mohammed's midnight journey to the seven heavens) and Mi'raj (Mohammed's ascension to the seven heavens from Jerusalem).

"After Palestine, the Zionists aspire to expand from the Nile to the Euphrates. When they will have digested the region they overtook, they will aspire to further expansion, and so on. Their plan is embodied in the "Protocols of the Elders of Zion," and their present conduct is the best proof of what we are saying."[15]

It is not difficult to see why Hamas is such a serious threat to Israel's continued security and why Israel would want to specifically target its leaders for assassination as it has done so effectively throughout 2002.

Organization and Structure of Hamas

Hamas has been heavily involved in the local political scene in Gaza by putting up candidates in local elections for union representatives and the board of trade. Its political opponent is the PLO. Hamas dates back to the mid-

Suicide Bombing. A Bomber with explosives strapped to his body blew up this crowded bus near Haifa, Israel, on April 10, 2002. (AP Photo/Herzel Shapira)

1980s, when it identified itself as a wing of the Palestinian Muslim Brotherhood. The Brotherhood had been seeking to establish a political wing for its organization, and in 1985 and 1986 it issued leaflets in Gaza to encourage a policy of civil disobedience. The leaflets were issued under names such as Harakat al-Kifah al-Musallah (Armed Struggle Movement), al-Murabitoon ala Ard al-Isra' (The Steadfast on the Land of al-Isra'), and Harakat al-Muqawama al-Islamiyya (Islamic Resistance Movement, IRM). As the tensions grew in the mid 1980s, these communiqués became more and more politicized and by 1988 the name Hamas began to appear.

The founders of Hamas were members of the Brotherhood, and the structure of Hamas reflects this. The military and intelligence wings of Hamas function independently. The intelligence wing gathers information and carries out surveillance operations on collaborators, drug dealers and other antisocial activities and metes out punishment ranging from warnings to executions. It also distributes literature about Israeli recruitment policy and methods of collaboration and warns the populace about complicity. The intelligence wing also monitors crime in the region.

The military wing has different but well-defined goals and objectives:

- establish *usar* (families) and underground cells;
- gather information on Israeli Defense Force activities for use in planned operations;
- carry out training programs in hand to hand combat;
- carry out military style operations against the IDF.

Hamas military strikes have continued predominantly against Israeli settlers in the territories and suicide attacks mainly against civilian targets in Israel. Tactics are of a hit and run nature, planting a bomb or a suicide bomb in populated areas of Jerusalem, for example. Despite the PLO agreements with Israel, the Hamas movement declares Arafat as a traitor for his (what are now viewed as failed) agreements with the Zionist enemy.

Hamas's response to these agreements has resulted in an increase in disputes with the PLO. Hamas receives its support from other Muslim countries, including Turkey, Iran, Afghanistan, Saudi Arabia and the Gulf States, Yemen and even Malaysia.

Hamas, although similar to the PLO, is willing to settle for a peace agreement with Israel, but has firm objectives which must be met before agreement can be reached. In 1994, Hamas proclaimed that it was not opposed to peace; however, for it to ". . .cease military operations in Gaza and the West Bank. . . ." the following conditions would have to be met:

1. complete Israeli withdrawal from the occupied territories;
2. disarming the settlers and dismantling the settlements;
3. placing international forces on the "green line" established in the occupied territories during the '48 and '67 wars;
4. free and general elections to determine true representation of the Palestinian people;
5. the Council, which will be composed of electoral victors, shall represent the Palestinians in any negotiations that determine their future and that of the occupied territories.

Many Palestinians lauded the Gaza-Jericho agreement of 1993, as they saw the prospect of establishing their own legitimate homeland. However, the slow progress since the agreement was reached and the continued development of the occupied territories by Israeli settlers has led to disillusionment by many Palestinians. This has led to internal strife between PLO and Hamas, with pro Arafat supporters being assassinated. Israel continued to wrangle over interpretation of sections in the agreement with the PLO throughout the remainder of the 20th century. It is no surprise that acts of terror aimed at Israeli settlements and at targets in the West Bank and Gaza Strip continued almost unabatted. As we know, no final accord has been brokered. As Yasir Arafat's position as leader of the PLO and the Palestinian political cause has become increasingly destabilized throughout the first six months of 2002, a natural successor organization would likely be Hamas. Hamas has been able to retain sufficient military strength to protect its interests against the Israelis and Hamas has a broad political constituency, especially among the young, due to the combination of its fundamentalist religious message and social welfare programs. Hamas' social programs, such as establishing clinics and schools, are an effective alternative to the PA's own social infrastructure, which was crumbling from corruption and mismanagement even before much of it was destroyed by the Israeli military. What's more, the recent negotiations between the Saudi government and Hamas lend the militant group an extra shot of international legitimacy. Saudi "sponsorship" of Hamas is in its embryonic stages, but should the relationship continue to develop, it would give Hamas another conduit to the outside world and a seat at high-level negotiations usually reserved for representatives of nation-states. Of course, such an arrangement would come at a price, as Hamas would be somewhat beholden to the Saudi government.[16] The current intifada, which has continued remorselessly since September 2000, has enabled Hamas to garner and maintain support from other Palestinian factions including Fatah, in what is becoming an unshakeable national consensus.[17] The military wing of Hamas, the Ezzedine al-Qassam Brigades, has continued to carry out suicide attacks against Israel in spite of the massive security operations to block all such attempts. Hamas declared an 'all out war' on Israel in January 2002 as a result of an Israeli incursion into the West Bank city of Tulkarem which saw Israeli commandos shoot dead four Hamas bomb makers and the West Bank leader of Hamas, Yousef Soragji.

Death of Elie Hobeika, former Lebanese Christian warlord. He was held responsible for the Sabra and Shatila massacres in 1982. His car was destroyed by a bomb in Beirut, January 24, 2002. (AP Photo/Osama Attar)

Suicide as a means to an end has been used before against the U.S. in the Middle East. The Beirut attacks against the U.S. Marine Corps barracks as well as the attack against the U.S. Embassy in West Beirut were the work of suicide attackers. The proximity of the Palestinians to the Israeli populous has made for somewhat easy pickings for the Hamas men of terror. The targets have usually been civilian centers in Tel Aviv, Jerusalem and other Israeli cities such as seaside resort towns like Netanya. Massive security clampdowns and numerous checkpoints on major arterial roads as well as street checks has not prevented repeated suicide missions by Hamas members. Each successful attack has resulted in a swift and ferocious response by Israel targeting 'suspected' militants in refugee camps in Palestinian territory. The cycle of violence has prevailed throughout 2002. Israel has also reverted to targeted assassination of 'suspected' militants mainly from Hamas. The method of the response has been to target residential buildings believed to house a specific suspect. On the night of July 23, 2002, an F-16 fighter aircraft dropped a one-ton bomb on a building in Gaza, which was the home of Hamas leader, Salah Shehadeh. The collateral damage in this attack was fourteen civilians. This can be deemed a form of terror being utilized by the Israelis. The Israeli response to the attack was that it had not intended to kill innocent civilians, however dropping a one-ton bomb in a residential neighbourhood would likely have just that effect. In times of war, civilians are often involved in 'mistakes.' The direct targeting of civilians as occurred in the WWII bombings of London by the Germans and Dresden by the allies can be deemed terror bombings and is considered an atroicity as it has no specific military objective or significance. In targeting terrorists hiding or living in a civilian environment makes such distinctions difficult. From a Palestinian viewpoint there is much to be gained in the propaganda war in showing dead civilians to eager news crews. What effect this style of reciprocal attack by Israel will have for peace is uncertain. Although calls for an investigation and wide criticism have ensued in the Israeli media, widespread condemnation has not been long lasting or that loud from the international community.

Palestine Liberation Front (PLF)

The **PLF** terror group split from the PFLP General Command in the mid 1970s and then again into pro-Syrian, pro-Libyan and pro-PLO factions. Its membership cadre is estimated to be between fifty and one hundred.[18]

The PLF's operations are now based in Iraq, having moved there from Tunisia after the attack on the cruise liner Achille Lauro and the murder of a wheelchair-bound U.S. citizen, Leon Klinghoffer. A longtime supporter of Yasir Arafat leads the PLF. Renounced terrorist Abu Abbas, born in a refugee camp in Syria in 1948, is a longtime Palestinian activist and terrorist. With a price on his head for his involvement in the Achille Lauro incident, he is wanted by the United States for the murder of Leon Klinghoffer. Abbas rose to prominence in the PLO and was elected to the powerful and influential Executive Committee of the PLO in 1982. Until 1985 he operated from Tunisia. After the Achille Lauro, the Italian authorities briefly detained him until he was flown to the Yemen. Now headquartered in Iraq he was an outspoken supporter of Saddam Hussein during the Gulf War.

Democratic Front for the Liberation of Palestine (DFLP)

A strong and vocal opponent to the Israeli peace accord with the PLO, this Marxist group split from the PFLP in 1969.[19] **DFLP** believes the Palestinians can only achieve their goals by mass uprising. Its political position in the early years of the 1980s was somewhere in between Arafat and the rejectionists. It again split into two more factions in 1991, one pro-Arafat and one hard-line group headed by Nayif Hawatmah. This group has suspended its membership in the PLO as it opposes the Declaration of Principles signed in 1993. The DFLP is estimated to have a membership totaling about 500 activists across both groups and has carried out its terror campaign mostly in Israel and the occupied territories. Since 1988 the DFLP has only been involved in cross border raids into Israeli areas. It receives its funding and logistical support primarily from Libya and Syria.

Palestinian Islamic Jihad (PIJ)

PIJ has its roots among the Palestinian fundamentalists in the Gaza Strip dating back to the 1970s. Its goals differ from the PLO and its aim is to achieve an Islamic Palestinian state through a holy war and the total destruction of Israel. This group strikes at both Arab and Jew alike. It has not limited its area of operation to the territories and the Gaza Strip like Hamas. It ranks the United States alongside Israel as one of its prime targets. Its acts of terror have been brutal and efficient. In 1991, PIJ attacked a tourist bus in Egypt killing eleven passengers, nine of them Israelis. Its method of attack in Israel and the occupied territories has been suicide bombings of bus stations and markets.[20] PIJ continues to front attacks in Israeli on targets both in Israel and the territories.

Kach and Kahane Chai

This organization was declared a terrorist organization by the Israeli government under the 1948 Terrorism Law, in 1994.[21] Binyamin Kahane, the son of an Israeli-American rabbi who was assassinated in the United States, leads this group. The aim of the group is to restore the biblical state of Israel. The **Kach and Kahane** were outspoken supporters for the terrorist attack on the al-Ibrahimi Mosque by Dr. Baruch Goldstein in February 1994. The group has threatened and attacked Palestinians and Arabs in Hebron and the West Bank and is an embarrassment to the Israeli government. The 1993 Declaration of Principles at the time seen as breakthrough agreement has staggered on with no outward resolution of the critical issues in the region, however it is important to list the main points of it below:

DECLARATION OF PRINCIPLES

Article VI: Preparatory Transfer of Powers and Responsibilities

1. Upon entry into force of this Declaration of Principles and the withdrawal from the Gaza Strip and the Jericho area, a transfer of authority from the

Israeli military government and its Civil Administration to the authorized Palestinians for this task, as detailed herein, will commence. This transfer of authority will be of a preparatory nature until the inauguration of the Council.

2. Immediately after the entry into force of this Declaration of Principles and the withdrawal from the Gaza Strip and the Jericho area, with the view to promoting economic development in the West Bank and Gaza Strip, authority will be transferred to the Palestinians on the following spheres: education and culture, health, social welfare, direct taxation, and tourism. The Palestinian side will commence in building the Palestinian Police Force, as agreed upon. Pending the inauguration of the Council, the two parties may negotiate the transfer of additional powers and responsibilities, as agreed upon.[22]

The above signaled a major breakthrough and a new hope for a definitive solution to the Palestinian question, even peace in the area that, of course, has not been realized. The full text of the Declaration of Principles is not included in this chapter, however its contents form the basis and fabric for both the Israelis and Palestinians to move toward the goal of a homeland for the displaced Palestinians. It has been a very bumpy road since 1993, and whether the two sides are able to fulfill the contents of the Declaration and meet all that is stipulated remains to be seen. There is considerable resentment in the territories and Gaza Strip of the slow pace toward meeting the goals of Principles. This has led to a rise in terror attacks, by members of Hamas in particular, and by dissident PLO member groups operating without the sanction of Yasir Arafat's council.

It is worthwhile to note that the Oslo strategy was to re-divide and subdivide an already fractured and fragmented Palestinian territory into three sub-zones, A B and C, in ways entirely devised and controlled by the Israeli side, as the Palestinians themselves were until very recently a map-less society. At the negotiations there were no Palestinian representatives with any geographical knowledge who could either argue or contest decisions.[23]

Recruitment and indoctrination into the terrorist cause is believed to continue unabated in the Gaza Strip as the next generation of terrorists are groomed and schooled in hatred aimed at their Israeli neighbors. Children as young as seven are seen to be parading with automatic assault weapons and singing patriotic Palestinian songs that glory in the destruction of Israel.[24] This is hardly a harbinger of a peaceful settlement in the years to come. The core of mistrust between the Palestinians and the Israelis, in both words and deeds, runs deepest in the occupied territories.

LEBANON

Lebanon has been in existence for centuries and is occupied by both Christians and Muslims. The Christians settled mainly in the mountainous regions while the Muslims inhabited the coastal region. Like most of the Middle East, the area was under the rule of the Turkish Ottoman Empire until the end of World War I. After the war, the French began to prepare the region for independent status. The French assisted in the creation and writing of the

Israeli tanks surround Yasir Arafat's compound in the West Bank town of Ramallah—September, 2002. (AP Photo/Brennan Lingley)

Lebanese Constitution. Lebanon gained its full independence in 1943 and, like its population, the government was designed to reflect the two majority religions, Christian and Muslim. From its very early days as an independent state Lebanon had close links to the western powers. In the 1950s and 1960s, Beirut was affectionately called the "Riviera of the Middle East." Its hotels and restaurants and vibrant market scene made it a popular spot for tourists and the wealthy. Its situation on the Mediterranean Sea helped it flourish as a port as well as a business center. Significant incidents brought about drastic changes in the Lebanese way of life, beginning with what must be termed an uprising. The first signs of trouble surfaced in 1958, when dissatisfied Muslims violently opposed the government strengthening its ties to the west. The uprising was tempered when U.S. forces were sent to the aid of Lebanon, and all seemed to return to relative tranquility in short order.

Palestinians Come to Lebanon

With the reversal in the fortunes of the PLO in 1969, which saw them being forcefully evicted by King Hussein's Jordanian Army troops, its members spilled into Lebanon in dramatic numbers. King Hussein's actions were in response to the rapidly growing number of confrontations between the PLO and Jordan's military. Support for the embattled King came by way of monetary contributions from the United States on a regular basis. Pressure was applied to the Jordanian king by tightening the purse strings, and the eviction of the PLO was imminent. The PLO were expelled from Jordan and relocated primarily to Lebanon. This move, which took place in September, gave rise to the Black September terrorist group, (who, as mentioned earlier, reached worldwide notoriety at the Munich Olympic Games in 1974). The Arab Muslim population in Lebanon swelled, but they were treated, at best, as fourth-class citizens. Many lived in the shabby refugee camps around Beirut International Airport. Sabra and Shatila remain in infamy as testament to the atrocities committed by Christian Militias, and in areas of southern Lebanon that were in easy striking distance of Israel. Terror campaigns of the PLO continued with strikes against Israel from these havens in south Lebanon. These actions further destabilized not only the government of Lebanon, but the country as a whole.

By 1975, the constant warring from incursions by the PLO into Israel and the retaliatory strikes by the Israeli air force against these Palestinian camps brought the country to civil war. The PLO in Lebanon was widely supported by the predominately Muslim Arabs, but were opposed by the Lebanese Christians. To the casual observer, Beirut and Lebanon have seen a never-ending cycle of violence perpetrated by warring factions from within its borders and unsympathetic neighbors such as Syria, Iran, Iraq and Israel. What for many was an "Orchid in the Mediterranean," turned rapidly into a patch of thistles and thorns, a lawless society with a feeble government unable to restore order or control either internal and external elements bent on its destruction.

The style and structure of terrorism to be played out in this theater of conflict can be viewed as political in nature. It is considered to be the oldest technique of psychological warfare. Political terrorism may be simply defined as coercive intimidation. It is the systemic use of murder and destruction, or the threat of murder and destruction, in order to terrorize individuals, groups, communities or governments into conceding to the terrorist's political demands.[25] While Syria had its own agenda and a desire to include Lebanon as a part of Greater Syria, far more sinister notions were spreading outward from the Persian state of Iran.

The last decade of the twentieth century saw relative calm return to the streets of Beirut. However, the city continues to echo the problems of a bygone decade. In January 2002, a car bomb killed a Lebanese Christian warlord, Elie Hobeika, who had a dubious past and was the militia leader, armed and equipped by the Israeli military under the control of Ariel Sharon. Hobeika may have led the assault on the refugee camps of Sabra and Shatila near Beirut International Airport in 1982, massacring Palestinian civilians. All this occurred with the knowledge and connivance of the Israeli military.

Hobeika had served as a Lebanese government minister until 1988, but as recently as 2001 he had agreed to give evidence against Ariel Sharon at the Belgian war crimes inquiry. Hobeika's record of involvement in the massacres is somewhat incomplete. Some say he directed operations of Christian fighters from the outside of the camps. An Israeli investigation, in 1983, into the massacres concluded that Sharon bore indirect responsibility and that Hobeika did not enter the camps. Who profits from the death of Hobeika? Many would wish him dead, and not least of all Palestinians. But also the finger could equally be pointed at Israel for the embarrassment his testimony in Belgium would have caused the Israeli government. The group claiming responsibility for his death calls itself the "Lebanese For a Free and Independent Lebanon," however, the group has not been identified by any mainstream opposition groups in the country and could well be a cover name for some other organization.[26]

Islam

Before we proceed to discuss the bloodbath which Beirut became, the student should understand some fundamental philosophies about the world of Islam. Islam is a religious faith much like any other. However, it is actually divided into two separate spheres of influence, the **Sunni** sect and the **Shi'a**. There are Five Pillars of Islam:

- *Shehada*—the statement in Arabic which says "There is no god but Allah and Mohammed is Prophet."
- *Salah*— prayer five times a day. Prayer in Islam is praise of God.
- *Zakat*—the paying of alms to the poor. This is traditionally calculated at 2.5%. Different Muslim countries have differing views on Zakat, now that income tax is a reality for many.
- *Ramadan*—the month of holy fasting. During Ramadan Muslims must not eat, drink or make love from sunrise to sunset.
- *Hajj*—pilgrimage to Mecca. This is an obligation of all Muslims who can afford it to make the trek to Mecca in Saudi Arabia once in their lifetime.[27]

Sunni Muslims account for about 90% of the world's Muslim population with the remaining 10% being the Shi'a Muslims. Struggles between the two groups date back as far as the seventh century. Both hold the Quran as their sacred text and Mohammed as the Last Prophet. The Shiites have and believe in their own version of Islamic Law and their own theology. The Shiites believe in a chain of leaders, or Imams, who came after Mohammed, and in a structure of spiritual authority through mullahs and a religious establishment.[28] Iran has the largest population of Shi'a Muslims in the world.

So, with an unstable government and warring factions fighting openly in the streets of Beirut, the country was ripe for the radicals to move in. With the Shah of Iran deposed and an Islamic Revolution underway, the actions of fundamentalists spread to the Middle East.

The Shi'a Sect in Lebanon

Imam Mousa el-Sadr, an Iranian-born cleric, was the undisputed leader of the Shi'a community in Lebanon by the end of the 1960s.[29] The Shi'a was not at this point involved in any type of terrorist activity. They were, however, aligned to politically defend and represent the poor of Lebanon. Together with Gregoire Haddad, a Catholic archbishop, they set up *Haraket el-Mahroumeen* or Movement of the Deprived. Its stated intention was to work within the Lebanese political system to achieve its political objectives. With the passing of time the Imam found it no easy task to reach his goals for the poor and oppressed so he changed his doctrine and approach to the government. His party would become rejectionist and take up the sword to fight the injustices. The group was known by the acronym Amal. In stark contrast to its near neighbors in Iran, the Shi'a sectarian movement continued to operate within the political system after the civil war of 1975. The Lebanese Shi'a community saw a significant ray of sunshine with the formation of a government out of the Iranian Revolution, particularly given the background and birthplace of the Imam. His contacts and involvement with the Iranian movement, as well as the leadership of Amal, was to end with his abduction and disappearance in 1978. A natural vacuum now ensued and the Amal became the Islamic Amal, with headquarters in the Bekaa Valley of Lebanon under the new auspices of Hussein el-Musawi. Islamic Amal was now foundering and Musawi joined forces to bring Amal under the umbrella of Hezbollah.

Hezbollah

The origins and development of the **Hezbollah** movement in Lebanon represent the most important and successful example of Islamic Iran's efforts to export its pan-Islamic brand of revolution beyond its border.[30] Hezbollah is also known as:

- Islamic Jihad
- Ansarollah
- Organization of the Oppressed
- Party of God
- Revolutionary Justice Organization

The goal of Hezbollah was and is to establish an Islamic state in Lebanon.[31] The establishment of the Hezbollah in Lebanon was supported and financed by the Revolutionary government of Iran, even members of the Revolutionary Guard were sent to the Bekaa Valley to join with the training cadres. Its is widely accepted that the Hezbollah is controlled and directed by radical Shiite clerics under the more central control of Iran through contacts in the Syrian capital of Damascus. Up until his death in 1989, the supreme guardian of revolutionary causes was the Ayatollah Khomeini, who called on "all oppressed Muslims to replace their governments with Islamic Fundamentalist ones." His brand of terror stretched far and wide and with sweeping ferocity he used terror as his instrument of punishment. His continued diatribes against the Great Satan,[32] his term for the United States, and his religious Fatwa (death sentence) against the British author Salman Rushdie for writing a novel called the *Satanic Verses* constantly stirred the boiling pot of the Middle East.

With their rise to prominence in 1982, they became a further embarrassment to the Lebanese Government. Prior to the Israeli invasion of Southern Lebanon, which led to the PLO retreating to Tunis, the streets of Beirut were governed by warring militia groups. These included the indigenous Druze populace of the hills around Beirut Airport. It was not uncommon for rockets and mortars to be fired over the airport at the Palestinian positions nearby. The damage and destruction this caused was tremendous.

Hezbollah's main targets are the Israeli Jews. Not restricted to only hitting Israel, they have also targeted the non-Islamic influences in Europe, the United States and Latin America. The United States is considered a legitimate target, as are other Western powers with United States alliances, and its Middle East policies. With the withdrawal of the Israeli army from Southern Lebanon, the Hezbollah have been able to prosper and recruit combatants for their "Holy War" against Israeli targets, most being military in nature. Carried on the Al-Manar TV network is a constant and objective view portraying the values of "martyrdom" (suicide). This network is broadcast across a wide expanse and is viewed by 25 million viewers in the Arab world. It is also broadcast into the occupied territories and viewed by countless thousands of Palestinians. The intentional objective of this TV network is ". . .to encourage people to martyr themselves" in the words of Nayef Krayem, chairman of the network.[33] Streets in Beirut under the control of Hezbollah are marked with flags displaying the images of martyrs that have completed their missions. Nevertheless, Beirut is still the temporary home to thousands of Palestinian refugees who are denied the same rights as the indigenous population and continue to live in abject squalor. Hezbollah has managed to garner prestige from the Arab states by being responsible for the ultimate Israeli withdrawal from Southern Lebanon. The messages being sent to the Gaza region through such methods as the Al-Manar network may sow the seeds for more martyrs from the Palestinian population but unlike the Hezbollah they are unable to retreat away in the hills of Lebanon to escape the wrath of the Israeli military. As it stands today the occupying Israeli forces totally surround the Palestinians.

Kidnapping

This is not a new tactic in the terrorist's arsenal, but the speed and efficiency with which Hezbollah executed kidnappings and executions in Beirut took the western world completely by surprise. The audacious kidnapping of Terry Waite, the Archbishop of Canterbury's special envoy to the Middle East was remarkable in that it was carried almost live on the major news networks. Hezbollah believed at the time that the envoy, Terry Waite, was working for the CIA. However, news bulletins, which showed Waite leaving an aircraft in Cyprus several steps ahead of Colonel Oliver North, provided ample incitement for the kidnappers to justify their actions. Both British and U.S. positions to not deal with terrorists or acquiescing to their demands resulted in

Terry Waite and others being incarcerated for several years in the suburbs of Beirut before their eventual release.

Structure and Development

From its original inception, Hezbollah operated like a "halfway house" for terrorists. It appears that Hezbollah received its direction from three different people within its hierarchy: Abu Musawi, Hassan Nasrallah and Sheik Mohammed Hussein Fadollah, the last being the Hezbollah's spiritual leader. As a former fighter with the Islamic Amal Nasrallah's role was to format a terrorist force for the Southern Lebanon region.[34]

As has been noted earlier, the Hezbollah were intent on establishing an Islamic state in Lebanon. This would undoubtedly not be welcomed by the style of government that had been established with the creation of Lebanon in the first quarter of the century, which assured that government would predominantly be in the hands of the Maronite Christian majority. As no census had been taken in the country decades, it was probable that the Maronite Christians were no longer in the majority, a fact not lost on the Beirut militia commanders. With so many different groups fighting for control of the streets and the government, the Hezbollah were not content to act like the PLO as an umbrella for other groups. With the death of Musawi, Nasrallah turned his terrorist forces toward the same style of revolution as had occurred in Iran and effectively created a regional militia movement. The many other groups had, by 1991, laid down their arms and signed a peace accord. Hezbollah, on the other hand, remained the one major force against the Israelis in Southern Lebanon and have been waging a terrorist campaign ever since.

Hezbollah used the human bomb to great effect, as did the Islamic Jihad. The Hezbollah are blamed for the suicide bomb attack on the U.S. Marine Barracks in West Beirut in October 1983. The suicide bomber drove a truck loaded with explosives and detonated it as he crashed into the camp. The impact was devastating, taking the lives of 241 U.S. Marines. The outcry in the United States was loud and clear: "What are our boys doing over there?" In spite of the carnage and outrage, the suicide attacks continued with spontaneous irregularity and with the same devastating results. Intelligence was scant at best on the group, and bringing any culprit to trial was almost impossible.

The terror tactics employed in Beirut significantly changed when on March 28, 1986, two British teachers were kidnapped in what, until this time, had been considered the "safe" area of West Beirut. The following month, Brian Keenan, a British national with dual nationality in the Republic of Ireland, was abducted, and the following week one of the Muslim militia groups operating in West Beirut announced that they had executed a British journalist, Peter Collett. The following day the three bodies of the Americans Peter Kilburn, Leigh Douglas and Philip Padfield were discovered, and another journalist, John McCarthy, was kidnapped. Beirut had become an extremely hostile place for Westerners. Hezbollah does not confine its attacks against the state of Lebanon exclusively to the Middle East theater; it is in fact a true international terrorist group with the ability to strike at Jewish targets throughout the world. Through local cell structures in South America it is believed to have been responsible for several large bomb attacks in Buenos Aires in 1994, as well as a car bombing in London.

Islamic Jihad

Not to be confused with the Palestinian Jihad, the Islamic Jihad is believed to be based in the Bekaa Valley of Lebanon and was an offshoot of the Muslim Brotherhood with Iranian influences. It is a shadowy organization believed to be under the control of the Syrians from Damascus. Much of its success is due to the inability of Western intelligence to accurately target the group. Its secrecy and very tight cell structure makes it difficult to infiltrate. Formed in 1981 under the leadership of Fathi Shekaki, it came under the umbrella of Hezbollah. It seems the Islamic Jihad tactics are to split and split again, in order to form impenetrable cells. Through this, they believe, a new form of terrorism would be born. The world of intelligence gathering and security is aimed at detection and prevention, provided it knows where to look and who and what to look for. Islamic Jihad chose a new weapon for its terror attacks against the Israelis and the West, the suicide or kamikaze bomber. The human bomb was a new phenomenon for the intelligence communities and the results of human bomb attacks are invariably devastating and on target.

SYRIA

Syria has been a major player in the issues involving Israeli/Palestinian problems, so we discuss it here in that context. Syria is a Muslim country with a population which is 90% Sunni Muslim. The country gained independence from France in 1946, and by the mid-1960s the Baath party rose to power with Hafez al-Assad as its president. Syria had for years been dominated by a succession of military governments. Assad, a former air force colonel, died in 2001 and his power passed to his son Bashar al-Assad, who continues much as his father did. Syria is a longtime supporter of the Palestinian cause and a sworn enemy of Israel. It has fought two unsuccessful campaigns against Israel and lost control of the Golan Heights on its southern border.

Although Syria is a sponsor and harborer of terrorists, it is likely that any terrorist acts perpetrated on its soil would quickly be suppressed. Assad himself shied away from the public and international eye and quietly assisted groups such as Islamic Jihad and Hezbollah by allowing Iran to re-supply them through Damascus. Assad's government was in open conflict with U.S. forces stationed in Lebanon and, in 1983, shot down an unarmed U.S. reconnaissance flight.

Syria tries to maintain some measure of control over Hezbollah and its actions. Syria continues to hedge its bets and maintains a thriving business in its support of training camps for expatriate terror groups such as the PFLP-GC, led by Ahmad Jibril, the Palestine Islamic Jihad and the Japanese Red Army. Not far away in the Bekaa Valley are members of the PKK, the Kurdish Workers Party, led by the university-educated Abdullah Ocalan, who spent part of his time in Syria before his capture and death sentence in Ankara in 2000.

Syria does not permit homegrown terrorists to perpetrate actions against the state, and Assad's government violently suppressed any attempts, particularly by Islamic fundamentalists, to disrupt the workings of the state. Not only terrorist and fundamentalist but other political factions are suppressed in the one-party state of Syria. This is not to say there have not been attempts by the Muslim Brotherhood to raise their banner in Syria. In 1982 an open revolt in the city of Hama by Islamic fundamentalists resulted in the Syrian Army taking immediate and decisive action to crush the uprising, the result being many deaths and casualties. Syria does, however, continue to provide a safe haven for terrorist groups that are currently active. Among those groups that have headquarters and training camps in Syria are the Popular Front for the Liberation of Palestine General Command (PFLP-GC) under Ahmad Jibril, and Palestinian Islamic Jihad (PIJ). In addition to bases in Syria, areas under its influence and military control in the Bekaa Valley of Lebanon also have camps for the Hamas, PIJ, PFLP-GC and the Turkish PKK. President George Bush included Syria in his list of countries forming an 'axis of evil' in 2002. Al-Assad has openly expressed support for the U.S. war against terrorism but has done little or nothing in support of it. Only time will tell whether the al-Assad has the capability and fortitude to weather pressure from the United States and take some decisive steps against Hamas, the PFLP and others that maintain close ties with the regime in Baghdad.

THE REST OF NORTH AFRICA

Now that we have examined the core of the terrorism problems in the Middle East, we will continue with the next ring of terror in North Africa with Algeria, Morocco, Libya, Egypt and others. The prospects for peace in the Middle East, which at one time looked promising, have turned ominously in the opposite direction since 1993, especially with extreme Islamic groups operating from Egypt.

MOROCCO

This North African country, neatly sandwiched between the Atlantic Ocean and Algeria has been remarkably adept at keeping terrorism at bay. The government has rigorously investigated all terrorist acts and threats and has been successful in countering any Islamic radicalism unrest within its borders. Morocco also arrested a member of the Algerian Islamic Salvation Front in December 1997.[35] Morocco gained its independence from French rule in 1955, after rioting broke out when the French sent the Sultan into exile. The uprising resulted in the Sultan being returned to his native Morocco. Sultan Mohammad V changed his title to that of King and established a constitutional monarchy to oversee and control all aspects of governing the country. On his death in 1961, his son Hassan assumed the mantle of King and also Prime

Minister. Since its independence, Morocco has laid claims to regions of the Saharan desert under Spanish mandate. Morocco and Mauritania both had claims on the region and had to contend with the Polisario Front, an indigenous group operating in the Sahara region. The Polisario Front wanted self-determination and was not likely to accept being consumed by either Mauritania or Morocco. Mauritania dropped its claim to the desert region and in its place Morocco claimed the whole area. In its efforts to stave off Morocco, the Polisario Front received military support from Libya and Algeria.

EGYPT

The history of Egyptian contributions to modern society is fascinating. Their feats of civil engineering, craftsmanship and overall attention to detail in developing a dynasty before most of the world became civilized is a matter of incredible historic record. The influences of the Egyptian people and the Pharaohs swept through Africa, the Middle East, and Mesopotamia dominating societies for centuries. Even now, the study of ancient Egyptian writings occupies the dedication of countless professors and universities. It is believed that the first Egyptian Pyramid was built 2500 years before the birth of Christ. Egypt became a part of the Roman Empire in 31 BC, and Roman rule dominated Egypt until approximately 395 AD, when the country was overrun and ruled by Muslims from the Arabian peninsula.

Twentieth-Century Politics

History sometimes repeats itself and that is the case with Egypt, which had been a country within the Ottoman Empire. The Muslim Brotherhood, which comprises a large percentage of native Egyptians, played a major part in the assassination of President Anwar Sadat in 1991. Sadat's readiness to make a peace deal with the Israeli government was as much about economics as anything else. Egypt was suffering from excessive military spending and Sadat had promised that this would be lessened with the signing of a peace treaty with the Israelis. At the latter part of the 1970s, Egypt was considered by Israel to be its most powerful enemy, as well as its next-door neighbor. A deal between the two countries was being brokered under the influence of U.S. President Jimmy Carter, and on March 29, 1979, in Washington DC, Menachem Begin and Anwar Sadat signed a peace accord. In hindsight this may have been the political action that lead to Saddat's untimely assassination. Immediately after the signing of the historic treaty, a summit of Arab League nations was held in Baghdad. The result was that Egypt was ostracized, both economically and politically from the Arab world. Under the terms of the treaty, the Israelis gave up the Sinai in return for a peace deal and financial support from the United States. Similarly, Egypt was now an outcast Arab state that was dependent on the United States for its aid. A large majority of Egyptians welcomed the accord.

The Muslim Brotherhood

Christians and Muslims have occupied Egypt for centuries. Egyptians who are born Christians are referred to as *Copts,* and number about 5 to 6 million. Formed in 1922 by Sheik al Banna, the Brotherhood stood solidly as President Nasser's most vitriolic of opponents in Egypt. There had been an attempt on his life by a member of the Brotherhood, which gave Nasser the excuse he needed to round up and jail the membership and proclaim a ban on the movement. The Brotherhood would see an about face by the Presidential office with the arrival of Sadat, and those factions of the Brotherhood willing to support Sadat against the extreme left opponents were themselves supported with large donations. The Brotherhood would eventually bite the hand that fed it, with considerable ferocity.

ANWAR SADAT 1919–1981

Over time Anwar Sadat's style of government became increasingly autocratic and though he had suggested that the country would benefit economically, there was no immediate change regarding military spending. In fact, spending in this area increased. Sadat was not gaining any allies among his Arab neighbors as he continued to attempt to keep the peace accord with Israel alive. Israel's attentions, by 1981, were diverted to the northeast and Lebanon. When the Israeli invasion of southern Lebanon began in 1982, the peace process with Egypt became mired in the sand. On the home front in 1981, Sadat was now facing increasing hostilities from the Muslim Fundamentalists of the Brotherhood. Far from supporting Sadat, the Brotherhood was now actively challenging his rule. In June 1981, fighting erupted between Muslims and Christians in Cairo, which resulted in massive property damage and a large number of deaths. Sadat began to suppress the Brotherhood and arrested 1500 members, including many of the organization's leaders.[36] Clearly out in the cold, Sadat's only close ally was the United States. This alliance fuelled the hatred of Sadat by the Muslim Brotherhood, and it was not aimed at the government but at Sadat himself. President Nasser was, by all accounts, mourned by an entire nation; not so with the passing of Sadat. The Sadat government was seen as increasingly corrupt, with the ordinary Egyptians suffering food shortages. Sadat's promise of a better life for Egyptians never seemed to materialize. At a military review on October 6, 1981, Sadat was taking the salute when he was cut down by a burst of machine gunfire from his own troops in a bloody twenty-five second rampage. The planning was meticulous and allowed the assassins to reach the dais. A three-ton military transport stopped in front of the grandstand and Lieutenant El-Sambouli and his co-conspirators opened fire on Sadat, killing him and six others in the grandstand instantly. Thirty others received injuries. There was no spontaneous eruption of violence, no revolution to carry the Muslim Brotherhood forward in Egypt, which had been the intention of the Muslim cell involved in the attack. Although the Western world leaders and governments mourned his passing, Egyptians seemed to breathe a collective sigh of relief and, to some extent, regarded Lt. El-Sambouli as a hero! With Islamic Fundamentalism on the rise throughout the Muslim world, it seemed probable that a revolt should occur, but this did not happen in Egypt. In elections in 1987, the Muslim Brotherhood, allied with two political parties, won 17% of the vote which translated into fifty-six seats in the Egyptian National Assembly.[37] In April 1982, El-Sambouli and his five co-conspirators were found guilty and executed for their crimes.

EGYPT'S ISLAMIC EXTREMISTS

Jamaat al-Islamiyya, and Egyptian Islamic Jihad, which are both radical and extreme Islamic groups, have long been associated with Egypt and made many attempts to violently attack and destabilize successive regimes. Mohammed Atta, the supposed leader of the 9–11 attacks, and an al-Qaeda member, was an Egyptian, and many of the al-Qaeda leadership come from this hot bed of Islamic extremism. The two groups gain much of their support from the slums of Cairo and the poorer regions of the state. Both have been responsible for the attacks mainly against foreign tourists in Egypt that decimated the Egyptian lucrative tourism economy. It has its roots going back to the Muslim Brotherhood and has been fighting for an Islamic state to replace the secular government of Hosni Mubarak.

Both groups are known to have sent members to Afghanistan for training with the mujahideen, which fought in Afghanistan against the Soviet Union. Many links exist between these two groups and al-Qaeda. To this end, the Mubarak government has suppressed both of them. Claims of torture by human rights groups, and criticism from the United States on the topic have not prevented extensive crackdowns on the extremist terror groups. The United States is a supporter of the Mubarak regime and pours considerable financial aid into the country. Of critical importance is the fact that Egypt continues to observe the terms of the 1979 Camp David accords, the first Arab peace treaty with Israel. Egypt's largest Islamic terror group is *Jamaat al-Islamiyya,* whose name means "the Islamic Group." *Jamaat al-Islamiyya* has a presence both in Egypt and worldwide. Its spiritual leader, the blind cleric Sheikh Omar Abdel Rahman, is serving a life sentence in the United States for his involvement in the 1993 attack on the World Trade Center. (In April 2002, the Justice Department charged that Abdel Rahman had tried to direct further terrorist operations from his cell in Minnesota.)

Following a violent campaign of attacks against governmental, Christian, and other targets in Egypt, *Jamaat al-Islamiyya* have largely honored a March 1999 cease-fire with the Egyptian government. Exiled members of Jamaat al-Islamiyya are known to have joined al-Qaeda and trained at its camps in Afghanistan.[38] The Islamic Jihad has close ties to bin Laden's al-Qaeda and continues its assault on the Egyptian government. Due to the repressive nature of the Mubarak regime the group has operated principally outside Egypt and has been turning its Islamic extremist campaign of terror towards U.S. targets. The philosophy of the fundamentalists is to overthrow the government and to replace it with a radical and extreme Islamic government similar to the former Taliban regime in Afghanistan. Over the last ten years, the Mubarak government's crackdown on the Islamic group has seen many militants either jailed or executed under military tribunals. Those in jail are believed to number more than 14,000.

The Egyptian government continues to support, in principal, the U.S.-led war on terror and is an ally of peace initiatives for the Middle East, however arms continue to be supplied to Palestinian groups through the Sinai Peninsula. Its crackdown on the extreme elements of the Islamic groups makes the leadership a prime target of bin Laden and his terror cells.

LIBYA

Libya is situated at the northern tip of Africa and has a northern border on the Mediterranean Sea. Its nearest neighbors to the east are Egypt and the Sudan, with Chad and Niger to the south and Algeria and Tunisia to the west and northwest, respectively. The country is made up of 97% Sunni Muslims or Arabian Berber tribesmen. In the 1930s, under Italian dominance, there was discrimination against Libyan Jews, who have been persecuted in Libya ever since. Libyans attacked the Jewish sector of Benghazi during World War II and about two thousand Jews were deported. By the time Libya had achieved independence in 1951, nearly all the remaining Libyan Jews had migrated either to Israel or Europe.[39]

COLONEL MUAMMAR EL-QADDAFI

Muammar el-Qaddafi is a man driven by hatred for the state of Israel, the United States, and any foreign power that supports them. The United States was for many years the second on the Libyan leader's hate list, with the United Kingdom not far behind. Libya, up until the late 1990s, did not limit itself to attacking the foreign governments, but also sought out and killed Libyan opponents of the Libyan leader.

Qaddafi came to power following a military coup that deposed King Idris in 1969, and has now achieved dictatorial status as leader of the Libyan People. His views are anti-Israeli, anti-Zionist and anti-semitic, although in his public statements he makes no distinction between them. As a mark of his hatred for the Jewish people, he seized all Jewish-owned properties and businesses in 1971. He rules with an autocratic style and ruthlessly "removes" all dissenters. His control of the government is absolute through the setup of people's committees. As a former military student and officer, he had never been cast in the secular role which he seems to have adopted in the 1990s. Reports out of Libya indicate that several attempts on his life have taken place, by a group calling itself the Libyan Militant Islamic Group.

Support for Terror

The phenomenon of state-sponsored terrorism applies most appropriately to Libya, Iran and Syria and forms part of what George Bush termed the "axis of evil." By far the most outspoken of the Arab world leaders, Qaddafi embarked

TERRORISM PLAYER 7–5

Muammar el-Qaddafi

Born in Libya in 1941, Muammar el-Qaddafi is a devout Muslim and follower of Islam and comes from a family of Bedouins. He trained as an officer at the Libyan Military Academy in Benghazi and also at the Royal Military Academy, Sandhurst, Berkshire, England. Denounced by many Western countries, Qaddafi has been strongly supported with military aid and hardware from the former Soviet Union, which supplied his air force with MIG fighter aircraft and tanks.

Attempts have been made on his life from different quarters. At home he has been the tar-get of several military coups by his own officers. In 1985, fifteen army officers were executed for attempting to assassinate him. On the international front the United States government under the Reagan Administration has attempted albeit unsuccessfully to target him with attacks by aircraft from the U.S. Navy in the Mediterranean. Since the events of 9–11, Qaddafi has been an outspoken supporter of the United States and the War on Terrorism—again, he is not one to support the Islamic fundamentalist cause, which he has managed successfully to suppress in his own country.

through the 1970s and 80s on what may be described as a reign of external terror against the United States and its citizens, specifically in Europe. The Libyans have supported other terror groups in Europe and have allowed them to train on Libyan soil. Libya has also provided weapons to such groups as the Provisional Irish Republican Army. In one notable incident, the Libyans supplied several tons of explosives and automatic weapons, which were seized by security forces in the Irish Republic. To Qaddafi, the PIRA are fighting a guerrilla war of independence from the dominance of an imperialist power. Security experts have not taken such actions lightly. Libya has been a home and terrorist training-ground for more than thirty terrorist organizations, such as Abu Sayeef from the Philipines. However, in order to get sanctions lifted among other actions taken Libya expelled members of the Abu Nidal organization in 1998.

There has been sufficient opposition to the Qaddafi regime to prompt him to unleash internal assassins to track down and coerce the dissidents into returning to Libya. Failure to return left only the option of death. In 1984 alone, more than thirty terrorist attacks were carried out by representatives of Libyan Revolutionary Committees on Libyans residing in Europe and the Middle East.[40] Not only did Qaddafi focus on his dissidents in Europe and the Middle East, he also sought them out in neighboring Chad and the sub-Saharan African states that were vociferously against his government.

Diplomatic Immunity

To circumvent the interference of foreign customs officials, Qaddafi used diplomatic privileges to move contraband weapons into and out of diplomatic missions in Europe. By the 1980s, Qaddafi had renamed the Libyan Embassies and was now referring to them as the Libyan People's Bureaus. The problems faced by the British government of Margaret Thatcher and public protests outside the Libyan People's Bureau in the St James's Park, London would result in the severing of diplomatic ties between the two countries. The following are extracts from the Vienna Convention on Diplomatic Relations: 1961

Article 22

1. The premises of the mission shall be inviolable. The agents of the receiving state may not enter them, except with the consent of the head of the mission.
2. The receiving State is under a special duty to take all appropriate steps to protect the premises of the mission against any intrusion or damage and to prevent any disturbances of the peace of the mission or impairment of its dignity.
3. The premises of the mission, their furnishings and other property thereon and the means of transport of the mission shall be immune from search, requisition, attachment or execution.

Article 29

The person of a diplomatic agent shall be inviolable. He shall not be liable to any form of arrest or detention. The receiving State shall treat him with due respect and shall take all appropriate steps to prevent any attacks on his person, freedom or dignity.

Comment: It is possible that a request made to the British authorities about the peaceful but vociferous protest outside the Libyan Peoples Bureau in April 1984 would have been covered by this section of the Vienna Convention.

Article 31

1. A diplomatic agent shall enjoy immunity from the criminal jurisdiction of the receiving State. He shall also enjoy immunity from its civil and administrative jurisdiction.
2. A diplomatic agent is not obliged to give evidence as a witness.

Comment: The actions occurring inside the Libyan People's Bureau as a result of gunfire from within the diplomatic mission would have been covered by this article

Article 45

If diplomatic relations are broken off between two States, or if a mission is permanently or temporarily recalled:

a. the receiving State must, even in case of armed conflict, respect and protect the premises of the mission, together with its property and archives;
b. the sending state may entrust the custody of the premises of the mission, together with its property and archives, to a third State acceptable to the receiving State;
c. the sending State may entrust the protection of its interests and those of its nationals to a third State acceptable to the receiving State.

News Networks in London, the BBC and ITN, showed the dramatic turn of events when gunfire erupted from the bureau into the crowd in the street.

The demonstrators were mainly exiled Libyan students protesting against Qaddafi. The gunfire killed a Metropolitan Policewoman, Yvonne Fletcher. The incident, which took place in the heart of the diplomatic center of London on April 17, 1984, and accounted for a dozen injuries to the demonstrators was not a random maniacal act but a deliberate attack on the demonstrators. Intelligence intercepts of messages between Tripoli and the London Libyan People's Bureau revealed that those inside were ordered to fire on the demonstrators. On the home front, the Libyan controlled press released a different story about the incident, stating that the police had stormed the building and describing the episode as a "barbarous outrage." The standoff at the Libyan People's Bureau ended on April 27, when the occupants agreed to be taken to the Civil Services College in Berkshire to be interviewed by police. Under diplomatic privileges to which they were entitled, they refused to help in the investigation and were returned to Libya. The events at St. James's Square were the culmination of a series of bombings and attacks against dissident Libyans in London and the northwest of England.

Qaddafi and the United States

Qadaffi sees himself as a latter day Abdel Nasser, with the ideology of leading and uniting the Arab nations. Fanatical and fundamentalist, he has targeted U.S. interests and personnel in Europe. Its is believed the attack on the La Belle discotheque in Berlin on April 5, 1986, which claimed the life of one U.S. serviceman and injured several scores of others, was the work of Libyan agents. This incident did not yield a particularly high body count, but the U.S. was in no mood to trifle with the Libyan government of Colonel Qaddafi. Death of U.S. personnel became the trigger the Reagan administration was searching for to launch a military response against Libya. American intelligence indicated that the disco bombing was planned and directed by "diplomats" from the East Berlin Libyan People's Bureau.

Operation El Dorado Canyon

International relations between the United States and Libya were at an all-time low by the middle of the 1980s. Behind the scenes at this time was the Soviet Union, which had been supplying weapons and aircraft to Libya. In a blatant effort to make the Libyans lose face, the United States began maneuvers with its Sixth Fleet in the Mediterranean off the north coast of Libya, in an area proclaimed by Libya as being an exclusion zone. The area in question was the Gulf of Sirte. These exercises began on March 24, 1986, and were calculated to intimidate the Libyan leader.

Far from intimidated, the result was the detonation of two bombs in Europe. The first, on April 2, 1986, exploded in the cabin of a TWA passenger jet in Greek airspace. Four Americans were killed in the blast, however the aircraft landed without further incident. Four days later a powerful explosion ripped through La Belle discotheque in West Berlin, killing an American serviceman. These two actions appear to have triggered a previously planned airstrike in Libya by U.S. forces. On April 14, 1986, aircraft from U.S. bases in the United Kingdom and from the U.S. Navy aircraft carriers in the Mediterranean attacked and bombed targets inside Libya. One could argue that the U.S. had violated the U.N. Charter and international laws with such a preemptive strike against a sovereign state.

Over one hundred aircraft took part in the raid in and around Tripoli and Benghazi, causing heavy damage and loss of life. It is believed that Colonel Qaddafi's adopted daughter was one of the fatalities. In all, more than one hundred lives were claimed. The U.S. actions analyzed in many different ways. Was the attack sending a message to other state sponsors of terrorism or was this strike designed to help topple or kill the Libyan leader and allow for a more moderate government to be formed in its place? This was the first time such aggressive military action had been aimed at a specific country in retaliation for terrorist attacks. Would other terrorist groups heed the example of the attack on Libya and cease activities against the United States? On the political front, members of the United Nations, including France and Italy, the two countries that had refused overflight clearances for strike aircraft from UK bases condemned the United States. Did the French and Italian governments fear some form of reprisal attack from the Libyan leader? The UK government on the other hand, the strongest American ally at the time, had already severed diplomatic ties with Libya. Whatever analysts may think, a far more serious terrorist attack was not far away, indicating that preemptive military actions may not be successful against determined and fanatical terrorist movements. Some thirteen years later, under a different U.S. administration, spy satellites and long-range smart bombs would again target terrorist sites but in Sudan and Afghanistan.

During the last decade, with the mounting pressure on his country from U.N. sanctions that were not lifted until 1999, the Colonel has had to reevaluate his position in the world. No longer does he have the support of the former Soviet Union and a period of appeasement was definitely the order of the day for survival. The concern to many is that Libya has small stocks of biological agents and the risk that those could fall into the wrong hands or, to be more specific, into the hands of al-Qaeda, has been a pressing issue for the United States. In May 2002 the U.S. State Department added Libya to the list of countries that were developing chemical and biological weapons of mass destruction. Certainly Qaddafi has no love for the Islamic extremists or al-Qaeda, and since 9–11 he has reportedly provided intelligence on Libyan militants outside of the country. This action would be of pure benefit to Qaddafi as he has maintained an iron-fisted approach to Islamic extremist inside Libya.

PAN AM 103

One of the most appalling terrorist attacks of the last fifty years has been the destruction of a Pan Am 747-200 over Lockerbie, Scotland, on December 21st 1988. The subsequent trial and conviction of a mid-level intelligence officer in the employ of the Qaddafi government still leaves the obvious question as to the complicity of the leader of the Libyan government in this atrocity. However, his recent overtures and offers to pay large sums of money to families has not helped his position, particularly in the eyes of a hostile American public. Forgiveness for these sins may not be quickly given or forgotten.

SUDAN

Sudan has been fighting an almost endless civil war between Muslims in the north and Christians in the south. Its government appears to have been devastated by the famine and poverty that has wrecked the nation. Sudan has, however, been on the U.S. State Department's list of countries which sponsor and support international terror groups. Safe haven and training grounds have been available to the Abu Nidal Organization, Hezbollah, Hamas and the PIJ. The U.N. Security Council passed several resolutions concerning the role of Sudan in sponsoring terror groups; not all have been complied with. One name stands apart from all others at the end of this decade: Osama bin Laden was ordered to leave the Sudan in 1997, but his legacy was to cause a military confrontation with the United States some twelve months later. Following the massive bombings of the U.S. embassies in the Kenyan and Tanzanian capitals which claimed hundreds of lives, the United States struck back. In a reaction similar to that of Ronald Reagan, the Clinton administration retaliated during the night of August 20, 1998.

In his address to the nation on August 20, President Clinton stated, "Today I ordered our armed forces to strike at terrorist-related facilities in Afghanistan and Sudan because of the imminent threat they presented to our national security . . . In recent history they killed American, Belgian and Pakistani peacekeepers in Somalia. They plotted to assassinate the Pope and the President of Egypt. They planned to bomb six United States 747s over the Pacific . . . their (terrorist) mission is murder and their history is bloody. The most recent terrorist events are fresh in our memory. Two weeks ago, twelve Americans and 300 Kenyans and Tanzanians lost their lives. Another 5,000 were wounded when our embassies in Nairobi and Dar es Salaam were bombed." The attack against a factory believed to be developing chemical weapons was carried out by a sea launched missile attack from U.S. naval ships in the Red Sea. The exact details of the strike were not confirmed; however, news reports seen on television indicate massive damage to the Al-Shifa Pharmaceutical Factory in Khartoum.

This attack will, in all likelihood, only harden the radicals' resolve to continue the fight. Throughout the Middle East and Asia, there were spontaneous demonstrations against the United States, and the action has probably given significant impetus to the Islamic extremist movement in Afghanistan. As in the 1986 strike against Libya, this kind of response is not seen as an effective deterrent. To many analysts, it is seen as having precisely the opposite effect.

ALGERIA

The People's Democratic Republic of Algeria (Algeria) emerged from its French colonial era through a nationalist movement that pitted the FLN (Fronte de Liberation National) against French security forces brutally aided by a pro-France terrorist organization known as the OAS (*Organisation Armie Secrete*). The terrorists' struggle lasted from 1954-62; one million Algerians and 17,500 French occupation forces were killed before the Evian Agreement of 1962 ended the FLN's campaign of assassination, bombing and sabotage and the French's ferocious counterinsurgency campaign of torture, death and repression.[41] The FLN emerged as victorious revolutionary heroes whose primary sense of political legitimacy lay in throwing out colonial suppressors. Algeria emerged from an effective two-pronged FLN campaign against the French: the guerrilla war in the cities and rugged countryside of Algeria, and a diplomatic campaign in European and African capitals. France agreed to a plebescite in 1962 on the issue of independence; 99% of the votes were cast in favor of Algerian independence. Ahmed Ben Bella, an FLN political leader during the war of independence, became the first president of independent Algeria. The FLN was in power from 1962 to 1992, when the civilian government was dissolved in a political coup.

Algeria remained officially a one-party socialist country for the three decades of 1962–1992, assisted by the French in oil and gas technology, capital fusions, and foreign aid. Population growth increased the size of the nation from nine million in 1962 to more than 28 million in 1995; 75% of Algerians are under age 25.

The subsequent rise of a radical Islamic movement in Algeria, which won a round of parliamentary elections in 1991, caused the FLN to abandon the election process and nullify the results. The party in question was the Islamic Salvation Front (FIS) and because of its radical Islamic goals was immediately banned by the FIS. Following the ban, its military wing commenced a campaign of attacks against government and security forces.

Economic Crisis

It can be argued that the FLN was ineffective in governing Algeria from 1962 to 1992.[42] A rapidly growing number of young persons eager to secure economic positions and hoping for a brighter future encountered bureaucratic inefficiencies of a socialist state economy, coupled with corruption and rigid attempts to control entrepreneurship. A severe housing shortage emerged, along with declining agricultural and industrial production and a devastating drop in oil prices. The economic situation was complicated by a lack of consumer goods, high unemployment and rising inflation. Servicing Algeria's huge foreign debt (more than $30 billion in 1995) requires almost all of the $9 billion in annual oil and gas revenues. In 1986, an austerity plan was imposed, in part to secure International Monetary Fund assistance.

October 1988 Riots.   The deteriorating economic situation shattered social and economic expectations. Riots ensued and the military responded with excessive repression, firing on and killing hundreds of protestors/demonstrators. Thousands were arrested, and shortly thereafter rumors began to circulate of security forces' torturing dissidents. Algeria's older citizenry, freedom fighters three decades before in the 1960–62 era, equated the military's torture to that of the "Colons" (the sometimes brutal French leaders of colonial days), a similarity that struck a cord and captured some Algerian hearts.

In late 1988, then President Chadli Benjedid undertook a democratic initiative and referendums were held in 1988 and 1989, changing the Constitution and including more respect for civil rights and a free press. Formation of political associations was permitted, and the one-party (FLN) system was abandoned.

By February 1989, at least fifty new political parties were formed, including the FIS (Front Islamic du Salat), recognized as legal in September 1989 (Alexander). The FIS was organized through mosques, and by late 1989 had at least three million adherents. FIS political themes included criticizing the state bureaucracy, widespread corruption, and western secular elites (French influences, primarily). Reflecting Islamic influences, subordination of women was advocated. The FIS sought an Islamic state, governed by Islamic law; it proposed to discriminate against ethnic and other minorities (Berbers, Jews, Christians, polytheists, etc.) and French-speakers ("the enemies of God"). Religious extremists sought imposition of *shari'a* law onto all social and political life.

These earlier political pronouncements, especially the proposed imposition of puritan codes (drinking, dress, calendar, etc.), alarmed the educated, business people and intellectuals. Minorities, French speakers, women and the more educated staged counter-demonstrations. Many secular parties boycotted the elections of Fall 1990.

In the June 1990 elections for municipal, department and provincial assemblies, the FLN was decisively defeated. The FIS won 54% of the popular vote cast, which totaled between 65–75% of the eligible voters. Since no elections had been held for national assembly, the FLN still controlled the national political scene and prepared for the June 1991 elections by gerrymandering to give more representation to FLN strongholds and districts. In this environment, one FIS leader (Abbassi Madani) called for a general strike, adoption of an Islamic state, and resistance through jihad and civil disobedience. The FIS was, interestingly, openly split over this call. Disruptive events occurred, but not mass revolution; the army declared a state of siege, and elections were rescheduled for December.

There is some suggestion that the FIS might not have fared well in the Fall 1991 elections, as they had not distinguished themselves at local, urban and municipal administration. It may have been that gerrymandering was an FLN provocation, and the FIS overreaction was triggered in part through infiltration of the FIS. In any event, the military declared a state of siege, banning meetings, publications, and demonstrations; suspending activities of political associations; and detaining civilian suspects. The military assumed local arrest authority and military tribunals conducted trials. FIS leaders were arrested en masse, and detained in camps and jails. By fall 1991, the state of siege was lifted to permit elections, scheduled by Chadli Benjedid for December 1991 and January 1992.

December 1991 Elections. In the December phase of the national election, the FIS won 189 of 231 National Assembly seats with 47% of the eligible vote; the rejection of the FLN was obvious. Faced with a certain FIS victory, the military pressured the president to resign. The National Assembly was dissolved, and the *Haut Comite d'Etat* (HEC) imposed. On January 11, 1992, the military coup was effected. The HEC banned the FIS (its principal opposition party), jailed almost all the known leaders, detained some 9,000–30,000 FIS members in five detention camps, and cracked down on the press. The latter included searching newspaper premises, expelling resident correspondents of European newspapers, arresting journalists writing for pro-fundamentalist papers, and jailing the editor of an independent weekly.

On January 22, authorities arrested the acting head of the FIS, radicalizing the movement and provoking widespread violence between FIS militants and security forces. A state of emergency was declared that continued until late 1995. By March 1992, the FIS leadership not in detention went underground or into exile, or migrated to adjacent countries. On May 5, military courts sentenced twelve FIS men to hang for the deaths of three army soldiers.[43] Five other Islamic extremist groups emerged and spread through Algeria: Armed Islamic Movement Group (an off-shoot of FIS), Armed Islamic Group, Hezbollah, Repentance and Emigration (al-Takfir wa'l Hijra), and Afghans (mostly veterans of the Afghanistan war). Actions were mostly decentralized acts of random terrorism and guerilla warfare. The volume of terrorist events increased sharply, and included attacks on security forces, assault on the navy headquarters, and attacks on foreigners.[44] Bombings, assassinations, and attacks on governmental representatives expanded to include slitting the throats of captured foreigners, FLN members and journalists. Disco dancers were killed by throat-slitting and shooting. Petroleum workers were shot and plants were bombed. In the countryside, with its rugged terrain and desperately poor inhabitants, guerillas controlled most of the mountain range. Satellite dishes were torn down, newspapers banned, women forced to wear traditional veils, men and women were segregated on buses, and Iranian-style enforcement of Islamic law prevailed. Eventually, an Air France airbus was hijacked, resulting in French security forces storming of the plane, rescuing of hostages, and killing of the hijackers.[45] Four nuns in Algiers were subsequently killed in retaliation. Iran and the Sudan provided arms and military training to the terrorists. To cut French support of the Algerian regime ($1.2 billion in annual aid to the Algerian government, intelligence and training), a series of bombings in Paris and other French cities was undertaken, resulting in deaths and casualties and putting a considerable dent in tourism as such attacks were widely reported by the media during 1995.

Algerian military undertook brutal and repressive actions in response to Islamic terrorism and violence. Military courts began to execute civilians convicted in the three courts that enforced the stringent antiterrorism law; executions began and a strict curfew was declared. Security forces known as "**Ninjas**"[46] arrested suspects who were found dead in public places. The next day pro-government death squads patrolled both rural and urban areas, and anti-FIS vigilantes took the law into their own hands. Villages formed self-defense groups to ward off FIS terrorism. Riots within prisons were fostered by FIS and other resistance members and were brutally repressed, along with the wholesale slaughter of detained FIS leaders.[47] The army was expanded through conscription, with mandatory military service of 18 months, and the military budget jumped 90% from 1992–93. The military elite appeared to become "eradicationalists," arguing that Islamic extremism could be stopped only by force.

By 1994, foreign investment had diminished to a trickle, families of diplomats were evacuated, embassies had been closed, the official unemployment rate had risen to 20%, the Algerian dinar (currency) had been devalued 50%, and servicing the international debt was consuming most of the petroleum-generated income. Efforts toward "national reconciliation" by national dialogue were made but failed, primarily by government intransigence in meeting directly with FIS leaders, or FIS boycotting of dialogues in other international sites. Even "secret meetings" appeared to have no appreciable ameliorative effect. It was in this environment that the military regime replaced the HEC with retired General Liamine Zeroual as President, signaling the direct movement of the military into the political arena.

The Armed Islamic Group (GIA)

This is an FIS splinter organization which continued the fight against the military regime. Since this North African country plunged into a civil war in 1992, the group has been linked to terrorist attacks in Europe and to the massacres of tens of thousands of civilians in Algeria. The crackdown by the government has been as fierce in Algeria as witnessed in Egypt and, in a similar vein, the GIA seek to overthrow the current regime and replace it with a radical Islamic one. Many GIA members have joined other groups in Algeria to continue attacks against the secular government. This group is also credited with the audacious hijacking of an Air France airliner from Algeria to France in 1994, in which the terrorists had planned to set off explosives over the French capital, Paris. The GIA have targeted their ex-colonial rulers in particular and have carried out limited bombing campaigns in France.

The French government has continued to support the military government in Algeria much to the opposition and ire of the GIA. Possible links to al-Qaeda could relate to Ahmed Ressam an Algerian national who attempted to cross from Canada to the U.S. with a bomb destined for Los Angeles International airport in what is termed the "millennium plot." Although Ressam is Algerian and is believed to have met with al Qaeda operatives this does not necessary widen the ties between the two groups. The GIA's aims are purely internal as it relates to the removal of the secular government, whereas the al-Qaeda objectives are truly international.

Many Algerians, grown tired of the poor standards of living, yearn to leave and join others. Most mainly in France, but many have fled to and sought refugee status in Canada. Their ability to speak French makes the Province of Quebec an ideal choice for settlement. In the aftermath of 9–11 there has been serious focus not only on immigration policies particularly in Canada but also on those Algerians that are currently resident inside the country and their possible involvement to al Qaeda.

SUMMARY

Marked changes have taken place in the Middle East and North Africa over the last seventy-five years or so. Israel's statehood became a reality, and Palestinian statehood did not. In spite of the Oslo accord of the last decade, peace seems as far away now as it has been for decades. Israel remains the major power broker in the region and is prepared to use its military might whenever and wherever it sees fit, to protect its nationhood. As for Palestine, the region remains locked in a time warp of refugees under strict controls from military doctrines of the Israeli government. In spite of any peaceful overtures from either side it is clear that as long as the hard liners from such groups as Hamas and Hezbollah are allowed free reign in the region, peace will most likely arrive only after much more bloodshed. The shadow of Osama bin Laden and his group hangs heavy over the region, particularly in Egypt where much of his support originates. The memory of Libya's involvement in the Pan Am disaster has not been allowed to fade.

TERMS TO REMEMBER

Abu Nidal	*fedayeen*	NMO
Al-Fatah	GIA	no solution
Ariel (Arik) Sharon (Shinerman)	Hamas	PFLP
	Hashemite Kingdom	PIJ
Balfour Declaration	Hezbollah	PLF
Black September	Jihad	PLO
Declaration of Principles	Kach and Kahane	Shi'a
	Libya Operation	Sunni
DFLP	"Ninjas"	Unit 101
FATAH		

REVIEW QUESTIONS

1. Discuss the importance of the Balfour Declaration and its influence on terrorism.
2. Describe the genesis of the PLO and what has been their role in the Middle East.
3. Discuss the destabilizing role of Hamas in the peace process.
4. Explain the role of the extreme right wing orthodox Jews in the peace process.
5. Why do you think that the Libyan president has kept such a low profile during the 1990s?

ENDNOTES

1. Council For the National Interest http://www.cnionline.org.
2. William Roger Louis, *The British Empire in the Middle East 1945–1951*, (Oxford: Clarendon Press, 1988) p. 439.
3. Mark Ethridge, U.S. member of the Palestine Conciliation report to State Department. Top Secret, NIACT, Beirut, March 28, 1949, FRUS 1949, pp. 876, 878.
4. Donald Neff, *Fallen Pillar*, U.S. Policy towards Palestine and Israel since 1945, (Institute for Palestine Studies, Washington, DC, 1995) p. 83.

5. The Foundation for Middle East Peace, *Report on Israeli Settlement in the Occupied Territories,* Special Report, July 1991 and Richard F. Nyrop (ed), *Israel: a Country Study,* 2nd Ed. (Washington, DC: U.S. Government Printing Office, 1979), p. XIX: Epp, p. 185.

6. Jody A Boudreault et al., (eds) *U.S. Official Statements: Israeli Settlements,* p. 15 (Washington, D.C.) Institute for Palestine Studies, 1992 p. 15.

7. Noam Chomsky, *The New Intifada, Resisting Israel's Apartheid, Verso,* London. Edited by Roane Carey 2001 p. 13.

8. "The beginning of the end of the Palestinian uprising?" *The Economist,* September 29, 2001 p. 50.

9. Yallop. *Tracking the Jackal,* David Yallop "Tracking the Jackal" Random House Inc. New York 1993, p. 335.

10. George Rosie. *The Directory of International Terrorism,* Paragon House, New York, 1987, p. 290.

11. Ibid p. 36.

12. Richard Clutterbuck. *Guerrillas and Terrorists,* Ohio University Press, 1980, p. 80.

13. Union of Palestine Relief Committees, "An Overview of the Gaza Strip", p. 3 issue # 25, March 1997.

14. This material was drawn from an article by Ahhmad Rashad, "The Truth about Hamas" on the Internet September 6, 1998. http://www.cyberus.ca/~baker/pac411.htm.

15. MidEastWeb for Coexistence R.A. - http://www.mideastweb.org.

16. STRATFOR (Strategic Forecasting) website, May 17, 2002 "Hamas vying to lead Palestinians." http://www.stratfor.com/standard/analysis.

17. "Hamas has the people's heart," *The Economist,* December 1, 2001, p. 43.

18. This material was drawn from MILNET articles maintained by George Goncalves, "Patterns of Global Terrorism," United States Department of State Publications 10321, 1997.

19. Ibid.

20. Ibid.

21. Ibid.

22. David Yallop *Tracking the Jackal* Random House Inc. New York 1993 p. 601.

23. Edward Said. "Palestinians Under Siege," p. 33. The New Intifada: Resisting Israel's Apartheid. Ed. Roane Carey. Verso London 2001.

24. Tom Gross. "Children are indoctrinated into terrorism," *The Weekly Telegraph,* London, Telegraph Group Inc. September 1, 1998, p. 20, Issue No 371.

25. Paul Wilkinson. *Terrorism and the Liberal State,* New York University Press, 1979, p. 49.

26. Slain Christian Warlord had no shortage of enemies. Article by Khaled Yacoub Oweis, Reuters with the daily telegraph. January 25, 2002.

27. The Internet. "The Five Pillars of Islam," *Political Islam Glossary.* http://www.megastories.com/islam/glossary/5pillows.

28. The Internet. "Sunnis and Shiites, the Great Schism," *Political Islam Glossary. Ibid.*

29. Ayala Hammond Schbley. "A Study of Some of the Lebanese Shi'a Contemporary Terrorism," *Terrorism an International Journal,* Taylor & Francis 1989, p.220, vol. 12 #4.

30. Magnus Ranstorp. "Hizballah's Command Leadership," *Terrorism and Political Violence,* Frank Cass, London, 1994, p.304 Vol. 6, #3.

31. Yonah Alexander. "Hizballah: The Most Dangerous Terrorist Movement" *Intersec,* Three Bridges Publishing Ltd. October 1994, p.393 Vol. 4, Issue 10.

32. Edgar O'balance. "Islamic Fundamentalist Terrorism." *Intersec,* Three Bridges Publishing Ltd. January 1995, p.14 Vol. 5 Issue 1.

33. Guy Lawson, *Time Magazine, A Few Good Martyrs.* January 2002. pp. 89–93.

34. Patterns of Global Terrorism: 1997 U.S State Department, Hellenic resources Network. http://www.hri.org/docs/USSD-Terror.

35. Jonathan R White. *Terrorism an Introduction,* Wadsworth Publishing Co. U.S.A. Second Edition, 1997, p. 141.

36. Heather Blearney and Richard Lawless. *The Middle East since 1945,* B.T. Batsford Ltd., London, 1989, p. 37.

37. Ibid. p.60.

38. International Policy Institute for Counter Terrorism. www.ict.org.

39. Libya. *Anti-Semitism World Report 1997* – The Internet.
40. Patterns of Global Terrorism: 1984, *Terrorism an International Journal,* Crane Russak & Company, Inc.1987 p. 419 vol. 9, number 3.
41. G Rosie, *The Directory of International Terrorism.* Paragon House, New York, 1986.
42. Martha Crenshaw, "Political Violence in Algeria," *Terrorism and Political Violence* 6/3 (1994): 261–280.
43. Youssef Ibrahim. "Algeria Sentences 12 Militants to Hang", *New York Times,* May 4, 1992. A–3.
44. Rachid Khiari. "Downtrodden Algeria Ruled by Death, Fear," *San Francisco Examiner,* April 4, 1994: A–9.
45. Thomas Sancton, "Anatomy of a Hijack," *Time Magazine,* January 9, 1995:54–57.
46. Christopher, Dickey. "The Ninjas Crack Down," *Newsweek,* June 19, 1995: 43–44.
47. Jesse Birnbaum, "The Prison of Blood" *Time Magazine* March 6, 1995.

8 The Persian Gulf

We suppose that humans are by nature wicked, the kindness and love need special explanation. If, on the other hand, we think that the depth of our soul knows only good we must provide and account of wickedness and violence.

John Lachs

OVERVIEW

Because of recent historical events in that area of the world, the Persian Gulf, the body of water that is surrounded by a number of Arab and Islamic states, is well known to most students. The oil crises, the exile of the Shah of Iran, the Iraq-Iran war, the hostages at the U.S. Embassy in Iran, the Gulf War and its continuing aftermath and other headline events have made the Persian Gulf a household term. But little is really known about this far away area of the world in regard to why it is the way it is today. Perhaps one of the most important areas of the world, especially when considering state-sponsored terrorism, the Persian Gulf is surrounded by some of the biggest players in the fields of terrorism. The student will be given a fast-moving tour through the history and background of the major political and religious events in this fascinating region. It will be shown how these countries are shaping the future of this region and how their past has influenced the present. These oil-rich countries have the power to bring modern technological societies to their knees, simply by cutting off the supply of that most critical commodity—oil. We begin our visit to the lands of the Arabian nights with the world's largest oil producer, Saudi Arabia.[1]

SAUDI ARABIA

The Kingdom of Saudi Arabia has borders with the Persian Gulf and on the Red Sea, north of Yemen. The kingdom is slightly more than one-fifth the size of the United States and only two percent of its land is considered arable. Bordering countries are Iraq, Jordan, Kuwait, Oman, Qatar, the United Arab Emirates and Yemen. Most of the country is a harsh, dry, mostly uninhabited sandy desert, with great extremes of temperature. Despite these conditions its petroleum, natural gas, iron ore, gold and copper have made Saudi Arabia a very rich nation. The Saudis' extensive coastlines on the Persian Gulf and Red Sea provide great leverage on shipping (especially crude oil) through the Gulf and the Suez Canal. With a population of only twenty million (which includes five million non-nationals), it is able to build and support the infrastructure for the kingdom in grand style. Ethnic groups are limited, with 90% being Arab and the remainder Afro-Asian. One hundred percent are Muslim and the official language is Arabic. As an Islamic monarchy, there is no constitution, but is governed according to Shari'a (Islamic law) as is the legal system.

King Abdul Aziz

The history of modern Saudi Arabia begins in the year 1902 when Abdul Aziz Al-Sa'ud and a band of his followers captured the city of Riyadh, returning it to the control of his family. **Abdul Aziz** was born about 1880 and spent the early years of his life with his father in exile in Kuwait. After the capture of Riyadh, he spent the next twelve years consolidating his conquests in the area around Riyadh and the eastern part of the country from where the Turks were expelled. The Arab tribes had never liked the Turks and they were only too willing to listen to a new ruler whose ambitions were aided considerably by the troubles of the Ottoman Empire. In 1933, the lands under the control of Abdul Aziz were renamed the Kingdom of Saudi Arabia and in 1936 a treaty was signed with Yemen marking the southern borders of the Kingdom.

The main preoccupations of Abdul Aziz were the consolidation of his power and the restoration of law and order to all parts of his recently created kingdom. To these ends, he developed a system whereby every sheikh was responsible for his own tribe under the authority of the king who was empowered to intervene to impose law and order. It was clearly understood that internal anarchy within the kingdom could quickly lead to foreign intervention. All were agreed that this was unacceptable. King Abdul Aziz died in 1953, after more than half a century as leader and king. Saud bin Abdul Aziz, his eldest son, succeeded him.

After eleven years, King Saud abdicated in favor of his brother, Faisal, the Crown Prince. In March 1975, King Faisal was assassinated in Riyadh by one of his nephews. The transfer of power, however, went smoothly and King Khalid bin Abdul Aziz took power, with Fahad bin Abdul Aziz being made Crown Prince. King Khalid continued most of King Faisal's policies that enjoyed great popularity. It was during King Khalid's reign that Saudi Arabia enjoyed the prosperity and enormous wealth of the so-called petro-dollar boom years.

King Khalid died in June 1982 and was succeeded by Crown Prince Fahad bin Abdul Aziz. King Fahad was well versed in the arts of government as he had served as the country's first Minister of Education. King Khalid had been in poor health for much of his reign, so Fahad had been ruling in all but title. Continuing development within the country and the infrastructure marked King Fahad's reign. On the political front, the open hostility from Iran toward Saudi Arabia led the government to strengthen its ties of defense with the United States, Britain and France.

Within days of Iraq's invasion of Kuwait in 1990, King Fahad allowed U.S. troops into the kingdom to help defend the country. In November 1990, King Fahad announced that plans were being made for the formation of Consultative Council; there was some feeling that this was done in response to criticism that he had not consulted widely enough before allowing foreign troops into the kingdom. In any case, in March 1992, the King announced that the Consultative Council would be appointed by year's end and he also made its duties clear. Like other such creations in the Gulf States, the Council is a purely consultative body with no legislative powers. Its formation, however, simply puts an official stamp on the long-standing system of consultation, which has long been a mark of Arab politics and society.

The Bush administration's most recently proposed Middle East peace plan will allow the United States to pursue its primary mission, which is hunting down the al Qaeda in the Gulf states. However, it will also strengthen Palestinian leader Yasir Arafat and widen the split with the Saudis, who will be forced to seek closer ties with Iran and Iraq. President George W. Bush made some tough statements on June 24, 2002, when he outlined the new United States plan for peace in the Middle East and set specific terms for dealing with the Palestinians. He again called on Palestinians to reform and promised that when the Palestinian people have new leaders, new institutions and new security arrangements with their neighbors, the United States of America will approve and support the creation of a Palestinian state whose borders, and certain aspects of its sovereignty, will be provisional until resolved as part of a final settlement in the Middle East.

Demanding that the Palestinians essentially replace Yasir Arafat, Washington has substantially improved Arafat's position. Anyone within the Palestinian community who now demands Arafat's resignation is open to the charge of collaborating with the Americans. The United States is aware of the consequences of its demand. By making reform and new leadership prerequisites for further American participation in a peace process, the United States has created the framework for its withdrawal from that process.

The U.S. president was, in effect, washing his hands of trying to solve the Israeli-Palestinian conflict. Washington's challenge, however, is not aimed at the Palestinians but at the country that pushed for greater U.S. involvement in the peace process—Saudi Arabia. Riyadh tried to shift U.S. attention from its war against terrorists and al Qaeda by making clear resolution of the Israeli-Palestinian conflict a key prerequisite for Saudi cooperation in hunting down Osama bin Laden's associates and financiers. Bush's actions are a warning to the Saudis that the conflict between Israel and the Palestinians can no longer serve as a distraction.

This could mean that a Saudi-U.S. confrontation may be on the horizon. By no longer taking responsibility for the Palestinians, Washington seems to be reaffirming its goal of destroying al Qaeda. To do this, it must strike at the network's center of gravity, Saudi Arabia. In response, the oil-rich kingdom may now seek to create alliances to resist American pressure. Worried about U.S. military deployments in Yemen and the surrounding Gulf states and unable to trust its strong ally in the region, Jordan, the Saudis might decide to move to strengthen ties with the two countries most committed to resisting U.S. dominance, Iran and Iraq.

From the Palestinians to Riyadh

Saudi Arabia inserted itself in the peace process when Crown Prince Abdullah used a column, written by *New York Times* writer, Thomas Friedman, earlier in 2002 in order to publicize his own newly created Middle East peace proposal.

Abdullah offered Israel complete normalization of ties with all the Arab states in exchange for Israel's full withdrawal to the 1967 borders. Though this was a promise Riyadh actually could not deliver, the tactic worked to buy time and direct the U.S. focus away, albeit temporarily, from Iraq and al Qaeda.

President Bush's new Middle East policy seems to make the United States appear eager to expand its involvement in the Middle East conflict. The president promised that the United States would, along with the international community, assist in organizing and monitoring fair, multi-party local elections by the end of 2002 and also help reform and develop the Palestinian economy.

It seems clear that the Bush administration will only be able to achieve any reforms if the Palestinians are willing to work with Washington. However, peace requires a new and different Palestinian leadership, if a Palestinian state can expect to be born. As no Palestinian politician or security chief would be able to cooperate with Washington without appearing to the Palestinian public to be a U.S. stooge, this issue is still up in the air. But President Bush has indicated that although Washington will continue to be engaged, its focus will change. Specifically, the Bush administration will try to segment its Middle East policy, placing the Israeli-Palestinian conflict in a box to free a policy to pursue its primary Middle Eastern goals, which are destroying the al Qaeda, displacing Iraqi President Saddam Hussein, and containing Iran. The single-most important piece of any U.S. strategy to annihilate bin Laden's terrorist network is to do something about Saudi Arabia. Since Riyadh has until now been a key U.S. ally in the Gulf, where the other two regional powers Iran and Iraq are decidedly anti-American, Washington has resisted placing any blame for 9–11 squarely on the Saudis.

KUWAIT

The State of Kuwait, a nominal constitutional monarchy, is slightly smaller than New Jersey, and lies between Iraq and Saudi Arabia, bordering the Persian Gulf. While its primary natural resource is petroleum, fish, shrimp, and natural gas are also plentiful. It is another Persian Gulf country with almost no arable land and no permanent crops. (About 75% of its potable water must be distilled or imported.) Kuwait has strategic value in its location at the head of Persian Gulf. The small population of only 1,834,269 includes 1,381,063 non-nationals. The ethnic mix is Kuwaiti 45%, other Arab 35%, South Asian 9%, Iranian 4% and other 7%. Muslims make up 85% of the religious followers, but are split: Shi'a 30%, Sunni 45%, other 10%. Christians, Hindus, Parsi and others make up the remaining 15%. While the official language is Arabic, English is widely spoken as Kuwait only gained its independence from the United Kingdom in 1961.

The Chief of State is Amir Jabir al-Ahmad al-Jabir Al Sabah (since December 1977) and the head of government is a prime minister. While there are no official political parties and leaders, several political groups act as de facto parties, (e.g., Bedouins, merchants, Sunni and Shi'a activists, and secular leftists and nationalists).

Kuwait has a small and relatively open economy with proven crude oil reserves of about 94 billion barrels, or roughly 10% of world reserves. Kuwait has rebuilt its war-ravaged petroleum sector; its crude oil production averages two million barrels per day. Petroleum accounts for nearly half of GDP, 90% of export revenues, and 75% of government income. Kuwait lacks water and has practically no arable land, thus preventing development of agriculture. With the exception of fish, it depends almost totally on food imports.

Because of its high per capita income, comparable with Western European incomes, Kuwait provides its citizens with extensive health, educational and retirement benefits. The bulk of the work force is non-Kuwaiti, living at a considerably lower level. Per capita military expenditures are among the highest in the world. The economy improved moderately since 1994, with the growth in industry and finance. The World Bank has urged Kuwait to push ahead with privatization, including in the oil industry, but the government will move slowly on opening up the petroleum sector. Relatively low petroleum prices can have a serious impact on the Kuwaiti economy. The civil telephone network suffered some damage as a result of the Gulf War, but most of the telephone exchanges were left intact. By the end of 1994 Kuwait had restored domestic and international telecommunications to normal operation and the quality of service is excellent.

In November 1994, Iraq formally accepted the U.N.-demarcated border with Kuwait that had been spelled out in Security Council Resolutions 687 (1991), 773 (1993), and 883 (1993). This formally ended Iraq's earlier claims to Kuwait and to Bubiyan and Warbah Islands. Saudi Arabia disputes ownership of Qaruh and Umm al Maradim Islands.

The present **Al-Sabah dynasty** was established in Kuwait in the mid-eighteenth century, about 1760. Kuwait was nominally a province of the Ottoman Empire, ruled from Constantinople. This was observed on paper but seldom in fact. In 1899 when the Turks threatened to take actual control of the country, the ruling sheikh sought and received British protection.

The Kuwait Oil Company discovered oil in Kuwait in 1938 but, because of World War II, it was not exported until 1946, after which time Kuwait's economy flourished. Kuwait remained a British protectorate until 1961 when it became independent under Sheikh Abdullah Al-Salem Al-Sabah. However, when Iraq claimed the emirate in the early 1960s, it once again received British protection. In July 1961 Kuwait joined the Arab League and in 1963 became a member of the United Nations. Also in 1963 the first legislative elections were held and Sheikh Abdullah, the Emir of Kuwait, inaugurated the first National Assembly in February 1963.

During the 1980s, Kuwait experienced several terrorist attacks by Shiite Muslim extremists, including one in 1985 that attempted to assassinate the emir. Kuwait, like most Arab states, supported Iraq in the Iran-Iraq War (1980–1988). Kuwait played a major role in establishing the **Gulf Cooperation Council** (GCC) consisting of Saudi Arabia, Kuwait, Bahrain, Qatar, the United Arab Emirates and the Sultanate of Oman in 1981. The Council held a firm position during Iraq's invasion of Kuwait on August 2, 1990, and its seven-month occupation of the Emirate.

When the oil industry was developed, the resources were used to tame the desert through construction and the planting of greenery. The oil resources were also used for the good of the Kuwaiti people and their brothers and sisters in developing countries around the world. Rather than befriend a tyrant or surrender to Saddam Hussein in the Gulf War, Kuwait stood firm in the heart of all the battles it faced. The battle of resistance against aggression was followed by the battle of extinguishing the oil fires and of rebuilding a ravaged nation. During the period of the Iraqi occupation, from August 2, 1990, to its liberation on February 26, 1991, the inhabitants of Kuwait once again gave evidence of their strength and fierce determination.

IRAQ

As this text goes into production, the debate continues as to how, when and with what to unseat Saddam Hussein. Time will tell if his removal from office, by any means, will open up a chance for calm in the Persian Gulf. The Republic of Iraq, which is slightly more than twice the size of Idaho, borders the Persian Gulf between Iran and Kuwait. Iraq gained independence from a League of Nations' mandate under British administration in 1932. Iraq has rich natural resources of petroleum, natural gas, phosphates and sulfur. Its population of a little more than twenty-two million is 75%–80% Arab, 15%–20% Kurdish with the remainder Turkoman, Assyrian or other. Iraq is 97% Muslim (Shi'a 60%–65%, Sunni 32%–37%) and 3% Christian or other. The official languages are Arabic and Kurdish. The chief of state and head of government is President Saddam Hussein. Political parties and activity are severely restricted.

The **Ba'thist regime** engages in extensive central planning and management of industrial production and foreign trade while leaving some small-scale industry and services and most agriculture to private enterprise. The economy has been dominated by the oil sector, which has traditionally provided about 95% of foreign exchange earnings. In the 1980s, financial problems were caused by massive expenditures in the eight-year war with Iran and damage to oil export facilities by Iran. This led the government to implement austerity measures and to borrow heavily and later reschedule foreign debt payments. Iraq suffered economic losses of at least $100 billion from the war. After the end of hostilities in 1988, oil exports gradually increased with the construction of new pipelines and restoration of damaged facilities. Seizure of Kuwait in 1990, and subsequent international economic embargoes, and military action by an international coalition beginning in January 1991 drastically changed the economic picture. Industrial and transportation facilities, which suffered severe damage, have been partially restored. Oil exports are at only 25% of the prewar level because of implementation of **United Nations Security Council Resolution 986** in December 1996. The U.N.-sponsored economic embargo has reduced exports and imports and has contributed to a sharp rise in prices. The Iraqi government has been unwilling to abide by U.N. resolutions so that the economic embargo could be removed. The government's policies of supporting large military and internal security forces and of allocating resources to key supporters of the regime have exacerbated shortages. In accord with a U.N. resolution, Iraq agreed to an oil-for-food deal in 1996, under which it would export $2 billion worth of oil in exchange for badly needed food and medicine. The first oil was pumped in December 1996, and the first supplies of food and medicine arrived in 1997.

Iran and Iraq restored diplomatic relations in 1990 but are still trying to work out written agreements settling outstanding disputes from their eight-year war concerning border demarcation, prisoners-of-war, and freedom of navigation and sovereignty over the Shatt al Arab waterway. In November 1994, Iraq formally accepted the U.N.-demarcated border with Kuwait that had been spelled out in Security Council Resolutions. This formally ended earlier claims to Kuwait and to Bubiyan and Warbah Islands. There is still dispute over water development plans by Turkey for the Tigris and Euphrates Rivers. Ironically, the area of the Middle East we now call Iraq, which we have seen in recent decades as a major source for state-sponsored terrorism and constant wars, is also where many scholars agree recorded history, as we know it, began.

In ancient times, the land area now known as modern Iraq was almost equivalent to Mesopotamia, the land between the two rivers (Tigris and Euphrates). The Mesopotamian plain was called the **Fertile Crescent.** This region was the birthplace of the varied civilizations that moved us from prehistory to history. An advanced civilization flourished in this region long before that of Egypt, Greece and Rome, for it was here in about 4000BC that the Sumerian culture flourished. Land was cultivated for the first time in this area, early calendars were used and the first written alphabet was invented there. Its bountiful land, fresh waters, and varying climate contributed to the creation of deep-rooted civilization that fostered humanity. Mesopotamia is suspected as the location for the Garden of Eden.

Hammurabi was the king and a great lawgiver of the Old Babylonian (Amorite) Dynasty. His law code was produced in the second year of his reign. Many new legal concepts were introduced by the Babylonians, and many have been adopted by other civilizations. These concepts included:

- Legal protection should be provided to lower classes;
- The state is the authority responsible for enforcing the law;
- Social justice should be guaranteed;
- The punishment should fit the crime.

A copy of the code is engraved on a block of black diorite nearly eight feet high. A team of French archaeologists at Susa, Iraq, formerly ancient Elam, unearthed this block, during the winter of 1901–1902. The block, broken in three pieces, has been restored and is now in the Louvre Museum in Paris.

Abu Ja'far Muhammad ibn Musa al-Khawarizmi (680–750 AD), a great scholar and mathematician, originated algebraic equations. And some credit him with the invention of the concept of zero. Al-Khawarizmi wrote ten math textbooks, which have survived the test of time. His *Kitab hisab al'adad al-hindi* was an arithmetic textbook, which introduced Hindu numbers to the Arab world. Now they are generally known as Arabic numbers. Christian Europeans at first rejected the Arabic numbers and declared them the work of Satan! His major work is entitled Kitab **(al-jabr)** w'al-muqabalah whose title gives us the word "algebra."

With a long and important history, Iraq developed into a major country on the Persian Gulf. In 1936, King Ghazi I formed the Pan Arab movement with the other Arab states, promising kinship and non-aggression. The first coup d'etat in the modern Arab world came in 1936 as well, led by General Baks Sidqi. This marked a major turning point in Iraq's long history, opening the door for further military involvement in politics. In 1945 Iraq became a founding member of the Arab League and joined the United Nations.

Iraq joined in the war with Israel in 1948, in which they allied with Jordan, in accordance with a treaty signed by the two countries during the previous year. The war had a negative impact on the Iraqi economy. Oil royalties paid to Iraq were halved when the pipeline to Haifa was cut off. The war led to the departure of most of Iraq's prosperous Jewish community. About 120,000 Iraqi Jews immigrated to Israel between 1948 and 1952.

In 1961, Kuwait gained its independence from Britain and Abdul-Karim Qassim immediately claimed the Emirate as originally part of the Ottoman province of Basrah. Britain reacted strongly by dispatching a brigade to the country to deter Iraq. Qassim backed down. In 1963, Iraq finally recognized the sovereignty and borders of Kuwait. (But this was not to be the last page of that story.)

In 1979, Saddam Hussein, who then assumed both of the vacated offices, replaced Ahmed Hasan Al-Bakr. Saddam purged political rivals in order to assure his position. Once more the political situation flared into hostilities with Iran. The Iran-Iraq War, which began in 1980, lasted for eight years and had a crippling effect on the economy of both countries. It was a monumental disaster and neither side gained any territory. But, an estimated total of one million lives had been lost. In July 1988, Iran accepted the terms of U.N. Resolution 598, and the cease-fire came about. Before Iraq had a chance to recover economically, Saddam once more plunged into war, with the invasion of Kuwait in 1990.

The United States got involved and declared its interest in keeping Saudi Arabia safe. In the ensuing months, the United Nations Security Council passed a series of resolutions condemning the Iraqi occupation of Kuwait, and applied total, mandatory economic sanctions against Iraq. A coalition of NATO nations as well as Arab states, subsequently provided support for Operation Desert Shield. In November, The U.N. Security Council adopted Resolution 678, permitting member states to use all necessary means, authorizing military action against the Iraqi forces occupying Kuwait, and demanding a complete withdrawal by January 1991.

Saddam Hussein failed to comply with this demand, and the Gulf War, **Operation Desert Storm,** began on January 17, 1991, with allied troops from twenty-eight countries. The combined air forces of Great Britain and the United States launched an aerial bombardment on Baghdad to start the battle. The war, which proved disastrous for Iraq, lasted only six weeks, but one hundred and forty thousand tons of munitions were dropped on the country and as many as 100,000 Iraqi soldiers were killed. Coalition air raids destroyed roads, bridges, factories, and oil industry facilities and disrupted electric, telephone, and water service. Finally, a cease-fire was announced on February 28, 1991. Iraq agreed to U.N. terms for a permanent cease-fire in April of that year, and strict conditions were imposed, demanding the disclosure and destruction of all stockpiles of weapons, including weapons of mass destruction (WMD).

Insurrections quickly broke out in southern Iraq and in Kurdistan in the north, where rebels took control of most of the region's towns. Units of Saddam's elite Republican Guard that had survived the conflict suppressed protest with extreme brutality to gain control in the Basrah, Najaf and Karbala regions. In the southern cities, rebels killed Ba'athist officials, members of the security service and other supporters of the Saddam regime. In **Kurdistan,**

October 14, 2002—Portrait of Saddam Hussein along with a hawk and the Lion of Babylon, in Baghdad. Below is a representation of the U.S. flag with skulls instead of stars, the Statue of Liberty holding a dagger, and a swastika. Portrait to mark Iraqi Referendum Day, October 15, 2002, when Iraqis overwhelmingly re-elected Saddam Hussein. (AP Photo/Jassim Mohammed)

Iraqi helicopters and troops regained control of the cities taken by the rebels and there was a mass exodus of Kurds to the Turkish and Iranian borders, fleeing from a possible repeat of the 1988 deadly chemical attacks. By the end of April, 2.5 million refugees had left Iraq.

The United States, attempting to prevent the genocide of the Marsh Arabs in southern Iraq and the Kurds to the north, established air exclusion zones north of the 36th parallel and south of the 32nd parallel. The attempted assassination of former President George Bush while in Kuwait prompted a swift military response on June 27, 1993. The Iraqi Intelligence Headquarters in Baghdad was targeted by twenty-three Tomahawk cruise missiles, launched from U.S. warships in the Red Sea and Persian Gulf.

In October 1994, Iraq again moved some Republican Guard units towards Kuwait, an act that provoked large-scale U.S. troops deployment to deter an Iraqi attack. The move was interpreted as a sign of Saddam's frustration with the continuation of stiff U.N. sanctions, but he backed down (establishing a pattern of behavior he is still using), and agreed to recognize the existence and borders of Kuwait. In the months that followed, his position appeared to become more precarious as dissatisfaction with his rule spread in the army and among the tribes and clans at the core of his regime.

In 1995, Saddam fired his half-brother, Wathban, as Interior Minister and in July demoted his notorious and powerful Defense Minister, Ali Hassan al-

Majid, to give more power to his two sons, Udai and Qusai. It became clear that Saddam felt more secure when protected by his immediate family members. Major General Hussein Kamil Hassan al-Majid, his Minister of Military Industries and a key henchman, defected to Jordan, together with his wife (one of Saddam's daughters) and his brother, Saddam (also married to one of the president's daughters), and called for the overthrow of the regime. In response, Saddam promised full co-operation with the U.N. commission disarming Iraq (UNSCOM) in order to pre-empt any revelations that the defectors might make. Not surprisingly, when the defectors were forgiven by Saddam and returned to Iraq, other clan members murdered them both, apparently, after they crossed the border.

The weakening of the internal position of the regime occurred at a time when the external opposition forces were as weak as ever, too divided among them to take any effective action. At the same time, France and Russia have pushed for an easing of sanctions. The United States and Britain's determination to keep up the pressure on Iraq has prevailed, however. In any case, the apparent weakening of the regime was illusory. In fact, during 1996, the regime's grip on power seemed to have significantly strengthened despite Saddam's inability to end the U.N. sanctions against it. Even as this is being written, there is now another major buildup of U.S. forces in the Gulf, as a result of Saddam's refusal to allow unrestricted inspections of suspected sites for storing weapons of mass destruction. It is clear that Saddam will continue to play

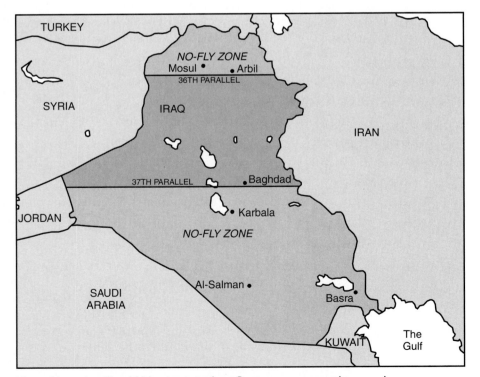

Map of Iraq detailing U.N. sanctioned no fly zones over northern and southern Iraq.

his unique game of cat and mouse with the world until he is eliminated, and war plans are said to be on the table to oust Saddam.

In May of 2002, on the eve of signing a historic U.S.-Russian nuclear arms reduction treaty, President Bush spoke strongly to President Putin of the Russian Republic, "If you arm Iran, you're liable to get the weapons pointed at you." Bush considers Russia's dealings with Iran the single greatest proliferation threat on the globe, a senior adviser said en route to Moscow. On a day that took him from the old East-West divide of Berlin to the heart of the former Soviet Union, a defiant Bush answered critics of his expanding anti-terror war plans. He denounced anyone who would appease terrorists or ignore threats to Europe.

Bush and Putin met to sign a ten-year treaty binding the nations to reduce their nuclear stockpiles by about two-thirds—to a range of 1,700 to 2,200 each. The three-page treaty has a preamble and just five articles. Hundreds of communists and leftists staged a noisy protest at the U.S. Embassy at the German capital. Bush responded to anti-war protesters who clogged city streets a day before—and to European leaders balking at his hopes of toppling Saddam.

President Bush came face to face with European opposition when three lawmakers from the ex-communist party of Democratic Socialism, seated about 20 feet away, held up a banner reading, Bush, Schroeder, Stop your wars. In a news conference before the address, German Chancellor Gerhard Schroeder declined to join Bush in pushing for a government change in Iraq. Separately, Defense Minister Rudolf Scharping suggested Germany did not have the resources to participate in military action against Saddam. We have no room for a new engagement, Scharping told German television. Nuclear proliferation is a sour point in a U.S.–Russia relationship that has flourished since 9–11. On another troubling issue, Bush said Putin understands that a loose nuke could affect his security and is doing what he can to prevent terrorists from getting nuclear materials from Russian stockpiles. As this edition goes to press, it is still unclear as to whether or not the United States will continue to prepare for and conduct another war against Iraq.[2]

BAHRAIN

The State of Bahrain is on a scattered archipelago in the Persian Gulf, east of Saudi Arabia. These landmasses are small, totaling only 3.5 times the size of Washington, DC. Bahrain has resources of oil, natural gas and fish. It is close to primary Middle Eastern petroleum sources, and located in a strategic position in the Persian Gulf. It has a very small population of 603,318 (including 221,182 non-nationals). Bahrain gained independence in 1971 from the United Kingdom.

The chief of state is Amir Isa bin Salman Al Khalifa (since 1961), and the head of government is the Prime Minister, Khalifi bin Salman Al Khalifa (since 1970). The cabinet is appointed by the amir. The amir is a traditional Arab monarch and political parties are prohibited. Political pressure groups and leaders are comprised of several small, clandestine leftist and Islamic fundamentalist groups. Following the arrest of a popular Shi'a cleric, Shi'a activists have fomented unrest sporadically since late 1994, demanding the return of an elected National Assembly and an end to unemployment.

In Bahrain, petroleum production and processing account for about 60% of export receipts, 60% of government revenues, and 30% of GDP. Economic conditions have fluctuated with the changing fortunes of oil since 1985, for example, during and following the Gulf crisis of 1990-91. With its highly developed communication and transport facilities, Bahrain is home to numerous multinational firms with business in the Gulf. A large share of exports consists of petroleum products made from imported crude. Construction proceeds on several major industrial projects. Unemployment, especially among the young, and the depletion of both oil and underground water resources are major long-term economic problems.

Bahrain has an ongoing international territorial dispute with Qatar over the Hawar Islands; maritime boundary with Qatar. The Sultanate continued to be plagued by arson attacks and other minor security incidents throughout 1997, most perpetrated by domestic dissidents. The most serious incident was an arson attack on a commercial establishment on June 13 that resulted in the death of four South Asian expatriates. One day later an abandoned vehicle detonated outside the passport directorate of Bahrain's Interior Ministry with no injuries. Bahraini courts in March convicted and sentenced to jail thirty-six individuals for being members of **Bahraini Hezbollah,** an Iranian-backed organization that sought the overthrow of the island's government. The jail sentences range from five to fifteen years. Some Bahraini Hezbollah members reportedly underwent terrorist training in camps in Iran and Lebanon.

The Sunni Muslim-led government in Bahrain is reforming the political system in order to pacify a vocal and increasingly discontented Shiite majority. However, these measures are limited in substance and may end up fueling more dissent and unrest in the country, a leading Persian Gulf banking center and U.S. Naval headquarters.

In February 2002, Bahrain's leader, Sheik Hamad bin Isa Al Khalifa, proclaimed himself king and declared his country a constitutional monarchy. Hamad also dissolved Bahrain's appointed consultative council, paving the way for the establishment of a bicameral parliament following elections scheduled for later in the year. Kuwait is currently the only Persian Gulf country with an elected parliament.

The government's transformation from the emirate system into a constitutional monarchy has been heralded as a step toward democracy. The feeling in the rest of the world is that it's not. Instead, it reflects the latest battle in an unresolved power struggle between Bahrain's minority Sunni Muslim-led government and the majority Shiite Muslim community. The shift will in the near term bring this struggle to the fore and could lead to another period of unrest in the tiny archipelago.

Instability in Bahrain could impact security and business in the entire Persian Gulf region. The country is not a major oil producer but does have a vital refining industry that imports crude from neighboring states. It is also an important financial hub for the region, with many foreign banks located in the capital Manama. Moreover, Manama is also headquarters for the U.S. Navy's 5th Fleet and a center for U.S. military operations in the Gulf.

Cooperation between Bahrain's two religious sects is critical to maintaining the island's calm. The situation in the country mirrors a historical contest between Islam's two largest sects throughout the Middle East and especially in the Persian Gulf. It also reflects two distinct communities' struggle for control over Bahrain's valuable resources.

OMAN

The Sultanate of Oman borders the Arabian Sea, Gulf of Oman, and Persian Gulf, between Yemen and United Arab Emirates. It is a country slightly smaller than Kansas with dry desert, and it is hot and humid along the coastal region. Although small, its natural resources include petroleum, copper, asbestos, some marble, limestone, chromium, gypsum and natural gas. This parched nation has no arable land and no permanent crops. Oman is strategically located on the Usandam Peninsula controlling the Strait of Hormuz, a vital transit point for world crude oil. The population of Oman, 2,264,590, is 75% Sunni Muslim, with the remainder Shi'a Muslim and Hindu. Oman is a sultanate, a monarchy which has been independent since 1650, when they expelled the Portuguese.

On November 6, 1996, Sultan Qaboos issued a royal decree promulgating a new basic law. Among other things, it clarified the royal succession, provided for a prime minister, barred ministers from holding interests in companies doing business with the government, established a bicameral Omani council, and guaranteed basic civil liberties for Omani citizens. The sultan is both the chief of state, the head of government and a hereditary monarch. Oman's economic performance is closely tied to the fortunes of the oil industry. Petroleum accounts for 75% of export earnings and government revenues and for roughly 40% of GDP. Oman has proven oil reserves of 4 billion barrels, equivalent to about 20 years' supply at the current rate of extraction. Agriculture is carried on at a subsistence level and the general population depends on imported food. The earliest settlements in Oman, as in the Arabian Peninsula generally, date from some time in the third millennium BC. Though at that time and for some hundreds of years more, Oman was on the edge of the trade routes linking ancient Mesopotamia to the Indus Valley, it does not appear to have profited a great deal from its location. Some centuries later, however, what is now Oman became of paramount importance to the ancient world.

The southernmost region of Oman, modern Dhofar, was responsible for the area's importance. It is one of the few spots in the world where frankincense trees grow. Frankincense is an aromatic gum from certain species of trees that grow only in southern Oman, the Wadi Hadhramaut in Yemen, and Somalia. The incense burns well because of its natural oil content. And in addition, it has medicinal uses. These two factors plus its relative scarcity made it an extremely sought after substance in the ancient world. (The gifts of the Magi to the Christ Child were gold, **frankincense,** and myrrh. At the time, gold was far less valuable than the other two.)

Frankincense was vital to the religious rites of almost every civilization in the ancient world. The great temples of Egypt, the Near East and Rome itself were all major consumers of the scarce commodity, not to mention the thousands of other temples found in every city, town and village. Indeed, the writer Pliny in the first century AD claimed that control of the frankincense trade had made the south Arabians the richest people on earth.

In the second century AD at the height of the trade, some 3,000 tons of frankincense were transported each year by ship from south Arabia to Greece, Rome and the Mediterranean world. The center of the trade was in a place now called Khor Rouri which the Greeks called Moscha. Though the trade went into a decline after the third century AD, it still managed to keep south Arabia relatively wealthy for another three centuries.

The tribes in the northern part of Oman were converted to Islam during the first generation of the Islamic era, the middle of the seventh century AD, and shortly thereafter came under the rule of the Umayyads whose center was in Damascus. About a century later, the Omanis revolted against the Umayyads and expelled them from their country. The Umayyads themselves had only a short time remaining as the leaders of the Muslim world, for the Abbasids whose capital was in Baghdad soon overthrew them.

Oman managed to remain free of the Abbasids and continued its adherence to Ibadi Islam, which is still dominant in the country today. Because of Oman's remoteness from other Muslims, the Ibadis survived as a group long after they had vanished from other parts of the Muslim world.

By the end of the eighteenth century, the Omanis were in control of an extensive empire. At its height in the nineteenth century, the empire ruled both Mombasa and Zanzibar and had trading posts much further down the African coast. (Oman's last colonial outpost—Gwadar, on what is now the coast of Pakistan—was not surrendered until September 1958, when Sultan Said bin Taimur allowed it to be re-integrated into Pakistan in return for a payment of £3 million.) In 1749 the first ruler of the present dynasty (Al-Busaid) gained power and in 1786 the capital was formally moved from the interior to Muscat. About this same time, the Al-Busaid adopted the title of Sultan that continues to this day.

The heyday of the Omani Empire occurred in the mid-nineteenth century under Sultan Said bin Sultan, who ruled from 1804–1856. He was responsible for bringing Dhofar under the Omani flag and he also extended Omani influence and control quite a way down the East African coast. He had an army of 6,500 men and a navy consisting of 15 ships. When he died, the empire split in two: one son became the Sultan of Zanzibar and the other the Sultan of Muscat and Oman. In the very name of the latter, the perceived difference between the interests of the coast and those of the interior was acknowledged. In fact, they were regarded, as two entities ruled by the same monarch, though the writ of the ruler in Muscat sometimes did not extend very far into the interior. Muscat's control depended very much upon the regard for the Sultan held by the tribes of the interior. In the early twentieth century, the sultan's power to control the interior of the country was felt to have decreased.

In February 1932, Sultan Said bin Taimur, father of the present ruler, came to power. When he tried to exercise his nominal control in the interior of the country in the early 1950s, the British, who believed there was oil, backed him. And in order to look for it, they needed the Sultan to have actual control of the area and for Oman's indefinite borders with Saudi Arabia and Abu Dhabi to be clearly defined and drawn. The ultimate result of this was a territorial dispute over the Buraimi oasis involving Oman, Saudi Arabia and Abu Dhabi. With British help and his own bravado, Sultan Said in the end was the winner and the Buraimi oasis is today firmly within the borders of Oman.

Sultan Said bin Taimur was, in the words of one British writer, an arch-reactionary of great personal charm. He wanted no change of any sort in Oman and did all that he could to isolate his country from the world. He issued all visas personally. He forbade travel to the interior by coastal residents and vice versa. Believing education was a threat to his power, he opposed it.

In general, Omanis were not allowed to leave the country and those who did were seldom allowed to return. The Sultan's only contact with the outside world was through his British advisers and Muscat's merchant families. He allowed these last to establish enormously lucrative monopolies for the import of goods, which he saw as crucial to his survival. In exchange, the merchants stayed out of politics and imported nothing which Sultan Said felt reeked of progress or the West (radios, books, eyeglasses). Through their customs receipts, the merchants provided the Sultan with most of the country's income. Aside from a few rich merchants, most of the population relied upon agriculture and fishing.

Oman has been Islamic since the seventh century. In about 1507, the city of Muscat and its hinterland came under Portuguese control. The Portuguese maintained their control until 1650 when the Omanis revolted and extended their influence as far south as the island of Zanzibar, off the African coast. The country was under Persian control for a short time (1741–1749) and then in 1798, a treaty of friendship was signed with Great Britain though Oman retained its independence. From 1932 to 1970, Oman was controlled by Sultan Said bin Taimur, a reclusive and repressive ruler whose policies finally resulted in revolt in Dhofar in 1965. In 1970 his son, the British-educated Qaboos bin Said overthrew him and embarked upon an ambitious modernization program. This small and tightly controlled country has been bypassed by most of the terrorism and violence in the region and is almost totally unknown in the rest of the world.

Oman, a key U.S. ally in the Middle East, is adjusting its budget to reflect its assistance to the War on Terrorism, but the oil-rich sultanate is actually reducing defense funding and shifting the savings into social welfare programs. Unlike many other governments in the region, Oman's regime has faced relatively little domestic opposition to its relationship with the United States. This is largely due to strong oil revenues and an extremely tolerant local segment of Islam. Even so, it appears the Omani leadership is investing in preventative measures to keep a lid on unrest, knowing that Washington will guarantee its external security. By addressing domestic security before it becomes an issue, Oman hopes to avoid the problems faced by neighboring Saudi Arabia, where extremist Muslims actively oppose the basing of U.S. military forces there. A pacified population will allow the Omani government to deepen its involvement with the U.S. military, which is likely re-examining its options in the anti-terror campaign.

The U.S. military currently uses at least three air bases in Oman as part of operations in Afghanistan. The Navy runs P-3 Orion aircraft patrols out of the Masirah air base, where at least one squadron of AC-130 gunships is based as well. Oman also hosts several Air Force pre-positioning sites, with enough equipment and fuel to maintain three air bases and 26,000 support personnel.

Its continuing support of the War on Terrorism makes Oman a key player in this global effort by the U.S. and the Coalition.

IRAN

One of the most controversial states in the Persian Gulf, the Islamic Republic of Iran borders the Gulf of Oman, the Persian Gulf, and the Caspian Sea, between Iraq and Pakistan. Iran is slightly larger than Alaska with large resources of petroleum, natural gas, coal, chromium, copper, iron ore, lead, manganese, zinc, sulfur. Its estimated population 67,540,000 includes 917,078 non-nationals with a broad base of ethnic groups (Persian 51%, Azerbaijani 24%, Gilaki and Mazandarani 8%, Kurd 7%, Arab 3%, Lur 2%, Baloch 2%, Turkmen 2%, other 1%) and religious affiliations (Shi'a Muslim 89%, Sunni Muslim 10%, Zoroastrian, Jewish, Christian, and Baha'i 1%). This broad spectrum is reflected in languages as well (Persian and Persian dialects 58%, Turkic and Turkic dialects 26%, Kurdish 9%, Luri 2%, Balochi 1%, Arabic 1%, Turkish 1%, other 2%). Iran is a theocratic republic and the constitution codifies Islamic principles of government.

Political pressure groups that generally support the Islamic Republic include *Ansar-e Hizballah*, *Mojahedin* of the Islamic Revolution, Muslim Students Following the Line of the Imam and the Islamic Coalition Association. Opposition groups include the Liberation Movement of Iran and the Nation of Iran party. Armed political groups that have been almost completely repressed by the government include Mojahedin-e Khalq Organization **(MEK)**, People's *Fedayeen*, Democratic Party of Iranian Kurdistan, and the Society for the Defense of Freedom.

Iran's economy is a mixture of central planning, state ownership of oil and other large enterprises, village agriculture, and small-scale private trading and service ventures. Under President Rafsanjani, the government adopted a number of market reforms to reduce the state's role in the economy, but most of these changes have moved slowly or have been reversed because of political opposition. In the early 1990s, Iran experienced a financial crisis caused by an import surge that began in 1989 and general financial mismanagement. In 1993–1994, Iran rescheduled $15 billion in debt, with the bulk of payments due in 1996–1997. The strong oil market in 1996 helped ease financial pressures, however, and Tehran has so far made timely debt service payments. In 1996, Iran's oil earnings—which account for 85% of total export revenues—climbed 20% from the previous year. Iran's financial situation remained tight through the end of the decade, and continued timely debt service payments depended, in part, on persistent strong oil prices during the following years, a prediction that has failed badly as petroleum prices plummeted in 1998.

Iran and Iraq restored diplomatic relations in 1990 but are still trying to work out written agreements settling outstanding disputes from their eight-year war concerning border demarcation, prisoners-of-war, and freedom of navigation and sovereignty over the Shatt al-Arab waterway. Iran is an illicit producer of opium poppy for the domestic and international drug trade, but net opiate importer and acts as a key trans-shipment point for Southwest Asian heroin to Europe.

TERROR BRIEF 8–1

Mujahedin-e Khalq Organization (MEK)

Also known as the National Liberation Army of Iran (NLA, the militant wing of the MEK) The People's Mujahedin of Iran (PMOI) Muslim Iranian Student's Society, the MEK was formed in the 1960s by the college-educated children of Iranian merchants, the MEK sought to counter what is perceived as excessive Western influence in the Shah's regime. In the 1970s, the MEK concluded that violence was the only way to bring about change in Iran. Since then, the MEK—following a philosophy that mixes Marxism and Islam—has developed into the largest and most active armed Iranian dissident group. Its history is studded with anti-Western activity, and, most recently, attacks on the interests of the clerical regime in Iran and abroad.

The MEK directs a worldwide campaign against the Iranian Government that stresses propaganda and occasionally uses terrorist violence. During the 1970s, the MEK staged terrorist attacks inside Iran to destabilize and embarrass the Shah's regime; the group killed several U.S. military personnel and civilians working on defense projects in Tehran. The group also supported the takeover in 1979 of the U.S. Embassy in Tehran. In April 1992, the MEK carried out attacks on Iranian Embassies in thirteen different countries, demonstrating the group's ability to mount large-scale operations overseas. Several thousand fighters are based in Iraq with an extensive overseas support structure. Most of the fighters are organized in the MEK's National Liberation Army (NLA).

In the 1980s, the MEK's leaders were forced by Iranian security forces to flee to France. Most resettled in Iraq by 1987. Since the mid-1980s, the MEK has not mounted terrorists operations in Iran at a level similar to its activities in the 1970s. Aside from the attacks into Iran toward the end of the Iran-Iraq war, and occasional NLA cross- border incursions since, the MEK's attacks on Iran have amounted to little more than harassment. The MEK has had more success in confronting Iranian representatives overseas through propaganda and street demonstrations. Beyond support from Iraq, the MEK uses front organizations to solicit contributions from expatriate Iranian communities.

Source: Patterns of Global Terrorism, 1997. United States Department of State, April 1998.

The 1979 Islamic revolution and the war with Iraq transformed Iran's class structure politically, socially, and economically. In general, however, Iranian society remains divided into urban, market town, village, and tribal groups. Clerics, called mullahs, dominate politics and nearly all aspects of Iranian life, both urban and rural. After the fall of Shah Palavi's regime in 1979, much of the urban upper class of prominent merchants, industrialists, and professionals, favored by the former Shah, lost standing and influence to the senior clergy and their supporters. Bazaar merchants, who were allied with the clergy against the Pahlavi Shahs, have also gained political and economic power since the revolution. The urban working class has enjoyed somewhat enhanced status and economic mobility, spurred in part by opportunities provided by revolutionary organizations and the government bureaucracy.

In 1961, Iran initiated a series of economic, social, and administrative reforms that became known as the Shah's White Revolution. The core of this program was land reform. Modernization and economic growth proceeded at an unprecedented rate, fueled by Iran's vast petroleum reserves, the third largest in the world. Domestic turmoil swept the country as a result of religious and political opposition to the Shah's rule and programs, especially SAVAK, the hated internal security and intelligence service. In January 1979, the Shah left Iran and died in exile several years after.

On February 1, 1979, exiled religious leader Ayatollah Ruhollah Khomeini returned from France to direct a revolution resulting in a new, theocratic republic guided by Islamic principles. Back in Iran after 15 years in exile in Turkey, Iraq, and France, he became Iran's national religious leader. Following Khomeini's death on June 3, 1989, the Assembly of Experts, an elected body of senior clerics, chose the outgoing president of the republic, Ali Khamenei, to be his successor as national religious leader in what proved to be a smooth transition. In 1989, an overwhelming majority elected Ali Akbar Hashemi-Rafsanjani the speaker of the National Assembly, President. He was re-elected June 11, 1993, with a more modest majority of about 63%; some Western observers attributed the reduced voter turnout to disenchantment with the deteriorating economy.

Iran's post-revolution difficulties have included an eight-year war with Iraq, internal political struggles and unrest, and economic disorder. The early days of the regime were characterized by severe human rights violations and political turmoil, including the seizure of the United States Embassy compound and its occupants on November 4, 1979, by Iranian militants. By mid-1982, a succession of power struggles eliminated first the center of the political spectrum and then the leftists, leaving only the clergy. There has been some moderation of excesses both internally and internationally, although Iran remains a significant sponsor of terrorism.

The Islamic Republican Party **(IRP)** was Iran's dominant political party until its dissolution in 1987; Iran now has no functioning political parties. The Iranian Government is opposed by a few armed political groups including the Mojahedin-e Khalq (People's Mojahedin of Iran), the People's Fedayeen, and the Kurdish Democratic Party.

Khomeini's revolutionary regime initiated sharp changes from the foreign policy pursued by the Shah, particularly in reversing the country's orientation toward the West. In the Middle East, Iran's only significant ally has been Syria. Iran's regional goals are dominated by wanting to establish a leadership role, curtail the presence of the United States and other outside powers, and build trade ties. In broad terms, Iran's Islamic foreign policy emphasizes:

- Vehement anti-U.S. and anti-Israel stances;
- Eliminating outside influence in the region;
- Exporting the Islamic revolution;
- Support for Muslim political movements abroad;
- A great increase in diplomatic contacts with developing countries.

Despite these guidelines, however, bilateral relations are frequently confused and contradictory due to Iran's oscillation between pragmatic and ideological concerns.

Iran's relations with many of its Arab neighbors have been strained by Iranian attempts to spread its Islamic revolution. In 1981, Iran supported a

Ministry of Security (SAVAK)

Shah-an-Shah [King of Kings] Mohammad Reza Pahlevi was restored to the Peacock Throne of Iran with the assistance of the Central Intelligence Agency in 1953. The CIA assisted in a coup against the left-leaning government of Dr. Mohammad Mossadeq, which had planned to nationalize Iran's oil industry. The CIA also provided organizational and training assistance for an intelligence organization for the Shah. With training focused on domestic security and interrogation, the intelligence unit was taxed with the mission to eliminate threats to the Shah.

Formed under efforts of United States and Israeli intelligence officers in 1957, SAVAK became an effective secret agency. General Bakhtiar was appointed its first director, only to be dismissed in 1961. He was assassinated in 1970 under mysterious circumstances. His successor, General Pakravan, was dismissed in 1966, failing to crush the opposition from the clerics in the early 1960s. The Shah then turned to his childhood friend and classmate, General Nassiri, to rebuild SAVAK to properly serve the monarchy. Mansur Rafizadeh, the SAVAK director in the United States throughout the 1970s, claimed that General Nassiri's telephone was tapped by SAVAK agents reporting directly to the Shah, an example of the level of mistrust pervading on the eve of the Revolution. SAVAK increasingly symbolized the Shah's rule from 1963–1979, a period of corruption in the royal family, one-party rule, the torture and execution of thousands of political prisoners, suppression of dissent, and alienation of the religious masses. The United States reinforced its position as the Shah's protector and supporter, sowing the seeds of the anti-Americanism that later manifested itself in the revolution against the monarchy.

Accurate information concerning SAVAK is not publicly available. Pamphlets issued by the revolutionary regime after 1979 indicated that SAVAK had been a full-scale intelligence agency with more than 15,000 full-time personnel and thousands of part-time informants. SAVAK was attached to the Office of the Prime Minister, and its director assumed the title of Deputy to the Prime Minister for national security affairs. Although officially a civilian agency, SAVAK had close ties to the military and many of its officers served simultaneously in branches of the armed forces.

Another childhood friend and close confidant of the Shah, Major General Hosain Fardust, was deputy director of SAVAK until the early 1970s, when the Shah promoted him to the directorship of the "Special Intelligence Bureau," which operated inside Niavaran Palace, independently of SAVAK.

Originally formed to round up members of the outlawed Tudeh, SAVAK expanded its activities to include gathering intelligence and neutralizing the regime's opponents. An elaborate system was created to monitor all facets of political life. A censorship office was established to monitor journalists, literary figures, and academics throughout the country; it took appropriate measures against those who fell out of line. Universities, labor unions, and peasant organizations, among others, were all subjected to intense surveillance by SAVAK agents and paid informants. The agency was also active abroad, especially in monitoring Iranian students who opposed Pahlavi rule.

SAVAK contracted Rockwell International to develop a large communications monitoring system called IBEX. The Stanford Technology Corp. (STC, owned by Hakim) had a $5.5 million contract to supply the CIA-promoted IBEX project. STC had another $7.5 million contract with Iran's air force for a telephone monitoring system, operated by SAVAK, to enable the Shah to track his top commanders' communications.

Over the years, SAVAK became a law unto itself, having legal authority to arrest and detain suspected persons indefinitely. SAVAK operated its own prisons in Tehran (the Komiteh and Evin facilities) and others throughout the country. SAVAK's torture methods included electric shock, whipping, beating, inserting broken glass and pouring boiling water into the rectum, tying weights to the testicles, and the extraction of teeth and nails. Many of these activities were carried out without oversight. At the peak of its influence under the Shah, SAVAK had at least thirteen full-time case officers running a network of informers and infiltration covering 30,000 Iranian students on United States college campuses. The head of the SAVAK agents in the United States operated under the cover of an attaché at the Iranian Mission, with the FBI, CIA, and State Department fully aware of these activities.

In 1978 the deepening opposition to the Shah erupted in widespread demonstrations and rioting. SAVAK and the military responded with widespread repression that killed 12–15,000 people and seriously injured another 50,000. Recognizing that even this level of state terrorism and violence had failed to crush the rebellion, the Shah abdicated the Peacock Throne and departed Iran in 1979. Despite decades of pervasive surveillance by SAVAK, working closely with the CIA, the extent of public opposition to the Shah and his sudden departure came as a considerable surprise to the U.S. intelligence community and national leadership.

The SAVAK organization was officially dissolved by Khomeini shortly after he came to power in 1979. However, it was no surprise that SAVAK was singled out as a primary target for reprisals, its headquarters overrun and prominent leaders tried and executed by Khomeini representatives. High-ranking SAVAK agents were purged and sixty-one SAVAK officials were among two hundred and forty-eight military personnel executed between February and September 1979.

Source: The Federation of American Scientists Website. A privately funded non-profit policy organization 1998 *www.fas.org.*

plot to overthrow the Bahrain Government. In 1983, Iran expressed support for Shi'ites who bombed Western embassies in Kuwait, and in 1987, Iranian pilgrims rioted during the **Hajj** (pilgrimage) to Mecca in Saudi Arabia. Nations with strong fundamentalist movements, such as Egypt and Algeria, also mistrust Iran. Iran backs Hezbollah, Hamas, the Palestinian Islamic Jihad, and the Popular Front for the Liberation of Palestine-General Command, all groups violently opposed to the Arab-Israeli peace process.

Relations with Western European nations have alternated between improvements and setbacks. French-Iranian relations were badly strained by the sale of French arms to Iraq. Since the war, relations have improved commercially but periodically are worsened by Iranian-sponsored terrorist acts committed in France. Another source of tension was Ayatollah Khomeini's 1989 call for all Muslims to kill Salman Rushdie, British author of **The Satanic Verses.** This is a novel many Muslims consider blasphemous to their Holy Scriptures. The United Kingdom has sheltered Rushdie, and strains over this issue persist. There are serious obstacles to improved relations between the two countries. The United States Government defines five areas of objectionable Iranian behavior:

- Iranian efforts to acquire nuclear weapons and other weapons of mass destruction;

- Its involvement in international terrorism;
- Its support for violent opposition to the Arab-Israeli peace process;
- Its threats and subversive activities against its neighbors;
- Its dismal human rights record.

The United States believes that normal relations are impossible until Iran's behavior changes. However, the United States has offered to enter into dialogue with authorized representatives of the Iranian Government without preconditions. The Iranian Government has not accepted this offer. The United States has made clear that it does not seek to overthrow the Iranian Government but will continue to pressure Iran to change its behavior. The continuing support by Iran of terrorists and terrorism creates continuing danger for Americans in Iran because of the generally anti-American atmosphere and Iranian Government hostility to the U.S. Government. American citizens traveling to Iran have been detained without charge, arrested, and harassed by Iranian authorities.[3]

YEMEN

The Republic of Yemen was established on May 22, 1990 with the merger of the Yemen Arab Republic (Yemen Sanaa or North Yemen) and the Marxist-dominated People's Democratic Republic of Yemen (Yemen Aden or South Yemen). The newly formed republic borders the Arabian Sea, the Gulf of Aden and the Red Sea, between Oman and Saudi Arabia. Yemen is slightly larger than twice the size of Wyoming, with borders to Oman and Saudi Arabia. There is an extraordinarily hot, dry, harsh desert on the east side of Yemen. Yemen has potential control of **Bab el Mandeb,** the strait linking the Red Sea and the Gulf of Aden, one of the world's most active shipping lanes. Estimates of its population run from 13.9 million to as high as 16.6 million people of Arab, Afro-Arab concentrations in western coastal locations, South Asians in the southern regions and small European communities in the major metropolitan areas. Muslims, including Sha'fi (Sunni) and Zaydi (Shi'a), plus small numbers of Jews, Christians, and Hindus practice their brands of religion.

The former Aden (South Yemen) gained independence from the United Kingdom in 1967. North Yemen had become independent in 1918 from the Ottoman Empire. The northern city Sanaa became the political capital of a united Yemen. The southern city Aden, with its refinery and port facilities, is the economic and commercial capital. Future economic development depends heavily on Western-assisted development of the country's moderate oil resources. Former South Yemen's willingness to merge stemmed partly from the steady decline in economic support with the demise of the Soviet Union. The low level of domestic industry and agriculture has made northern Yemen dependent on imports for practically all its essential needs. Once self-sufficient in food production, northern Yemen has become a major importer. Land once used for export crops such as cotton, fruit, and vegetables, has been turned over to growing a shrub called qat, whose leaves are chewed for their stimulant effect by Yemenis but which has no significant export market.

British and Turkish Domination

The British conquered Aden (Southern Yemen) in 1839 and it became known as the **Aden Protectorate.** The British also made a series of treaties with local tribal rulers, in a move to colonize the entire area of Southern Yemen. British influence extended to Hadhramawt by the 1950s and a boundary line, known as the violet line, was drawn between Turkish Arabia in the north and the South Arabian Protectorate of Great Britain, as it was then known. (This line later formed the boundary between northern and southern Yemeni states in the 1960s.)

In 1849 the Turks returned to the Yemen and their power extended throughout the whole of that region not under British rule. Local insurrection against the Turks followed and autonomy was finally granted to the Zaydi imam in 1911. By 1919 the Turks had retreated from the Yemen for the last time and the country was left in the hands of Imam Yayha, who became the country's king. Britain recognized Yemen's independence in 1925.

Separate States and Unification

In the late 1960s, the British presence in southern Yemen was minimal outside of Aden itself. Intense guerrilla fighting throughout the mid-sixties resulted in British withdrawal from Aden in 1967. With the closure of the Suez Canal, Yemen's economy was on the verge of ruin, and the new People's Republic of South Yemen, which came into being in 1967, relied heavily on economic support from Communist countries. It became, in effect, the first and only Arab Marxist State. In 1970 the republic's name was changed to the People's Democratic Republic of Yemen or PDRY.

Mutual distrust between the two Yemens characterized the seventies, and tensions flared into a series of short border wars in 1972, 1978 and 1979. Two presidents of the **YAR** were assassinated during this period. But under the Presidency of Ali Abdullah Salah of the Hashid tribe, in the late seventies/early eighties, the stability of the YAR steadily improved. By the end of 1981 a constitution had been drafted in order to implement a merger between the two states. Attempts to consolidate this, however, were delayed by political instability in the PDRY and it was not until 1990 that the merger was made official.

The new country was named the Republic of Yemen. The border was opened and demilitarized, and currencies were declared valid in both of the former countries. A referendum sealed the unification of the Yemen, and today's Yemen is probably more accessible than it has been throughout its history. Although there is no major tourist industry, visitors are now welcomed on a modest scale, and Yemeni society is fast becoming modernized.

Sanaa took major steps during 1997 to improve control of its borders, territory, and travel documents. It continued to deport foreign nationals residing illegally, including Islamic extremists identified as posing a security risk to Yemen and several other Arab countries. The Interior Ministry issued new, reportedly tamper-resistant passports and began to computerize port-of-entry information. Nonetheless, lax implementation of security measures and poor central government control over remote areas continued to make Yemen an attractive safe haven for terrorists. Moreover, Hamas and the PIJ maintain offices in Yemen.

A series of bombings in Aden in July, October, and November of 1997 caused material damage but no injuries. No group claimed responsibility. The Yemeni Government blamed the attacks on Yemeni opposition elements that had been trained by foreign extremists and supported from abroad. A principal suspect confessed in court he was recruited and paid by Saudi intelligence, but this could not be independently verified. Yemeni tribesmen kidnapped about 40 foreign nationals, including two U.S. citizens, and held them for periods ranging up to one month. Yemeni Government officials frequently asserted that foreign powers instigated some kidnappings, but no corroborating evidence was provided. All were treated well and released unharmed, but one Italian was injured when resisting a kidnap attempt in August. The motivation for the kidnappings generally appeared to be tribal grievances against the central government. The government did not prosecute any of the kidnappers.

SUMMARY

If there were any students now reading this text who had never heard of the tinder box states of the Persian Gulf, they have now gotten a glimpse. This is an extremely important area to the modern world, primarily because of oil, and it is constantly in turmoil over religious and power issues. Most of these nations were not even nations at the turn of the twentieth century and most were living as they had for thousands of years. In the second year of the twenty-first century, these oil-rich countries seem to be calling the shots with the EEC, Japan and the United States. The religious conflicts between and among the Islamic nations has cost millions of lives. It is not surprising that Iraq attempted to take over Kuwait's oil fields, as all of them except Saudi Arabia can see the oil gauge plunging to empty. Few of the rich citizens of those states would want to return to riding camels instead of Mercedes cars.

Many of these Persian Gulf states are individually active in sponsoring terrorists and terrorism in areas around the world, but are consolidated when it comes to sponsoring it against Israel, and lately the United States, on its own soil. The stumbling and staggering peace process between Israel and the PLO may ultimately result in a different arrangement of pieces on the Persian Gulf chessboard. Religious hatred in places like Iran and Iraq runs deep, however, and an incredibly scary scenario would be for those two countries to combine their efforts against the rest of the Persian Gulf. Saddam Hussein continues to play cat and mouse with the rest of the world because he knows that oil is so important to any modern Western economy. Perhaps there will finally be a new source of non-fossil fuel energy discovered in the early decades of the new millennium, but for now the Persian Gulf is probably the most valuable land on earth. In the next chapter, we shall take the student on an exploration of the central and southern areas of the Dark Continent of Africa, an area that is rife with racial and tribal divisions that have led to terrorism and genocide in many of their strife-torn countries.

TERMS TO REMEMBER

Abdul Aziz	Fertile Crescent	MEK
Aden Protectorate	frankincense	Operation Desert Storm
al-jabr	Gulf Cooperation Council	The Satanic Verses
Al-Sabah dynasty	Hajj	United Nations Security Council Resolution 986
Bab el Mandeb	IRP	YAR
Bahraini Hezbollah	Kurdistan	
Ba'thist regime		

REVIEW QUESTIONS

1. Why is there such hatred and a split between the Shi'a and Sunni Muslim sects?
2. Which of the Persian Gulf states has the most oil reserves and what kind of governmental system does it have?
3. How was the present state of Yemen assembled and how is it ruled?
4. The Gulf War was fought over what issue?
5. Describe the way the state of Oman is ruled and its importance in the Gulf.
6. Why does President Bush want to attack Iraq and throw Saddam Hussein out of office?

ENDNOTES

1. Most of the background data contained in this chapter . . . and woven into and throughout this book were extracted from Web sites such as: The U.S. State Department of State. *Patterns of Global Terror* Report; The U.S. Department of State *Country Reports on Human Rights Practices;* The U.S. Department of State *Background Notes: Geographic Entities and International Organizations;* http://www.state.gov. The U.S. Central Intelligence Agency *World Factbook* http://www.cia.gov/ and other government sources. We remain grateful for the presence of these sources and the information they have provided.
2. Bush Throws Gauntlet at Saudis with Middle East Plan. Extracted from *STRATFOR RE-PORT,* June 25, 2002, www.stratfor.com.
3. United States Department of State. Public Affairs Washington, DC, July 1994 http://www.state.publicaffairs.gov.

9 Northeast, Central and Southern Africa

Political power grows out of the barrel of a gun.

Chairman Mao's Little Red Book

OVERVIEW

In this chapter, the reader will be introduced to a different source of terror, one that has evolved, over time, into the state against its ethnic, religious and historic tribal enemies. In the central and southern regions of Africa to be in power often means for a ruler to use almost any measures, including **genocide,** whatever the current despot sees fit. This chapter delves into the rise and fall, and some terror methods used, from the despicable, modern day tactician, Field Marshall, President For Life, Idi Amin Dada. Further south we shall examine the historical roots and progression to modern times in places like Mozambique, Zimbabwe, the Republic of Congo, South Africa and others, each with its own significant and unique issues that need evaluating. We start our safari for facts in Ethiopia.

ETHIOPIA

Ethiopia has undergone some major and dramatic changes since the overthrow of **Emperor Haile Selassie** "the Lion of Africa," in 1974. In 1935 the country became the object of Italian colonialism, and the emperor fled the country to live in exile in England. During World War II the British, with the help of the Ethiopians, evicted the Italians from the country and returned Haile Selassie to the throne.

Eritrea is a region that lies to the north of Ethiopia, along the Red Sea coast, which had been under Italian control and influence since the 1880s. The Ethiopian government took over control of Eritrea in 1961 and ever since has been fighting an unending battle with Eritrean Nationalists seeking independence. Extremely poor living conditions coupled with resentment of the Selassie regime's autocratic methods and corrupt government gave rise to a military coup led by Lt. Colonel Mengistu in 1974. Trouble also flared in the south of the country in a region known as the **Ogaden,** which was claimed by neighboring Somalia. Many of the inhabitants of that region were Somalians, and the resulting invasion of the region by Somalia's military in 1977 has been an ongoing and festering sore between the two nations.

By the latter half of the 1980s, the military rulers were making a turn toward an elected civil government under a new constitution. Although elections were held, the military continued to control the country. On May 28, 1991, the Ethiopian People's Revolutionary Democratic Front **(EPRDF)** toppled the authoritarian government of Mengitsu Haile-Mariam and took control in Addis Ababa. A new constitution was promulgated in December 1994 and national and regional popular elections were held in May and June 1995. The main issues facing Ethiopia at the end of the decade are that of rebuilding the crumbling infrastructure of the country following years of civil war.

Ethiopia and Somalia continue to squabble over the Ogaden region in the southern half of the country. The country is also a staging post for the transshipment of illicit drugs from Asia destined for Europe and North America and cocaine for the markets of South Africa.

SOMALIA

Much inter-clan fighting and a weakened military from the fighting in Ethiopia left the country in desperate straits. In 1969, the clans within Somalia felt that the distribution of wealth only benefited a small number of people and clans. The control of the country reverted to military rule under the **Somali Revolutionary Socialist Party,** led by Major General Said Barre. All forms of the economy, banks, schools, and land came under the direct control of the military government. This action coincided with one of the major famines in the twentieth century and the ruling party did nothing to aid the sick, starving, and dying Somalians.

Resistance and uprisings finally came in the formation of the United Somali Congress (USC) that ousted **Said Barre** on January 27, 1991. However, since that date, the country deteriorated even further, with no functioning government and anarchy throughout, marked by inter-clan fighting and banditry. One of the poorest countries in Africa continued to stumble forward blindly with no functioning administration as the various clans vied for power, until the transitional government of Ali Khalif Galaid was voted into power in 2000—and as quickly out again in a no-confidence vote a year later. The interim government was recognized by the United Nations but was not held in high esteem by the Somali populace. The country remains spilt down old tribal lines with warlords controlling the major city of Mogadishu. This country is all about turf wars and any possibility of a leader able to bring the country out of the Middle Ages seems somewhat remote.

After its military successes in Afghanistan, speculation was that America's next target might be Somalia, as it seemed to fit the bill of a lawless state, drawing terrorists like a magnet. Sudan and Somalia remain the only regional countries not allied to the United States. Friendly relations with Kenya, Tanzania, Ethiopia and Eritrea seem secure, despite some recent wars.

Since the U.S. missile strikes on Sudan after the two U.S. Embassy bombings, (which resulted in Osama bin Laden being deported), and especially since 9–11, Africa's largest state has been attempting to shed its image as a "sponsor of terrorism" and thus stop U.S. support for the southern rebels.

The defining moment in relations between the two countries in the last decade was the 1993 killing of eighteen American marines in the capital Mogadishu, and the subsequent evacuation of U.S. forces from Somalia, (a battle made famous by the movie "Blackhawk Down," in which hundreds of Somalis also died). This was portrayed as Somali rejection of a peacekeeping mission, but in fact the deaths were a direct result of a seventh botched attempt to capture the warlord Mohammed Aideed.

Most reports claim that Ethiopia has long been Somalia's main rival in the region and its foreign policy, always aimed at keeping Somalia weak and divided. Ethiopia has been urging the United States to extend the "War on Terrorism" to Somalia since 9–11. Ethiopia invaded Somalia in 1996 and 1999 (capturing and killing hundreds of Somalis). And again, in 2002, Ethiopia supported anti-government rebels such as the Rahanwein Resistance Army. In August 2000, however, a peace conference ended in the nearest thing that Somalis have ever had to a broad-based national government. Ethiopia, however, seems actively trying to destabilize its ruined neighbor.

The only impartial party on the ground, the United Nations, says there is no terrorist activity in Somalia. President Abdiqasim Salad Hassan, a vocal supporter of multiparty democracy, has also stated this to be so. Some may doubt his sincerity, but his government has invited the United States to carry out investigations. Transport Minister Abdi Guled Mohamed stated, "If there are terrorists here, then we will put them in prison, put them where they belong. We will work with the Americans to fight terrorists."

Washington has also declared the Somali Islamic movement, al-Itihaad, a terrorist organization. Al-Itihaad emerged in 1991 as one of numerous warring militias, and its aim was the establishment of an Islamic state. However, its military operations ended with defeat in 1997 by invading Ethiopian troops. Since then, it has become Somalia's leading provider of education, judicial, health and welfare services, all scarce and badly needed in a country experiencing an extensive drought in the south and facing severe food shortages. The Somali government and the United Nations deny that al-Itihaad undertakes terrorist operations or has any links with al Qaeda.

But U.S. resolve may be driven by its success in Afghanistan. After all, the United States found and courted enthusiasm for its war in Afghanistan among the Central Asian states, in particular neighboring Uzbekistan and Tajikistan, which support anti-Taliban Afghan forces and are fighting their own Islamic insurgents. Thus when one sees the regional gains made by the United States in its wars against Iraq and Afghanistan, it is not difficult to draw parallels to Somalia, and to understand the deep-rooted fear and suspicion in the Arab and Muslim worlds that behind the "War on Terrorism" is a strategy of attaining regional dominance and compliant allies regardless of consequences. The Somalis are basically distraught and mistrusting of the tribal politics that is modern Somalia. The last government set a course to appease the warlords by offering olive branches in the form of cabinet posts. Some 15,000 militiamen were given positions as police officers. This has cost the government most of its money, and it still dare not deploy the new policemen throughout Mogadishu for fear they will return to their former warlord masters.[1]

UGANDA

Located in Central East Africa and bordering on Lake Victoria in the south, Uganda as we know it today went through a turbulent period in its most recent history. Uganda gained its independence in 1962 from Britain, and elected **Milton Obote** as its first Prime Minister. The country's president, **Sir Edward Mutesa II,** and Obote were at odds with each other on political issues, and so in 1966 Obote overthrew Mutesa, who went into exile in Britain, and established a new constitution that would encompass all the regions in the area including Buganda (a separate tribe from the same origins). Obote assumed the role of President of Uganda. Political stability did not last long in that turbulent African state, and by 1971 the Ugandan Army under the control of General Idi Amin Dada led an overthrow of the government of Milton Obote, sending him into exile.

For Ugandans, the 1970s were turbulent indeed, at a time when **Idi Amin Dada,** Uganda's self-proclaimed "President for Life" might well have coined the modern phrase **'ethnic cleansing.'** The sheer scope of the terror that this man committed on his own people, during very dark days from 1972–1979, is almost unbelievable in the present times. His avowed praises of the work carried out by Adolph Hitler to exterminate the Jews, and his open hostility and espoused demands for the destruction of Israel spewed from the mind of a deranged psychopath. To try and understand any ideology that Amin may have had is a difficult task. He was extremely temperamental and prone to changing his mind quickly.

What is not in question is the length he went to purge that benighted country of all his opponents both political and social. His first move was to cleanse the country of foreign influence and return Uganda and its wealth to the native Ugandans. The son of a witch doctor, Amin's appetite for wealth knew no boundaries and the lengths he would go to get it were incredible. Obote made him responsible for military control of the northern region of Uganda.[2] To achieve his wealth he engaged in smuggling and murder, or to put it the old-fashioned way: "rape, plunder and pillage," was the order of the day.

One of the first actions Amin took on his route to terrorizing his own nation was the creation of a bureaucracy of state-sponsored terrorism to carry out his own bizarre personal kinds of terror and torture. He established two secret state police organizations, **the Public Safety Unit** and **the Bureau of State Research**. The Public Safety Unit was empowered to shoot to kill anyone on mere suspicion. The Bureau of State Research carried out interrogations and torture, usually also resulting in the death of any hapless prisoner. The actual numbers of Ugandan citizens killed during Amin's reign have never been accurately accounted for, but are believed to be as many as 500,000 . . . or more. As is too often the case in other regions of the African continent, tribal rivalries and old hatreds have a great part to play in the business of selective genocide. Uganda, under Amin (a member of the **Lugbara** tribe), set in motion the calculated elimination of all the Lugabaras' historical tribal enemies, especially the Acholi and Langi tribes. Hand-picked secret police and interrogation units from his native Lugbara tribe were at the point of this state-sponsored genocide.

On many occasions Amin would observe or indulge in torture and other excesses personally. His presidential palace was linked by a series of tunnels connecting it to the Bureau of State Research in an adjoining building in the capital city of Kampala. He surrounded himself with a team of specially trained Palestinian bodyguards. When it came to executions, one of the methods employed was to provide a hammer to one prisoner who was then commanded, at gunpoint, to hammer the skull in of the prisoner next to him. This process of execution was then continued until the last prisoner was dispatched with a gunshot. Many executed prisoners were returned in mutilated condition to their families or dumped in rivers and in forests for the predators. Among other atrocities practiced by Amin and his tribesmen was **cannibalism.**

Killings in the army, where Amin's tribesmen were engaged in a systematic massacre of Acholi and Langi tribesmen, were the first signs to a watching public of the madness to follow. The expulsion of the Israelis in 1972 was ultimately a result of their refusal to supply arms to Uganda. The Asian exodus was one of the most significant events in Uganda's history. It scarred Uganda for the rest of its national life, only now beginning to heal, after over a quarter of a century. The reason for the expulsion is not clear; certainly Amin was under significant internal pressure to "deliver the goods" of post-liberation euphoria and expectation, not just from the civilian population but also his army.

Asians and the British owned and controlled over half of Uganda's wealth, and expelling them was his short cut to achieving what was expected. In addition, Amin bore some motives for revenge on the British and wanted to teach the British a lesson they would never forget. According to Amin, the reason for expelling the Asians was revealed to him in a dream, where God decreed that if he didn't do it, the country would be ruined.

Though Amin continued to exercise free license to murder anybody he perceived to be a threat, people seemed to get on with fearful conditions. In 1978 he invaded Northern Tanzania in an effort to boost failing morale and wipe out more enemies. The retaliation was supported by expelled Ugandan fighting troops, including the Front for National Salvation (FRONASA) that was lead by Yoweri Museveni. Their advance on Kampala was swift against the demoralized, though heavily armed, troops of Idi Amin. The Tanzanian and Ugandan liberators arrived in Kampala in April 1979 under the banner of the Uganda National Liberation Army (UNLA). Once again the chorus of jubilation echoed around the streets. After a short period of indecision, the Uganda National Liberation Front (UNLF) was formed from an amalgam of several Ugandan political and military groups. Not for the first time in Uganda's history, the people had united against a common enemy.

Once again Obote, who returned from exile, would contest elections as leader of the UPC (Ugandan Political Coalition). A third major political party emerged to do battle with the DP (Democratic Party) and UPC. It was the Uganda Patriotic Movement (UPM) and once more Yoweri Museveni's name was prominent in Ugandan affairs. Milton Obote won the election with a comfortable, though dubiously attained margin and was sworn in as President on December 11, 1980. Obote's army, under Major General Tito Okello, returned him to power anxious for revenge on those who supported Amin in 1979. Worst of all for Ugandans, Obote had no control over the army, whose senior officers systematically plundered government coffers, and whose ranks looted and raped without restraint.

Dissatisfied with the election results, Yoweri Museveni and twenty-six young men, retreated into the Luwero Triangle and started what was to be a long campaign of guerrilla warfare. The National Resistance Army (NRA) was formed under the banner of the National Resistance Movement (NRM). The turning point in the long bush war was the death of the UNLA commander, Oyite-Ojok, who was Obote's cousin. He was a powerful figure and his death demoralized Obote's troops and caused a power struggle within the Langi and Acholi army factions. Obote's men continued to run riot in the city and towns, frustrated at the lack of success against the NRA. Obote consistently resisted appeals to negotiate with the NRA and he gradually alienated the Acholi who felt they were fighting alone against the NRA. This feeling finally lead to Obote's being removed from power.

The constitution was suspended, Parliament dissolved and Major General Tito Okello was sworn in as President in July 1985. But violence and lawlessness remained. Gradually the NRA gained more support and more control in crucial areas. Museveni and Okello met in Kenya and signed peace agreements for a new, equally represented government. Within a month of the agreement the war intensified and the NRA moved closer to Kampala, and on January 26, 1986, the NRA overran Kampala.

Yoweri Kaguta Museveni was sworn in as President of Uganda on January 29, 1986. Museveni announced that his takeover represented a fundamental change in the affairs of Uganda and not a "mere change of guards." He proclaimed a ten-point program where NRM would "usher in a new and better future for the people of Uganda." The ten points included issues ignored or maligned by the previous seven presidents, such as democracy, security, and elimination of corruption. To mixed reactions, a large, broad-based cabinet was appointed with friend and foe alike. In an effort to unite every corner of Uganda under one government, Museveni included representatives of previously antagonistic political parties, tribal groups and religious factions in the government of the day.

Museveni extended personal invitations to exiled Ugandans, offering key government advisory or corporate positions. A significant brain drain had taken place during the war years and Museveni was anxious that these individuals help rebuild a fragmented and broken country. When the NRA arrived in Kampala, serious resistance was not encountered. The victorious soldiers were disciplined and friendly; this army was within the law, not above it.

The task that lay ahead in 1986 was immense. The weird and violent policies of a whirlwind of governments had left Ugandans without belief in their leaders. National pride and identity was essential to rebuild the battered country, one of Museveni's most painful and arduous tasks. Convincing the people that a democracy would emerge from a military takeover was difficult. The country was in a mess and only a slow, systematic and transparent examination of the damage might set wrongs to right. The NRA re-established law and order everywhere in Uganda, except the north and northeast that remained bastions of discontent and insecurity. The sporadic lawlessness in the north has been a constant problem to the NRM, and until a national identity emerges the issue will remain.

Infrastructure in every aspect of life, whether the judicial system, the constitution, roads, agriculture, health, education or tourism, had broken down. Infrastructural redevelopment was the starting point for the new government. In addition, a system of local government through locally elected officials was put in place from the very beginning. Every Ugandan is a member of at least one legislative body that gives him a voice in everyday affairs. This was to be the foundation on which national identity would be built.

The personification of Uganda's malaise has been the magnitude of the AIDS crisis. Uganda was one of the first countries in Africa to recognize and begin to deal with the disease. The results have been very positive. Education and awareness have been the key areas targeted by the programs initiated. Museveni, who is 52, has been active since his student days at **Ntare School,** Mbarara; he studied political science and economies at the **University of Dar-es-Salaam,** graduating in 1970 with a Bachelor of Arts.

Although, Yoweri Museveni is a man with strong opinions and a keen sense of right and wrong, the reality of the chaotic situation that he found in Uganda when he took power in 1986 meant that he had to accommodate people with views and attitudes which sometimes ran directly counter to his own.

As recently as August 2002, humanitarian agencies and Ugandan authorities were working out an emergency plan following a Lord's Resistance Army (LRA) attack on a refugee camp in northern Uganda, which forced thousands of Sudanese refugees to flee into the bush. The office of the U.N. High Commissioner for Refugees (UNHCR) said plans were in hand to move the at least 24,000 Sudanese refugees who had fled from the camp to a safer location, following the Monday morning LRA attack on the Acholi-Pii refugee settlement in Pader District. UNHCR's information officer for Uganda, reported that Ugandan authorities had, at an emergency meeting between humanitarian agencies and senior government officials, agreed to relocate the refugees to a safer location yet to be agreed upon, preferably in Yumbe, Hoima or Nebii districts, all in western Uganda.

The International Rescue Committee (IRC) for Uganda said it was also planning a response, which would involve transporting food to Rachkoko from neighboring Kitgum District. This was the second LRA attack in a week on the Acholi Pii Camp. The LRA group had first attacked the camp on July 31 2002, but government soldiers repulsed the attackers, UNHCR said. Earlier, on July 8, LRA fighters had attacked the Maaji refugee settlement, in nearby Adjumani District, killing six refugees and putting another 8,000 to flight. The number of casualties incurred in the Monday attack remains unclear. Maj Shaban Bantariza, the Ugandan army spokesman, told the BBC that about 200 LRA fighters had killed four soldiers and eight civilians, losing eleven of their own in the process. The magnitude of the attack was an indication that the Ugandan government was no longer able to guarantee security in northern Uganda, where humanitarian assistance was becoming increasingly dangerous as a result. The IRC had earlier withdrawn most of its staff from the camp, following the first attack, but re-deployed them there after receiving assurances from the Ugandan authorities guaranteeing their security. The LRA since June 2001 has intensified attacks on northern Ugandan districts, in response to the pressure exerted on it in southern Sudan. About 500,000 displaced Ugandans and some 155,000 Sudanese refugees live in camps in northern Uganda, according to the refugee agency.

Uganda has approximately 8,000 of its troops in the Democratic Republic of Congo (DRC). Again, this is a consequence of the rich reserves of timber and diamonds. A form of trade was developed in the border regions, with shipments, transferred through Uganda under the control of the Ugandan military.

There is no vested interest for the Ugandans to see any ceasefire or peace within the DRC. Much of the spoils in this conflict originate in the northern city of Kisangani.

ZIMBABWE

Many black African states were looking to shed the yoke of the British Empire in the 1960s and 1970s. White rule in Rhodesia, under Ian Smith, ended in 1980 when the country gained its independence and Robert Mugabe became the country's first prime minister. But Mugabe and his government faced violent opposition mainly from the region of Matabeleland. Mugabe's ruling party, the Zimbabwe African National Union **(ZANU)** was also strongly opposed by the Zimbabwe People's Revolutionary Army **(ZIPRA)** and the Zimbabwe African People's Union **(ZANPU).** Mugabe used what can easily be termed state terror on the peoples of Matabeleland to ensure his own position in Zimbabwe. To do this he used the Zimbabwe Army Fifth Brigade as a vehicle to control, repress, restrict, torture, interrogate and execute all armed opponents in Matabeleland.

The UDI

November 11, 1965, is the date when Ian Smith declared a **Unilateral Declaration of Independence** (UDI) for Rhodesia. If one were to look to the north about the same time as scenes were being played out in the name of independence you might find the view far from gratifying. Millions were dead in Nigeria and the Congo, more than 500,000 in the Sudan and over 200,000 in Rwanda and Burundi. In nearly all instances it was black man killing black man, and the countries were in the hands of blood-crazed dictators.[3] Unfortunately for the Ian Smith rebel government, the rest of the world, including Britain and the United Nations, would not recognize the new breakaway state and instead enforced strong economic sanctions on the country. In the years preceding the UDI, most forms of terrorism and similar violent criminal action were well under the control of the authorities. In that era, when there was a perception of weakness and an opportunity arose to destabilize a region in Africa, the undertones of communist involvement were never far away.

So, too, it was with Rhodesia. Many of the young blacks were lured out of the country on promise of "scholarships" in Zambia and Tanganyika. In fact, these young men were being sent for communist indoctrination and weapons training in camps in North Korea and the former USSR. They were returned via such ports as Dar es Salaam on the coast of Africa and then infiltrated back into Rhodesia to fight against the Smith government.

With so many ways to define terrorism would these men be viewed as terrorists, insurgents, freedom fighters or just violent criminals? The answer to these definitions is not easy. From the Rhodesian standpoint they were certainly seen as terrorists, so the Smith Government used the Rhodesian Special Air Service Regiment to good effect in destroying these "terrorists." The task from the military standpoint was almost hopeless, given the make up of the borders that surrounded the country. The only friendly region lay to the south with the South African Government. The numbers of terrorists and insurgents continued to grow in the same manner as that faced by the United States as they fought an impossible war in Vietnam.

The politics of the day did nothing to inhibit the violence in Rhodesia. On the contrary, to most people in Rhodesia, both black and white, it seemed that the terrorist forces had the tacit support of the British government in the name of African Nationalism. The two leaders of the terror groups, **Joshua Nkomo** and **Ndabaningi Sithole,** were openly supported in Britain, even though they were leaders of the two parties banned by the Smith government. The black nationalists, Robert Mugabe being one of them, formed ZANU as a result of a split with the Nkomo leadership. Nkomo formed the opposing ZAPU movement. Formed along tribal lines, Nkomo's support came principally from the Ndebele tribes of Matabeleland in the west, while Mugabe's support lay in the tribes of Mashonaland in the east of the country.

On March 20, 2002, the announcement from London was that Zimbabwe will be suspended from the Commonwealth for twelve months. The leaders of South Africa, Australia and Nigeria made the decision on behalf of the 54-nation group, after studying an observer mission report on Zimbabwe's appalling presidential elections. Announcing the decision in London, Australian Prime Minister John Howard said he hoped the international community would encourage reconciliation in Zimbabwe between the main parties.

Howard and the presidents of South Africa and Nigeria, Thabo Mbeki and Olusegun Obasanjo, were appointed to decide what, if any, action the commonwealth should take against Zimbabwe at a summit staged before the Zimbabwe election. The ballot in Zimbabwe saw the re-election of incumbent President Robert Mugabe amid allegations of violence, terrorism and intimidation against the opposition Movement for Democratic Change, led by Morgan Tsvangirai. Western governments have severely criticized the fairness of the

Zimbabwean President Robert Mugabe at Independence Day celebrations in the capitol, Harare, April 18, 2002. (AP Photo)

election, while African governments have been less willing to condemn Mugabe.

The commonwealth observer group accused Mugabe of using state powers and institutions to steal his victory. The United States, Britain and the European Union condemned the elections as "unfair and not free." Before leaving Australia for London, Howard said, "This is quite a moment of truth for the Commonwealth . . . it's not something that can be swept under the carpet."

Mbeki and Obasanjo held talks with Mugabe, to try and seek a compromise. Among the proposals speculated on was a government of national unity, but both Mugabe and Tsvangirai, have cast doubt on the plan. Tsvangirai said: "We arrived at the conclusion that the objective conditions do not exist for meaningful discussion because (Mugabe's party) ZANU-PF is embarking on mass retribution against our members in the rural areas."

Mugabe, who has been in power since 1980, was sworn in for another six-year term. He took the victory as a mandate to pursue his land reform program. Zimbabwe's main labor federation called for a three-day general strike to protest against what it called post-election harassment of workers.

The Harare meeting came on the same day that a white farmer was shot dead by suspected ruling party militants. Terry Ford was the first white farmer killed since Mugabe was re-elected and the tenth killed since militants began often-violent occupations of white-owned land two years ago. Denmark, which is not a member of the Commonwealth, announced it was closing its Harare embassy and ending further developmental aid to the country, and stated that reports from national and international observers clearly show that it was not a free and fair election. Therefore Denmark withdrew its embassy staff from Harare that summer.

Zimbabwe continues to reel under the effects of Mugabe's dictatorship with millions facing certain death from disease, starvation and state-sponsored violence and yet Mugabe's message to the nation was a promissory note for more misery and death. This year's (2002) National Heroes' Day proved to be no exception.

However, the illegitimate ZANU-PF government has routinely turned this somber national occasion into an indecent partisan junket to spread a message of violence and hatred. Mugabe fails to connect with the primary concerns of the people of Zimbabwe, which are food, jobs, health and an end to poverty. He instead concerns himself primarily with rhetorical nationalism. In fact, Zimbabwe now is a country where everything is in short supply except misery, starvation and death. The regime has reduced innocent citizens to the level of scavenging animals.

Where Zimbabweans expect a message of hope and decisive leadership to confront the problems bedeviling the country, they are told that their daughters and sons will be forcibly drafted into the so-called National Youth Service and be transformed into killing machines for the perpetuation of Mugabe's dictatorship. Change in Zimbabwe is inevitable no matter how many innocent citizens are slaughtered by the regime.

Evidence at hand demonstrates, beyond any reasonable doubt, the regime's culpability in widespread and systematic incidences of murders, tortures, rape, abductions, arsons and many other forms of well-organized political violence that have taken place with impunity over the past twenty-seven months. The partisan public media has neither exposed nor condemned ZANU-PF violence, but defended it. The police force on the other hand has mastered the art of selec-

Body of farmer Terry Ford covered by a blanket—shot at his farm by ruling party militants, March 18, 2002. (AP Photo)

tive harassment, arrests and prosecution of the opposition when ruling party criminals who are guilty of heinous crimes are walking scot-free.

In addition to the above acts of barbarism that have been perpetrated with state sanction and impunity, the regime has sought to legalize the harassment of political opponents and to control what the people read, hear or see through the enactment of legislation with severe democratic deficits, like Jonathan Moyo's Access to Information Act and John Nkomo's Public Order and Security Act. What is blatantly disturbing and unacceptable about the behavior of the regime is, that at a time when the nation has an avalanche of a political and economic crisis at its hands for which the regime is responsible, the regime's ministers, such as John Nkomo, Joseph Made and Jonathan Moyo, are busy trying to outdo each other in their daily television appearances competition. The regime's ministers have become obsessed with little things at a time when they should be answering questions about more serious things like the whereabouts of salt for Zimbabwean families.

The United Nations has condemned Zimbabwe, Uganda and Rwanda for actions in the DRC. These three countries initially intervened in the DRC to stabilize the area in the aftermath of the overthrow of Mobutu Sese Seko by Laurent Kabila and the subsequent chaos that took place in the eastern half of the former Republic of Zaire. Uganda and Rwanda support the rebels in the east and Zimbabwe supports the government. However, the U.N. report accuses Zimbabwe, Uganda and Rwanda of perpetuating the war for their own financial gain, as they exploit the country's rich mineral resources. The DRC is one of the richest countries in the world in mineral terms. It has gold, copper, diamonds, cobalt, coltan (a metal ore for use in aerospace telecommunications industries) and timber.

In the rebel-controlled areas, Rwanda is accused of exporting coltan, which it mines inside the DRC, and Uganda is accused of gold smuggling activities, while Zimbabwe allegedly engages in joint ventures with DRC government officials, which benefit only the ruling elite back in Harare. The armed forces of the DRC have been pushed into the western half of the country, unable to penetrate the areas held by the Tutsi-backed rebels in the areas where these three countries' armies are operating, despite receiving military aid from Zimbabwe, Angola and Namibia.

The governments of Rwanda and Uganda reject the claims that they are prolonging the war for their own gain. Although a cease-fire has been established, which U.N. forces monitor, there is still fighting between rival armed groups. The result, as is the usual case in Africa, is paid for in civilian suffering and lives. Infant mortality stands at 40%, there are reportedly two million displaced persons and sixteen million people classified as not receiving the basic nutritional levels as stipulated by the United Nations.

In the clinical sense, starvation has not set in yet in Zimbabwe. But the signs are there, with stick-like arms and legs and swollen bellies that it is on its way. AIDS is wiping out a whole generation of parents. Thousands upon thousands of small children barely exist with no food, no family income, no medicines and no answers. Over a third of these children have HIV or AIDS themselves. It is not life they are living; they just are waiting to die. Zimbabwe is facing a major famine that may decimate half of the country's population.

From Harare, the word from Zimbabwean officials is that "white farmers will live to regret" their defiance of government orders to abandon their land. This follows nearly 3,000 white farmers being ordered to leave their property as part of a plan to seize white-owned lands and turn them over to poor blacks. No serious measures have been taken yet against farmers who have defied the deadline, which changes often.

But Co-Vice President Joseph Msika, head of Zimbabwe's land-reform task force, told state television about the farmers refusing to leave their land: "Those who are not going to work within the laws of Zimbabwe have nobody to blame but themselves. The law will take its course." A powerful local government minister, said, "All the excuses by the farmers show what an arrogant and racist bunch they are. It shows they want to derail the land- redistribution program by any means . . . they will not succeed," according to the state-run Herald newspaper. Vice President Simon Muzenda warned that authorities would act firmly against farmers opposing the "irreversible" land program. "You are told by government what we want done and you simply do that," he told state radio. In Washington, DC, the U.S. State Department denounced Zimbabwe's attempt to evict the farmers and thousands of farm workers as "a reckless and reprehensible act."

THE DEMOCRATIC REPUBLIC OF CONGO (DRC)

In 2001, South Africa's National Treasury made the Democratic Republic of the Congo a $73 million bridge loan to help Kinshasa meet its International Monetary Fund liabilities. This will allow the DRC to draw on resources from the IMF's poverty alleviation facility. Throughout much of the DRC's nearly four-year-old civil war, Pretoria somewhat obliquely supported Rwanda in its

REWARD NOTICE

Substantial rewards will be paid by Government to any person who volunteers information, to the Security Forces, which leads to the death or capture of terrorists or their supporters, or to the recovery of terrorist weapons. This information will be kept secret.

Rewards can be paid in cash, or into a Post Office savings account, bank savings account, or building society savings account. The payment of such reward money will be kept secret by Government.

LISTED BELOW ARE THE REWARDS:

$5 000 Not less than $5 000 FOR INFORMATION LEAD-ING TO THE DEATH OR CAPTURE OF A SENIOR TERRORIST LEADER.

$2 500 Not less than $2 500 FOR INFORMATION LEAD-ING TO THE DEATH OR CAPTURE OF A TERRORIST GROUP LEADER.

$1 000 Not less than £1 000 FOR INFORMATION LEAD-ING TO THE DEATH OR CAPTURE OF ANY TRAINED TERRORIST.

$500 Not less than $500 for EACH anti-vehicle mine, heavy weapon of war.

$300 Not less than $300 for EACH full box of small arms ammunition, grenades, anti-personnel mines, OR EACH light personal weapon.

A substantial reward will be paid for INFORMATION LEAD-ING TO THE ARREST of any person who voluntarily houses, feeds, associates with or helps terrorists.

These rewards will not be payable to a civil servant who is engaged on duties concerned with anti-terrorist activities or to a member of the Security Forces, unless he obtained the information while he was off-duty.

BY ORDER OF THE GOVERNMENT OF RHODESIA

Reward poster dropped by air over Rhodesia.

fight against the government in Kinshasa. But now, with the conflict winding down and DRC President Joseph Kabila winning friends in Europe and the United States, Pretoria wants to re-engage its past rival. The bridge loan may signal an initial success in that strategy, as well as a shift in South African-DRC relations. Such foreign policy initiatives are intended to advance South Africa's stature as a leader on the subcontinent. However, mounting problems at home will undermine Pretoria's regional aspirations.

Since the end of apartheid, South Africa's economy has been on the decline. This is despite its having the most developed economy in Africa—with $125.9 billion in GDP—as well as abundant natural resources, a globally recognized stock exchange and well-developed communications, defense, energy, financial and transportation sectors. It also attracts more foreign direct investment than the rest of sub-Saharan Africa as a whole. Yet about one-third of the workforce is unemployed, it has one of the world's highest crime rates and nearly 20 percent of adults are infected with HIV/AIDS. The ruling African National Congress (ANC) has suffered one political scandal after another, and President Thabo Mbeki has little political credibility at home and abroad. Government plans to cut state spending and privatize state-owned industries have stalled due to massive unemployment, widespread strikes and opposition from labor unions.

The conflict between the DRC government's foreign policy goals and domestic realities has yet to come to a head. For example, Pretoria's support for Zimbabwe's President Robert Mugabe's controversial land reform persisted, despite the negative impact on the South African economy due to Zimbabwe's own economic decline. Eventually, however, Pretoria will find it hard to pursue policies like lending millions to other African states when its own domestic situation continues to worsen. States usually have a cornucopia of carrots and sticks to use as foreign policy tools, but in South Africa's case, that range of options is narrowing.

SOUTH AFRICA

For the past half of the century, South Africa operated under a white government using apartheid as an official method to control the actions, activities and opportunities of native black, colored and African Asians in the Republic of South Africa. The main political party set up to fight apartheid was the **African National Congress (ANC).** Strangely the party started on a political platform and moved towards armed confrontation with the South African Government.

Color alone by no means carries with it a unity of belief, purpose or ambition. The most virulent and persistent of hatreds in Africa is between people of the same color. The black population of South Africa is divided into at least seven distinct ethnic groups, each with its own written language and home area, and each resolved to retain its own identity. That way they could develop separately and still remain apart. The South African governments of the forty years up to the early 1990s set out to regulate this problem by the establishment of separate, self-governing "homelands" for each group.[4] To most people from the outside looking in, apartheid has always had an evil connotation. Although this text is not intended to be a forum for debating the pros and cons of segregation of ethnic groups in South Africa, it is relevant to the South African experience with terrorism.

Britain's involvement in the Cape Colony dates back three centuries when the region along the cape was important as a refueling and trading post for shipping to and from the orient and India. The Cape Colony was also home to Dutch migrants from Europe who had settled the colony in 1652. From the middle of the sixteenth century, the Dutch East India Company had executive powers over the colony and all its inhabitants but was allowing Dutch settlers to leave the company and start their own farms. These people became known as "Boers." With the migration inland, the white farmers fought the tiny San Tribes people (bushmen) and either killed or enslaved them for work on the farms.

The Dutch government formally turned the Colony over to Britain in 1834. The first British settlers had arrived in the Cape in 1820, and so with control going to Britain the unpopular decision was made to end slavery. Britain established English as the official language of the Cape to the extreme resentment of the Boers in the colony. Unhappy with British rule, the Boers began to move north and settle in regions farther away in the Transvaal, the Orange Free State and Natal. The move north became an historic event for the Boers and is generally referred to as the **"Great Trek."**

With the discovery of diamonds in the Kimberley region and gold in the Johannesburg areas, Anglos and Boers would fight the first Anglo-Boer war. Overwhelming force of arms allowed the British to defeat the Boers by 1902, thus bringing about the Orange Free State, Transvaal and Natal under British rule. This rule, not surprisingly, included all the black tribes, most of which submitted peacefully to their new masters. As in most matters, there is an exception to a rule, and the South African exception was the Zulus. A warlike tribe, they would submit to nobody and in 1879 defeated and destroyed a well-trained British regiment at Isandhlwana. Overwhelming superiority of forces and firepower eventually defeated the Zulus, and by 1888 none of the black African tribes retained their independence.

Afrikaner Nationalism

Two famous Boer Generals, Louis Botha and Jan Smuts, had a great part to play in the rise of Afrikaner nationalism in South Africa. General J. Hertzog formed the Nationalist Party, which had the ideology that the Boers had a right to rule South Africa and to unite the Anglos and Afrikaners. With a nationalist government coming to power in South Africa for the first time in 1922, they began the changes to shape the united South Africa of their dreams. This included the recognition of Afrikaans alongside English as the official language and also the development of industry less dependent on Great Britain. With the outbreak of World War II and South Africa already an independent nation within the British Commonwealth, there was considerable debate as to which side, if any, to support. Hertzog favored neutrality while the Boer General Smuts sided with the British against Germany.

Apartheid

During the war years, the Nationalist party underwent a rebirth and change of direction under the inspiration of D.F.D. Malan, a strong supporter of the Nationalist South African cause. Under his guidance the adoption of segregation along racial lines **(apartheid)** was developed and instituted as part of government policy with sweeping police powers of enforcement. The government had created the power to direct the masses on where to live and where to work. The struggle against apartheid, or racism as some observers prefer to call it, became a part of the South African struggle and terrorism for fifty years.

Extreme Right Wing Afrikaner Movement

Extremism in South African politics emerged at the end of the 1960s from splinter groups that had split off from the National Party and called themselves the *Herstige Nasionale Party* (HNP). By 1971 all the hard-liners of Afrikaner Nationalism had been forced out from the National Party and thus formed the ***Afrikaner Weerstandsbeweging*** **(AWB, The Afrikaner Resistance Movement).** The AWB became known principally for its menacing but flamboyant leader Eugene Terre'Blanche. Likened to Adolph Hitler, his speechmaking skills were legendary. This ability allowed him to attract large crowds of supporters to his meetings. Not only was he a consummate politician and orator but an accomplished sportsman. He served in the South African Police Service as a warrant officer. After leaving the police service he went on to form the AWB in July 1973 with another former police colleague, Jan Groenewald. The early movement was extremely small and the meetings were secret for fear of drawing the attention of the **Bureau of State Security (B.O.S.S.).** When the group first came to public view, it portrayed all the same trappings and uniform style complete with swastika as the German Nazi movement. Albert Hertzog, a former cabinet member of the National Party and founder of the HNP, was at this time outside the party hierarchy following the party's disastrous showing in the general election, and was looking for a cause to support. That support, together with his business acumen went to Terre'Blanche and the AWB. Although the 1970s were the formative years for the AWB, no specific acts of terror can be attributed to the organization. With the dismantling of the apartheid system in South Africa, that would change over the following seventeen years.

The AWB became labeled by many observers as a neo-Nazi organization. Although the leadership of the AWB vehemently denied the label, their flamboyant uniforms did not easily dispel this viewpoint. Still searching for its true identity, the AWB went through several different scenarios, usually linked to storm trooper and motorcycle gang-style images with fearsome sounding names like the Lightening Falcons or Storm Falcons. Most were burly and surly men outfitted with jack boots and helmets.

The first signs of violence came in 1985 when Terre'Blanche proclaimed that the AWB would form into units of guards. These groups were called the "Sentinels" or ***"Brandwag"*** and were formed mainly along the Northern Transvaal border with Zimbabwe. The white farmers in the border areas formed Brandwags to protect against incursions from across the border with

Zimbabwe. The AWB equipped itself with its own bodyguard of heavies to "control" and monitor meetings. Most of the white farmers in the remoter regions of the Transvaal were also local commando (army) members so it was not surprising that they would be well armed with sophisticated weapons. With the extreme right wing sympathy and sophisticated weapons now in their hands, the aims of the AWB were ready to make sure black groups and political organizations would not become targets for action from the AWB. What made the AWB so popular was their belief in preserving their claims to land and their demands for an Afrikaner Nation to be formed out of the former Boer Republics.

By the end of the 1980s, it became clear that the enemy of the AWB apart from left wing politicians was also the African National Congress (ANC). Over the years that led up to the first ANC-elected government and the ending of the apartheid system in South Africa, AWB members and supporters carried out various terrorist acts to destabilize the ANC and the elected government. The AWB had hoped to escalate the violence into a full-scale civil war. As we now know, that was not to be the case. However, the bomb attacks were directed mainly at black civilian targets as were the indiscriminate use of bombs in the major cities. The bombing campaign resulted in many AWB arrests and convictions; in 1996 the AWB—still under the control of Terre'Blanche—announced that the movement would operate underground.

The AWB symbol is the eagle, the meaning of which it details in its official guidebook. "This emblem enables the AWB to give its full acknowledgement to the symbolism of the eagle which epitomizes the protection of the Lord: Like an eagle that stirs up its nest, that flutters over its young, spreading out its wings, catching them, bearing them on its pinions." (Deuteronomy 32: 11.)

The Future

With the general acceptance of the new government and South Africa's recognition once again by the United Nation and the rapidly lifting of the international sanctions, it is difficult to see the AWB or a similar nationalist movement emerging in any major fashion for the near future. As long as Afrikaner nationhood is alive and well, however, there will always be the opportunity and threat for a different generation to take up where Terre'Blanche has left off.

The African National Congress (ANC)

This quasi-political movement dates as far back as 1912 and has consistently, along with other liberal groups, opposed the nationalists and their apartheid policies. Garnering support for any action, given the overwhelming numbers— 75% of the population is black and 14% white, with the balance being made up of Asians—would not be difficult. Probably the most famous name connected to the movement is that of the current president of South Africa, **Nelson Rolihlahala Mandela.** Born in 1918, the son of a tribal chief, he received an excellent education and became a lawyer, and towards the end of World War II joined the African National Congress. An outspoken opponent of apartheid, Mandela led protests and demonstrations against apartheid and police brutality during the 1950s, for which he was charged with treason. The charge was not proven, however, and he was acquitted. He was arrested again in 1962 and charged with terrorist offenses and sentenced to life in prison. His release thirty-two years later would become the harbinger of the new South Africa and a black majority government. The role of the ANC and various acts of terrorism in South Africa are intertwined. The ANC contention is that they had been driven to acts of criminal violence, bombings, shootings and murder because they lacked any political alternative. With the apartheid firmly in place and their leader firmly in jail, the ANC embarked on a terror campaign aimed at the state, the white minority and their own black brothers who failed to support them. Inter-tribal fighting has been a hallmark of fighting in the south, however some of the forms and the brutality used are quite gruesome to describe. One favored most of all in killing recalcitrant blacks was the **"necklace,"** with a victim beaten and then placed in a stack of used car tires and set on fire.

The ANC received external support in their campaign from communist sources from outside the South African borders. This led to the government reducing and diminishing the effects of apartheid on the black and colored communities. The ANC has a military wing that advocates revolutionary violence. It further advocated the kind of communist revolution that swept into Russia at the start of the century. A 1987 quote from **Winnie Mandela,** wife of the imprisoned Nelson Mandela, clearly defines the communist goals for the ANC: "The Soviet Union is the torchbearer for all our hopes and aspirations. In Soviet Russia, genuine power of the people has been transformed from dreams into reality." Since the middle of the 1980s, the Republic of South Africa has undergone drastic political changes and with it came to fruition the dreams of the overthrow of the regime and the system of apartheid. Having been banned since 1961, the ANC had been headquartered outside the country in neighboring Zambia. To this extent one may assume material support was given by the Zambians to ANC terrorists crossing into South Africa. The South African Police and military were very effective in patrolling and controlling border incursions from neighboring African countries, hostile to the apartheid regime. The neighboring countries of Lesotho, Mozambique and Botswana have been at varying times the locations for terrorist training bases for the ANC which were supported by Russian technicians. The external location did not prevent the South African security forces from taking preemptive actions in those countries against the training base locations. The ANC also aided in defining the term terrorism by declaring in the 1980s that the South African government was a terrorist government and that the ANC was acting in self-defense.

Robben Island University (Isle of Purgatory)

Many historic landmarks have formed the center points for penal servitude around the world. Well known among those landmarks are Wormwood Scrubs in London, England, the Island of Elbe, Devil's Island and Alcatraz. Not so well known to the world is Robben Island, situated off the southern coast of Africa, at Cape Town, but with a splendid view of Table Mountain. This island has served as a dropping off point for Cape traders in the sixteenth century. It has been a leper colony, a hospital for the insane, an armed garrison and the long-time residence of Nelson Mandela and other banned and convicted members of the ANC. Today it is a national monument and tourist attraction. The island was turned over to the South African Department of Prisons when the South African Artillery School vacated it in 1959. The first African political prisoners arrived at the prison to serve their sentences in 1962 along with members of the Pan-African Congress activists as well as soldiers from an armed group called "Poqo." Members of the ANC, including Nelson Mandela, arrived soon after. Many arrived in a state of general illiteracy, however B Section, which housed Mandela and his cohorts, became known as **"Robben University."** Many were able to learn and further their political debates and beliefs. A prison code was observed by the ANC "students," which required that they maintain their commitment to changing South African society and to find positive development through their term of imprisonment. The code also required that none were to leave the prison without education. The last prisoners left the island in 1991 after the ANC finally received political recognition.

Winnie Madikizela-Mandela

The estranged wife of Nelson Madela, the first black president of South Africa, Winnie has been described as the **"Mugger of the Nation."** During the political build-up to her husband's dramatic release from his life sentence on Robben Island, in true charismatic fashion, Winnie surrounded herself with a phalanx of bodyguards. As the ex-wife of the president her actions and that of her bodyguard have been questioned. Just how far her involvement in any specific crimes or terrorist activities committed by her bodyguard is still in question. Known as the **Mandela United Football Club,** they have been involved in beatings of blacks in the townships. Mandela herself was convicted of kidnapping in 1991.[5] The "football team" was made up of a group of tough youths from the Soweto Township and was led by the coach Jerry Richardson, who was convicted of murder.

Is South Africa out of the shadow of terrorism? Presumably not, as was demonstrated by the 1998 bombing of the Planet Hollywood in Cape Town. The passage of time and the removal of the white-dominated South African government have not seen the sudden improvement in everyday living conditions hoped for by the millions of African blacks. Questions are now coming to the table about corruption and incompetence of the highest order under the government of Nelson Mandela. What this will mean in terms of terrorist activity in the republic is that the ground will be fertile and the borders no longer strictly controlled and external influences and tensions will be brought into play. Weak governments in the African continent have been susceptible to terrorism. However, until recently South Africa had a strong democratic system of government and had control of its borders and also an effective security force. It seems probable that the Rainbow of Nations in South Africa and their neighbors may pale. As whites leave the country in ever-increasing numbers for a safer life outside the Republic, the fabric and wealth of South Africa may suffer from instability.

KENYA

Myriad tribal groups, spread throughout the land, have populated Kenya for centuries. The Kikuyu, being one of the largest tribes of the region, work the land alongside the Kamba, Masai, and Luo tribes. The beginnings of colonialism in the nineteenth century saw the erosion of the tribal rights in Kenya and Britain was granted title over what is now called Uganda and Kenya. Uganda became a British Protectorate in 1885 and Kenya followed shortly after in 1893. Britain in those days was interested primarily in the rich natural resources of Uganda and constructed a railway system between Kampala and Mombaspa. Much of the labor was done by imported labor from the Indian subcontinent. Most of the merchants of Kenya and Uganda are the descendents of these railway workers. By 1915, British settlers had claimed the fertile highland regions for growing crops for export and displaced the tribes of the region. African and Asians were prohibited from being landowners.[6] The British, unprepared to deal with the native issues in Kenya, permitted the growth of black nationalist movements and in 1929 one of the most prominent African leaders of this century, Jomo Kenyatta, went to England to negotiate for land rights on behalf of the Kikuyu Central Association. With the onset of World War II, Africans were conscripted, and this provided a trained cadre for what became the Mau Mau terrorist group.

In relation to its nearby neighbors, the population of Kenya has been relatively free of terrorist activity and atrocities. Insurrection or uprisings in Kenya have been perpetrated in living memory by what is still considered one of the most shadowy organizations to gain a foothold on the African subcontinent, the Mau Mau. This almost mythical, shadowy and mysterious organization in Kenya came to prominence again as a result of what may be construed as a colonial land grab. In fact, the tribes of Kenya were land farmers and cattle herders who considered the land "everyone's land." But much of their area was now "owned" by white families. Kenya became part of Britain's far-flung empire, bringing with it taxation as well as education to the natives of the region. Britain and the settlers were of an unshakable belief that the land was the sole property of the tribal government and therefore the colonial government had rights to the land. Naturally such an assumption did not sit well with the tribes of Kenya. The land grab instigated a rebirth of the Mau Mau. Although the specific aims of the organization have never been detailed, the group flourished in the tribal lands of Kenya.

One of the best-educated tribes of the region was the Kikuyu and it was from this environment that the Mau Mau found its roots. The Kikuyu, like the other tribes, had been reduced almost to the levels of third-class citizens or serfs in their own country. In a region of the world where superstitions and magic have a considerable foothold, the groundswell of support for a secret society to fight for them quickly became apparent. The **Mau Mau** had sworn an oath, which was taken extremely seriously by the Kikuyu, for the total removal of all whites and those that supported the colonial British Government. In the early 1950s, the Mau Mau began attacking white settlers on their farms in Kenya. The attacks came to a full-scale rebellion in 1956, which was finally forcibly crushed by the British. Many tribesmen were sent to detention camps or were hunted and killed. The Mau Mau leader at the time was Dedan Kimathi, who was executed for leading the uprising.

The Mau Mau campaign had a softening effect on the British and sincere efforts were made to stabilize the country; however, from 1956–1960 the country was under a 'state of emergency.' The **Kenyan African Union (KANU),** led by Jomo Kenyatta, sought independence for the country. In 1963, Britain granted full independence to Kenya and Kenyatta became the country's first president.

International Terrorism in Central Africa

With the emergence and spread of Islamic fundamentalism throughout the Middle East and as well into regions of Northern and Southern Africa, it is not surprising that a 'soft' target such as an embassy of a foreign super power would suffer the brunt of a terrorist attack.

That attack came against the U.S. embassy in Nairobi, Kenya, in early August 1998. The U.S. embassy in Nairobi certainly did not have the levels of security protection afforded to other U.S. legations, particularly in the Middle East. The embassy was considered below the acceptable standards for security, particularly after the bombing of the U.S. Marine Corps barracks in Beirut in 1984 which claimed the lives of 242 U.S. Marines. Recommendations to beef up security had not included Kenya, presumably the threat assessment was considered low for this region of the world. With lax security and the location of the building being in the center of Nairobi, it became too good a target for the determined terrorist to miss. A massive car bomb decimated the embassy building and caused extensive damage to the surrounding buildings. The bomb claimed one hundred and seventy lives, mostly Africans, and wounded several thousand. The object of the attack was the U.S. administration and not Kenya. This attack demonstrates how a determined terror unit can attack at will and without warning and press home its vengeful message to a nation.

The prime suspect in this attack was Osama bin Laden, a Saudi Arabian dissident with operational training bases believed to be in Pakistan and Afghanistan, a man whose name would be associated with infamy for the 9–11 attacks on the United States.

Politically Expedient Response

The attack in Nairobi will be viewed as history repeating itself in almost the same vein as similar catastrophic terror events. At the time of this action, the terrorists caught the Clinton administration almost totally unprepared for a problem of such magnitude, and at a time when the president was facing serious personal and legal problems of his own. The outrage that this attack caused had the same kind of political and military response as the Libyan attack on U.S. servicemen in Germany. That incident quickly resulted in President Reagan ordering an attack on Libya, even though there was no confirmed evidence that the Libyans were in fact responsible.

If retribution or retaliation is to be meted out, and it seems to have been in this case, governments must be cautious about the levels of violence and the message that they are sending—not only to a small group of determined terrorists, but also to whole nations that have become the target for retribution.

The effects of retaliatory attacks against the Sudan and Pakistan have been determined, in this tit-for-tat approach, marginal at best. Do these counter attacks result in a diminished number of terror attacks against the United States or other Western governments? Since 9–11, it is fair to wonder. The answer to this question is not simple, nor is it easy to quantify.

The police crackdown after the IRA bombings on the British mainland in the early 1970s and their success in bringing the supposedly wrong people to trial for the Guildford Pub Bombings did not deter whole generations from becoming immersed in terrorist activities, both on the mainland and in Northern Ireland. The attacks against Libya did not deter the bombers from destroying a TWA airliner over Lockerbie, Scotland, in 1988. On the other hand, the suicide attack against the U.S. Marines in Beirut did not deter President Reagan from ordering his Marines to invade the tiny Caribbean Island of Granada some short time later, responding to fears of an alleged Cuban takeover of the island.

ANGOLA

Angola had been the prize jewel of Portugal in Africa for more than 500 years. The land was first claimed for Portugal by the Portuguese navigator Diego Cam, who landed in 1482 and left his mark in the traditional Portuguese shape of the cross. Over the centuries, the Portuguese exploited little if any of the natural wealth of a country that was rich in mineral deposits. With colonial development happening all around, Angola continued in its quiet slumber. All this was to change on March 15, 1961, when a cross-border incursion by gangs of guerrillas loyal to Holden Roberto raided villages in northern Angola. They killed the inhabitants and committed atrocities during the raids on both the living and the dead. At one location, the victims were put through a sawmill while still alive.[7] They attacked men, women and children and hacked limbs from bodies and heads from torsos. This one act, over the next decade, spurred Angolan economic development to a fever pitch. It also brought with it communist factions bent on controlling the country and removing the Portuguese influence.

TERROR BRIEF 9–1

Sharpeville Massacre

On March 21, 1960, a massacre marked the turning point in the attitude of the international community towards the apartheid government of South Africa and caused the sting of economic sanctions against it. One of the requirements of the apartheid laws was for all blacks to carry ID cards. In protest, blacks went to police stations without their cards and waited to be arrested. The same scene was played out in many locations, however in Sharpeville the police opened fire with automatic weapons, and killed 67 and wounded over 200 blacks. From this one incident the ANC formed its military wing the *Umkonto We Sizwe* (Spear of the Nation).

Source: George Rosie, *The Directory of International Terrorism*, Paragon House, New York, 1986, p. 265.

TERRORISM BYTE 9–1

Independence for Angola and Mozambique

On April, 25, 1974 as a result of a coup d'etat in Portugal, independence was granted to the Portuguese colonies of Mozambique and Angola. This effectively opened up a further 700 miles of hostile rugged frontier to guard against increasing "insurgent" infiltration. Rhodesia now had an 1800-mile hostile border and only a 125-mile friendly stretch with South Africa.

Source: Barbara Cole, "*The Elite. The story of the Rhodesian Special Air Service,*" Three Knights Publishing, Transkei, 1984, p. 436.

Popular Movement for the Liberation of Angola (MPLA)

This popular movement started in the late 1950s, in the Angolan capital of Luanda, and by 1961 had begun to fester into a civil war throughout the country. In the northern region of Angola, the Front for the Liberation of Angola **(FNLA)** was formed, and in 1966, the National Union for the Total Independence of Angola **(UNITA)** appeared. The warring factions continued sporadic fighting over the years; however, the overthrow of the Portuguese government in Lisbon by the military in 1974 led to Angola's eventual independence a year later.

With the guerrilla army's spread throughout the country, neither of the sides could agree as to which would eventually lead the new government, and so fighting resumed. The MPLA was receiving considerable aid from both the USSR as well as Cuba. The Russians supplied weapons, training and support and Cuba supplied the fighters to help with the guerrilla war.

By 1976, the battles were over and the Marxists dominated and influenced the MPLA. With a Marxist government so close to the northern border of Namibia, formerly South West Africa, the South African government continued to provide support and weapons to the UNITA rebels fighting against the Marxist government forces of the MPLA. Many of those fighting with the UNITA were South African mercenaries as well as former British soldiers. A cease-fire eventually came into being in May 1991 and lasted until October 1992.

At that time UNITA refused to accept the election results and fighting resumed again between UNITA and the MPLA government. Sporadic fighting continued over the next two years and finally, in 1994, it was agreed that UNITA guerrillas would merge with the Angolan Army. All this took place under the watchful eye of U.N. peacekeepers, and although the transition was slow the new Government of National Unity came into office in April 1997. Since that time the U.N. forces have pulled out of Angola.

However, the ongoing decades of violence since independence from Portugal have now seen a dramatic shift in the fortunes of one of the main protagonist groups, namely the ongoing battle with UNITA, the National Union for the Total Independence of Angola. In February of 2002, government troops engaged in a fierce firefight with UNITA rebels led by their patriarchal leader, Jonas Savimbi. During this one action, Savimbi was killed when troops attacked his stronghold in the southern region of the country. The short- and long-term effects of his death will likely mean that there will be a vacuum, and those inside will likely concentrate on a power struggle, thus fracturing UNITA. Whether this means the end of UNITA, it is too early to say. Much of the funding support for UNITA came from its illegal trade in diamonds. No doubt the trade will still continue and arms will still be traded for them. Savimbi's movement has not benefited from the end of the Cold War when much of his support network came from the Democratic Republic of the Congo, headed up by Mobuto Sese Seko.

MOZAMBIQUE

Sandwiched between Tanzania and South Africa, this other legacy of Portuguese colonialism bears the ravages of civil war and is today one of the poorest nations in Africa. Much of Mozambique's problems stem from its nearby neighbors, South Africa and Zimbabwe, the former Rhodesia. Organized along the lines of a one-party state, the current government moved out of the realm of a guerrilla/terrorist organization and become a political party. In the early 1960s, many inhabitants were becoming increasingly frustrated with the Portuguese rule and the Front for the Liberation of Mozambique **(FRELIMO)** was formed.

The movement carried out operations against the Portuguese until 1974, when the country was finally granted independence. FRELIMO was a strong Marxist regime opposed to the white minority rule (apartheid) of South Africa in the 1980s and also of the Ian Smith minority independence government of Rhodesia. When independence was declared, FRELIMO closed its western border with Rhodesia and many dissidents from Rhodesia set up bases in Mozambique to attack the Smith government, assisted by the Russian-supported FRELIMO. As the ideological focuses of the surrounding states changed so did Mozambique. The Samora Machel government in Maputo supported the banned ANC movement in South Africa and supplied weapons, training and support to terrorists fighting cross-border battles with the South African Security forces.

Mozambique also had its own internal strife at this time and South Africa supported the Mozambique National Resistance (RENAMO) movement with its guerrilla war with the Marxist government. By 1984, agreement had been reached between South Africa and Mozambique to stop supporting terrorists and guerrillas in each other's own country. However, this did not stop the RENAMO from continuing its war against apartheid with the FRELIMO. The RENAMO tactics were aimed at totally destabilizing the country and it began to destroy even schools and medical institutions. Over 1,800 schools were destroyed, and 500 health centers. Added to that total, nearly 100,000 people were killed in the countryside villages. By 1992, an uneasy peace was agreed between the two sides and called for an election process that would include RENAMO on the ballot. When voting took place in 1994, FRELIMO had 44% of the vote and RENAMO 33%.

Death of Samora Machel

In 1986, President Samora Machel met his death in an untimely fashion when his Russian-made Tupolev aircraft and Russian crew crashed into a hillside on the South African side of the border. What is uncertain about this crash is the manner in which it occurred. Was it an accident or an planned assassination? There has been much speculation since the crash that there was a high-level South African plot to eliminate Machel. Evidence from the crash suggests that external influences somehow tampered with the directional systems of the Tupolev 134A-3 aircraft. Because it was so wildly off course, it is suspected that a decoy navigational beacon was activated to redirect the aircraft onto a crash course into a hilltop. South Africa covertly supported the increasing number of RENAMO raids into Mozambique and had increasingly angered Machel. Whether South Africa was involved or not, it is known that there were raised tensions in the previous weeks before the crash, including threatening signals from the SA Defense Ministry. This led to extreme tension between the two countries and continued distrust on both sides.

RWANDA

A small landlocked African state, Rwanda has become infamous with the death of Dian Fossey, the naturalist of silver-backed gorilla fame. And in the sixties, others knew of it for its fabulous and pictorial postage stamps that graced many a philatelist's collection. But, in 1994 it became a killing ground for the native Hutus who massacred well over 500,000 Tutsi.

Rwanda has for centuries been a land of farmers occupied by the Hutu tribesmen and Pygmy hunters. In the thirteenth century, the warrior Tutsis invaded and took control of the Hutus. To the casual onlooker it might seem logical to assume that the Hutu and Tutsi were sworn enemies. That could not be further from the truth; in fact, Hutu and Tutsi had lived side by side and inter-married for hundreds of years.

It is not possible to denote the difference in any physical characteristics between the two tribes. They look the same, pray to the same gods and have peacefully coexisted for centuries. So the question one has to ask is: What happened to cause the genocide that took place in 1994? One must first look at the role played by the colonial forces of Belgium who ruled up to the early 1960s. The Belgian authoritarian control in Rwanda decided to organize and institutionalize the ethnic stereotypes in the country. As it was impossible to physically distinguish between Hutu and Tutsi the Belgian decreed a system that sounds like it came out of the dark ages, to define which ethnic group a person belonged to. Amazingly, it used these criteria; if a farmer owned nine cows or less he was issued an identity card stating he was a Hutu; if he owned ten or more cows he was a Tutsi. The Belgians had overnight created a class structure dependent on the details of an identity card—and this has been the basis for a social division of the two since the 1930s.

Now that the Belgians had created a minority elite, they gave them privileges and positions on the Belgian colonial administration structure. The Belgians ruled by the grace of the Tutsi minority in Rwanda, who had been schooled and educated by the Belgians. As they grew more powerful they sought to throw off the mantle of colonialism and demanded independence for their country. To counter the Tutsi demands, the Belgians began to switch their allegiance to the Hutu majority, producing enough hatred against the Tutsi to start a popular uprising. The uprising brought the Hutu into government and over 100,000 Tutsi were killed. A similar number, fearing further atrocities, fled to neighboring Uganda in the north where they remained in exile. It was this exiled group and their descendents that returned to begin the civil war in 1990. The group had formed in exile the Rwandan Patriotic Front (RPF), which was made up of displaced Tutsis, and Hutus dissatisfied with the Hutu government. The aims of the RPF were to replace the oppressive and repressive government with a new democratic styled order.

The Hutu-dominated government of President Habyarimana was determined not to be removed from power and to achieve that end they engaged and planned to eradicate the Tutsi in methods not dissimilar to the Nazi genocide perpetrated against the Jews in Germany. The tools of the trade in this instance were propaganda. As most of the Hutus were illiterate farmers, the government began to systematically bombard the population with radio announcements that were deliberately and openly anti-Tutsi.

It went beyond just denouncements of the Tutsi, but actively demanded that the civilian Hutus kill any and all Tutsi they came across. Terror and threat, terror and threat were repeated over and over in efforts to sow the seeds of total annihilation for the Tutsi. In a format reminiscent of South American Death Squads, the Hutu government set up civilian militia and trained them in weaponry and hand-to-hand combat and methods to quickly kill their enemy. This organization was called the *Interahamwe* which means, "those who attack together." The Hutu militias began killing Tutsi wherever they found them, and soon it became apparent that to kill a Tutsi would not be considered a crime in that country, just eliminating a form of vermin. However, after three years of the civil war and slaughter, a cease-fire was finally reached between the two sides in 1993. Then, under the auspices of the United Nations in 1994, the devastated country prepared to set up some form of transitional government. What was also occurring was that the Hutu continued to arm and train their civilian militia openly, under the noses of U.N. observers. It is still not clear to the international community why the United Nations made no effort to either report these facts or seek any clarification on how to handle the issues.

Death of a President

Uprisings often need a "trigger mechanism" to set them off. In April 1994, the plane carrying President Habyarimana was shot down as it approached Kigali, the Rwandan capital. The President died and this one incident became the green light for the genocide to begin again. Within hours of his death the attacks and killings of Tutsi began and within a month nearly half a million lay dead and the rest scattered throughout the country. Those that were able to do so escaped to neighboring countries. The United Nations stood by during the genocide and has been criticized for its failure to intervene to stop the massacres.

It was through the death of President Habyarimana that the world came to hear about the genocide being perpetrated on the Tutsi as graphic and horrifying pictures and accounts in newspapers emerged worldwide. Two months into the killings, the United Nations finally passed a resolution to send in a U.N. peacekeeping force of around 5,000 troops. With the killings all but over and the RPF advancing from the north, many of the Hutu militia and military escaped across the border to Tanzania and refugee camps set up inside the border. The point may have been missed in newspaper articles in regard to the goings-on in Rwanda, and the need for urgent humanitarian aid for the refugees. But most of the refugee camps held only the murderous members of the Hutu as nearly all the Tutsi had been caught and killed in the preceding six-week period. A long rebuilding process has begun but how long the scars will take to heal is anyone's guess.

Unique in world history is the country's demand that the Hutu and Tutsi reintegrate within Rwanda. Genocide, civil war, refugee flight, abundant hate propaganda, a culture of impunity and ongoing insurgency and atrocities, these are the stories in Rwanda. The most telling and difficult question is whether the people of Rwanda can rewrite a social contract that will be acceptable to any functioning society. Can they overcome their mutual suspicion and live as neighbors and fellow countrymen again? For the Hutu returning to Rwanda they fear retaliatory actions being meted out against them, the same as to the Tutsi in 1994.

In recent history, such a reintegration has never happened. It certainly did not take place in Germany, causing the international community to create Israel, a sovereign Jewish state. Fleeing from the killing fields of Cambodia, the people of those regions resettled in other countries. Similarly, following the Armenian genocide early this century, a separate nation was carved out for them. Rwanda today is still a dangerous and suspicious place, and terror and atrocities continue to take place, as old and not so old scores are settled.

BACKGROUND ON THE DEMOCRATIC REPUBLIC OF CONGO

Located in the center of Africa and straddling both the equator and the mighty Congo River, with a population of around 40 million, the DRC is rich with mineral resources of gold, copper, zinc and diamonds to name but a few. It was discovered by Henry Stanley in the 1870s, who was asked to set up Belgian trading posts along the Congo River in 1878 by King Leopold of Belgium. The King ruled this African country as his own private fiefdom and it only fell under the control of the Belgian government in 1908. It was called at that time the Congo Free State.

By the last years of the 1950s, the colonial Belgian rule was coming to an end and, on June 30, 1960, the Belgian Congo became the independent Republic of Congo. The first president of the new Central African Republic was Joseph Kasavubu with the legendary Patrice Lumumba as his prime minister. Unluckily for the young, communist-inspired Lumumba, his position was extremely tenuous in the eyes of the West, particularly the United States. At the height of the Cold War and intent on reducing and eliminating any Soviet involvement in mineral-rich central Africa, the CIA conspired with factions that were anti-communist to overthrow the Lumumba government and install a pro-West regime.

This was achieved by infiltrating mercenary elements into the country. The CIA had worked out a plan to poison Lumumba, however prior to his assassination, the army mutinied. In July and again in September of 1960, Desire Mobutu, a colonel in the army announced the suspension of all political parties and took control of the country. In November 1960, Lumumba was arrested and handed over to rebel forces, who executed him on January 17, 1961. For the next four years the government was in turmoil, until the military coup of Mobutu. For the next thirty-two years Mobutu Sese Seko ruled the country with an iron fist. His leadership was violently anti-communist and strongly pro-West, which suited the situation in the Cold War years.

Mobutu Sese Seko

Mobutu's tyrannical reign was all about pillage and plunder in a twentieth-century format. He was estimated to be one of the five richest men in the world, and was president of one of the poorest nations and standard of living in Africa, or the entire world for that matter. In a country of such enormous mineral wealth it is not very difficult to establish where the wealth had gone. Mobutu had a lavish lifestyle and had plush villas throughout Europe. One of the earliest uprisings against the Mobutu regime came in 1964, in the area of the eastern Congo and led by a young rebel of Marxist trappings, Laurent-Desire Kabila, who would later return to lead the civil war against the Mobutu regime. Much of what took place in the Congo was a result of outside influences and internal disputes between the many ethnically diverse tribes that had settled in the region or were refugees from rebel actions and atrocities in neighboring countries.

Hutu and Tutsi differences from the genocide in Rwanda played a significant part in the eventual rebellion and civil war that overtook the DRC. Insurgent rebellion was prevalent throughout the long dictatorial reign of Mobutu, but he had always managed to put down the uprisings either by force or by proclaiming presidential or legislative reforms. The country existed as a one-party state under Mobutu, so challenges to his rule were frequent. Citizenship issues and land rights also added to the tensions of the DRC. The complications of the various regions of the DRC are interwoven with the ethnic groups, who vie for power. The principal groups are located in the province of Kivu, which has a long history of ethnic violence; these groups are the Hunde, Nande and Banyarwanda people.

Banyarwandans are a collection of displaced Rwandans who arrived in the region courtesy of their colonial Belgian masters to work the land, and comprise both Hutu and Tutsi. This group was not considered to be citizens of Zaire under Mobutu's rule, and that has not changed with the transition to Kabila's government in 1997. The local chiefs in Northern-Kivu province had rented most of the land occupied by the Banyarwandans to them. The Banyarwandans by 1993 were pushing for reforms and an end to injustices against them. What was to complicate the situation in Zaire was the mass and sudden exodus of Hutus from Rwanda, which included the local militia Interahamwe that had been involved in the genocide in Rwanda after the death of the Rwandan president.

An uprising in 1993 escalated into yet another a full-scale ethnic battle. Most of those killed were Banyarwandan. The situation was not improved by the arrival of the Hutu refugees from the fighting in Rwanda. The uprising spread and soon became a national movement to overthrow Mobutu. The rebel forces consisted mainly of Tutsi warriors, and soon Laurent Kabila became their revolutionary leader.

Widespread disillusionment in the Zaire army led to the eventual capitulation of the Mobutu government. On May 16, 1997, with only his personal bodyguard remaining in Kinshasa and the rebel forces on the doorstep, Mobutu left quietly for the safety of Morocco where he lived in exile until his death in September 1997, from prostate cancer. However, since Kabila came to power the ethnic violence between the factions has not ceased, and with unprotected borders the DRC has seen an increase in rebel attacks from outside. From within, the fighting and massacres have continued particularly in the North and South Kivu provinces. Hutu and Tutsi continue to kill each other. An end to this violence is not expected anytime soon. Much of Kabila's support comes from the army that has been dominated by Rwandan Tutsis.

The country has seen the military involvement of six foreign countries as well as ten guerrilla movements. War-torn Congo took a tentative step toward peace with a settlement in April 2001 that would bring the two main sides in this conflict to a peaceful settlement. The Democratic Republic of the Congo (DRC), currently under the leadership of Joseph Kabila, would hand the post of prime minister under a new government to the leader of the Movement for Congolese Liberation (MLC), Jean Pierre Bemba. The presidency would remain with Joseph Kabila. The MLC has been one of the major guerrilla movements fighting to grab power in this mineral-rich country and what this accord will do is severely curtail the actions of the remaining rebel groups.

NIGERIA

The rise of Islam in Nigeria is not something that should necessarily be a surprise, particularly to the Nigerian public. The country has been subjected to years of government squandering and corruption, so much so that Muslim regions have turned to the strict Shira to enforce laws. After 9–11, there were sporadic outbreaks of violence between Muslims and Christians, which included burning and looting of Christian-owned shops and restaurants that served alcohol, in retaliation for attacks by Christians on a mosque. In the many decades since the retreat of colonial powers, Africa has been an unsettled and volatile land. So is it very surprising that radical Islamic fundamentalism would have some magic appeal in developing as well as underdeveloped nations in Africa? Does the rise of Islam also mean that there is likely to be an increase in fundamentalist attitudes towards Western democracies and values? Certainly a minority would seek to use religion as a cover for subversive operations against either the host state or to assist in propagating the fundamentalist movement in other regions. Lawlessness and crime are an everyday problem for most nations of the world; however, the activities noted in Nigeria lend a new twist to the meaning of crime fighting. The Bakassi Boys are a group of young men who have taken some measure of control over the lawless southern city of Onitsha. The Bakassi Boys operate a kind of terror subculture working outside of the established law. The Boys' brand of terror is to snatch victims, usually suspects in some crime or wrongdoing, and subject them to interrogation and in many cases instant execution. The Anambra State Governor Chinwoke Mbadinuju has financed the group and provided them with weapons and even police vehicles. Quite clearly, law and order has broken down, and regional southern states have turned to vigilante operations to suppress crime. This can quickly lead to wider regional implications for the formation of private armies to do the bidding of their financial backer.

SUMMARY

The turbulent passage to independence for many northeastern, central and southern African countries has led to wide-spread violence. The establishment of an apartheid-free South African nation under the presidency of Nelson Mandela had its fair share of violence perpetrated by both sides. South Africa is still considered one of the richest and most powerful nations in Africa and its influence on its neighbors over the coming years will be of considerable interest to students.

The troubles plaguing the regime of Robert Mugabe and the struggle that brought him to power in Rhodesia/Zimbabwe were all typical characteristics of gaining nationhood in southern Africa. Many of the fledgling countries that fought for independence have suffered under the thumb of tyrannical dictators, whose only real interests were to use capital and foreign investment in their respective countries for bankrolling their personal lifestyles. The influences of communist involvement in the region over the past forty years have been considerable and destabilization seems to continue in one form or another. This extremely vast area is at the same time rich in resources, but impoverished in the human sense. The devastation caused by intertribal wars, genocide and revolutions has been supplemented and exacerbated by the devastation caused by AIDS and famine. This region of the world holds great promise and should be followed in detail as we move deeper into the twenty-first century. In the following chapter we will chart the rise of terrorism on the Indian sub-continent and beyond.

TERMS TO REMEMBER

African National Congress (ANC)	**Afrikaner Weerstands-beweging (AWB, The Afrikaner Resistance Movement)**	**apartheid** *Brandwag*

Bureau of State Security (B.O.S.S.)

cannibalism

EPRDF

Emperor Haile Selassie

ethnic cleansing

FNLA

FRELIMO

genocide

"Great Trek"

Idi Amin Dada

Joshua Nkomo

Kenyan African Union (KANU)

Lugbara

Mandela United Football Club

Milton Obote

"mugger of the nation"

Ndabaningi Sithole

necklace

Nelson Rolihlahala Mandela

Ntare School

Ogaden

the Mau Mau

the Public Safety Unit and the Bureau of State Research

Robben University

Said Barre

Sir Edward Mutesa II

Somali Revolutionary Socialist Party

Unilateral Declaration of Independence

UNITA

University of Dares-Salaam

Winnie Mandela

ZANPU

ZANU

ZIPRA

REVIEW QUESTIONS

1. What was so important about the fact the Nelson Mandela became the first black man to become president of South Africa?

2. Describe the reign of Idi Amin Dada and tribal rivalries in Uganda.

3. Explain the manner in which Cecil Rhodes influenced the development of terrorism in Rhodesia.

4. Discuss why apartheid was able to be maintained for so long in South Africa.

5. Present an argument as to whether you think there will be peace in that region in the near future.

ENDNOTES

1. Somalia's government and warlords—A patchwork of fiefs. *The Economist*. November 3, 2001.

2. Bruce Quarrie. "The World's Secret Police," Octopus Books Ltd., London, 1986, p. 104.

3. Douglas Reed. "The Siege of Southern Africa," Macmillan, South Africa, 1974, p. 45.

4. Ibid. p. 95.

5. Peter Hawthorn. "Mugger of the Nation." Time, Canada Limited, December 8, 1997, p. 37.

6. Kenya. Capsule History. http://www.africanet.com.

7. Douglas Reed. "The Siege of Africa," Macmillan, South Africa, 1974, p. 25.

10 Southern and Southeast Asia

. . . regional instability is exacerbated not by a general sort of "ethnic conflict," as many claim, but rather by a number of entertwined issues relating to ethnicity, nationalism, religion, economic inequality, environment degradation and popular belief.

Richard H. Shultz and J. Marlow Schmauder

OVERVIEW

Nowhere outside Northern Ireland or the Middle East are the words quoted above more appropriate than in Southern Asia. In this part of the world, the splits between religions and factions within the same religion are longstanding and deep. To add to that delicate situation, two of the major powers are known to have nuclear weapons. This is one of the most misunderstood parts of the world to Westerners. The region is continuously faced with terrorism and violence. This chapter will acquaint the student with some of the major problem areas in the most troubled countries, from enormous India to tiny Sri Lanka. The student will become aware of ongoing battles for autonomy and freedom fought largely by terrorism and insurrection. It will be shown how difficult it is to separate the problems of this vast region into neatly defined categories. In addition, we will take a critical look at the potential threat of the Islamic efforts to unite into a global power stretching from the Persian Gulf to the eastern parts of the Russian republic. We will start with South Asia and examine the history of ancient, mysterious India.[1]

SOUTH ASIA

India

It is important for the student to have some historical background on the Indian subcontinent and its bordering states, which have long been the crossroads of Southern Asia. It some ways this area is like the Balkans, with many cultures passing through on the way east and west. The Indian subcontinent has had a civilization since 2500 BC, when the inhabitants of the Indus River Valley developed a culture based on commerce and sustained by agricultural trade. During the second millennium BC, pastoral Aryan-speaking tribes migrated from the northwest into the subcontinent and settled in the middle Ganges River Valley. A brief history of this region is essential to understanding its development on many levels, to include religious discord, violence and terrorism. The map of ancient and medieval India was made up of many kingdoms with fluctuating boundaries. In the fourth and fifth centuries AD, northern India was unified under the Gupta Dynasty. During this period, known as India's Golden Age, Hindu culture reached new heights.

Islamic influences spread across the subcontinent over a period of 500 years. Starting in the tenth and eleventh centuries, Turks and Afghans invaded India and established sultanates in the areas around Delhi. Descendants of Genghis Khan swept across the Khyber Pass in the eleventh century and established the Mogul Dynasty, which lasted from the eleventh to the fifteenth centuries. During this period, there were two major cultural and religious systems, those of the Hindus and Muslims. These cultures had centuries of mutual contact and lasting influences upon each other.

The British appeared on the subcontinent in 1619, and by the middle 1800s controlled most of present-day India, Pakistan and Bangladesh. In 1857, a bloody rebellion in north India led by mutinous Indian soldiers resulted in the transfer of all political power to the British Crown, which began administering most of India directly and controlling the rest through treaties with local rulers.

By the late 1800s, the first steps had been taken toward self-government. The British viceroy established provisional councils comprised of Indian members to advise the Crown. The British subsequently widened Indian participation in such legislative councils. By 1920, the Indian leader Mahatma Gandhi had transformed the **Indian National Congress** political party into a powerful movement against British colonial rule. Following Gandhi's concepts of nonviolent resistance, the party used both parliamentary means and non-cooperation to compel the British to award India its independence. In 1947, India was awarded Commonwealth status and Jawaharlal Nehru became the first prime minister. A period of continuing and escalating bloody conflicts, between Hindus and Muslims, led to the British partition of India. This division, created on the basis of religion, resulted in forming East and West Pakistan, where there were Muslim majorities. These groups were forcibly moved, Muslims north and Hindus south, creating animosity that continues to the present. After partition, India became a republic and a full member of the Commonwealth on January 26, 1950.

Always volatile, present-day relations between India and Pakistan took a downward plunge when both acquired nuclear weapons capability. Recent tests seem more calculated to divert attention from economic and international issues than to "rattle nuclear sabers." India has long complained about continuing foreign interference from Afghanistan and Pakistan, with the menace of escalating terrorism in the region. For years, the most ruthless Islamic and other terrorist organizations have been known to use Afghanistan as a base for recruiting, training and harboring terrorists to carry out operations abroad. On many occasions, India has drawn the attention to the presence of training camps in neighboring **Kashmir and Afghanistan**. There terrorists are trained and equipped to carry out operations in India, particularly in the states of Jammu and Kashmir. Many hundreds of thousands of refugees from the war in Afghanistan are easily recruited by their protectors in Pakistan and are used to foment terrorism and to pressure India to grant even more territory in the Kashmir.

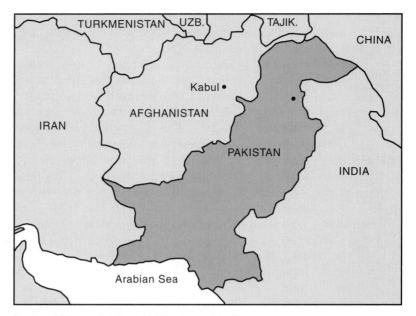

Regional Map—Pakistan/Afghanistan border.

PAKISTAN

India remains a strong supporter of the United State's worldwide War on Terrorism, despite some minor conflicts with its nuclear neighbor, Pakistan, over the disputed province of Kashmir. Diplomatic contacts with both these nuclear powers have been a major effort by the Bush Administration to keep a peace while fighting the battles in Afghanistan.

America has followed India's concern over Pakistan-sponsored cross-border terrorism in Jammu and Kashmir carefully. The U.S. government has expressed continuing concern over the fate of the four remaining western hostages kidnapped in Kashmir in 1995. Of the six original hostages, one managed to escape and another was killed in captivity. But the fates of the remaining four, Keith Mangan and Paul Wells (U.K.), Donald Hutchings (U.S.) and Dirk Hasert (Germany) remain unknown. The kidnappings did, however, reveal and highlight the involvement of the Pakistan-sponsored *Harakat-ul-Ansar* (**HUA**), which was branded a terrorist organization by the U.S. Government in 1997 under the Anti-Terrorism and Effective Death Penalty Act of 1996. It is difficult to separate the issues of terrorism between India and external terrorism by surrounding Muslim states. Therefore, we shall now examine the most prevalent of these issues.

In November 1997, the Pakistani driver and four U.S. employees of Union Texas Petroleum were murdered in Karachi when the vehicle in which they were traveling was attacked near the United States Consulate. Shortly after the incident, two separate claims of responsibility for the killings were made, one by the *Aimal Khufia* Action Committee, a previously unknown group, and one by the **Islami Inqilabi Mahaz,** a Lahore-based group of Afghan veterans. Both groups cited as the motive for the attack the conviction of Mir Aimal Kansi, a Pakistani national who was tried in the United States in November for the murder of two CIA employees and the wounding of three others in 1993. Kansi was found guilty and sentenced to death. Ramzi Ahmed Yousef, who was extradited from Pakistan to the United States in 1995, was also convicted in New York in November 1997 for his role in the 1993 World Trade Center bombing in New York City.

Deadly incidents of sectarian violence, particularly in Punjab Province, surged in 1997. According to press reports, two hundred people died during that year. In addition, five Iranian air force technicians were killed in Rawalpindi. *Lashkar i-Jhangvi,* a violent offshoot of the anti-Shiíte, Sunni group called *Sipah i Sahaba Pakistan,* claimed responsibility. In Iran, the government-controlled press held Pakistan responsible for failing to stop the attack and accused the United States of conspiring in the murders.

Security problems persist in India as a result of insurgencies in Kashmir, in the primarily Sikh Punjab, and in the northeast. The violence has also spread to New Delhi, where there were more than twenty-five bombings in 1997, mainly in the marketplaces and on the public buses of old Delhi, leaving ten killed and more than two hundred injured. These attacks appeared to be designed to spread terror among the public rather than cause casualties. Nearly one hundred bombings with similar characteristics took place elsewhere in India, most with no claims of responsibility. Although foreigners were not the primary targets of these attacks, foreign tourists were injured in a train bombing outside Delhi.

Most recently, massive anti-Muslim mob violence has been taking place in Gujrat State, the ruling party of the state and of the country, has been accused of allowing the violence, if not fomenting these riots where the local police and Army have been seen witnessing the killings of hundreds of Muslims without taking action. To date about 5000 Muslim men, women and children have been killed, many by being burnt to death; rapes are rampant. Over 100,000 Muslims have been made refugees when they fled their villages.

This cycle of violence began when some Muslims rioted and attacked and burned a train in which 300-400 Hindus were killed. The Muslim riots were instigated against Hindu extremist takeover of the Ayodhya Mosque site and the beginning of construction of a Hindu Temple; the mosque had been destroyed earlier by Hindu extremists. The Hindus claim the Mosque had been built on the site of a Hindu temple some centuries ago. The Muslim extremists in turn claim the site was holy to Muslims.

Pakistan, Afghanistan and Islam

As can be seen above, religious differences and a long history of violence and hatred among former brothers and fellow countrymen separate India and Pakistan. Sponsoring international terrorism, separatist subversion and insurgency is not new to either side. Since the 1970s, Pakistan has also trained rebel Sikh and other Indian separatist movements. The *Shironami Gurudwara Prabandhak Committee* [**SGPC**], is the major Sikh terrorist organization in India. It began to establish a tight control over the culture and economy of the Indian State of Punjab in the early 1980s. The SGPC forced Sikh traditionalism and conservatism on Punjabi society. Pakistan was quick to recognize this as an opportunity to exploit any further divisions in India.

India's nuclear weapon test explosions have rocked Washington as few other events have in recent years. Among senior officials, there is a palpable sense of outrage at having been deceived by the new BJP-led government. "We were told privately and publicly that India would continue to show restraint in the nonproliferation field, and would do nothing to surprise us," Assistant Secretary for South Asian Affairs Rick Inderfurth told a Senate committee on May 13, 1998.

This time around, it is still by no means clear that India now knows what it wants to achieve with nuclear weapons, or how it is going to get there. But the world in the meantime has changed a great deal. The idea that a more convincing demonstration of India's nuclear weapon capabilities will somehow boost India's international standing is so out of step with the times that it could almost be considered quaint if it were not also so damaging to the very cause of disarmament that India professes to support. The Cold War ideological rivalries that spawned the nuclear arms race are gone, nuclear arsenals are in steep decline, and something of a global consensus has emerged that the interests of international security are best served by halting the proliferation of nuclear weapons while reducing existing arsenals and building the international norms and institutions that can eventually displace the role of nuclear deterrence in the international system.

While American policymakers have long understood that India does not accept this framework for coping with the nuclear danger, the Clinton Administration thought it was working towards a new understanding with India. India's stealthy preparation and conduct of the recent test series has wiped out what was to have been a cooperative effort at mutual accommodation, and it has sowed seeds of distrust that may continue to sprout for years to come.

As for the nuclear threat from Pakistan, exactly how does detonating five nuclear explosives control, reduce, or in any way mitigate this threat? Think about it. Pakistan does not pose a conventionally superior military threat to India, so Indian nuclear weapons are not "needed" for this purpose. And it is absurd to think that Pakistani leaders must be actively "deterred" from deliberately launching a "bolt out of the blue" nuclear attack for the unprovoked and purely genocidal purpose of killing millions of Indians, including millions of fellow Muslims.

Today the Cuban missile crisis is widely acknowledged as involving supremely irresponsible risk-taking by both national leaderships. Without either leadership actually willing it, the crisis could well have culminated in inadvertent nuclear war. Reducing, but by no means eliminating this risk, through robust nuclear command and control systems, survivable basing, and nuclear options short of immediate Armageddon, while still seeking the deterrent benefit of nuclear weapons in conventional military confrontations with another nuclear weapon state, requires the expenditure of billions of dollars. Is India really prepared to go down this road? If not, India may wind up with the worst of both worlds — a nuclear "deterrent" that emboldens and then ensnares the national leadership in crisis situations, but ultimately provokes rather than deters nuclear attack.

If the Test Ban Treaty TBT ultimately unravels as a result of India's ill-considered actions, and nuclear explosions once again rock the earth in the five declared weapons states and other states as well. It is unlikely that the rest of the world will find much consolation in the notion that India was ostensibly acting in accordance with its "principled" stand against "nuclear discrimination." And in favor of a "timebound disarmament." The international community will remember a nation whose long delayed and now utterly improbable nuclear ambitions came cloaked in the rhetoric of disarmament, and it won't be fooled again.

Source: Extracted from an article by Christopher E. Paine, Senior Researcher and Co-Director, Northern Region Developmental Center Nuclear Program. May 18, 1999.

Members of the national Akali Dal burn an effigy of Islamic terrorist Osama bin Laden near Pakistan High Commission—New Delhi, September 13, 2001. The members were demanding the extradition of bin Laden, whom they say was being sheltered by Islamic nations. (AP Photo/Prakesh Hatvalne)

The Sikh struggle for an independent state attracted Pakistan's attention. Pakistan had long held claims to Kashmir and saw possible benefit from encouraging the formation of a Sikh state, **Khalistan**, in the Punjab, as this would weaken India's defense of the remaining portion of Kashmir. Pakistan looked to exploit the tensions in Kashmir in order to destabilize India. Pakistan began to provide training and military assistance, and terrorist actions of the Sikh militants increased. The Sikhs began to represent such a potential threat that India launched an assault on the Golden Temple at Amritsar, one of the holiest places for Sikhs, in July 1984. That event started an unprecedented bloodletting between Sikhs and Punjabis, with casualties far exceeding all Sikh terrorism efforts combined to that point. Ultimately, the escalation of Sikh separatist terrorism resulted in the shocking assassination of Indira Gandhi, the prime minister, and daughter of Mahatma Gandhi. The Sikhs' armed insurrection escalated, as high quality weapons became available. The arsenal included sophisticated bomb-making techniques and better training for Sikh terrorists of the *Dal Khalsa* separatist movement in the Afghanistan Mujahideen camps. The long reach of Sikh terrorism resulted in the bombing of the Air India jet from Toronto that blew up over the coast of Ireland, killing 329 passengers. (See Chapter 3).

A corresponding ideological development in Indian Kashmir then occurred. Almost overnight, the prevailing popular sentiment in Indian Kashmir was the belief that because the targets of Indian security forces were Muslims, Islam was in danger. This had a galvanizing effect on the youth of the Kashmir region, and they formed new cadres of terrorists. The extent of Pakistani and Afghan influence on the Islamist transformation of the Kashmir insurgency was profound and deadly.

The **ISI** (Pakistan Intelligence) then assumed quite a different role from its behind the scenes maneuvers. It seemed to appear they were taking over direct control of the Sikh movement. The ISI made the city of Darra, in Pakistan, the primary source of weapons for the Sikh, Tamil and Kashmiri liberation movements. The escalation of terrorism by the Karachi-based organizations rejuvenated the domestic Darra market and the Pushtan population in Karachi became the storefront for the regional arms market.

The availability of weapons, primarily supplied by America to the Afghan resistance turned the major cities of Pakistan into centers for international terrorism weapons. Such trade was suspected of involving Palestinians and people from India, Nepal, Afghanistan, Burma, Thailand, Sri Lanka, the Philippines, and Africa. These were Muslims who lived in Karachi, providing manpower for the planning and development of terrorist operations. Having witnessed the initial impact of the Islamist message in Indian Kashmir, Pakistan began to broaden its horizons and set it sights higher. In 1986, with growing experience in training, organizing and operations with Afghan Mujahideen, and with military supplies available, Pakistan began expanding its operation to sponsor and promote separatism and terrorism, primarily in Kashmir, as a strategic long-term program. Among the most crucial activities of the ISI were the following:

- Religious radicalism was propagated in small, but lethal doses to promote separatism and communal outlook.

- Training and indoctrination of selected leaders from the Kashmir Valley was arranged to create militant cadres.

- A large number of youths from the Kashmir Valley and Poonch Sector were given extensive training in the use of automatic weapons, sabotage and attacks on security forces. Automatic weapons and explosives were now issued to these people.

- Special teams were trained to organize disruption and engineer incidents to damage the myth of a democratic and secular image for India and Kashmir.

The head of the ISI Political Section developed a long-term program called K-2, aimed at castigating the Kashmiri and Sikh subversion efforts by making them appear to be under one umbrella of Sikh and Kashmiri extremists and Muslim fundamentalists. These groups would clearly not become allied with each other because of long-held hatreds among them. This would then intensify acts of violence in Punjab, Jammu and Kashmir, and the Terai region of Uttar Pradesh. Escalation of terrorism and subversion since the early 1990s is widely believed to have been a direct outgrowth of the ISI's implementation of the K-2.

After their revolution, Iran had a special commitment to the Islamist struggle in Kashmir. The maternal branch of the family of the Ayatollah Khomeyni had lived in Kashmir since the eighteenth century. The Khomeyni-based branch of the family had continued to maintain relations with their relatives in Kashmir, and in the twentieth century, the Persian Khomeini have cared for children of Shia Kashmiris sent for higher religious learning in Qom and Najaf. Ayatollah Khomeyni still retained contacts with the main branch of his Kashmiri family and had emotional ties to its cause.

Sikh terrorists were increasingly smuggling their weapons from the Jammu and Kashmir area or from Ganganagar in Rajasthan, where the ISI had its own bases. Clandestine ISI support for the Sikh rebels continued to improve. Eventually, Sikh terrorists in Punjab were reportedly receiving instructions from Pakistan-based leaders for an intensification of terrorist operations, which, as pointed out before, seems highly improbable. More likely the support was from Pakistan. Sikh terrorists received additional explosives and small arms from Pakistani stockpiles, as well as antiaircraft guns and recoilless rifles, sniper rifles and, "the latest weapons" for special operations. These weapons now dominate the insurgency in the Rajasthan area. By 1992, the ISI was operating thirteen permanent, eighteen temporary and eight joint training camps for Kashmiris in Pakistan and Kashmir alone. Thus, while these Kashmiris failed to incite or stir up a popular war, they did establish wide and solid enough popular backing to embark on the second phase, namely a direct and violent confrontation with the Indian security forces, whom they consider to be occupiers. That would not have been possible without Pakistani and other Islamist support.

Many of the factions involved in the Afghanistan civil war included large numbers of Egyptians, Algerians, Palestinians, and Saudis. Many of these factions continue to provide haven to terrorists by facilitating the operation of training camps in areas under their control. The factions remain engaged in a struggle for political and military supremacy over India. The Indian and Pakistani governments each claim that the intelligence service of the other country sponsors bombings on its territory. The government of Pakistan acknowledges that it continues to provide moral, political, and diplomatic support to Kashmiri militants but denies allegations of other assistance. Reports continued from Indian intelligence, in 1997, of official Pakistani support to militants fighting in Kashmir. In Pakistan, deadly incidents of sectarian violence, particularly in Sindh and Punjab Provinces, continued throughout 1997. Pakistan accuses India of being the instigator of these incidents. There continue to be credible reports of official Pakistani support for Kashmiri militant groups that engage in terrorism, such as the HUA (Harakat Ul-Ansar).[2]

KASHMIR

Over the decades, there has been a continuous state of declared and undeclared war between India and Pakistan with an ever-increasing enmity between the two countries. Protagonists of each country are emphatic about their claim to Kashmir and stand firm that they will never give up the claim. This article hopes to explore another possibility which is usually left ignored by both sides: that of letting Kashmiris have control over their own fate.

The Kashmir problem was created towards the end of the British rule in India and lies at the heart of the instability between Pakistan and India; this issue even affects Afghanistan. In the last years of British rule it was decided by all parties to divide India into a Hindu-majority country called India and a Muslim-majority country called Pakistan. Pakistan took its first form as East Pakistan (now Bangladesh) and West Pakistan about 1100 miles apart on either side of India.

TERRORISM BYTE 10-1

Sikh Terrorism

Sikh terrorism is sponsored by expatriate and Indian Sikh groups who want to carve out an independent Sikh state called Khalistan (Land of the Pure) from Indian territory. Active groups include Babbar Khalsa, International Sikh Youth Federation, Dal Khalsa, Bhinderanwala Tiger Force. A previously unknown group, the Saheed Khalsa Force, claimed credit for the marketplace bombings in New Delhi in 1997.

Sikh attacks in India are usually against Indian officials and facilities, other Sikhs, and Hindus. They include assassinations, bombings, and kidnappings. These attacks have dropped markedly since 1992. Indian security forces killed or captured many of the senior Sikh militant leaders and extremist groups. Many low-intensity bombings that might have been due to Sikh extremists occur without subsequent claims of credit. Sikh militant cells are active internationally and extremists gather funds from overseas Sikh communities. Sikh expatriates have formed a variety of international organizations that lobby for the Sikh cause overseas. Most prominent are the World Sikh Organization and the International Sikh Youth Federation.

Source: Patterns of Global Terrorism, 1997. United States Department of State, April 1998.

TERRORISM BYTE 10-2

The Harakat Ul-Ansar (HUA)

The Harakat ul-Ansar (HUA), an Islamic militant group based in Pakistan and operating primarily in Kashmir, was formed in October 1993 when two Pakistani political activist groups—Harakat ul-Jihad al-Islami and Harakat ul-Mujahedin — merged.

The HUA has carried out a number of operations against Indian troops and civilian targets in Kashmir. It has been linked to the Kashmiri militant group Al-Faran that kidnapped five Western tourists in Kashmir in July 1995; one was killed in August 1995, and the other four reportedly were killed in December of the same year. The HUA has several thousand armed supporters located in Azad Kashmir, Pakistan, and in the southern Kashmir and the Doda regions of India composed of mostly Pakistanis and Kashmiris, but includes Afghans and Arab veterans of the Afghan war. The HUA uses light and heavy machineguns, assault rifles, mortars, explosives, and rockets.

The HUA is based in Muzaffarabad, Pakistan, but HUA members have participated in insurgent and terrorist activities primarily in Kashmir. The HUA trains its militants in Afghanistan and Pakistan. The HUA collects donations from Saudi Arabia and other Gulf and Islamic states and from Pakistanis and Kashmiris. The source and amount of HUA's military funding are unknown.

Source: Patterns of Global Terrorism, 1997. United States Department of State, April 1998.

Other areas not contiguous to the two wings of Pakistan were the states of Hyderabad Deccan (which opted for self-government) and the State of Junagadh and Manavadar which opted for Pakistan. Hyderabad was attacked by Indian forces in November 1947, a period of cease-fire followed and it was finally forced to accede to India a year later. Junagadh opted for Pakistan but was forced to accede to India on November 8, 1947; Manavadar was forced to accede on February 15, 1948. Portuguese territories (Daman, Goa, Mapuca, etc.,) were overrun by Indian forces and annexed by India in installments from 1954-1961; the French gave up their territories to India (Chandernagore, Pondicherry, Karikal, etc.) also in installments from 1950–1954.

The state of Kashmir was close to the heart of Jawaharlal Nehru, the first Prime Minister of Independent India; he did not wish to give it up to Pakistan in spite of its Muslim majority. The departing British under Lord Mountbatten made no secret of their dislike for the nascent state of Pakistan and for its leader, Mohammed Ali Jinnah. Mountbatten joined Nehru in persuading the Hindu Raja of Jammu and Kashmir to accede to India which the Raja did at Independence. In order to afford India with a contiguous connection to Kashmir and make it defensible, the British granted the adjoining Gurdaspur district to India instead of Pakistan as was originally planned.

The Muslim majority of Kashmir has been unwilling to have Indian rule over Kashmir and has been involved in an escalation of resistance to India since independence in 1947. As a result, India has had more troops and other security forces per capita in Kashmir then any other nation has had anywhere. The Kashmiri resistance is being referred to as "terrorists" by the Bush Administration. Had it not been so tragic it would have been funny that Bush and Russian President Putin stood side by side as they jointly told Pakistani President Musharraf to stop aiding terrorists crossing the ceasefire line into Indian Kashmir. George Bush was obviously ignoring his companion Putin who is responsible for almost 100,000 Chechens killed and still counting. It is also a sad fact that the United States only defines "terror" as something done by individuals and groups and not by nations unless, of course, the nation has the misfortune to be on our list of nations to despise. In Kashmir, the fact is that Indian forces have held a reign of terror from the beginning. Kashmiri Muslims disappear after being "detained" by Indian security forces; if they are lucky enough to return it is only after suffering severe torture, and many are killed either "while resisting arrest" or while "attempting to escape," euphemisms applied with impunity by the occupying forces.

No sooner had India and Pakistan become independent than hostilities began between them for the possession of Kashmir. It is said that the Kashmir dispute has been the cause of two wars between India and Pakistan. In fact the Kashmir dispute has been the cause of a 55-year war between India and Pakistan; the two nations have hardly ever had a week without exchange of fire along the cease-fire line that lies between the Indian Kashmir and the Pakistani Kashmir. Huge numbers of soldiers have been killed and wounded but each side keeps its losses secret. Billions and billions of dollars have been spent in pursuit of warfare between the two nations just to get the upper hand in the battle for Kashmir. At the same time, millions of people constantly face death by starvation and preventable diseases. Things as simple as drinkable water and sewage systems are nonexistent; illiteracy is the rule and populations are booming to catastrophic proportions. It is unacceptable that people do not have food for the family but each nation has enough nuclear weapons to destroy the other's land for hundreds of years.

The only problem in Kashmir that gets any attention is the human rights situation there, but it is far more complex. India regards Kashmir as a part of India and therefore has pride and honor involved; for Pakistan it is a matter of survival because the only major river of Pakistan originates in Kashmir.

At the time of Independence, there were six major rivers flowing through Pakistan. Except for Indus River, five of them flowed through the province of Punjab ("five waters") in North Eastern Pakistan. These five rivers were Ravi, Sutlej, Beas and Chenab all flowing from Indian East Punjab and Jhelum flowing from Kashmir. In the 1950s, India drew up plans to divert some of the rivers that flowed through Pakistan. Nine years of negotiations later an agreement was made which resulted in the Indus Waters Treaty of 1960. This treaty gave up three of the rivers, the Ravi, Beas and Sutlej for India's exclusive use while Indus, Jhelum and Chenab were to be shared with Pakistan.

The mighty Indus which was used for fishing as well as for river commerce is no longer mighty. In fact, during the dry months it becomes almost stagnant in the South, permeating the air with the smell of rotten vegetation. Over a hundred miles upstream, one may cross this now slow river on foot without ever dampening one's knees.

Small wonder Pakistan feels insecure if India should control the headwaters of the Indus, the Jhelum and the Chenab.

Currently, Pakistan is accused of supporting the "terrorists" in Kashmir. These are largely Kashmiris supported by Pakistanis who are struggling to remove Indian rule from Kashmir. Pakistan does support them by giving them protection, shelter, and some military support. This is no different from Indian support of rebels in areas of Pakistan like Baluchistan, North-West Frontier Province, etc. In fact the largest support India has given to any rebel movement in Pakistan (that pales in comparison with anything Pakistan has done in India) was to the Bangladesh freedom fighters. This support first began in 1971 as providing shelter to the Mukti Bahini, the Bangladesh liberation army. The support continued to escalate until finally war was declared between India and Pakistan resulting in the independence of Bangladesh. In hindsight, this was a just war for India to be involved in; the Bengalis were oppressed and near-genocidal action was being taken against them by the (West) Pakistan Army. One could make a similar argument for the Kashmiris of today and for support of their liberation movements.

Since independence, India has dissolved at least three popularly elected state governments of Kashmir. The Muslim governments of Kashmir failed to toe the Indian line by demanding more and more autonomy so India imposed presidential rule over them, each time lasting for years. During the last fifty-five years of war and terror between India and Pakistan, only a few voices have been heard demanding Kashmir for Kashmiris and both sides ignored them. Why not vacate Kashmir and leave it for the Kashmiris to rule? Such a step would lead to the first rapprochement between the two warring nations. It would also allow the beleaguered Kashmiris their first opportunity to live and prosper in peace.

In such a scenario, Kashmir would be a neutral independent state. In the beginning, both India and Pakistan could provide a tiny fraction of their military billions and help build a viable economic infrastructure in Kashmir with help from the rich West. A Kashmir with open borders would give people from India and Pakistan opportunities to meet, promote mutual understanding and invest there in joint ventures. With the elimination of tensions in Kashmir would come a scaling back of arms and perhaps demilitarized borders. From there, it may only be a small step towards a closer relationship and perhaps even the initiation of a loose federation involving India, Pakistan and Bangladesh. All three nations spring from the same source; families have been split between the three sides and even culturally, the similarities far outweigh the differences. Is there really a reason why the three countries cannot follow the European Community model to come together?

Resolving the Kashmir issue may be the first and greatest step in preventing many future wars and separatist movements in South and Central Asia. The removal of tension may even help bring democracy to Pakistan where the "security" is the catchword for all sorts of repression by successive governments, civilian and military.[3]

SRI LANKA

The Democratic Socialist Republic of Sri Lanka (short form Sri Lanka) is an island in the Indian Ocean, south of India, which is slightly larger than West Virginia and was known as Ceylon until 1972. It was the center of Buddhist civilization in the third century BC and remains a strong Buddhist majority at

69%, with minority representation by Hindu 15%, Christian 8% and Muslim 8% among an estimated population of more than 18,700,000. The Portuguese first settled it in 1505, followed by the Dutch in 1658. The British arrived in 1796 and it was made a colony in 1853. It was finally granted independence in 1948. The Ceylonese government resisted an insurrection by terrorists attempting its overthrow in 1971. It commands a strategic location near major Indian Ocean sea lanes.

There have been hostilities between the Sri Lankan government by armed Liberation Tigers of Tamil Elam (**LTTE**) and other smaller Tamil separatist groups since the mid-1980s. Several hundred thousand Tamil civilians have fled the island, and as of late 1996, 63,068 were housed in refugee camps in south India. Another 30,000-40,000 lived outside the Indian camps, and more than 200,000 Tamils have sought political asylum in the west. The Sri Lanka Tamils initially received support from India and Indian Tamil groups in South India.

Drought, slow economic reform, and civil war, in 1996, exacted a heavy economic toll. Insufficient monsoon rains caused power cuts that hurt industrial and agricultural production, and the stepped-up LTTE insurgency reduced foreign investment and tourism, Sri Lanka's two key sources of foreign exchange. Meanwhile, the government counterinsurgency efforts caused defense expenditures to overrun budget targets by 42%. In 1997 and 1998, agricultural production should improve, but industry will still be hampered by high real interest rates, slow improvement in foreign investment inflows, and stalled progress on privatization. The government's main challenge will be to curb defense and social welfare spending to cut the budget deficit as a percentage of GDP in half by year-end 1998, as stipulated in its deficit reduction program.

The LTTE continued its terrorist activities in 1997, attacking government troops, economic infrastructure targets, and assassinating political opponents. The LTTE's most spectacular terrorist attack in 1997 was a truck bombing directed at the newly opened **Colombo World Trade Center** on October 15. The explosion injured more than one hundred persons, including many foreigners, and caused significant collateral damage to nearby buildings. Eighteen persons—including LTTE suicide bombers, hotel security guards, and Sri Lankan security forces—died in the explosion and aftermath. Sri Lankan authorities shot two of the terrorists as they tried to escape, and another three killed themselves to avoid capture. One of the bombers lobbed a grenade into a monastery as he fled the scene, killing one monk. In two separate incidents in June in the Tricomalee area, the LTTE assassinated two legislators and nine other civilians.

During the summer months, naval elements of the LTTE conducted several attacks on commercial shipping, including numerous foreign vessels. In July LTTE rebels abducted the crew of an empty passenger ferry and set fire to the vessel. The captain and a crewmember—both Indonesian—were released after three days. The LTTE stormed a North Korean cargo ship after it delivered a shipment of food and other goods for civilians on the Jaffna Peninsula, killing one of the vessel's 38 North Korean crewmembers in the process. The Tigers freed its North Korean captive's five days later and eventually returned the vessel. Sri Lankan authorities charged the LTTE with the July hijacking of a shipment of more than 32,000 mortar rounds bound for the Sri Lankan military. In September the LTTE used rocket-propelled grenades to attack a Panamanian-flagged Chinese-owned merchant ship chartered by a U.S. chemical company to load minerals for export. As many as Twenty people, including five Chinese crewmembers, were reported killed, wounded, or missing from the attack.

In August, a strange group calling itself the Internet Black Tigers (IBT) claimed responsibility for e-mail harassment of several Sri Lankan missions around the world. The group claimed in Internet postings to be an elite department of the LTTE specializing in "suicide e-mail bombings" with the goal of countering Sri Lankan Government propaganda disseminated electronically. The IBT stated that the attacks were only warnings.

The Sri Lankan Government strongly supports international efforts to address the problem of terrorism. It was the first to sign the International Convention for the Suppression of Terrorist Bombings in January 1998. The goverment was quick to condemn terrorist attacks in other countries and raised terrorism issues in several international venues, including the U.N. General Assembly and the Commonwealth heads of government meeting in Edinburgh. No confirmed cases of LTTE or other terrorist groups targeting U.S. citizens in Sri Lanka occurred in 1997.

In Sri Lanka, the LTTE showed no signs of abandoning their campaign to cripple the Sri Lankan economy and target government officials. The group retains its ability to strike in the heart of Colombo, as demonstrated by an October bomb attack on the World Trade Center in the financial district that was reminiscent of the January 1996 truck bomb attack that destroyed the Central Bank. The LTTE was designated a foreign terrorist organization in October pursuant to the Antiterrorism and Effective Death Penalty Act of 1996.[4]

Other known terrorist front organizations:

- The Liberation Tigers of Tamil Eelam (LTTE)
- World Tamil Association (WTA)
- World Tamil Movement (WTM)
- Federation of Associations of Canadian Tamils (FACT)
- The Ellalan Force
- The Internet Black Tigers (IBT)[5]

Of all these organizations, the LTTE is the most powerful Tamil group in Sri Lanka and uses covert and illegal methods to raise funds, acquire weapons, and publicize its cause of establishing an independent Tamil state. Founded in 1976, The LTTE began its armed conflict with the Sri Lankan government in 1983 and relies on a guerrilla strategy that includes the use of terrorist tactics. The group's elite Black Tiger squad conducts suicide bombings against important targets, and all rank-and-file members carry a cyanide capsule to kill themselves rather than allow themselves to be caught. The LTTE is very insular and highly organized with its own intelligence service, naval element (the Sea Tigers), and women's political and military wings.

The LTTE has integrated a battlefield insurgent strategy with a terrorist program that targets key government and military personnel, the economy, and public infrastructure. Political assassinations include the suicide bomber attacks against Sri Lankan President Ranasinghe Premadasa, in 1993, and Indian Prime Minister Rajiv Gandhi, in 1991, (the group's only known act out-side Sri Lanka.). The LTTE has detonated two massive truck bombs directed against the Sri Lankan economy, one at the Central Bank in January 1996 and another at the Colombo World Trade Center in October 1997. The LTTE also has attacked infrastructure targets such as commuter trains, buses, oil tanks, and power stations. They prefer to attack vulnerable government facilities then withdraw before reinforcements arrive, or to time its attacks to take advantage of security lapses on holidays, at night, or in the early morning. The LTTE has recruited approximately 10,000 armed combatants in Sri Lanka, with about 3,000 to 6,000 forming a trained cadre of fighters. The LTTE also has a significant overseas support structure for fundraising, weapons procurement, and propaganda activities.

The Tamil Tigers control most of the northern and eastern coastal areas of Sri Lanka but have conducted operations throughout the island. Headquartered in the Wanni region, LTTE leader Velupillai Prabhakaran has established an extensive network of checkpoints and informants to keep track of any outsiders who enter the group's area of control. The LTTE's overt organizations support Tamil separatism by lobbying foreign governments and the United Nations. They also use its international contacts to procure weapons, communications, and bomb-making equipment. The LTTE exploits large Tamil communities in North America, Europe, and Asia to obtain funds and supplies for its fighters in Sri Lanka. Information obtained since the mid-1980s indicates that some Tamil communities in Europe are also involved in narcotics smuggling. It should be obvious to the student that the LTTE has learned well from the tactics employed by the IRA in Northern Ireland.

AFGHANISTAN

Islamic extremists from around the world—including large numbers of Egyptians, Algerians, Palestinians, and Saudis—continued to use Afghanistan as a training ground and home base from which to operate in 1997. The Taliban, as well as many of the other combatants in the Afghan civil war, facilitated the operation of training and indoctrination facilities for non-Afghans in the territories they controlled. Several Afghani factions also provided logistic support, free passage, and sometimes passports to the members of various terrorist organizations. These individuals, in turn, were involved in fighting in Bosnia and Herzegovina, Chechnya, Tajikistan, Kashmir, the Philippines, and parts of the Middle East.

Saudi-born terrorist financier, Osama bin Laden, who was originally recruited by the CIA in efforts against the Soviet occupation and war in Afghanistan, relocated from Jalalabad to the Taliban's capital of Kandahar in early 1997 and established a new base of operations. He continued to incite violence against the United States, particularly against U.S. forces in Saudi Arabia. Bin Laden called on Muslims to retaliate against the U.S. prosecutor in the Mir Aimal Kansi trial for disparaging comments he made about Pakistanis, and praised the Pakistan-based Kashmiri group HUA in the wake of its formal designation as a foreign terrorist organization by the United States. According to the Pakistani press, following Kansi's rendition to the United States, bin Ladin warned the United States that, if it attempted his capture, he would "teach them a lesson similar to the lesson they were taught in Somalia."

The realities of the War on Terrorism and the Afghanistan campaign that filtered out after the ouster of the Taliban have punctured the mood that prevailed in October 2001. The idea that the Afghanistan campaign vindicated a new strategy of warfare, based on the employment of massive precision-guided airpower with little commitment of ground troops is now being revisited. Large numbers of Afghan civilians apparently died, owing to less-than-precise bombing, and scores of people allied to the United States were targeted and killed by U.S. forces acting on sometimes faulty intelligence. Relying on Afghan mercenaries to do the fighting on the ground for the U.S. resulted in Osama bin Laden's escape from the Tora Bora Mountains. And when U.S. troops did engage in close-quarters fighting with the Taliban/al Qaeda forces in the Gardez area near Pakistan in early March, 2002 an enemy that was assumed to be on the run bloodied them.

Though it has not achieved its prime objective of capturing bin Laden or dismantling the al Qaeda network, Washington thinks it has the strategic initiative. It seems to be the case, however, that it has launched itself into a multi-front war of attrition where it cannot consolidate victory on any front. The momentum is also being lost on the political front. As the military campaign lessened in intensity in Afghanistan, the United Nations was brought in to broker a political settlement that would usher in representative democracy while the European Union was dragged in to police the peace via a British-led armed contingent. It has become clear, however, that the centralized authority that had been forged by the Taliban has given way to a return of warlords' taking the power roles in different parts of the country, and the role of the security force is increasingly to keep the ex-partners in the Northern Alliance from cutting each other's throats. The current Karzai government seems to be steadily losing support because it is being perceived more and more as a front for U.S. control. This became more suspicious when American forces replaced the Pushtun security guarding Karzai. As Afghanistan slides into anarchy again Pakistan's President, General Musharraf, has been destabilized and delegitimized by American pressure to take sides in the war against terror. The prestige of Islamic extremists among the population is now probably greater than before the 9–11 events. Saudi Arabia is seething with discontent, and Washington faces the unpleasant prospect of having to serve ultimately as a police force between an increasingly isolated Saudi elite and a restive youthful population that regards Osama bin Laden as a hero or prophet.

Washington's tilt towards Israel has not helped in shoring up the legitimacy of its Arab allies, including Egypt's Hosni Mubarak, among their people. Israel is the great spoiler of the U.S. effort to manage the Middle East, and it can get away with it because it can rely on its massive support in the U.S. Congress to blunt pressure from the U.S. executive branch, as the brazen Israeli moves to destroy the Palestinian Authority in defiance of Washington recently demonstrated.

Indeed, the Afghan fiasco and Israeli intransigence, it can be argued, have combined to make Washington's strategic situation in the Middle East and the Persian Gulf worse rather than better. Nor have there been any political or military gains in Southeast Asia, with Indonesia maintaining its distance from Washington and the U.S. buildup in the Philippines becoming more controversial by the day. The introduction of U.S. forces in some of the Central Asian republics — the so-called "Stans" — may, on the surface, seem to be a strategic plus, especially when one takes into consideration the energy reserves of the area. However, with the failure to achieve decisive military or political victory on any front, Washington's Central Asian deployment may actually be a case of overextension.

The impressions (real or imagined) that the United States is actually working to undermine Islam is being strengthened by U.S. support of regimes in Uzbekistan and Turkmenistan. These regimes like America's other ally, Turkey, are brutal in their suppression of Muslims and any practice of Islam. As the negative image of the United States grows throughout non-extremist Islam, so do acts of terrorism against Americans and U.S. facilities in Islamic regions.[6]

The big question in 2003, in terms of international drug control efforts, is how to prevent the 2002 opium poppy harvest in Afghanistan from reaching global drug markets. And the more important question that follows is the one of how to end decades of Afghanistan's dependency on opium growing? To fully understand the importance of the issue, one only needs to know that as recently as in the year 2000, Afghanistan accounted for 70% of global production of opiates as well as for up to 90% of all heroin found in European markets.

In July 2000, the then ruling Taliban authorities issued a ban on opium poppy cultivation, declaring it "un-Islamic." This ban resulted in a considerable decrease of opium production in 2001. There are plenty of theories as to the motivation of that oppressive regime's decision. Some believe that they wanted to escape a threat of new sanctions, while others speculate that they wanted to please the international community and relax their isolation. Many have said that the reason for the ban was that the Taliban simply wanted to increase the price of existing stockpiles from the record harvest in 1999, which was 4,600 metric tons, and "next-to-the-best harvest" in 2000 of 3,300 metric tons. Whatever their motivation, the Taliban ban was effective. In 2001, the areas under opium poppy cultivation were reduced by 91 percent. If the ban had been maintained for another year, the existing stockpiles (estimated to amount to 2–3 years of production) would have melted down with all the predictable consequences. . .a gradual shortage of heroin in European markets, increase in prices, decrease in purity of the heroin offered, and an even a higher demand for treatment. That historic opportunity in international drug control efforts is now in danger of being missed or at least delayed.

The period following the events of September 11, 2001 and the subsequent fall of the Taliban regime coincided with the opium poppy planting season in Southern and Eastern Afghanistan. There were indications that Mghani farmers that had been hard hit by years of the draught and Taliban ban on their livelihood had resumed opium poppy cultivation. To verify anecdotal evidence about the resurgence of poppy cultivation in the country and to try and forecast the likely extent of opium poppy cultivation in 2002, the United Nations Drug Control Program (UNDCP) Country Office for Afghanistan, with the support of the UNDCP Illicit Crop Monitoring Program, implemented a pre-assessment survey. Conducted from February 1–10, 2002, the results of the UNDCP pre-assessment survey has confirmed those indications.

Present and Future Challenges

Some people, looking at the figures on the expected production in 2002, have even been tempted to speculate whether, at least on this issue of drug control, one would be better off if the Taliban were still in place. The answer is clearly no. It was exactly that regime that, profiting from the drug business for years and making Afghanistan a safe haven for international terrorist masterminds, created conditions for drug traffickers in the first place.

The Taliban regime seized control of the major opium producing areas of Afghanistan in 1996 and regularly collected taxes from the drug business (10% from producers and 20% from traders). It is difficult to imagine that in such a tightly controlled society, production and stockpiling of thousands of tons of opium could have gone on throughout the 1990s without the complicity of' the Taliban authorities. A further proof of the regime's involvement in the growth of opium production over the past decade is the fact that there were no recorded drug seizures in that country, while 90% of global seizures of heroin took place in neighboring Iran. On January 17, 2001, Afghanistan's new interim authority head, Dr. Hamid Karzai, issued a ban even more comprehensive than the one issued by the Taliban. His decree bans not only cultivation, but also processing, and illicit use, smuggling and trafficking of opium. Although, at the time of the ban, most opium poppy fields had already been sown.

The commitment of Afghanistan's interim authorities to drug control has been widely recognized, but the facts are that after decades of devastation of their country, the interim government still does not have the capacity to enforce its ban. That is why the international community needs to assist them in building that capacity. In the short term, the challenge for the international community is how to assist Afghanistan's authorities in preventing this year's harvest from reaching the world markets. The ideas raised in an ongoing debate range from destroying the opium poppy crops to compensating farmers by buying 2003 harvest and then destroying it. Proponents of this latter formula argue that buying opium from producers, at the farm-gate prices which average about $30 per kilo, is still much less expensive than allowing it to get into the hands of the traffickers who sell it, depending on the region, for $230-$300 per kilo. Whatever course of action is finally decided, destroy, buy or something else, it is a decision that needs to be made on the ground, in full coordination with Afghanistan authorities and international representatives. This short-term strategy also needs to include a tightening of the security measures against drug traffickers countries like Iran, Pakistan, Tajikistan and Turkmenistan. Now that the basic conditions for establishing lasting drug control in Afghanistan are being put in place, a cooperative government committed to drug control, and an international community engaged in the reconstruction of the country coordinated by the United Nations, there is an emerging consensus among all involved that unless effective drug control is actually exercised, everything else being done in Afghanistan might be in vain.[7]

BURMA

Burma is a Southeast Asian land about which most people know very little. Veterans of World War II may recall the Burma Road or the Flying Tigers, but probably know nothing of the Burma of today. Images of shining pagodas, elephants, and flying fish at play along the mighty Irrawaddy River and Rudyard Kipling's famous "Road to Mandalay" may come to mind. But Burma's reality today has little in common with romantic legends. For most of its modern history following independence from Britain in 1948, in classic state terrorism style, Burma has been run by an army-controlled socialist regime that isolated the country, wrecked its economy, and repressed its diverse ethnic populations.

A massive and peaceful "people power" movement demanded an end to dictatorship in 1988. The army reacted violently and quickly to repress this movement and maintain the status quo. A new junta, the State Law and Order Restoration Council (**SLORC**), seized direct power to quell any movement toward democracy. Crowds of peaceful protesters were machine-gunned by troops and thousands died. For a few days, events in Burma captured world headlines, but were soon replaced by other world events in more familiar locales. Global attention briefly picked up again in December 1991, when Daw Aung San Suu Kyi, the detained democracy advocate and leader, was awarded the Nobel Peace Prize.

Still, to most of the world, Burma remains mysterious and unknown. To further confuse the situation, the SLORC generals changed the country's official name in English to "**Myanmar**," a transliteration of the country's Burmese language name. This change, done by decree and without public consultation, was rejected and has not been recognized by Burma's democratic opposition. More confusion came when, in November 1997, the generals renamed their own junta the State Peace and Development Council (**SPDC**), in hopes of improving their international image.

The people of Burma suffer under one of the planet's most brutal and repressive regimes. The United Nations, world religious leaders from Pope John Paul to the Dalai Lama of Tibet, many governments, and human rights groups have urged an end to human rights violations in Burma. The military regime's response so far has been intensified abuse, such as murder, torture, rape, political imprisonment, and forced labor. There is no free expression or freedom of association in Burma, and the junta does not allow Burmese citizens a voice in the shaping of their own future.

The military regime allows and perhaps participates in an explosion of heroin production. Cease-fires with several ethnic opposition armies that have long traded drugs have allowed an estimated increase of nearly 400% in Burma's heroin production since the junta took power in 1988. Around the world, this flood of cheaper and purer heroin is causing a vast new wave of addiction. In recent years, approximately 60% of the heroin reaching the United States has been of Burmese origin. And in Burma itself, an estimated half million addicts are spreading an AIDS epidemic at a rate equaling the areas in Central Africa.

Burma plays a pivotal role is Asia's security, due to its strategic position linking South and Southeast Asia and bordering the continent's two most populous countries, China and India. Independent Burma had long pursued a policy of neutrality. To the alarm of many countries, the military regime is now increasingly dependent on China as a political ally and arms supplier. Fear of Chinese military influence in Burma is helping to spur a costly regional arms race, which diverts funds desperately, needed for human development.

Pressing for increased international involvement with the military regime are people who argue that trade and tourism can promote respect for human rights. Some claim that "constructive engagement" could convince the junta to fight drug trafficking and to reduce their reliance on China. A few declare simply that business and human rights are separate issues that should not be mixed. The junta itself, backed by a few Asian autocrats, asserts that it respects human rights in an "Asian" or "Burmese" context and those internationally recognized standards do not apply. Among these critical human rights issues is the detention of opposition figures by the SPDC. This was discussed in a 1998 United States Department of State Briefing:

> Resolution of the political impasse in Burma will require real, substantive dialogue with the democratic opposition, including Aung San Suu Kyi and representatives of the ethnic groups. Arbitrary detentions are unjustifiable and will only worsen rather than solve the political crisis.
> We have protested these actions to the Burmese Government through our embassy in Rangoon. We will continue to work with likeminded countries to press the Burmese Government to take positive action, including the release of the individuals and the initiation of a genuine dialogue with Aung San Suu Kyi and other NLD leaders.[7]

The explosion in April of a parcel bomb at the house of a senior official in Burma's military-led government was the most significant terrorist event in Burma in 1997. The blast killed the adult daughter of Lieutenant-General Tin Oo, Secretary Number Two of the ruling State Law and Order Restoration Council. No group or individual claimed responsibility for the attack, but the Government of Burma attributes the act to Burmese antigovernment activists in Japan; the package bore Japanese stamps and postmarks. The Burmese expatriate and student community in Japan denies any involvement in the incident.

Accounting for about 90% of Southeast Asian production and about half of the world's supply, Burma is the world's leading producer of illicit opium. Recent reports suggest an increase in methamphetamine production and distribution from Burma as well. Although the Burmese government has expanded its counter-narcotics efforts over the past few years, the impact has been limited. While part of the problem is that the Burmese government does not control many of the ethnic groups that traffic in drugs, the government also does not make sufficient effort at interdiction. There is also some evidence of corrupt elements in the military that may be aiding the traffickers, and there are signs that the Burmese encourage traffickers to invest in a multitude of development projects throughout the country.

> The U.S. remains concerned about the commitment of the Burmese government to fight narcotics and about the potential damage that opium cultivation in Burma can inflict on the United States and the

Burma, The South Africa of the Nineties: Does Constructive Engagement Work?

Investments in Burma, by companies who claim that they can only influence the Burmese regime by investing in the country are under attack. South African Bishop, Desmond Tutu, who was refused entry to Burma in 1993 along with six other Nobel Prize winners, including the Dalai Lama, had the following to say on the subject of **constructive engagement**:

"As a South African, I can claim some expertise on the subject of constructive engagement. For years, some governments claimed that the best way to deal with the apartheid regime in South Africa was by continuing to talk and trade. This gradualist approach, they said, would persuade the white-minority regime to share power and end its flagrant abuses.

"Today the world knows what a failure that policy was. These ties gave the apartheid regime the political will and economic sustenance to continue its repressive policies. Only when serious sanctions started to take a significant economic toll on my country did the road to real reform begin."[8]

United States President Clinton transmitted to Congress a required report on conditions in Burma and U.S. policy toward Burma for the period from March 28, 1998, to September 28, 1998. U.S. statute (Public Law 104–208) requires that such reports be given to Congress every six months. That Congressional report, as summarized below, was highly critical:

Plan for Implementation of Section 570 of Public Law 104–208 (Omnibus Appropriations Act, Fiscal Year 1997)
CONDITIONS IN BURMA AND U.S. POLICY TOWARD BURMA FOR THE PERIOD MARCH 28, 1998 - SEPTEMBER 28, 1998

"The people of Burma continue to live under a highly repressive, authoritarian military regime that is widely condemned for its serious human rights abuses," the report says.

"The reorganization and renaming of Burma's ruling military junta in November 1997, through which the former State Law and Order Restoration Council (SLORC) became the State Peace and Development Council (SPDC) did not herald significant policy changes."

"The regime has made no progress in the past six months in moving toward greater democratization, nor has it made any progress toward fundamental improvement in the quality of life of the people of Burma. To the contrary, conditions have worsened with the regime rounding up and detaining over 900 opposition National League for Democracy (NLD) officials and supporters, including 200 Members-elect of Parliament," the report continues.

According to the report, the Burmese economy is deteriorating due to "SPDC economic mismanagement, combined with spillover effects from the Asian financial crisis."

"The government is reportedly virtually bankrupt with regard to foreign exchange reserves, holding an amount equal to only several weeks of imports. Inflation is increasing, while the kyat continues its downward slide against the dollar. Imported foodstuffs are growing more and more difficult to obtain. Both gasoline and diesel fuel are rationed to three gallons per vehicle per day. The military junta continues to dominate the political, economic and social life of the country in the same oppressive, heavy-handed way that it has since seizing power in September 1988 after harshly suppressing massive pro-democracy demonstrations," the report says.

"As a result of sanctions and the ongoing financial crisis in much of the rest of Southeast Asia, approvals of new foreign direct investment in Burma fell by 65 percent in FY 97/98, contributing to the financial collapse of the Burmese economy. U.S. and European investors continue to pull out of Burma due to the unfavorable political situation. While the government's own mismanagement contributes to the problem, the SPDC is unlikely to find a way out of the crisis unless political developments in Burma permit an easing of restrictions on lending by international financial institutions," the report continues.

U.S. policy toward Burma seeks progress in three key areas: democracy, human rights, and counter-narcotics, the report states.

"We have taken strong measures to pressure the SPDC to end its repression and move towards democratic government," the report says. "Since 1989, the United States has been unable to certify that Burma has cooperated in efforts against narcotics. The U.S. has suspended economic aid, withdrawn Burma from the General System of Preferences (GSP) and Overseas Private Investment Corporation (OPIC) programs, implemented an arms embargo, successfully opposed assistance from international financial institutions, downgraded our representation from Ambassador to Charge, d'Affaires, imposed visa restrictions on senior officials and their families, and instituted a ban on new investment by U.S. persons."

The United States remains engaged in multilateral diplomacy to encourage the Association of Southeast Asian Nations (ASEAN), Japan, Korea, China, the European Union (EU), and other nations to take similar steps and/or other actions to encourage progress by the SPDC, according to the report.[9]

rest of the world. Against this backdrop, we have supported a small program, the Old Soldiers Project of 101 Veterans, Inc., in Burma to replace opium poppy cultivation with substitute, economically viable alternative crops. Despite impressive strides in a short period of time the Old Soldiers Project has not received permission from the Burmese Government to continue, and the project was suspended on September 15.[10]

Burma is a poor country, with an average per capita GDP of approximately $406, at a weighted exchange rate, perhaps double that in terms of purchasing power parity. Progress on market reforms has been mixed and uneven. Beginning in 1988 the government partly opened the economy to permit expansion of the private sector and to attract foreign investment. Though modest economic improvement ensued, since 1993 the pace of economic reform has slowed, and major obstacles to further reform persist. These include disproportionate military spending, extensive overt and covert state involvement in economic activity, state monopolization of leading exports, a bloated bureaucracy prone to arbitrary and opaque governance, poor education and physical infrastructure. In addition, due to international opposition and to the SPDC's unwill- ingness to cooperate fully with the IMF, SPDC access to external credit from the IMF, World Bank, and Asian Development Bank continues to be blocked by sanctions. In September 1998, the World Bank announced that Burma had defaulted on its loan repayments. The laundering of drug profits in Burma's legitimate economy is thought by some analysts to be extensive.

At the ASEAN meetings in Manila, in July 1998, U.S. Secretary of State Albright, with Foreign Minister McKinnon of New Zealand, led a discussion of the political impasse in Burma, which included representatives from Austria, Australia, Canada, Germany, Korea, Japan, the U.K. and Burmese Foreign Minister Ohn Gyaw. The ministers expressed their concerns over the deteriorating conditions in Burma and demanded a speedy, peaceful resolution to the situation and pressed for the immediate commencement of an SPDC dialogue with the democratic opposition, to include Aung San Suu Kyi. Secretary Albright continued to actively promote international engagement with the SPDC toward an improved human rights climate.

It is clear that the SPDC is not eager to release its chokehold on the Burmese people, and the world's attention is often drawn away from such remote areas. The report to the U.S. Government is seen a good first move in a game of chess that seems to be using the people of Burma as pawns. It is to be seen whether or not peroccupation with problems in Bosnia, Israel and Iraq will distract prompt diplomatic action by the major powers to right the situation in Burma.

In South Asia, many of the factions involved in the Afghanistan civil war, including large numbers of Egyptians, Algerians, Palestinians, and Saudis continued to provide haven to terrorists by facilitating the operation of training camps in areas under their control. The factions remain engaged in a struggle for political and military supremacy over their countries and regions.

SOUTHEAST ASIA

Incidents of terrorism in Southeast Asia increased in 1997. Continuing defections from the Khmer Rouge to Cambodian forces reduced the threat from the terrorist group, but guerrillas in the Cambodian provinces have been responsible for deadly attacks on foreigners. The unstable political situation in Cambodia has led to marked political violence, and the most significant example of terrorism there was a grenade attack on an opposition political rally in 1998, which left nineteen persons dead and more than one hundred injured, including a U.S. citizen. In October, the Secretary of State designated the Khmer Rouge as a foreign terrorist organization pursuant to the Antiterrorism and Effective Death Penalty Act of 1996.

CAMBODIA

Cambodia is located on the Gulf of Thailand, between Thailand and Vietnam. It is a tiny country, slightly smaller than Oklahoma. The country is a land of paddies and forests and dominated by the Mekong River. It has a population of about 11 million, ethnically composed of Khmer (90%), Vietnamese (5%), Chinese (1%), and other (4%) distribution. The religious preference is overwhelmingly Theravada Buddhist (95%). Cambodia was called Kampuchea under the disastrous rule of the Khmer Rouge.

The Cambodian economy has been virtually destroyed by decades of war, but it is slowly recovering. Government leaders are moving toward restoring fiscal and monetary discipline and have established good working relations with international financial institutions. Growth, starting from a low base, was strong between 1991–96. Despite such positive developments, the reconstruction effort faces many tough challenges because of the persistence of internal political divisions and the related lack of confidence of foreign investors.

Rural Cambodia, where 90% of about 9.5 million of the Khmer live, remains mired in poverty. The almost total lack of basic infrastructure in the countryside hinders development and contributes to a growing imbalance in growth between urban and rural areas over the near term. Moreover, the government's lack of experience in administering economic and technical assistance programs and rampant corruption among officials slows the growth of critical public sector investment. The decline of inflation from the 1992 rate of more than 50% is one of the bright spots in Cambodia's return to a peacetime period. In a somewhat interesting and unusual move, the Khmer Royal Armed Forces (**KRAF**) was created in 1993 by the merger of the Cambodian People's Armed Forces and the two noncommunist resistance armies. (KRAF is also known as the Royal Cambodian Armed Forces or RCAF.)

Offshore islands and sections of the boundary with Vietnam remain in dispute and the maritime boundary with Vietnam is not clearly defined. Also, parts of the border with Thailand are now in dispute, as its boundaries are also not clearly defined. *Golden Triangle,* where Cambodia, Thailand, and Vietnam have mutual borders, heroin being routed to the West gives Cambodia the possibility of becoming a major money-laundering center. High-level narcotics-related corruption reportedly involves the government, military, and police. There are small-scale opium, heroin, and amphetamine production operations in Cambodia, and a larger production system of high-grade marijuana for the international market.

Hard-liners based in the Khmer Rouge stronghold at Anlong Veng regularly launched guerrilla-style attacks on government troops in several provinces. Guerrillas are also suspected in two deadly attacks against ethnic Vietnamese civilians in Cambodia, but they have denied playing a role in the disappearance of two Filipino and two Malaysian employees of a logging company in 1997.

The death of former **Khmer Rouge** leader Pol Pot on April 15, 1998, in the Thai-Cambodian border area brought to an end one of the most chilling and bloody chapters of the twentieth century. During Pol Pot's three and a half years of rule over Cambodia, from 1975 to 1978, the Khmer Rouge killed as many as two million people through mass executions, starvation and slave labor. The genocide in Cambodia was the outcome of a complex historical development in which the pernicious ideological influence of Stalinism came together with the military bloodbath carried out against the people of Indochina. Pol Pot will be little mourned by the people of Cambodia.

The fate of British mine-clearing expert Christopher Howes, allegedly kidnapped by the Khmer Rouge in March 1996, remains unresolved. Unconfirmed reporting suggested Howes was with forces loyal to Pol Pot, and some Cambodian officials expressed fears publicly that he had been killed. In May, Khmer Rouge leader Khieu Samphan denied any knowledge of Howes' whereabouts.

Incidents of terrorism in East Asia increased in 1997. Continuing defections from the Khmer Rouge to Cambodian forces reduced the threat from the terrorist group, but guerrillas in the Cambodian provinces have been responsible for deadly attacks on foreigners. The unstable political situation in Cambodia has led to marked political violence. In October, the Secretary of State designated the Khmer Rouge as a foreign terrorist organization pursuant to the Antiterrorism and Effective Death Penalty Act of 1996.

The Khmer Rouge is a communist insurgency that is trying to destabilize the Cambodian Government. Under Pol Pot's leadership, the Khmer Rouge conducted a campaign of genocide in which more than 1 million people were killed during its four years in power in the late 1970s. The Khmer Rouge is still engaged in a low-level insurgency against the Cambodian Government. Although its victims are mainly Cambodian villagers, the Khmer Rouge has occasionally kidnapped and killed foreigners traveling in remote rural areas. One to two thousand members of the Khmer Rouge operate in outlying provinces in Cambodia, particularly in pockets along the Thailand border. The Khmer Rouge may not be considered by many as a serious threat to destabilization of Cambodia yet again. But, some seventeen years and three Cambodian regimes later, the National Army of Democratic Kampuchea, as the Khmer Rouge military is known, continues to wage warfare and terrorism from scattered jungle bases of operation in an attempt to regain control of Cambodia and resume their utopian experiment. Although there have been large-scale defections from the Khmer Rouge to Cambodian Government forces since 1996, and the group suffered a significant split in 1997, it still may be considered dangerous.

THAILAND

The ancient Kingdom of Thailand (sometimes referred to as Siam) borders on the Andaman Sea and the Gulf of Thailand. Southeast of Burma, it is slightly more than twice the size of Wyoming. This peaceful country has a population of almost 60 million; the ethnic groupings are Thai 75%, Chinese 14%, and other 11%. Religious affiliations are Buddhism 95%, Muslim 3.8%, Christianity 0.5%, Hinduism 0.1%, other 0.6%, who all seem to be harmonious together. Thailand has had independence since 1238 AD and has never been colonized. A new constitution was approved in 1991 and amended in 1992.

One of the more advanced developing countries in Asia, Thailand depends on exports of manufactured goods, including high-technology goods and the development of the service sector to fuel the country's rapid growth, averaging 9% since 1989. Most of Thailand's recent imports have been for capital equipment and raw materials, although imports of consumer goods are beginning to rise. Thailand's 35% domestic savings rate is a key source of capital for the economy, and the country is also benefiting from rising investment from abroad. Prime Minister Chawalit's government is Thailand's seventh Government in six years. It will probably continue Bangkok's pro-business policies and reemphasize Bangkok's traditional fiscal austerity.

The new government is beginning to address Thailand's serious infrastructure bottlenecks, especially in the transport and telecommunications sectors. Over the longer term, Bangkok must produce more college graduates with technical training and upgrade workers' skills to continue its rapid economic development. Thailand is a minor producer of opium, heroin, and marijuana. It is, however, a major illicit transit point for heroin en route to the international drug market from Burma and Laos. Eradication efforts have reduced the area of cannabis cultivation and shifted some production to neighboring countries, and opium poppy cultivation has also been reduced. A drug money-laundering center, Thailand has a rapidly growing role in amphetamine production for regional consumption as well as increasing indigenous abuse of methamphetamine and heroin.

While there is little terrorism to report in this placid country, an appeals court in Thailand upheld the conviction and death sentence passed on an Iranian convicted of a 1994 plot to bomb the Israeli Embassy in Bangkok. The defendant, Hossein Dastgiri, has appealed to the Supreme Court. Also, Muslim separatist groups in southern Thailand carried out a series of bombings and other violent attacks in 1997. Bomb attacks in October killed seven persons, and a bombing of a Chinese religious festival in December killed three and wounded fifteen. Government authorities credited separatist groups with assassinating eleven policemen in a two-month period and blowing up a railroad in May.

VIETNAM

The Socialist Republic of Vietnam is a communist state made up from the former North and South Vietnams so well remembered from the Vietnam War. This country, war-torn for decades, is in Southeastern Asia, bordering the Gulf of Thailand, Gulf of Tonkin, and South China Sea, between China and Cambodia. It is slightly larger than New Mexico. After consolidation at the war's end, Vietnam has a population of over 75 million. The ethnic population distribution is: Vietnamese 85%-90%, Chinese 3%, with MuongTai, Meo, Khmer, Man and Cham making up the balance. Religious affiliations are (in descending order) Buddhist, Taoist, Roman Catholic, indigenous beliefs, Islam, Protestant, Cao Dai, Hoa Hao. Vietnam won its independence from France in 1945, when the French colonial forces were defeated. Its new constitution was approved in 1992.

Vietnam is a poor, densely populated country that has had to recover from the ravages of decades of war, the loss of financial support from the old Soviet bloc, and the rigidities of a centrally planned economy. Substantial progress has been achieved over the past ten years in moving forward from an extremely low starting point. Economic growth continued at a strong pace with industrial output rising by 14% during 1996 and real GDP expanded by 9.4%. Foreign direct investment rose to an estimated $2.3 billion for the year, up by about 30% from 1995. These positive numbers, however, masked some major difficulties that are emerging in economic performance. Many domestic industries, including coal, cement, steel, and paper, reported large stockpiles of inventory and tough competition from more efficient foreign producers. Vietnam's trade deficit widened to $4 billion in 1996, up over 80% from just the previous year. While disbursements of aid and foreign direct investment have risen, they are not large enough to finance the rapid increase in imports and it is widely believed that Vietnam may be using short-term trade credits to bridge the gap. That is a risky strategy, one that could result in a foreign exchange crunch in the near term. Meanwhile, Vietnamese authorities continue to move very slowly toward implementing the structural reforms needed to revitalize the economy and produce more competitive, export-driven industries. Privatization of state enterprise remains bogged down in political controversy, while the country's dynamic private sector is denied both financing and ac-

TERRORISM PLAYER 10-1

Pol Pot

The political activity of **Pol Pot** (Saloth Sar) (d. 1998) began in post-World War II France, when Cambodia was part of its Indochina colony. The son of a relatively well-off peasant family, he received a government scholarship in 1949 to study in Paris, where he gravitated with a number of his friends to the Stalinist circles around the French Communist Party. He returned to Phnom Penh in 1953, worked as a teacher and was involved in the start of the embryonic Communist Party in Cambodia. Police repression under the government of Prince Norodom Sihanouk, the country's first post-colonial ruler, forced the party leaders to flee the capital in 1963 and seek sanctuary in the remote rural areas of the country.

It was only after the American intervention in Cambodia during the Vietnam War, that Pol Pot and the Khmer Rouge began to get wider support. From a badly organized, rag-tag force of less than 5,000 men in 1970, the Khmer Rouge expanded to an army of around 70,000. In April 1975, the Lon Nol dictatorship collapsed and Pol Pot came to power.

The peasant-based army and Khmer Rouge leaders carried out policies of a anti-working-class character, which had far more in common with fascism than socialism. With an economy in shambles, Pol Pot was unable and unwilling to organize the feeding of the cities; He ordered the evacuation of Pnomh Penh and other towns. The entire urban population of workers, intellectuals, civil servants, small shopkeepers and others were driven into the countryside to labor under very harsh conditions on irrigation schemes and other grandiose projects aimed at elevating agricultural production.

As highlighted by the film, "The Killing Fields," hundreds of thousands died of overwork, hunger and disease. Many more were executed in the course of the pogroms against all culture and intellectual life. Others died in the vicious factional disputes that erupted within the Khmer Rouge when its economic plans fell to pieces.

Shattering, urban economic life and even traditional peasant agriculture finally led the Khmer Rouge to rely more on culturally and socially primitive layers of those living an essentially tribal existence. Under Pol Pot's leadership, the Khmer Rouge conducted a campaign of genocide in which an estimated more than 2 million people were killed during its four years in power in the late 1970s.

Source: An extract for "The Death of Pol Pot." SAIS/Asia Society Cambodia Policy Study Group. Internet, 1998, http://www.fiv.edu/~fcf/polsdead 41698.html.

cess to markets. Reform of the banking sector is proceeding slowly, raising concerns that the country will be unable to tap sufficient domestic savings to maintain current high levels of growth. Administrative and legal barriers are also causing costly delays for foreign investors and are raising similar doubts about Vietnam's ability to maintain the inflow of foreign capital. Ideological bias in favor of state intervention and control of the economy is slowing progress toward a more liberalized investment environment.

Vietnam has disputes over maritime boundaries with Cambodia and is involved in complex negotiations over the Spratly Islands in the South China Sea. These are ongoing with China, Malaysia, the Philippines, Taiwan, and possibly Brunei. There are also unresolved maritime boundaries with Thailand and with China in the Gulf of Tonkin, disputed ownership of the Paracel

TERROR BRIEF 10-2

The Old Guard Prevails

He may have won the war, but General Giap seems to have lost the plot. Now in his late 80s, the Vietnamese military hero who vanquished first the French and then the Americans recently told an audience that "caring for the nation and fighting foreign invaders are the duties of every generation" of Vietnamese. Like many of Vietnam's older generation, he probably finds it difficult to adjust to change. And yet he was called as a keynote speaker at an academic conference on international co-operation. The event, held in Hanoi in mid-July 1998 with the help of a $200,000 grant from America's Ford Foundation, was the first of its kind to be organized inside Vietnam.

More than three hundred foreign scholars turned up. The foundation hopes it will open up debate in a communist country where Marxism-Leninism and "Ho Chi Minh thought" are still taught to schoolchildren. Yet General Giap's remarks were not the only sign of how far that debate still has to go. Apart from the standard summary of 4,000 years of Vietnamese history, the participants also heard from local professors about Ho Chi Minh's poetry and his "initial study on the way of writing foreign proper nouns." Foreign delegates, with their irritating tendency to come to conclusions at odds with the party line, were mostly ignored.

An American studying suburban development in Ho Chi Minh City was told that she could not hope to research the subject because she was not Vietnamese. Another American comparing rural resistance in China and Vietnam to economic reform was told there was no such thing in Vietnam-despite renewed unrest last year in the northern province of Thai Binh.

Foreigners felt that they had been invited merely to provide window dressing for a feast of cultural self-congratulation. The conference overlapped with a meeting of the Party's powerful Central Committee, which concentrated on a future national cultural policy. After ten days of discussions, it declared that the object of all cultural activities was "to preserve Vietnam's cultural identity . . . for the building and defending of the socialist homeland."

Despite Vietnam's attempts at economic integration with the region, it remains constrained socially and politically by the Communist Party. For example, Vietnam's universities have no political-science departments and no real experts on international relations. As a result, Vietnam is unable to take part in the academic forums on security that are increasingly a part of confidence building in East Asia. The hope is that, with growing opportunities for Vietnamese scholars to travel abroad, and with more foreign research under way in Vietnam, that will change. Indeed, even five years ago it would have been impossible to hold any sort of international academic conference in Vietnam.

Yet the risk is that such progress will be slowed by a faltering economy: Vietnam has cut its target for economic growth this year, from 9% to under 7% because of the Asian turmoil. The signs are that the party will now try to bolster support through even more introspection the contemplation of past glories, and with a call for a new campaign that would culminate in some sort of national conference in 2000. The subject will be national heroes, General Giap would be proud.

Source: Editors, "Uncle Ho's Legacy." *The Economist.* (Economist Newpapers, London. July 25, 1998) p. 39.

Islands in the South China Sea, which occupied by China but claimed by Vietnam and Taiwan. Offshore islands and sections of boundary with Cambodia are in dispute as well.

Key growing areas in Vietnam cultivated 3,150 hectares of poppy in 1996, producing twenty-five tons of opium, making it a major opium producer and an increasingly important transit point for Southeast Asian heroin destined for the United States and Europe. Vietnam has a growing opium addiction problem, plus possible small-scale heroin production in-country. While there is little known terrorism in Vietnam, a Vietnamese court sentenced two persons to death and three others to life in prison for carrying out a grenade attack on the waterfront in Ho Chi Minh City in 1994, in which twenty persons, including ten foreigners, were injured. The five were part of the Vietnam Front for Regime Restoration, an antigovernment exile group based in the United States.

SUMMARY

The terrorism and violence generated in the areas we have covered in this chapter span the whole menu of scenarios. These range from individual acts (assassination of two presidents named Gandhi), religious hatred (the Hindus and Muslims and Sikhs), political genocide (Khymer Rouge), state terrorism (Burma) and all the way up to conventional and nuclear war possibilities. This strange and mysterious region has huge potential but many problems. Thailand alone stands calm and stable in the midst of such violence and terror. The former Indochina has suffered from wars, terror and destruction for over four decades and are beginning to make some progress, but with fits and starts. The situation between India and Pakistan, the nuclear armed giants of this region seem to be the biggest problem to face. Time will tell if these great nations, facing a situation every bit a dangerous as any in the Middle East can eventually come to some accommodation. The incredibly long history of most of the nations in the region has created very long memories, great hatreds and grudges. In the next chapter the student will observe a lot of the same issues and problems, which have been exacerbated by a serious economic problem on the Pacific Rim.

TERMS TO REMEMBER

Afghanistan Mujahideen
Colombo World Trade Center
constructive engagement
HUA
Indian National Congress
ISI
Kashmir and Afghanistan
"Khalistan"
Khmer Rouge
KRAF
LTTE
Myanmar
Pol Pot
SGPC
SLORC
SPDC

REVIEW QUESTIONS

1. Describe the conditions in the past that created the hatred between India and Pakistan.

2. How does Afghanistan stand in the friction between Pakistan and India on the Kashmir issues?

3. What is the major religion in Sri Lanka and how does that relate to strife in the region?

4. Why do you think that Cambodia had to go through such a horrible time of "the killing fields" from the Khmer Rouge?

5. Discuss the situation in existence in Burma and elaborate on the United State's stance regarding that problem.

ENDNOTES

1. Much of the background data contained in this chapter. . . and woven into and throughout this book were extracted from web sites such as: The U.S. State Department of State. *1997 Patterns of Global Terrorism* Report; The U.S. Department of State *Country Reports on Human Rights Practices;* The U.S. Department of State *Background Notes: Geographic Entities and International Organizations;* The U.S. Central Intelligence Agency *World Factbook* and other government sources. We are, again, grateful for the presence of these sources and the information they have provided.

2. *Patterns of Global Terrorism, 1997.* United States Department of State, April 1998. http//www.state.gov.

3. The authors are grateful, again, to our friend and consultant, Jafar Siddiqui, who provides us with a different view of the region.

4. *Patterns of Global Terrorism, 1997.* United States Department of State, April 1998. http//www.state.gov.

5. Press Statement by James P. Rubin, Spokesman September 8, 1998 http//www.state.gov.

6. *Walden Bello,* 29 April 2002 http//www.state.gov.

7. Editors, *Intersec,* March 3, 2002, *Afghanistan's 2002 Opium Harvest,* 78–81.

8. Bishop Desmond Tutu, press statement on the subject of constructive engagement. http//www.state.gov.

9. The White House. Office of the Press Secretary October 27, 1998 http//www.state.gov.

10. The Secretary of State's Office's report to Congress. "Conditions in Burma and U.S. Policy Toward Burma for the Period March 28, 1997 to September 28, 1998. http//www.state.gov.

11. *Patterns of Global Terrorism, 1997.* United States Department of State, April 1998. http//www.state.gov.

11 The Pacific Rim

"Efforts to categorize terrorism as a class or form of political violence are complicated by the fact that violence occurs on different levels of political interaction."

Martha Crenshaw

OVERVIEW

The Pacific Rim contains those countries that sweep in a long arc from Australia to Japan, many of which have been suffering massive financial crises. As major trading partners to the United States and European Economic Community, many of these countries have brought the world turmoil. Most of these countries have been suffering from wars, insurgencies, corrupt governments and right and left wing terrorists for decades.

Mixed in with this problem is the impact on the major countries of this region and what financial and political chaos can do the make opportunities for terrorist groups to take advantage of such opportunities and turmoil to forward their own causes. This chapter will build on the previous analysis of Southern and Southeast Asia, and discuss individual countries are reacting in terms of their backgrounds and histories of terrorist actions. We start with the biggest country, in terms of population and production . . . China.

CHINA

Discussion of the Far East and the Pacific Rim cannot begin without first referring to the People's Republic of China (**PRC**). Following the fall of the Soviet Union, the PRC has become the world's #2 superpower. Bordered on the water by a coastline of over 10,000 miles that includes the East China Sea, Korea Bay, Yellow Sea, and South China Sea. China is only slightly smaller than the United States. It protects borders along over 14,700 miles that include the countries of Afghanistan, Bhutan, India, Kazakstan, North Korea, Kyrgyzstan, Laos, Macau, Mongolia, Nepal, Pakistan, Russia (northeast), Russia (northwest), Tajikistan, and Vietnam. China is the world's fourth-largest country (after Russia, Canada, and the United States), with a population of one and quarter billion. The ethnic makeup of this world giant is: Han Chinese 91.9%, Zhuang, Uygur, Hui, Yi, Tibetan, Miao, Manchu, Mongol, Buyi, Korean, and "other" make up the remainder.

While China is officially atheist, it is traditionally pragmatic and eclectic and Daoism (Taoism), Buddhism, Muslim religion is unofficially practiced by 2%–3% of the population, and Christians number about 1%.

China is an ancient and scattered society that was unified under the Qin or Ch'ing Dynasty 221 BC. The Ch'ing Dynasty, the last, was replaced by the Chinese Republic in 1912. The People's Republic of China was established in 1949. Beginning in late 1978, the Chinese leadership began trying to move the economy from a sluggish Soviet-style centrally planned economy to one that is more market-oriented but still within a rigid political framework of Communist Party control. To this end the authorities switched to a system of household responsibility in agriculture in place of the old collectivization, increased the authority of local officials and plant managers in industry, permitted a wide variety of small-scale enterprise in services and light manufacturing, and opened the economy to increased foreign trade and investment.

The result has been a quadrupling of China's GDP since 1978. Agricultural output doubled in the 1980s, and industry also posted major gains, especially in coastal areas near Hong Kong and opposite Taiwan, where foreign investment helped spur output of both domestic and export goods. On the darker side, the leadership has often experienced in its hybrid system the worst results of socialism (bureaucracy, lassitude, corruption) as well as of capitalism (windfall gains and stepped-up inflation). Beijing thus has periodically backtracked, re-tightening central controls at intervals. In 1992–96 annual growth of GDP accelerated, particularly in the coastal areas—averaging more than 10% annually, according to official figures.

In late 1993, China's leadership approved additional long-term reforms aimed at giving still more play to market-oriented institutions and at strengthening Beijing's control over the financial system. State-controlled enterprises would continue to dominate many key industries in what was now termed "a **socialist market economy**." In 1995–96 inflation dropped sharply, reflecting tighter monetary policies and stronger measures to control food prices. At the same time, the government struggled to:

- Collect revenues due from provinces, businesses, and individuals;
- Reduce corruption and other economic crimes;
- Keep afloat the large state-owned enterprises, most of which had not participated in the vigorous expansion of the economy and many of which have been losing the ability to pay full wages and pensions.

It is estimated that from 60 to 100 million surplus rural workers are adrift between the villages and the cities, many subsisting through part-time low-paying jobs. Another long-term threat to continued economic growth is the deterioration in the environment, notably air pollution, soil erosion, and the steady fall of the water table especially in the north. China continues to lose arable land because of erosion and economic development; furthermore, the regime gives insufficient priority to agricultural research. The next few years will witness increasing tensions between a highly centralized political system and an increasingly decentralized economic system.[1]

China is a major trans-shipment point for heroin produced in the Golden Triangle and is experiencing a growing domestic drug abuse problem. There were no reported incidents of international terrorism in China since 1997, but **Uygur separatists** continued a campaign of violence. The Uygurs are a Chinese Muslim ethnic minority group concentrated in the Xinjiang Autonomous Region in Far Western China. In February 1997, Uygur separatists conducted a series of bus bombings in Urumqi that killed nine persons and wounded seventy-four. Uygur rioting earlier in the month in the city of Yining caused as many as two hundred deaths. Uygur exiles in Turkey claimed responsibility for a small pipe bomb that exploded on a bus in Beijing in March, killing three persons and injuring eight. In August, Uygur separatists were blamed for killing five persons, including two policemen. The Chinese Government executed several individuals involved in both the rioting and bombings. Beijing claims that support for the Uygurs is coming from neighboring countries, an accusation these countries deny.

In the calm since 1991, China seems to be pretty much free from terrorist acts today, mainly because the society is so tightly controlled. As the mighty country becomes less and less tightly controlled, and if the Asian economies are slow in recovering, the dissidents now in hiding may be the seeds from which future discord or insurgent acts will bloom. With 60–100 million people wandering without work, that potential is great. This huge, ancient country bears careful tracking in the near future.

Falun Gong

While, as noted above, there is little reported terrorism in China, members of the *Falun Gong* spiritual group have created waves in the tight control in Mainland China's aging leadership. The government's anti-Falun Gong propaganda, a new phase in the battle between the group and the government could pose a bigger threat to the Communist Party if the country's urban unemployed rise up in support of the group. They hacked into Chinese government television broadcasts in Yantai, Shandong province, and briefly aired a message saying, "Falun Gong is good." The incident was the latest in a string of broadcast hijackings that have hit six cities in six months, primarily in the country's northeastern "rust belt," where unemployment and labor unrest are growing. The effort is trying to counter the government's massive anti-Falun Gong propaganda campaign, which centers on the January 2001 self-immolation attempt by a group of followers in which two died. The new tactic reveals the group's technological savvy and may point to a shift in focus. Since most of the Falun Gong broadcasts focused on China's northeast, the government fears groundwork for a new showdown with them, one that could draw on urban unemployed. By hacking into state television to take its case directly to the people, the Falun Gong is confronting China's central leadership—a new strategy that has thus far used peaceful demonstrations, appeals for dialogue and attention from foreign media to try to convince Beijing to lift its ban. The government's inability to crush the group has only reinforced Beijing's perception that the Falun Gong is a threat to its authority. Although the group simply could have moved underground after the government outlawed it in 1999, it chose to fight for its rights—which has led it down the current path toward confrontation.

The Falun Gong first emerged as a semi-religious exercise group in the early 1990s, growing rapidly and across socio-economic classes, filling a spiritual void in China in a time of rapid change. In April 1999, after a run-in with a local government, the Falun Gong confronted Beijing directly in one of the most impressive displays of civil action in China since the 1989 Tiananmen

Square incident. More than 10,000 followers converged along the street outside the government compound in Beijing in a daylong silent vigil. This Gandhi-inspired peaceful demonstration, which faded quietly into the night, had precisely the opposite effect on the Chinese government. Rather than persuade China's leaders to legitimize the group, it sparked confusion among the country's elite. The protest showed the Falun Gong's very well-developed command and communications structure as massive and pervasive across Chinese society. After a brief respite, Beijing banned the group and began a massive crackdown, rounding up and detaining thousands of Falun Gong'sThe Falun Gong quickly began to appeal for international help. It turned to foreign supporters and drew international media attention at a time when China was petitioning for entry into the WTO and bidding to host the 2008 Summer Olympics. Falun Gong began appearing in Tiananmen Square, in peaceful protest. The cruel crackdown by Chinese security forces that followed was captured on foreign media and broadcast worldwide.

In January 2001, the group's strategy fell apart after a group of alleged Falun Gong practitioners arrived in Tiananmen Square and lit themselves on fire. Whether these were overzealous members of the Falun Gong or a group of people misled by government infiltrators to take extreme measures, the self-immolation proved a propaganda coup for the Chinese government.

Whereas previous government claims that the Falun Gong was evil and dangerous were brushed aside by many Chinese who felt Beijing was overreacting, the pictures of half-burnt young girls on national television leant credence to the government's argument. Once again the Falun Gong altered its strategy. Foreigners, rather than Chinese followers, in Tiananmen Square, increasingly carried out protests. Also, wherever the Chinese leaders traveled in Europe or Asia, supporters of the Falun Gong were there. In January 2002, the Falun Gong began its new tactic of pirate attacks on government television. The first incident took place on January 1 in Chongqing, Sichuan province, and was followed a month later on February 16 in Anshan, Liaoning. In Anshan, three Falun Gong activists tapped into the local cable line but were caught in the process, and security forces shot at least one.

On March 5, Falun Gong activists managed to hack into eight channels in Changchun, Jilin province, the hometown of Falun Gong founder Li Hongxi. They broadcast two 20-minute films contradicting the self-immolation story and extolling the virtues of the Falun Gong. On April 21, they struck in Harbin, Heilongjiang province, reportedly airing pro-Falun Gong material for more than an hour.

The two most recent cases, on June 21 in Laiyang and on June 25 in Yantai, both in Shandong province, were shorter broadcasts, simply relaying the message that "Falun Gong is good." But in these cases, rather than hacking into cable lines, the Falun Gong managed to hijack the government satellite broadcasts—according to Chinese security officials cited by the *South China Morning Post*—something quite a bit more sophisticated than splicing a VCR into cable lines.

There are three key characteristics of these most recent Falun Gong actions. First, they all suggest that what appeared to be a headless organism has a centralized planning and organization structure. Second, the attacks indicate a technological savvy, particularly if the group managed to pirate the satellite system. The similarity of the attacks and their dispersal also suggest there is an active training network inside the Falun Gong. Finally, the TV hijackings primarily took place in China's northeast rust belt. Heilongjiang, Jilin and Liaoning provinces have been the sites of active labor protests for months, and large-scale demonstrations have rocked Daqing and Liaoyang and broken out in Fushun and Anshan. Although this could be a coincidence—the area is the traditional support base of the Falun Gong—it also could be an attempt to bridge a gap between the group and the large pool of unemployed former state workers there.

There appears to be a realization among the Falun Gong leadership that the Chinese government will not, and perhaps cannot, change its position on the group now, particularly after a three-year nationwide campaign denouncing it as an evil cult and a socially destabilizing element. There is no way to regain the rights to practice Falun Gong through persuasion or dialogue with the current regime. The only way to re-legitimize the Falun Gong, then, is through a regime change in China—and tapping into the disgruntled masses of unemployed former state workers may be the first step.

This presents a very troubling picture for China's leadership, particularly as the government prepares for a change in leadership at the end 2002. China's economic travails as it transitions from a centrally planned economy into one more acceptable to its fellow WTO members have triggered massive unemployment and ripped the longstanding social contract between the country's workers and the Communist Party-led government.

Since the leadership compound was surrounded in 1999, China's leadership has been frightened of the Falun Gong—and not without good cause. China has faced threats from similar quasi-religious organizations in its past—particularly in times of economic stress, weak central government and increasing foreign pressures.

In 1774, martial arts expert and herbalist Wang Lun, who drew on Buddhist folklore, led the White Lotus Rebellion. Its support came from restless barge-pullers and coolies on the Grand Canal in Shandong province, and it was triggered not so much by specific political or social repression but more by general dissatisfaction with the dominant forces in the kingdom and by a desire to perpetuate a spiritual cause.

In the 1840s, another semi-religious sect led what became the 1853–1864 Taiping Rebellion, the longest and deadliest rebellion in Chinese history. This group was led by Hong Xiuquan, a failed Confucian scholar who, after coming into contact with Western Christian missionaries, dreamt that God and Jesus instructed him to slay demons, in this case the ruling Manchus. Hong attracted the marginalized and disenfranchised, such as poor peasants and laborers, ethnic minorities, criminal gangs and ex-soldiers, as well as artisans and professionals.

In 1900, China faced another group of semi-religious martial arts practitioners, the Boxers. They first appeared in Shandong province, attracting peasants and workers hurt by the poor economic conditions created by drought and then floods. Partly out of fear, Beijing sided with the Boxers, who rebelled by attacking primarily foreigners and Chinese converts to Christianity. The outcome was disastrous for the Chinese leaders, as a combined foreign army entered Beijing, destroyed the Boxers and sent the ruling elite on a flight to central China.

While none of these precisely match the current situation, the volatile mix of zealous Falun Gong believers and hundreds of thousands of disgruntled unemployed is something the government can't ignore. If the organizational structure of the Falun Gong can harness the manpower of the unemployed, China could be in for another rebellion, one that could hasten the end of Communist Party rule if it goes unchecked.

Hong Kong

Hong Kong returned to its former status as a province of China on July 1, 1997. High-flying Hong Kong businesspeople and others had fled in droves from the island when this move was first announced several years ago, but many are returning to be where "the action is" in Asia. In a joint declaration, China promised to respect Hong Kong's existing social and economic systems and lifestyle. Hong Kong borders the South China Sea and Mainland China and is about six times the size of Washington, DC, scattered over more than two hundred islands. The six and a half million people are an unbalanced ethnic mix of Chinese 95%, other 5%. They practice religion in an eclectic mix of local religions 90%, Christian 10%.

Hong Kong has long been the a major and dynamic business and financial center of mainland Asia and a bustling free market with few tariffs or nontariff barriers. Natural resources are limited, and food and raw materials must be imported. Manufacturing and construction account for about 18% of GDP. Goods and services exports account for about 50% of GDP. Real GDP growth averaged a remarkable 8%. A shortage of labor continues to put upward pressure on prices and the cost of living. Prospects remain bright so long as major trading partners continue to be reasonably prosperous and so long as investors feel China will continue to support free market practices after the takeover. While terrorism has been virtually nonexistent, Hong Kong is a hub for Southeast Asian heroin trade, involved with trans-shipment and money laundering. There is also an increasing problem with indigenous amphetamine abuse.

TAIWAN (REPUBLIC OF CHINA)

The Republic of China (usually called Taiwan) borders the East China Sea, Philippine Sea, South China Sea and Taiwan Strait. It is north of the Philippines. It is a large island off the southeastern coast of China, slightly smaller than Maryland and Delaware combined. The population of 21,699,776 is composed of Taiwanese 84%, Mainland Chinese 14% and aborigine 2%. Religion is based on a mixture of Buddhist, Confucian, and Taoist 93%, Christian 4.5% and other 2.5%. Political pressure groups include Taiwan independence movement, various environmental groups. Debate on Taiwan independence has now become acceptable within the mainstream of domestic politics on Taiwan. Political liberalization and the increased representation of the opposition Democratic Progressive Party (**DPP**) in Taiwan's legislature have opened public debate on the island's national identity. Advocates of Taiwan independence, including within the DPP, oppose the ruling party's traditional stand that the island will eventually reunify with mainland China. Goals of the Taiwan independence movement include establishing a sovereign nation on Taiwan and entering the U.N. Other organizations supporting Taiwan independence include the World United Formosans for Independence and the Organization for Taiwan Nation.

Taiwan has a dynamic capitalist economy with considerable guidance of investment and foreign trade by government officials and partial government ownership of some large banks and industrial firms. Real growth in GDP has averaged about 9% a year during the past three decades. Export growth has been even faster and has provided the impetus for industrialization. Inflation and unemployment are low. Agriculture contributes less than 4% to GDP, down from 35% in 1952. Traditional labor-intensive industries are steadily being moved off-shore and replaced with more capital and technology-intensive industries. Taiwan has become a major investor in China, Thailand, Indonesia, the Philippines, Malaysia, and Vietnam. The tightening of labor markets has led to an influx of foreign workers, both legal and illegal.

Taiwan is involved in a complex dispute over the Spratly Islands with China, Malaysia, Philippines, Vietnam, and possibly Brunei; Paracel Islands occupied by China, but claimed by Vietnam and Taiwan. The Japanese-administered Senkaku-shoto (Senkaku Islands/ Diaoyu Tai) are also in disputed claims from China and Taiwan. The island nation is tightly controlled and there is very little terrorism of any scope. Taiwan is considered an important heroin transit point and there seems to be a major growing problem with domestic consumption of methamphetamine and heroin.

JAPAN

The ancient kingdom of Japan is a constitutional monarchy that became an independent state in 660 BC through the efforts of Emperor Jimmu. It is located in Eastern Asia, an island chain between the North Pacific Ocean and the Sea of Japan, east of the Korean Peninsula and is slightly smaller than California. Japan's appetite for fish, with a population of over one and a quarter million, is contributing to the depletion of these resources in Asia and elsewhere. Ethnic diversity is literally unknown in Japan, with; Japanese 99.4%, other 0.6% (mostly Korean). Religions are similarly broken out with those who observe both Shinto and Buddhist 84%, other 16%.

Japan Government-industry cooperation, a strong work ethic, mastery of high technology, and a comparatively small defense allocation (roughly 1% of GDP) have helped Japan advance with extraordinary rapidity to one of the most powerful economies in the world. One notable characteristic of the economy is the working together of manufacturers, suppliers, and distributors in closely-knit groups called **keiretsu**. A second basic feature has been the guarantee of lifetime employment for a substantial portion of the urban labor force, but this guarantee has been slowly eroding. Industry, the most important sector of the economy, is heavily dependent on imported raw materials and fuels. The much smaller agricultural sector is highly subsidized and protected, with crop yields among the highest in the world. Usually self-sufficient in rice,

Japan must import about 50% of its requirements of other grain and fodder crops. Japan maintains one of the world's largest fishing fleets and accounts for nearly 15% of the global catch.

For three decades overall real economic growth had been spectacular: a 10% average in the 1960s, a 5% average in the 1970s, and a 4% average in the 1980s. Growth slowed considerably in 1992–95 largely because of the after effects of over investment during the late 1980s and contradictory domestic policies intended to wring speculative excesses from the stock and real estate markets. Growth picked up in 1996, largely a reflection of simulative fiscal and monetary policies as well as low rates of inflation and social disorder. As a result of the expansionary fiscal policies and declining tax revenues due to the recession, Japan currently has one of the largest budget deficits as a percent of GDP among the industrialized countries. The crowding of habitable land area and the aging of the population are two other major longterm problems.

The trial and after-effects of the leader of Aum Shinrikyo, the group responsible for sarin gas attacks on the Tokyo subway system in 1995, has created an ongoing discussion as just how to define terrorism in Japan. A government panel decided not to invoke the Anti-Subversive Law to ban **Aum Shinrikyo**, concluding that the group poses no future threat, although the group continued to operate and to recruit new members. The U.S. Secretary of State designated Aum Shinrikyo as a foreign terrorist organization pursuant to the Antiterrorism and Effective Death Penalty Act of 1996. In addition to the murder charges stemming from the March 1995 sarin nerve gas attack on the Tokyo subway system, Asahara faced 16 other charges, ranging from kidnapping and murder to illegal production of drugs and weapons. Nine former Aum members pleaded guilty or received sentences from twenty-two months to seventeen years for crimes they committed on behalf of Asahara, one Aum member was acquitted of forcibly confining other cult members.

Despite the legal proceedings against Asahara and other members, what remained of Aum following the arrests of 1996 continued to exist, operate, and even recruit new members in Japan. A government panel decided not to invoke the Anti-Subversive Law against Aum Shinrikyo, which would have outlawed the sect. The panel ruled that Aum posed no future threat to Japanese society because it was financially bankrupt and most of its followers wanted by the police had been arrested.

Several members of the Japanese Red Army **(JRA)** terrorist organization were arrested in 1997. Five members were convicted in Lebanon on various charges related to forgery and illegal residency and sentenced to three years in prison. Another member, Jun Nishikawa, was captured in Bolivia and deported to Japan where he was indicted for his role in the 1977 hijacking of a Japanese Airlines flight. Four of the five JRA members arrested in remain in custody in Lebanon. The Japanese Government is seeking extradition of the five to Tokyo to face terrorism and other charges upon their release.

Tsutomu Shirosaki was captured in 1996 and brought to the United States to stand trial for offenses arising from a rocket attack against the U.S. Embassy in Jakarta, Indonesia, in 1986. He was convicted in Washington, DC, of assault with the intent to kill, attempted first degree murder of internationally protected persons, and attempted destruction of buildings and property in the special maritime and territorial jurisdiction of the United States. He was also convicted of committing a violent attack on the official premises of internationally protected persons. (In February 1998 he was sentenced to 30 years in prison.) Seven hardcore JRA members remain at large.

The battle against Aum Shinrikyo is an uphill one. Thousands of young Japanese have attended Aum Shinrikyo meetings; some have paid up to thousands of yen in joining fees. The cult may also be active in Russia, where it is banned. It is possible that young people are still joining Aum because all the factors that created Aum's membership in the first place still exist. Japan is still a rigid society that stifles individualism and Aum exploits this, as it does the general sense of unease generated by Japan's stagnant economy. It seems remarkable that Aum Shinrikyo's revival is based on selling exactly the same product as before. Armageddon remains the cult's pivotal concept. We are now living in an age when "evil of all kinds thrives," Araki explains. "This evil will be shed in a "catastrophic discharge" made manifest in wars and natural disasters, such as the Kosovo conflict or a storm in Sydney in 1999 with hailstones the size of golf balls."

Could Aum Shinrikyo again develop the potential to give this catastrophe a nudge? In 1999 Japanese police unearthed Sarin precursor chemicals hidden by Aum in mountains north of Tokyo, raising the question of what else the cult was hiding. A few months before that a self-declared Aum member threatened to release gas at eleven Moscow subway stations.

In its continuing crackdown, police have confiscated more than half a million leaflets. Not surprisingly, Aum Shinrikyo has never apologized or expressed remorse for its past actions. An apology is vital if the cult expects any chance of a normal relationship with Japanese society, but the cult's six leaders have not come to the same conclusion. The Japanese authorities could have outlawed Aum Shinrikyo using a draconian 1952 law against subversive activities, but decided the sect did not pose an "immediate and obvious threat" to public safety. Meanwhile clumsy policing and political paralysis may continue to provide the conditions for Aum Shinrikyo to thrive.

Taro Takimoto is one person dedicated to putting the brakes on Aum Shinrikyo's current resurgent growth. He runs a support network for more than a hundred ex-Aum Shinrikyo cultists called the Canary Group. It is named after the canaries used by police as sarin-detectors during raids on the cult's compounds in 1995. Fifty of the group's members have now got jobs or college places, says Takimoto, while the rest are still recovering from years of physical and mental abuse. "Only a handful have really got over it," he says. Takimoto himself narrowly escaped assassination in 1994 when a teenage Aum member injected sarin into his car.[2]

The Japanese economy is still shaky at this writing and the financial and political situation, while somewhat calmed, is ripe for more anti-government and dissatisfaction with high potential for sophisticated attacks on travelers and leaders. On a more frightening level, Liberal Party President Ichiro Ozawa's recently made statements that Japan could easily build a nuclear arsenal and outgun China, which elicited little debate inside Japan. The question of a nuclear Japan is not one of technology but of political will, and the muted reaction of the country's politicians and public points to the rapid shift in Japanese thinking on issues of defense over the past few years.

Recent statements by the president of Japan's opposition Liberal Party about the country's nuclear arsenal were less significant in what was said than in how the country responded. Ichiro Ozawa said, on April 6, 2002, that Japan could easily produce several thousand nuclear weapons, and gain the upper hand on China, if it was challenged by Beijing.

The comments by Ozawa, known for his strong views on Japan's national security, were not particularly astonishing. Neither, quite frankly, is the idea that Japan is technically capable of producing nuclear weapons. What is interesting is the mild reaction to his remarks inside Japan. There seems to be a steady political evolution taking place in Japan, and since overcoming the once taboo issues of military deployments, constitutional changes and nuclear weapons no longer elicit a massive uproar from the politicians or the public.

Ozawa was not exaggerating when he said Japan was capable of producing several thousand nuclear devices. The country by some estimates has enough weapons-grade plutonium from its fast-breeder reactors to build as many as 6,000 weapons, and there is little doubt about Japan's technical ability to build such weapons. A nuclear program in Japan then is not limited by technology, as it may be in countries like Pakistan and North Korea, but by political will. And resistance to changes in Japan's defensive posture is fading.

The non-reaction to Ozawa's comments contrast sharply with the domestic and international outcry that followed comments by former Vice Minister of Defense Shingo Nishimura in a 1999 interview, in which he said "if Japan armed itself with nuclear weapons it may be better off." The minister was forced to resign, and the public outcry nearly broke apart the fledgling coalition between the ruling Liberal Democratic Party and Nishimura's Liberal Party. Other "provocative" statements by Japanese politicians have been similarly received. Japanese Defense Agency Chief Fukushiro Nukaga resigned in 1998, ostensibly over an agency procurement scandal, though his statement that a pre-emptive strike on North Korean missile sites could be considered "defense" under Japan's constitution did little for his political longevity. Other politicians in Japan sometimes suggest that Japan's constitution was U.S.-imposed pacifism and forced Japan to remain defenseless.

With the 1998 North Korean missile launch over Japan, and East Timor's referendum for independence from Indonesia a year later, Japan's military policy slowly began to evolve. The 9–11 attacks, and The United State's global anti-terrorism campaign have accelerated this evolutionary change.

On June 17, 2002, Japanese naval ships were dispatched to the Indian Ocean. In November they were placed under U.S. command and control, according to an article in the Asahi Shimbun daily. The paper cited Japanese government sources, who said officers of the Maritime Staff Headquarters accepted U.S. control over the ships during a meeting at the U.S. Central Command fleet headquarters in Bahrain. The move violated the government's interpretation of Japan's Constitution, which prohibits the right of collective self-defense, using Japan's military to protect another country or its interests. Over 60,000 people gathered in Yoyogi Park in Tokyo to protest the defense measures.

This changing shape of Japan's military role in the twenty-first century world bear watching carefully. But, even more frightening, is the thought that fanatical groups like the Japanese Red Army, or the Aum Shinrikyo, or terrorists from outside rogue states may find ways to up the ante on their terrorism and get at the stockpiles of enriched plutonium to build a dirty bomb. The world continues to change, in the wake of 9–11.

PHILIPPINES

The Republic of the Philippines is situated in Southeastern Asia, on a long archipelago between the Philippine Sea and the South China Sea. It is east of Vietnam and is slightly larger than Arizona. The scattered population of more than seventy-six million has an ethnic mix of Christian Malay 91.5%, Muslim Malay 4% Chinese 1.5%, and other 3%. The major religions are: Roman Catholic 83%, Protestant 9%, Muslim 5%, Buddhist and other 3%

The Philippine economy, primarily a mixture of agriculture and light industry, continued its fourth year of recovery in 1996, led by growth in exports and investments. Officials targeted 7.1%–7.8% growth for 1997 after achieving an estimated 5.5% growth in 1996. The government is continuing its economic reforms to enable the Philippines to move closer to the development of the newly industrialized countries of East Asia. The strategy includes improving infrastructure, overhauling the tax system to bolster government revenues, and moving toward further deregulation and privatization of the economy.

In the Philippines, implementation of a peace agreement with insurgent groups has reduced fighting with government forces, but former members of these insurgent groups and members of Philippine terrorist organizations continued attacks. Foreigners number among their victims. In 1998, the United States Secretary of State designated one of these terrorist organizations, the **Abu Sayyaf Group**, as a foreign terrorist organization pursuant to the Antiter-

Heavily armed members of Abu Sayyaf terrorist group. (AP Photo/STR, File)

rorism and Effective Death Penalty Act of 1996. In China and Indonesia, separatist violence not targeted against foreigners but having the potential to claim foreigners as collateral victims continued.

The Philippine Government began implementing terms of a peace agreement signed with the Moro National Liberation Front (**MNLF**) in 1996 and continued efforts to negotiate a peace agreement with the Moro Islamic Liberation Front (**MILF**). The government began the process of integrating former MNLF rebels into the Philippine military. A cease-fire with the MILF reduced the fighting that peaked in the first half of 1997, but the two sides failed to agree on a more comprehensive arrangement. The MILF and the smaller Abu Sayyaf Group continue to fight for a separate Islamic state in the southern Philippines.

Muslim rebels in the southern Philippines conducted several attacks against foreigners in 1997. A Japanese businessman and three Filipino boys were kidnapped in June by members of the Abu Sayyaf Group. A rescue operation by the Philippine military freed the Japanese hostage. A German businessman was abducted in September by former members of the MNLF and was released in December only after his family agreed to pay the kidnappers some $100,000 in ransom. In separate incidents in October and November, former MNLF members abducted priests—one Irish and one Belgian—and demanded payment of funds owed them under a government rehabilitation program. The captives were released after the government agreed to expedite disbursal of the funds.

The government had mixed results in its efforts against communist rebels in 1997. Philippine police captured some key communist personnel. The government again suspended negotiations with the political arm of the communist New People's Army (**NPA**) in late 1997 following an upsurge in small-scale attacks by the NPA on police and government units. In May, communist guerrillas ambushed a vehicle owned by a subcontractor of a major U.S. firm, killing two Filipino employees. In December, New People's Army rebels ambushed two army detachments and abducted twenty-one paramilitary troops in Davao City in Mindanao. The government pledged to revisit the issue of a dialogue with the communists if acceptable circumstances could be met. Another communist rebel group, the Alex Boncayao Brigade, is not participating in peace talks with the government.

In September a previously unknown group calling itself the Filipino Soldiers for the Nation claimed responsibility for grenade attacks at bus terminals in Manila and Bulcalan City that killed six persons and wounded sixty-five. Press reports indicated the group claimed to favor a constitutionally prohibited second term for President Ramos. The Ramos government strongly condemned the attacks and blamed them on unknown provocateurs.

The Philippine Government continued its strong support for international cooperation against terrorism and actively sought to build a multilateral approach to counterterrorism in regional and other forums. The government cooperated in providing additional personnel to protect likely targets and to identify, investigate, and act against likely terrorists. The government quickly responded when a U.S. company experienced what appeared to be an NPA attack on one of its subcontractors in Quezon, and officials at the cabinet level met with company executives to discuss what could be done to improve security.

TERROR BRIEF 11–1

Philippine Cronyism Is Back

Much of East Asia is trying to rid itself of signs of "crony capitalism," the Philippines, which has long delighted in being different, is engulfed in a storm over the resurgence of some old cronies under its new president, Joseph Estrada. Many Filipinos are still haunted by the corruption and brutality of Ferdinand Marcos, the dictator toppled by a "people power" revolution in 1986. Hence concern rose at the sight in 1999 of Eduardo Cojuangco sweeping up to the head office of the country's brewing and food giant, San Miguel, in a Mercedes to reclaim his post as chairman after a boardroom coup. Cojuangco was Marcos's main chum and during his rule assembled a vast business empire. The two were so close that when Marcos fled Manila, Cojuangco left in the helicopter with him. Though exiled to the political wilderness by two subsequent presidents, Corazon Aquino and Fidel Ramos, Cojuangco has not only moved back into the boardroom of San Miguel but is also fighting for control of a large block of shares in the company. These were seized from him in 1986 by Aquino's administration after allegations that they had been acquired illegally through his links with Marcos. Many believe the tycoon will soon have his shares back.

Although Estrada says the affairs of San Miguel have nothing to do with him, it is hard for him to avoid the controversy. Cojuangco was the chief financier behind Estrada's expensive election campaign and is now head of the president's political party. The two are so close that many wonder who is calling the shots. Estrada has also been criticized for his efforts (so far unsuccessful) to have Marcos's body moved from cold storage in the dictator's home town of Batac, in the northern Philippines, and buried in Heroes' Cemetery in Manila. The president has also said he would try to seek a settlement with the Marcos family—led by his redoubtable widow, Imelda—to recover money plundered from government coffers. This creeping rehabilitation of the Marcos family worries many Filipinos. Imelda's daughter Imee now serves as a congresswoman, and her son Ferdinand, who is usually known as "Bong Bong," is a newly elected provincial governor.

Estrada's officials have added to the controversy by saying they want to reach a settlement over a 25.6 billion pesos ($611 million) tax-evasion case against Lucio Tan, a Chinese-Filipino tycoon also once linked to Marcos. The secretive Tan is widely reckoned to be the country's richest man. He owns Philippine Airlines, Asia Brewery, Fortune Tobacco and Allied Bank. Tan was also a financial backer of Estrada's presidential campaign. But, as Edgardo Esdpiritu, the finance minister, admits, the pressure on the government to reach agreement with Tan is clear: it faces a budget deficit of 70 billion pesos and Tan's contributions would come in useful.

The problem of how to deal with the Marcoses and their cronies is turning into a far more awkward issue than many expected. One of the reasons given by Estrada for abolishing the Presidential Commission on Good Government, a body established by Aquino to reclaim assets believed to have been acquired illegally during the Marcos years, is compelling—it has not worked. Even the influential Roman Catholic Church believes it is best to draw a line under the Marcos years and move on. But having the old dictator's family and their cronies restored to positions of power and influence may prove too much even for forgiving Filipinos.

Source: "The Marcos Mob is Back." *The Economist.* (Economist Newpapers, London. July 25, 1998) pp. 38–39.

The Moro Islamic Liberation Front rebels handed over Italian priest Luciano Benedetti to Philippine government officials in Maguindanao, Mindanao, several hours after he was released by his captors to MILF forces.

The guerrilla arm of the Communist Party of the Philippines (CPP), an avowedly Maoist group formed in December 1969 with the aim of overthrowing the government through protracted guerrilla warfare. Although primarily a rural group, the NPA has an active urban infrastructure to carry out terrorism, and uses city-based assassination squads called sparrow units. It derives most of its funding from contributions of supporters and so-called revolutionary taxes extorted from local businesses. NPA is in disarray because of a split in the CPP, a lack of money, and successful government operations. With the U.S. military gone from the country, NPA has engaged in urban terrorism against the police, corrupt politicians, and drug traffickers. The NPA has an estimated strength of several thousand members operating throughout the Philippines. It is unknown whether it receives any external aid.

The Philippines has had a long and complex dispute over the Spratly Islands with China, Malaysia, Taiwan, Vietnam, and possibly Brunei. It has also laid claim to the Malaysian State of Sabah. The Philippine growers export locally produced marijuana and hashish to East Asia, the U.S., and other Western markets and serves as a transit point for heroin and crystal methamphetamine to Western countries.

INDONESIA

Indonesia, the former Dutch East Indies is situated in Southeastern Asia, on an archipelago between the Indian Ocean and the Pacific Ocean. It has a varied population of almost two hundred and ten million in land area of slightly less than three times the size of Texas. Independence from the Netherlands came in 1949, when Indonesia became legally independent from the Netherlands. The combined islands of Indonesia have the largest Muslim population in the world.

Indonesia enjoyed a decade and a half of peace in the 1950–1960 timeframe, but it's political fortunes shifted significantly in 1965, following a leftist coup attempt against President Sukarno, the republic's first leader. Within days, the army executed the leaders of the coup, but its aftermath brought a wave of violence. Rightist gangs, encouraged by military commanders, killed tens of thousands of alleged communists. By 1966, an estimated 500,000 people had been killed in the unrest. The events of 1965 and 1966 left President Sukarno severely weakened. In 1966, he was forced to transfer key political and military powers to then General Suharto, who had led the military defeat of the coup. In 1967, the legislative assembly named Suharto acting president, removing Sukarno from power.

With the backing of the military, Suharto quickly proclaimed a "New Order" in Indonesian politics, concentrating on policies of economic rehabilitation and development. Using advice from Western-educated economists, Indonesia grew steadily, transforming itself from an agricultural backwater to a highly diversified manufacturing and export-driven state. Per-capita income levels rose from $70 in 1966 to $900 in 1996, while the proportion of the population living below the poverty line declined from 60% to an estimated 11% over roughly the same period. The government instituted further economic reforms in the early 1980s, liberalizing trade and finance and expanding foreign investment and deregulation. Trade and investment boomed as a result; Indonesia's economy grew more than 7% annually from 1985 to 1996.

Suharto, his family, and his friends benefited greatly from the economic expansion. Critics claim the president regularly used his position to provide subsidies and regulatory relief for the companies of his children and friends. Suharto's family controls an empire valued anywhere from $16 billion to $35 billion in industries ranging from hotels and transportation, to banks and automobiles.

The country's economic prosperity, however, did little to affect the political freedom of the average Indonesian. Beginning with the 1965 coup, Suharto's security forces jailed hundreds of activists for speaking out against the government; many were eventually tortured and killed in prison.

In the mid-1970s, Suharto moved quickly to stop what he saw as a leftist move to make the colony of East Timor independent after Portugal abandoned the territory. Fearing creation of a state that could destabilize surrounding provinces, Suharto sent in troops to crush the movement and annexed East Timor. Thousands of people died during the fighting or later starved to death.

The United States cut off some military assistance to Indonesia in response to a November 1991 shooting incident in East Timor, involving security forces and peaceful demonstrators. In 1996, government forces swept through East Timor again, this time after a series of guerrilla attacks on security personnel. The government takeover of Indonesian Democratic Party's East Timor headquarters in July of that year triggered serious rioting in Jakarta. Human rights officials say that five died and 149 were injured in the attack. Twenty-three people were reported missing.

Despite the corruption and human rights abuses, Suharto continued to stay in power into 1998. His grip on power started deteriorating the year before, when Thailand announced the devaluation of the baht in July 1997, a move that caused the value of Indonesia's currency–the rupiah–to drop as much as 80% at one point. Foreign investors fled and many companies, adversely affected by the currency devaluation, went bankrupt. Like other Asian countries, Indonesia's banks were hit especially hard; by January 1998, sixteen banks had their operations suspended. As the country negotiated with the International Monetary Fund over the terms of its $43 billion bailout package in early 1998, riots began to erupt over rising food prices, gradually intensifying despite violent police efforts to put them down.

The **People's Consultative Assembly**, a legislative body largely appointed by the president himself, reelected Suharto to a seventh term. Student protests broke out, and calls mounted for him to step down. In May, riots and looting turned violent as tens of thousands of students demonstrated in Jakarta and other parts of the country. Hundreds perished in clashes with security forces in Jakarta. In a show of resistance, students occupied the country's parliament grounds, demanding the president's resignation. On May 21, Suharto bowed to the pressure and resigned, naming Vice President B.J. Habibie as his successor.

Within days, Habibie pledged to lift restrictions on political parties and hold open elections as part of a package of reform measures intended to liberalize life in Indonesia and revive political activity that had been stifled for more than four decades.

The moves, however, did little to quell the unrest. Throughout the summer of 1998, student demonstrators continued to demand the resignation of President Habibie, claiming that the government had done little to stem the country's economic crisis or spiraling high prices.

In November 1998, massive student-led protests for greater democracy in Jakarta turned violent after a harsh crackdown on demonstrators killed at least five students and two others. Rioting ensued as demonstrators burned shops across the city and set cars ablaze. At least sixteen killed were killed over a period of several days.[3]

To add to the mounting problems in this troubled country, a thousand fires were burning at the end of February 1998 in the rainforests of East Kalimantan, the Indonesian part of the island of Borneo. It was only three months since monsoon rains finally put out the last set of devastating fires on the island. Those fires burned from July to November 1997, destroyed 15,000 square kilometers of forest and covered a huge area of Indonesia, Malaysia, Singapore and Brunei with choking smog. The pollution forced schools and airports to close and made thousands of people ill with breathing problems. Every one of these fires has been started deliberately. It was a man-made disaster, but by whom, and why?

In another major problem, the United States welcomed the Indonesian Government's establishment of a broad-based fact-finding team in 1999 to investigate the causes of the may riots and the rapes of ethnic Chinese women. In November the team, which included representatives from the government, the Indonesian military (**ABRI**), the police, and non-government organiza-

A massive car bomb destroys a night club in Bali, killing 200 mainly foreign tourists and injuring 300, October 13, 2002. (AP Photo/Jack Hamilton)

tions, released their report. Despite "reservations" registered by some members, and the fact that investigators, victims, witnesses, and family members face anonymous death threats and other forms of intimidation, the fact-finding team issued a credible, balanced report under difficult circumstances.

The report found three patterns to the riots, ranging from local and spontaneous, to riots aggravated by provocateurs and other more obviously deliberately stimulated. This included involvement by elements of the military. The report called for further investigations and recommended that Lt. Gen. Prabowo and all others involved in cases of kidnappings of political activists be brought before a military court. The report also verified that eighty-five acts of violence targeted against women occurred, including rapes, torture, sexual assaults, and sexual harassment during the riots, most against ethnic Chinese.

It was declared crucial, in order to restore credibility and confidence, that the Indonesian Government implement the team's recommendations, including further investigation of military leaders and others alleged to be involved in fomented or participating in the violence. It was further strongly urged that the Indonesian Government take steps to prevent intimidation and threats of violence against investigators, witnesses, and their families and that those responsible for all these acts should be held accountable.[4]

Sovereignty over Timor Timur (East Timor Province) is disputed by Portugal and not recognized by the United Nations and two islands are in ownership dispute with Malaysia. Indonesia is an illicit producer of cannabis largely for domestic use, with a possible growing role as trans-shipment point for Golden Triangle heroin. Separatist groups in East Timor apparently continued to target non-combatants and were involved in several bomb-making activities in 1997. In Irian Jaya, an attack allegedly by the separatist **Free Papua Organization** against a road surveying crew, in April 1997, left two civilians dead. Indonesia, if it can't get its economic situation straightened out, is a powder keg and may have serious state and opposing groups committing escalated violence and terrorism.

AUSTRALIA

Located on the Oceania continent, the Commonwealth of Australia is slightly smaller than the United States. It is the world's smallest continent but sixth-largest country. Its population (18,438,824) lies concentrated along the eastern and southeastern coasts. The ethnic makeup is: Caucasian 95%, Asian 4%, aboriginal and other 1%. Religious affiliations are: Anglican 26.1%, Roman Catholic 26%, other Christian 24.3%, and balance unknown. Australia became an independent member of the Commonwealth in1901.

Australia has a prosperous, Western-style capitalist economy, with a per capita GDP above the levels in highly industrialized West European countries. Rich in natural resources, Australia is a major exporter of agricultural products, minerals, metals, and fossil fuels. Commodities account for about 60% of the value of total exports, so that a downturn in world commodity prices can have a big impact on the economy. The government is pushing for increased exports of manufactured goods, but competition in international markets continues to be severe. Australia has suffered from the low growth and high unemployment characterizing the commonwealth countries in the early 1990s,

The Al-Mukmin school in Solo, Java. The sign reads "America is the world terrorist." (AP Photo/Yusuf Gunawan)

but the economy has expanded at reasonably steady rates in recent years. In addition to high unemployment, short-term economic problems include a balancing of output growth and inflationary pressures and the stimulation of exports to offset rising imports.

Australia has had very little terrorist activity on an annual basis and it not too difficult to explain some of the possible reasons for this. Not the least is the fact that it is a huge country with pockets of population that would not in any way be considered dense by world standards. This means that the population is a tight community and any attack tends to be known quickly by all. Crime events are so low and there is difficulty in attackers "melting into the background." Travel away from the scene of crime or terrorism with any speed is limited to planes and their sophisticated checks. To go by car is slow and relatively easy to track down.

There have been a few terrorists attacks, by our definitions, which have occurred in the past. Among them was the assassination of Turkish Consul General Sarik Ariyak in December 1980. Then there was the 1982 bomb extortion against Woolworth, a retail chain, and before that, a bombing outside the Hilton Hotel in 1978 where the Commonwealth heads of government were staying. A letter bomb campaign from the Middle East in 1975 injured a press secretary at the Queensland State Premier's office and back in 1966, a premature explosion of a parcel bomb in a Melbourne mailroom believed intended for a major pro-Yugoslav supporter occurred.

Tasmania, an island to the south of Australia, is one of the world's major suppliers of licit opiate products. The government maintains strict controls over areas of opium poppy cultivation and the output of poppy straw concentrate.

SUMMARY

The Pacific Rim has become a major trading block, import and export, for the rest of the world. The importance of this group of nations is reflected by its impact on the trading exchanges around the globe from the recent financial crises that are occurring. There are such a variety of governments and economies in this vast area of island and continental based nations. The giants like China and Japan and Korea are changing and feeling the effects on their populations. The next chapter will take the student on a tour of Central and South America, where the terrorism strikes closest to the United States. While religious and left-wing terrorism seems to prevail in the other hot spots we have discussed, the dictatorship of right wing leaders seems to be the "*plate de jour*" for the Latin American countries.

TERMS TO REMEMBER

ABRI	**JRA**	**PRC**
Abu Sayyaf Group	**keiretsu**	**socialist market**
Aum Shinrikyo	**MILF**	**economy**
DPP	**MNLF**	**Uygur separatists**
Filipino Soldiers for	**NPA**	
the Nation	**People's Consultative**	
Free Papua	**Assembly**	
Organization		

REVIEW QUESTIONS

1. Explain why there is so little terrorism in China.
2. Describe the organization and operations of Aum Shinrikyo and what it is most famous for.
3. What do you think will ever happen in regard to Taiwan becoming rejoined with China.
4. The Philippines are seeing a resurgence of terrorism. What is the reason?
5. Australia has almost no terrorism. What do you think are the reasons for that?

ENDNOTES

1. U.S. Department of State, Secretary Albright "Meeting the Far East Crisis: What Should Governments Do?" http//www.state.gov.
2. Andrew Marshall co-author of, "The Cult at the End of the World: The Incredible Story of Aum."

3. Geoge Wehrfritz, Newsweek, April 13, 1998, pp. 24–30.

4. Tim Ito, washingtonpost.com October, 1998 The Washington Post Company.

5. U.S. Department of State Office of the Spokesman. Press Statement by James P. Rubin, spokesman November 4, 1998. *Indonesia-Report by Fact-Finding Team* http//www. state.gov.

12 Latin America

"Individually and collectively we will deny terrorist groups the capacity to operate in this hemisphere. This American family stands united."

Declaration by the Organization of American States,
September 21, 2001

OVERVIEW

In our attempts to define terrorism, the experience of the Central and South American countries tends to have significant differences from those activities found in countries located in Western Europe and the Middle East. Many of the Latin countries have suffered from what was described as state terrorism, using death squads that have been brought into play by extreme right wing, authoritarian governments. A definition worth considering is that put forward by the United States Department of Defense: ". . . the calculated use of violence or the threat of violence to inculcate fear intended to coerce or to intimidate governments or societies in the pursuit of goals that are generally political, religious, or ideological."

This definition was carefully crafted to distinguish between terrorism and other kinds of violence. The act of terrorism is defined independently of the cause that motivates it. People employ terrorist violence in the name of many causes. Insurgency, freedom-fighting or just plain terrorism from both the left and the right continues unabated in Colombia. The tendency to label as terrorism any violent act of which we do not approve is erroneous. Terrorism is a specific kind of violence. It therefore begs the question about the state involvement in systematic abuse of human rights and the tacit support given to unofficial death squads by military juntas in many Central and South American countries. The so-called **Banana Republics,** joked about in the early part of the twentieth century, became serious problems when they experienced revolutions and insurgencies in the 1970s and 1980s. The former Soviet Union and other communist causes often backed these efforts to destabilize the area and break the support of dictators by the United States.

This chapter will start with the most prominent terror movements in Central America, from their developmental stages after the Mexican revolution of 1910 to the changes in typical terror tactics in South America. Massive drug dealings by the Colombian, Mexican and other drug cartels (referred to as narco-terrorism), the oppressive regimes in Uruguay, El Salvador, Argentina and others will be discussed. The horrors associated with Latin American death squads will be explored, along with the conditions, tactics and distinctive characteristics of Latin American terrorism.

CENTRAL AMERICA

MEXICO

We start with the United States' closest neighbor to the south, Mexico. At the dawn of the twenty-first century, this country is a far cry from that of a century ago. The Revolutionary Party had been in power since the revolution of 1910, the country had undergone economic growth and seen rapid social and economic advances for middle and upper class members of Mexican society. A major issue facing the Mexican government has been the land dispute surrounding the Chiapas region in southern Mexico. Mexico has experienced almost unprecedented economic growth in the past few decades, but there has been a clear failure to equitably distribute that wealth due to a lack of social reform. As a result, Mexico remains a country of "haves and have nots." In addition to Chiapas, other regions have experienced guerrilla warfare or, as the Mexican government portrays them, terrorist movements. These are located in the regions of Oaxaca, Hidalgo, Vera Cruz and Puebla. Immortalized from the days of the revolution, Emilio Zapata, killed in 1919, is still lauded by the peasantry of southern Mexico as their true hero. Using Zapata as a symbol of revolutionary righteousness, the Zapatista movement continues to wage an armed struggle for land rights in the Chiapas region.

Zapatista National Liberation Army (ELZN)

By far the best known of the groups operating within Mexico, the Zapatista violently appeared on the world scene in 1994, by fomenting an armed uprising against the Mexican government to protest the distribution of land in the region. This movement better fits the definition of a guerrilla movement than a subversive terror organization. But the group uses terror tactics to achieve notoriety as well as political aims. The ELZN burst on to the national scene as a result of the political and economic alliance between Mexico, the United States and Canada. In the latter two countries, the pros and cons of the **North American Free Trade Agreement (NAFTA)** were hotly debated. In Mexico, however, some went to war over it. As we have seen in so many similar conflicts, the primary issue surrounding the uprising was land. Mexicans who farmed the land and eked out their living in that fashion had been granted land for their families. This ended with NAFTA, when the Mexican government stopped the land distribution program. Armed and angry men from Chiapas came out of the hills and attacked the cities. The response from the Mexican government to this localized and popular uprising was to send in the military. Chiapas became a region patrolled and controlled by the Mexican Army. Many of the problems facing Mexico revolved around the stumbling economy in 1994 and the slow rate of recovery. The erosion of the ruling Institutional Revolutionary Party's (PRI) erosion of power has not helped and contributes to the continuing unrest.

In 1995, 30,000 Mexican soldiers intent on the destruction of the **ELZN** guerrillas invaded the region of Chiapas. The exercise was an abject failure.

The ELZN simply disappeared into the hills of Chiapas, much like the Viet Cong, who also knew their regions so well. The soldiers continued to surround Realidad, believed to be the center of Zapatista operations. To appeal for their rights to the land and a cessation of the violence, Bishop Samuel Louis Garcia has acted as a mediator between the ELZN, the people of Chiapas and the Mexican authorities. **Chiapas** is still a region in conflict and one of the main reasons for the fall of the long-ruling PRI in Mexico. The PRI lost both the presidency and the governorship of the Province of Chiapas in 2000. The new President, Vicente Fox, began his term with the intention of bringing an end to the rebellion in that region. The talks foundered and the zones controlled by the Zapatista rebels, although much quieter now, continue to remain off limits to government control.[1]

Right Wing Violence

More disturbing are extreme right wing attacks against the ELZN and its supporters by a movement calling itself "Peace and Justice." This group pledges its support to the Institutional Revolutionary Party and operates as a death squad in the Chiapas region. The viciousness of the right wing attacks seems to have the support of the military as well as the local police authorities, and this has led to beatings, murders and the mass evacuation of entire villages. Active units pledging support for the government and finding support from the police have the same goals as state-sponsored terrorism. The student will recall that this involves the systemic and purposeful creation, by a political regime, of mass fear by violent means, and/or by the threat of such violence. The purpose of the systematic exercise of such publicly visible violence is to maintain, legitimize, or strengthen the social and administrative control of the state. The activities of Peace and Justice seem destined to be part of the fabric of Mexican society for this region. By generating significant fear, this right wing group is able by force of presence and the generation of fear to influence the predominantly Mayan Indian people of Chiapas.

Popular Revolutionary Army (EPR)

The **EPR** organization probably ranks second in strength to the Zapatista movement. With its base and origins in the southern states of Oaxaca and Guerrero, it gains support from the mainly poverty-stricken villages of those areas. The topography of the region, forested mountains and rugged terrain, makes an ideal home base for a guerrilla force. The EPR is a left wing group and considered by the Mexicans to be several diverse movements operating under a single banner. EPR attacks have been sporadic and often without a clearly understood or defined objective. Armed ambushes against federal police and military convoys are the primary tactics of EPR. Their strength and size has yet to be determined with any precision, but the group claims over 20,000 guerrillas operating in the southern states. Support for the group has also come from an outside source, which may well be responsible for arming them with modern Russian-made weaponry. In response to the logistics and training it has received from Peru's Marxist Shining Path, the EPR set up a Mexican Support Committee for the Popular War in Peru. Sustained operations have been difficult and whether the group has the ability to employ any effective tactics to disrupt or alter government policy is questionable. Attacks on the outskirts of Mexico City have occurred and communiqués have been issued to target the "fat cat" capitalist businesses located there.

Other movements are surfacing in the poorer regions of Mexico as a result of the country's economic woes and the perception that the poor are getting poorer and the rich getting richer. Such groups as the Revolutionary Army of Popular Insurgence, and the Armed Front for the Liberation of the Marginalized People of Guerrero may be following the Zapatista uprising as means for gaining concessions from the government. It is unclear whether the Mexican military can contain more than one guerrilla army at a time. Currently fully occupied with the Chiapas region, it would seem incapable of handling yet another.

The Twenty-First Century

As Mexico entered the new millennium, the growing discontent and trouble from insurgent groups, especially in the poorer regions of the country, cannot be discounted. Unrest has begun to reach the cities, where the abuses of paramilitary police produce the same results in cities as the Zapatista have done in the rural areas. Mexico currently has neither an effective means to deal with violence and corruption within the ranks of its police force, nor the capability to deter any terror organizations with any significant measures of success. Mexico also is rife with a healthy drug trade and associated with that comes the inevitable violence with cartels settling scores among themselves. Much of the killings tend to be within the cartels but bribery of police and judiciary is also commonplace.

GUATEMALA

Outside communist influences in Guatemala during the last forty-five years have done much to further the violations of human rights to the individuals opposed to the many dictatorships and juntas that have come to power. During the Cold War years, this influence was particularly strong. The United States assisted in the military overthrow of Guatemala's communist regime in 1954, but the series of right wing military governments that followed did nothing to initiate reforms in the region. Rather, they focused on campaigns against communist infiltration. With so much oppression in the country the peasantry began to retaliate with such movements as the **Rebel Armed Forces (FAR)**, which began to take shape in the early 1960s and which was the precursor to the Guatemalan National Unity (URNG), was established in 1982. The military had little success in repressing such movements and, with the arrival of **URNG**, embarked on a vicious campaign of state-sponsored terror.

The military was unleashed, and death squads were formed and operated clandestinely, while military and security police openly committed murder and torture. The resulting exodus from the region gradually gained international attention. The military leaders of Guatemala were desperate to remain in power, and to this end they increased the tactics of state-sponsored terror against their own people. A scorched earth policy was employed in many instances and whole villages, their lands and crops were destroyed. Torture of suspected communists was commonplace and the methods of torture were gruesome in the extreme. Human rights in Guatemala and past U.S. support for the regime are issues for the student to ponder, as are questions regarding the level of involvement by the U.S. government in such political murders, torture and human rights abuses.

Impunity

The abuses and atrocities perpetrated by, and in the name of, the Guatemalan state have rested on a system of impunity, which can be defined "freedom from accountability for criminal wrong doing. . .or freedom from other legal sanctions." The impunity system in Guatemala is conducted by several simple mechanisms. Primarily, the state denies any state-sponsored violence and secondly, those that would have made claims of torture and rights abuse have simply been "disappeared." Such disappearances make it difficult to bring any judicial action against Guatemala. In the sixteen years leading up to 1990, it is estimated that more than 100,000 Guatemalans were killed and possibly another 40,000 disappeared without a trace. The government has a very thin veneer of democracy, but its ability to control the powerful military is doubtful, especially when it comes to human rights abuses. The peace accord, finalized in 1996, brought an end to thirty-six years of internal fighting, and Guatemalans began returning to their villages from the neighboring countries.

State-sponsored terrorism in Guatemala has fostered a populace with a shared set of experiences of systemic human rights violations. It is a populace

---

TERRORISM BYTE 12–1

Gerardi Condera Assassination

Monsignor Juan Gerardi Condera

Guatemala and its rebels signed a peace deal in 1996, however this did not eradicate all the violence that permeates the country. On Sunday, April 26, 1998, two days after Monsignor Juan Gerardi Condera released a report on human rights violations, he was beaten to death by a lone assailant as he returned to his home. Gerardi was the Bishop of Guatemala and the coordinator of the Archbishop's Human Rights Office (ODHA). Monsignor Gerardi was the driving force behind the project for the Recovery of Historical Memory (REMHI), which he had created to shed light on the war's human rights violations. The killer had access to his house and car and his colleagues believe he was the subject of a death squad attack. Witnesses saw unknown men in two trucks hanging around the parish house the night of the killing, another trademark of the death squads that had killed with impunity during the 36-year conflict. Geradi's report entitled *"Guatemala: Never Again"* documented 55,021 cases of human rights abuse occurring during the conflict, placing 80% of the responsibility on the Guatemalan Army.

Source: War Called Peace, "Death of a Bishop," Piet van Lier 1998, Internet, http://zena.secureforum.com/znet/LAM/zGuatemala.html.

not only cynical of the formal, institutional applications of justice, but one that has experienced extralegal "justice" in the fight for social control and social transformation of Guatemalan society.[2]

The Civil War

The first thorn in the side of successive oppressive military governments was the Rebel Armed Forces (FAR), which began limited guerrilla operations as far back as 1962. Over the years, the movement grew among the indigenous groups and expanded to include the Guerrilla Army of the Poor (EGP) in 1972 and the Organization of People in Arms (OPRA). With the merging of these three guerrilla movements, all with the same causes and complaints, the Guatemalan National Unity Group (URNG) was formed. Many villages were totally destroyed and entire populations killed in operations conducted by the military. In some part, their actions typified those used in the Vietnam War, collectively called pacification. A scorched earth policy was employed. By targeting the civilian population in the Guatemalan countryside, the military assumed they would stop support of the guerrilla army. Since the signing of the 1996 Peace Accords, there have been many attempts to bring justice to bear in Guatemala. Amnesty International has been prominent in detailing human rights abuses believed perpetrated by the military and the death squads. This has led to attacks against prominent church leaders in Guatemala to try to silence such criticism.

By the end of 1998, climatic changes in the region prompted the government to suspend parts of their constitution. Following the distinctive impact of Hurricane Mitch, which decimated several Central American countries, including Guatemala, the government of Alvaro Arzu suspended two articles of the country's constitution, Article Six and Twenty-Six. This is believed to be a direct result of the looting and violence in the cities following the hurricane and the government's fear of a resurgence of terrorism.[3] Article Six protects Guatemalans from detention or imprisonment without cause or in the absence of a court order and Article Twenty-Six guarantees the right of freedom of travel. Such severe measures threaten to return Guatemala to a repressive government. This volatile country should be carefully watched over the next decade.

HONDURAS

As has been evidenced throughout most of Central America, the paranoia that gripped the United States during the Cold War years of the 1960s was played out in its support of countries ripe for communist influence. Honduras has benefited from decades of military support from the United States, and was involved, throughout the 1980s, in fighting with the invading Sandinistas and in hunting down rebel contra bases.

Morazanist Patriotic Front (FPM)

This small, extreme left wing terror group was violently opposed to U.S. intervention and support of the right wing political government in Honduras. It has targeted the United States for attacks. The group, small and not particularly well organized, is believed to have been supported by Cuba. It has carried out bomb attacks on military buses carrying U.S. service personnel and, in 1989, claimed responsibility for such an incident in which three U.S. servicemen were wounded. Attacks since then have been sporadic and ineffectively executed.[4]

EL SALVADOR

As in Mexico, the natives of El Salvador have been engaged in an ongoing demand for land reform and rights, dating back nearly seventy years. Much of El Salvador's economy was based on its coffee production and export, which was controlled by a select and influential group of families. The first sign of protest dates back to the first quarter of the twentieth century and a campaigner from the Central American Communist Party, Augustin Farabundo Marti. His goal, like that of the Chiapas of Mexico, was not the overthrow of the government but the redistribution of wealth from the land on an equitable basis. By 1930, the country was under the military control of General Martinez, who sided with the society elite and coffee owners. Marti was arrested in a military crackdown on his movement and was subsequently executed by firing squad. The peasants were not organized in sufficient numbers to mount any sort of insurgent response. The military sought to purge the country of peasant "subversives" and went on a massive killing spree, that accounted for more than 30,000 deaths. In 1981,there were 12,501 murders reported in El Salvador.

El Salvador in the late 1960s and 1970s provided yet another example of extreme right wing terror being used as a government tool to eradicate opposition. Again death squads became the norm and two specific groups were formed, one covert and the other overt, to protect wealthy landowners and to spread fear among the peasants. The commander of the El Salvador National Guard in1968[5] formed the ORDEN. This was an intelligence gathering organization to amass information. It went beyond information gathering; it was also kidnapping and murdering peasants. In attempting to analyze and define terrorism some scholars believe that the actions of death squads are not terroristic in nature. However, the subversive actions of a terrorist or guerrilla organizations spread fear, disorder and uncertainty within the ruling government and the country as a whole. In the same way repression by death squads or paramilitary groups has the identical effects.

Periods of relative peace were interrupted by violence against the peasantry mainly by the death squads, which operated both clandestinely and openly. The violence was brought to a halt in 1992 with a peace agreement. Liberal views made anyone a target for death squads, and even priests and nuns were murdered. Also targeted were outspoken labor leaders as well as politicians. Throughout the 1980s, fear was pervasive throughout El Salvador.

NICARAGUA

This small Central American country of 4.5 million has been embroiled in what can best be described as a struggle between superpowers. Nicaragua has had a leadership that boasts close ties to the United States and its military

TERRORISM BYTE 12–2

Kidnappings

Kidnappings remain one of the most pernicious problems in Central and Latin America. Nineteen U.S. citizens were kidnapped in Latin America in 2002, including four in Mexico, and five in Colombia. Counterterrorism units in Colombia arrested fifty people in connection with the abduction of five U.S. oil workers in Ecuador and the subsequent murder in January 2001 of U.S. hostage, Ron Sander.

training institutions for the better part of the twentieth century. This country has also been involved in the sale of drugs for weapons, and brought into disrepute the dealings of the Central Intelligence Agency (CIA). The National Guard of Nicaragua was modeled after and trained by the United States military in the years prior to World War II. The United States provided support to the regime of Anastasio Garcia and successive generations of his family up until 1979. It seemed of no particular concern to U.S. administrations what political ideology was being espoused, so long as it was not communist. In fact, he held power with corrupt associates and used repression to great effect. He was also an avid anti-communist, which very much appealed to the United States in the Cold War years.

Anastasio's corrupt government, and the repressive tactics used, was eventually overthrown by a communist-inspired revolutionary movement called the **Sandinista.** The Sandinista's National Liberation Front (FLSN) had been waging a guerrilla war against Samoza Anastasio since the start of the 1970s. The Cold War was not a distant memory for the United States and military assistance was provided to the Anistasio government to fight the Sandinistas. The Sandinistas, with Soviet assistance, seized power from Anastasio in 1979. Now the stage was set for the United States to support what the Nicaraguan government would call rebels, while the Soviet bloc would support the Sandinista government. The Reagan administration was committed to eliminating any communist influences on its doorstep and promptly poured aid into the rebel Contra movement in its attempt to dislodge the Sandinistas.

Fund Raising

Aside from the problems of the guerrilla war in Nicaragua, a far bigger scandal was being unraveled in the halls of the Pentagon. Questions arose concerning the level of involvement by the government of the United States in drug trafficking in exchange for weapons to the **Contras.** There have been many sensational journalistic pieces, pointing a finger at the CIA and the administration. The Kerry Committee Report of April 1995 holds some interesting facts in its findings. The sub-committee found that the Contra drug links included:

- Involvement in narcotics trafficking by individuals associated with the Contra movement.

- Participation of narcotics traffickers in Contra supplies operations through business relationships with Contra organizations.
- Provision of assistance to the Contras by narcotics traffickers, including cash, weapons, planes, pilots, air supply services and other materials, on a voluntary basis.
- Payment to drug traffickers by the United States State Department of funds authorized by the Congress for humanitarian assistance to the Contras, in some cases after the traffickers had been indicted by federal law enforcement agencies on drug charges, in others while traffickers were under active investigation by these same agencies.[6]

There is no doubt that those involved in these drug schemes on the U.S. side hoped to expunge any pending legal indictments in return for assistance to the rebel Contras. The level of exploitation by the drug traffickers was purely self-serving and certainly not ideologically driven.

When examining the infrastructure that was in place in the 1970s, for the movement of illegal narcotics through Central America to the United States, it was a simple shift to include weapons into this operation's mix. This was a method used by the Sandinistas to bring Cuban weapons into Nicaragua. Supply and staging areas abounded along the Nicaraguan border with Costa Rica, and most of the neighboring governments, which supported the actions of the Sandinistas, offered them safe haven and the opportunity to transfer drugs and weapons for their cause. When the Sandinistas gained power, the gun running did not cease. In fact all that changed was the end user. The suppliers now had El Salvadoran rebels as customers, and not the Sandinistas.

One name has become synonymous with the Contras in the 1980s, Lieutenant Colonel Oliver North, who at the time "managed" Contra operations on the Southern Front. Evidence in the Kerry findings relates also to a U.S. national living in Costa Rica. John Hull, was an Indiana farmer who moved to Costa Rica, and bought up large tracts of land. The area was known as Hull's Ranch, and happened to include six airstrips that were ideal for drugs and weapon smuggling. Hull helped the CIA with military shipments to the Contras and was also heavily involved in transshipments of drugs from Colombia. Added to this was the fact that the state department was actively signing contracts with companies and their principals that were either under investigation or had been indicted on narcotics-smuggling charges. These companies were used to make military hardware drops to the Contra rebels.

PANAMA

Formerly under Spanish rule, this tiny strip of land between the Pacific and the Atlantic first became a province of Colombia, before gaining its independence in 1903. Famous for the Panama Canal, which was under the control of the United States until the late 1970s, Panamanians have been a largely rural nation. The country has seen many varied forms of military governments over the past century but the most notorious was that of General Manuel Noriega, who became president of Panama in 1983. From the time he came to power, he ran a corrupt government and made millions of dollars from drug trafficking to the U.S. and from diverting aid funds. He controlled the public with strong-arm tactics and death squads. In 1988, he was indicted by a Florida grand jury on charges of racketeering and drug running. Up until 1989, Noriega continued to act with impunity. However, after the death of a U.S. Marine officer, and Noriega's overturning the results of a democratic election, President George Bush gave the almost unprecedented order for U.S. troops to invade Panama and restore the elected president. The paratroopers also seized Noriega and handed him to U.S. Marshals. He then stood trial and was sentenced to forty years in federal prison, where he languishes today. Some think the effort to restore democracy in Panama was more about trying to stem the endless flow of drugs into the United States and to bring Noriega to trial for his drug trafficking.

SOUTH AMERICA

COLOMBIA

The 40-plus million inhabitants and the democracy of the State of Colombia are under assault by three narco-terrorist groups—the revolutionary **Armed Forces of Colombia (FARC), the National Liberation Army (ELN)** and the **United Self-Defense Forces of Colombia (AUC).** Between them, they are capable of providing over 25,000 combatants. FARC and AUC have a pronounced involvement at all levels of the drug trade and derive considerable income from it. Estimations run to $300 million annually. In 2001, the AUC killed two Colombian legislators, while FARC kidnapped six; between the three groups, they accounted for the assassination of twelve mayors.[7]

To most students, the name Colombia conjures up several simple words: drugs, kidnapping, rebels. The U.S. Department of State characterizes the country as one of the most dangerous in the world to visit and that is still a fact at the start of the new millennium. Marijuana, cocaine, and kidnappings have been products of Colombia for the past forty years, but the market for drugs did not take off until the wealthy and middle classes in the United

TERRORISM BYTE 12–3

Remote-Controlled Airplane Bombs

On August 26, 2002, the Colombian military seized nine remote-controlled toy airplanes during an early morning raid on a FARC-controlled cocoa production facility. The military believes the rebels intended to load the toy planes with explosives and use them as improvised explosive devices against nearby oilfield targets and an army base. Each airplane was capable of carrying two-three pounds with an effective range of 1.5 miles. This is the second time in 2002 that the military has discovered materials being assembled for an aerial attack.

Source: Air Security International Hot Spots, 8/27/02, Air Security International Intelligence Sources, http://toolbox.airsecurity.com.

States began abusing them. Cocaine became the drug of choice, and the opportunity for expansion into a North American market was huge. Drugs in Colombia are controlled in two regions of the country, Medellin and **Cali.** These two drug cartels control nearly 80% of Columbia's distribution. Terrorist groups in Colombia have been fully involved in the sale and supply of narcotics for financial support for the bitter fight against successive Colombian governments.

Violence and intimidation in Colombia has focused around the drug trade. Terrorism, therefore, becomes a byproduct of the drug trade and a means of control and power. Extortion, kidnapping, and murder are all hallmarks of the drug cartels. In a country where the economics are dictated by drug barons, anarchy is not far away. It is difficult to appreciate the enormous wealth that comes from the machinations of the drug trade. Drug barons are known to have utilized outside "sources" to assist their own internal security services. The economy of Colombia seems to be drug dependent, and eradicating the drugs from the region would be simpler if there was a legal economy able to produce an income similar to the drug trade. Several have been attempted, but the demand for drugs makes growing cocoa a better alternative. Colombia also has to contend with an insurgent group of left wing rebels/revolutionaries/ terrorists that have plagued the state for close to forty years with little or no sign of resolution.

Revolutionary Armed Forces of Colombia (FARC)

This terror group is considered the largest and best equipped of the terror organizations in Colombia. An extreme left wing, communist-inspired movement, the FARC aspires to the overthrow of the Colombian government and little else. It first came to notice in 1966 as a military wing of the Colombian

Year	Potential cocaine hydrochloride production (metric tons)	Coca leaf cultivation (hectares)	Coca leaf eradication (hectares)
1987	*	22,960	460
1988	*	34,230	230
1989	*	43,400	640
1990	*	41,000	900
1991	*	38,472	972
1992	60	38,059	959
1993	65	40,493	793
1994	70	49,610	4,910
1995	230	59,650	8,750
1996	300	72,800	5,600
1997	350	98,500	19,000
1998	435	115,450	13,650
1999	521	135,900	47,000
2000	580	183,200	43,246

*Data not available
Source: Us States Department, *International Narcotics Control Strategy Report,* March 2001

Colombian Cocoa Production 1987–2000. (U.S. State Department)

Communist Party. Formed on rough military outlines, its members engage in a broad scope of activities. In a country where kidnapping is as commonplace as drinking a cup of coffee and might be considered the largest growth industry, the FARC targets the government, military, locally elected municipal mayors, police and civilians. Much of FARC's income is derived not only from drug trafficking, but also robbery, kidnapping and extortion. FARC is rabidly anti-United States and its campaign resembles that of Cuban-style revolution. Its campaign against the Colombian governments has not specifically detailed or promoted attacks outside of the country. For foreign visitors, particularly American businessmen, a trip to Colombian is one to be avoided at all costs. FARC's membership of active terrorists is believed to number around 16,000, with support in rural areas from the indigenous population. It has definite links to organized drug trafficking and also carries on external activities in Ecuador, Panama and Venezuela.[8]

The high number of attacks on the judiciary, military police, civil servants and members of government has given rise to a movement of death squads. Unable to effectively control the terrorists and drug barons by democratic process, some police and military officers have formed underground units, by way of a response, to target and destroy the terrorists. Colombia's drug cartels have had assistance in training their private security teams provided by mercenaries from Britain and Israel in paramilitary style training schools uncovered by the Colombian Secret Police (DAS) near Puerto Boyaca.[9] FARC's central demands are not considered realistic by most observers; their demands for the ending of privatization and reduction of the 20% unemployment and other reforms seem hopelessly futile. On the political front the Colombian government of President Andreas Pastrana, in 2001 the year leading up to the elections, had made slow headway with negotiating a peace deal with FARC. As negotiations became bogged down, the Pastrana government threatened to end the deal that had created a demilitarized zone (DMZ) in southern Colombia, an area approximately the size of Switzerland that had been occupied by FARC. Since the events of 9–11, the Colombian government has been fortified with U.S. aid and military hardware for the express purpose of combating the drugs trade in the country. This aid has given significant impetus to the Colombian military to go on the offensive against FARC, something of a novelty for Colombia's military which has traditionally fought in defensive mode against FARC. Operation Black Cat, which commenced in February 2002 was a military offensive directed against FARC with the use of aircraft and helicopters. At the same time, Pastrana annulled the FARC's political status and issued arrest warrants for its leaders. In the February 12 attack, the Colombian military struck so far into FARC territory that it was taken totally by surprise. The area attacked was the town of Barrancomina in eastern Colombia, an area where the 16th Front of FARC had been able to operate with complete impunity. The significance of the attack showed that the Colombian military had the skill and support intelligence and the military know-how to attack FARC. In the coming months, this will no doubt be a deciding factor in peace talks—if they ever resume. FARC's resilience has never really been in question, the organization is a survivor. You cannot call it a truly communist-inspired movement, even though committed communists are included in its membership. FARC is also involved in the drug trade, although it cannot be considered a drug cartel, but it is involved in narco-terrorism. Because it flourishes in the deep rural and jungle regions of the state, it may be considered a peasant army. In some respects this may be true but because of its wide-ranging terror attacks, it cannot be termed as the vanguard of the peasant populous. FARC's appeal to the peasantry could be rationalized as it offers a level of employment when there is no prospects elsewhere. After thirty-eight years, a new leadership will become self-evident. The failures of the group's participation in government representation may spawn an organization that will feed off the lucrative trade in drugs, kidnappings and extortion.

FARC will likely continue to become more marginalized as it sees itself up against the United States-backed Colombian military, and an ever-growing number of paramilitary forces arrayed against it. In this context, it is expected that now that it has been hit systemically in areas it once operated in with freedom, it will have to reconsider its actions and adapt, to survive in this new environment.

FARC and ELN (National Liberation Army) have become bitter enemies. Agreements between the two on sharing the spoils in kidnapping ransomes have been violated and FARC is again licking its wounds. With FARC temporarily on the run it makes itself a better target for the Colombian military, and the fact that FARC has no international support or a conduit for a supply of arms and weapons will make its response all the more dangerous. Its ability to strike against both the local political apparatus and the civilian population is well documented and this is exactly what has happened since February 2002. With the arrival of the new president, Alvaro Uribe, who has committed to destroying FARC in his term of office, there is little doubt that further attacks will continue. The new president also has some unfunished business with the rebels, who have tried on at least fifteen occasions to kill him, but more than that—the FARC rebels killed his father in 1983. The new president hails from the Antioquia Province where he was the governor from 1995–97. During his term as governor, he promoted the 'self-defense' groups, some of which evolved into paramilitary groups that, like the rebels they supposedly battle, are blamed for numerous civilian massacres.

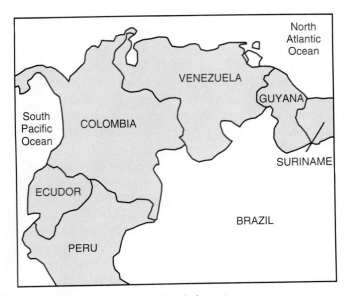

Regional Map—Northern South America.

National Liberation Army (ELN)

Formed in 1963, the ELN, smaller and less organized than FARC, carries on a campaign against the government. It is predominately a Marxist-inspired group with membership of about 3,000 fighters. Similar to FARC the group is anti-United States, and frequently engages in the profitable tactic of kidnapping. Usually the target is a businessman from a foreign company working in Colombia. In addition it targets U.S. and foreign installations for bomb attacks. ELN's operations are focused on the Colombian northwestern border with Venezuela and central and northwestern regions habitually growing cannabis and poppy opium. ELN and FARC have both systematically targeted Colombia's oil facilities and in 2001, the government suffered nearly $500 million in lost revenues. To this end, the United States has supplied $6 million in Foreign Military Funds (FMF) to start the training of Colombian military units to protect the Cano Limon pipeline that has been repeatedly bombed by both groups. Other methods employed by ELN have been and continue to be the practice of kidnappings for ransom. Since 1992, FARC and ELN have kidnapped a total of fifty-one U.S. citizens and murdered ten.[10]

Right Wing Death Squads

The rise to prominence of the death squads in Colombia appears to have had the tacit support of both the government and military. Many of these defense groups sprang up in the 1960s and 1970s in response to terrorist activities against wealthy landowners by the FARC. Over the years the groups, which tended to operate in select areas, moved from defensive to offensive strategies

A necklace explosive device, used by FARC guerrillas to extort money. This device exploded, killing the victim and a bomb disposal technician, May 15, 2000. (AP Photo)

and began to attack suspected members of FARC and to intimidate peasant villagers believed to be helping the FARC.[11] In regions such as Central Magdelena, drug cartels began buying up rich tracts of land, and this was most directly responsible for transforming the self-defense units into right wing death squads.[12]

The student should not lose sight of the real issue in the rise of death squads and the necessary need for terrorist actions in this country. For the Colombian drug lords, the end most certainly justifies the means. In a country so heavily dependent on the production and export of drugs, the methods used, which terrorize the populace, are not intended as means to overthrow or replace a political system. Their efforts are aimed at maintaining the status quo for their own benefit and dissuading police, judges and politicians from legal approaches to dealing with drug traffickers. The rise of the right wing death squads and paramilitaries dates back thirty years when rich landowners, farmers and the drug cartels adopted their own small and very private protection forces. These have grown into a sort of loose coalition known as the United Self-Defense Forces of Colombia (AUC). AUC and the other two organizations have been responsible for in excess of 2800 kidnappings and the deaths of more than 3000 Colombians. AUC has publicly stated that it gains most of its support and income from the lucrative drug trade. The allegations of human rights abuses abound around the AUC, which has been linked on more than one occasion to senior members of Colombia's military elite. The methods of intimidation used by AUC has meant that more than 340,000 Colombians were forcibly evicted from their homes and land by groups such as AUC bringing the total number of displaced persons to more than two million in the last decade.

International Links

America's most wanted terrorist, the Saudi dissident millionaire Osama bin Laden, is not known to have links with Latin American terrorist groups. However one of his associates, a member of Egypt's largest militant group, Jammaa Islamiyya, was arrested in Bogota, Colombia, in early November 1998. He was subsequently released by the Colombian authorities and deported back to his country of origin, Ecuador. The question to carefully consider is, why would such a high ranking and high profile terrorist be in Latin America? It may be assumed that he was either studying the U.S. embassy as a potential target or negotiating meetings with FARC or ELN to set up trade deals involving drugs for weapons. FARC and its connections to Irish paramilitary groups came dramatically to a head when the Colombian authorities arrested several senior IRA members in 2001. Prior to their arrest, the Colombian authorities revealed that the IRA men had been involved in training members of FARC in military tactics, the use of explosives and the manufacture of arms as stated by General Tapias, Chairman of the Joint Chiefs of Staff, the Armed Forces of Colombia, in his testimony before the U.S. House International Relations Committee on April 24, 2002. The types of attack mounted in 2002 showed a higher level of sophistication than had previously been the case with FARC attacks. The level of sophistication in attacks is similar to those used by the IRA. The reason and background for IRA involvement is not clear but of course there is plenty of

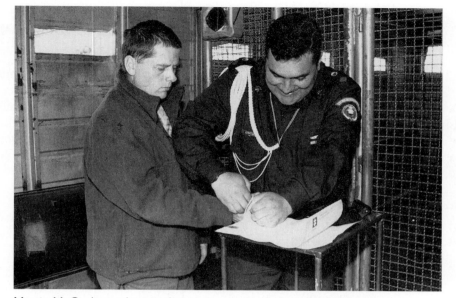

Martin McCauley and two others were arrested by Colombian military in August 2001. All are believed to be members of the Irish Republican Army providing tactical training to FARC members. (AP Photo)

speculation from the various security organizations. In Britain the suggestion is that the IRA was paid $2 million for the training in explosives that they provided to FARC, and of course the U.S. concern is that it may be a case of a much broader coalition of international terror relationships, but there is no hard evidence available. And for the official response to the IRA arrests, the usual comment came from Gerry Adams, the leader of Sinn Fein, when he refused to testify before the International House Relations Committee. In response to the chairman of the committee, Henry Hyde, he wrote, "Let me state again that neither I, nor anyone else, in the Sinn Fein leadership were aware that the three men were traveling to Colombia."[13] Of course, the careful wording in this statement cannot be construed that Sinn Fein was not aware of their involvement—no doubt good enough reason not to testify. It seems highly probable that FARC is delving deeper into drugs trafficking in exchange for military hardware and much-needed cash reserves for its fight.

PERU

Peru is often remembered only for its fabulous Inca villages and high mountains. History tells us that an Inca chief named Tupac Amaru and his Inca followers overcame their colonial Spanish masters in the latter half of the seventeenth century. The country has been under the control of military juntas throughout much of the twentieth century, but civilian rule returned to Peru in the 1980s. Peru suffers from two sources of indigenous terrorism with the Sendoro Luminoso **(Shining Path)** and the Tupac Amaru Revolutionary Movement **(MRTA)**.

TERRORISM BYTE 12–4

U.S. Embassy Car Bomb

A car bomb exploded outside the U.S. Embassy in Lima Peru in March 2002. The bomb had been placed in a car outside the Banco de Credito opposite the U.S. Embassy and in a crowded shopping area. The bomb detonated at 10:45 P.M. and killed nine and injured more than thirty. The bomb is likely the work of the Shining Path guerrillas who have managed to maintain some operational capability in spite of the arrests of its founder and most of the leadership.

Source: Reuters, Associated Press, and www.ict.org.

Sendoro Luminoso (Shining Path)

The Shining Path movement has its origins in the university city of Aucayacu, in the upper Huallaga region. It was led by **Abimael Guzman,** who received his indoctrination and training in China in 1965, at the start of the Chinese Cultural Revolution. His time in China taught him how to set up and organize clandestine political and terrorist activities against the democratic state. On his return home, he became the leader of the pro-Maoist faction of the Peruvian Communist Party. Guzman was working high in the Andes Mountains as a university lecturer studying the exploitation suffered by Peru's Indians. He had no trouble drawing parallels with the Chinese peasants who fought for Mao Tse Tung three decades earlier. He recruited his students into the Maoist Party and sent them to agitate in the Indian villages.[14] His movement went underground in 1976 and began its campaign of terror and insurgency in 1980.

In 1976, while the Peruvian Government was trying to restore the democratic processes and the economy of the country, Guzman and his Shining Path followers were training with automatic weapons. He and his followers were of the belief that the Peruvian society had to be torn down, and a classless society formed to replace it. Guzman and his followers started out as the saviors of the poor of Peru. That was to quickly change as their Marxist style became similar, in his approach to the natives, to that of the Khmer Rouge in dealing with the Cambodians. In merging the extreme teachings of Chairman Mao with the philosophy of Che Guevara,[15] a dangerous hybrid emerged. Like the Khmer Rouge, Guzman and his guerillas set about the destruction of the country by intimidating villagers into joining his movement. Those who refused were killed. The group quickly became a cult of mass murderers, feared for their savagery throughout Peru. Guzman aimed to overthrow the democratic government and replace it with a Marxist dictatorship built in his own image. Over the next fourteen years, their reign of terror took the lives of 25,000 Peruvians and resulted in over $20 billion in damage to the country's infrastructure.

Shining Path terrorists include a number of female operatives, and they have been known to use children to deliver bombs to public buildings and police stations. Guzman's philosophy and ideals spread farther than just Peru; he had goals of reuniting the old Inca Empire, and his terrorists threatened not only Peru, but Ecuador, Colombia, and Bolivia. Guzman was believed to be invincible by his supporters and was called the Fourth Sword of Marxism due to this belief.[16] This belief was to be dispelled by his capture in September 1992. During the 1980s, terrorist activity was so prevalent that villagers were fleeing to the urban slums of big cites such as Lima to escape the ravages of Shining Path. International observers feared that the democratic government in Peru would not be able to deal with the onslaught from the Shining Path.

Following Abimael Guzman's capture in 1992, the movement stumbled and began to disintegrate but within the ten years since his arrest it has started a return to action. The Peruvian government of President Fujimori was determined to overcome both narcotics trafficking and terrorism in Peru and seemed to have the overwhelming support of the people. Prior to Guzman's capture, several other key members of Shining Path were behind bars. No doubt information gathered during their interrogations assisted in Guzman's apprehension. Fujimori's democratic administration and revival of the country's economy had done much to defeat the terrorist threat, which considering the meager level of counterinsurgency training available to the barely equipped security police is quite surprising. Shining Path, in spite of the setbacks of the late 1990s, is still a credible force and problem to Peruvian authorities. In 2001, the U.S. State Department Patterns of Global Terrorism report indicates that in that year alone the number of terrorist acts were standing at one hundred and thirty. Most of the incidents in Peru were relegated to the more remote areas of the country and were invariably related to the drug trade and trafficking. However the fact remains that Shining Path is still in existence and has attempted to mount a bombing campaign against U.S. targets in Lima, most notably a failed attempt to bomb the U.S. Embassy.

Tupac Amaru (MRTA)

The second of Peru's terrorist movements takes its name from the previously mentioned legendary Inca leader. With the country heading towards elections in 1993, the levels of terrorism began to pick up, and by 1996 both MRTA and Shining Path were resorting to campaigns of terror once again. The Shining Path was not able to deliver the same number of guerrillas to the campaign as previously and the numbers of combatants was significantly lower. Following the principles of Carlos Marighella, written three decades previously, the level of urban terrorism was beginning to take shape.

Victor Polay formed the Tupac Amaru in 1985. A traditional Marxist/ Leninist movement, its goal was the overthrow of imperialism in Peru. The group had no external support and its membership was considerably less than that of Shining Path. Polay, however, was captured in 1992 and sentenced to life in prison. In a spectacular display of support and solidarity for Polay, Tupac Amaru terrorists attacked the Japanese ambassador's residence in Lima during a diplomatic Christmas celebration in December of 1996. They took hundreds of guests, mainly diplomats, as hostages. In front of the world press corps assembled outside, Tupac Amaru demanded the release of Polay. With the strong support of the population, Fujimori stood his ground and did not give way to the threats from the terrorists. Through pressure from the government of Japan for a quick resolution to the impasse, everyone settled down to wait.

The assault on the ambassador's residence took place when about 400 guests were starting a meal. The celebration was short lived, as more than a dozen heavily armed guerrillas stormed the grounds, firing weapons in the air. The attackers were calling themselves the Edgar Sanchez Special Forces, commanded by Comrade Edigirio Huerta. The assault began at about 8:00 P.M. on December 17, 1996. The situation was delicate, as a large number of foreign dignitaries and ambassadors were being held hostage, including the ambassadors of Austria, Brazil, Bulgaria, Cuba, Guatemala, Panama, Poland, Romania, South Korea, Spain and Venezuela—a truly significant group. The government of President Fujimori would be put to the test as they had steadfastly refused to negotiate with terrorists, so both political and economic implications would rest on the outcome.

The terrorist demands were as follows:

1. They would shoot hostages unless their demands were met;
2. Release of their imprisoned comrades totaling up to 500;
3. Transfer of freed prisoners and hostages to a jungle hideout, with the last hostage to be released at the final destination;
4. Payment by the Peruvian Government of a "war tax" of an unspecified amount;
5. An economic program to aid the Peruvian poor.[17]

The End of the Crisis

After dragging on for four months, the drama was eventually brought to its climax when the Peruvian special security forces tunneled into the compound and rescued the hostages. Up until the middle of March, negotiations had been proceeding well, and the numbers of hostages had dwindled down to seventy-one, as concessions and counter concessions were made. However Fujimori would not budge on the main demand, which was for the release of the imprisoned members of Tupac Amaru. At 3:20 P.M., April 22, 1997, the rescue began. The Peruvian government had authorized a rescue mission: tunneling, which had taken weeks was now completed, allowing security forces to gain entry for a surprise strike. Explosions and gunfire were heard from inside the compound and plumes of smoke curled up from the residence windows. Within forty minutes, the one hundred and forty-man rescue team had secured the residence, all fourteen guerillas were dead and twenty-five hostages were injured. Two members of the rescue team died in the operation. This incident brought congratulations to the Fujimori government for his stance against terrorism from leaders around the world. But it was also a harsh reminder of the vulnerability of political leaders to terrorist attacks.[18] In overall terms, the Peruvian authorities have seen some considerable success go their way in the war on domestic terrorism. In 2001, they had captured more than 259 suspected terrorists, and since the 9–11 attacks Peru presented itself as a strong regional leader in the fight against terrorism and has participated in the U.S. State Departments Antiterrorism Training Assistance program.

BOLIVIA AND BRAZIL

Neither of these two South American nations has suffered from any significant domestic terrorism problems. But, Brazil has become a hot-bed region for kidnappings and extortion, some of which may be politically motivated. Reported kidnappings in 2001 amounted to a total of 307 in Sao Paulo compared with only 63 the previous year.[19] Although Bolivia has a subversive and anti-Western group called the Tupac Katari Guerrilla Army (EGTK), its actions have been extremely limited. Like so many other Latin areas, Bolivia and Brazil saw military governments during the 1960s and 1970s result in repression. Both countries have been almost free of both government terror and international terror. Human rights violations continue to occur in both countries, as these states have the apparatus in place for torture and confinement. Efforts to bring any wrongdoers to task for repressive activities have thus far failed. Brazil has a democratic constitution, which prohibits the inhumane treatment of prisoners and detainees. When a military coup toppled the Bolivian government in 1980, the usual array of journalists, opposition politicians and trade unionists were detained by the secret police, the *Servicio Especial Seguridad* (SES). However, most detainees were only held for a short period of time.

Politically motivated assassinations have also taken place in recent months. An outspoken member of the Socialist Workers Party was kidnapped in January 2002, and his tortured and bullet-riddled body was found two days later. Much of the violent activities of gangs is laid at the door of former groups involved in urban guerrilla activities in Chile. One of the main protagonists in the gang problems in Brazil is Mauricio Norambuena, a leading figure in the Manual Rodriguez Patriotic Front (FPMR), which is now believed to have its base in Montevideo, Uruguay.

Brazil is famous in international terrorist circles for the pamphlet, *Mini-Manual of the Urban Guerrilla,* which was written by Carlos Marighella in 1969. On Tuesday, November 4, 1969, he was assassinated in Sao Paulo. On that day, two missions were simultaneously interrupted. The first was the life of a man who for nearly forty years had been shaping theories in the struggle against the dominant system. The second was that of a determined **urban guerrilla.** Marighella was killed in an ambush as he was just about to begin rural guerrilla warfare, the next step in his liberation cycle. He had the unique position of having made valuable contributions to the revolutionary cause in both theory and practice. During the last year of his life, as a parallel to the action he undertook, he wrote intensively to support his theories about the liberation of Brazil.

The Mini-Manual of the Urban Guerrilla, which is presented, in part, as a Terrorism Brief in this chapter has special importance. The work examines the conditions, characteristics, necessities, and methods of guerrilla war and the urban guerrilla, and demonstrates his sense of detail, organization, and mental clarity. It also shows, in passing, that Marighella was endowed with inexhaustible confidence and a youthfulness that belied his fifty-eight years. For the experiences described in its pages and for its detailed foresight, the *Mini-Manual of the Urban Guerrilla* became one of the principal books of every man who, in the inevitable battle against the bourgeoisie and imperialism, takes the road of armed rebellion.[20]

TERROR BRIEF 12–1

The Mini Manual of the Urban Guerrilla

Mini-Manual of the Urban Guerrilla

The chronic structural crisis characteristic of Brazil today, and its resultant political instability, are what have brought about the upsurge of revolutionary war in the country. The urban guerrilla is a man who fights the military dictatorship with arms, using unconventional methods. A political revolutionary and an ardent patriot, he is a fighter for his country's liberation, a friend of the people and of freedom. The area in which the urban guerrilla acts is in the large Brazilian cities. There are also bandits, commonly known as outlaws, who work in the big cities. Many times, assaults by outlaws are taken as actions by urban guerrillas. The urban guerrilla however differs radically from the outlaw. The outlaw benefits personally from the action, and attacks indiscriminately without distinguishing between the exploited and the exploiters, which is why there are so many ordinary men and women among his victims. The urban guerrilla follows a political goal and only attacks the government, the big capitalists, and the foreign Imperialists, particularly North Americans.

Another element just as prejudicial as the outlaw and also operating in the urban area is the right-wing counterrevolutionary who creates confusion, assaults banks, hurls bombs, kidnaps, assassinates, and commits the worst imaginable crimes against urban guerrillas, revolutionary priests, students, and citizens who oppose fascism and seek liberty. The urban guerrilla is an implacable enemy of the government and systematically inflicts damage on the authorities and on the men who dominate the country and exercise power. The principal task of the urban guerrilla is to distract, to wear out, to demoralize the militarists, the military dictatorship and its repressive forces, and also to attack and destroy the wealth and property of the North Americans, the foreign managers, and the Brazilian upper class.

The urban guerrilla is not afraid of dismantling and destroying the present Brazilian economic, political, and social system, for his aim is to help the rural guerrilla and to collaborate in the creation of a totally new and revolutionary social and political structure, with the armed people in power. The urban guerrilla must have a certain minimal political understanding. To gain that he must read certain printed or mimeographed works such as:

- *Guerrilla Warfare* by Che Guevara
- *Memories of a Terrorist*
- *Some Questions about the Brazilian*
- *Guerrilla Operations and Tactics on Strategic Problems and Principles*
- *Certain Tactical Principles for Comrades Undertaking Guerrilla Operations*
- *Organizational Questions*
- *O Guerrilheiro,* newspaper of the Brazilian revolutionary groups.

Personal Qualities of the Urban Guerrilla

His bravery and decisive nature characterize the urban guerrilla. He must be a good tactician and a good shot. The urban guerrilla must be a "person of great astuteness to compensate for the fact that he is not sufficiently strong in arms, ammunition, and equipment. The career militarists or the government police have modern arms and transport, and can go about anywhere freely, using the force of their power. The urban guerrilla does not have such resources at his disposal and leads a clandestine existence. Sometimes he is a convicted person or is out on parole and is obliged to use false documents.

Nevertheless, the urban guerrilla has a certain advantage over the conventional military or the police. It is that, while the military and the police act on behalf of the enemy, whom the people hate, the urban guerrilla defends a just cause, which is the people's cause.

The urban guerrilla's arms are inferior to the enemy's, but from a moral point of view, the urban guerrilla has an undeniable superiority. This moral superiority is what sustains the urban guerrilla. Thanks to it, the urban guerrilla can accomplish his principal duty, which is to attack and to survive. The urban guerrilla has to capture or divert arms from the enemy to be able to fight. Because his arms are not uniform, since what he has are expropriated or have fallen into hands in different ways, the urban guerrilla faces the problem of a variety of arms and a shortage of ammunition. Moreover, he has no place to practice shooting and

marksmanship. These difficulties have to be surmounted, forcing the urban guerrilla to be imaginative and creative, qualities without which it would be impossible for him to carry out his role as a revolutionary.

The urban guerrilla must possess initiative, mobility, and flexibility, as well as versatility and a command of any situation. Initiative especially is an indispensable quality. It is not always possible to foresee everything. And the urban guerrilla cannot let himself become confused, or wait for orders. His duty is to act, to find adequate solutions for each problem he faces, and not to retreat. It is better to err acting than to do nothing for fear of erring. Without initiative there is no urban guerrilla warfare.

Source: Carlos Marighella. *Mini-Manual of the Urban Guerrilla.* (Pamphlet, 1969) pp. 1-2.

From the U.S. and international perspectives the specter of **Lebanese Hezbollah** and **Hamas** may be a subject for consideration. The areas of Brazil that border Argentina and Paraguay are also home to a large Arab population, and although any links to the al Qaeda have not yet been uncovered, there is significant interest in the financial support systems in place for Hezbollah and Hamas activities.

URUGUAY, PARAGUAY

In comparison to other Latin American states, Uruguay seemed to have an advantage with a prosperous economy, built upon its sugar growing and its export market. However, as has been evidenced in other regions of the world, the onset of severe economic downturns have led to the rise of worker parties, student revolts and such. This was the scenario with Uruguay, when the economy crashed in the late 1950s. With the collapse came unrest, high unemployment and inflation. The sugar workers had already organized labor unions to speak on their behalf, and by the end of the 1950s the union was being led and influenced by extreme elements demanding social reforms and justice. Confrontation was the ultimate result.

National Liberation Movement (MLN): The Tupamaros

This movement grew out of the disillusionment of unionists, who marched on Montevideo, the capital, in 1962. The confrontations with police in the capital ended in numerous arrests. The government was unsympathetic to union demands, and rather than listen to their claims, portrayed them as insurgents and guerillas. A law student who was arrested during one of the clashes rose to form the MLN. Raul Sendic emerged from a brief spell in prison bitter and determined to fight back. The government imposed more restrictions on rights and freedoms, which forged the beginnings of terrorism in Uruguay. Largely an agricultural country, Uruguay is situated on the Atlantic Ocean and borders the River Plate. To mount an effective campaign, the group decided that its base and battleground would be the streets of Montevideo. The aim of the MLN was not to replace the government, but to force issues and change policy for the redistribution of wealth. Although the MLN espoused Marxist theories, it did not engage in rhetoric at the expense of support from the public. By the end of the 1960s, the Tupamaros had grown significantly, and were believed to number more than 2,000. The combatants had no doubt studied the *Mini-Manual of the Urban Guerrilla* for their approach and their tactics tended to mirror Marighella's teachings. For support and supplies they depended on bank robberies and kidnapping officials for ransom. Their methods became an example for other terror groups operating in urban centers of the world.

The police in Uruguay were unable to stop the growing surge of the Tupamaros. With the democratic fabric now in tatters, the police resorted to torture to extract information and to deter would-be Tupamaros. Many suspected members of the MLN ended up in the country's top security prison, the Penal de Libertad under the control of the county's secret police, the Organismo Coordinador de Actividades Anti-Subversivas.[21] Methods of torture were cruel, inhuman and effective, and included rapes, burning, electrical shocks and sleep deprivation.

The end for the Tupamaros was not as might have been expected. The chaos they had brought to the cities forced the government into a more vigorous application of repressive measures. In other words, in classic fashion, the Tupamaros' brand of terror forced the government to respond with its own brand of terror. However, the Tupamaros sought respectability and began to align with left wing political movements to replace the government at the polling booth. This was a disaster, as left wing constituents did not favor terrorism and the bid for a socialist ticket failed. As socialists, they should have expected support from the working classes but MLN was made up mainly of middle-class Uruguayans. With the failure of the political movement, a strong right wing military government came into power. Its draconian measures in curbing the Tupamaros were endorsed by the populace, and resulted in mass arrests and the end of MLN. The kidnapping of the British ambassador, Sir Geoffrey Jackson, in Montevideo in 1972 ultimately shattered the myth that the Tupamaros were invincible. Shortly after his release from captivity, a general election was held and the *Frente Amplio* (Broad Front) a strong political supporter of the Tupamaros was decimated at the polls. The government was returned to office with a clear mandate to end terrorism.

The Tupamaros served as an example of how to organize an effective strike force of terrorists in an urban environment, using the city for cover, following the advice of the *Mini-Manual of the Urban Guerrilla*. Other such terror groups have profited from this example in Northern Ireland and in West Germany. The tactics employed by these middle-class terrorists, as saviors of the poor of Montevideo, did not translate into popular support for the movement. To some extent their organization was built on small independent units, and a cell-like structure, also a hallmark of the Irish Republican Army.

Internationally, countries in South America could become havens for Middle East and North African terrorist groups, not just a sanctuary but a fertile recruiting, logistical and financing center. Uruguay does not figure on the world map of terrorism but is an outspoken supporter of antiterrorism conventions in the region. The presence of al-Said Hassan Mokhles, a suspected Armed Islamic Group (GIA) member, was discovered in Uruguay and his presence immediately brought a request for extradition from Egypt where he was wanted on terrorist offences. GIA does have links with al Qaeda and many Algerians have migrated to North America, in particular Canada, over the last two decades. Uruguay has also become a home base for the Chilean urban Marxist guerrilla movement the Manuel Rodriguez Patriotic Front.

ARGENTINA

Argentina has suffered through systematic human rights violations, under the political will and control of strict military juntas since the mid 1970s. In order to escape the problems at home, the Argentine military government called on the historic claims of the nation to the Malvinas Islands (Falkland Islands) deep in the South Atlantic. Argentina had for the past century claimed title to the islands, which were populated by British families. Before the battle for the Falklands, Argentine's military had attempted to "remove" all political opponents to its regime. This was achieved by clandestine arrests, which were followed by the complete disappearance of those arrested. Bodies that had been dumped in the ocean were pulled up in fishing nets showing signs of brutalization and torture.

Before World War II, Argentina had close ties to Germany. However, in 1945 the new government of General Farrell severed its links and joined the allies in the defeat of Germany. Two of the most celebrated names associated with South American politics are those of Colonel Juan Domingo Peron and his equally famous wife, Eva. Peron was almost certainly responsible for initiating the use of what is now termed "death squads" in Argentina. His vision on coming to power as president in 1946 was to industrialize the nation at the expense of the agricultural industry, which had been the economic mainstay of for most of the century. With industrialization and heavy government spending came inflation at a staggering rate never before seen in Argentina. Left wing political opposition to Peron's activities mounted, and as the 1950s arrived, Argentina was sliding down a dangerous slope, where food shortages and protests were the order of the day. In response, Peron nationalized the press and took total control over what was printed in the media. In 1949, he had created his own secret police force known as the **CERT**. CERT and its later version, the Division de Informacion Politicas Antidemocratic (DIPA) hid within its ranks a group designed for torture and repression called the Triple A or the Argentine Anti-Communist Alliance. Peron was deposed in 1955, three years after the death of Eva Peron.

The Triple A (AAA)

This was an extreme right wing death squad that functioned clandestinely at the beginning of the 1970s and consisted of members of the Argentine military and police. Many people suspected of being left wing sympathizers were abducted, usually in the very early hours of the morning. The captors would explain that they were government agents. Death camps were set up apart from the normal prison structures of the country, making it almost impossible for relatives to locate those taken, let alone establish the agency that had detained them. There were forty-seven of these secret camps, which were similar to the concentration camps built by the Nazis.[22] As the years of unceasing military repression grew, so did the pressure from the Red Cross and Amnesty International to make the military juntas accountable for those missing. In a remarkable piece of legislation passed by the Argentine government in 1979, those who were missing were presumed legally dead unless it could be proved otherwise!

Montoneros

One of the military junta's main targets were the **Montoneros** and their supporters. Set up as a left wing Peronist movement after the death of Juan Peron, they were active from 1975–1979. The Montoneros were violently opposed to the military takeover of the Argentine government. They attempted to organize the union movement as a cohort in their activities, but a brutal crackdown by the junta prevented any effective action in the cities and the group had to settle for actions in the countryside. Their tactics were hit-and-run, using bombings and shootings. By 1979, the group had been totally destroyed.[23] This is yet another example of how an extreme right wing military government resorting to terrorism of its own to remain in control, by using torture, murder and widespread intimidation.

CHILE

As a sad century of military dictatorships in Central, Southern and Latin America drew to a close, the only active terror group in Chile was a splinter group called the Manuel Rodriguez Patriotic Front (FPMR). Active in the 1980s was the Lautaro Youth Movement, which was a mixed bag of disillusioned youths, leftist elements, and criminals.

One of the most significant influences in Chile over the past twenty years was General Augusto Pinochet, a military dictator of fascist principles, who is today considered by many in Chile to be an elder statesman of the country. Few dictators ever successfully reach happy retirement, but Pinochet is an example of one who has "gone the distance," despite the appalling acts during his tenure. Pinochet swept to power during a bloody military coup in 1973, which removed the Marxist regime responsible for the mismanagement of the country and its economy over a three-year period.

The Marxist leader Salvador Allende was the first democratically elected Marxist president to head a nation in the western Hemisphere. Allende came to power in 1970, on a ticket promising social programs for Chileans. His government took immediate control of the country's copper mines and banking system. His huge increase in the minimum wage structure and attempts to keep the cost of consumer products at a low level fueled runaway inflation. Inflation between 1971 and 1973 rose by nearly 400%! The government was besieged on all sides. Violent protests began in the streets of Santiago. The military, assisted by the CIA, overthrew the Allende government on September 11, 1973. Allende was arrested and died in custody. Reports on the circumstances of his death vary from torture, execution and suicide.

The Pinochet Years

The military takeover followed by the installation of yet another junta was not widely accepted. Fighting broke out between right wing supporters of Pinochet and the extreme left communist elements. The junta cracked down hard on all opposition by dissolving congress, restricting the freedom of the press, and privatizing what had formerly been nationaled industries. Pinochet banned all political opposition parties and ran the country as a dictatorship. The trigger point for the attempted coup was not a momentary aberration on the part of Pinochet, in fact many of the high-ranking military generals actually served in the Allende Cabinet. What caused the problems for the military was the inclusion of left wing extremism into the fabric of Chile's society. Allende had placed communist reactionaries in the armed forces to incite rebellion, and over 14,000 foreign agitators moved into Chile. These included Cuban DGI agents, who were in Chile to reorganize internal security for Allende, as well as Soviet, Czech and North Korean military instructors and arms suppliers and hard-line Spanish Communist Party members. Their intent was to organize revolutionary brigades to take on the established military. The 1970s were a decade of change for Central and South America, and insurgent terror groups and guerrilla movements were on the move from Montevideo to Managua.[24]

To stem the flow of left wing subversives, the Pinochet junta carried out mass arrests and used torture to gain both information and confessions. He arrested not only Chileans, but also foreign subversive elements. These are the actions for which the international communities want him held accountable. Executions were commonplace in Chile, and the targets were leftist politicians, trade unionists, and other activists. Many simply disappeared, never to be heard from again. The junta engaged a semi-official death squad organization to do some of its dirty work. The Avengers of the Martyrs was a fascist paramilitary movement comprised mainly of military and police/security personnel. To make sure the security and paramilitary groups could conduct business in an unfettered manner, a decree was passed by the military to effectively denude the legal process and protection of the public. The Decree Law on Amnesty gave total and unequivocal immunity from arrest and prosecution for all security forces since Pinochet's coup.

The Pinochet military regime laid the foundation for a vibrant South American economy and passed it on to a democratic government that followed. Pinochet had turned Chile from a second-rate, Third-World country into a strong market economy, one that is being emulated in the 1990s. Military dictators usually leave in the same violent manner by which they arrived in power, but **General Pinochet** is considered by many in Chile to be a hero of the people—and to a great many others as a despot and murderer.

In 1998, on a visit to Britain for back surgery, General Pinochet was arrested in his hospital bed. Now into his eighties, he faces claims of torture inflicted by his regime and requests for his extradition. The highest court in Britain dealt a stunning blow to Pinochet, and in a stand for international law and justice, the British have hammered a nail into a portion of his coffin. Pinochet and the democratic government of Chile claimed he had diplomatic immunity as a former head of state and was therefore not subject to arrest and extradition. In the majority decision handed down in November 1998, Lord Nicholls commented that "the Vienna Convention on diplomatic relations may confer immunity in respect of acts performed in the exercise of functions which international law recognizes as functions of a head of state irrespective of the terms of his domestic constitution." Lord Nicholls further commented that "it hardly needs saying that the torture of his own subjects, or of aliens, would not be regarded by international law as a function of a head of state."[25] Reactions to the decision in Santiago have led to waves of protest as well as outpourings of relief. Whether the democracy that Pinochet has resurrected in Chile can survive remains to be seen. Certainly any frailty of the system may invite left wing advances on the power base of government and a return to Marxism. Pinochet subsequently returned to Chile and stood trial in what was termed the "Caravan of Death" political killings that were orchestrated soon after he swept to power in 1973 and unleashed death squads to systematically execute political prisoners and subversives throughout the country. A ruling came down in March 2001 which was then appealed to the Chilean Supreme Court which in July 2002 accepted the findings of the earlier ruling that the former dictator was mentally unfit to stand trial. Now in his eighties, the former General suffers from senile dementia as well as having had several strokes. To many his passing will be a fitting end to his regimes horrendous abuse of civil liberties. On the international terror front Chile experienced two terror-related incidents. In the wake of the 9–11 attacks, the U.S. Embassy received a functional letter bomb, and an anthrax-laced letter was sent to a doctor's office, however the composition of the anthrax did not match with those in the domestic U.S. attacks. In a wider investigation, the Government of Chile began to take a serious interest in the activities of Lebanese businessman Assad Ahmed Mohamed Barakat. It is suspected that Barakat is involved in financial holdings and money transfers for the Lebanese Hezbollah terror group.

VENEZUELA

Venezuela might be considered a democratic oasis in a desert of military dictatorships. Unlike much of Latin America, this country has had a history of democratic government since 1958, with lessening interference by the military. Venezuela suffers minor incursions by Colombian terrorists in the border villages and towns. Kidnapping and extortion are the main activities of both the National Liberation Army (ELN) and the Colombian Peoples Liberation Army (EPL).

Since the independence movement led by Venezuela's favorite son, **Simon Bolivar,** in the early 1800s, the country had been the home to a succession of military dictators. Venezuela began to prosper with the discovery of petroleum, which became its main source of revenue. Mismanagement and corruption ended the military dictatorship of General Gomez in 1935, when the democratic movement, supported by the army, overthrew him and established a democratic government. The country has been ruled by two parties since 1958, the Accion Democratica (AD) and the Christian Democratic Party (COPIE). Each has had its share of periods in office. However, economic downturns have stalled government action on behalf of the many poverty stricken Venezuelans. Although there is no active terror movement in the country, there are definite signs that reforms will be needed if democracy is to endure. The government has utilized severe measures to control the country in tough economic times and the former leader of the 1992 military coup, Lieutenant Colonel Hugo Chavez, has made a successful leap into the current political system. General elections were held in December 1998, and Chavez won the presidency with a plurality of 56.5%, for a five-year term.[26]

Many of the problems facing the existing government involve corruption at the highest levels as well as drug smuggling and money laundering. The United States is one of Venezuela's main import and export partners and has, on the surface, made some effort to deter the drug traffic. With poverty so widespread and little light at the end of the economic tunnel, a different style of government as emerged. There are also problems associated with cross border incursions from Colombia and the probability that the Venzuelan government has been turning a blind eye to such actions. For the landowners and ranchers in the border regions this has meant reliance on vigilante squads and support from AUC in Colombia to combat the FARC incursions into Venezuela. The embattled President Hugo Chavez has had to contend with a coup attempt in April 2002, which briefly saw him ousted from power. The probability of a further military coup has subsided but the worries for the middle classes especially in the capital Caracas continue to persist. They fear that another coup will see the poorer elements in Venezuela rise and target the mainly middle-class and wealthy suburbs of the capital. What will likely then happen is a civil uprising with the middle classes being protected by the military—such events can only lead to a civil war in Venezuela.

By the end of 2002, the country's middle class population had become increasingly disturbed by the Chavez Government. A general strike was called in November 2002, which shut down Venezuela's oil industry. Noticeably the television news coverage by U.S. broadcast media had failed to note that this strike was not being led by the working class masses but by the middle class management populous. In its attempt to unseat Chavez the Opposition party has attempted to illicit support for a coup from the United States, however the Bush government was more concerned with global issues involving Iraq and North Korea to pay too much attention to Venezuela. Chavez has managed to retain control of the military and will likely continue to do so as long as the government does not attempt to use force against the strikers. The opposition has also launched a campaign to discredit the government by stating Chavez close association and ties to Cuban President Fidel Castro. They have alleged that Cuba has been reinforcing troops loyal to Chavez. This type of rhetoric has failed to impress the United States and neither has comments that Chavez's government sent financial aid to the Taliban and al Qaeda. With the general strike beginning to falter the best hope for opposition groups is as much violence as possible, and that is an action that the Chavez government have skillfully managed to avoid. The outlook for the country remains bleak and much will depend on the military and how long it will support the peoples President.

ECUADOR

Ecuador is not a region well known for terrorism and insurgency and in the last years of the last decade remained relatively calm with the exception of the October 12, 2000, kidnapping of eight oil rig workers by armed men that lasted into early 2001. The hostage takers executed one of the U.S. hostages named Ron Sander. A little-known group calling itself the Revolutionary Armed Forces of Ecuador has taken credit for two bombs that exploded recently in the coastal city of Guayaquil. The FARE could be a front for the Revolutionary Armed Forces of Colombia (FARC) or a stand-alone group. Either way, its emergence suggests the Colombian conflict soon will affect U.S. personnel and assets outside Colombia. In August 2002, a bomb attack on a McDonalds restaurant was claimed to be the work of an unknown terror group calling itself the FARE. The FARE state they are a prodigy of the Revolutionary Armed Forces of Colombia (FARC), and that it threatens more violence and assassination. At this juncture very little is known about the group, its make-up or its aims, however there is a probability that this could be a breakaway faction of the FARC, and could be setting up in Ecuador to make the politicians wary of being aligned with the U.S. war on narcotics in the region. Elections scheduled for October 2002 could also be a focal point for the FARE if its wish is to influence any political outcome. Authorities have previously reported the presence of FARE, but no terror attacks have been previously attributed to the group—which authorities say may number several hundred members from both Ecuador and Colombia. The FARE do not appear to be linked to drug trafficking, however if they are actually FARC by another name, then narcotics trafficking may soon be on their agenda.

SUMMARY

Central and South America have been under strong right wing military rule for many decades of the twentieth century. They have also suffered the ravages of death squads. In studying the causes of terrorism and guerrilla activity throughout Latin America, there are trends which become apparent. In Mexico, El Salvador, Chile and Uruguay, much that took place was related to land claims, where the few wealthy landowners had immense influence in the ruling political and military governments. In protecting those interests, the extreme right death squads operated with impunity. Violations of human rights and the prosecution of those responsible continue to the present. General Pinochet, the former Chilean dictator has escaped the possibility of trial due to his senility. Argentina is recovering from the stringent rule of the military juntas of the 1980s and crushing humiliation and defeat in the Falkland Islands at the hands of the British. The loss of loved ones to death squads will continue to plague the citizens of new democracies as they strive to move forward. The 38 years of Colombian terrorism seems likely to continue with an upsurge in attacks by FARC and an ever-increasing number of paramilitaries ranged against it and its supporters. South American countries still lead the way in kidnappings and extortion. The presence of Lebanese Hezbollah and Hamas members as well as the GIA will prompt U.S. power brokers to keep close watch on developments to ensure that international terrorism with aims of attacking the United States and U.S. interests is not played out in the region.

TERMS TO REMEMBER

Abimael Guzman

Armed Forces of
Colombia (FARC)

"Banana Republics"

Cali

CERT

Chiapas

Contras

ELZN

EPR

General Pinochet

Hamas

Lebanese Hezbollah

Montoneros

MRTA

North American Free
Trade Agreement
(NAFTA)

Rebel Armed Forces
(FAR)

Sandinista

Shining Path

Simon Bolivar

the National Liberation
Army (ELN)

United Self-Defense
Forces of Colombia
(AUC)

urban guerillas

URNG

REVIEW QUESTIONS

1. Discuss the insurgency issues and why the Mexican Government has been unable to settle the problems in the Chiapas region.
2. Describe how the death squads were used and the reasons for them in Venezuela.
3. Who were the Sandinistas, and how were they a factor in the United States policy in Central America?
4. Discuss the reasons for the increase in paramilitary groups in Colombia.
5. Discuss the threat to U.S. security from Middle East terror groups based in South America.
6. Trace the origins of the Shining Path in Peru and their methods for influencing the government and bordering states.

ENDNOTES

1. *The Economist,* January 12, 2002, Mexico, Post Rebellion Pains, p. 35.
2. Frank M. Afflitto. Abstract from a paper presented at the Conference of the American Society of Criminology, November 20, 1997. San Diego, California.
3. Global Intelligence Update. http://www.stratfor.com/standard/analysis.
4. *Patterns of Global Terrorism,* United States Department of State, Publication 10321. http://www.stratfor.com.
5. Jonathan R. White. *Terrorism an Introduction,* Brooks Cole Publishing: Belmont, California, p. 157.
6. *Kerry Committee Report,* April 19, 1995.
7. U.S. State Department International Information Programs, Grossman Outlines Terrorist Threat to Colombia. Testimony by Ambassador Marc Grossman, Under Secretary of State for

Political Affairs before the Senate Committee on Foreign Relations Sub-committee for Western Hemisphere Affairs. April 24, 2002, http://usinfo.state.gov/topical/pol/terror.htm.

8. *Patterns of Global Terrorism, 1997.* United States Department of State, April 1998. http://www.state.gov/s/ct/rls/pgtrpt/1998.htm.

9. Stan Yarbo, "Death Squads Seek Negotiations," *The Christian Science Monitor,* June 18, 1990, p. 3.

10. *National Post* May 27, 2002 "Alvaro Uribe father was killed by guerrillas in 1983." Reuters, Agence France-Presse Report.

11. Stan Yarbo, *The Christian Science Monitor,* November 18, 1998.

12. Ibid.

13. U.S. Department of State International Information Programs April 25th 2002. U.S., Colombia Investigate Expansion of Terrorist Alliances. Charlene Porter Washington, File Staff Writer. http://usinfo.state.gov/topical/pol/terror02042500.htm.

14. Sam Dillon, "As Peru Votes, Insurgents Mystique Casts Shadow." *Miami Herald,* June 10, 1990, pp. 1A, 26A.

15. Jonathan R. White, *Terrorism an Introduction* (West/Wadsworth Publishing Co, Belmont Ca. 1998) p. 82.

16. "The Shining Path comes back," *The Economist,* August 17, 1996, p. 35.

17. Gabriel Escobar, "Peruvian guerrillas hold hundreds hostage." Washington Post, Foreign Service. December 19, 1996.

18. CNN Interactive World News, "One hostage killed in daring Peru rescue." CNN, April 22, 1997, http://www.cnn.com/world19704/22/peru.update.late.

19. Strategic Forecasting, Stratfor.com, Feb. 27th 2002 http://www.stratfor.com.

20. N. A. Keck, CPP, ASIS presentation paper, May 16th, 1996, American Society for International Security paper.

21. Bruce Quarrie, "*The World's Secret Police,*" (Octopus Books Ltd., London 1986), p. 48.

22. Ibid.

23. White, *Terrorism an Introduction,* p. 48. Terrorism an Introduction. Jonathan R. White, Brooks/Cole, USA 1991, p. 49.

24. Arnaud de Borchgrave, "Demonized for killing a left-wing plot," *The Washington Times,* October 27, 1998, p. A-15.

25. International News, *The Globe and Mail,* Canada Thursday November 26, 1998.

26. Steven Gutkin, *Associated Press,* November 28, 1998.

PART THREE
Counterterrorism

Airport security upgrades, Washington Ronald Reagan Airport, October 2001. (AP Photo/Doug Mills)

13 Countering Terrorism

"What is coming to the Americans, will not, by the will of God, be less than what has come."

Sulayman Abu Ghayth, al Qaeda spokesman,
on Al-Jazeera Radio broadcast, June 23, 2002.

OVERVIEW

We have heard so many times that since 9–11 our lives have changed forever. In many respects that is true. The way we have responded to security needs and our overall concern for our safety has become a discussion topic for almost everyone. Many might use the famous French saying in regard to airport security, *"tous le change, tous le meme chose,"* meaning "the more things change the more things stay the same." To underscore the reasons that countering terrorism is so vital to democratic survival is also found in the insatiable appetite of the media. **"The War on Terrorism"** was carried on major networks twenty-four hours a day and seven days a week for more than nine months after the attacks in New York and Washington. Every small-bladed knife that gets through a security check at an airport, or unattended bag is suddenly a cause for headline news. The public is now conditioned more than ever before to be cognizant of security. The faults, the failings and the endless debates continue: what to do next, where will the next attack come from, how will we respond, are we equipped to defend against it, will it be biological, nuclear or chemical, does the United States go after Saddam Hussein or not? All have had extensive airing on the audio, visual and written news media. In this chapter we will examine the special types of organizations that concerned countries have established as the up-front forces to specifically deal with hostage takings and terrorist-related events. Nations use different tactics and methods to deal with terrorist issues and we will see how the democracies of the world mix military with civilian police operations. The methods used to gather information about suspected terror groups and individuals will also be discussed, along with some of the most effective and recognized response units for countering terrorism.

The student will be shown how difficult it is for covert operations by forces against terrorism to respect suspected terrorists' civil liberties, and how easily such efforts conflict with their mission in a democratic society this fact was graphically emphasized by the news pictures of al Qaeda/Taliban fighters under guard at Guantanamo Bay. The need for inter-agency and intra-agency cooperation and the free flow of information between those agencies will be examined, particularly in the aftermath of the events of 9–11, where the failings of the intelligence community have been exposed.

The student will understand the need for nations to develop a trained and specifically designated organization that can be held responsible for responding to terrorist incidents while maintaining civil liberties on a scale acceptable to the public in general. We will examine the important part that the media plays, as does the public, in the critical intelligence-gathering role. The student will gain an appreciation of how an effective counterterrorism agency must gain the acceptance of the public it serves in order for its efforts to stem the flow of terrorist activity. Questions surrounding the security of aviation and other forms of transport and transportation will also be looked at, some of the failings will be discussed along with the history behind aviation security and the dangers we continue to face from terrorism in the aviation arena.

THE ROLES FOR COUNTERTERRORISM

Are the actions of subversive groups and insurgents terrorist or criminal? In many countries legislation has been enacted not only to ban membership in terror organizations, but to sometimes allow for certain suspensions of civil rights to facilitate law enforcement and intelligence activities. To implement such actions successfully in a western democracy requires that the government ensure that such legislation requires renewal on a regular basis. In the United Kingdom, the legislation restricting the Irish Republican Army and other terrorist groups required the government to regularly justify its need for such drastic powers, because without such justification it would automatically lapse.

The tactics of the terrorists that strike fear in the public for political gain are well documented. This has been clearly shown in the United Kingdom, where the Provisional IRA has waged a continuous campaign of indiscriminate violence against the authorities and innocent civilians. One of the earliest terror incidents in Great Britain was an attack on the Parachute Regiment Officers Mess in Aldershot, which is located about fifty miles southwest of London. It was viewed by many as reprisal for the Bloody Sunday massacre by British paratroopers in Northern Ireland. (Refer back to Chapter 4.) The reaction depicted in local and national press coverage and on the television news was complete outrage at such a senseless act. Immediately after the bombing, there were sporadic incidents against local Irish families, who were intimidated and even assaulted. The same reaction occurred after the Guilford and Birmingham bombings. Calls for restraint from both ends of the British political and religious spectrum, went out quickly, and diffused a major outpouring of hatred against the several million Irish citizens who have coexisted peacefully alongside their English counterparts and Welsh and Scottish neighbors. In the same vein, the events of 9–11 allowed a frantic American public to think that every Muslim or Arab was a terrorist in waiting; and the way we viewed our ethnically different neighbors suddenly changed. It would most certainly be incorrect to cast a suspicious eye at every "Muslim-looking" person. In the same way, we cannot characterize any group purely by their religious beliefs. Every Catholic is not by any stretch of the imagination a supporter of the Provisional Irish Republican Army and neither must we now make the mistake that every Middle Eastern person is branded as an Islamic extremist. Immigration came under specific scrutiny in both the United States and Canada, and also the methods by which student and visitor visas were issued and how checks are made. Our problem as Americans, if in fact it is considered a problem, unlike some less than democratic countries, is that we enjoy a free and open democracy, where we value the freedom of speech, the freedom of association and our ability to travel without hindrance. This is in stark contrast to many countries where such liberties are not available. The events of 9–11 were perpetrated by people who took advantage of those freedoms and liberties that we hold dear, and they would attempt to destroy those values and freedoms.

Maintaining Order

The example of the Irish Troubles has been remarkable in many respects. In Britain and Northern Ireland, the role of the police had always been very public, and the typical British "Bobby" was always on hand to assist. During the

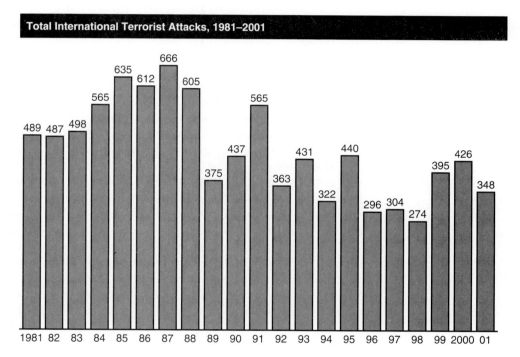

Total International Terrorist Attacks, 1981–2001

In past years, serious violence by Palestinians against other Palestinians in the occupied territories was included in the database of worldwide international terrorist incidents because Palestinians are considered stateless people. This resulted in such incidents being treated differently from intraethnic violence in other parts of the world. In 1989, as a result of further review of the nature of intra-Palestinian violence, such violence stopped being included in the US Government's statistical database on international terrorism. The figures shown above for the years 1984 through 1988 have been revised to exclude intra-Palestinian violence, thus making the database consistent.

Investigations into terrorist incidents sometimes yield evidence that necessitates a change in the information previously held true (such as whether the incident fits the definition of international terrorism, which group or state sponsor was responsible, or the number of victims killed or injured). As a result of these adjustments, the statistics given in this report may vary slightly from numbers cited in previous reports.

Source: Patterns of Global Terrorism. US Department of State. Statistical Reviews *2001.*

International Terrorist Attacks, 1981–2001. (U.S. Department of State)

terrorist campaign of bombing on the mainland of Britain, the police did not resort to a system of rigid rules and control. As has been evidenced in many Latin American countries, threats and intimidation by terrorist actions have too often been met by even harsher measures inflicted by military police. In the British experience, terror against the public in general reached almost epidemic proportions in the 1970s. But order and calm prevailed and the public outrage was contained. Rather than form vigilante groups to hunt down suspected terrorists, the public and media were fully supportive of the police actions. The police were shown, on TV news coverage, as the front-line troops, always the first on the scene of whatever new atrocity that had been perpetrated by the IRA. London in the 1970s became a virtual battleground, but sound police tactics and investigative techniques did far more to bring the criminal terrorists to justice than the suspension of any civil liberties might have.

In many countries throughout the world, armed and aggressive police are a reality. That norm was not the case in Great Britain, where police were unarmed throughout the IRA crisis. The police adhered to their role of identifying, tracking down and apprehending terrorists as they would any criminal. Police investigations are all about the necessity to gather information, intelligence and ultimately evidence. Britain's Special Branch, which deals with terrorists, took the lead gathering intelligence on subversive Irish groups operating in Northern Ireland and Great Britain. Success for such efforts, however, must be a result of cooperation between police, the public and the media. As has been seen in the United States, cooperation between agencies can be strained. Some jealously guard not only sources, but information as well. Usually, the public is the last to know the true story. There are no simple right or wrong tactics in combating terrorists. There are, however, many examples of how and how not to deal with terrorist situations.

The **Balcombe Street** siege was a botched IRA action in which a group of armed terrorists held an elderly couple hostage in their central London home. The Metropolitan Police handled the stand-off, which was captured by television for all to see, effectively and decisively. What may also have caused the terrorists to give up was the leaked briefing to the press that the Special Air Service (SAS), Britain's elite military counter terrorist unit, were en route to assist the police, and the terrorists wanted nothing to do with that elite paramilitary organization. (The SAS will be discussed later on in this chapter.) The most open display of police weaponry is seen at London's Heathrow Airport, which has been the site of numerous false alarms as well as actual bombings and mortar attacks. The message is clearly sent that the police are ready to respond with overwhelming force.

Repression

To determine whether repressive actions by the state against terror are effective, one only has to examine the Soviet Union before the fall of the communist regime. Very few, if any, terrorist attacks were either recorded or reported in the former Soviet Union, which had a thriving community of secret police and thousands of informers in every sector of business and society. This made it very difficult, if not impossible, for subversive ideas to become reality. The KGB would almost certainly snuff out such plots before they became action.

Yet, with the break-up of the Soviet Union we have witnessed criminal activity as well as terrorism on a massive scale. The question to be asked is why did that happen in this society? The fall of the Soviet Union was so sudden, the Russian Federation of States underwent such rapid change, that it brought about the collapse of their structured and well-supported police service. In a vast empire that had relied on a state police for all forms of investigations and tactics, both overt and covert, there was now chaos. Now the time was right for criminal and subversive elements to move in and take advantage of weak controls. The drastic reduction in the need for nuclear weapons capability created a ready illegal market in which radical terroristic governments could acquire nuclear technology and even devices, especially if they could bid at the highest prices.

Great Britain since the 1990s is a very different battleground altogether. With ever-increasing demands on civilian police forces, they have adopted a significant "Big Brother" approach to their duties, maintaining a watchful eye on the communities they serve. Closed-circuit television cameras to monitor the heart of the major cities, as well as the network of major motorway systems, have aided in the search for serious criminals and terrorists. Civil libertarians and extreme left wing agitators may argue that is an invasion of privacy, but the police have had indisputable success in tracking down terrorists in London who abandon vehicles packed with explosives.

To many observers, it would have been an acceptable solution in the wake of the IRA bombing campaign to unleash the army against what were perceived to be vicious and callous terrorists. One must keep in mind that an army's main role is that of national defense, not policing. The use of the U.S. Marines in Somalia demonstrated the futility of policing with a military combat unit. In Northern Ireland, when the local (formerly) Royal Ulster Constabulary was unable to protect Catholics from Protestant terrorism, the army was called in to "assist." That assistance to the Catholic community was also the rallying call for the under-equipped Irish Republican Army of the day. As matters further deteriorated at the end of the 1960s, the army was brought into a policing role that involved searches of houses for weapons. At the very least, their actions were heavy handed, and the soldiers became the objects of hatred and scorn for the local Catholics they were attempting to protect.

Military responses to terror events have also been graphically emphasized by the Israeli use of heavy armor, helicopters and fighter aircraft to attack elements of Hamas in the West Bank and Gaza regions. The effect of the campaign by Israel in 2002 was to identify locations where suspected terrorist leaders were, and then hit them with extreme force. The issue with this is that Israel is actually targeting areas where civilians will become part of the damage ratio. Collateral damage can always occur where terrorists are concerned, however firing rockets into densely packed apartment buildings with the express intention to kill one suspected terrorist will invariably result in the deaths of many innocent civilians. The international community questions these actions by Israel. Of note here is that it has been neither a total success in curtailing the never-ending cycle of violence both in Israeli cities nor the Palestinian areas of the West Bank and Gaza Strip. From Israel's perspective their intelligence network has become so efficient in targeting suspected terror elements that it is self-evident that targeting civilian areas will continue as a means of routing out the terrorists.

Northern Ireland

Without using the ultimate weapon of imposing martial law in Northern Ireland, the British government used a statutory instrument to control the lawlessness of the terror groups operating against the security forces in the province. Special powers to deal with the present emergency came into effect in 1973. The Northern Ireland (Emergency Provisions) Act empowered the military to have a greater impact in dealing with the urban terrorists. "No go" areas in parts of Belfast and Londonderry had been springing up and fostering terrorists and supplying safe houses. The Emergency Provisions gave sweeping powers that would permit the searching of houses without the necessity of warrants from the civil courts. These searches were authorized to take place at any time and the security forces could detain and question anyone for up to four hours. These methods allowed the military to build up a significant database of information about the people of Northern Ireland. In the years from 1972 to 1976, nearly 250,000 houses were searched by the army, uncovering 5,800 weapons and 661,000 rounds of ammunition. Added to these powers was the internment of active members of terrorist organizations. Hundreds of Irishmen were interned in the 1970s and, in hindsight, brought the Provisional IRA to the brink of defeat. Nearly all its executive and operations groups are either serving prison sentences or interned.[1] The IRA's call for a Christmas truce in 1974 was made from a position of extreme weakness. After all, there was no way IRA demands for the total withdrawal of the British from Northern Ireland and general amnesty for all convicted terrorists would be met. It would be another twenty-four years before the IRA terrorists would walk out of prison as part of the Good Friday Agreement of 1998.

Legislation

Many operational methods and legislated practices can be put into place, but in a true and solid democracy there is the necessity to ensure that civil liberties are not abrogated to such an extent that the public is duly effected by its restrictive nature. Over the past thirty years there have been significant pieces of legislation and internationally recognized conventions aimed at curbing the activities of terrorists as well as countering their actions. The first major terror attacks attracting attention on a global scale involved hijacking of commercial airlines by terrorists from the PLO. Those attacks and the ineptitude of most governments in handling such crises prompted international anti-hijacking legislation to be drafted. These terrorist acts also prompted a more fundamental approach by one of the target states, Israel.

Israel was one of the first states to provide trained and armed **"sky marshals"** on all their aircraft around the world. Wherever there was an El Al flight, specially trained staff carried out stringent physical and profile security checks on every passenger boarding the flight. So effective was the El Al approach to handling security issues that the terrorists had to find a "soft underbelly" to attack. This, in several instances, was a ground level attack at airport check-in counters. There were also attempts to shoot down the aircraft by means of RPG-7 rockets, as was the case with the failed attack by Black September terrorists at Orly Airport in France.

The fundamental principle of international legislative instruments, such as the **Chicago Convention** and in particular **Annex 17,** was that they required member states to safeguard global air transportation from acts of unlawful interference. The Convention applied a common set of standards for the security of international civil aviation.

Terrorism and Aviation

9–11 opened the festering weaknesses so many have been used to seeing in our daily travels in North America: the inadequacies of the security program (or lack thereof) for protecting to any degree passengers flying out of international airports in the United States. It is our view that throughout the 1990s following the **President's Commission** findings that the FAA, which has the responsibility for safety of civil aviation and has an excellent body of staff with immense expertise, were severely hampered in their ability to make the changes needed to protect civil aviation from terror attacks inside the United States. This is in part due to funding issues for research and development of new technology and the powerful U.S. aviation lobby. Aviation now finds itself in the front line in the war against terrorism, a position it has actually been occupying since 1968!

It is important to appreciate that there are international conventions that cover protocols for dealing with hijackings and the like aside from the criminal statutes that nation states have promulgated to deal with individual criminal acts. The enacting of international treaties covers the issue of international terrorism and the hijacking of aircraft. The most significant conventions are as follows:

- **The Chicago Convention—December 1944**

  This convention was entered into force on April 4, 1947.[2]

  This treaty paved the way for the creation of the International Civil Aviation Organization (ICAO)—ICAO was designed to establish the standards for which international aviation and airports would comply and this would continue development through agreements that would be formed to cover hijackings in particular and also acts of interfering with the operation of aircraft both on the ground and in the air.

- **The Tokyo Convention—enacted September 14, 1963, and in force December 4, 1969**

  This convention stipulated the authority of the Captain of the flight and his authority to act: "if he had reasonable grounds to believe that an act has been or is about to be committed which is a threat to safety or good order and discipline on board the aircraft."

- **The Hague Convention December 16, 1970—Convention for the Suppression of Unlawful Seizure of Aircraft, in force October 1971**

  This agreement between the signatory states determined the process for investigation and detention of those involved in hijackings or attempted hijackings of aircraft. Agreement on cooperation between the state receiving the hijacked aircraft as well as the jurisdiction of registration is also covered in this convention.

- **The Montreal Convention September 23, 1971**

  This convention targets sabotage and destruction of aircraft and aviation facilities. It specifies, "Unlawfully and intentionally to perform an act of violence against a person either when that person is on board an aircraft in flight and the act is likely to endanger the safety of the aircraft or that person is at an airport serving international civil aviation and the act is likely to cause serious injury or death, to destroy an aircraft in service or to so damage it as to make the flight unsafe or impossible; to place or cause to be placed on board an aircraft in service by whatever means a substance likely to destroy it or so to damage it that it cannot fly or that its safety in flight is likely to be endangered; to destroy, damage, or interfere with the operation of air navigation facilities if it is likely to endanger the safety of an aircraft in flight; to communicate knowingly false information thereby endangering the safety of such an aircraft; to destroy or damage the facilities or an airport serving international civil aviation or damage aircraft not in service located on such an airport or disrupt the services of such an airport."

The formidable task for providing reasonable aviation security is well documented and no more graphically so than in a statement before the House of Representatives' Government Activities and Transportation Subcommittee in September 1989–one year after the Pan Am disaster over Lockerbie in Scotland. In this incident there were many human failings, which we will discuss later. However Homer Boynton Security Director of American Airlines stated to the Subcommittee that ". . . In 1988 ICAO estimated that worldwide 1.1 billion passengers flew on board 1100 commercial aircraft, on 38,000–40,000 flight segments. During this period one explosive device caused the awful aviation disaster over Lockerbie, Scotland. If one looks at these statistics in their totality, security personnel were seeking one explosive device carried by one passenger among 1.1 billion passengers.[3]

Taking Boynton's comments in the context of the tragic 9–11 events seems to underscore the point that even though security is there, they are not necessarily going to find anything. Unfortunately the U.S. system has been so deplorable for the last two decades it is almost surprising that such an event has not happened earlier. In addition, Boynton's comments would seem to point the finger at security screeners missing a bomb in baggage, when in fact that was not the specific case in Pan Am 103, as there were more factors to the inherent risk that passengers were taking by flying Pan Am in 1988. The President's Commission on Aviation and Terrorism concluded in 1990 that Pan Am was basically an accident waiting to happen and the incident was preventable. What are undisputed facts in this case are that a terrorist was able to place a bomb in a suitcase on board Pan Am 103, which detonated at 31,000 feet

TERRORISM BYTE 13–1

Hijacking in Europe, February 1972

Five Palestinians on a flight from Delhi to Greece hijack a German airliner belonging to Lufthansa Airlines. The hijackers divert the aircraft to Aden, in southern Yemen and release their hostages in exchange for $5 million. The authorities in turn released the hijackers after taking $1 million of the ransom.

killing 259 persons on the aircraft and 11 on the ground. If this was preventable perhaps it is important for the student at this point to understand how easy it was in 1988 for human elements to come into play. The FAA inspected Pan Am's operation at Frankfurt, West Germany, and they were concerned with the lack of a verifiable tracking system for interline bags, i.e. bags transferring from other airlines and the confused state of the passenger screening process. The FAA inspector wrote, "The system, trying to control approximately 4,500 passengers and 28 flights per day, is being held together only by a very labor-intensive operation and the tenuous threads of luck." The inspector then went onto condone the actions by adding, "it appears the minimum FAA requirements are being met." Luck however was not on the side of passengers of Pan Am 103. Among the many questions being asked after Lockerbie was "how did the interline bag get onto the flight?" It seems the answer to that is "With ease" given the vagaries of the systems at that time.

Reconciliation of passengers and baggage is a central issue. The requirement being that an aircraft on an international flight will only carry bags onboard for the passengers it has checked in. In other words, if a passenger transfers with baggage from another flight there must be a method to reconcile that passenger and his baggage; if the passenger does not fly, then neither does the bag. The other problem for Pan Am was that the processes for screening interline baggage was by an X-ray detection system. Even with the X-ray technology in place, the system was not capable of detecting the semtex explosive used in this attack. What could have been detected were the sources used to detonate the explosive and thus human error played a part as well as a lack of sufficient technology to detect this specific explosive. In Pan Am's defense they informed the President's Commission that the FAA Director of Aviation had given the airline verbal approval to X-ray interline bags rather than searching or reconciling them with passengers, which not surprisingly was denied by the FAA.

There are some eerie similarities to the intelligence failings in 1988 with what went wrong 13 years later on 9–11. Prior to the bombing of **Pan Am 103,** the intelligence community had received warnings that trouble was brewing in Europe. A total of nine security bulletins that could have had relevance to the Pan Am tragedy were issued between June and December 1988. One bulletin described how a Toshiba radio cassette player, containing a fully primed bomb together with a barometric trigger, was found by the West German police in a vehicle belonging to a member of the PFLP-GC. The FAA cautioned airlines that the device found by the West German authorities ". . . would be very difficult to detect via normal X-ray," and informed U.S. airlines that **passenger/baggage reconciliation** procedures should be rigorously applied." The specific threat received by the U.S. Embassy in Helsinki on December 5, 1988, detailing a threat that a woman would carry a bomb on board a Pan Am flight from Frankfurt in the following two weeks, was released by the FAA and was then redistributed by the U.S. State Department to U.S. Embassies. The U.S. Embassy in Moscow made the information public to the 2,000-member community of U.S. citizens including Moscow news media.[4]

Although there has been no evidence to link that threat with the actual bombing it is surprising that the Pan Am management and their security were not paying specific attention to baggage reconciliation. In view of the threat assessment by the FAA, there were significant lapses in stringent applications of the reconciliation process at Frankfurt on that fateful day in 1988. It is also important to know how impotent the FAA was in dealing with Pan Am's security problems. Even after the Lockerbie disaster, the FAA found numerous security discrepancies by Pan Am at both Frankfurt and London's Heathrow Airport. Almost six months after Lockerbie the FAA found major discrepancies at Pan Am's Frankfurt operation. The inspector's report on June 9, 1989, stated, "The posture of Pan Am is considered unsafe, all passengers flying out of Frankfurt on Pan Am are a great risk."[5] Concerning the attacks on the World Trade Center and the Pentagon, an anxious public is now fully aware the plot to attack aviation was brought to the attention of the FBI from flight training academies inside the United States, and from reports from its own agents. The failure of any resource to follow up on such intelligence is but one issue that led to the destruction on 9–11.

Security improvements in the 1990s, particularly in the light of the aforementioned President's commission, fell woefully short. The viewpoint of the FAA was basically that **'it won't happen here';** hijacking aircraft is not a North

Weapons removed from carry on baggage during routine passenger screening. (Courtesy CSI)

American problem and it is more fitted to the European and Eastern European regions of aviation. After all is said and done, no one has been injured by an act of terrorism against airliners flying within or from the United States. Cathal Flynn stated ". . . that in the decade since (Pan Am 103), amid attacks on other carriers no U.S. aircraft has been successfully attacked and not one person harmed on U.S. flag flights anywhere in the world, despite terrorist's determined efforts. This owes a great deal to strengthened intelligence and law enforcement efforts and to international cooperation in fighting terrorism, both airport and carrier programs have been key factors."[6]

Passenger Screening

There are many issues surrounding passenger screening and the related training of security operatives. In the United States and Canada, the aviation regulations have made the airlines responsible for security of passengers and screening baggage prior to boarding a flight. In other regions of the world, governments make the airports responsible. As we saw on 9–11, passengers were able to board aircraft with small-bladed knives and it seems likely that these were used to gruesome effect to crash aircraft into the World Trade Center and the Pentagon.

The screening process and the need to do it developed as a response primarily to attacks by Middle Eastern and European terrorist groups hijacking airliners and taking hostages. In the late 1960s, the threat posed was from gun- and explosives-toting terrorists gaining access to the aircraft. Their intent was not specifically to kill anyone but to use their hostages as bargaining chips for the release of prisoners held in jails, primarily in Israel and Europe. The training and equipment for passenger screening has not changed that much since those early days. The message was clear to the terrorists: "that so long as aviation security measures were not in place then aviation was a lucrative, media grabbing and sensational target." And it continues to be so today.

Tombstone Technology

When the body count becomes too much for an administration to bear then the cost of fixing the existing problems gets the necessary funding it should have had in the first instance. We like to refer to this as **"tombstone technology."** The facts remain that 9–11 could have been and most probably should have been prevented. This may be a bold assertion, but one we know we are definitely not alone in making. In North America the airlines were tasked up until 2002 with the security of passengers. Costs are always an issue for airlines, and in the United States, security companies regularly were required to bid on these security-screening contracts. The successful bidder was almost always the lowest bid. Your security when traveling was entrusted to low-paid, low-skilled, often untrained, poorly motivated individuals, and often—new immigrants. This is and has been the case in the United States for the last two decades. The level of training and the types of test items that the staff used for training were totally out of context with the types of weapons and cutting devices available on the market. In Canada, at least the government had created a standard and training course requirements that even fifteen years ago exceeded that of any training for U.S. screeners. So it is not incorrect to state that there are still significant holes in the screening process both in the United States and elsewhere. Inconsistency is also another issue. We have all been through airports where different items attract attention at one airport but not another.

A major flaw in the process and most noticeably in the United States had been that passengers and the general public could go through security screening, but all this did was raise the obvious prospect of breaches and items getting through the process. For the security screener on his minimum wage, he has about seven seconds to determine what he is viewing on the X-ray monitor. Added to this, most passengers before 9–11 took the view that security was a hindrance and the abuse suffered by low-paid screeners from irate passengers and airline staff is legend. In many cases, the issue surrounding whether a passenger could take a specific item would be referred to an airline supervisor for a decision as to whether it can be carried. Most decisions would be made in favor of the fare-paying passenger. This did little for the moral of the screener and even less for security in flight. To underscore this, we refer the reader/student to such documents as the 1994 **U.S. General Accounting Office** report to Congressional Committees on Aviation Security. In that report, which disseminated the President's Commission Report, the Commission raised concerns about screeners' efficiency, mail and cargo, and the coordination of security between law enforcement and airport personnel. As you can see, little has changed in the intervening years. Shutting the door after the horse has bolted is a term that adequately describes what has taken place since 9–11. Responsibility for airport security has now passed to a new agency the TSA (Transportation Security Administration) federalizing all airport security screeners by the end of 2002 and creating a long-awaited level of training for those employees. Added to this is the requirement to screen all hold baggage by the end of 2002. This is not a practicality and the end of 2003 will be more realistic, but no doubt very problematic. The 100% screening of hold baggage has been a reality in the United Kingdom since 1998. Both North America and some European countries are far behind. Since 9–11 massive funds are now earmarked and being provided to support the security functions at U.S. airports, however this may be too little too late. The opportunity existed prior to 9–11 for terrorists to openly observe the screening processes at the nation's airports, to assess where the weak points were, how the screeners searched and what items were being taken from passengers. It is not improbable to suggest that they had done dummy runs with similar objects, and even if they had

TERRORISM BYTE 13–2

Airport Attack, Rome 1973

On December 17, 1973, five members of the youth movement of the Palestinian Liberation Organization kill thirty-three Pan Am passengers in the terminal at Rome's Leonardo Da Vinci International Airport and then hijack a Lufthansa aircraft to Kuwait where they surrender and are handed over to the PLO.

been detected the outcome would not have brought them to the attention of the authorities.

HIJACKINGS

The 1970s and 1980s were the decades of hijackings and the preferred mode of attack for terrorists. As effective security was moved against that threat, the sophistication of the terrorists shifted to other areas of aviation that were considered to be weak. Pan Am 103 is one example. To many people, the attacks against civil aviation tend to get lost in the mists of time and few remember specific threats and attacks particularly when they occur in other regions of the globe. We list here some specific examples where the threat is from explosive devices either placed in the hold or carried on as cabin baggage. A Pan Am 747 had a bomb explode on board on a flight from Tokyo to Honolulu in August 1982, and also the same year an improvised explosive device **(IED)** was discovered on a Pan Am 747 at Rio de Janeiro airport. In December of the same year a piece of checked luggage was removed from an Alitalia (Italian Airlines) flight when the passenger did not board the aircraft. The passenger was checking the bag through to a Pan Am flight to New York. Police discovered a bomb inside the bag.[7]

The terrorist hijackings by the **PLO,** and subsequently, many other terrorist groups with connections to the Middle East, which occurred at the end of the 1960s, changed the face of aviation for the next twenty years. For the terrorists, a hijacked aircraft became a way to attract the worldwide media coverage that the group craved. This allowed them to present an agenda or message about their cause instantly and universally. For the respective governments and the traveling public, the horror became too much to deal with. Measures to counteract these depredations were hastily drawn up and passenger screening for hand-carried baggage was born. Security is in many ways a reactive function and this is clearly seen in the aviation industry.

Airports, as everyone is aware, are busy and often-cramped locations designed and built in the decades before security of passengers and aircraft had been considered an issue. Even newly built facilities in the United States over the last five years of the twentieth century did not factor in a hardening of the facility for security purposes, especially the screening areas, or incorporating

---

TERRORISM BYTE 13–3

Bombing, Leonardo Da Vinci Airport, 1985

On July 1, 1985, seven days after the Air India disaster in the Irish Sea which claimed 329 people, fifteen baggage handlers were injured when a bomb exploded. The explosion occurred in an open-air baggage bay underneath the main terminal building, shattering glass and causing minor structural damage. Because the baggage had not been sorted at the time of the explosion, authorities were unable to determine the suitcase's point of origin or destination.

sophisticated detection devices into the baggage sorting/conveyor systems. A demand had now added an additional layer of baggage security to an already overtaxed system. The biggest problem facing the airlines was, who is going to pay for all this? In the long run, it would of course be the traveling public as it always is. After the bombing of Pan Am 103 in 1988 developing effective explosive detection equipment that could handle the massive baggage throughput was also part of the immediate challenge for airports and aviation security experts. Screening hold baggage had not been a priority for North America in spite of the President's Commission Report in 1990. In North America, resolution to this problem has once again reared its ugly head. The integration of systems to check baggage has been available—after all it's more than thirty-five years since we put a man on the moon—so why not the capability to screen 100% of bags for explosives in an efficient and timely fashion? North America as well as many European countries have failed to provide 100% screening of hold baggage, on the other hand, post Pan Am 103 the United Kingdom went on an aggressive and determined track to ensure **100% screening.** The screening of baggage in the United Kingdom has been a reality since 1998, but it is nowhere near to reality for North America. We now hope to see a new breed of security screener—one that is well equipped to perform an arduous function. But is that where the story ends for passenger security and terrorists? Unfortunately, the answer is a resounding "no." That soft underbelly still exists and until all airlines and governments come to terms with the need to secure hold baggage, mail and freight, the opportunity to introduce a bomb in checked luggage is more feasible now than at any time in the last thirty years. Many will argue about the cost of attempting to provide 100% security and many would argue that it is impossible. The events of 9–11 have shown the world that we cannot afford <u>not</u> to provide the highest levels of security and protection to aviation. Travel by air is an international mode of transportation and the will to make the changes to civil air security involves all respective governments and agendas and attitudes must surely change. or there will surely be another attack against aviation.

Suicide as a means to impress terrorism on the unsuspecting has been used to great effect particularly in the Middle East by both Hamas in Israel and Hezbollah in Lebanon. In the past, the aim of such attacks was to get a specific response from the specific suicide attack. In the case of the U.S. Marine Corps bombing, it had the desired effect and the Americans vacated Beirut. As for the utilization of aircraft as flying bombs, a plan originating with World Trade Center bomber Ramzi Yousef, who was the earlier architect of the Manila plots to destroy eleven U.S. airliners. The very sobering message we now get from the terrorists is that they want NOTHING from us. They only want our destruction. Hussein Mussawi, former Hezbollah leader stated, "We are not fighting so that the enemy may offer us something. We are fighting to wipe out the enemy." This also meets exactly with the goals of Osama bin Laden's al Qaeda terrorist organization.

Airport Facilities

Airports are, by their very nature, open and public places. As a result, the opportunity for terrorists to leave bombs in such public places always exits. Only awareness, vigilance and response by the public and police can help prevent disaster. But what about security in other sectors of the aviation industry?

TERRORISM BYTE 13-4

Richard Reid: The Shoe Bomber, December 22, 2001

Three months after the events of 9–11, a massive security failure took place in Europe. Englishman Richard Reid had converted to Islam while serving time as a young offender and had also spent time in the same London mosque as Zacarias Moussaoui. Reid attempted to board an American Airlines flight from Paris to Miami and during the flight attempted to ignite a fuse to a sophisticated bomb in the heel of his trainer-style shoe. The crew and passengers overpowered him and fighter aircraft immediately escorted the aircraft to Boston. Reid had boarded the flight with a ticket paid for with cash and had no luggage. At a time of high security, it is inconceivable that he was not the subject of a stringent screening process. In Boston on January 30th 2003, Reid was sentenced to life in prison by U.S. District Judge William Young. He was sentenced on eight charges including attempted use of a weapon of mass destruction, placing an explosive device on an aircraft, and attempted murder.

What about mail and airfreight carriers? How secure is that? Millions of tons of freight are handled and moved by airlines throughout the world and a large percentage travels without any serious screening in the holds of passenger aircraft. At the present time this area of airline operation is open to serious risk and exposure. Furthermore, many countries including the United States do not make specific security checks a requirement to work in restricted areas of an airport. This means that access to the aircraft, by catering facilities, etc., must receive serious attention if the sterility of the aircraft is to be maintained. It is of little benefit to any operation if passengers are fully screened for weapons and airport workers are allowed almost unrestricted access without checks. Without stating the obvious, the opportunity must therefore exist for airport workers to secrete weapons or even bombs on an aircraft. A comprehensive system must be employed to assure the integrity of all those persons requiring access to restricted areas of the airport and also the bags and items that they carry in with them.

In the United States arena, the threat as it has already been evidenced in Europe can also extend to passengers in the line-ups to airline check in counters. For airports and security these areas require consideration and attention. Even at times of heightened security—and the United States most certainly was on guard on July 4, 2002, the United State's Independence Day—when a man of Middle East descent opened fire on passengers at the El Al check-in desks at Los Angeles International airport. What do we learn from such events as this? El Al, the Israeli national airline, which prides itself on its stringent security systems and profiling approach to complete prevention, is a model for all to observe. In addition, the concern also needs to focus on other such methods of terror attack such as a suicide truck or car bomb targeting the front of an airport terminal. A broader view will then have to be taken of the amount of glass in airport terminals and how to protect and reduce the injuries from blast damage to those facilities with large areas of partitioned glass.

In the United Kingdom, we have seen such incidents as the attempt by Irish terrorists to fire mortars from outside the airport perimeter onto runways and terminal buildings in the early 1990s. For the first time police and intelligence had to be concerned not only with the airport facility and its protection but also to evaluate the threat from areas surrounding the airport. The better use of closed circuit television systems (CCTV) and better intelligence on who owns the lands and buildings in close proximity to airport facilities now had to be viewed in the overall risk assessment for an airport. Following the terrorist attacks on 9–11, there was considerable concern about the use of and the availability of **Stinger** missiles against U.S. and U.N. targets. While there is no evidence to suggest that any Stinger missiles are in the United States, it is important to note that a U.S. military fact sheet details the Stinger in this manner, "The missiles' complexity can be accommodated by almost any potential user nation or group."

The Stinger missile is five feet long and weighs in at thirty-four pounds. It is manufactured by Raytheon and can be fired from a distance of five miles and has a vertical range of 10,000 feet. A Stinger would be a lethal weapon when used against a conventional civilian airliner. Stingers were originally sent to Afghanistan as part of the campaign to arm the local mujahideen against the Soviet invasion. At the time of the transfer there were advocates against such a move with the outright fear that the Islamic fundamentalist who dominated the Afghan mujahideen had about as much love of the West as they did for the Soviets. The opportunity for some to be traded to terrorist organizations was a genuine and highly conceivable proposition. As for other countries that have Stinger missiles they include: Somalia, Iraq, United Arab Emirates, Qatar, Zambia, North Korea.[8]

A People Issue

In the United States, the problem exists as to who has access to the restricted areas of airports, and the same problem exists in Europe. While passenger security screening may be increased, what measures can be taken to make sure airport workers, baggage loaders, refuellers, aircraft cleaners and the like have undergone sufficient background checks to assure the authorities of their integrity? News reports out of the United Kingdom in early September 2002 indicated that at least fifteen illegal aliens were employed cleaning aircraft at London's Heathrow Airport. The problem, as we can see, is not restricted to U.S. civil aviation. Passenger screening agents from contract security companies in the United States have already come under the same scrutiny and have been found wanting. Federalizing the operations will change that and require security clearances for everyone working in restricted areas of the operation.

To sum up the main failings that led to 9–11:

- The insufficient training and the lack of a definable training program for security screeners at U.S. airports;
- The failure of the U.S. FAA administration to resolve long-standing issues of an inadequately functioning civil aviation security program;
- The ongoing failure by some U.S. carriers to apply any consistent level of security processes and procedures;
- The significant failings that have been evident since the U.S. President's Commission in 1990 to implement and adopt and adapt to new technologies into the screening process;

TERROR BRIEF 13–2

IRA Attack at Heathrow

The Heathrow Experience

1st Attack: On Wednesday March 9, 1994, between 5:00 P.M. and 5:30 P.M., using a recognized code word, telephone calls were received by various news organizations warning of:

- Bombs at Heathrow
- In terminals and runways in one hour

Just before 6:00 P.M., there was an explosion in a car, in the parking lot of the Excelsior Hotel, on the north side of the airport. Several cars were engulfed in flames and four mortars were found near the northern runway.

- None had exploded on impact.
- No damage or injury occurred.
- The hotel parking lot had in the past been utilized as an evacuation point.

2nd Attack: On the following day between 5:30 P.M. and 9:45 P.M., a number of similar calls were received. At midnight, four more bombs were fired from wasteland beyond the perimeter on the southern side of the airport near Terminal Four. Again there was no explosion, damage or injury. The launcher was free-standing, purposely built apparatus, placed in undergrowth and concealed with plastic sheeting and branches.

3rd Attack: Three days later on Sunday, March 13, 1994, there were again a series of similar calls between 6:00 A.M. and 6:40 A.M. Flights were diverted from the southern runway and just after 8.00 A.M., rockets were again fired towards Terminal Four, from the opposite direction. One landed on the terminal without causing damage.

4th Attack: Between 6:45 P.M. and 7:30 P.M. on that same Sunday, coded calls were received, giving the same unspecific information, stating that bombs had been placed at Heathrow and Gatwick. Contingency plans were implemented at both airports, but this was found to be a hoax. It is properly described as an attack because the disruptive effect was equal to that at earlier incidents.

Source: Commander David Tucker—London Metropolitan Police. AVSEC World 94 Proceedings, Chicago, U.S., October 23–26, 198.

- Too much reliance on an intelligence system that the U.S. administration would get adequate warnings of significant threats to civil aviation.

The above failings are as relevant to civil aviation in the U.S. in 2001 as they were post-Pan Am 103 in 1988. U.S. President George Bush announced in September 2001 following 9–11 that his administration would:

- Establish new standards for security operations;
- Supervise the passenger and baggage security at the 420 commercial passenger airports in the United States;
- Ensure that intensive security and background checks were carried out and that enhanced and effective security training programs would be in place for security screeners and other security staff;
- Provide new and more sophisticated equipment;

- Oversee the patrolling and monitoring the quality of the access controls at airports;
- Develop a **Department of Homeland Security** to facilitate the coordination.

In the light of the failings at U.S. airports, the FAA specifically targeted Boston's Logan International, Newark, New Jersey, and Dulles Airport in Washington and found that these airports had the lowest detection rate for weapons among the twenty-five largest U.S. airports. Even prior to 9–11, the **Gore Commission**—after the loss of TWA 800 off Long Island New York in 1996—made many recommendations in regard to airport security including the positive bag matching for domestic passengers on domestic flights. From this, the airlines insisted that the cost in delays was unacceptable, and came up with a proposal to use the **Computer Assisted Passenger Profiling.** This would permit the airlines to identify from a set of parameters those passengers that might pose a threat. The four hijackings of 9–11 have shown how devoid of any value that system turned out to be. Since 9–11, we have been led down the path that security is much tighter at airports with the new Transportation Security Administration making all security screeners federal employees. However, as we approached the one year anniversary of 9–11, the new TSA reported that all was not well and revealed that screeners at thirty-two of the largest U.S. airports failed to detect weapons and explosive devices in approximately 25% of the tests carried out in June 2002. In airports such as Cincinnati, Jacksonville and Las Vegas, the newly monitored screeners failed to detect at least half of the tests, and at Los Angeles International the failure rate was 41%.[9]

European Civil Aviation Conference (ECAC)

Nations are responsible for implementing effective aviation security systems for flights leaving their country. Terrorism is an international issue striking anywhere within hours by modern air transport. Therefore, it is necessary to have an international body to work with governments to develop measures, standards and recommended practices. That body is the **ECAC** and operates with the active support of the International Civil Aviation Organization (ICAO). ECAC, formed more than twenty years ago, has the following three principles in the area of aviation security:

1. That the threat of unlawful interference with civil aviation in its many forms of violence is likely to persist;
2. That **ICAO** Standards and Recommended Practices in aviation security have to take into account the widely varying provisions available for their implementation in more than 180 Contracting States of ICAO;
3. Mutual understanding and close and constant co-operation between all State authorities concerned are necessary to achieve and maintain a high standard of aviation security.[10]

Combating Terrorists

One of the first considerations any would-be hijacker would have looked for during the last two decades of the twentieth century was the amount of mass media publicity he or she could hope to achieve for the 'cause.' Certainly hi-

The Nazer Hindawi Incident

By the spring of 1986 the world was well accustomed to the specter of airport delays caused by security checks. Heathrow is no exception. The traveling public was subjected to monotonous lines waiting for hand luggage to be searched, blissfully ignorant that the suicide or mule bomber even existed. There had, at this juncture, been no recorded attempts to destroy an aircraft by suicide bombing. This was to change dramatically on April 17, 1986. Terminal One at Heathrow International was the hub for the British Airways European and domestic arrivals and departures. However, on several days of the week it was also the terminal used by Israel's El Al Airlines for their Boeing 747 flight to Israel. At mid-morning, with the El Al 747 on the jetty at Gate 23, passengers for that flight and also the BA flight to Tel Aviv, coincidentally being checked in and boarded at the adjacent departure gate 21, were coming through the pre-boarding security checks. All passengers leaving the United Kingdom in 1986, and specifically those with checked baggage, were asked a series of questions:

- Is this your baggage?
- Did you pack it yourself and are you taking any packages for somebody else?
- Have you left your baggage unattended at any time?

After the questions the passengers would proceed to an immigration desk for passport inspection, not far from the watching eye of Metropolitan Police Special Branch officers.

On this particular day a young girl from the Republic of Ireland had answered all the questions had had her passport checked and her hand luggage and hold baggage screened by X-ray. The girl unwittingly proceeded to the El Al boarding gate with her single piece of carry-on baggage. The bag was of nylon construction with an expanding compartment at the base, a type of bag used by millions of travelers. El Al airline, which prides itself on being one of the most secure airlines in the world, with good reason, conducts a secondary manual security check and questioning of every passenger. El Al's own security team conducts this. The young lady who was pregnant with her boyfriend's baby was apparently going to visit his family in the Middle East; he, however, was not traveling. The security staff thought this a strange story, and while doing the physical check on the bag noticed that even when it was empty it seemed overly heavy for its construction. At that point, a police explosive search dog passed by, and immediately reacted to the bag. Further inspection revealed several sheets of plastic explosive wired to a calculator and battery. The bomb was in a false bottom of the bag. The boyfriend, Nazer Hindawi, had befriended the girl, gotten her pregnant and was sending her to her death. A Jordanian Palestinian sponsored by Syria, he had gone to remarkable lengths and considerable planning to pull this attack off. He was sentenced to forty-five years in prison.

Source: Author's private papers.

jacking an aircraft and demanding it be flown to JFK Airport in New York, or to London's Heathrow Airport, would gain worldwide media attention. And because of the size and complexity of these airports, the ensuing chaos and disruption to the traveling public would be horrendous. Consider that in combating a hijacking it is imperative to have the option to 'direct' the hijacked aircraft to an airport of choice. Authorities must be able to handle the incident without disrupting the major airports and airline systems of the world.

Blue "Trolley Bag"

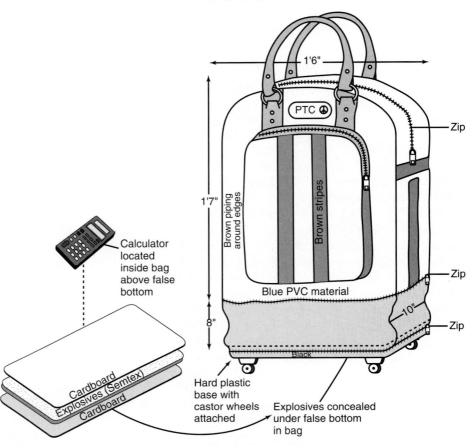

Trolley bag bomb intended to blow up EL-AL flight at London's Heathrow Airport, 1986. Explosive was hidden in false bottom of carry-on bag. (Authors' private papers)

Aircraft Hijack Response Location—Stanstead Airport, UK

London's third airport is little known to the international traveler, who will normally arrive at the gateway airports of Heathrow, on the outskirts of London, or Gatwick, about one hour south of London. Stanstead, located to the east of London, has become the venue of choice for the authorities in dealing with a hijacked aircraft. This supposes, of course, that they are able to hoodwink the terrorist into believing the plane is actually landing at Heathrow. The airport was first used to receive a hijacked aircraft in 1975, when a BAC1-11 was hijacked on an internal flight between Manchester in the North of England and London. The hijacking took place as the aircraft was approaching Heathrow and the pilot managed to divert, without the hijackers' knowledge, to Stanstead. The hijacker then demanded money and to be flown to France. By the time the pilot had flown around and then landed at Stanstead, the hijacker was convinced he was in France. Few police were available in those days to cover Stanstead airport, and the lessons they learned as a result were incorporated into the training of the Special Air Service (SAS) Regiment for dealing with terrorist hijackings in the future. Security operations were lacking in:

- Numbers of police on hand to deal with an emergency of this magnitude;
- Designated emergency rendezvous points for emergency services;
- Communications between pilot and ground;
- A designated command post for the operation.

The requirement to train and maintain a level of response became of great importance. A second hijacking, originating in central Africa in 1982, ended up with an Air Tanzania Boeing 727 landing, after a circuitous route around Europe, at Stanstead. On this occasion, the response was a combined police and military operation with the elite SAS in attendance to mount a hostage rescue if police negotiations failed. While police negotiated, a team of SAS embarked on similarly configured British Airways 737 and flew directly from Heathrow to Stanstead. As a result of protracted negotiations involving the Tanzanian High Commissioner, the siege was brought to a peaceful conclusion some twenty-four hours later. What was also apparent in this incident was the role of the media and its release of sensational and newsbreaking pictures to an eager public. However, images of armed police laying near the aircraft could have been a considerable problem for the negotiators had they reached the hijackers. In any democratic society, the value of the press and its principle focus of news gathering must be weighed against the impact on the situation at hand. Close cooperation with the media is an issue that must be addressed in terror and hijacking incidents where they are present.

In August 1996, a Sudan Airways A310 Airbus, which originated in Khartoum, had been hijacked by an Iraqi group demanding the plane be flown to Italy. Because of insufficient fuel, the aircraft had to land in Cyprus, refuel and then take off for London. Stanstead, having learned valuable lessons of the last twenty years, was ready and waiting to receive the aircraft. This particular hijacking was to end peacefully, and again Stanstead remains the airport of choice for receiving terrorist-controlled flights into the United Kingdom.[11]

The Media Angle

Interfering with the media's "right to know" is of course frowned upon. However, there must be limits placed on the release of pictures and information while the incident is still ongoing. As preservers of order in the fabric of democracy, the police and military are bound to come into conflict with the media about the control and dissemination of information. One example of such a conflict occurred during the Falklands War, when the media were given briefings by the government and the content of news was tightly censored so as not to give critical information to the enemy. During the Gulf War, the commander himself, General Norman Schwarzkopf, conducted press briefings. These briefings contained the diluted information that the military chiefs allowed for media release. The press was not allowed on the field of battle during the invasion operations. In a terror incident taking place in a city, it is not possible to control media coverage in the first phase of the action. The bombing of the Federal Building in Oklahoma City brought the television crews to the scene at almost the same time rescue and police services were arriving, some even quicker. The graphic television coverage of the heroic deeds of fire fighters and police officers goes a long way toward winning the public's acceptance of the methods they may subsequently use to catch terrorists. Police are seen as the front line against terrorism as part of the community and therefore better appreciated.

Media coverage can also have negative effects in combating terror, even when the government censors have neutralized the information. A disastrous media mistake involved a hijacked American airliner at Beirut International Airport in 1985. A rescue unit of Delta Force commandos was dispatched to the region, only to be thwarted by news coverage of their imminent arrival, which allowed the hijackers time to hide and move their captives throughout Beirut. Many analysts have discussed and reviewed the effects of media coverage on terrorist actions. And many conclusions both for media coverage and against can surely be reached. The media however must understand that they should remain at arms length so as not to become a tool of the terrorist. Much media coverage is aimed at showing the horrors of the unfolding situation. The motivational drives of the terrorists are seldom considered, and search for the dramatic effect of horror the coverage becomes the main goal. Without intention, the media begins presenting the terrorist side of issues. When that happens, the media inadvertently serves the purposes of the terrorists, giving them precisely the attention they seek.

After all, as mentioned in several chapters, terrorist actions are all about sending a message. Their preferred method of sending the message is via the broadest media coverage possible. No doubt studies might conclude that sensational pictures of terrorist events do nothing to get "the message" out to the public but may, in fact, fuel public anger. In a free society, the media and government will invariably clash on what should get coverage and what should not. However, much of what is reported will generally be acquired through government sources, who may appear to be manipulating the media. No one has suggested that the media were manipulated on 9–11. We believe that the media coverage awoke a nation to the true and cowardly nature of terrorists and their despicable acts—so often perpetrated against civilians. In this instance, live news footage of the World Trade Center attack as the second plane crashed into the second of the twin towers was more vivid than any Hollywood portrayal. The cataclysmic events of 9–11 were also viewed and broadcast in Middle East countries and the following day newsprint articles and television news coverage showed joyful Palestinians dancing in the streets. To most people that was abhorrent, but it needed to be shown. Censorship of the press and restrictions placed on them is undoubtedly a common practice in many countries, especially where military dictatorships and totalitarian governments are in power. A good example is the tactics and laws imposed by the Robert Mugabe government in Zimbabwe, which makes it a criminal offense to criticize the government and its ministers.

Policy

As the second millennium continues, the reaction of Western governments to terrorist activity has been to come up with methods of responding to them swiftly and effectively. The use of military and spy satellites to track down the terrorist have enhanced this effort. Is the problem of defining and dealing with terrorism a police or military problem? Certainly the bombing of U.S. embassies in Nairobi and Dar es Salaam in the summer of 1998 was very difficult for the local police to deal with. In trying to come to terms with an enemy not residing within its own borders, the United States decided on a preemptive military strike at the bases of suspected terrorists in both the Sudan and Pakistan. Were they violating sovereign territory of two other countries? The primary target was Osama bin Laden and his al Qaeda network, who were suspected of being behind the two bombings as well as the subsequent attacks against the USS Cole in Yemen. As a result of the two bombings, and the retaliatory strikes by the United States, we wondered who would fire the next shot in anger. We now know the next shot was from the Islamic extremists of bin Laden's al Qaeda terror organization deep into the heart of the American public in New York, Washington and Pennsylvania.

International cooperation in dealing with world terrorism was previously addressed at the **Lyon Summit** Conference in 1996. Ministers responsible for state security agreed on a framework of some twenty-five measures. The agreement focussed on the following main points:

1. Adopting internal measures to prevent terrorism, by improving counter terrorism cooperation and capabilities. By adopting this strategy, governments could focus on training of counterterrorism personnel to prevent all kinds of terrorism actions including the use of chemical, biological and toxic substance attacks;

2. Accelerating the research and development of methods to detect explosives and other harmful substances that cause death or injury, and also to develop standards for marking explosives in order to identify their origin in post-blast investigations;

TERRORISM BYTE 13–5

Egypt Air 648

The incident at Malta Airport in 1985 is an example of what can go wrong even with a well-trained and equipped anti-terror unit. The lessons learned from this debacle, which ended with fifty-four dead passengers, is testament to the paramount need to have as much intelligence as possible about the target group before an assault is mounted. In addition, snipers outside the aircraft mistook escaping passengers for terrorists and gunned some of them down. In September 1985, an Egypt Air flight was hijacked to Malta and the Egyptian government dispatched Force 777 to the island to assist with the hostage rescue operations. The Maltese government gave the go-ahead for Force 777 to take action against the terrorists. The assault began at about 8:00 P.M. and lasted for more than a minute and a half, which is nearly four times longer than most anti-terror groups will take to storm an aircraft and release hostages. The series of mistakes, miscalculations, and lack of intelligence and planning resulted in the death of the passengers.

Source: Extracts from Leroy Thompson, "The Rescuers, The World's Top Anti-Terrorist Units." Paladin Press. pp. 20, 1986.

3. In respect to prosecution and deterrence, the agreement noted that where sufficient justification existed according to national laws, that states must investigate organizations, groups and associations, including those with charitable social or cultural goals, used by terrorists as a cover for their operations. (An example of such a group would be NORAID, which supports and collects funds for the IRA in the United States.)

4. Adopt laws for the restriction and control of weapons and explosives including export controls, to prevent their use by terrorist organizations;

5. Review and amend all current anti-terror legislation;

6. In dealing with political asylum issues, states must ensure that the rights and freedoms of a country are not taken advantage of by terrorists who seek to fund, plan and commit terrorist acts;

7. Facilitate the exchange of information through central authorities to provide speedy coordination of requests. Direct exchange of information between competent agencies should be encouraged;

8. The exchange of information should specifically identify:

   • The actions and movement of persons or groups suspected of belonging to or being connected with terrorist networks;

   • Travel documents suspected of being forgeries;

   • Trafficking in arms, explosives or sensitive materials;

   • The use of communications technologies by terrorist groups;

   • The threat of new types of terrorist activities including those using, chemical, biological, or nuclear materials and toxic substances.[12]

U.N. Security Council Resolution 1373

After the terror attacks of 9–11, the General Assembly of the United Nations, by consensus of the 189 member states, called for international cooperation to prevent and eradicate acts of terrorism on a worldwide basis. The United Nations also held accountable the perpetrators and those states who harbor and support them. The Security Council Resolution was unanimously adopted on September 28, 2001, under Chapter VII of the U.N. Charter. Resolution 1373 is a legally binding resolution on all member states. It defines the new international campaign to deal with terrorism. It requires among other things that all member states prevent the financing of terrorism and deny safe haven for terrorists. **1373** makes it imperative for all states to review and strengthen their border security operations, banking practices, customs and immigration procedures, law enforcement and intelligence cooperation and share pertinent information with respect to these efforts. The full implementation of 1373 will require each member state to take specific measures to combat terrorism; most will have to make changes to laws, regulations and practices.

The following steps were taken by the United States:

• September 23, 2001. Executive Order 13224 froze all the assets of twenty-seven foreign individuals, groups and entities linked to terrorist acts or supporting terrorism and authorized the freezing of assets of those who commit or pose a significant threat of committing acts of terrorism.

• September 28, 2001. The United States sponsored the U.N. Security Council resolution 1373, calling on all U.N. members to criminalize the provision of funds to all terrorists, effectively denying terrorists safe financial haven anywhere.

- October 5, 2001. The U.S. Attorney General redesignated twenty-five terrorist organizations to include al Qaeda as foreign terrorist organizations pursuant to the Anti-terrorism and Effective Death Penalty Act 1996. Giving material support or resources to any of these foreign organizations is a felony under U.S. law.

- October 12, 2001. Under Executive Order 13224 thirty-nine names were added to the list of individuals and organizations linked to terrorism or terrorist financing.

- October 26, 2001. The United States enacted the USA Patriot Act, which significantly expanded the capability of U.S. law enforcement to investigate and prosecute persons who engage in terrorist acts.

- October 29, 2001. The Foreign Terrorist Tracking Task Force was created and aimed at denying entry into the United States of persons suspected of being terrorists and locating, detaining, prosecuting and deporting terrorists already in the United States.

- November 2, 2001. The United States designated twenty-two terrorist organizations located throughout the world under Executive Order 13224, thus, highlighting the need to focus on terrorist organizations worldwide.

- November 7, 2001. The United States added sixty-two new organizations and individuals, all of whom were either linked to the Al Barakaat conglomerate or to the Al Taqwa Bank, which have been identified as supplying funds to terrorists.

- December 4, 2001. The United States froze the assets of the Holy Land Foundation in Richardson, Texas, whose funds are used to support the Hamas terrorist organization, and two other entities, bringing the total to 153.

- December 5, 2001. The Secretary of State designated thirty-nine groups as terrorist organizations under the Immigration and Nationality Act, as amended by the USA Patriot Act.[13]

International Policing

International police cooperation has existed through the efforts of the International Criminal Police Organization **(Interpol)** for several decades. Terrorism is considered by Interpol to be, "a crime, characterized by violence or intimidation, usually against innocent victims in order to obtain a political or social objective." Interpol considers and distinguishes between terrorism and organized crime by commenting that organized crime has a profit motive, whereas terrorism's goals are not primarily for financial, but rather for ideological, gains.

INTELLIGENCE GATHERING

Intelligence gathering for terrorist offenses is the domain of police forces throughout the world. Many forces grudgingly share information, and when some spectacular IRA attacks occurred in London in the early 1990s, the intelligence-gathering operations were transferred from the police to the arm of British intelligence known as MI5. MI5's analysis encompassed not only IRA terrorists, but also all groups that could pose a threat. In March 1996, the British Government published a report by the Parliamentary Committee on Security and Intelligence that detailed that about 39% of resources went toward compiling data on membership, infrastructure and methods used by terrorist groups through long-term penetration. The risk when cases of terrorism are brought to trial on evidence painstakingly gathered by both police and MI5, would be counterproductive for a spy to appear on the witness stand to give testimony. Cooperation between these agencies is essential, and there has been successful cooperation between the British police and the intelligence community.

In the United States, following 9–11, much was made of perceived intelligence failings on the part of the U.S. intelligence community. It is of course easy to be critical after the event has taken place, however there were indicators that were missed and reports in this instance that were not followed up on. In order to determine the problems, we should first make an analysis of the current and historic state of the U.S. intelligence services. It could be said and has been said that the United States has the greatest intelligence in the world; however, if the right people do not listen and react to the information, it just becomes another secret file to be uncovered in future decades. Many U.S. intelligence agencies have been engaged in focusing on prevention of large-scale conflicts. Obviously there is a serious need for such intelligence, however, the risk from modern terrorism trends and unconventional attacks does not appear to have the same resources. The Cold War era of intelligence by comparison is viewed as a simpler mode as it was easier to train covert operators to operate in the former Soviet Union than it is to train operatives to go native and assimilate into Arabic cultures and communities, mainly due no doubt to the constraints of culture, religion and self-identification.

Budget constraints on human intelligence **(HUMINT)** can be traced as far back as the 1970s when the United States began spending huge sums on improving the eyes and ears of the intelligence community with modern technology and satellite programs. On the other hand the field operative has the capability to make judgments that are specific to a designated target country or culture that an analyst located thousands of miles distant would be unable to achieve. An example of such a failing in a military context was the inability of the U.S. administration to have adequate intelligence about what Iraq's intentions were prior to its invasion of Kuwait and similarly it may also have been important to have intelligence targeting the activities of the Pakistan Inter-Service Intelligence (ISI) agency and their support of the Taliban and Osama bin Laden's mujahideen.

In addition to the lack of HUMINT resources there is a balance in signals intelligence (SIGINT) between developing new systems and technologies to penetrate more sophisticated communications without forgetting how to decode the old systems of encryption. Since 9–11, the fear of "sleeper cells" has become a threat to the nation's security and this becomes a challenge for the forces charged with protecting domestic security. Quite obviously, any Islamic extremist elements would likely conceal themselves in regions where other members of the same ethnicity reside. The ability of the sleeper to elude possible detection relates to the likely communications gap between the U.S. State Department that controls and issues visas, the Immigration and Naturalization

Service (INS), with responsibility for investigating and deporting illegal immigrants, and the Federal Bureau of Investigation (FBI), the organization tasked with domestic counterintelligence. The massive bureaucracies that have developed have also been the impeding factor in creating an effective means of performing counterterrorism operations and investigations within the United States. Harry S Truman for this very reason combined the country's intelligence efforts under the Central Intelligence Group, the forerunner to the CIA more than fifty years ago. However with the speed of the development of technology and the vying for political influence and budgetary constraints, the notion of a synergistic approach to the development of intelligence has been overlooked.[14]

COUNTERTERRORISM UNITS

GREAT BRITAIN

In the world of counterterrorism operations, few are as effective as the British SAS. Terrorism in the twentieth century has taken place primarily in the fifty-year period after World War II; and therefore counterterror and counterinsurgency units have also developed since the war. However, an eccentric Scot, David Stirling, formed the SAS during World War II. A commando officer, Captain Robert Laycock, ably assisted him. Conventional army theoreticians during the war frowned upon the activities being proposed by the unconventional Stirling. At 6' 5", he was an impressive figure of a man, and he believed passionately that there was an important role for "special operations" behind enemy lines. Once in Egypt, he teamed up with a Welsh Guardsman, an Australian named Jock Lewis, and these three men created the Special Air Service. Protocol was the order of the day, and for Second Lieutenant Stirling to communicate his ideas to the general commanding Middle East operations would require going through a long chain of command. Stirling thought the war would be over before his ideas reached the general. By fortuitous accident, he met with the Deputy Commander, General Ritchie, who was so impressed with the Lieutenant's ideas that they were soon put into practice for operations behind German lines in North Africa. This first unit was named "L Detachment, Special Air Service Brigade" and the SAS was born.

Special Air Service (SAS)

The SAS of the 1990s is a far cry from that of the war years, and it has developed into what is arguably one of the best counterterror units in the world. Many counterterrorism organizations around the world have been modeled after the SAS. The SAS regiment is headquartered in Hereford in the west of England, but with government spending cuts, it is destined for a new home at Royal Air Force base at Creedenhill. The Special Air Service is made up of a Special Projects Team, and it is from this team that the Counter Revolutionary Warfare Squadron has been formed to handle both foreign and domestic terrorism issues. Training for the SAS is constant, with one squadron always on

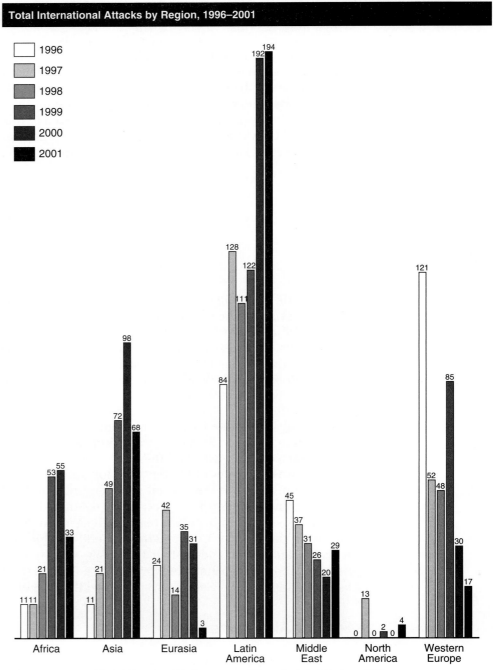

Total International Attacks by Region, 1996–2001

- □ 1996
- ▨ 1997
- ▨ 1998
- ▨ 1999
- ■ 2000
- ■ 2001

Africa: 11, 11, 21, 53, 55, 33
Asia: 11, 21, 49, 72, 98, 68
Eurasia: 24, 42, 14, 35, 31, 3
Latin America: 84, 128, 111, 122, 192, 194
Middle East: 45, 37, 31, 26, 20, 29
North America: 0, 13, 0, 2, 0, 4
Western Europe: 121, 52, 48, 85, 30, 17

Source: *Patterns of Global Terrorism*. U.S. Department of State. Statistical *Reviews 2001*.

International Terrorist Attacks, 1996–2001. (U.S. Department of State)

standby to leave at a moment's notice to deal with a terrorist situation. An Operations Research unit supports all SAS projects and has developed weaponry specific to the needs of the Regiment. This unit developed the stun grenade that is widely used by counterterrorism units around the world. They also developed night vision goggles and special ladders for aircraft and train assaults.

As a peacetime unit, the SAS has been primarily involved in dealing with the IRA. The Provisional IRA referred to the British application of the SAS in Northern Ireland as death squads sent to terminate Irishmen. Unfortunately for the Provisional IRA, the SAS was extremely effective in the urban warfare of Northern Ireland. The speed and efficiency with which the unit carried out operations stunned the Irish terrorist community.

SAS activity is not restricted to just the United Kingdom, however, and it is believed that the regiment has been involved in operations against Libya. Adding to the mystique surrounding this elite regiment is the anonymity that surrounds its members. A hostage drama at the Iranian embassy in London was covered by a plethora of news cameras from around the world, which captured live the sudden and dramatic rescue by armed men dressed in black fatigues. The success of that raid, which led to the death of all but one of the terrorists, placed Britain firmly in the spotlight as a country that did not deal lightly with terrorists and was prepared to use whatever force was necessary to end a crisis. It is important to note that this operation had been under the control of the civil police authorities until the go ahead was given for the SAS assault. This was the first time the public saw the SAS in action, and although there was an outpouring of indignation from extremists, the vast majority of Britons strongly supported the actions of the elite SAS team.

The SAS has been used against the IRA throughout Europe. An IRA unit had been followed to Gibraltar in 1988, where intelligence sources indicated the terrorists would detonate a bomb during a military parade. The SAS carried out an attack on the three IRA members, and according to witness reports gunned them down in cold blood. The subsequent outcry seemed too much for a democracy to handle with claims of a "shoot to kill" policy being adopted by the government. The IRA now had their "martyrs" to bury at home in Northern Ireland and the opportunity to haul the British government before the European Court of Justice, which condemned the assault. This court decision showed that caution was required, lest the counterterrorist forces go too far. Of course, for the IRA it meant they had the right to not only to shoot first, but to kill as well! The SAS is on good terms with numerous countries, as it has actively assisted in training so many antiterrorism units around the globe. It is believed that the SAS is present, either officially or unofficially, at every terror incident to view how it was handled and to determine what went well and what went wrong. Thorough debriefs are held, and every minute detail of the operation is analyzed. The SAS were present and provided assistance to the Peruvian government when terrorists took control of the Japanese ambassador's residence in Lima in 1996.

Special Boat Squadron (SBS)

The British Royal Navy has its own counterterrorism unit to rival the SAS. This unit is highly trained to respond to maritime acts of terrorism, though it has not been widely used. The unit responded with the SAS, most notably during the bomb threat to the ocean liner Queen Elizabeth II in the North Atlantic. Specifically designed for naval operations, the unit was deployed prior to the arrival of the Naval Task Force off the Falkland Islands at the outbreak of the war between Great Britain and Argentina.

SAS ASSOCIATES

Because of the proven effectiveness of the regiment and its legendary exploits since World War II, other commonwealth countries have modeled their counterterrorism units on the SAS. The Australian SAS and the New Zealand SAS have even adopted the same name as the British regiment.

AUSTRALIA

Tactical Assault Group (TAG) and Special Air Service Regiment (SASR)

The above units were originally formed in 1957, and comprise Australia's response to any outbreak of domestic terror. The Australian SAS was originally a single company. By 1964, two additional companies had been added and the unit was renamed the Special Air Service Regiment. The regiment saw military action in Borneo, and with the outbreak of the Vietnam War, was instrumental in training the Australian army for its role in Southeast Asia. By the time the Vietnam War ended, the SASR had achieved some impressive results in the area of "special operations." Since the Vietnam War, Australia has not seen terrorist activity at home and the unit has been scaled down. Like its British counterpart, SASR engages in training and assists other units in the west. SASR has staff based at Fort Bragg and Little Creek in the United States. A specialist unit is also available for sea-borne counterterror response called the Offshore Installations Assault Group (OAG). Since its creation the SASR has lost a total of seventeen men; six were killed on active duty in Vietnam, three in operations in Borneo, and eight were killed during a training exercise near Townsville in 1996.

RHODESIA

Rhodesian SAS

The Rhodesian SAS is part of the original regiment which was disbanded at the end of World War II. That regiment was so effective that German radio stations referred to David Stirling with respect and fear. Rhodesians have a long and proud history of engagements on foreign soil. One World War II Rhodesian, Mike Sadler, served with the SAS in North Africa and was considered to be the best navigator in the vast Western Desert.[15] When the war was over, the members of the SAS were returned to their respective countries. The regiment was almost disbanded, but survived as a territorial unit.

After the war with Germany and Japan was won, the next problem facing the allied powers was the rise of communism in the Far East. It was the Malayan crisis of 1951 which established the reasons for retaining a Rhodesian SAS regiment for actions at home and abroad. The Commonwealth countries were asked to supply volunteers for a force to be dispatched to Malaya to handle the entrenched Communist terrorists in the region. It was commanded by Major "Mad Mike" Calvert, who had been given the go-ahead to form a self-sustaining warfare unit, trained in jungle conditions to operate for long periods of time. Its mission would be to deploy for continually harassment and disruption of communist terrorist activity. Major Calvert flew to Rhodesia to meet with the contingent of one hundred men and briefed them on the Malayan operation. The unit from Rhodesia would become C Squadron 22 SAS (Malayan Scouts).[16]

The Malayan emergency was to last until the end of that decade, and the Rhodesian SAS remained on station for two years. On returning to Africa, the unit was disbanded and the men returned to their civilian lives. However, the lessons learned in that Far East operation were of value in the country's development, as it struggled for its identity and independence in the 1960s. Rhodesia's army was in need of specialized expansion and development. Following an assessment, it was decided that the Special Air Service Squadron would be established as a branch of the Rhodesian army. Training would be conducted under the auspices of the British SAS at Sterling Lines in Hereford, England. The Rhodesian military had a long and successful history of graduates at the Sandhurst Military Academy in Berkshire, England, and several cadets have been awarded the coveted Sword of Honor. Among those selected to join the newly formed Rhodesian SAS were remnants of the old Malaya task force of C Squadron.[17]

The Rhodesian SAS was exceptionally well trained and schooled in jungle warfare techniques and were also accomplished paratroopers. The squadron assisted the 22 SAS Regiment in operations with the British army in the Crater District of Aden (now Yemen) during that crisis. The 1960s were a time of rationalization and decolonization. Great Britain was divesting itself of major parts of its Empire and Africa was in massive turmoil, as other European empires were doing the same. The break-up of parts of Rhodesia began, the northern part becoming Zambia, and Nyasaland became independent Malawi. In 1964, Ian Smith, a Rhodesia-born former WWII fighter pilot, became prime minister of the country, determined to take Rhodesia to full independence from Britain. Politics would play a major role in the gradual demise of the SAS in Rhodesia. When Ian Smith was unable to convince the British government to grant independence to Rhodesia, he declared a Unilateral Declaration of Independence (UDI). This resulted in sanctions by Britain and a full trade embargo by the United Nations. The following fourteen years of turmoil in the region would end with a Black Nationalist government in power and the dissolution of the SAS. On December 31, 1980, the Rhodesian SAS disbanded and its members fled south to South Africa, taking with them the memorial to their war dead.

REPUBLIC OF IRELAND

The Army Ranger Wing (ARW) is classified as an elite counter terror force and the Republic's front line against terrorism. Not as well known as its British counterparts the SAS, the ARW has an impeccable reputation. The unit is made up of approximately one hundred members and is subordinate to the

Chief of Staff, Army. Like its SAS neighbors, it has some of the same basic responsibilities including:

- Hostage rescue in extreme situations such as hijackings both maritime and aircraft;
- Search and rescue operations;
- Providing close protection security details to VIPs and selected government officials;
- Ongoing maintenance of contingency planning processes for terrorist attacks.

Although there are no current details of actions undertaken by the group, the unit has maintained close ties with many of the European counterterrorism units including the French GIGN and the German GSG9. ARW has been involved in peace-keeping operations through the United Nations in Somalia, Bosnia and Lebanon.

SPAIN

Grupo Especial de Operaciones (GEO)

Spain, which has had problems with the ETA terrorist group, and also GRAPO, was late in establishing an effective counterterrorism unit. In 1978, following the successes of the German GSG-9, Spain sought help from Germany in setting up GEO. One of Spain's difficulties was finding fiscal and political resources with which to staff the unit. Spain has both left wing and right wing terrorist problems, so there was a desperate need for apolitical members of any elite unit for this type of activity. Spain's GEO is not well known outside that country, but is a highly trained and effective force. Although Spain has a thriving munitions industry of its own, the GEO use the same close assault weapons as their counterparts in GSG-9, favoring the Heckler and Koch MP5. As secretive as their comrades in both the SAS and GSG-9, GEO has had some unsung successes in dealing with terrorists. In May 1981, twenty-four right wing terrorists had occupied the Central Bank of Barcelona and taken over 200 hostages. The bank was stormed by GEO using their standard assault weapon, the MP5. Only one of the hostages was injured, and ten of the terrorists were captured and one terrorist was killed. The remainder fled the bank with the hostages in the ensuing confusion.[18]

Guarda Civil

Spain's second unit, which handles hostage taking and terrorist activity, operates within the structure of the *Guarda Civil* (National Police). The *Unidad Especial de Intervencion* (UEI), is responsible to the ministries of the interior and defense and forms part of Spain's national police force. Like the GEO, it is deployed across the country and has had notable successes in rescuing kidnap and hostage victims from both ETA and Grapo.

THE PERSIAN GULF

Cobras (Sultan of Oman Special Forces SSF)

Continuing traditions, with close ties to the Royal Military Academy at Sandhurst, the SAS provided training and logistical support for friendly Middle East countries. The tiny sultanate of Oman has seen very little terrorist activity but, when the region started to destabilize with pro-communist guerrillas under the Popular Front for the Liberation of Oman (PFLO), the sultan requested assistance from Britain. The rebellion in Oman lasted almost thirteen years between 1962–1975. During that time, the British SAS was actively involved in counterterrorism operations with the sultan's army. However, the sultan was not prepared for the kind of terror and insurgent tactics the guerrillas would use. The SAS was more than happy to oblige and was instrumental in bringing down the opposition forces opposing the sultan. When the fighting was over, Sultan Qaboos made the decision that his country would never again be without a response unit for insurgency and terrorism.

The British SAS gave support and training in setting up the SSF for the sultan. The Cobras, based in Dhofar, are now considered the most elite force in the Persian Gulf region. Cobra teams are set up along the same military lines as the SAS, and are on constant fifteen-minute standby. From their bases in Dhofar and Muscat, they have provided assistance to neighboring Kuwait. In a peculiar setup, the Cobras are seconded to the Omani police, who are less well equipped and trained. The police retain jurisdictional control of incidents. Jealousy and inter-service rivalry have not helped efforts to maintain this effective force in the Gulf.

FRANCE

Groupment d'intervention de la Gendarmerie Nationale (GIGN)

Unlike the British SAS, this elite counterterrorism response force in France was formed following the terrorist attacks at the Munich Olympic Games and the takeover of the Saudi Embassy in Paris. The GIGN is a police unit, not military. The recruits to this unit come from the ranks of the paramilitary police service, the *Gendarmerie Nationale* (National Police). All members undergo eight months of rigorous training similar to that of the SAS, to include parachute qualification. On successful completion they are based at the Maison Alfort near Paris. As a police unit, the GIGN is called on to deal with criminal incidents as well as terrorist attacks. The unit is heavily armed with Heckler and Koch MP5 sub-machine guns as well as an assortment of sophisticated handguns. The GIGN are also trained in negotiating skills and recognizing psychological weaknesses and changes in the state of mind of the terrorist. Like the SAS, GIGN shuns publicity. They have had remarkable success in rescuing kidnap victims. Their most widely known and spectacular action was the storming of an Air France Airbus at Marseilles, which resulted in the death of all thirteen hijackers.

NETHERLANDS

Bijondere Bijstands Eenheid (BBE)

Qua Patet Orbis (The Whole World Over) is the motto of the Netherlands Marine Corps. "Sending in the marines" has always been an option for Western governments and is an often-used phrase. In the case of the Netherlands, that is exactly what takes place in handling hostage taking and terrorist actions. The Netherlands has one of the oldest military organizations in the world with the Dutch Marine Corps, which was founded on December 10, 1665. Today's modern Royal Netherlands Marine Corps numbers about 2800. The corps is split into two separate areas for operational purposes, one group in the Netherlands for NATO duties and the other stationed in Aruba in the Dutch Antillies. The Marines represent a strike force that can respond to any terrorist situation that presents itself. A section of the Marine Corps is devoted to counterterrorism functions and is called the BBE. Translated, this has the literal meaning, "different circumstances unit." The Dutch government, like other west European countries, does not negotiate with terrorists, and though the country is not beset with severe terrorist problems. One incident that happened that resulted in conflict relates to Dutch colonialism in Indonesia. The region known as South Molucca, seeking independence from Indonesia, put pressure on the Dutch government by hijacking a train in 1975. The hijackers were members of the Free South Moluccan Youth Organization (VZJ).

The Netherlands' response was to send in the marines (BBE). On this occasion, as with others involving the South Moluccans, the siege was ended by extreme force resulting in the death of the terrorists and minor injuries to the rescuers and the rescued. Each attack unit of the BBE consists of two thirty-three-man platoons, each comprised of four assault teams. They are further broken down into five-man units. The unit's functions are similar to those of the British SAS and is assisted with maritime operations from the 7th Special Boat Squadron, another elite unit made up of four six-man intervention teams.

NORWAY

Forsvarets Spesialkommando (FSK, Special Defense Commando)

Norway's elite military response unit was formed in 1982, primarily as a defensive unit to deal with terrorist attacks against its many North Sea oil rigs. It is also responsible for the close protection of the Norwegian Royal Family, the national assembly and other government officials. The FSK is a branch unit of the Norwegian Army Jegercommand. This is another unit that has used the example of the SAS, and the start-up of the unit involved five years of close involvement with them. The two units have continued to maintain close ties and often train together on exercises. The close nature of the two units brought the FSK some unwanted publicity when it was reported in the Norwegian press that they had been involved in SAS operations against the IRA in Northern Ireland in 1994, a report that has been strenuously denied by both governments. FSK has also seen service overseas when it was dispatched to the Kashmir to help locate a Norwegian being held captive by Al-Faran guerrillas.

GERMANY

Grenzschutzgruppe 9 (GSG9)

GSG9 stands alongside the major elite terrorist responders in the world today as one of the most successful units. The unit was formed following the disaster at the Munich Olympic Games. After the horrendous events of the Olympics, the Germans were not prepared to allow such atrocities to happen again. In the case of the Olympics, it was the soft target with worldwide media coverage that the Black September movement was after. In the two decades after the end of the war, Germany had taken pains not to produce any elitist forces for any purpose. This unit was formed and fully operational by April 1973, six months after the Munich massacre. Unlike the SAS, this unit would become part of the Federal Border Police service and not part of the German military. Membership has the requirement that each is a volunteer and a member of the Border Police. Those in the German army who wish to volunteer must first resign from the army and join the Border Police.

The group is split into three definable units, each with fifty members: GSG-9/1, with one hundred members, is responsible for counterterrorism; GSG-9/2 for maritime counterterrorism; and GSG-9/3 deals with airborne issues. The federal government supplies GSG-9 with the best and most advanced equipment available. They operate in five-man units, and are outfitted with two sets of combat gear, one for day and the other for night-time operations.

TERRORISM BYTE 13–6

Colonel Ulrich Wegener

Ulrich Wegener joined the Federal Border Police in 1958, and his impeccable credentials made him the obvious choice to lead GSG-9. His training with both the FBI and the Israeli Secret Service gave him expert knowledge on terrorism. He is believed to have been involved with the Israeli raid at Entebbe in 1976. Wegener's orders had been to create a small and highly flexible anti-terrorist unit that could be used and deployed at a moment's notice. Following his success at Mogadishu, he was promoted to Brigadier and given ultimate control over the whole of the Federal Border Police.

Source: Leroy Thompson, GSG-9. Leroy Thompson: The Resources, The World's Top Anti-Terror Units. Paladin Press, 1986, p. 64.

ISRAEL

Sayeret Mat'Kal

Sayeret Mat'kal is also known as the General Staff Reconnaissance Unit 269 and was founded in 1957. This unit has been in the forefront of every anti- and counterterrorism strategy since its inception. It is the unit that is also dedicated to handling hostage-taking incidents. In wartime, this unit takes on the role of intelligence gathering. The *Sayeret Mat'kal* actively does the bidding of the Israeli government and has hunted down and executed known terrorists. After the Munich massacre it was mandated to track down and kill those involved.

CZECH REPUBLIC

URNA is the counterterrorist and crime-busting force of the Czech Police. URNA is modeled to be similar to its elite counterparts in the German GSG-9 and the French GIGN. URNA is the republic's rapid response force to fight serious crime and terrorism in the country. It has specific responsibilities and as such is tasked directly from the Ministry of the Interior to include the protection of foreign heads of state, security of major sporting events against sabotage and assisting the police in drugs and serious crime interdiction. By far its most important role is its intervention in extreme terrorist situations including hostage takings and hijackings. Although not as well known as other western European counterterror units, URNA is considered one of the elite reaction units and is held in very high regard.

Hostage Rescue Units (HRU)

These types of units are in operation throughout the world. Most countries have teams designated, trained and equipped to deal with hostage-taking crises, and the protection of VIPs and government officials. Units have been

---

TERRORISM BYTE 13-7

Operation Spring Youth

The Sayeret Mat'kal is also an offensive anti-terror unit and has used every possible means at its disposal in the protection of Israeli interests. It carries out actions that for nearly every other Western power would be unacceptable, however to the embattled Israelis their actions are accepted as a requirement in the protection of the state. On April 9–10, 1973, Sayeret infiltrated Beirut, which had to be considered extremely hostile territory, and assassinated the leaders of the Black September organization. This action was carried out successfully at three separate locations in West Beirut.

formed in the Philippines named the Aviation Security Commando (AVESCOM). In Thailand, it is the responsibility of the Royal Thai Air Force. In India, the extremely efficient and well-trained Special Counterterrorist Unit (SCU) is considered to be the best in Asia. Malaysia uses the Special Strike Unit of the Royal Malay Police, and Sri Lanka has the Army Commando Squadron. In the Middle East, Bahrain and Saudi Arabia have units trained by the British SAS and the French GIGN respectively. The Hashemite Kingdom of Jordan maintains the 101st Special Forces Battalion, which also provide sky marshals for Alia, the national airline of Jordan. Egypt has had a colorful history of failures in hostage rescue in recent decades. Both of the incidents occurred in the Mediterranean. Egypt uses the Saiqa unit for counterterrorism operations, as well as Force 777, created in 1978.

The countries of Latin and South America use sections of the military and federal police services for HRU functions in most cases.

UNITED STATES OF AMERICA

The United States has only in the last decade begun to experience at home what most European and Middle East countries have been experiencing for nearly four decades. Hostage rescue, kidnapping and their negotiation have long been the province of the Federal Bureau of Investigations (FBI), assisted by special police squads that are formed in almost every jurisdiction in the United States. These units are termed Special Weapons and Tactical Units (SWAT). The FBI is the U.S. federal agency responsible for information and intelligence gathering at home, which is not as many believe the domain of the Central Intelligence Agency. The CIA is mandated for intelligence and field operations outside the United States and for protecting her interests. With varying gun laws throughout the United States, weapons offenses are a daily diet for the state police, with SWAT teams regularly called upon to deal with many criminal activities, particularly bank hold-ups. With the hostage crisis in Tehran in the 1970s, the need arose to have dedicated and well-trained tactical teams to deal with subversive activities both at home and abroad.

Delta Force was the brainchild of Charles Beckwith in the 1970s. Beckwith realized that the United States did not have the same capability for hostage rescue and counterterrorism response as the Europeans and proposed establishing an elite unit from the ranks of the U.S. Special Forces. Selection began, using the same harsh and disciplined methods as the SAS, which Beckwith himself had experienced with the SAS in the 1960s. The seizure of the U.S. embassy in Tehran, in November 1979, placed the Delta Force on standby to handle the rescue and evacuation of the hostages. Considerable intelligence gathering and logistical planning went into the plans to rescue the hostages, which would use the Delta team front and center. The mission was to fail due to dust storms and with one of the helicopters crashing into a C-130, carrying munitions, resulting in the death of eight members of the Marine Corps.

The members of Delta Force managed to escape injury and returned to the United States without completing their mission. After the abortive mission to Iran, a Special Operations Group was initiated, and from that came the creation in 1980 of SEAL Team Six. SEAL Team Six is the Navy's equivalent to the Delta Force and responsible for handling counterterrorism in any maritime environment. Its beginnings relate directly to the failure of the Tehran operation that had been designated by the code words "Eagle Claw." The name SEAL Team Six was chosen as a ploy to confuse the Soviets as to exactly how many SEAL units the United States had in operation at the time. All of the SEAL platoons were trained in counterterrorism. SEAL Six went through an extensive training regimen that involved training overseas with members of the SAS, GSG-9, GIGN and other counterterrorism organizations. Seal Team Six would undergo further changes to its structure, including a name change due to its poor reputation within the Navy. SEAL Team Six was embarrassed by its founding member, Commander Richard Marcinko, who was charged with an assortment of offenses, ranging from fraud to bribery, and he was sentenced to a brief term of imprisonment. Following this fiasco, the unit designation was changed to The Naval Special Warfare Development Group. Structured on the same lines as the SAS and numbering approximately two hundred men, the NSWDG covers a wide spectrum of abilities, much the same as the SAS and the SBS. Unlike their European counterparts, they have not had the opportunity to prove themselves, as the SAS had at Prince's Gate or the GSG-9 had at Mogadishu, although they have been in both covert and overt operations since the 1980s.

In 1985, they were on standby in the Mediterranean during the Achille Lauro hijacking that claimed the life of Leon Klinghoffer, but they were not called into use. In the same year the unit was used during the U.S. invasion of Grenada to rescue the governor of the island, Sir Paul Scoon. During that operation, four SEALs were drowned during the helicopter insertion offshore. In a more criminal response operation for the U.S. government, they were involved alongside the Delta Force to locate and capture Manuel Noriega from Panama in 1990. Following a coup in Haiti in 1991, it is believed the unit was involved in rescuing deposed President Aristide. The SEALs were used for the initial landings in Somalia in 1992, when they came ashore in scuba gear to a throng of media with video cameras and floodlights which broadcast their invasion, live, around the world. This was a prime example of poor understanding between operational forces and the media.

The United States has also used, in domestic situations, the Alcohol Tobacco and Firearms (ATF) unit for dealing with criminals stockpiling illegal weapons. A major operation was covered for weeks by the news media when the ATF went to execute a warrant against the Branch Davidians, led by David Koresh, in Waco, Texas. The ensuing gun battle and a long standoff later resulted in an assault by the ATF during which all inside the compound were incinerated. It was discovered after the event, however, that many had been killed or committed suicide before flames overtook the buildings.

PIRACY

"*Robbery, kidnapping or violence committed at sea or from the sea without lawful authority, especially by one vessel against another.*" This definition is from the Oxford English Dictionary and from the International Maritime Bureau Piracy Center there is a more recent definition of piracy: "*The act of boarding any vessel with the intent to commit theft or other crime and with the capability to use force in the furtherance of the act."*

Article 101 of the United Nations Convention of the law of the sea defines piracy as:

Piracy consists of any of the following acts:

a. Any illegal acts of violence or detention, or any act of depredation, committed for private ends by the crew or the passengers of a private ship or a private aircraft and directed:

    (i)   On the high seas, against another ship or aircraft, or against persons or property on board such ship or aircraft

    (ii)   Against a ship, aircraft, persons or property in a place outside the jurisdiction of any State

b. Any act of voluntary participation in the operation of a ship or of an aircraft with knowledge of facts making it a pirate ship or aircraft;

c. Any act of inciting or of intentionally facilitating an act described in sub paragraph a or b.

For the reader/student it is also important to examine a less well-known topic but nonetheless very serious threat that continues to exist throughout the shipping world. Sea piracy has been in existence for centuries and to many conjures up an almost romantic or exotic event. The truth is far from that and also has a major economic and security threat attached to it. The worst areas of the globe affected by sea piracy are located in the waters of the Far East—the South China Sea, the waters surrounding Indonesia and the Philippines. Frequent attacks on shipping go virtually unnoticed in the news media, however crew deaths are not an uncommon result of sea piracy. In earlier days, almost all trade around the globe went via ships, and the lucrative routes between the Middle East and the Far East were the hunting grounds for myriads of pirates. The well-known, sixteenth-century English sea captain Sir Francis Drake could also be likened to a pirate. His ships' targets were invariably those belonging to Spain. Britain had been on and off at war with Spain and the seizing of Spain's ships was not considered to be piracy, at least not by the British. Drake was deemed to be a **"Privateer,"** and his many countrymen operated under the same royal protection. However the Spanish Government considered Drake and Walter Raleigh to be dyed in the wool pirates. Piracy on the high seas has developed and become more sophisticated with the passage of time and with obviously higher risks and greater rewards for the pirates.

The International Maritime Organization has defined three types and levels of piracy:

1. An attack on a ship operating close to shore, often an opportunist attack, by pirates in small high-speed seagoing craft, with the intent to steal cash and personal valuables from the crew and the ship's safe. This is Low Level Armed Robbery **(LLAR).**

2. Medium Level Armed Robbery and Assault **(MLAAR)**—this level attack is invariably a deadly assault on the ship's crew and/or passengers, often by well-armed and equipped pirates. This type of attack has often been coordinated with the aid of a mother ship enabling the attack to take place in international waters.

3. The most serious level defined by the organization—Major Criminal Hijack **(MCHJ)**—invariably involves international criminals who are well equipped and trained. These groups will either take total control of the vessel, stealing the vessel's entire cargo and offloading it to another ship, or casting the crew adrift and re-manning and renaming it.

What makes sea piracy so lucrative in this century is that a large number of states have depleted their navies, thus making them unable to have a presence to deter pirate attacks on ships both in international and territorial waters. Add to this a dimension of high technology where many vessels are now dependant on much smaller operating crews, then you have an opportunity for pirates to operate unhindered. Shipping in international waters is protected by the 'flag' of the country in which it is registered. Many countries adopt a 'flag of convenience' for their vessels, this means that a vessel owned in one country, the United States or Great Britain can be registered in Panama, Liberia, or Cyprus, thus avoiding international safety and taxation regulations. Nearly ninety percent of ocean-going cargo ships entering United States ports' are operating under foreign flags. Many of these ships, such as Greek-flagged and flag of convenience ships, officially called "open registry ships" operating out of Piraeus employ low-wage seamen from the developing countries of Pakistan and the Philippines. Flag of convenience countries are often unwilling to take any significant diplomatic action against countries from which pirates are operating. The International Maritime Bureau has a piracy center located in Kuala Lumpur, Indonesia, that has responsibility to provide information around the clock on piracy activities in all the regions of the globe and provides information updates.

The legal aspects of piracy and maritime hijacking are somewhat convoluted and complex. The international community recognizes that an Act of Piracy can only be committed in international waters and must therefore be dealt with under international law. Should the commission of a sea-borne attack on a maritime vessel occur inside territorial waters then the responsibility for pursuing and prosecuting the incident as robbery falls to the state which claims the territorial right over that region of the ocean. International law requires any warship or government vessel to *repress piracy on the high seas'* and to come to the aid of any vessel under attack. The rules of engagement for sea piracy as it affects government vessels are that force should only be used as a means of self-defense against piracy. There are in fact no listed rules of engagement for sea piracy. The action of individual member states navies is governed therefore by that state.

Historical data on piracy does not date back much more than the last two decades of the twentieth century. However some areas of the globe have suffered from acts of piracy to such an extent that action had to be taken. The Nigerian ports of Lagos and Bonny in the early 1980s were particularly targeted. Ships at anchor and waiting to berth were targeted by pirate groups that would attack after dark and break into containers onboard. The eventual outcome was a concerted crackdown by Nigerian police and customs to root out the pirates and also their bases of operation. Piracy has also been highly prevelant in the Far East in the Straits of Malacca, one of the busiest shipping lanes

TERROR BRIEF 13-2

The Achille Lauro Incident

On October 7, 1985, four Syrian-backed members of the Palestine Liberation Front hijacked the Italian cruise ship, Achille Lauro. The hijack coincided with joint Palestinian/Jordanian talks in London formulated by then British Prime Minister Margaret Thatcher. Abul Abbas masterminded the hijacking. It took place in the Mediterranean shortly after 8:00 A.M. when four young Palestinians burst into the cruise ships dining area firing automatic weapons. Their demands were simple: the release of fifty captive Palestinians for the release of the ship, its crew, and more than 400 passengers. When negotiations began to turn sour they executed an elderly American Jew. Leon Klinghoffer and his wheel chair were tossed overboard. The ship attempted to dock at the Syrian port of Tartus but was turned away. It came to Port Said, Egypt, on October 10, where the hijackers agreed to surrender to Egyptian authorities. The four hijackers plus Abu Abbas, the leader of the PLF, were flown to Tunisia. In a show of strength, F14 fighters from the USS Saratoga intercepted the aircraft over the Mediterranean and forced the Egyptian aircraft to land at a NATO air base in Sicily. They were arrested by Italian police but not before diplomatic wrangling between the United States and Italy was eventually resolved by the intervention of President Reagan. It is believed the intended target was not the cruise liner. In fact the terrorists were planning a raid in Egypt when they were discovered on the Achille Lauro with weapons and explosives.

In August 1997, the family of Leon Klinghoffer reached a legal settlement with the PLO for damages. The family of Klinghoffer and the travel agents that had booked the cruise liner sued Arafat and the PLO for damages. Although it is not known what that settlement was, it appears that restitution has been paid for the family's suffering, as a result of Klinghoffer's murder.

Source: George Rosie. *The Directory of International Terrorism,* Paragon House, New York, 1987, p. 39.

in the world. In efforts to contain and minimize the attacks against commercial and other shipping, the International Maritime Organization established a working group to study the problem and come up with a methodology and recommendations. The results of the study were that the underreporting of acts of piracy be discouraged and that masters should immediately report acts and attempted acts of piracy. Probably the most significant effort would be the assistance of technology through the International Telecommunications Union and the International Mobile Satellite Organization (Inmarsat) by the inclusion of a "Piracy/armed robbery attack" as a category of distress message which ships are now able to transmit through Digital Selective Calling (DSC) or using Inmarsat by depressing a button.[19] The message will be received automatically by ships and shore stations in the area. Maritime piracy continues in many regions of the world and particularly in areas where it is easy for pirates to escape without detection. The vastness of the South China Sea is testament to that, and there are attacks on fishing vessels around the many islands of the Philippines. In these attacks, pirates take the fish and any other valuables on board or take the entire vessel. Due to the rapid rise of piracy in the 1980s, the International Maritime Board created the Piracy Reporting Center located in Kuala Lumpur.

TERRORISM BYTE 13–8

The U.N. Convention of the Law of the Sea Article 105

The seizure of a pirate ship or aircraft: on the high seas, or in any other place outside the jurisdiction of any State, every State may seize a pirate ship or aircraft, or a ship or aircraft taken by piracy and under the control of pirates, and arrest the persons and seize the property on board. The courts of the State which carried out the seizure may decide on the penalties to be imposed, and may also determine the action to be taken with regard to the ships, aircraft or property, subject to the rights of the third parties acting in good faith.

Source: http://www.un.org/Depts/Cos/Conventies.agreements.htm.

The Piracy Reporting Center works around the clock and provides daily commentary and bulletins to shipping on pirate activity throughout the globe. The center is actually supported on an annual basis by voluntary contributions towards its funding from shipping lines and insurance companies. The worldwide use of such modern technological breakthroughs as global positioning and tracking systems has enabled shipping companies to adopt such innovations as the SHIPLOC system, which is an inexpensive method of using satellite technology and the Internet to track an individual ship. Irrespective of technology and the will to combat the scourge of piracy, it is likely to continue and the pirates themselves will likely become more sophisticated in their modus operandi. Whether a ship will be used in a wider terrorist attack such as the destruction of a passenger cruise liner with massive loss of life is no doubt on the list of scenarios being looked at by the security and intelligence communities at large.

SUMMARY

The abhorrent attacks on September 11, 2001, show us how little had been done to protect civil aviation particularly in North America and in reviewing this chapter it is clear that not enough was done in the preceding decades to fully protect the traveling public. This lapse was caused in part by complacency, cost and expediency—all of which must be viewed in the full context of the event. The counterterrorism units of the world will continue to have a significant role to play, however, the need for human intelligence will also play a part in our defense. Some salient points to remember are that the authorities have immense power at their fingertips and need to use it cautiously and judiciously. Specialized counterterrorism units have been used as a response mechanism and may be viewed as a well-advertised deterrent by governments unwilling to deal with terrorists. As can be seen with Northern Ireland, both police and specialized units have been deployed in the common cause of fighting terrorism. Special military powers to restrict, control, search and intern suspected members of illegal or proscribed organizations have also been instituted. In democracy, specialist units like the SAS, GIGN, GSG-9 can operate effectively and have the support of the government and the public they serve. It is also necessary and prudent to have strict guidelines and controls for the use of such counterterrorism units. In Northern Ireland, the accusations of a "shoot to kill" policy and "death squads" were hurled by the IRA in a desperate attempt by that subversive group to halt the activities of a response mechanism that was too effective for their purposes. Piracy is a topic not previously touched on, but which shows that there are regions of the globe susceptible to this type of rabid activity and the dangers it poses to the international community. Many ships containing extremely hazardous cargoes circumnavigate the globe, and the risks to nation states and the opportunity for terrorists to take advantage must not be discounted. In the final chapter we will be looking at weapons of mass destruction as well as chemical and biological weapons and future prospects for the use of such horrific weapons against civilian targets.

TERMS TO REMEMBER

Balcombe Street	**Interpol**	**President's Commission**
Chicago Convention	**'it won't happen here'**	**Privateer**
Computer Assisted Passenger Profiling	**LLAR**	**sky marshals**
	Lyon Summit	**Stinger**
Department of Homeland Security	**MCHJ**	**The War on Terrorism**
	MLAAR	**tombstone technology**
ECAC	**Pan Am 103**	**U.S. General Accounting Office**
Gore Commission	**passenger/baggage reconciliation**	
HUMINT		**100% screening**
ICAO	**PLO**	**1373**
IED		

REVIEW QUESTIONS

1. Describe the reasons for establishing counterterrorism specialized units in England and Ireland.
2. Discuss the three Conventions established to protect civil aviation from acts of terrorism.
3. Discuss the role of the European Civil Aviation Conference (ECAC) and how it acts to protect the air traveler.
4. Discuss some of the reasons for the security failures at U.S. airports on 9–11.
5. What are the three levels of piracy defined by the IMO?
6. Discuss the United Nation's role in establishing controls over piracy on the high seas.
7. Discuss some of the failings of the Computer Assisted Passenger Profiling System, established by the airline industry in the United States.

ENDNOTES

1. Paul Wilkinson. *Terrorism and the Liberal State,* New York University Press, 1977, p. 155.

2. Treaties and other International Acts Series. Washington, DC. Government Printing Office 1946. http://www.jurisint.org/pub/01/en/doc/192_3.htm.

3. *Terrorism* (Volume 13 #4 & 5 July-October 1990) Aviation Terrorism Air Carrier Security Programs: Statement before the U.S. House of Representatives, Vol 13 pp. 353–357. Government Activities and Transportation Sub committee, Homer Boynton, Taylor and Francis, 1990.

4. Report of the President's Commission on Aviation Security and Terrorism, 1990 http://www.frac.com/presrprt.htm.

5. Ibid.

6. Cathal Flynn, "Aviation Security is Tight," *USA Today,* March 19, 1999. p. 14A.

7. Billie Vincent, Aviation Security and Terrorism, *Terrorism an International Journal* December 1990. Vol. 13. p. 404.

8. Political Science Monitor. 1999.

9. Jane's Terrorism and Security Monitor 2002. Ed Stephen ULph, James Information Group, London. UK.

10. Alan Pangborn. "How Far Has Europe Come Since Pan Am 103?" *Intersec,* Three Bridges Publishing, May 5, 1996), Vol. 6, p.195.

11. Gerry Edwards. "Hijackers' Gateway." *Intersec,* Three Bridges Publishing, April 1998 Vol. 8, Issue 4, p. 168.

12. Summary of the Ministerial Conference on Terrorism, Paris, France, July 30, 1996. http://www.efc.ca/pages/doc/g7.html.

13. Report to the United Nations Security Council Counter Terrorism Committee December 19th 2001. http://www.fas.org/irp/threat/unsc.html.

14. Sean Hill, The Complexity of Intelligence Gathering, *Sam Houston University, Crime and Justice International* Vol. 17 #56 Oct/Nov 2001 pp. 5.

15. Barbara Cole. *The Elite: The Story of the Rhodesian Special Air Service,* Three Knights Publishing, Transkei, 1984), p.6.

16. Ibid. p, 9.

17. Ibid. p, 15.

18. Leroy Thompson. *The Rescuer.* Paladin Press, Colorado, 1986, p. 84.

19. The Maritime Safety Division, International Maritime Organization web site. http://www.imo.org/home.asp.

14 Terrorism in the Twenty-First Century

Predicting stuff is difficult, especially when it's about the future.

Pogo Possum

OVERVIEW

The quote above, by cartoonist Walt Kelly, in the 1950s from his great comic strip, is so perfect in the turbulent and changing world of today that we had to share it with students who may have never heard of that great satirist. In the world of terrorism intelligence, predictions are more often wrong than correct. After the first attack on the World Trade Center, in 1993, the authorities were concerned about the fact that the terrorists had not succeeded in destroying the entire building . . . as had obviously been their intention. There was also serious concern that they had also intended it to be a biological attack. So much for predicting the future! When we began writing the first edition of this book, the hopes for future peace between Northern Ireland and Britain were high, and an accord was even written and signed. By the time this new edition is off the presses and in the bookstores, who knows where that situation will stand? The Israelis and the PLO, who at one time may have seemed near to a peace plan, seem now almost at opposite ends of the spectrum in that regard. The best we can hope for is to give the student a valid picture of what has happened in the past involving serious terrorism and violence, hoping this background will provide some clues about the future from a social, economic, religious, psychological, political and economic standpoint. While the past may often be prologue, trying to plan for the future by using only the past as a guide is as dangerous as driving a truck by looking only in the rearview mirror. You are probably going to be in for one helluva crash!

How do we conclude a book that has engrossed our minds and our time for so long? It seems that all we can do now is examine what we see as some of the most critical issues that have emerged in regard to terrorism and make some modest comments as to the warning signs. Many of these statements are extensions of those we have covered in the thirteen previous chapters. What is remarkably clear to us in regard to the future is that more than 50,000 terrorists were trained in the camps in Afghanistan, and many are now hidden and blending into the civilian populous of more than sixty nations, and this indicates there could be many thousands of sleeper cells lying dormant in European countries and the United States.

TERRORISM GETS A LARGER STAGE

United States Embassies Become Targets

Osama bin Laden is alleged to control a personal fortune estimated at over $250 million and spends it freely on his personal war against America and the Western democracies that he despises. He has combined financial muscle with religious extremism, a deadly cocktail. Bin Ladin and a coalition of Islamic extremist groups even issued a fatwa, (similar to that issued on Rushdie in Iran). Its wording is chilling: "To kill the Americans and their allies, civilian and military, is an individual duty for every Muslim who can do it, in any country in which it is possible to be done." These words were carried in our first edition of *Terrorism Today*, and we now know that he meant what he said and will continue to take his war with the West to wherever and with whatever means he can find, to include chemical, nuclear and biological weapons of mass destruction.

Prior to 9–11, our angers and fears were focused on terrorism committed in far-off lands like Tanzania and Kenya—of course we refer to the bin Laden-sponsored attacks on the two U.S. embassies in Africa. The result of such terror attacks was defined and targeted, but limited to bombing attacks by the U.S. on bases in the Sudan and Afghanistan. As we noted above, however, predicting the future is difficult and analyzing the past is a lot easier. The al Qaeda, as we now know it, is probably more predictable than we might have imagined. Over the last four years they have responded to every U.S. operation mounted against them. Or, it may be more correct to state, that the U.S./U.N. teams have responded to their attacks. The passage of time between attacks by bin Laden seems to be due in part to the planning that goes into each mission/assault. Planning the attack is not left to chance and it is apparent that when the attack is put at risk the perpetrators retreat until the timing is correct—from intelligence sources there are indications that on September 11, 2001, there were other terrorists in the air that fateful day that could not or did not follow through with their mission.

As for the future, the United States has already developed and submitted to Congress a proposal for cabinet-level Homeland Security Department responsible to the Office of the President of the United States.[1] One can only hope that the United States has not created an additional level of bureaucracy that will seriously encumber the mission of counterterror and intelligence organizations. This major reorganization of the government was preceded by the almost immediate establishment of the Office of Homeland Security after 9–11.

As we become further removed from the horrific events of 9–11, and people move on with their everyday lives, the terrorist threat may grow dimmer in the eyes of many Americans. But the world is just as dangerous today, if not more so, than it ever was. The threat is real—as real as it was in 2001. In fact, it is a permanent condition to which all of us must adapt permanently. But, it's important to remember that we can adapt—we can do something about it.

We already know what the terrorists want to do to us. We have it from their missing or dead leader, Osama bin Laden, in his own words, from a December 2001 videotape, broadcast by the Arabic television news station Al Jazeera.

- "Our terrorism is against America. Our terrorism is a blessed terrorism . . ."
- "It is very important to hit the U.S. economy with every available means. . . . [It] is the base of its military power."
- "If their economy ends, they will busy themselves away from the enslavement of oppressed people. . . . It is important to concentrate on the destruction of the American economy."

Clearly, they want to take innocent lives and destroy the American way of life.

The very first "mission" in the President's Executive Order creating The Office of Homeland Security reads: "to develop and coordinate the implementation of a comprehensive national strategy to secure the United States from terrorist threats or attacks." Former Governor, Tom Ridge, takes every word of that Executive Order seriously. The Office of Homeland Security will help build the consensus—but the action will happen on the front lines, carried out by people who have the experience and expertise to get the job done—and who prove it every single day. The Office of Homeland Security, (and the new cabinet-level agency), must wrap its arms around every aspect of homeland security. Our strategy must not be just to raise questions, but to provide answers and solutions. National strategy is not federal. That means the states and localities, the private sector and academia, and the American people must work together to make it happen. Securing the United States means preserving a physical, financial and electronic infrastructure, our people, our freedoms and our way of life. Securing them is the core responsibility of government. Anticipating all threats or attacks is critical and means we must not only improve our preparedness, but we must preempt and deter attacks at their source, whether in Afghanistan, Europe or in our own backyard.

A comprehensive national strategy will prioritize our long-term needs. It will reveal what we need to protect and how to protect it. It will outline the resources available to us, and point the way for their best use and institutionalize our response over the course of several years. Put another way, it will answer three questions often asked, "Whose job is it? What do we need to do it? Who pays for it?" Homeland security requires a new way of governing, a new way of looking at things. We have to think anew, and in the business vernacular of today, "Think outside of the box." To respond to terrorist threats, we have to anticipate their moves. We cannot be everywhere at once, all the time. Our resources won't allow it. More importantly, our freedoms won't allow it. Our national strategy will be guided by an overarching philosophy of "risk management," focusing limited resources where they will do the most good, to achieve the maximum protection of lives and property. We will play both offense—massing our resources to meet the most immediate threats—and defense, working to fill our most glaring gaps.

To that end, the current Office of Homeland Security is undertaking a large-scale review of our nation's critical infrastructure. They are working with the states and the private sector—which owns more than 80 percent of that infrastructure—to map in detail this infrastructure, examining risks, probabilities and consequences, so priorities can be set in providing protection. The challenge is vast. It encompasses so much: oil and gas refineries, power plants and electrical substations, water treatment plants and reservoirs, dams and pipelines, to name just a miniscule fraction. Add to that our schools and hospitals, our banks and financial institutions, our airports and seaports, our bridges and highways. But take a second look. We can turn these vulnerabilities into strengths.

- Our public health system can save lives in a bioterror attack, and issue early warnings to prevent an outbreak from spreading.
- Our banks and financial institutions can be used to help investigators stop money laundering and take terrorists' dollars out of their pockets.
- Our roads and rail systems can be used to make potential targets more mobile and less visible.
- Our ports and harbors, airports and border entry points can be transformed from vulnerabilities into barriers against terrorism.

It has already begun, by refocusing the mission of the Coast Guard to homeland security. It's working to deter more than terrorism. Some indicators show a significant reduction in crime as a result of the homeland security measures taken at ports.

If we secure the hometowns, we will secure the homeland. And, that too is happening. Great work is being done, much of it by neighbors, the firefighters and police officers, the doctors and EMTs, the border guards and businessmen. This is work that began well before 9–11. These are the folks on the front lines. They're the ones who will respond to and recover from a crisis and who will influence key budget decisions in the city halls, county commissions and state legislatures.

The Office of Homeland Security of Homeland Security has created a two-way flow of ideas and information with them. There is strong support for the President's four budget initiatives: first responders, biodefense, border security and information sharing. The four were chosen because of risk management.

- Our first responders initiative will help reduce the risk of injury and death in an attack.
- Bioterror has one of the highest rates of consequence, and our preparedness has historically lagged behind the threat.
- We're building "smart borders" of the future—focusing our technological and human resources on separating high-risk traffic from low-risk and no-risk traffic.

With federal funds, El Paso and Detroit are busy developing new initiatives to protect America from terrorists.

- The Office of Homeland Security is developing an entry-exit visa database to monitor short-term visitors to this country, especially those who overstay their welcome—reducing the risk that we'll lose track of the few who seek us harm.
- And the president's budget increases cyber-security funding by 64 percent. This will include a Cyberspace Warning Intelligence Network to link government and the private sector so we can reduce the risk of damage caused by

cyber-terrorists or hackers. Technology can help make us more secure—but security must extend to technology.

States and localities are eager to work with the Office of Homeland Security, and they want direction and support, not micromanagement. The Office of Homeland Security encouraged them to join regional mutual aid compacts and develop interoperable communications systems. We're asking them to hold regular drills and simulations; the more we practice, the more we reduce the risk. And, above all, we've asked state and local officials to work together on a single, integrated, statewide anti-terrorism plan. We are encouraged by their response. Some of you may have caught the phrase "our freedoms and our way of life" in the list of things we must protect. It's the truth—and a responsibility that the Office of Homeland Security takes very seriously.

The answer to an attack on our freedom is more freedom, not less. Freedom is not vulnerability, but strength. In the 1940s, American businesses built an "arsenal of democracy" to win the war. Today they're building an "arsenal of security"—exciting, nimble, cutting-edge products that can cut our response time and save lives. The Office of Homeland Security needs this innovation and imagination. And businesses need the opportunity—the opportunity to do well by doing well. It can give us not just a safer, more secure America, but also a more competitive and prosperous America. Many of these products are designed to improve communication and speed the flow of information. Attorney General Ashcroft has said that, "Information is the best friend of prevention."

The Office of Homeland Security is going to knock down the information "stovepipes" throughout government and turn them into pipelines. That's one reason why we created the Homeland Security Advisory System. One lesson of 9–11 is that when information doesn't get to the right people in time, it can be just as dangerous as when it falls into the wrong hands.

CHEMICAL, BIOLOGICAL, AND NUCLEAR WEAPONS OF MASS DESTRUCTION

Even greater threats to national and western security are the potential for biological, chemical, and nuclear attacks. The United States is making alliances around the world, not just to track down the pockets of al Qaeda, but also to identify those countries that are amassing the materials to construct such weapons of mass destruction.

A July 2000 report by the U.S. General Accounting Office showed:

- Investigators from the GAO visited nineteen military sites in Europe, the Middle East and the Pacific. Their report cited several inadequacies in protection and procedures and gave examples without disclosing the facilities' locations. The GAO report said: "Significant security and procedural anti-terrorism/force protection problems continue at many installations."

- Congressional investigators report that U.S. military forces around the world remain vulnerable to terrorist attack despite improvements made after a truck bomb killed nineteen Americans at a U.S. military complex in Saudi Arabia four years ago. A Pentagon spokesman stated that the General Accounting

Office (GAO) report contained errors and did not reflect its strong commitment to combat terrorism. Officials did agree with some recommendations.

A further report to the Senate Intelligence Committee in February 2002, through the GAO, reports CIA Director George Tenet's comments, in a detailed briefing on national security threats in which Tenet outlined the key dangers:

- The al Qaeda is working on "multiple-attack plans" and putting cells in place to carry them out.
- Iran continues to support terrorist groups and has sent arms to Palestinian terrorists and the group Hezbollah. Tenet said: "Tehran also has failed to move decisively against al Qaeda members who have relocated to Iran from Afghanistan."
- Terrorists could attack U.S. nuclear plants or chemical industry sites using conventional means "to cause widespread toxic or radiological damage."
- Al Qaeda cells in major European and Middle Eastern cities could launch attacks, and al Qaeda is connected with groups in Somalia, Yemen, Indonesia, and the Philippines.
- There are fears that al Qaeda and other terrorists will attack using nuclear, chemical or biological weapons. Director Tenet said: "Terrorist groups worldwide have ready access to information on chemical, biological, and even nuclear weapons via the Internet, and we know that al Qaeda was working to acquire some of the most dangerous chemical agents and toxins."
- Tensions between India and Pakistan remain high over a December 13, 2001, terrorist attack on the Indian parliament, and the two nations could resort to nuclear weapons. Tenet said: "We are deeply concerned that a conventional war, once begun, could escalate into a nuclear confrontation."
- Terrorists could attempt to attack the United States by conducting cyber-strikes designed to cripple U.S. electronic-based infrastructures. Countering the terrorist threat and determining the response will present the biggest challenge challenges for the coming months, and for years to come.

A NEW GULF WAR?

In the ten years since the Gulf War ended, Iraqi President Saddam Hussein has stated that he has always considered himself at war with America. And during that time, the United States has always considered him a threat. While America's military has unleashed its might against the Taliban and al Qaeda, powerful forces in Washington and the president are considering attacking a much bigger target. The events of 9–11 have re-energized Saddam's strongest opponents in Washington. The weekend following the suicide attacks on the World Trade Center and the Pentagon, President George W. Bush met at Camp David with his top advisers. "There was a lively debate about Iraq policy."

As the War on Terrorism in Afghanistan begins to wind down, more and more speculation as to what to do about Iraq is building. U.S. Secretary of State Colin Powell says the Bush administration is examining a full range of options on Iraq, and, "It is the most serious assessment of options that one might imagine." The following is the latest on this prickly situation and what the Secretary of State Powell and Secretary of the Army have to say about it. By the time this edition has been printed and released, the decision to wage war will have been made or rejected, but President Bush is "leaving no stone unturned as to what we might do," Powell said, in dealing with Iraqi President Saddam Hussein's refusal to permit U.N. international weapons inspections to resume.

"The president is examining a full range of options of how to deal with Iraq," the secretary said, during testimony before the House International Relations Committee on February 6, 2002. The committee was conducting a hearing on the administration's request for $25,300 million for U.S. international affairs spending in fiscal year 2003. Secretary of State Powell declined to elaborate on the extent of the options under consideration by the Bush administration. However, he said there is no doubt that Iraq is pursuing a nuclear weapons program. "The best intelligence we have suggests that it isn't something they have ready to pop out with in the next year or so. It would take them a bit longer," Powell said. To accomplish the U.N.-mandated inspections effectively, Powell stated that the Iraqi government must allow the international inspectors unfettered access.

"The president is determined to keep this on the front burner and is looking at all the options that are available for him to deal with this in a decisive way," Powell said. "We still have a U.S. policy of regime change because we believe Saddam Hussein should move on and that the Iraqi people deserve better leadership." Powell suggested "regime change is something the United States . . . might have to do alone." At a separate hearing before the Senate Select Intelligence Committee, CIA Director George Tenet said "Saddam remains a threat, and the Iraqi leader is determined to thwart U.N. sanctions imposed for failing to permit international weapons inspectors in the country." "Iraq continues to build and expand an infrastructure capable of producing WMD [Weapons of Mass Destruction]," Tenet said. He added, "Iraq retains a significant number of nuclear scientists, program documentation, and probably some dual-use manufacturing infrastructure that could support a reinvigorated nuclear weapons program."

Secretary of Defense Donald Rumsfeld asserts that, "previous weapons inspections inside Iraq were often ineffective and relied upon defectors. Any new inspections program, he added, must be much stronger and more intrusive to end Saddam Hussein's efforts to build weapons of mass destruction." Speaking on CBS-TV program "Face the Nation" February 24, 2002, Rumsfeld said, "The Iraqis have had more time to go underground. They've had lots of dual-use technologies that have come in. They've had lots of illicit things that have come in. They have advanced their weapons of mass destruction programs." As a result, Rumsfeld pointed out, "If you try to use the old regime, it wouldn't work. You would have to have a much more intrusive regime and many more inspectors and the Iraqis not controlling when they could come in, where they could go, what they could do." Rumsfeld praised the efforts of Pakistan's President Musharraf in finding the killers of journalist Daniel Pearl, but refused to speculate as to whether the murder might be related to al Qaeda. Without giving numbers, Rumsfeld confirmed that many members of al Qaeda and Taliban leadership have been captured or killed. "And clearly," he said, "there are more that we're still looking for." Secretary Rumsfeld denied reports that a new Pentagon office might deliberately provide misinformation to the news media and foreign publics. "Clearly, this Secretary and the people that work with me are not going to engage in misinformation to the

TERROR BRIEF 14–1

Strengthening Homeland Security Since 9–11

Immediately following the tragic events of September 11, departments and agencies from across the federal government took steps to strengthen the safety and security of the American people. At the federal level, a total of $10.6 billion from the fiscal year 2002 Emergency Budget Supplemental was dedicated to homeland security. The challenge is large, and much more remains to be done, but the foundation for a stronger, more secure America has been put in place:

Law Enforcement Activities

- Established the Homeland Security Advisory System (HSAS), which is designed to be the foundation for building a comprehensive and effective communications structure for the dissemination of information regarding the risk of attacks to all levels of government and the American people.
- Deployed more than 4,000 FBI special agents and 3,000 support staff to the international investigation of the September 11 terrorist attacks the largest criminal investigation in history.
- Responded to more than 8,000 cases of anthrax attacks or hoaxes.
- Implemented the USA Patriot Act which, among other things:
  a. Updated federal laws to reflect the rapid and dramatic changes that have taken place in recent years in communications technology;
  b. Required the Department of the Treasury to require financial institutions to verify the identities of persons opening accounts, granted immunity to financial institutions that voluntarily disclosed suspicious transactions, and increased the penalties for money-laundering;
  c. Broadened the terrorism-related definitions in the Immigration and National-

ity Act, expanded the grounds of inadmissibility to include aliens who publicly endorse terrorist activity, and required the Attorney General to detain aliens whom he certifies as threats to national security;
  d. Authorized grants that will enhance state and local governments' ability to respond to and prevent terrorism, and expanded information-sharing among law enforcement authorities at different levels of government.
- Established 56 Joint Terrorism Task Forces and nearly 100 Anti-Terrorism Task Forces to coordinate the investigations and improve communications among federal, state, and local law enforcement.
- Launched Operation Green Quest to dry up sources of terrorist funding. To date, the assets of 192 individuals and organizations connected with the al-Taqua, al-Barakaat, and Hamas organizations have been frozen.
- Established a web site and toll-free hotline for citizens to report suspected terrorist activity.
- Adopted new, stronger encryption standards to safeguard sensitive, non-classified electronic information such as financial transactions, and ensure the privacy of digital information ranging from medical records and tax information, to PIN numbers for millions of Americans.

Border and Port Security

- Proposed INS regulations to eliminate the current minimum six months admission period for B-2 visitors for pleasure, replacing it with "a period of time that is fair and reasonable for the completion of the purpose of the visit."
- Immediately required individuals planning to attend school in the United States

to obtain the proper INS student visa prior to their admission to the country.

- Proposed INS regulations to reduce the maximum visa extension from one year to six months. Additionally, the visitor must prove there are adequate financial resources to continue to stay in the United States and that he or she is maintaining a residency abroad.
- Placed the nation's air, land, and seaports of entry on Alert Level 1 following September 11, ensuring a more thorough examination of people and cargo.
- Created the new Customs Trade Partnership Against Terrorism (Customs-TPAT) initiative to enhance security throughout the entire import-export process.
- Launched the Container Security Initiative, which establishes a tough new international security standard for cargo containers.
- Deployed approximately 1,600 National Guardsmen to assist in securing the nation's borders.
- Increased National Park Service personnel and upgraded security equipment and the procedures at highly visible national monuments, such as the Statue of Liberty in New York, the National Mall in Washington, the Liberty Bell and Independence Hall in Philadelphia, the Gateway Arch in St. Louis, and other sites in the 384-unit National Park System.

Transportation Security

- Recruited thousands of federal security personnel to perform screening duties and other functions at commercial airports.
- Significantly expanded the Federal Air Marshal program.
- Announced the first group of Federal Security Directors. These experienced law enforcement officers will be directly responsible for security at airports and provide a clear and direct line of authority.
- Developed new passenger boarding procedures and trained pilots and flight crews for hijacking scenarios.

- Required all airport personnel to undergo background checks.
- Limited airport access points and implemented secondary screening procedures.
- Deployed more than 9,000 National Guardsmen to help secure the nation's airports.

Health and Food Security

- Aided thousands of rescue workers involved in the September 11 recovery activities through Disaster Medical Assistance Teams (DMATs).
- Identified more than 750 victims of the World Trade Center attacks through Disaster Mortuary Operational Response Teams (DMORTs).
- Dispensed antibiotics to thousands of persons potentially exposed to anthrax mail attacks.
- Acquired more than a billion doses of antibiotics and signed agreements for the procurement of the small pox vaccine.
- Distributed $1.1 billion to help states prepare for bioterrorism attacks.
- Strengthened systems to prevent, detect and eliminate threats to agriculture and the food supply, including $328 million for pest and animal disease prevention, food safety, research, laboratory upgrades and stepped up security at key facilities.
- Distributed $2 million in grants to 32 states to bolster emergency animal disease prevention, preparedness, response and recovery systems.
- Improved inspection and testing of products destined for consumer markets in the United States.
- Provided millions of dollars through the Food Stamp and Women, Infants, and Children (WIC) programs to families of victims and displaced workers of the September 11 attacks.

Environmental and Energy Security

- Provided security training to drinking water and wastewater utility companies.

TERROR BRIEF 14–1

Strengthening Homeland Security Since 9–11 (continued)

- Provided security guidance and support to private sector chemical and pesticide manufacturers.
- Conducted vulnerability assessments of energy infrastructure throughout the country.
- Created a 24-hour network to ensure energy producers have up to date information from law enforcement information.
- Provided 24 hour-per-day, 7 day-a-week security at 348 dams and reservoirs and 58 hydroelectric power plants, including Hoover, Grand Coulee, Glen Canyon, and Shasta Dams.
- Constructed biological, radiological, and nuclear mobile detection capability to conduct threat-based searches.
- Placed nuclear power plants across the nation on the highest level of security.
- Developed pocket radiation detector for first responders.
- Engaged in a top-to-bottom security review of nuclear facilities, including plant vulnerability to aircraft.

Citizen Engagement

- Established Citizen Corps to enable Americans to participate directly in

homeland security efforts in their own communities. These components include:

- *Medical Reserve Corps:* Enables retired healthcare professionals to effectively augment local health officials' capacity to respond to an emergency.
- *Operation TIPS (Terrorist Information and Prevention System):* Allows millions of American transportation workers, postal workers, and public utility employees to identify and report suspicious activities linked to terrorism and crime.
- *Community Emergency Response Teams (CERT):* Enables individual Americans to participate in emergency management planning in their communities and prepare to respond to disasters and other emergencies.
- *Neighborhood Watch Programs:* Enhances the program by incorporating terrorism prevention into its mission.

Developed the "Patriot Readiness Center" to help federal retirees return to active service. More than 15,000 people have responded.

Source: Office of the Press Secretary, Office of Homeland Security, April 11, 2002.

American people or to foreign public," Rumsfeld said. "We are simply not going to do it. That's not what we do."[2]

THE NEW DEPARTMENT OF HOMELAND SECURITY

On January 24, 2003, at 1:20 P.M. EST, President George W. Bush announced the formation of, and unanimous congressional approval of the new "Department of Homeland Security." This first new cabinet department since the Pentagon, retained and confirmed as its first Secretary, former Pennsylvania Governor Thomas Joseph Ridge. Homeland Security becomes the 15th executive department in the Bush cabinet. The President stated that it begins a vital mission in the defense of our country. Vast oceans no longer protect us from the dangers of this new era. This government has a responsibility to confront the threat of terror wherever it is found. And at home we are taking every measure to protect the American people against a serious and ongoing terrorist threat. The Department of Homeland Security will lead a comprehensive and unified effort to defend this nation within its own borders and its near shorelines. The Department will analyze threats; guard our borders and airports; safeguard critical infrastructure and coordinate the response of our nation to future emergencies.

Under the leadership of Tom Ridge, more than 170,000 dedicated Americans, and professionals, will have the overriding mission of protecting their fellow Americans. The White House Office of Homeland Security now has broader reach and authority. Secretary Ridge earned an unanimous vote of confirmation by the United States Senate. This new Department will face many challenges in the year to come. The President assured the American people it can be certain that the mission of homeland security will be carried out with focus and resolve, with the resources the task requires.

Organization of the Department of Homeland Security

Terrorists today can strike at any place, at any time, and with virtually any weapon. This is a permanent condition and these new threats require our country to design a new homeland security structure.

The United States faced an enormous threat during the Cold War. We created a national security strategy to deter and defeat the organized military forces of the Soviet bloc. We emerged victorious from this dangerous period in our history because we organized our national security institutions and prepared ourselves to meet the threat arrayed against us. The United States is now under attack from a new kind of enemy—one that hopes to employ terror against innocent civilians to undermine their confidence in our institutions and our way of life. Once again America must organize and prepare ourselves to meet a new and dangerous threat.

Mission of the New Department

The mission of the Department of Homeland Security would be to:

- Prevent terrorist attacks within the United States;
- Reduce America's vulnerability to terrorism;
- Minimize the damage and recover from attacks that do occur.

The Department of Homeland Security would mobilize and focus the resources of the federal government, state and local governments, the private sector, and the American people to accomplish its mission.

Organization

The creation of the Department of Homeland Security would empower a single Cabinet official whose primary mission is to protect the American homeland from terrorism. The Department of Homeland Security would have a clear, efficient organizational structure with four divisions.

- **Border and Transportation Security**
- **Emergency Preparedness and Response**
- **Chemical, Biological, Radiological, and Nuclear Countermeasures**
- **Information Analysis and Infrastructure Protection**

Even after creation of the new Department, homeland security will still involve the efforts of other Cabinet departments. The Department of Justice and the FBI, for example, will remain the lead law enforcement agencies for preventing terrorist attacks. The Department of Defense will continue to play a crucial support role in the case of a catastrophic terrorist incident. The Department of Transportation will continue to be responsible for highway and rail safety, and air traffic control. The CIA will continue to gather and analyze overseas intelligence. Homeland security will continue to require interagency coordination, and the President will still need a close adviser on homeland security related issues. Accordingly, the President intends a strong continuing role for the White House Office of Homeland Security and the Homeland Security Council.

Tom Ridge is sworn in as Director of Homeland Security.

WEAPONS OF MASS DESTRUCTION (WMD)

Nations of the world and, more particularly, Western democracies have had to come to the sudden realization that future threats from terrorists may come from the unthinkable, the use of chemical and biological agents as a means of mass destruction. Let's not forget that bin Laden wants nothing except destruction! There is much talk of the countries that have the desire and capacity to build components for WMD. First we look at Iraq, a country led by a despotic leader for the last 25 years and which has field-tested chemical agents to grisly effect against the Kurds in the northern-most areas of Iraq in the 1980s. There are probably more than twenty-eight countries around the globe with the ability to build chemical agents and some are not deemed friendly states. The chilling words of Ambassador Ekeus, who led the United Nations Special Commission to Iraq, when he referred to what Iraq had not admitted to possessing as being, "an unparalleled level of deception, fraud, cheating and intimidation." If there is any doubt of the capacity of what the Iraqi regime is up to, we can refer backwards to an UNSCOM official report in 1991. The Commission found over 46,000 munitions filled with chemical agents, of these 20,000 were 120mm CS-filled bombs, 14,000 contained mustard gas, and 11,000 with sarin. Later discoveries were made near Saddam Hussein's Tikrit base, including 200 Anthrax bombs. The fears for the future are real. U.N. inspectors have been kept out of Iraq for years and there is little doubt that development and production have continued in secret unabated. Will any U.N. inspection teams find the evidence when and if they are admitted? Has Iraq passed on any of its deadly technology or hardware to Islamic extremists with desires to continue attacks against the west and the United States in particular?

U.N. Security Council Resolution 688 demands that Iraq unconditionally accept the destruction and removal, under international supervision, of all chemical and biological weapons and furthermore it unconditionally agrees not to acquire or develop nuclear weapons. Saddam Hussein is not renowned for his response to dictates from the U.N. Security Council. Iraq is also believed to have training bases for international terror groups, including Palestinian terror organizations. Saddam Hussein also pledges the equivalent of $25,000 to the families of suicide bombers martyring themselves in Israel. Is Iraq a threat to our future? Undoubtedly his avowed hatred for both the United States and Great Britain, and his disdain for the United Nation make him a very unpredictable threat in an already unstable region of the globe.

As for the chemical threat from the Iraqi regime, this is again evidenced from UNSCOM which states that the Iraqi regime is in every likelihood producing and stockpiling chemical agents such as Sarin, Cyclosarin, and mustard gas. In addition, UNSCOM states that Iraq has not accounted for hundreds of tons of chemical precursors, to include material for warheads for its SCUD missiles. It has also not accounted for at least 15,000 artillery rockets, armaments that have been the regime's preferred method of delivering nerve agents. That Iraq has also hugely understated its chemical weapons program must lead us to the conclusion that Iraq not only has produced and stockpiled WMD it is likely at the point where it will be able to deliver it on a suitably equipped missile against its foe.

As for other rogue states: North Korea, according to a 1996 U.S. DOD report "has the ability to produce limited quantities of traditional infectious biological-weapon agents or toxins" and a 1988 comment by Iran's parliamentary speaker Hashemi Rafsanjani said, "Chemical and biological weapons are poor mans' atomic bombs and can easily be produced. We should at least consider them for our defense." Syria is also considered to have one of the largest chemical warfare capabilities in the Middle East. So is the threat of an attack by chemical or biological a credible threat? In the context of the 9–11 attacks, the next most likely scenario is just such an attack. If the aim of terror groups and individuals like bin Laden and al Qaeda is destruction then it behooves all of us to be cognizant of the risk of such an attack in the future.

NUCLEAR THREATS

The threat of a terrorist attack with nuclear weapons may be the least likely threat from WMD. Although there has been much international concern about security of facilities in the former Soviet Union throughout the last decade and the accessibility of materials for nuclear weapons, preparing and constructing a nuclear device is no mean feat to achieve. It requires a large investment as well as considerable technical expertise. Osama bin Laden has the wealth to achieve the goal for acquiring a nuclear weapon, but the next problem would have to be in the method of delivery. He would appear to be a terrorist on the run if in fact he is alive, and with no fixed base to work at creating his nuclear WMD. The main constituent of a nuclear weapon is highly enriched uranium (HEU) or plutonium. The quantities located around the globe amount to around 2,000 tons plus an additional three hundred tons of plutonium. Building a nuclear warhead can be achieved with as little as 25 pounds of HEU. Without the sophisticated machine tools, electronic circuitry and triggering devices needed to make a proper nuclear weapon, merely blowing up a lump of plutonium or HEU with conventional high explosives could cause widespread and deadly radioactive pollution.[3]

CHEMICAL AND BIOLOGICAL THREATS

In 1972, 103 countries signed the Biological Weapons Convention, which prohibited the development of biological and chemical weapons, including their use. Iraq as we know has not complied with this Convention. We now know that the risks of biological and chemical attacks are very real—the anthrax attacks against U.S. public officials and their offices after 9–11 showed how easy it was for a relatively insignificant amount of 'white powder' to turn a public to mass panic and hysteria, presumably one of the aims of that specific terrorist. The anthrax attacks of 2001 made whole governments sit up and take notice of the threat and also notice how unprepared they were to respond to such deadly threats and attacks. It is important to have a brief understanding of how chemical and biological weapons work. Biological weapons are created in naturally occurring organisms that create disease. Two of the most common examples are the bacteria *Bacillus anthracis,* which produces a toxin and smallpox, a viral disease that is highly infectious. Chemical weapons are poisons, such as the nerve gas sarin and mustard gas that was used in trench warfare in the 1914–1918 World War. The anthrax bacterium most often affects grazing cattle. The bacteria produces shell-like spores allowing the bacteria to lie dormant in soil. When anthrax is used as a biological weapon, the spores usually enter the human body via the lungs and then enter the blood stream. The spores become active, and reproduce in large numbers and release a devastating toxin that is lethal to cells. When enough spores have been inhaled, then the anthrax will kill. Anthrax may not be fatal to those who have been vaccinated and after exposure receive antibiotics. However someone who has not received any vaccine will likely die within thirty-six hours of exposure. Smallpox on the other hand was virtually eradicated worldwide by the end of the 1970s after an aggressive two decades of vaccination. This highly infectious viral disease could be used against a generation that has not been so vaccinated, and the unvaccinated death rate would likely be at the level of 30%. The only known remaining smallpox cultures kept under tight security are in Kosovo, Russia, and Atlanta, Georgia. Starting up a biological weapons laboratory requires a person with full knowledge of microbiology and a few thousand dollars worth of equipment. Development may be one issue but the control of the culture would be a significant issue for the would-be terrorist. Probably one of the most significant reasons that we have not witnessed broad attempts at biological terror is the issue of containing the culture. Bacteria and viruses do not discriminate between the terrorist and his intended targets and the biological effects of the agent affecting the one who releases it is a common occurrence.

On the chemical front sarin gas, which was used by the Japanese Aum Shinrikyo terror group to attack a Tokyo subway, has a devastating effect. The gas is odorless and colorless and attacks the central nervous system. Death can occur within 2–15 minutes. Cyanide, a more commonly known chemical agent, is a gas that is produced in massive quantities with apparent ease. Cyanide acts almost instantly and the target ingesting it is usually dead in seconds. This gas was used in World War I and also by Saddam Hussein against the Kurds in northern Iraq. The agent tabun is a nerve agent that has been around since the 1930s and has been used as a pesticide and can be found in many regions of the world. Like many other nerve agents it is absorbed via the skin. Tabun is resistant to heat and can be delivered in aerosol format, which would make it deliverable by artillery shell.[4]

An audit by the U.S. General Accounting Office in 1991 indicated that nine chemical sites visited in the United States were potentially vulnerable to aerial attack, and that four of the sites may be susceptible and vulnerable to ground attack. Since 9–11, no doubt much attention has been given to security at these sites in the United States. The use of chemical and biological agents may be restricted to those organizations bent purely on destroying democracy, rather than those that are using terrorism to 'bargain' for their own styles of democracy.

HOLY TERROR

Terrorism motivated by religious imperatives is growing quickly, increasing the number of killings and reducing the restraints on mass, indiscriminate murder. So great is this change, according to Bruce Hoffman, an advocate for woman's choice, that we may have to revise our notions of the stereotypical terrorist organization. Hoffman explained that traditional terrorist groups could be characterized as groups that engage in conspiracy as a full-time avocation, living underground and constantly planning and plotting terrorist attacks, perhaps under the direct control or at the behest of a foreign government. What we viewed as an amateurish attack on the World Trade Center in 1993 now reveals to us the kind of individual/terrorist groups that we must contend with in the future. From that investigation it seems evident that Islamic extremists in that case had not completed the attack. It was, however, completed eight years later by their brothers-in-arms in the suicide attacks of 9–11. This new breed of terrorists represents an even greater threat than its predecessors have.

"Holy terror" and the purely so-called "secular terror" have radically different value systems, mechanisms for justifying their acts, and concepts of morality. For the religious terrorist, violence is a divine duty. Whereas secular terrorists generally regard indiscriminate violence as immoral and counterproductive, religious terrorists view such violence as both morally justified and necessary. Also, whereas secular terrorists attempt to appeal to a constituency composed of sympathizers and the aggrieved people they claim to speak for, religious terrorists act for no audience but themselves. This absence of a constituency, combined with an extreme sense of alienation, means that such terrorists can justify almost limitless violence against virtually any target who is not a member of their own religious belief or sect.

Religious or ethnic extremism could more easily allow terrorists to overcome the psychological barriers to mass murder than a radical political agenda has in the past. Many white supremacists actually welcome the prospect of nuclear war or terrorism. They see it as an opportunity to eliminate their avowed "enemies" and permit the fulfillment of their objectives to create a new world order peopled exclusively by the white race. Any doubts about the seriousness of such hate groups were dispelled when police and federal agents raided a white supremacist compound in rural Arkansas in April 1984, and discovered a stockpile of some thirty gallons of cyanide to be used to poison municipal water supplies. The targets and tactics of "holy terror" operations that have occurred or been attempted during the past decade lead to the possibility of far more destructive acts. Ominous examples already abound:

- Poisoning of water supplies of major urban centers—not only American white supremacists, but also terrorists in India are alleged to have made such plans.
- Dispersal of toxic chemicals through internal building ventilation system, which has been attempted by white supremacist "skin heads" in Arizona.
- Indiscriminate, wanton attacks on busy urban centers—accounting for 1,400 injuries and deaths in Bombay last winter—alleged to be the work of Muslim terrorists.
- Attacks on power grids to disrupt electrical service to large population areas—conducted by a Black Muslim sect in Colorado.
- Poisoning of food—undertaken in Oregon by followers of the Baghwan Rajneesh to influence a local election.

As the millennium approached, the fears became real when Ahmed Ressam was intercepted entering the United States from Canada with a bomb planned for Los Angeles International Airport. While our attention is now fully averted towards terrorist cells possibly at large in the cities and the countryside, one should not discount the threats that could still pose a significant danger. If we ignore the militias and the network they have across the nation, we do so at our own peril. It is clear that this movement is growing rapidly. The student need only type in the word "militia" on the browser and they will find dozens of the examples like those discussed in earlier chapters.

TECHNO TERRORISM

While the Internet offers great opportunity for good and is the fastest growing business sector the world has ever seen, it must be aligned with commercial market forces and operate on an international basis. Some observers believe that encryption software must be developed so that industrial and other espionage is prevented. The proliferation of strong encryption will have the opposite effect of that envisioned by the administration. That is, it will help fight crime by keeping information secure in the new borderless world.

Testifying before a Senate committee, Jerry Berman, executive director of the Center for Democracy and Technology, thinks that data security demands strong encryption to foil threats wherever they are in the world. And good data security and privacy policies must recognize that the Bill of Rights in the U.S. Constitution is nothing more than a local law. As the Internet user reaches the unnerving conclusion that terrorism, like the Internet, recognizes no national boundaries, law enforcement officials will seek more ways to ferret it out and take preventive actions.

In the past, investigators have wielded telephone wiretaps against terrorists, but the Clinton administration points to the recent use of encrypted files by child pornographers, militia members and spies to avoid discovery. Grave crimes, such as a plot to shoot down several airliners over Chicago, have been foiled by the use of wiretaps. Had the FBI been unable to read those transmissions, a major tragedy might have occurred. Strong language calls for regulation of Internet content, such as the Clinton administration's ill-fated attempt to curb child pornography via the Communications Decency Act.

Senator Dianne Feinstein, (D-California) introduced a bill that would make it illegal to distribute explosives-making information "by any means" including online, if the distributor intends or knows the information would be used in committing a crime. Perhaps this will become an important law enforcement tool. Encryption that is difficult to decipher should not be distributed to anyone. It's almost the same argument as that for gun control. The good citizen doesn't need a background check, but how can you tell that person from a bank robber without one? This area is another that must be watched closely, since the vast network of right wing militias and racist organizations can be used covertly and encrypted today.

PRO-LIFE TERRORISM

On January 3, 1997, the peace of the new year was shattered by bomb blasts and injuries at the Northside Family Services Clinic in Atlanta, Georgia, rekindling fears and memories of the bombing at the Summer Olympics in that stately southern city. The first blast occurred at 9:30 a.m., while the second blast was set and deliberately delayed to catch federal agents, firemen, ambulance attendants, and clinic workers as they responded to the scene forty-five minutes later. The second blast resulted in major and minor injuries and serious damage to the five-story building less than a week before the twenty-eighth anniversary of the Supreme Court's decision in *Roe v. Wade,*[5] which had legalized abortion. Was this explosion simply individual rage and violence or was it a terrorist act? This question will be the major thrust of this section.

The Task Force on Terrorism concluded that terrorism is a technique, a way of engaging in certain types of criminal activity, so as to attain particular ends. This would be a process by which a group would create "an overwhelming fear for coercive purposes," such fear to be raised not only in the immediate victims but also within the audience of community or society. It seems that this definition fits nicely within the parameters of the violence against abortion clinics by extremist members of the Pro-Life movements across the nation. The technique used in the Atlanta bombings is one well known from the efforts of terrorist groups like the Irish Republican Army. This method is referred to by experts on terrorism as the "congregate effect." The goal is to get people to gather around or near the first bombing and then explode the second or third device with devastating impact. Such planning is not typical of a random act of violence by a single dissident.

As we discussed in Chapter 1, terrorism is defined by the FBI as, "the unlawful use of force or violence against persons or property to intimidate or coerce a government, the civilian population, or any segment thereof, in furtherance of political or social objectives." Again, the acts of violence against abortion clinics by those who wish to have the Supreme Court reverse *Roe v. Wade* seem to fall neatly within this definition as well.

"Limited political" or "sub-revolutionary" terrorism are the terms usually applied to those acts in which the goal is to influence, through coercive fear, certain public policies or practices. While violence, harassment, disruptions, arson and bombings, demonstrations and action plan documents *in toto* squarely fit the Federal Bureau of Investigation's definition, the Department of Justice has concluded that abortion clinic violence is not terrorism and that there is no national conspiracy to engage in terrorism. It is not clear whether the FBI addressed the question of regional or local conspiracies in this decision, although the Justice Department continues to investigate the alleged conspiracy among anti-abortion activists and to indict activists on federal conspiracy and arson charges.

A Social Construction of Abortion Clinic Violence/Terrorism

The United States has been undergoing a religious revival since at least 1977, in part due to the passage of the millennium and in part due to a reactionary movement fueled by fear of crime, anti-Semitism, racism, political demagoguery, and a desire to make the past become the future. The New Right has emerged with its goal of political and cultural hegemony in the United States. Anti-abortionists, in particular, define abortion as a "violation of their moral precepts." The movement gained momentum in the 1980s, with the election of pro-life presidents Reagan and Bush.

The movement can be characterized as:

- Adopting a "pro-family" stance;
- Stressing parental rights;
- Emphasizing strong families;
- Expressing moral indignation of abortion, perceived as murder;
- Stressing the patriarchal family as the ideal model;
- Emphasizing a fear of changes occurring in the family systems;
- Decrying the alleged decline in the traditional American family.

Thus, this is a backlash movement, and the heart of the effort is to fight the shifts and changes underway in American culture by focusing concerns on reproductive control, including abortion, women's rights, and male domination over women's bodies. For pro-life extremists, those not holding the same moral and religious beliefs are viewed in dualistic terms: good-bad, saved-damned, chosen-evil, God's children-spawn of Satan. Such moral absolutes permit causal attribution, assigning to one's opponents both malicious intent as well as evil character. Such a mind-set encourages and validates the use of force against opponents ("sinners"). Indeed, it is a moral requirement to punish offenders using whatever force necessary to restrain the wicked and make them virtuous. This could include violence against persons and property, as well as threats of violence (verbal statements, confrontations at abortion clinics, telephoning a mother of an abortion clinic patient and stating that her yet unborn grandchild is going to be killed by the pregnant daughter, etc.).

The anti-abortion movement and the New Right interact and network in many ways, including media evangelists, workshops, books, training sessions, Bible colleges, and demonstration events. While some movement speakers state that their followers ought not to engage in violence, they also argue that it is to be expected, since "truly moral" people have no other recourse, having been pushed to these extremes. Thus one could argue that frustration and anomie are underlying causes of abortion clinic violence and demonstrations.

Abortion and Religious-Political Organizations

Although abortion clinic demonstrators come from a wide swath of society, it could be argued that most demonstrators are middle-class, religiously influenced and motivated by millenarianism, post-millennium eschatology, the *parousia* (second-coming), and a long-range hope for the revitalization of the Church and re-Christianization of American society. The four major religious strategy groups are the Lambs of Christ, Operation Rescue, Pro-Life Action League, and Missionaries to the Pre-Born. Other groups exist (Rescue America, for example), but no one knows the relative composition or influence of these groups. Since academic study of the more radical factions of the pro-life movement is at best scanty, research lags behind events, although written diverse materials are abundant.

The major groups, their seminal leaders, and examples of their strategic literature are:

- Lambs of Christ, founded by "Father Doe" (Father Norman Weslin);
- Operation Rescue, founded by Randall Terry;
- Pro-Life Action League, headed by Joseph Scheidler;
- Missionaries to the Unborn, headed by Joseph Foreman with Matt Trewhella as chief strategist.

The basic concern is with abortion clinic bombings, killings and disturbances. But we call attention to the fairly coherent body of literature and existing personal narratives that have not been carefully examined by scholarly inquiries or students of terrorism, writer and researcher, Jeffrey Kaplan, being one exception to this criticism.

Abortion Clinic Violence and Disruption

The National Abortion Federation compiles national statistics forwarded by family planning programs and abortion service providers. Relying on voluntary reporting creates many of the same problems associated with the Uniform Crime Reports and data should be interpreted as minimal estimates of the extent of abortion clinic violence and disruptions. For example, data are gathered on "stalking," defined as the "persistent following, threatening, and harassing of abortion provider, staff member, or patient away from the clinic." Stalking may be so frequent that some staff may relegate it to "routine behavior" and not report the incidents. Harassing calls at any hour of the day or night may also be underreported. There is no equivalent of the National Crime Victimization Survey to permit estimates of the extent of underreporting.

Examples of anti-abortion activities likely to be underreported in the data gathered by the National Abortion Federation include the following:

- Beheading of a cat of a clinic worker;
- Spray painting the van of a county councilwoman with the word "baby killer" to coerce her to vote to terminate the lease of a Planned Parenthood agency;
- Poisoning dogs of a physician who performs abortions in his office;
- Threatening a clinic worker by holding a sledge hammer over her head;
- Holding red meat up before a physician's children while asking why their father "kills babies";
- Shooting a judge;
- Picketing physicians' and council members' homes;
- Slashing tires of clinic workers;
- Telephoning patients in the middle of the night and yelling "baby killer";
- Calling parents of clinic patients to accuse their daughters of sexual and moral misconduct ("whore" "tramp" "slut" "pin cushion" "Ms. Community Chest", etc.).

It is estimated that many similar such acts go unreported.

Such harassment techniques are aimed at inducing fear. Private practices and public policies are influenced by such coordinated efforts. It would not exceed the limits of logic to argue that religious-political terrorists are attempting to impose their moral beliefs and religious practices on a nation by the use of and the threat of the use of violence to gain sufficient power to affect political institutions, especially local and state lawmaking bodies.

There is evidence of persistent action against abortion providers, and some suggestion of decline in overall incidents in the last two years. Murder and attempted murder are more recent developments; invasion and vandalism are down in numbers. A summary statement might be that such incidents have been influenced by *Roe v. Wade,* the U.S. Supreme Court's later reaffirmation of that case, and a 1994 federal law guaranteeing access to clinics that provide abortions (Freedom of Access to Clinic Entrances), as well as a 1994 U.S. Supreme Court decision upholding the legality of "buffer zones" to keep protesters away from clinics. Violence and disruptions continue but at a reduced level of incidence.

Future Scenarios

It is clear that after a somewhat calmer period after 1996, the level of violence at abortion clinics and providers may be rising again. There was a drop in incidents of violence against abortion providers since the peaks of the early 1990s, but a sharp increase in the number of incidents of disruption. When you combine these two categories, it becomes clear that the total increase in incidents is *threefold.*

Protesters in general have undertaken new strategies for removing abortion providers and reducing opportunities for abortion. After having failed to secure a reversal of *Roe v. Wade* and facing U.S. Supreme Court affirmation of buffer zones, anti-abortion strategists may have concluded that more might be gained by focusing activities on local and state governments. These include challenging the tax-exempt status of Planned Parenthood organizations by searching for legal flaws in the wording of charters and bylaws, seeking revocation of property-tax exemptions of nonprofit organizations, pushing local statutes and ordinances, and encouraging passage of anti-abortion laws. The National Abortion Federation points out that there is no evidence that militant anti-abortion activism has stopped women from having abortions. Nonetheless, it has caused untold trauma, unnecessary and unconscionable health risks, and the loss of personal dignity and privacy for hundreds of thousands of women. It also points out several factors at work in the 21% decline in anti-abortion violence in 1996:

- The deterrent effect of the passage and enforcement of the Freedom of Access to Clinic Entrances Act;
- Control of both Houses of Congress and many state legislatures by conservative forces which advanced an anti-choice agenda, which may have appeased some anti-abortion extremists;
- Increased expenditures by abortion providers on security systems, programs, and staff training;
- Utilization of legal tools such as injunctions, buffer zones, and restraining orders.

Editors of *The New York Times* were less sanguine on the erosion of the constitutional right to choose abortion, noting that hospital abortion is now so expensive that women must go to physician's offices or specialized abortion clinics. Protesters' harassment and violence have led many physicians to stop performing abortions and a spate of new laws may have further closed off a woman's right to choose abortion. The changing legal environment on local and state levels cited by the editors included:

- Some 84% of counties in the nation do not have abortion providers;
- Eleven states require women to undergo a bifurcated procedure: physician counseling and a 24-hour waiting period before abortion. (This could permit local activists to trace license plate numbers after the first visit and contact families of the patients before they come in for the abortion.)
- In 1995, legislators in twenty-two states introduced legislation requiring mandatory waiting periods;
- Twenty-eight states require women under age eighteen to get consent of one or both parents. (This could contribute to teenagers deferring abortions until later when abortions would be more complicated and potentially more dangerous to patient's health.)
- Thirty-seven states deny Medicaid coverage for abortions, even if necessary to preserve the woman's health;
- Mississippi requires both the bifurcated process as well as consent of both parents, and that physicians who advertise abortion services (and perform more than nine a month) to widen their hallways and hire more staff to qualify as surgical centers. Physicians must also provide patients with color photographs of fetuses at two-week stages of development.[6]

The editors argued that pro-life think tanks are continuously drafting proposed new laws, which state legislators introduce around the country. They conclude that such development in the states has received little attention since middle-class women's access to abortion has largely been unhampered, but such efforts have heavily impacted poor, young, small-town and rural women who cannot afford to overcome the bifurcated hurdle, track down absent fathers to secure permission for abortion, find overnight baby sitters, and commute to a large city and pay for hotel costs. Anti-abortion activists no doubt take comfort in achievements to date to limit constitutional rights to choose.

The battlefield in America's abortion struggle may be redrawn with the introduction of RU-486 (mifepristone), which was approved in 1996, for nonsurgical abortion in the very early stage of pregnancy (and by women who would not choose a surgical termination). The treatment protocol would require three visits to the physician's office (first for counseling and mifepristone, a second visit 36–48 hours later for administration of prostaglandin, and a third visit to assure the abortion is complete). It is likely that middle-class women might follow this protocol, but that poorer women still face hurdles in their efforts to seek abortion. Alternative markets have arisen to provide the pills, but poorer women often opt to avoid the confirmation (third) visit to the physician's office.

There is little reason to suspect that anti-abortion activists, currently with ready access to names and addresses of license plate owners, will not also have ready access to names of physicians willing to administer the RU-486 non-surgical abortion option. As Rebecca Lindstedt of the American Life League stated: "it won't be difficult to find out who is prescribing RU-486 in Topeka, Kansas." Presumably these physicians (and the pharmaceutical manufacturers) would then receive the attentions of anti-abortionists.

Our concern has been with the use of violence and threat of use of violence to induce fear among targeted victims and a larger audience to achieve limited social and religious goals. We postulate that these acts, in the aggregate, are not only unlawful but should be defined as domestic terrorism. Persistent abortion clinic violence, ranging from arson, to murder of staff, to the carefully planned terrorist-style bombing of the Atlanta clinic seems to us to clearly fit the definition of terrorism as enunciated by the Federal Bureau of Investigation. The FBI, however, has decided that antiabortion violence is not terrorism, possibly for political or other reasons. To be more generous, this may be for such administrative reasons as wanting to focus attention on international or offshore terrorism, or to downplay the real or imagined existence of domestic terrorists to the public. By not defining abortion clinic violence as terrorism, the FBI has shifted responsibility for bombing and arson investigation to the Department of the Treasury and the Bureau of Alcohol, Tobacco and Firearms, a smaller agency with considerably fewer resources than the FBI. Perhaps the federal government can now begin to refocus attention on this extremely violent behavior as a true form of domestic terrorism.

Finally, we raise the question of subversion of constitutionally guaranteed federal rights. The Fourteenth Amendment of the U.S. Constitution defines residents as being citizens of both the federal government and the state in which they reside. It expressly forbids states from making any ordinance, law or regulation that abridges the federal rights of citizens. If there is a constitutional right to abortion and the effects (whether by "color" or "usage") of local, county or state government clearly abridge that right, is there a colorable issue that might be considered by federal courts? If one defines anti-abortion terrorism as an effort to impose a set of religious beliefs on others, is there a colorable question of separation of church and state? Students of constitutional history may later consider these early millennium years as an odious period of challenge to and denial of liberty.

TERRORISTS FOR SALE OR EXCHANGE

In an ideal world, governments would deal with any terrorists they apprehended themselves. Alternately, if requested to do so and good reason was given, they would hand them over to the government of the country where their crimes had been committed, for trial with the barest of formalities or delays. And, they should fully expect reciprocal treatment. Unfortunately, this seldom happens, because one man's terrorist is another man's freedom fighter, and suspicious governments seldom give away something for nothing. All want to retain a few bargaining terrorist chips, just in case. A terrorist in hand often has value.

Years ago, the expression "he has a price on his head" was clearly understood: it meant that a person was "wanted" by the justice authorities, for either escaping from legal custody, or on the run for allegedly having committed a crime. A cash reward was offered for his apprehension and conviction, especially in the days before modern police forces, to induce the public to bring the criminal to justice. Cash rewards for these purposes brought about bounty hunters, a practice which still lingers on in some countries. Nowadays, the expression that "every government has its price" might be more apt, particularly when dealing with the extradition of terrorists.

Extradition has always been a delicate subject, touching as it does on national sovereignty, seeming at times to be regarded more as a personal favor to the government asking for it, than a routine moral, international transaction. One has long suspected that there must be secret exchange channels, as all such transactions are carried out with the utmost discretion, and are publicly denied.

Cash Will Do Nicely

In August 1994, the French government "bought" the notorious Carlos the Jackal from the Sudanese government for a reputed $2 million. The French only admitted that he had been arrested "outside the legal framework." Carlos (Ilyich Ramirez Sanchez) was a star terrorist captive, wanted for killing eighty-three people in a series of terrorist attacks, several in France. In December 1975, he had led the terrorist team that kidnapped eleven OPEC oil ministers in Vienna.

Carlos had long been sheltered in Middle Eastern states, courtesy of the KGB, but with the ending of the Cold War he became an embarrassment. He was subsequently ejected from Syria, refused entry by Yemen and Libya, and forced to accept asylum in Sudan. Carlos now resides in a French prison, having just been convicted for killing two gendarmes. The French thought they made a good bargain; perhaps so did the Sudanese government.

The Carlos incident established the fact that terrorists have a monetary value. We may be able to look forward to "transactions" involving other elderly, redundant former active international terrorists, such as Abu Nidal or bin Laden and others of his generation, who made international headlines in the 1970s, 1980s and 1990s. Bringing them to trial for a price, when certain governments still sheltering them need a cash infusion could be tempting. Such show trials provide a major boost to the morale of national security services. Lower profile terrorists might be obtained for lower prices, a process that might have been in operation for some time for all we know, as secrecy surrounds it. Either the media were well ahead of the diplomats in the Carlos case, or the French government deliberately sought publicity.

During the Western hostage saga in Lebanon (1984–1992), most of those held were eventually ransomed. Often huge sums of money were paid for the release of employees by wealthy international concerns, since is against government policy to deal directly with terrorists. The last two German hostages (Kemptner and Strubig) were only freed after the two Hamadei Brothers, who had been involved in hijacking and kidnapping, were released from German detention—a person for person exchange. In June 1995, the German government paid a reputed $1 million to the poverty-stricken Yemeni government for the extradition of Johannes Weinrich, a colleague of Carlos in his heyday.

After twenty years on the run, he was wanted for murder and explosions in Berlin, and is now in prison in Germany. One wonders who may be next.

Bounty Hunting

While the much-publicized Carlos incident may have alerted the world to the cash value of a terrorist, some states, especially the United States had long been offering cash rewards for the apprehension of criminals in order to tempt bounty hunters, many of which have been successful. No film about the Old West is complete without its "Wanted: Reward" poster in the background.

In October 1985, the Italian cruise ship the Achille Lauro was hijacked in the Mediterranean, and one United States citizen was killed. The situation was resolved with the help of the Egyptian government, which provided an aircraft for escaping terrorists. Under President Reagan's "you can run but you can't hide" policy, U.S. aircraft forced the plane down in Italy, where the leader, Abu Abbas, a Palestinian terrorist mastermind, was allowed to escape to Yugoslavia. The other terrorists involved stood trial and were convicted in Italy. One, Magied al-Mulkil, was sentenced to thirty years imprisonment and later jumped his parole for good behavior, whereupon the U.S. government immediately offered a $2 million reward for his recapture. After the terrorist massacre at Luxor (Egypt) in November 1996, the Egyptian government condemned the British government for harboring Islamic fundamentalist terrorist leaders thought to be responsible. The pot often calls the kettle black.

The United States offered a reward of $2 million (which seems to be the going rate for a top terrorist) for the apprehension of Ramzi Ahmad Yousef. He was the mastermind and "evil genius" behind the conspiracy to blow up the World Trade Center, in New York, and other buildings and bridges. He was thought to be in Pakistan. Yousef was located by the CIA, which issued thousands of small green (an Islamic color) matchboxes, with his likeness on one side of them and details of how to obtain the reward on the other. They smoke a lot in Pakistan, and this did the trick. Yousef is now in an American prison.

One hopes that the CIA will issue its green match boxes by the hundreds of thousands in Afghanistan, where many Islamic fundamentalist terrorists, including bin Ladin, are reputed to have sought refuge with the Taliban. This would be in the hope that money, lots of it, may overcome religious scruples. Now that the Taliban's income from drug trafficking is much reduced, it is becoming short of ready cash and may have some Islamic fundamentalist terrorists to sell. As of this writing there have been no takers for the $25 million reward offered for the capture or body of Osama bin Laden.

The Exchange Market

Through fact and fiction during the Cold War, we came to accept that spies were sometimes exchanged, so why not "wanted" terrorists too? In the turbulent Middle East, terrorists have sometimes been selectively exchanged under cover of Red Cross prisoner-of-war transfers. Exchanging hostages is an ancient military custom, revived during the Lebanese Civil War (1975–92), when warring factions had their own private prisons where hostages were held as security insurance, for vengeance and for selective exchange.

Israel has, on occasion, indulged in kidnapping raids on occasions to seize terrorist leaders, including Sheikh Abdul Rahman Obeid and Mustafa Dirani. This practice is known locally as "cross-border terrorism." According to the Israeli press, the Israeli government offered to release forty-seven Palestinians, including certain political prisoners loosely referred to as terrorists, for the freeing of one captured Israeli soldier. There have been other instances when "Arab guerrillas," meaning terrorists, have been released in exchange for Israelis who have been taken prisoner.

Two Mossad agents were caught after failing to assassinate Khaled Mishal, a Hamas leader in Amman (Jordan), and four others took refuge in the Israeli Embassy in Amman, all with forged Canadian passports. In exchange for the safe return of the Mossad agents, Israel had to release Sheikh Ahmad Yassin, imprisoned spiritual leader of the Hamas terrorist organization, which had been exploding suicide-bombs in Israel: their star prisoner. Israelis have made a few selective key terrorist exchanges over the years, censorship invariably concealing precise details.

A Sliding Scale

High prices have been demanded and obtained for the release of certain terrorist-held hostages, but the success of these extortion plans depended on someone's ability to pay large sums of money, governments excepted. Wealthy commercial concerns might be prepared to meet a terrorist's demands for the release of one of their employees, but would hesitate to embark upon such an illegal and secretive process. However, a few have done so, but as indirectly as possible. Not all were wealthy, but many were able to raise lesser sums of money, so it is probable that there was a terrorists' sliding scale of ransom demands, a sort of actuary's table, understood only by terrorist masterminds and their intermediaries.

Comparatively few hostages are killed, as lucrative prospects seem to out-weigh political scruples and vengeance. This unfortunately does happen sometimes, particularly when terrorists quarrel amongst themselves over possession of the hostage: and what to do with him or her. On occasion, one terrorist group will snatch a kidnapped hostage from another. Generally, terrorist groups more often quarrel with each other over spoils and territory than political dogma.

Occasionally, hostages have been sold or bartered between groups. One example, is that of Rod Arad, an Israeli airman shot down over Lebanon, and taken hostage by a small Shia terrorist group known as the Faithful Resistance. Led by Mustafa Dirani, the group, according to some intelligence sources, held Arad for two years before selling him to the Iranian Pasdaran organization for $300,000. Hopes are that Arad may still be alive somewhere in Iran.

Shelf-Life Expired

In 1999, when the Lebanese army was reasserting its control over parts of the lawless Beka'a Valley, it cleaned out a nest of miscellaneous international terrorists, including five members of the Japanese Red Army. They were all former prisoners of the Israelis who had been freed in a mass Red Cross-organized Arab-Israeli exchange. One was Kozo Okamoto, the surviving terrorist of the May 1972 massacre at Lod Airport, in which over twenty people had been killed and more than eighty injured. Another was Kazuo Tohira, the group's master passport forger. The JRA members had disappeared from public view and notice.

Japan showed no interest in them at all, as their shelf-life had expired and Japanese authorities were reluctant to resurrect the emotions of past terrorist dramas. In July 1999, the Lebanese government was reduced to charging the five JRA terrorists with illegal entry into Lebanon, and they were sentenced to three years imprisonment, after which they were to be deported. The Lebanese government seems to be the loser, having to pay for their upkeep in prison, and probably also an airline ticket, if it can persuade the Japanese government to eventually accept them.

Open Negotiation

Communications between terrorist hostage-takers and those who ultimately pay the ransoms is invariably shrouded in secrecy. An exception seems to be the case in Chechnya, where a twenty-one month separatist war (1994–1996) between Russia and Chechnya left an open expanse of No Man's Land between the two hostile military forces, across which illicit contacts and trade flourish. Russian mothers seeking missing soldier sons have been placing notices on general information boards in the area, giving details and asking for information about them. These well-read notice boards are also being used by terrorist go-betweens for communication (not always in code), quoting demands for ransom and how negotiations may begin.

Terrorist leaders in Chechnya have already kidnapped several international aid and humanitarian workers, demanding food, medical supplies and money in return for their release. An unofficial exchange of military prisoners seems to be conducted through the medium of the general information notice boards, while military authorities look the other way, as the end result is often to their own benefit. Russian authorities admit that a prosperous market in kidnapping for ransom exists in Chechnya. What of the future? Sadly, one must forecast more of the same, with governments forever seeking to extradite wanted terrorists, and terrorists forever seeking valuable hostages. Market forces influence the prices and we can predict a lot more terrorists being turned in for thirty pieces of silver.[7]

As we look to the future we continue to look back over our shoulders at what has taken place. If September 11, 2001, was a watershed for the West, what effect did it have on the aspirations of the Islamic extremist movements? We continue to believe that the Islamic terror threat emanates from Osama bin Laden and al Qaeda. Al Qaeda has not made inroads into any political organizations around the world and everywhere we view the Islamic threat, their support and activities are both on the wane. In countries like Sudan, Egypt, Kashmir, and Indonesia we have witnessed attempts by Islamic groups to organize and destabilize the political road map of those countries. In each we have witnessed failure and in each there have been somewhat spectacular acts of violence. If bin Laden and his cronies expected a popular uprising from the millions of Muslims around the world it has not happened, nor is it likely.

After the coalition invasion of Afghanistan there were no calls from Muslim clerics to declare a holy war against an infidel West. Silence! Not only silence, but there have even been calls from other extreme agents of Islam against the actions of al Qaeda. In Egypt the imprisoned leader of al-Gama'a al-Islamaya issued a public declaration distancing his organization form the extreme activities of bin Laden and al Qaeda—hardly a recommendation for a worldwide holy war!

As to whether Osama bin Laden is alive or dead we can only speculate. Many of his henchmen are likely still at large around the globe and with superhuman efforts by the United States and Great Britain and the pressure of an intensive and cohesive intelligence campaign the next attack could possibly be averted. The opportunity always exists for single crazies to make a short and bloody statement with a random act of terror, which unfortunately may be a scenario the west will continue to live with.

SUMMARY

Well, we have come to the end of the tale we have spun for you, the student. There was no realization prior to 2001 that we would see the West at war with terrorism. The risks, the dangers and the threats from groups hell-bent on the destruction of Western democracies are now at hand. Can they produce another 9–11? As is clear, we have only touched the tip of the iceberg and have not used nearly as much material as we would liked to have done. Events often move faster than we can get them down on paper. In this chapter, we have touched on just a few of the issues facing our tottering world, as it stumbles ahead into the twenty-first century and the probable threats for the future. It will be up to the next generation to try to find ways to eliminate the conditions that separate people, ethnically, religiously, racially, tribally, politically, traditionally and, last but not least, economically. We know that worldwide we have failed to gather all the available intelligence, or analyze and spot the signs to interpret them. This will change, and the wheel will turn. We hope that this book has opened a window through which the student will view the evening news from a far different perspective. If we have whetted the student's appetite for knowing more about how violence and terrorism came about, we are pleased and will feel that all this writing has been worth it.

In conclusion, the words of General Barry R. McCaffrey U.S. Army, Retired seem to us to be most pertinent, "Osama bin Laden suggested that nineteen boys in four domestic airliners had brought powerful America to her knees. The terrorists reasoned that America had been unable to tolerate the blood of 350,000 Americans casualties in Vietnam, had withdrawn its fleet when U.S. Marines were slaughtered in Beirut, and had been humbled and forced to leave Somalia by the number of Ranger casualties. The al Qaeda calculus was clear: these American people are powerful in material but weak in spirit; they are politically divided; they have no real allies."[8] A serious miscalculation by bin Laden and al Qaeda? We shall wait and see!

ENDNOTES

1. International Atomic Energy Agency, http://www.iaea.org/worldatom/Press/Focus/IaeaIraq/index.html.
2. U.S. State Department Report, *Powell on Iraq*, February 6th, 2002, www.state.com.
3. Paul Cornish "Sabotage by Sarin," *Intersec: The Journal of International Security*. Three Bridges Publishing, Surrey. Volume 7, Issue 9, September 1997.
4. Taken from www.milnet.com.
5. Bruce Hoffman. Winter 1994 issue of the RAND Newsletter.
6. Harry E. Allen and Clifford E. Simonsen. "Abortion Clinic Violence and Terrorism." Paper prepared for presentation at the annual meeting of the Southern Criminal Justice Association, September 27, 1996, Savannah, Georgia.
7. Edgar O'Ballance. "Terrorists for Sale or Exchange." *Intersec: The Journal of International Security*. Three Bridges Publishing, Surrey. Volume 8, Issue 1, January 1998, pp. 9–10,12.
8. General Barry R. McCaffrey USA-Retired, Challenges to U.S. National Security, *Armed Forces Journal International*, February 2002.

Index of Internet Web Sites

The following is a short list of government agencies, think tanks and other organizations involved in the theories and academic research into terrorism. We have included sites that discuss chemical and biological issues as well as prevention and preparedness for chemical and biological incidents.

WEB SITE NAME	WEB SITE ADDRESS
FEMA, Terrorism site	www.rris.fema.gov
Office of Justice Programs	www.ojp.usdoi.gov/new.htm
National Security Institute	www.nsi.org/terrorism.html
The Network of Terrorism	http://usinfo.state.gov
Strategic Forecasting	www.stratfor.com
Rand Corporation	www.RAND.org
FEMA Terrorist incident planning guidelines	www.fema.gov/pte/ pte052101htm
US Department of Defense	www.defenselink.mil/other_info/terrorism.html
Federation of American Scientists	www.fas.org
Janes Terrorism and Security	http://intelweb.janes.com
Israeli Intelligence	www.debka.com
Terrorism Research Center	www.terrorism.com/Ctgroups.html
American Civil Liberties Union	www.aclu.org
Amnesty International	www.amnesty.org
Anti Defamation League	www.adl.org
Human Rights Watch	www.hrw.org
Centre for the Study of Terrorism and Political violence	www.st-and.ac.uk
Federal Bureau of Investigation	www.fbi.gov
International Policy Institute	www.ict.org
Southern Poverty Law Center	www.splcenter.org
US Department of State Office of the Coordinator for Anti Terrorism	www.state.gov/www/global/terrorism/index.html
Center for Democracy and Technology	www.cdt.org
First Amendment Foundation	www.floridafaf.org
DOJ ODP	www.ojp.usdoj.gov/odp/
NDPO	www.ndpo.gov
National Institute of Justice "Center for Civil Force Protection"	www.nlectc.org/ccfp
Chemical and Biological Analysis Center	www.cbiac.apgea.army.mil
Center for Disease Control	www.cdc.gov

FEMA Terrorism Incident	www.fema.gov/r-n-r/frp/frpterr.htm
Chemical Emergency Preparedness	www.epa.gov/swercepp/cntr-ter.html
Harvard University Kennedy School of Gov't Executive Session of Domestic Preparedness	http://ksgnotes1.harvard.edu/BCSIA/ESDP.NSF/www/Home
US Department of Defense	www.defenselink.mil/other_info/terrorism.html
The Markle Foundation	www.terrorismanswers.com/home/
Public Affairs Section US Embassy Belgium	www.uspolicy.be/Issues/Terrorism/terrorism.htm
BBC News Background on Terror	http://news.bbc.co.uk/hi/english/in_depth/world/2001/war_on_terror/
The National Commission on Terrorism	http://www.fas.org/irp/threat/commission.html
Department of Transportation	http://www.oig.dot.gov/
Special Report–Afghanistan	http://www.pbs.org/newshour/bb/asia/afghanistan/index.html
CIA World Fact Book	http://www.pbs.org/newshour/bb/asia/afghanistan/index.html
Islamic Studies	http://www.arches.uga.edu/~godlas/
IslamiCity	http://www.islam.org/
Arab American Anti Discrimination Committee	http://www.adc.org
Arab American Institute	http://www.aaiusa.org/index.htm
ArabNet Iraq	http://www.arab.net/iraq/iraq_contents.html
UN Monitoring Inspection and Verification Committee	http://www.un.org/Depts/unmovic/index.htm
Aviation Security International	www.avsec.com
International Terrorism Program	www.ipg-protect.com/doc102.htm
The Nizkor Project	www.nizkor.org

The above list of websites is intended to offer the student opportunities for further research in the areas of terrorism and counter terrorism. The authors do not specifically recommend any websites and the student should check the authenticity of any materials being utilized from any website.

Index

A

Abbas, Abu, 198, 403
Abdullah, Crown Prince (of Saudi Arabia), 227–228
Abortion clinic violence
    bombings, 17
    terrorism, defining as, 17–18
Abu Nidal, 25, 185–186, 186, 187
Abu Sayyaf Group, 320
Acebes, Angel, 116
Achille Lauro, 198, 403
Action Direct, 119–120
Adams, Gerry, 73, 77, 79
Aden Protectorate, 246
Afghanistan
    civil war, 287
    Islamic extremism, 294–295
    opium trade, 296, 297
    Pakistan operations for terrorism, 286
    Soviet invasion, 154
    terrorist training, 211, 294
Afrikaner Weerstandsbeweging, 264, 265
Agca, Mehmet Ali, 168
AIDS crisis, in Uganda, 255
Air India bombing, 59, 189
Airline security. See aviation security; counterterrorism
Airplane bombs, remote controlled, 339
Al Khalifa, Hamad bin Isa, 236
Al Khalifa, Salman, 235
Al Qaeda, 15
    France, operations in, 122
    Germany, operations in, 131
    infiltration into Iran, 35
    Spain, operations in, 116–117
    spread of influence, global, 103–104
    Sudan, haven in, 28
Al-Asifa, 183–185
Al-Assad, Bashar, 28, 207
Al-Assad, Hafez, 207
Al-Busaid dynasty, 238
Al-Fatah, 183–185
Al-Gama'a al-Islamiyya, 28
Al-Khattab, Ibn, 158
Al-Megrahi, Abdelbasset Ali Mohmed, 27
Al-Sabah dynasty, 229
Albania, 166, 167
Alexander II, Czar, 151
Alfred P. Murrah Federal Building, 46
Algeria
    Algerian Islamic Salvation Front, 208
    economic crisis, 218–221
    Ninja security forces, 220
    overview, 217–218
    riots, December 1991, 219–221
    riots, October 1988, 218–219
Algerian Islamic Salvation Front, 208
Amaru, Tupac, 345
Amin, Idid, 252, 253
Angola, 270–272, 271
Angry Brigade, 100, 101–102
Animal rights militia, 102–103
ANO. See Abu Nidal organization
Ansarollah, 204
Anthrax attacks, 38, 420
Apartheid, 262–263, 264. See also South Africa
Apprentice Boys, 88

Aquino, Corazon, 322
Arab League, 231
Arab Liberation Front, 26
Arab Revolution, 127
Arab Revolutionary Brigades, 185
Arab Revolutionary Council, 185
Arad, Rod, 432
Arafat, Yasir, 177, 178, 181, 183, 196–197
Arbuckle, Victor, 78
Argentina, 353–354
Arguello, Patrick, 190
Aristide, Jean-Bertrand, 65
Armed Islamic Group, 221
Armed Proletarian Nuclei (NAP), 136
Armee Republicaine Bretonne, 120
Armenian terrorism in Turkey, 145
Arzalluz, Xavier, 114
As Aqsa Martyrs Brigades, 188
Assassination, 15–16
Assassins, word origin, 22
Atlanta Olympic Games, bombing, 18
AUC. See United Self-Defense Forces of Colombia (AUC)
Aum Shinrikyo, 317, 318
Auschwitz, 125
Australia, 326–327, 392
Aviation security, 370, 380. See also counterterrorism; hijackings
Aziz, King Abdul, 226–227

B

Ba'thist regime, 230
Baader Meinhof Gang, 126, 127, 184
Baader, Andreas, 126, 127
Bab el Mandeb, 245
Bahrain
    government, 235–236, 236
    instability, 236
    overview, 235
    petroleum production, 236
    religious sects, tension between, 237
    territorial dispute, with Qatar, 236
Bahraini Hezbollah, 236
Bakunin, Mikhail, 152
Balfour Declaration, 172
Balfour, James, 173
Barak, Ehud, 177
Barre, Said, 250
Basque Nationalist Party
    in 21st century, 114–115
    opposition, 115–116
    origins, 112–114
    public support, 115
    training from PFLP, 114
Basque separatism, 111
Battle of the Boyne, 70
Beckwith, Charles, 399
Begin, Menachem, 209
Bekr, Abu, 31
Belgium
    CCC, 146–147
    FRAP, 146
    Mad Killers, 146
    neo-fascist groups, 146
    overview, 145–146
    violence in, 146
Belsen, 125
Bemba, Jean Pierre, 277

Ben Khamais, Sami Essid, 137
Benito, Eustakio Mendizabel, 113
Berlin, La Belle Discotheque bombing, 27, 215
Berman, Jerry, 423
Bernadotte, Folke, 175
Beruit, 202, 203
    kidnapping/killings, 206
    safety, lack of, for Westerners, 206
Biden, Joseph, 16
Big Seven (state supporters of terrorism), 23–24
Bijondere Bijstands Eenheld (BBE), 396
Bin Laden, Osama, 15. See also September 11
    assassination of, legality of, 16
    CIA recruitment, 294
    embassy bombings, role in, 46
    fortune, 408
    inability to capture, 295
    Latin American terrorist ties, 344
    Moussaoui, Zacarias, association with, 122
Bin Taimur, Said, 238
Biological Weapons Convention, 420
Black and Tans, 72
Black September, 184, 185, 202, 368
Blair, Tony, 77, 92
Blanco, Carrero, 114
Bloody Sunday, 152
BMW (car as used by terrorists), 126
BO. See Boevaya Oranisatsia
Boccacci, Maurizio, 136
Boevaya Oranisatsia, 151–153
Bolivar, Simon, 356
Bolivia, 349, 351
Bolsheviks, 153
Border security. U.S., 414–415
Bosnia, 166
Botha, Louis, 263
Brandwag, 264
Brazil, 349, 351
Britain
    animal rights militia, 102–103
    counterterrorism units, 389–391
    Islamic terrorist groups, based in London, 103–104
    Libya, severing of diplomatic ties with, 214–215
    overview of terrorist acts there, 100–101
    right-wing groups, extreme, 107
    soccer club attacks, 107
    Special Air Service (SAS), 389–391
    Special Boat Squadron, 391
    terrorism, response to, 105–106, 389–391
Brotherhood of Assassins, 22
Buchenvald, 125
Bulgaria, state-sponsored terrorism, 167–168
Burma, 298–299, 300–303
Bush, George Herbert, 30
Bush, George W., 23, 235

C

Caesar, Julius, 22
Cairo Gang, 71
Caliph, 31

Cambodia, 299, 302, 303, 306
Canada
    border security, 61–62
    overview, 59
    terrorism, 59–60, 62
Cannibalism, in Uganda, 253
Card, Francis, 77
Carette, Pierre, 147
Carlos the Jackal, 118, 127, 157, 175, 430
Carter, Jimmy, 209
Castro, Fidel, 17
    childhood, 63–64
    leadership, length of, 63
    September 11th, stance on, 24
Catholic Reaction Force, 82–83
Celik, Oral, 168
Centennial Olympic Park, 18
Central Intelligence Agency, assassination
    plots, 17
Chartist Movement, 100
Chavez, Hugo, 357
Chechnya
    deterioration, 161
    historical overview, 160
    present-day status, 162
    rebels, 155, 158, 160
    Russian military action, 161
    treaties, 160–161
Cheka, 154
Chemical/biological threats, 420–421
Chemical/biological weapons, 411–412
Chernomyrdin, Viktor, 155
Child pornography, encryption of, 423
Chile, 354–356
China
    economy, 311
    ethnic makeup, 310
    Falun Gong. (see Falun Gong)
    Hong Kong. (see Hong Kong)
    overview, 310–311
    religions, 310
    Taiwan. (see Taiwan)
    terrorism within, 311–312
    workers, rural, 311
CIA. See Central Intelligence Agency
CIRA. See Continuity Irish Republican
    Army
Citizenry, role in homeland security, 416
Clinton, William Jefferson, 17
    Burma, position on, 300–301
    Sudan, attack on, 217
Cobras (Sultan of Oman Special Forces
    SSF), 395
Coco, Francesco, 134
Cojuangco, Eduardo, 322
Collett, Peter, 206
Collins, Michael, 71, 72
Colombia
    drug lords, 344
    drug trade, 339–340
    National Liberation Army (ELN). (See
        National Liberation Army (ELN))
    Revolutionary Armed Forces of
        Colombia (FARC). (see Revolution
        ary Armed Forces of Colombia
        (FARC))
    right-wing death squads, 343–344
Colombo World Trade Center, 292
Colon, Rafael Hernandez, 56
Combs, Cindy C., 3
Comradeship evenings, 129

Condera, Juan Gerardi, 334
Congregate effect, 18
Connolly, Niall, 79
Constitution, 50
Continuity Irish Republican Army, 81
Contras, 337, 338
Corsican separatists, 120
Cosa Nostra, 49
Cosgrove, William, 72
Counterterrorism
    airport security, 376–378
    aviation security, 369–373
    bounties and rewards, 430–433
    in Australia, 392
    in Britain, 389–191
    in Czech Republic, 398–399
    in France, 395
    in Germany, 397
    in Ireland, 393–394
    in Israel, 398
    in Norway, 396–397
    in Persian Gulf, 395
    in Rhodesia, 392–393
    in Spain, 394
    in the Netherlands, 396
    in United States, 399–400
    intelligence gathering. (see intelligence
        gathering)
    international policing, 387
    legislations, 368, 369
    Lyon Summit conference, 385–386
    of piracy, 400–404
    order, maintaining, 365–366
    overview, 363–364
    passenger screening, 373
    passenger/baggage reconciliation,
        371–372
    policies of Western governments,
        384–386
    repression, 366–367
    roles for, 364–365
    United Nations Security Council Reso-
        lution 1373, 386–387
Courtailler, David, 122
Courtailler, Jerome, 122
CRF. See Catholic Reaction Force
Crimes against humanity, defining, 34
Croatia, 165, 166
Crusades, 30, 32–33
Cuba. See also Castro, Fidel
    Castro's stance on September 11th,
        24
    economy, 62–63
    ethnic makeup, 62
    FPMR, harboring of, 24
    location, 62
    terrorist detention at Guantanimo Bay,
        24
Curcio, Renato, 134
Curtis, Robert, 78
Cyprus, 141–142
Czech Republic, 398–399

D
Dachau, 125
Dalai Lama, 298
Dawson Field Hijackings, 118
De Codex, Juan Carlos Delgado, 116
De Gaulle, Charles, 60
De Valera, Eamon, 72
Declaration of Principles, 183

Delta Force, 399
Democratic Front for the Liberation of
    Palestine, 199
Democratic People's Republic of Korea,
    27
Democratic Progressive Party (Taiwan),
    315
Democratic Republic of Congo, 255–256,
    260, 262, 275–277
Department of Defense
    construct of terrorism, 10–12
    definition of terrorism, 10
Department of Homeland Security, 379, 408,
    409, 410, 411
    divisions, 418
    formation, 416–417
    mission of, 417
    organization of, 417, 418
Depression, Great, 124
Desert Storm, 143, 232
Dev Sol, 143–144
DFLP. See Democratic Front for the Libera-
    tion of Palestine
Dirani, Mustafa, 432
Diversity of modern society, 21
DOD. See Department of Defense
Domestic terrorism
    Americans view of compared to for-
        eign, 47–48, 52–53
    growth of, 53
    left wing, 54
    overview, 47–48
    right wing, 54
    special interest extremists, 55
Dominican Republic, 64–65
Douglas, Leigh, 206
Dozier, James, 135, 168
DPP. See Democratic Progressive Party (Tai-
    wan)
DPRK. See Democratic People's Republic of
    Korea
Drake, Sir Francis, 401
Drive-by shootings, street gangs, 49
Drug trade, worldwide, 298
    Afghanistan, 296
    Colombia, 339–340, 344
    Mexico, 333
    Nicaragua, 337–338
    Tasmania, 327
    Vietnam, 305–306
Dumont, Lionel, 122
Duvalier, Francois "Papa Doc," 65
Duvalier, Jean-Claude "Baby Doc," 65
Dzhugashvoili, Josef Vissarionovich. See
    Stalin, Joseph

E
Easter Rebellion, 72, 78
Ecuador, 358
Edgar Sanchez Special Forces, 348
Egypt
    historical overview, 209
    Islamic extremists in, 211–212
    twentieth-century history, 209
Egypt Air 648 hijacking, 385
El Salvador, 336
El-Qaddafi, Muammar, 212, 213, 215, 216.
    See also Libya
El-Sambouli, 210, 211
ELA. See Espanastatikos Laikos Agonas
Eldad, Israel, 174

Embassy targets
    bin Laden, Osama, embassy bombings, role in, 46
    Federal Bureau of Investigations involvement in solving, 16
    growth in U.S. embassies as targets, 408–411
    Kenya, 11, 46
    Peru, 346
    Tanzania, 11, 16, 17, 46
Emigrants, the (student group), 103
Energy security, 415–416
Ensslin, Gudrun, 126
Environmental security, 415–416
EOKA, 141–142
EPRDF. See People's Revolutionary Democratic Front
Espanastatikos Laikos Agonas, 140
Estonian guerrilla movement, 156–157
Estrada, Joseph, 322
ETA. See Euzkadi Ta Azkatasuna
ETA-Military, 112
Ethiopia, 249–250
Ethnic cleansing, 33. See also genocide
    in Bosnia, 166
    in Uganda, 252
European Civil Aviation Conference, 380
Euzkadi Ta Azatasuna, 111–112
Euzkadi Ta Azkatasuna, 6
Ezzedine al-Qassam Brigades, 197

F
FACE. See Freedom of Access to Clinic Entrances
Fahad, King (of Saudi Arabia), 226
Faisal, King (of Saudi Arabia), 226
Falun Gong, 312–315
FARC. See Armed Forces of Colombia (FARC)
Fardust, Hossain, 243
Fatah Revolutionary Council, 185
Fatah-the Intafata, 29
Fatwa, against Salmon Rushdie, 25
FBI. See Federal Bureau of Investigations
Fear, as result of terrorism, 11–12
Federal Bureau of Investigations
    construct of terrorism, 10
    coordination of investigations into terrorism, 10
    definition of terrorism, 10
    embassy bombings, investigations into, 16
    role in hostage-taking situations, 15
Feinstein, Dianne, 16, 17, 423
Ferdinand, Franz, 165
Fernandez, Ronald, 57
Fertile Crescent, 231
Fifteenth (15th) of May organization, 26
Fillisteen al-Muslima, 103
Final Solution, 125
Finsbury Park Mosque, 104
FLN. See Fronte de Liberation National
FLQ. See Front de liberation du Quebec
Ford, Gerald, 17
Fossey, Dian, 273
FPMR. See Frente Patriotico Manuel Rodriguez
France
    Action Direct, operations in, 119–120
    Corsiacan separatists, 120

Executive order 13224 (assets frozen of terrorists), 121
    Groupment d'Intervention de la Gendarmerie Nationale (GIGN), 395
    Japanese Red Army, operations in, 119
    Orly Airport rocket attack (by PLO), 120–121
    Popular Front for the Liberation of Palestine, bases in, 118–119
    post 9–11 stance against terrorism, 121
    revolutionary terrorism. (see French Revolution)
Franco, Francisco, 111
Frankincense, 237
FRAP. See Frente Revolucionario Anti-Fascista Y Patrotico
Free Papua Organization, 326
Freedom fighters, 6, 7
Freedom of Access to Clinic Entrances, 55
Freeh, Louis, 16
French Revolution, 20, 117
Frente Patriotico Manuel Rodriguez, 24
Frente Revolucionario Anti-Fascista Y Patrotico, 116, 146
Friedman, Thomas, 227
Front de la Liberation Nationale de la Corse, 120
Front de liberation du Quebec, 59, 60–62
Fronte de Liberation National, 217–218

G
Galiad, Ali Khalif, 250
GAP, 135–136
Gastarbeiter program, 128
Gaza Strip, 191, 196, 200
Genocide
    definition, 30, 33–35, 166
    vs. "ethnic cleansing" term, 166
    word origin, 33, 166
GEO. See Grupo Especial De Operaciones
George, David Lloyd, 173
Germany
    al Qaeda operations in, 131
    anti-Semitism, present-day, 129
    counterterrorism, 397
    Gastarbeiter program, 128
    GSG9, 397
    immigration policies, 128, 130
    labor, restrictions on, 128–129
    law enforcement, 131
    post-WWII politics, 125–126
    Red Army Faction, 126–128
    religious freedom law, 131
    terrorist groups, rise of, 123–124
    unification, 129–131
Gerry, Elbridge, 52
Gestapo, 124
Ghazi I, King, 231
GIA. See Armed Islamic Group
Giap, General, 307
Gligorov, Kiro, 166
Good Friday Agreement, 69, 75, 94, 95
Gorki, Maxim, 150
Goulding, Cathal, 76
Government of Ireland Act, 72
GRAPO. See Grupo De Resistencia Antifascista Primo
Great Britain. See Britain
Greece

Cyprus. (see Cyprus)
    ELA. (see Espanastatikos Laikos Agonas)
    minor terrorist cells, 141
    Pasok party, 140
    police as targets for terrorists, 139
    Revolutionary Cells. (see Revolutionary Cells)
    Revolutionary Organization November 17. (see November 17 Group)
Grenzschutzgruppe 9, 397
Grievance, perceived, 21
Griffith, Arthur, 70
Group retaliation, 20
Grupo De Resistencia Antifascista Primo, 116
Grupo Especial De Operaciones, 115
Guatamala, 333–335
Guevara, Che, 64, 346, 350
Gulf Cooperation Council, 229
Gulf War, 232–233
    Kuwait stance, 229–230
    new, 412–413
Gun-control legislation, 54
Gurion, Ben, 174
Guzman, Abimael, 346, 347
Gypsies, extermination of, 35

H
Habash, George, 29, 175, 187, 188
Habibe, B. J., 324
Haddad, Gregoire, 204
Haganah, 36
Haiti, 65–66
Hajj, 203, 244
Hall, John, 301
Hamas
    charter of, 191, 192–194
    Latin American links, 351
    organization/structure, 194–198
    popularity, 191
    state support for, 23, 24
    Sudan, haven in, 28
    support sources, 196
    Syria, haven in, 29
Hammurabi, 231
Hamza, Abu, 104
Harakat ul-Ansar, 282, 289
Hashemite Kingdom, 181
Hassan, Abu, 181, 182
Hassan, King (of Morocco), 208–209
Health and food security, 415
Herri Batasuna Party, 114–115
Hertzog, J., 263
Hezbollah
    alternate names for, 204
    goals, 204
    Latin America links, 351
    origins, 204
    state support for, 23, 24
    structure and development, 206–207
    Syrian haven, 29
    targets, 205
Hijackings, 189–190, 369–373
    airport facilities (openness), 376–378
    combatting/response, 380, 382–383
    Egypt Air 648, 385
    overview, 375
    Stanstead Airport incident, 382–383

Hitler, Adolf
    birthday, celebration by European
        Nazis, 146
    Final Solution, 125
    labor camps. use of, 154
    power, rise to, 124
    terror tactics, 124–125
Hobeika, Elie, 202–203
Hoffman, Bruce, 7
Holocaust, 33, 34
    atrocities, 125
    concentration camps, 125
    denial of, 48
Home Rule Bill, 71–72
Homeland Security, Department of. See De-
    partment of Homeland Security
Honduras, 335–336
Hong Kong, 315
Hongxi, Li, 313
Hostage-taking
    international law definition, 14
    legal issues, 15
    price demands for, 432
    US government policy toward situa-
        tions, 14, 15
HUA. See Harakat ul-Ansar
Huebner, Frank, 129
Hume, John, 73
Hussein, Saddam, 144
    Gulf War aggression against Kuwait,
        229–230
    money given to suicide bombers' fami-
        lies, 419
Hutus, 35, 273, 274, 275, 276

I
Independent Commission on Policing in
    Northern Ireland, 99
India
    Air India jet bombing, 286
    Kashmir, conflicts over border, 281
    Kashmir, fight over, 290
    nuclear weapons, 284–285
    overview, 280–281
    Pakistan, conflicts with, 281, 282,
        283
    Sikh struggle for independence, 283,
        286, 287, 288
Indian National Congress, 281
Indonesia, 323–326
INLA. See Irish National Liberation Army
Intifada, support for in Iran, 25
Intelligence gathering, 387–389
Intent, formation of, 21
International Maritime Organization, 400,
    401–402
International terrorism. See also specific
    countries and terrorist groups
    overview, 55
Interpol, 387
IRA. See Irish Republican Army
Iran
    anti-Americanism, 245
    assassins, origins of, 22
    economy, 240
    infiltration by al Qaeda, 35
    infiltration by Taliban, 35
    intifada, support for, 25
    Iraq, relationship between, 230–231,
        240
    Islamic revolution, 242, 244

Khomeini, Ayatollah. (see Khomeini,
    Ayatollah)
    overview, 240
    political groups, 240
    population statistics, 240
    Shah, fall of, 241
    state-sponsored terrorism, 23, 24–25
    US complaints against, 244–245
    White Revolution, 241–242
Iraq
    Arab League, founding of, 231
    economy, 230
    Gulf War. (see Gulf War)
    history, ancient, 231
    Iran, relationship between, 230–231,
        240
    overview, 230
    regime, 230
    sanctions against, 234
    September 11, attitude and stance to-
        ward, 25
    state-sponsored terrorism, 23
    terrorist bases in, 25–26
Ireland. See also Troubles, the
    Army Ranger Wing (ARW), 393–394
    British occupation, 73–75
    civil liberty issues, 87–88
    decomissioning of terrorist weapons,
        69, 95, 97
    historical overview, 70–72
    lessons learned from, 106
    marching season, 88–90
    peace process, 93–99
    political overview, 75–78
    sectarian violence, 90–91
Irgun, 36, 38
Irgun Zvaileumi (NMO, National Military
    Organization), 178
Irish Free State, 72
Irish National Liberation Army, 82–83, 86
Irish Republican Army, 6, 7, 72. See also
    Provisional Irish Republican Army
    Balcombe Street siege, 366
    British attempts to maintain order,
        365–366
    Latin American terrorist ties, 344–345
    membership, number, 78
    overview of activities, 78–80
    repression by Britain, 367, 368
    tactics, 364
IRP. See Islamic Republican Party
Islam
    Nigeria, rise in, 277–278
    overview, 203
Islami Inqilabi Mahaz, 282
Islamic Front, 103
Islamic Jihad, 24, 28, 204, 207
    Eqyptian, 28
    Palestine, 28, 29
Islamic Liberation Party, 103
Islamic Republican Party, 242
Islamic Revolutionary Guard Corps, 24
Islamic Salvation Front, 103
Israel
    historical overview, ancient, 172
    political history, 172–174
    Sayeret Mat'kal, 398
    settlements in Palestinian Authority
        areas, 171–172, 175, 176, 196
    sky marshals, 368
    Stern Gang. (see Stern Gang)

    terrorist acts by, 174, 176, 177
    terrorist attacks on, 178. (see also spe-
        cific terrorist organizations)
    UN Partition plan, 172
    Unit 101, 174, 179
    US monetary support, 171, 295
Italy
    9–11, reaction to, 137
    government style, 133
    international terrorism in, 137
    kidnapping, high rate of, 135
    Leonardo Da Vinci Airport assault,
        187, 374
    Mancino law, 136
    Red Brigade. (see Red Brigade)
    Rome cyanide threat, 133
    Skinheads in, 136, 137
    terrorism links, 132–133
    Vienna Airport attack,
        187

J
Jackal, Carlos the, 118, 127, 157, 175, 430
Jacobins, 5, 20
Jamaat al-Islamiyya, 211
Japan
    agricultural sector, 316–317
    economy, 316–317, 318
    military, 319–320
    national security, 319
    overview, 316–317
    politics, 318, 319
    Red Army. (see Japanese Red Army)
    religions, 316
    Sarin attacks, 318, 421
Japanese Red Army
    arrests, 317
    French operations, 119
    in Syria, 207
Jarrah, Ziad Zamir, 132
Jenkins, Brian, 9
Jews, persecution/genocide, in Nazi Ger-
    many, 35
Jihad, definition, 32
John Paul II, Pope
    assassination attempt on, 168
    Burma human rights issues, speaking
        out on, 298
Jordan, 188–189
Juan Carlos (king of Spain), 116

K
Kach and Kahane Chai, 199–200
Kansi, Mir Aimal, 282
Kaplan, Metin, 132
Karlin, Elizabeth, 55
Kasavubu, Jospeh, 275
Kashmir
    Muslim majority, 289
    refugees, 281
    resistance, 289, 291
    terrorists, 290
Keenan, Brian, 206
Keiretsu, 316
Kelly, Walt, 407
Kemal Ataturk, 142–143
Kemal, Mustafa, 142
Kennon, George, 36
Kenya
    cruise missile strike following embassy
        bombing, 17

embassy bombing, 11, 46
embassy bombing, FBI investigation
    into, 16
overview, 268–269
political response, 269–270
terrorism, international, 269
Khaled, Leila, 190
Khmer Rouge, 299, 302–303, 306
Khmer Royal Armed Forces, 303
Khomeini, Ayatollah, 22, 25. See also Iran
    ascendancy to Iran's religious leader-
        ship, 242
    Paris demonstrations in support of,
        120
Kidnapping
    by Hezbollah, 205–206
    Colombian, 339
    in Brazil, 349
    in Central and Latin America, 337
Kikuyu, 268
Kilburn, Peter, 206
Killing Fields, The, 306
Kimathi, Dedan, 268
King, Jr., Martin Luther, 49
KINTEX, 168
Kirov, Sergei, 156
Kitab, 231
KKK. See Ku Klux Klan
Klein, Hans-Joachim, 127
Klinghoffer, Leon, 198, 403
Knesset, 179
Koresh, David, 48
Kosovo Liberation Army, 166
Kostov, Vladimir, 168
Kristallnacht, 125
Krushchev, Nikita, 156
Ku Klux Klan, 48, 49, 54
Kurdistan, 232–233
Kurdistan Workers' Party, 25, 28, 103,
    144–145, 207
Kuwait
    Al-Sabah dynasty, 229
    Chief of State, 228
    economy, 228–229
    Gulf War stance, 229–230
    oil, 229
    overview, 228
    terrorist attacks on, 229
Kuwait Oil Company, 229

L
La Belle Discotheque bombing, 27, 215
Lachs, John, 21
Laporte, Pierre, 60
Laqueur, Walter, 9
Laycock, Robert, 389
Lebanon
    historical overview, 200–202
    Palestinian refugees, 202–203
Leizaola, Jose Maria, 119
Lemkin, Raphael, 33, 34
Letter bombs, 38
Leumi, Irgun Zvai, 36
Lewis, Jock, 389
Lewis, John, 48
Liberation Tigers, 103
Liberation Tigers of Tamil Elam, 292, 293
Libya
    diplomatic immunity, as guise to move
        weapons, 213–215
    Operation El Dorado Canyon, 215–216

overview, 212
Pam Am 103. (see Pan Am Flight 103
    bombing)
Pan Am Flight 103 bombing, involve-
    ment in, 27, 31
September 11, reaction to, 27
state-sponsored terrorism, 23
terror support, 212–213
terrorism support, 27
US interests, as terror targets, 215
Libyan Militant Islamic Group, 212
Lindstedt, Rebecca, 429
Linton, David, 78
Lord's Resistance Army, 255
Lowney, Shannon, 55
Loyal Orange Institution, 90
Loyalist Volunteer Force, 86
LTTE. See Liberation Tigers of Tamil
    Elam
Lun, Wang, 314
LVF. See Loyalist Volunteer Force
Lynch Law, 49

M
Machel, Smaora, 273
Macheteros, 57
Mackey, Francie, 82
Made, Jospeph, 259
Madikizela-Mandela, Winnie, 266, 267
Madison, James, 50
Mahler, Horst, 126
Majid, Ali Hassan, 233–234
Manama, 236
Mancino law, 136
Mandela United Football Club, 267
Mandela, Nelson, 267
Mandela, Nelson Rolihlahala, 265–266
Mandela, Winnie, 266, 267
Marcos, Ferdinand, 322
Marcos, Imee, 322
Marcos, Imelda, 322
Marighella, Carlos, 134, 347, 349
Markov, Georgi, 168
Martin, Leo, 77
Marx, Karl, 152–153
Marxist Shining Path, 332
Maskhadov, Aslan, 161
Mau Mau, 268
Maze Prison, 85
Mbeki, Thabo, 257, 258
McCarthy, John, 206
McCauley, Gerald, 78
McCauley, Martin, 79
McCloskey, Francis, 78
McGuiness, Martin, 69, 75, 77
McKee, Billy, 77
McKevitt, Bernadette Sands, 82
McStiofain, Sean, 77
McVeigh, Timothy, 54
Mecca, 244
Media
    Oklahoma City bombing coverage,
        383–384
    right to know in terror incidents,
        383–384
    War on Terrorism coverage, 363
Meinhof, Ulrike, 126, 127
Meir, Golda, 181
MEK. See Mujahedin-e-Khalq
Mexico
    drug cartels, 333

overview, 331
Popular Revolutionary Army (EPR),
    332–333
present/future situation, 333
right-wing violence, 332
Zapatista National Liberation Army
    (ELZN), 331–332
Militia of Montana, 50, 51–52
Militias, Oklahoma City bombing, 46
Milosevic, Slobodan, 166, 167
Mini Manual of the Urban Guerrilla, 349,
    350–351, 352
Ministry of Intelligence and Security
    (MOIS), 24–25
Missadeq, Mohammad, 243
Mogadishu, GSG-9 attack, 127
Mohammad (prophet), 31
Mohammad V. King (of Morocco), 208
MOIS. See Ministry of Intelligence and Se-
    curity (MOIS)
Monaghan, James "Mortar," 79
Morazanist Patriotic Front, 335–336
Moro Islamic Liberation Front, 321
Moro, Aldo, 135
Morocco, 208–209
Motivations for terrorism
    antisocial, 12
    culture of violence, 13
    internal, 12–13
    outsider status, 13
    psychological, 12
    religion, 14
Moussaoui, Zacarias, 104, 121, 122
Moyne, Lord, 175
Moyo, Jonathan, 259
Mozambique, 271, 272–273
Msika, Joseph, 260
Mubarak, Hosni, 295
Mugabe, Robert, 256, 257, 258
Mujahedin-e-Khalq, 25, 241
Munich Olympic Games massacre,
    181–182, 184, 189, 202
Musa, Abu, 28
Museveni, Yoweri, 253, 254, 255
Muslim Brotherhood, 208
    in Egypt, 209, 210
Mutesa II, Edward, 252
Myanmar, 298

N
Nairac, Robert, 76
NAP, 136
Narco terrorists, 55, 339–340, 344
Narodnaya Volya, 150–153
National Abortion Federation, 427
National Guard, vs. constitutional unorga-
    nized militia, 50
National Liberation Army (ELN), 339, 342,
    343
National Liberation Army of Iran, 241
National Military Organization. See Irgun
    Zvaileumi (NMO, National Military Or-
    ganization)
NATO. See North American Treaty Organi-
    zation
Nazer Hindawi incident, 381
Nazis
    children conscripted to youth parties,
        124–125
    genocide, 33, 34
    rise of party, 124

Nazis (*cont.*)
spy tactics, 125
Nehru, Jawaharlal, 281
Neo-Nazis, 48, 54
in Britain, 107
in Germany, 129, 130
Netanyahu, Benjamin, 179
Netherlands counterterrorism unit, 396
New People's Army (Philippines), 321
New World Order, 54
Nicaragua, 336–338
Nicholas I, Czar, 152
Nichols, Lee Ann, 55
Nichols, Terry, 54
Nigeria, 277–278
Nkomo, John, 259
Nkomo, Joshua, 257
NMO. See Irgun Zvaileumi (NMO, National
Military Organization)
Noriega, Manuel, 338–339
North American Free Trade Agreement,
331
North American Treaty Organization
as terror target, 119, 138–139
North Korea terrorist activities, 27–28
North, Oliver, 338
Northern Ireland. See Ireland
Northern Ireland Emergency Provisions Act,
87
Northside Family Services Clinic, 17
Norway counterterrorism unit, 396–397
November 17 group, 110
ideology, 138
operations, pervasive, 138
origins, 138
NPA. See New People's Army (Philippines)
Nuclear threats, 420
Nuclear weapons, 411–412
Nuremberg Trials, 34

O
O'Brady, Rory, 77
O'Neill, Juliet, 59
Obasanjo, Olusegun, 257, 258
Obote, Milton, 252
Ocalan, Abdullah, 207
Ogedan, 249
Ojeda Rios, Filiberto, 57
Okello, Toto, 254
Oklahoma City bombing, 11, 46, 383–384
Okomato, Kozo, 184
Okrano, 36
Omagh bombing, 90
Oman, 237–240
OPEC. See Organization of Petroleum Ex-
porting Countries
Operation Black Cat, 341
Operation Desert Storm. See Desert Storm
Operation El Dorado Canyon, 215–216
Operation Spring Youth, 398
Opium trade, 296, 301, 305–306, 327
Orange Order, 90
Orange Volunteers, 86
Orangeism, 88
Organization of Petroleum Exporting Coun-
tries, attack against, 118,
127
Organization of the Oppressed, 204
Orly Airport rocket attack (by PLO),
120–121, 368
Ortiz, Arnoldo, 114

Ortiz, Jose, 113
Oslo peace accord, 183
Outsider status, 13
OV. See Orange Volunteers

P
Padfield, Philip, 206
Paisley, Ian, 94
Pakistan
India separatists training camps, 283,
287
India, conflicts with, 281, 282, 283
inteligence operations, 286–287
Kashmir, fight over, 290
security problems, 283
terrorism, cross-border,
282
Union Texas Petroleum murders,
282–283
violence, cycle of, 283
Palestine Liberation Front, 198
Palestine Liberation Organization, 6, 7
origins and overview, 180–183
Paris operations, 120
recognition by international commu-
nity, 181
Palestinian Islamic Jihad, 199
Palestinian Muslim Brotherhood, 195
Pan Am Flight 103 bombing, 27, 31, 189,
216–217, 370, 371
Panama, 338–339, 339
Papendreou, Andreas, 139
Paraguay, 351, 352, 353
Parti Quebecois, 60
Partisan Action Group (GAP), 135–136
Party of God, 204
Patrice Lumumba University, 157
Patten, Chris, 99, 100
Pearse, Patrick, 72
Peel, Robert, 100
People's Consultative Assembly, 324
People's Liberations Army, 82
People's Republican Army, 82
People's Revolutionary Democratic Front,
250
Peron, Eva, 353
Peron, Juan, 353
Persia, 22
Peru
embassy, U.S., car bomb, 346
hostage rescue, 348
Japanese ambassador's house, attack
on, 347–348
overview, 345
Shining Path. (see Shining Path)
Tupac Amaru Revolutionary Move-
ment (MRTA). (see Tupac Amaru
Revolutionary Movement (MRTA))
PFLP. See Popular Front for the Liberation
of Palestine
Philippines, 320–321, 322, 323
PIJ. See Palestinian Islamic Jihad
Pinochet, Augusto, 354, 355–356
PIRA. See Provisional Irish Republican
Army
Piracy, 400–404
PKK. See Kurdistan Workers' Party
PLA. See People's Liberations Army
Planned Parenthood, 427
PLF. See Palestine Liberation Front
PLO. See Palestine Liberation Organization

Poland, James M., 9
Polay, Victor, 347
Politics, religion, relationship between, 22
Popular Front for the Liberation of Palestine,
25–26, 29
France, bases in, 118–119
origins, 187
Syria base, 208
training of Basques, 114
Popular Front for the Liberation of Pales-
tine-General Command, 28, 29, 208
Popular Movement for the Liberation of An-
gola (MPLA), 271–272
Popular Revolutionary Army (EPR) (Mex-
ico), 332–333
Pot, Pol, 299, 306
Powell, Colin, 412
PRA, 82
Preval, Rene, 66
Prisoner-of-war exchanges, 431–432
Privateers, 401
Pro-life terrorism
future scenarios, 427–429
overview, 424
religious-political organizations,
425–426
social construction of, 424–425
violent acts, 426–427
Provisional Irish Republican Army, 69, 74.
See also Irish Republican Army
attacks of, 77
British response to, 105–106
evolution, 80
organization, 80
Ptrovskaya, Sophia, 151
Puerto Rican terrorist groups, 54, 56–58
Putin, Vladimir, 235

Q
Qatada, Abu, 122

R
Rabin, Yitzak, 176
Radio Free Iraq, 26
Rafizadeh, Mansur, 243
Ramadan, 203
Ramos, Fidel, 322
Real Irish Republican Army, 82
Rebel Armed Forces (FAR), 333
Red Army Faction, 119, 126–127, 126–128
Red Brigade
extortion, 134
kidnapping, 134, 135
members, founding, 133
Mini Manual of Urban Terrorist,
134
origins, 132, 133
structure, 134–135
Red Hand Defenders, 85–86
Regime de la Terreur, 4–5
Reid, Richard, 122, 377
Reign of Terror, 4–5
Relief Agency for National Political Prison-
ers and their Dependants, 129
Religion. See also religious terrorism
as terrorist motivation, 14, 421–423
politics, mixture, 22
Religious terrorism
Crusades. (see Crusades)
historical overview, 30–32
Holy Terror, 421–423

overview of numerous conflicts, 33
Renaissance, 33
Republic of China. See Taiwan
Republican Sinn Fein, 82
Ressam, Ahmed, 104, 117
Revolutionary anarchism, 36
Revolutionary Armed Forces of Colombia (FARC), 339, 340–342
Revolutionary Cells, 140–141
Revolutionary Front for Proletarian Action (FRAP). See Revolutionary Front for Proletarian Action (FRAP)
Revolutionary Justice Organization, 204
Revolutionary Nuclei. See Revolutionary Cells
Revolutionary Organization of Socialist Muslims, 185
Rhodesia, 256, 392–393. See also Zimbabwe
Richard, King, 32
RIRA. See Real Irish Republican Army
Robespierre, Maximillen, 118
Rockwell International, 243
Rogue states, 23
Rosie, George, 9
Rossello, Pedro J., 56
Royal Ulster Constabulary, 73, 99
RSF. See Republican Sinn Fein
RUC, 73
Rumsfeld, Donald, 413
Rushdie, Salmon, 25, 244
Russia
    Afghanistan, invasion of, 154
    Bloody Sunday, 152
    Boevaya Oranisatsia, 151–153
    Bolsheviks. (see Bolsheviks)
    church, role of the, 153
    Cold War, actions during, 167–168
    Cold War, end of, 158
    Estonian guerilla movement, 156–157
    free-market economy, 158–160
    freedom of press, 157–158
    Georgia region, 162–163
    Great Terror, 156
    Kaspiysk, bombing of, 151
    KGB, 157, 158, 159, 366–367
    Killer College, 157
    Mafia, rise of, 158–160
    Moscow apartment bombings, 159
    N-bombs, suitcase, missing, 155
    Narodnaya Volya, 150–153
    Pankisi Gorge area, 162–163
    Pushkin Square bombing, 162
    repression, 366–367
    secret police (Cheka), 154
    state terrorism, 153–154
    terrorism, early twentieth century, 151
Russian Federation, 161
Rwanda, 273–275

S
Sabri al-Banna, 185
Sadat, Anwar, 209, 210–211
Saladin, 32
Salemeh, Ali Hassan, 181, 182
Salvi, John, 55
Sanchez, Illich Ramirez, 118, 127, 157, 175, 430

Sandanistas, 338
Sands, Bobby, 82
Sarin gas, 421
Sarin toxin, 38
Satanic Verses, The, 244
Saudi Arabia
    overview, 225–226
    peace process, involvement with, 227–228
    royal family, 225–226
SAVAK, 243, 244
Savasta, Antonio, 168
Sayeret Mat'kal, 398
Schlayer, Hanns-Martin, 128
Schmid, Alex, 7
Schroeder, Gerhard, 235
Schwarzkopf, Norman, 383
Scotland, nationalism, 102
Scottish Nationalist Party, 102
Scranton, William W., 175–176
SEAL teams, 399–400
Seko, Mobuto Sese, 276–277
Selassie, Haile, 249
September 11, 189
    airport security following, 363–364
    Bush's speech to joint session of Congress following, 23
    Castro's stance on, 24
    ease of which carried off, 11
    fear following, 15–16
    homeland security following, 414–416
    impact on views of terrorism, 3
    Libyan reaction to, 27
    prevention, possibility of, 373
    security failings that contributed to, 378–380
    Syrian reaction to, 28
    unexpectedness of, 6
Serbia, 165, 166, 167
Serno-Solovevich, Alexander, 36
Servants of Islam, 132
Shah of Iran, 120
    exile, 242
    fall of, 241
    White Revolution of, 241–242
Shaimiev, Minitimir, 160
Shakhrai, Sergei, 160
Shamir, Yitzhak, 174
Shankhill Butchers, 87
Sharia, 161
Sharon, Ariel, 174, 178, 179
Sharpeville massacre, 270
Shehada, 203
Shi'a sect, 203, 204
Shining Path, 103, 345, 346–347
Shirosaki, Tsutomu, 317–318
Shoe bomber, 122, 377
Shuqeiri, Ahmad, 180
Sikh terrorism, 283, 286, 287, 288
Sinn Fein, 70–71
    election results, 73
    PIRA, relationship between, 74
    terrorist links, 77, 92–93
Sithole, Ndabaningi, 257
Six-Day War, 172, 175
Skinheads, 48
    in Britain, 107
    in Germany, 129, 130
    in Italy, 136, 137
Sky marshals, 368

SLA. See Symbionese Liberation Army
Smallpox, 421
Smith, Ian, 256
Smuts, Jan, 263
Social groups, 4
Somalia
    as terrorist harbor, 250
    historical overview, 250
    marines, killing of ("Blackhawk Down"), 250–251
Soragji, Yousef, 197
Sossi, Mario, 134
South Africa
    African National Congress, 265–266
    Afrikaner nationalism, 263
    apartheid, 262–263, 264
    British settlers, 263
    Bureau of State Security, 264
    diamonds, 263
    future of, 265
    right-wing Afrikaner movement (extreme), 264–265
    Robben Island University (Isle of Purgatory), 266–267
Soviet Union. See Russia
Spain
    Basque separatism, 111
    Euzkadi Ta Azatasuna.
    Grupo Especial de Operaciones (GEO), 394
    Guarda Civil, 394
    overview of region, 110–111
    post 9–11 police actions, 116–117
    terrorism, efforts at combating, 115–116
Special Air Service Regiment, 106
Special Weapons and Tactical Units (SWAT), 399
Specter, Arlen, 16
Spraly Islands, 316
Sri Lanka, 291–294
Stalin, Joseph, 153–154
Stanstead Airport, United Kingdome, hijack response, 382–383
Starovoitova, Galina, 159
State-supported terrorism. See also specific countries
    advantages (for terrorists), 29–30
    genocide, 33–35
Stephenson, John, 77
Stern Gang, 141, 174–177
Stern, Avraham, 174
Stinger missiles, 378
Stirling, David, 389
Sudan, 28, 217
Suez Canal, 173–174
Suharto, General, 323
Suicide bombers, 5
    Hamas, carried out by, 197, 198
    money given to families of, 419
    profile of Palestinian, 184
    victims of, 11
Sunni sect, 203
Swierczek, Michael, 129
Symbionese Liberation Army, 47
Syria
    as harbor for terrorists, 207, 208
    as terrorist haven, 28–29
    overview, 207
    September 11, reaction to, 28
    training camps, 207

T
Taiwan, 315–316
Takimoto, Taro, 318
Taliban, infiltration into Iran, 35
Tanzania, embassy bombing, 11, 46
    cruise missile strike following, 17
    FBI investigation into, 16
Takfir wal Hirja, 122, 124
Target selection, 8
Task Force on Violence Against Abortion
    Providers, 55
Task Force, U.S. Vice-President's, 9–10
Tasmania, 327
Techno terrorism, 423
Terrorism
    cyclical nature of, 35–36, 38
    definition, 3, 5, 6–7, 9–10
    domestic (U.S.). (see domestic terror-
      ism)
    emotional response to, 9
    historical roots of, 38–39
    international. (see international terror-
      ism)
    motivations for. (see motivations for
      terrorism)
    objectives of, for groups/persons com-
      mitting, 8–9, 10–11, 12–14
    pro-life. (see pro-life terrorism)
    religious. (see religious terrorism)
    state-supported. (see state-supported
      terrorism)
    techno. (see techno terrorism)
    use of term, first, 4–5
    vs. other types of crimes, 7
Terrorist incident, definition, 3
Terrorists
    governments treatment of, 429–430
    motivations. (see motivations for ter-
      rorism)
    negotiations with, 433–434
    semantic labels for, 6
    vs. other types of criminals, 7
Thailand, 304
Tiedermann, Gabrielle, 127
Tito, Josip, 165
Tolstoy, Leo N., 150
Tombstone technology, 373–374
Townson, Liam, 76
Transportation security, 415
Trimble, David, 80
Trochmann, Randy L., 52
Troubles, the. See also specific terrorist
    groups in Ireland; Ireland
    civil liberties issues, 87–88
    killed, number of people, 94
    overview, 86
    turf wars, 86–87
Trudeau, Pierre, 60
Truman, Harry S., 172
Tse-Tung, Mao, 113
Tsvangirai, Morgan, 257
Tunnel vision, 22
Tupac Amaru Revolutionary Movement
    (MRTA), 345, 347–348
Tupamaros, 351–352
Turkey
    Armenian terrorism, 145
    Dev Sol. (see Dev Sol)
    historical overview, 142
    Istanbul airport attack, 143

Kemal Ataturk, 142–143
    Turkish Revenge Brigade, 145
    war on terror, support of, 144
Turkish Revenge Brigade, 145
Turks, Crusades, role in, 32–33
Tutsis, 35, 273, 274, 275, 276
Twomey, Seamus, 77

U
UDA. See Ulster Defense Association
UDI. See Unilateral Declaration of Indepen-
    dence
UDLP. See Ulster Loyalist Democratic Party
UDP. See Ulster Democratic Party
UFF. See Ulster Freedom Fighters
Uganda
    AIDS crisis, 255
    Bureau of State Research, 252
    cannibalism, 253
    Entebbe, Raid on, 253
    ethnic cleansing, 252
    historical overview, 251–252
    infrastructure redevelopment, 254–255
    Public Safety Unit, 252
    terror acts against own people,
      252–253
Uganda National Liberation Front, 253
Uganda Patriotic Movement, 253
Ulster Defense Association, 84–85
Ulster Democratic Party, 84
Ulster Freedom Fighters, 84, 86
Ulster Loyalist Democratic Party, 84–85
Ulster Volunteer Force, 83–84, 86–87
UN Convention for the Suppression of the
    Financing of Terrorism, 27
UN Convention of the Law of the Sea Arti-
    cle 105, 404
UN security Council Resolution 1373, 28
Unilateral Declaration of Independence,
    256
Union of Russian Men, 36
United Nations Drug Control Program, 296
United Nations Security Council Resolution
    1373, 386–387
United Nations Security Council Resolution
    688, 230
United Nations Security Council Resolution
    986, 230
United Self-Defense Forces of Colombia
    (AUC), 344
UNSCOM, 234, 419
Urban guerrillas, 349
Uruguay, 351, 352, 353
USS Cole, bombing, 11
Uygar separatists, 311–312

V
Van der Graaf, Volkert, 147
Venezuela, 356–357
Victims of terrorism, randomness, 11
Vietnam
    maritime boundaries, 305
    overview, 304–305
    poppy/opium trade, 305–306
    poverty, 305
    rulers, 307
Violence
    addictive nature of, 22
    in early man, 20–21
    paradigm of, 20

progression of, 21
    sectarian, 106
Von Hindenburg, Paul, 124

W
Waco Massacre, 48
Wales, terrorism, 102
War
    exhileration of, 21–22
    horrors, 21
War Crimes Tribunal, 33
War on Terrorism. See also September 11
    Castro's stance on, 24
    Iraqi crisis, 26
    media coverage of, 363
    realities of, 295
Warfare, terror as by-product of, 5
Weapons of mass destruction, 28, 419–420
Wegener, Ulrich, 397
Weldon, Curt, 155
Western Hostage Saga, 430
Whitaker, Vincent, 55
White Lotis Rebellion, 314
White Revolution (in Iran), 241–242
William III, 71
Woolsey, James, 17
Worch, Christian, 129
World Trade Center, 11. See also September
    11
    1993 bombing, 45–46
Wright, Billy, 85

Y
Yablokov, Alexei, 155
Yellin-Mor, Natan, 174
Yeltsin, Boris, 155, 157, 160
Yemen
    Aden bombings, 247
    British domination, 246
    economy, 245
    overview, 245
    qat, 245
    Republic of, 246
    states, 246
    Turkish domination, 246
    unification, 246–247
Young, Andrew, 49
Yousef, Ramzi Ahmad, 431
Yugoslavia
    economic crises, 165
    ethnic splits, 165
    historical overview, 164–165
    problems, present-day, 165–167

Z
Zaire. See Democratic Republic of Congo
Zakat, 203
Zapatista National Liberation Army
    (ELZN), 331–332
Zimbabwe
    communist indoctrination camps,
      256–257
    minerals, 259
    overview, 256
    starvation/famine, 258
    state-sponsored terrorism, 258–259
    terror groups, 257
    whites, ordered to abandon farms, etc.,
      260
Zurich Airport attack, 118